New York City SHSAT Prep 2019-2020

Second Printing

PUBLISHING

New York

SHSAT (Specialized High Schools Admissions Test) is a test administered by the New York City Department of Education, which was not involved in the production of, and does not endorse, this product.

Published by Kaplan Publishing, a division of Kaplan, Inc.
750 Third Avenue
New York, NY 10017

10 9 8 7 6 5 4 3 2

ISBN-13: 978-1-5062-4951-3

Kaplan Publishing print books are available at special quantity discounts to use for sales promotions, employee premiums, or educational purposes. For more information or to purchase books, please call the Simon & Schuster special sales department at 866-506-1949.

TABLE OF CONTENTS

Part 4: Ready, Set, Go!

Part 5: Practice Tests

AVAILABLE ONLINE

For Any Test Changes or Late-Breaking Developments

kaptest.com/publishing

The material in this book is up-to-date at the time of publication. However, the NYC Department of Education may have instituted changes in the test or test registration process after this book was published. Be sure to read carefully the materials you receive when you register for the test.

If there are any important late-breaking developments—or any changes or corrections to the Kaplan test preparation materials in this book—we will post that information online at kaptest.com/publishing. Check to see if any information has been posted there for readers of this book.

HOW TO USE THIS BOOK: THE CLASSIC PLAN

Ideally, you should take a couple of months to work through this book, though it's certainly possible to read it in far less time. Here's how you should go about prepping with it:

1. Read through each chapter completely, learning from the example problems and trying the practice problems.
2. Read the section entitled "Ready, Set, Go!" to set the stage for your preparation and testing success.
3. Take Practice Test 1 under strictly timed conditions to get a sense of your strengths and areas of opportunity.
4. Before taking Practice Test 2, review your greatest areas of opportunity.
5. Give yourself an evening of rest right before Test Day.

If you have time, complete two or three chapters a week, and be sure to take some time off from your SHSAT preparation when you need a break. Giving yourself a few days away from your preparation will help you resume your studies with greater energy and focus.

HOW TO USE THIS BOOK: THE EMERGENCY PLAN

Maybe you have only two or three weeks—or even less time than that. Don't worry! This book has been designed to help students in your situation, too. If you go through a chapter or two every day, you can finish this book in a couple of weeks. If you have limited time to prepare for the SHSAT (less than six weeks), we suggest you do the following:

1. Take a slow, deep breath. Read the "Ready, Set, Go!" section to maximize your study and testing time.
2. Read "Section 1: The Basics."
3. Complete as many Practice Set problems (located at the end of each chapter) as you can.
4. Take both of the practice tests under timed conditions.
5. Review your results, with special attention to the questions you missed.
6. Give yourself the day before the test off.

SHSAT Emergency FAQs

Q: It's two days before the SHSAT and I'm clueless. What should I do?

A: First of all, don't panic. If you have only a day or two to prepare for the test, then you don't have time to prepare as thoroughly as you may like. But that doesn't mean you should just give up. There's still a lot you can do to improve your potential score. First and foremost, you should become familiar with the test. Read "Section 1: The Basics." And if you don't do anything else, take one of the full-length practice tests at the back of this book under reasonably test-like conditions. When you finish the practice test, check your answers and look at the explanations for the questions you didn't get right.

Q: I don't feel confident. Should I just guess?

A: There is no wrong-answer penalty, so you should definitely fill in an answer for every question. However, this does not mean that you should always guess randomly. Whenever you can eliminate wrong answers, you increase your chances of guessing correctly. Therefore, you should guess strategically whenever possible.

Q: What's the most important thing I can do to get ready for the SHSAT quickly?

A: In addition to Math and English Language Arts skills, the SHSAT mainly tests your ability to take the SHSAT. Therefore, the most important thing you can do is to familiarize yourself with the directions, the question types, the answer grid, and the overall structure of the test. Make sure you know how to get to your testing location and so forth. Read every question carefully—many mistakes are the result of simply not reading thoroughly.

Q: So it's a good idea to panic, right? RIGHT?

A: No! No matter how prepared you are for the SHSAT, stress will hurt your performance, and it's really no fun. Stay confident and don't cram. Just breathe, stay calm, and do your best.

A SPECIAL NOTE FOR PARENTS

The nine specialized high schools in New York City are Fiorello H. LaGuardia High School of Music and Art and Performing Arts; Bronx High School of Science; Brooklyn Latin School; Brooklyn Technical High School; High School for Math, Science and Engineering at City College; High School for American Studies at Lehman College; Queens High School for the Sciences at York College; Staten Island Technical High School; and Stuyvesant High School. The Specialized High Schools Admission Test (SHSAT), administered once a year, is required for admission to all of these schools except for Fiorello H. LaGuardia High School of Music & Art and Performing Arts. If a student is applying only to LaGuardia, then admission is based on an audition and a review of academic records. However, if a student is applying to LaGuardia and any of the other schools, he or she must take the SHSAT.

Approximately 30-40,000 applicants apply for about 2,000 spots at just three of the specialized New York City schools each year (Stuyvesant, Brooklyn Tech, and Bronx Science).

You have the opportunity to play an important role in your child's preparation for the Specialized High Schools Admissions Test. The SHSAT is difficult and the stakes are high, so your child may be feeling quite a lot of stress. You are the best judge of how much supervision and structure he or she needs in order to prepare. Similarly, since you know how your child handles stress, you are the best person to reassure and motivate your child during his or her preparation.

Much of the information that follows can be found elsewhere in this book. However, the information most salient for parents has been summarized here so that you don't have to search for it.

Getting Started

If you do not have it already, you should get a copy of the *Specialized High Schools Student Handbook*. This is published by the Department of Education and is available on their website. It should also be available in your son or daughter's guidance office. Get this handbook early and spend some time reading through it. Additionally, it's worth your while to do a little research into the individual schools. Take some time to learn the features and strengths of each.

Bronx High School of Science

75 West 205th Street
Bronx, NY 10468
(718) 817-7700
www.bxscience.edu

Brooklyn Latin School

223 Graham Avenue
Brooklyn, NY 11206
(718) 366-0154
www.brooklynlatin.org

Brooklyn Technical High School

29 Fort Greene Place
Brooklyn, NY 11217
(718) 804-6400
www.bths.edu

Fiorello H. LaGuardia High School of Music & Art and Performing Arts

100 Amsterdam Avenue
New York, NY 10023
(212) 496-0700
www.laguardiahs.org

High School for Math, Science and Engineering at the City College of New York

240 Convent Avenue
New York, NY 10031
(212) 281-6490
www.hsmse.org

High School of American Studies at Lehman College

2925 Goulden Avenue
Bronx, NY 10468
(718) 329-2144
www.hsas-lehman.org

Queens High School for the Sciences at York College

94-50 159th Street
Jamaica, NY 11451
(718) 657-3181
www.qhss.org

Staten Island Technical High School

485 Clawson Street
Staten Island, NY 10306
(718) 667-3222
www.siths.org

Stuyvesant High School

345 Chambers Street
New York, NY 10282
(212) 312-4800
www.stuy.edu

The SHSAT

Format and Timing

The test is broken into two sections, English Language Arts and Math. The English Language Arts contains 57 multiple-choice questions, with 37 Reading Comprehension questions and 20 Revising/Editing questions. The Math Section contains 57 questions—52 are multiple-choice questions and 5 are grid-in questions.

Timing

Test takers have 180 minutes (3 hours) for the entire test. The recommended time for each section is 90 minutes. However, test takers can break up the time however they choose.

Scoring

The English Language Arts and Math sections contribute equally to the final score. The test contains 114 questions. 94 of the questions are worth 1 "raw" point and 20 are experimental questions that aren't scored. The maximum Raw Score is therefore 94. The Raw Score is multiplied by a formula known only to the Department of Education to arrive at a scaled score. Test takers receive a scaled score for each section and a Composite Score for the entire test. The highest possible Composite Score is 800.

Admission

Admission is determined exclusively by test takers' scores on this 800-point scale. Essentially, roughly the top 5,500 scorers are admitted to the eight specialized high schools requiring the SHSAT. It is impossible to know what the "cutoff" scores will be for each school, since this depends on the number of test takers and their overall performance.

Things to Keep in Mind

The test is the sole criterion for admission.

Other test scores, grades, and connections do not help. If your child does not have straight A's, he or she can still gain admission to one of the specialized high schools. If your child does have straight A's, he or she may not get in. It may seem unfair—and it certainly puts a lot of pressure on the test takers—but it's the most objective method the Board of Education could devise to open the admissions process to all applicants.

Only students prepared to attend one of the specialized science high schools should take the SHSAT.

Your child should *not* take the SHSAT just to see how he or she would do. Only students who are serious about attending one of the specialized high schools should take the test. Any student who is admitted to one of these schools is expected to attend. Make sure that your child is serious about this commitment before taking the test.

Applying to more than one specialized high school increases your child's chances of admission.

The application asks the applicant to rank his or her choices of schools. If your child is interested in all of the schools, he or she should indicate an order of preference. Obviously, applying to six schools increases an applicant's odds of being admitted into one. However, this does not mean that all applicants should apply to all of the schools. Consider issues such as location and school size when making this decision. Think very seriously about how long a commute is acceptable.

How to Help Your Son or Daughter Prepare for the Test

Help your child identify his or her priorities.

There are two reasons to do this. First, it's a good to idea to verify that your child actually wants to attend one of the specialized high schools and is prepared to make the accompanying commitment. Second, if your child identifies what she or he wants from this process, his or her motivation is likely to be clearer. Consequently, she or he may feel more control over the application and test-taking process.

Help your child design and maintain a study schedule.

This is a self-study book. Self-study requires a lot of self-discipline—not a quality for which eighth graders are generally known. Creating a schedule will increase your child's chance of working through and deriving the benefit from the entire book. You know your child and consequently know how much supervision she or he needs to stick to the schedule. A little supervision and prodding can help keep a lot of students on track. Of course, too much oversight can become oppressive for all parties.

Let your child know that you understand that this process is stressful.

The bottom line is that this is a difficult, high-stakes test. Preparing to take it can be extraordinarily stressful. While the high stakes can provide motivation, they can also induce fear—which can be paralyzing. Encourage your child to read "Ready, Set, Go!" Make sure that your child realizes that it will be disappointing, but not the end of the world, if he or she does not gain admission to one of the specialized high schools.

PART 1

The Basics

CHAPTER 1

SHSAT Mastery

CHAPTER OBJECTIVES

By the end of this chapter, you will be able to:

- Answer common questions about the Specialized High Schools Admissions Test
- Take advantage of the test's structure
- Approach the questions strategically

You're using this book because you're serious about attending high school at Brooklyn Latin, Stuyvesant, Bronx Science, Brooklyn Tech, City College, Lehman College, Staten Island Tech, or York College. You probably already know that if you want to go to one of these specialized high schools, you have to take the Specialized High Schools Admissions Test (SHSAT). Fortunately, there are some steps you can take to maximize your score. Essentially, you need to:

- Understand the structure of the test
- Hone your Math and English Language Arts skills
- Develop strategies and test-taking techniques
- Practice what you've learned

The Specialized High Schools Admissions Test (SHSAT) is a standardized test. It's certainly not easy, but it is a fairly predictable test. This means that you can prepare for the content and question types that you'll see on Test Day.

Before delving into the specific content and strategies you will need to perform well on the SHSAT, you should know some basic information about the test. Here are answers to some common questions about the test.

COMMON QUESTIONS ABOUT THE SHSAT

Why Should I Take the SHSAT?

If you want to attend high school at Brooklyn Latin, Stuyvesant, Bronx Science, Brooklyn Tech, City College, Lehman College, Staten Island Tech, or York College, you must take the SHSAT. It is the sole criterion for admission. This means that your grades, extracurricular activities, and so on play no role in the admissions process. **Do not take the test if you are not serious about attending one of the schools!** If you score high enough to be accepted at a school, you will be expected to attend.

Who Administers the Test?

The New York City Department of Education administers the test. The Department of Education is composed of teachers and administrators who decide what students at New York City high schools need to learn.

> **✔ What Does SHSAT Stand For?**
>
> The full name of the test is the Specialized High Schools Admissions Test. SHSAT is just a wee bit easier to say.

Why Is the Test the Sole Criterion for Admission?

Having one test be the only factor that determines whether you are accepted at the school of your choice is rough. However, more than 30,000–40,000 students apply for admission, and the Department of Education needs a way to pare down that number to roughly 5,500. A multiple-choice test given to all applicants is a very efficient way to make the cut because it subjects all applicants to the exact same standard and is very easy to grade. You might not be thrilled about this process, but it is not going to change before October. Therefore, regardless of your personal feelings about standardized tests in general or this test in particular, you need to take some time to prepare for the SHSAT.

Is There *Any* Other Way to Get into the Specialized High Schools?

A limited number of students may be eligible to participate in a Discovery Program, which is designed to give disadvantaged students who have demonstrated high potential a chance to enroll in a specialized high school program. For more information about this program, see the *Specialized High Schools Student Handbook*.

How Is the Test Scored?

Composite Score

The Composite Score is based on 800 points. The number of correct answers from the Math and English Language Arts (ELA) sections determines the Composite Score. In calculating the Composite Score, the Math and ELA sections are weighted equally.

Raw Score

The Raw Score is the sum of the correct answers from each section. There are 57 questions per section; however, 10 questions per section are experimental. The experimental questions are not scored. Therefore, the maximum number of scored answers per section is 47. Overall, the highest Raw Score for the total test is 94. The Raw Score is converted to the 800-point scale to determine the Composite Score.

Experimental Questions

The 10 experimental questions per section are mixed in with the scored questions. You will not know if a question is experimental or scored. Therefore, you should answer all questions as if they were scored.

What Is a "Good Score"?

That's a good question. Unfortunately, there's really no answer to it. Admission works like this: The Department of Education identifies the number of places available at each school. If there are 500 spaces available at Stuyvesant, the Board of Education accepts the top 500 scorers who identified Stuyvesant as their first choice. Therefore, there is no magic number for admission.

What Should I Bring to the Test?

You need your admissions ticket, two or more No. 2 pencils, an eraser, and a watch that does not contain a calculator. You may not bring a calculator to the test.

TAKING ADVANTAGE OF THE SHSAT'S STRUCTURE

You can be confident that the test will look very similar to the test-like practice in this book. Therefore, you can take advantage of the test's predictability and use what you know about the structure to raise your score.

You Do Not Need to Answer the Questions in Order

Usually when taking a test, you automatically answer the questions in the order that they're written. However, there are a lot of questions on the SHSAT, and you may be able to make it easier on yourself by doing the questions you find easier first. For example, if you're good at Reading Comprehension questions, build your confidence and grab some quick points by doing them first. Or if you have a tough time with coordinate geometry, skip the coordinate geometry questions and go back to them when you have time.

You Can Go Back to the English Language Arts Section Once You've Finished the Math Section

Most standardized tests don't let you move between sections. On the SHSAT, however, you can go back to the English Language Arts section after you've finished the Math section.

There Is No Penalty for Wrong Answers

Don't leave anything blank on the SHSAT. A correct answer is a correct answer. It makes no difference to your score if you get the question correct by solving the question or by guessing. Of course, you should solve the questions you know, but there's no harm in guessing when you don't know how to answer a question or are running out of time. Remember, you have a 0 percent chance of getting a question correct if you leave it blank. Your chances of getting it correct if you guess are at least 25 percent. Go with the odds.

> ✔ **Don't Leave It Blank**
>
> **Don't leave any questions blank! There's no penalty for wrong answers, so a guess can only help and will never hurt.**

Gridding In Your Answers

Don't lose valuable points on the test by misgridding! The answer choices are labeled A–D and E–H to help you keep track of answers.

Always Circle Questions You Skip

Whenever you choose not to answer a question, circle the entire question in your test book. This can help you in two ways. The first is that it will be easier to find the questions you skipped if they're circled. The second is that you are less likely to misgrid when you skip questions if you clearly mark the ones you skip. Anything that will help you approach the test efficiently is worth doing. Circling questions that you skip is relatively effortless and can save you time and get you points.

Always Circle The Answer You Choose

A great way to avoid careless gridding errors is to circle your answers in the test book. If you circle your answers, you can quickly check your circled answers against your gridded answers to make sure that you did not misgrid. Additionally, if you have time to recheck your answers, it's easier to do this if the answers are circled.

Grid Your Answers In Blocks of Five

Don't grid in each answer after you answer each question. Instead, grid in your answers after every five questions. As you're entering the answers into the grid, silently say, "1, A," "2, G," and so on. This will help you to avoid any omissions. Since questions alternate between A–D choices and E–H choices, you should be able to catch a mistake if you have skipped a question or entered answers onto the wrong line.

> ✔ **Grid Smart**
>
> **Instead of gridding in each answer as you finish the question, circle the answer in your test book and grid in the answers after every five questions.**

APPROACHING SHSAT QUESTIONS STRATEGICALLY

As important as it is to know the setup of the SHSAT, it is equally important to have a system for attacking the questions. You wouldn't venture onto the subway for the first time without looking at a map, and you shouldn't approach the SHSAT without a plan. Remember, the more knowledge you have about the test and the questions, the better you'll be able to take control of the test. The following is the best way to approach SHSAT questions systematically.

Think About the Questions Before You Look at the Answers

It's hard to emphasize strenuously enough precisely how important this strategy is. Basically, IT'S REALLY, REALLY IMPORTANT! One of the most damaging mistakes that students make when taking the SHSAT is that they jump immediately from the question to the answers without stopping to think first. This is particularly true with the Reading Comprehension questions, but it is a problem with most question types. Here's what will happen if you read the questions and then go directly to the answer choices: you will be confronted with very tempting, but very wrong, answer choices. If you take the time to think before looking at the choices, you will be much less likely to fall for the traps.

> ✔ **Think Before You Answer**
>
> **Try to predict the answer—or at least think about it before you look at the answer choices. If nothing else, you may realize what the answer won't be. This will help you to avoid the tempting "traps" set by the test maker.**

Use Backdoor Strategies and Guess

You'll learn more about backdoor strategies later, but the gist of them is that sometimes there are shortcuts to solving problems and guessing strategically. No one sees your work, so you do not have to solve problems the way you would in school. Any method that gets you the correct answer is the "right" way on the SHSAT. Additionally, because there is no penalty for wrong answers, don't leave any answers blank!

> **✓ Go for the Points**
>
> **You don't gain any points for leaving questions blank, and you don't lose any points for getting them wrong. You're better off guessing than leaving questions blank.**

Pace Yourself

The SHSAT gives you a lot of questions in a relatively short period of time. To get through the test, you need to be in control of your pace. Remember, although you should enter an answer for every question, you don't have to answer *every* question correctly to score well. There are a few strategies you can employ to take control of your pace.

- Don't spend too much time on any one question. You can always circle a question and come back to it later.
- Give yourself a rough time limit for each question—move on if you run out of time.
- Be flexible—you can answer questions out of order.
- Don't spend more than 3–4 minutes on any one Reading Passage—keep reading and move on. Remember, your points come from answering the questions.
- Practice under timed conditions.

> **✓ Take Control**
>
> **Taking control of your pace will help you take control of your testing experience.**

Locate Quick Points If You're Running Out of Time

Some questions can be answered more quickly than others. Some are simply amenable to shortcuts. For example, a Reading question that contains a line number or asks for the meaning of an *italicized* word may be easier to answer more quickly than one that does not give you a clue. Other questions will be easier because of your particular strengths. For example, if you're comfortable with geometry and are running out of time, look for the geometry questions.

> **✓ Know Thyself**
>
> **You know your strengths and weaknesses better than anyone else. Use this knowledge to work efficiently.**

CHAPTER 2

Inside the SHSAT

CHAPTER OBJECTIVES

By the end of this chapter, you will be able to:

- Describe the structure of the test, how it is scored, and the timing of each section
- Pace yourself effectively during the test

The SHSAT is a standardized test, which means that it is predictable. Therefore, you can take control and build your confidence by knowing what to expect. When you sit down to take the test, you should know what the test will look like, how it will be scored, and how long you'll have to complete it.

STRUCTURE OF THE TEST

There are two sections on the test: English Language Arts and Math. The English Language Arts section has two question types: Reading and Revising/Editing. Though the Math section has only one question type, you can expect to see arithmetic, algebra, geometry, and other math topics on the test.

English Language Arts Section

The English Language Arts section is the first section on the test. It contains 57 questions and accounts for one-half of your total points on the SHSAT. The suggested time for the section is 90 minutes, or 1 hour and 30 minutes. All 57 questions will be multiple choice.

The breakdown of the English Language Arts section is as follows:

English Language Arts Sub-Section	Sub-Section Breakdown	Total Number of Questions
Revising/Editing Stand-Alone Questions	3–5 questions	9–11 questions
Revising/Editing Passages	1 passage with 6–8 questions	
Reading Comprehension	6 passages with 6–10 questions each	46–48 questions

✔ Know the Test's Structure

You'll see 57 English Language Arts and 57 Math questions on the test. The English Language Arts and Math sections are equally weighted.

Math

The Math section is the second section on the test. It contains 57 questions and accounts for one-half of your total points on the SHSAT. The suggested time for the section is 90 minutes, or 1 hour and 30 minutes.

The breakdown of the Math section is as follows:

Math Sub-Section	Total Number of Questions
Grid-In Questions	5 questions
Multiple-Choice Questions	52 questions

SCORING

Scoring for the SHSAT is a little strange. It's not that the scoring is difficult to understand; it's just that individual scores matter only to the extent that they are above or below a cutoff line.

Here's how the scoring works. First, you get a Raw Score based on the number of questions you answer correctly. The test contains 114 questions. 94 of the questions are worth 1 "raw" point, and 20 are experimental questions that aren't scored. The maximum Raw Score is therefore 94.

Next, your Raw Score is multiplied by a formula known only to the Department of Education to arrive at a scaled score. You receive a scaled score for each section and a Composite Score for the entire test. The highest possible Composite Score is 800.

Admission to all specialized high schools (except LaGuardia) is based solely on your Composite Score. The way this works is that all of the students are ranked from high score to low score and then assigned to the school of their first preference until all the available seats are filled. For example, if Stuyvesant had exactly 500 spaces available and the top 500 scorers all picked Stuyvesant as their first choice, all 500 scorers would be admitted. If the 501st scorer listed Stuyvesant as her first choice and Bronx Science as her second choice, she would be assigned to Bronx Science. In other words, if 500 students were admitted to Stuyvesant and the 500th highest score was 560, then 560 would be the "cutoff" score for Stuyvesant. Therefore, scores are relative; it matters only whether they are above the cutoff, but there is no way of accurately knowing what the cutoff score will be. All you know is that it will likely be a little higher than last year's cutoff because the test becomes increasingly competitive every year.

SHSAT TIMING

When the test begins and you open to the first page, here's what you'll see:

PART 1—English Language Arts

Time—90 Minutes

57 Questions

The most important thing to remember about SHSAT timing suggestions is that they are just that—**suggestions!**

Here's the way it works. You'll have 180 minutes to complete the entire test. It is recommended that you spend approximately half the time (90 minutes or 1 hour and 30 minutes) on each section. However, if you finish the English Language Arts section early, you can move on to the Math section without waiting for the 90 minutes to end. Similarly, if you finish the Math section with time to spare, you can go back over both the Math and English Language Arts sections of the test.

What this means is that you have both the freedom to structure your time and the responsibility to use your time wisely. While you can spend more than 90 minutes working on the first section, it may not be wise to do so. However, the flexibility you have in skipping around and going back to one section after finishing the other gives you ample opportunity to play to your strengths.

PACING

You are responsible for setting your own pace on the test. This is a big responsibility that you should take very seriously. Here are some rough guidelines to follow.

English Language Arts	**Revising/Editing** (11 questions)	$1\text{–}1\frac{1}{2}$ minutes per question
	Reading (6 passages, 46 questions)	2–3 minutes reading each passage, $1\text{–}1\frac{1}{2}$ minutes per question
Math	57 questions: 5 grid-in, 52 multiple-choice	$1\frac{1}{2}$ minutes per question

Remember that these guidelines are estimates. You will spend more time on some questions and less time on others. However, you must be aware of time if you want to maximize your score. If you're casual about it, you could find yourself unexpectedly running out of time.

THE SCHOOLS

In addition to preparing for the test, you should be doing some research about the schools. Remember, if you get accepted into a school, you will be expected to attend. Therefore, you want to make an informed decision here. The best way to get information about the schools is to contact them or check out their websites. Here's the contact information for each school:

Bronx High School of Science
75 West 205th Street
Bronx, NY 10468
(718) 817-7700
www.bxscience.edu

Brooklyn Latin School
223 Graham Avenue
Brooklyn, NY 11206
(718) 366-0154
www.brooklynlatin.org

Brooklyn Technical High School
29 Fort Greene Place
Brooklyn, NY 11217
(718) 804-6400
www.bths.edu

Fiorello H. LaGuardia High School of Music & Art and Performing Arts	100 Amsterdam Avenue New York, NY 10023 (212) 496-0700 *www.laguardiahs.org*
High School for Math, Science and Engineering at the City College of New York	240 Convent Avenue New York, NY 10031 (212) 281-6490 *www.hsmse.org*
High School of American Studies at Lehman College	2925 Goulden Avenue Bronx, NY 10468 (718) 329-2144 *www.hsas-lehman.org*
Queens High School for the Sciences at York College	94-50 159th Street Jamaica, NY 11451 (718) 657-3181 *www.qhss.org*
Staten Island Technical High School	485 Clawson Street Staten Island, NY 10306 (718) 667-3222 *www.siths.org*
Stuyvesant High School	345 Chambers Street New York, NY 10282 (212) 312-4800 *www.stuy.edu*

Do some research. Talk to your parents, teachers, and guidance counselor. Some factors that you may want to consider are these:

- Location
- Age and condition of facilities
- Class size
- School size
- Areas of concentration
- Advanced Placement courses
- Research programs

- Availability of hands-on tech courses
- College courses offered
- Extracurricular activities

Additionally, here are a few trivia facts that you may or may not know about some of the specialized high schools:

- Brooklyn Tech is one of the ten largest high schools in the country, according to *U.S. News and World Report*.
- Stuyvesant was recognized by the President's Commission on Excellence as one of the best schools in the country.
- Five Nobel Prize winners attended Bronx Science: Leon Cooper, 1972; Sheldon Glashow, 1979; Steven Weinberg, 1979; Melvin Schwartz, 1988; Russell A. Hulse, 1993.
- Brooklyn Latin, which opened in 2006, features a curriculum that is focused on the humanities.

TEST DATE

The test is administered during a weekend in late October for eighth graders and during a weekend in late October or early November for ninth graders.

Log on to schools.nyc.gov for updated information.

PART 2

SHSAT English Language Arts

CHAPTER 3

Introducing SHSAT English Language Arts

CHAPTER OBJECTIVES

By the end of this chapter, you will be able to:

- Identify the format and timing of the SHSAT English Language Arts section
- Apply tips and strategies to the SHSAT English Language Arts section

ENGLISH LANGUAGE ARTS OVERVIEW

The English Language Arts section is the first section on the test. It contains 57 questions and accounts for one-half of your total points on the SHSAT. The suggested time for the section is 90 minutes, or 1 hour and 30 minutes.

The breakdown of the English Language Arts section is as follows:

English Language Arts Sub-Section	Sub-Section Breakdown	Total Number of Questions
Revising/Editing Stand-Alone Questions	3–5 questions	9–11 questions
Revising/Editing Passages	1 passage with 6–8 questions	
Reading Comprehension	6 passages with 6–10 questions each	46–48 questions

THE QUESTION TYPES

Revising/Editing Stand-Alone Questions

The beginning of the Revising/Editing section will look like this:

REVISING/EDITING

QUESTIONS 1–11

IMPORTANT NOTE

The Revising/Editing section (Questions 1–11) is in two parts: Part A and Part B.

REVISING/EDITING Part A

DIRECTIONS: Read and answer each of the following questions. You will be asked to recognize and correct errors in sentences or short paragraphs. Mark the **best** answer for each question.

The SHSAT English Language Arts sections include 3–5 Stand-Alone Questions. You will be asked to apply your knowledge of Sentence Structure and Formation; Punctuation; Usage; Knowledge of Language; Organization, Unity, and Cohesion; and Topic Development to answer questions.

Revising/Editing Passages

The beginning of the Revising/Editing Part B section will look like this:

REVISING/EDITING Part B

DIRECTIONS: Read the passage below and answer the questions following it. You will be asked to improve the writing quality of the passage and to correct errors so that the passage follows the conventions of standard written English. You may reread the passage if you need to. Mark the **best** answer for each question.

There is one Revisinq/Editinq Passage with 6–8 questions. You will be asked to apply the same Conventions of Standard English and Knowledge of Language skills you'll use to answer Revising/Editing Stand-Alone Questions.

Reading

The beginning of the Reading section will look like this:

READING COMPREHENSION

QUESTIONS 12–57

DIRECTIONS: Read each passage below and answer the questions following it. Base your answers **on information contained only in the passage**. You may reread a passage if you need to. Mark the **best** answer for each question.

The Reading questions don't exactly test your ability to read. They test your ability to comprehend what you've read. You'll get 6 Reading passages, each of which will be followed by 6–10 questions.

The passages will appear on a variety of topics such as science, social studies, humanities, poetry, and literary fiction.

The 4 Reading question types—Global, Detail, Inference, and Function—test your understanding of what you've read in the passages, so it's crucial to refrain from using outside information when answering questions.

HOW TO APPROACH SHSAT ENGLISH LANGUAGE ARTS

To do well on the SHSAT English Language Arts section, you need to be systematic in your approach. In other words, you need to know how you are going to deal with each question type and the section as a whole before you open the test booklet. You need to know your strengths and weaknesses. For example, if you find Revising/Editing Passages questions easiest, you can jump directly to them and get some quick points. Or you can leave them in the middle to break up the section. It's up to you. You have to be aware of timing. Six Reading passages are a lot. You have to be aware of your time and plan it well. If you spend an hour making certain that all your Revising/Editing Passages questions are correct, you're going to have a difficult time answering the rest of the questions in the remaining 30 minutes.

CHAPTER 4

The Kaplan Methods for Revising/Editing Text & Sentence Structure and Formation

CHAPTER OBJECTIVES

By the end of this chapter, you will be able to:

- Apply the Kaplan Method for Revising/Editing Paragraphs
- Apply the Kaplan Method for Revising/Editing Passages and Sentences
- Identify and correct Sentence Structure and Formation errors

THE KAPLAN METHODS FOR REVISING/EDITING TEXT

You will use the Kaplan Methods for Revising/Editing Text to boost your score on the SHSAT English Language Arts section. Be sure to use these methods for every Revising/Editing question you encounter, whether practicing, completing your homework, working on a Practice Test, or taking the actual exam on Test Day.

There are two Kaplan Methods for Revising/Editing Text: the Kaplan Method for Revising/Editing Paragraphs and the Kaplan Method for Revising/Editing Passages and Sentences.

The Kaplan Method for Revising/Editing Paragraphs

The Kaplan Method for Revising/Editing Paragraphs has two steps:

Step 1: Read the text and identify the issue

Step 2: Select the sentence that should be revised

Let's look at each step.

Step 1: Read the text and identify the issue

Each Revising/Editing Paragraph question will include four sentences. Read each sentence systematically, checking for errors.

Step 2: Select the sentence that should be revised

Only one of the four sentences will include an error. Select the sentence with the error and move right along to the next question.

Try It Out

DIRECTIONS: Read and answer each of the following questions. You will be asked to recognize and correct errors in sentences or short paragraphs. Mark the **best** answer for each question.

1. Read this paragraph.

> (1) Llamas make excellent pets, it is because they are very friendly and are well liked by their owners as a result. (2) In various parts of the world, people have herded llamas in flocks. (3) In South America, llamas helped the Andean civilization thrive in the high mountains. (4) Llamas provide not only wool but also a mode of transportation.

Which sentence should be revised to correct a run-on issue?

A. sentence 1
B. sentence 2
C. sentence 3
D. sentence 4

2. Read this paragraph.

> (1) Given that they often spend a lot of time engaged in solitary pursuits, house cats have gained a reputation for being aloof. (2) Although they can be extremely sociable and affectionate with other felines and humans, cats almost never live in groups as adults. (3) They form dominance hierarchies and refuse to accept new cats. (4) Cats also protect its territory by leaving markings, monitoring their surroundings, and chasing away intruders, and therefore are perceived as nonsocial.

Which sentence contains a usage error and should be revised?

E. sentence 1
F. sentence 2
G. sentence 3
H. sentence 4

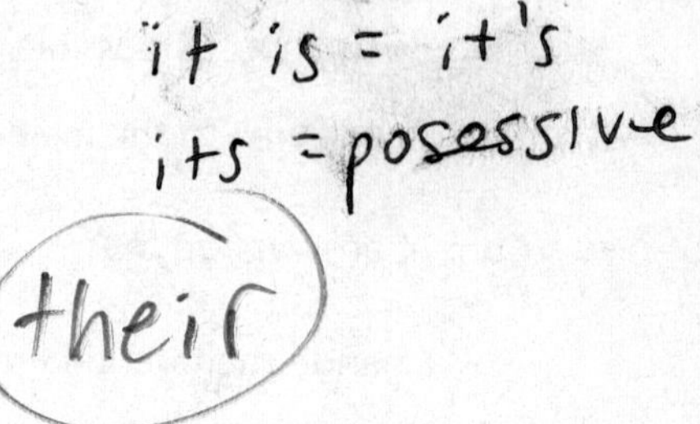

The Kaplan Method for Revising/Editing Passages and Sentences

The Kaplan Method for Revising/Editing Passages and Sentences has three steps:

Step 1: Read the text and identify the issue

Step 2: Eliminate answer choices that do not address the issue

Step 3: Select the choice that creates the most correct, concise, and relevant text

Let's take a closer look at each step.

Step 1: Read the text and identify the issue

Revising/Editing Text questions test Sentence Structure and Formation; Usage; Knowledge of Language; Organization, Unity, and Cohesion; and Topic Development issues. Read until you have enough information to identify the issue.

Step 2: Eliminate answer choices that do not address the issue

Eliminating answer choices that do not address the issue increases your odds of getting the correct answer by removing obviously incorrect answer choices.

Step 3: Select the choice that creates the most correct, concise, and relevant text

Correct, **concise**, and **relevant** means that the text will:

- Make sense when read with the correction
- Be as short as possible while retaining the information in the text
- Relate well to the main idea of the sentence, paragraph, or passage

Correct answers do NOT:

- Change the intended meaning of the original sentence, paragraph, or passage
- Introduce new grammatical errors

Try It Out

DIRECTIONS: Read and answer each of the following questions. You will be asked to recognize and correct errors in sentences or short paragraphs. Mark the **best** answer for each question.

1. Read this sentence.

For the last two weeks in my science class, we have studied how volcanoes are formed, how scientists predict eruptions and how lava and magma differ.

Which edit should be made to correct this sentence?

A. insert a comma after ***studied***

B. insert a comma after ***volcanoes***

C. insert a comma after ***eruptions***

D. insert a comma after ***lava***

2. Read this sentence.

After graduating from high school, Kaylee's plan to attend college in Vermont and to study American literature.

Which edit should be made to correct this sentence?

E. change ***Kaylee's plan*** to **Kaylee plans**

F. change ***Kaylee's plan*** to **Kaylee's plan is**

G. change ***Kaylee's plan*** to **Kaylee's plan will be**

H. change ***Kaylee's plan*** to **Kaylee's plans**

DIRECTIONS: Read the passage below and answer the questions following it. You will be asked to improve the writing quality of the passage and to correct errors so that the passage follows the conventions of standard written English. You may reread the passage if you need to. Mark the **best** answer for each question.

Questions 3–9 refer to the following passage.

Languages

(1) Many native English speakers think that it is pointless to learn a second language because so many people worldwide speak English. (2) It is true that, in many countries, children begin to learn English in elementary school. (3) Also, many adults abroad find that they need to learned English to succeed, particularly in business and the arts.

(4) These facts, while true, not being an excuse for native English speakers to speak only English. (5) There are three main reasons for this. (6) First, one can't fully experience another country in translation. (7) Most native English speakers, when they visit France, can simply speak English with the French. (8) But they would experience so much more if they spoke French. (9) Moreover, we even come to understand our own language and culture better when we learn others.

(10) Second, not everyone speaks English. (11) Many villages in Latin America don't have the funds to teach children to read, let alone to speak English. (12) A native English speaker would need to use Spanish to communicate there.

(13) Finally, and perhaps most importantly, it is arrogant to assume that English is the only important language. (14) In fact, English is not even the most widely spoken language in the world. (15) What does it say about native English speakers that we make everyone cater to us instead of doing our part to meet people halfway, sharing the burden of communication?

(16) Some people understand these concerns and are beginning to realize the benefit of really speaking another language well, so they have created language immersion schools. (17) These schools teach children as young as kindergarten age to speak fluently in a language other than English. (18) In Los Angeles, California, the most popular languages in dual-language schools are Spanish, Korean, and Chinese/Mandarin. (19) Parents for whom these are their native languages often send their children to language immersion schools so they learn their parents' language. (20) There are also many students whose parents' native language is English, but who want their children to learn another language and be as fluent as a native speaker. (21) Children in schools like these not only learn a second language but also a more global and sympathetic view of other nations and people.

3. Which edit is needed to correct sentence 3?

   A. change ***abroad*** to **internationally**

   B. change ***find*** to **have found**

   C. change ***they*** to **foreigners**

   D. change ***to learned*** to **to learn**

4. Which edit is needed to correct sentence 4?

   E. change ***These facts*** to **This fact**

   F. change ***not being an excuse for*** to **are not excuses for**

   G. change ***speak*** to **speaking**

   H. change ***only*** to **just**

5. What is the best way to combine sentences 7 and 8 to clarify the relationship between ideas?

   A. For example, since most native English speakers that visit France can simply speak English, the visitors would experience so much more if they spoke French.

   B. Most native English speakers visiting France could simply speak English, they would experience so much more if they spoke French.

   C. For example, although most native English speakers who visit France can simply speak English, they would experience so much more if they spoke French.

   D. Most native English speakers visit France to only speak English but they would experience so much more if they spoke French.

6. Where is the best place to insert the following sentence?

   However, as a native English speaker I would like to express my disagreement.

   E. after sentence 1

   F. after sentence 3

   G. after sentence 4

   H. after sentence 7

7. Which transition should be added to the beginning of sentence 11?

   A. For instance

   B. However

   C. Despite this

   D. Afterward

8. Which transition should be added to the beginning of sentence 16?

   E. Centuries from now
   F. Afterward
   G. Years ago
   H. Today

9. Including a paragraph on which of the following would most strengthen the writer's argument?

   A. the deteriorating facilities of schools in developing nations
   B. the high percentage of non-native English speakers who do not learn English
   C. examples of arrogance among the very rich
   D. examples of foreign business leaders using English

SENTENCE STRUCTURE AND FORMATION

Fragments and Run-ons

Fragments and run-ons create grammatically incorrect sentences. The SHSAT requires you to apply the specific rules governing sentence construction to Revising/Editing questions.

Fragments

A complete sentence must have a subject and a predicate verb in an independent clause that expresses a complete thought. If any one of these elements is missing, the sentence is a fragment. You can recognize a fragment because the sentence will not make sense as written.

Missing Element	Example
Subject	*Running down the street.*
Predicate verb	*Seth running down the street.*
Complete thought	*While Seth was running down the street.*

Run-ons

If a sentence has more than one independent clause, the clauses must be properly joined. Otherwise, the sentence is a run-on. There are four ways to correct a run-on sentence like this one: *I know how to write a few basic commands in code, I plan to try more difficult programming soon.*

To Correct a Run-On	Example
Separate the clauses into two sentences.	*I know how to write a few basic commands in code**.** I plan to try more difficult programming soon.*
Use a semicolon.	*I know how to write a few basic commands in code**;** I plan to try more difficult programming soon.*
Make one clause dependent.	***Now that** I know how to write a few basic commands in code, I plan to try more difficult programming soon.*
Add a FANBOYS conjunction: *For, And, Nor, But, Or, Yet, So.*	*I know how to write a few basic commands in code, **and** I plan to try more difficult programming soon.*

Try It Out

DIRECTIONS: Read and answer each of the following questions. You will be asked to recognize and correct errors in sentences or short paragraphs. Mark the **best** answer for each question.

1. Read this paragraph.

> (1) Before 1972, colleges could give greater support to men's sports teams; today, women's and men's teams must receive equal funding. (2) Title IX of the Education Amendments prohibits gender discrimination at colleges and other federally funded institutions. (3) Resulting in more money in athletic departments allocated for women's sports. (4) This has led to more interest in these sports, more college scholarships, better competition, and improvements in the quality of athletics for women.

Which sentence should be revised to correct a fragment issue?

A. sentence 1
B. sentence 2
C. sentence 3
D. sentence 4

2. Read this sentence.

> White roses signify unity, yellow roses signify friendship, and red roses signify love however, many people believe red roses are the most cherished flower within that flora.

Which edit should be made to correct this sentence?

E. insert a semicolon after ***signify***
F. insert a comma after ***signify***
G. insert a comma after ***love***
H. insert a semicolon after ***love***

Modifiers

A modifier is a word or a group of words that describes, clarifies, or provides additional information about another part of the sentence. Modifier questions on the SHSAT require you to determine if sentences place appropriate modifiers in grammatically correct locations. In many cases, an introductory phrase or clause will modify the first noun that follows. Use context clues in the passage to identify the correct placement of a modifier; a misplaced modifier can cause confusion.

Modifier/Modifying Phrase	Incorrect	Correct
nearly	*Andre* ***nearly*** *watched the play for four hours.*	*Andre watched the play for* ***nearly*** *four hours.*
in individual containers	*The art teacher handed out paints to students* ***in individual containers.***	*The art teacher handed out paints* ***in individual containers*** *to students.*
A scholar-athlete	***A scholar-athlete****, maintaining high grades in addition to playing soccer were expected of Maya.*	***A scholar-athlete****, Maya was expected to maintain high grades in addition to playing soccer.*

Try It Out

DIRECTIONS: Read and answer each of the following questions. You will be asked to recognize and correct errors in sentences or short paragraphs. Mark the **best** answer for each question.

3. Read this sentence.

> After studying intensively for exams all week, Alexandra's eagerness was great for the upcoming weekend and her family's planned trip to the lake.

Which edit should be made to correct this sentence?

A. change ***intensively*** to **intensive**

B. change ***intensively*** to **intense**

C. change ***Alexandra's eagerness was great*** to **very eager was Alexandra**

D. change ***Alexandra's eagerness was great*** to **Alexandra was very eager**

4. Read this paragraph.

> (1) Most gems are crystallized minerals, but amber, coral, and pearls come from organic material. (2) Amber's buoyancy suggest organic origins; unlike most gemstones, this ancient fossilized resin floats in water. (3) Coral is a discarded limestone skeleton found in the sea. (4) Oysters take several years to form white, black, or pink pearls, which cover them with layers of coating.

Which sentence should be revised to correct a misplaced modifier issue?

E. sentence 1

F. sentence 2

G. sentence 3

H. sentence 4

The following practice sets provide an opportunity to apply the concepts and strategic thinking covered in this chapter. While many of the questions pertain to Sentence Structure and Formation, some touch on other English Language Arts concepts to ensure that your practice is test-like, with a variety of question types. To practice Test Day timing, follow the suggested timing guidelines for each section.

PRACTICE SET

Suggested Timing: 25 minutes

QUESTIONS 1–7: Revising/Editing in a Passage

DIRECTIONS: Read the passage below and answer the questions following it. You will be asked to improve the writing quality of the passage and to correct errors so that the passage follows the conventions of standard written English. You may reread the passage if you need to. Mark the **best** answer for each question.

Archerfish

(1) Few fish find their food outside of the water. (2) Even fewer find their food several feet above the surface. (3) And only one fish hits its food with a concentrated stream of water, thereby knocking its prey into the water. (4) That fish is called the archerfish. (5) They are generally small, from five to ten centimeters, they are capable of growing as large as 40 centimeters.

(6) The archerfish patrols the brackish waters of Southeast Asia and Australia to prey on insects that stray too close to the surface. (7) Lurking just below the surface, the archerfish uses its tongue to send a stream of water up into the air. (8) Elder archerfish have been documented hitting insects six feet away.

(9) The fact that they can shoot a stream of water is impressive, but the accuracy of their shots is astounding. (10) Sending out an accurate shot means that the archer must compensate for both gravity and the refraction of light in water. (11) Gravity is a constant, both underwater and on land, light, however, changes its wavelength as it enters the water. (12) An archerfish looking up at an insect on a branch will not see them where they actually are. (13) Archerfish either compensate for the refraction or shoot from a position directly below an insect, thereby eliminating the angle of refraction altogether.

(14) Interestingly, accurate aiming is not instinctual in the archerfish. (15) As evidenced by young fish that frequently miss the target. (16) To make it better, young fish hunt in small clumps to up the odds that at least one archerfish will be able to do a good job. (17) Archerfish hunting in schools are often far more successful than those that attempt lone pursuits. (18) Accuracy comes with experience, and in one study, was shown to be enhanced by watching older archerfish performing. (19) Archerfish have also been known to actually jump out of the water and catch prey with their mouths if the prey is within reach of how far the fish can jump and catch it. (20) The mantis shrimp is another animal which hunts in a strange way, using its powerful claws to smash its prey.

Practice Set

1. Which edit is needed to correct sentence 5?
   - A. change ***are*** to **is**
   - B. change ***small*** to **minute**
   - C. change ***they*** to **but they**
   - D. change ***growing*** to **grows**

2. Which sentence would best follow and support sentence 6?
   - E. Brackish water is a mixture of salt and freshwater.
   - F. These insects include moths, beetles, and grasshoppers.
   - G. Archerfish do not eat shellfish.
   - H. Archerfish prefer live prey.

3. Which edit is needed to correct sentence 11?
   - A. change ***is*** to **are**
   - B. change ***land,*** to **land;**
   - C. change ***its*** to **it's**
   - D. change ***as*** to **for**

4. What edit is needed to correct sentence 12?
   - E. change ***looking*** to **looks**
   - F. change ***an insect*** to **insects**
   - G. change ***see*** to **seeing**
   - H. change ***they*** to **it**

5. What is the best way to combine sentences 14 and 15?
   - A. Interestingly, accurate aiming is not instinctual in the archerfish; as evidenced by young fish that frequently miss the target.
   - B. Interestingly, accurate aiming is not instinctual in the archerfish but as evidenced by young fish that frequently miss the target.
   - C. Interestingly, accurate aiming is not instinctual in the archerfish, as evidenced by young fish that frequently miss the target.
   - D. Interestingly, accurate aiming is not instinctual in the archerfish, young fish that frequently miss the target.

6. Which revision of sentence 16 uses the most precise language?

   E. To make it better, young fish hunt in small groups to increase the odds that at least one archerfish will be able to do a good job.

   F. To make it better, young fish hunt in small groups to increase the odds that at least one archerfish will be able to catch prey.

   G. To compensate for this, young fish hunt in small clumps to up the odds that at least one archerfish will be able to do a good job.

   H. To compensate for this, young fish hunt in small groups to increase the odds that at least one archerfish will be able to catch prey.

7. Which sentence is irrelevant to the passage and should be deleted?

   A. sentence 17

   B. sentence 18

   C. sentence 19

   D. sentence 20

Questions 8–20: Revising/Editing Stand-Alone Items

DIRECTIONS: Read and answer each of the following questions. You will be asked to recognize and correct errors in sentences or short paragraphs. Mark the **best** answer for each question.

8. Read this paragraph.

> (1) Al Hirschfeld, whose caricatures were often featured in the *New York Times*, became famous for incorporating into all of his drawings his daughter's name, which is Nina. (2) In the 1920s, he began drawing political cartoons for newspapers and magazines, which captured readers' attention. (3) When he drew Broadway performers and other celebrities, he conveyed his interest in people and their expressive faces. (4) Famous museums now display some of the artistic creations that Hirschfeld produced over the course of at least 65 years.

Which sentence should be revised to correct a misplaced modifier issue?

E. sentence 1
F. sentence 2
G. sentence 3
H. sentence 4

9. Read this sentence.

> The amount of water used by Americans can be reduced by turning off faucets when not in use, decreasing time spent in showers and running washing machines less frequently.

Which edit should be made to correct this sentence?

A. insert a comma after ***Americans***
B. insert a comma after ***faucets***
C. insert a comma after ***showers***
D. insert a comma after ***machines***

10. Read this sentence.

> The student council officers agreed to meet in two weeks in the schools library to discuss a number of issues affecting the community.

Which edit should be made to correct this sentence?

E. change ***officers*** to **officers'**
F. change ***weeks*** to **weeks'**
G. change ***weeks*** to **week's**
H. change ***schools*** to **school's**

11. Read this sentence.

> Winter weather provides us with the opportunity to do so many outdoor activities, we can ski down mountains, skate on ice, make snowmen, and glide downhill on a snowboard.

Which edit should be made to correct this sentence?

A. replace the comma after ***activities*** with a semicolon

B. replace the comma after ***mountains*** with a semicolon

C. replace the comma after ***ice*** with a semicolon

D. replace the comma after ***snowmen*** with a semicolon

12. Read this sentence.

> The professor, after distributing samples of igneous lava explained that this type of rock is initially liquid magma and is formed under intense heat and pressure deep within the earth.

Which edit should be made to correct this sentence?

E. insert comma after ***lava***

F. insert comma after ***explained***

G. insert comma after ***intense***

H. insert comma after ***deep***

13. Read this sentence.

> At my favorite restaurant, the waiters sing as they serve the food, their tips are much higher than those of servers at other restaurants.

Which edit should be made to correct this sentence?

A. remove the comma after ***restaurant***

B. remove the comma after ***food***

C. replace the comma after ***food*** with a semicolon

D. insert a comma after ***servers***

Practice Set

14. Read this sentence.

> The electric fan was an ingenious invention for keeping people cool during the summer it was popular only briefly, however, until the air conditioner was invented.

Which edit should be made to correct this sentence?

E. insert a semicolon after ***invention***

F. insert a comma after ***invention***

G. insert a comma after ***summer***

H. insert a semicolon after ***summer***

15. Read this sentence.

> Miss Adams, our swim team coach chose Sarah to swim the final lap of the three-person relay race at last week's competition in Brooklyn.

Which edit should be made to correct this sentence?

A. delete the comma after ***Miss Adams***

B. insert a comma after ***coach***

C. insert a comma after ***lap***

D. insert a comma after ***competition***

16. Read this sentence.

> My classmate, Jacob said that yesterday's basketball practice involved several sets of intense long running drills.

Which edit should be made to correct this sentence?

E. insert a comma after ***classmate***

F. insert a comma after ***said***

G. insert a comma after ***basketball***

H. insert a comma after ***intense***

17. Read this sentence.

> When asked to name my favorite baseball team, the Yankees is my choice because they always have amazing players and have an impressive history.

Which edit should be made to correct this sentence?

A. change ***the Yankees is my choice*** to **I choose the Yankees**

B. change ***the Yankees is my choice*** to **the Yankees**

C. change ***amazing*** to **amazingly**

D. change ***impressive*** to **impressively**

18. Read this sentence.

> The special effects used in todays movies would have been unimaginable as recently as ten years ago.

Which edit should be made to correct this sentence?

E. change ***effects*** to **effect's**

F. change ***todays*** to **today's**

G. change ***movies*** to **movies'**

H. change ***years*** to **year's**

19. Read this sentence.

> The successful fundraising campaign for the school's field trip continued for a week teachers counted money every morning with growing amazement.

Which edit should be made to correct this sentence?

A. insert a comma after ***successful***

B. insert a comma after ***week***

C. insert a semicolon after ***week***

D. insert a semicolon after ***money***

20. Read this sentence.

> In his speech to the whole school, our principal announced that we would have more exciting enjoyable field trips this year than last year.

Which edit should be made to correct this sentence?

E. insert a comma after ***speech***

F. insert a comma after ***principal***

G. insert a comma after ***exciting***

H. insert a comma after ***enjoyable***

ANSWERS AND EXPLANATIONS

The Kaplan Method for Revising/Editing Paragraphs

1. A

Category: Sentence Structure and Formation

Getting to the Answer: When the paragraph includes a complex sentence, be sure that it is not a run-on. In **(A)**, two independent clauses are improperly joined by a comma. **(B)**, **(C)**, and **(D)** have grammatically correct sentences.

2. H

Category: Usage

Getting to the Answer: When a sentence includes a pronoun, check to see if it matches the antecedent (the noun to which it refers). The pronoun "its" is singular, but the antecedent "[c]ats" is plural, so **(H)** is correct. Sentence 4 should have the plural pronoun "their" to match the plural antecedent "[c]ats." **(E)**, **(F)**, and **(G)** reflect correct usage.

The Kaplan Method for Revising/Editing Passages and Sentences

1. C

Category: Sentence Structure and Formation

Getting to the Answer: When a sentence has a list of three or more items, check that commas follow each item before the conjunction "and." In this sentence, since there is a list of three items, a comma is needed after "eruptions." **(C)** is correct. **(A)** is incorrect because no pause is needed after the verb "studied." **(B)** wrongly places a comma after "volcanoes," interrupting the phrase "how volcanoes have formed." **(D)** is incorrect because if there are only two items in a list, such as "lava" and "magma," a comma is not needed.

2. E

Category: Usage

Getting to the Answer: When a sentence has an introductory phrase, make sure it is followed by what the phrase logically describes. As written, the phrase "after graduating from high school" logically describes "Kaylee" rather than "Kaylee's plan." **(E)** corrects the error by changing the possessive form "Kaylee's" to the subject "Kaylee." **(F)**, **(G)**, and **(H)** are all incorrect because the introductory phrase is still followed by "Kaylee's plan."

Languages

3. D

Category: Usage

Getting to the Answer: The verb phrase "to learned" is incorrect—the sentence requires the present tense verb "learn." **(D)** fixes the error. **(C)** is unnecessary; "they" clearly refers to "many people abroad." **(A)** also makes an unnecessary change; either word is correct. **(B)** is inappropriate; the logic of the sentence is that these adults currently "find" this to be true; and even if you thought the idea could be in the past tense, there would be no reason for the perfect tense.

4. F

Category: Usage

Getting to the Answer: The *–ing* form of a verb by itself can never be a sentence's predicate verb. Sentence 4 is a fragment; it has no verb. Only **(F)** corrects the error.

5. C

Category: Organization

Getting to the Answer: The relationship between the sentences needs to be clarified. Sentence 7 makes a statement and sentence 8 explains why people should not adhere to the statement. **(C)** shows this relationship with the contrasting transition word "although," removes the plural noun "French [speakers]" from the first clause (so "they" clearly refers to the English speakers), and uses "who" in reference to people. **(A)** incorrectly uses the causal transition word "since." **(B)** omits "for example," which clarifies the relationship with sentence 5, and omits a contrasting transition word. **(D)** changes the meaning to say that English speakers visit France to speak English.

6. E

Category: Organization

Getting to the Answer: The sentence expresses disagreement, so it must contrast with the preceding sentence. The writer argues that native English speakers should learn a second language, so she disagrees with sentence 1, and **(E)** is the correct choice. There is nothing in the passage to suggest that the author disagrees with sentence 3, as **(F)** would indicate. **(G)** is a statement that the author makes and therefore agrees with. **(H)** would interrupt the idea in sentences 7 and 8 that English speakers miss out by speaking only English in France.

7. A

Category: Organization

Getting to the Answer: Sentence 11 provides an example of the statement presented in Sentence 10. "For instance" provides a perfect transition, making **(A)** correct. **(B)** and **(C)** are contrast transitions, and **(D)** implies a sequence the writer does not mention.

8. H

Category: Organization

Getting to the Answer: Sentence 16 introduces current feelings about learning multiple languages, so **(H)** is the appropriate transition. **(E)**, **(F)**, and **(G)** do not make sense in context.

9. B

Category: Topic Development

Getting to the Answer: The passage argues that native English speakers should learn foreign languages and gives three specific reasons why. **(B)** would add statistics to bolster the second reason—that not everyone speaks English. **(A)** and **(C)** are Out of Scope; the writer doesn't discuss deteriorating schools, and the writer argues that native English speakers, not rich people, are arrogant. **(D)** expands on details from the passage that do not affect the argument.

Sentence Structure and Formation

1. C

Category: Sentence Structure and Formation

Getting to the Answer: A complete sentence should have a subject and a predicate verb and express a complete thought. Sentence 3 lacks a predicate verb, so the answer is **(C)**. **(A)**, **(B)**, and **(D)** are complete sentences.

2. H

Category: Sentence Structure and Formation

Getting to the Answer: Two independent clauses within a sentence need to be properly joined with a conjunction or a semicolon; otherwise, the sentence is a run-on. In this sentence, the first independent clause ends with the word "love," so a semicolon should be placed after "love." **(H)** is correct. **(E)** and **(F)** are incorrect, since either a semicolon or a comma after "signify" creates an awkward pause. **(G)** is incorrect because adding a comma after the independent clause does not fix the run-on problem.

3. D

Category: Sentence Structure and Formation

Getting to the Answer: When a sentence has an introductory phrase, make sure it is followed by what the phrase describes. As written, the phrase "after studying intensively for exams all week" logically describes "Alexandra" rather than "Alexandra's eagerness." **(D)** correctly places "Alexandra was very eager" after the introductory phrase. **(A)** results in the awkward phrase "studying intensive." Likewise, **(B)** results in the awkward phrase "studying intense." **(C)** does not fix the issue because "Alexandra" should come right after the opening phrase.

4. H

Category: Sentence Structure and Formation

Getting to the Answer: Modifiers should be close to the words they modify. In the last sentence, "which cover them" could refer either to oysters or pearls. Instead, the sentence could begin with "Oysters cover pearls with layers." **(E)**, **(F)**, and **(G)** have clear sentences, so **(H)** is correct.

PRACTICE SET

Archerfish

1. C

Category: Sentence Structure and Formation

Getting to the Answer: Sentence 5 is a run-on, combining two independent clauses ("They...10 centimeters" and "they...40 centimeters") with just a comma. **(C)** fixes the error by adding the coordinating conjunction "but" after the comma. None of the other answer choices addresses the issue.

2. F

Category: Topic Development

Getting to the Answer: Any additional sentence has to make sense in context, and, in this case, support the previous sentence. Sentence 6 notes that archerfish prey on insects, and **(F)** identifies these insects, directly supporting the sentence. The other answer choices do not fit in context.

3. B

Category: Sentence Structure and Formation

Getting to the Answer: **(B)** correctly uses a semicolon to separate the two independent clauses. **(A)**, **(C)**, and **(D)** do not fix the run-on error.

4. F

Category: Usage

Getting to the Answer: As written, the plural pronouns "them" and "they" do not agree with the singular antecedent "insect." **(F)** corrects the error by changing "an insect" to the plural word "insects." The other choices not only do not fix the error but also introduce new issues.

5. C

Category: Sentence Structure and Formation

Getting to the Answer: Sentence 15 is a fragment. Joining it to Sentence 14 with a comma creates a grammatically correct sentence, so **(C)** is correct. **(A)** incorrectly joins an independent clause and a dependent clause with a semicolon. **(B)** joins the two sentences with a coordinating conjunction ("but"), which creates one long fragment. **(D)** combines the two clauses with a comma but does not include the phrase "as evidenced by," which creates a fragment.

6. H

Category: Knowledge of Language

Getting to the Answer: Sentence 16 uses vague and imprecise language and needs to be corrected. **(H)** is the only choice that consistently uses precise and specific language.

7. D

Category: Topic Development

Getting to the Answer: Read each of the answer choices in context to find one which is not on the same topic as the entire passage. The information about the mantis shrimp, **(D)**, while interesting, is off topic and should be deleted. The other answer choices are all relevant to the passage's topic of the archerfish.

8. F

Category: Sentence Structure and Formation

Getting to the Answer: Modifiers should be close to the words they modify. In the second sentence, the cartoons, newspapers, or magazines could be the things "which captured readers' attention." In **(F)**, the sentence could include "he captured readers' attention when he began." **(E)**, **(G)**, and **(H)** do not have issues.

9. C

Category: Sentence Structure and Formation

Getting to the Answer: When a sentence has a list of at least three items, check that commas follow each item before the conjunction "and." In this sentence, since there is a list of three things people can do to reduce the amount of water they use, a comma is needed after "showers." **(C)** is correct. **(A)** is incorrect because we do not need to pause between the noun "Americans" and the verb "can." **(B)** wrongly places a comma after "faucets," interrupting the phrase "turning off faucets when not in use." Likewise, **(D)** is incorrect because no pause is needed after "machines."

10. H

Category: Sentence Structure and Formation

Getting to the Answer: Possessive forms of nouns show ownership. Be on the lookout for nouns that should be made possessive. In this sentence, "schools library" should be changed to the possessive form "school's library." Choice **(H)** is correct. **(E)** is incorrect because we cannot put a possessive before the verb "agreed." **(F)** and **(G)** wrongly turn "weeks" into possessive forms when no ownership follows.

11. A

Category: Sentence Structure and Formation

Getting to the Answer: Two independent clauses within a sentence need to be properly joined with a conjunction or a semicolon. If independent clauses are joined only with a comma, the sentence is a run-on. In this sentence, the first independent clause ends after the word "activities." Choice **(A)** correctly replaces the comma after "activities" with a semicolon. In the second independent clause, we have a list of winter activities. Items in a list should be separated with commas rather than with semicolons, making **(B)**, **(C)**, and **(D)** incorrect.

12. E

Category: Sentence Structure and Formation

Getting to the Answer: If a phrase within a sentence is not essential to the sentence structure, it should be set off with commas. The phrase "after distributing samples of igneous lava" should be set off with commas since it can be separated from the rest of the sentence. **(E)** is correct since it provides the necessary comma after "lava." **(F)** wrongly adds a comma after the verb "explained." **(G)** and **(H)** insert commas that interrupt the flow of the sentence.

13. C

Category: Sentence Structure and Formation

Getting to the Answer: Sentences with two independent clauses need to be properly joined with a conjunction or a semicolon. If independent clauses are joined only with a comma, the sentence is a run-on. **(C)** is correct because it replaces the comma after "food" with a semicolon. **(A)** is incorrect because a comma is needed after an introductory phrase. **(B)** is incorrect because removing the comma does not fix the run-on problem. **(D)** adds a comma after "servers," interrupting the flow of the second clause.

14. H

Category: Sentence Structure and Formation

Getting to the Answer: Two independent clauses within a sentence need to be properly joined with a conjunction or a semicolon; otherwise, the sentence is a run-on. In this sentence, the first independent clause ends with the word "summer," so a semicolon should be placed after "summer." **(H)** is correct. **(E)** and **(F)** are incorrect since either a semicolon or a comma after "invention" creates an awkward pause. **(G)** is incorrect because adding a comma after the independent clause does not fix the run-on problem.

15. B

Category: Sentence Structure and Formation

Getting to the Answer: If a phrase within a sentence is not essential to the sentence structure, it should be marked off with commas. The phrase "our swim team coach" should be set off with commas since it can be separated from the rest of the sentence. **(B)** is correct. **(A)** makes the sentence harder to read by deleting the comma after "Miss Adams." **(C)** and **(D)** insert commas in wrong places, interrupting the flow of the sentence.

16. H

Category: Sentence Structure and Formation

Getting to the Answer: When a sentence has multiple adjectives to describe a noun, check to see if a comma is needed between the adjectives. In this sentence, the "running drills" are both "intense" and "long," so we need a comma between "intense" and "long." **(H)** is correct. **(E)** is incorrect because we do not pause between "classmate" and "Jacob." Likewise, **(F)** wrongly places a comma after "said." The comma in **(G)** creates an awkward pause between "basketball" and "practice."

17. A

Category: Sentence Structure and Formation

Getting to the Answer: When a sentence has an introductory phrase, make sure it is followed by what the phrase logically describes. As written, the opening phrase describes a person rather than the team "the Yankees." **(A)** fixes the problem by replacing "the Yankees is my choice" with "I choose the Yankees." **(B)** does not address the mistake because "the Yankees" follows the opening phrase. **(C)** and **(D)** wrongly change the adjectives "amazing" and "impressive" to adverbs.

18. F

Category: Sentence Structure and Formation

Getting to the Answer: Possessive forms of nouns show ownership. Be on the lookout for nouns that should be made possessive. In this sentence, "todays movies" should be changed to the possessive form "today's movies." **(F)** is correct. **(E)** and **(G)** turn the wrong nouns into possessives since "effects" and "movies" are each followed by verbs. **(H)** makes "years" possessive, but that is incorrect since "ago" cannot be possessive.

19. C

Category: Sentence Structure and Formation

Getting to the Answer: Independent clauses must be joined by an appropriate conjunction or a semicolon; otherwise, the sentence is a run-on. As written, "The successful fundraising campaign for the school's field trip continued for a week" and "teachers counted money every morning with growing amazement" are two independent clauses improperly joined. **(C)** correctly places a semicolon between them. **(B)** only inserts a comma after "week," which results in a run-on sentence. No comma is needed after "successful," making **(A)** incorrect. **(D)** is incorrect because no punctuation is necessary after "money."

20. G

Category: Sentence Structure and Formation

Getting to the Answer: When a sentence has multiple adjectives to describe a noun, check to see if a comma is needed between the adjectives. In this sentence, the "field trips" are both "exciting" and "enjoyable," so we need a comma between "exciting" and "enjoyable." **(G)** is correct. **(E)** inserts a comma after "speech," which interrupts the flow of the phrase "In his speech to the whole school." **(F)** incorrectly places a comma between the subject "principal" and the verb "announced." **(H)** is incorrect because it places the comma after the adjectives "exciting" and "enjoyable" rather than between them.

CHAPTER 5

Punctuation & Usage

CHAPTER OBJECTIVES

By the end of this chapter, you will be able to:

- Apply the Kaplan Methods to answer Punctuation questions
- Identify and correct Punctuation errors
- Apply the Kaplan Methods to answer Usage questions
- Identify and correct Usage errors

PUNCTUATION & USAGE

Punctuation

The SHSAT requires you to identify inappropriate commas, semicolons, colons, dashes, and apostrophes when they are used to indicate breaks in thought within a sentence. When you identify a Punctuation question, check to make sure the punctuation is used correctly in context.

Commas

Use commas to...	Example
Separate independent clauses connected by a FANBOYS conjunction (*For, And, Nor, But, Or, Yet, So*)	*Jess finished her homework earlier than expected, so she started a project that was due the following week.*
Separate an introductory or modifying phrase from the rest of the sentence	*Knowing that soccer practice would be especially strenuous, Tia spent extra time stretching beforehand.*
Set off three or more items in a series or list	*Jeremiah packed a sleeping bag, a raincoat, and a lantern for his upcoming camping trip.*
Separate nonessential information from the rest of the sentence	*Professor Mann, who is the head of the English department, is known for the extensive assignments in his courses.*
Separate a dependent and an independent clause	*When it started to thunder, the lifeguards quickly ushered swimmers out of the pool.*
Separate coordinate adjectives	*Yogurt is a tasty, nutritious snack that is a good source of probiotics.*

✔ Expert Tip

When deciding if you need a comma between two adjectives, make sure you can (1) replace the comma with the word "and" and (2) reverse the order of the adjectives without altering the meaning of the sentence.

Semicolons

Use semicolons to...	Example
Join two independent clauses that are not connected by a FANBOYS conjunction	*Gaby knew that her term paper would take at least four more hours to write; she got started in study hall and then finished it at home.*
Separate items in a series or list if those items already include commas	*The team needed to bring uniforms, helmets, and gloves; oranges, almonds, and water; and hockey sticks, pucks, and skates.*

Colons

Use colons to...	Example
Introduce and/or emphasize a short phrase, quotation, explanation, example, or list	*Sanjay had two important projects to complete: a science experiment and an expository essay.*

Dashes

Use dashes to...	Example
Indicate a hesitation or a break in thought	*Going to a history museum is a good way to begin researching prehistoric creatures—on second thought, heading to the library would likely be much more efficient.*
Set off explanatory elements within a sentence	*Rockwell's Space Transportation Systems Division handled all facets—design, development, and testing—of the reusable orbiter.*

Apostrophes

Use an apostrophe to...	Example
Indicate the possessive form of a single noun	*My oldest* ***sister's*** *soccer game is on Saturday.*
Indicate the possessive form of a plural noun	*My two older* ***sisters'*** *soccer games are on Saturday.*
Indicate a contraction (e.g., *don't, can't*)	***They've*** *won every soccer match this season.*

✔ Expert Tip

To check whether *it's* is appropriate, replace it in the sentence with *it is* or *it has*. If the sentence no longer makes sense, *it's* is incorrect.

The tree frog blends perfectly into its surroundings. When it holds still, it's nearly invisible.

Try It Out

DIRECTIONS: Read and answer each of the following questions. You will be asked to recognize and correct errors in sentences or short paragraphs. Mark the **best** answer for each question.

1. Read this sentence.

> Unable to decide between a career in law and one in medicine Jemma combined her two interests and studied forensic medicine.

Which edit should be made to correct this sentence?

A. insert a comma after ***law***

B. insert a comma after ***medicine***

C. insert a comma after ***interests***

D. insert a comma after ***forensic***

2. Read this paragraph.

> (1) Often, the winner of an election is the candidate who best masters the art of the political advertisement. (2) Most voters have a stake in the issues of the day but cannot make sense of the rules and rhetoric of the real processes of government. (3) The thirty-second commercial on prime-time television—making sense out of technical political jargon plays a crucial part in the political process. (4) Those who wish to speak for an electorate must make their case to that electorate, and the political advertisement is the most direct and effective way to achieve that goal.

Which sentence should be revised to correct a punctuation error?

E. sentence 1

F. sentence 2

G. sentence 3

H. sentence 4

3. Read this paragraph.

> (1) Bicycling is a mainstream form of transportation in Japanese cities. (2) Nearly every type of person uses a bicycle, blue-collar workers, well-dressed businesspeople, parents toting babies, and students. (3) In the United States, however, bicycling is more often seen as a recreational activity or form of exercise than as a means of transportation. (4) The single exception is among American children, who often rely on bikes, given their more limited transportation options.

Which sentence should be revised to correct a punctuation error?

A. sentence 1

B. sentence 2

C. sentence 3

D. sentence 4

4. Read this sentence.

> Although the statue was intended, in ancient times, to tower above the landscape, it's presence is now dominated by the enormous skyscrapers that came with the city's modernization.

Which edit should be made to correct this sentence?

E. change ***Although*** to **However**

F. change ***above*** to **through**

G. change ***it's*** to **its**

H. change ***by*** to **with**

Usage

Agreement

Subject-Verb Agreement

A verb must agree with its subject in person and number:

Singular: *The apple tastes delicious.*

Plural: *Apples taste delicious.*

The noun closest to the verb is not always the subject: *The chair with the cabriole legs is an antique.* The singular verb in this sentence, *is*, is closest to the plural noun *legs*. However, the verb's actual subject is the singular noun *chair*, so the sentence is correct as written.

Only the conjunction *and* forms a compound subject requiring a plural verb form:

Saliyah and Taylor are in the running club.

Either Saliyah or Taylor is in the running club.

Neither Saliyah nor Taylor is in the running club.

Pronoun-Antecedent Agreement

A pronoun is a word that takes the place of a noun. Pronouns must agree with their antecedents not only in person and number but also in gender.

Gender	Example
Feminine	*Because Yvonne had a question,* ***she*** *raised her hand.*
Masculine	*Since* ***he*** *had lots of homework, Rico started working right away.*
Neutral	*The rain started slowly, but then* ***it*** *became a downpour.*
Unspecified	*If a traveler is lost,* ***he*** *or* ***she*** *should ask for directions.*

Modifier Agreement

A modifier is a word or group of words that describes, clarifies, or provides more information about another part of the sentence.

Adjectives are single-word modifiers that describe nouns and pronouns: *Ian conducted an* ***efficient*** *lab experiment.*

Adverbs are single-word modifiers that describe verbs, adjectives, or other adverbs: *Ian* ***efficiently*** *conducted a lab experiment.*

Verb Tense and Pronoun Case

Verb Tense

Verb tense indicates when an action or state of being took place: past, present, or future. Each tense has three forms: simple, progressive, and perfect. Don't worry about the names of verb tenses, just their correct usage.

	Past	Present	Future
Simple: Actions that occur at some point in time	*She **studied** two extra hours before her math test.*	*She **studies** diligently.*	*She **will study** tomorrow for her French test.*
Progressive: Actions that are ongoing at some point in time	*She **was studying** yesterday for a French test today.*	*She **is studying** today for her math test tomorrow.*	*She **will be studying** tomorrow for her physics test next week.*
Perfect: Actions that are completed at some point in time	*She **had studied** two extra hours before she took her math test yesterday.*	*She **has studied** diligently every day this semester.*	*She **will have studied** each chapter before her physics test next week.*

Pronoun Cases

There are three pronoun cases, each of which is used based on the context of the sentence.

Case	Pronouns	Example
Subjective: The pronoun is used as the subject	I, you, she, he, it, we, you, they, who	*Rivka is the student **who** will lead the presentation.*
Objective: The pronoun is used as the object of a verb or a preposition	me, you, her, him, it, us, you, them, whom	*With **whom** will Rivka present the scientific findings?*
Possessive: The pronoun expresses ownership	my, mine, your, yours, his, her, hers, its, our, ours, their, theirs, whose	*Rivka will likely choose a partner **whose** work is excellent.*

✔ Expert Tip

When there are two pronouns or a noun and a pronoun in a compound structure, drop the other noun or pronoun to confirm which case to use. For example: *Leo and me walked into town.* Would you say, "Me walked into town"? No, you would say, "I walked into town." Therefore, the correct case is subjective, and the original sentence should read: *Leo and I walked into town.*

Try It Out

DIRECTIONS: Read and answer each of the following questions. You will be asked to recognize and correct errors in sentences or short paragraphs. Mark the **best** answer for each question.

1. Read this sentence.

> The most successful scientists are often theorists who sees beyond the facts and speculate about the general principles that underlie them.

Which edit should be made to correct this sentence?

A. change ***are*** to **is**

B. change ***sees*** to **see**

C. change ***speculate*** to **speculates**

D. change ***them*** to **it**

2. Read this paragraph.

> (1) Sandstone, limestone, and shale are three of the most common water-made rocks, and it all can play a role in fossil creation. (2) Shale is composed of mud, often distinct layers that have dried together, and usually it is formed by erosion from landmasses. (3) By contrast, sandstone and limestone often come from the ocean bottom. (4) Sandstone is made up of grains of sand that, with the help of water, have adhered to one another over time, often trapping and fossilizing simple sea creatures and plants in the process.

Which sentence should be revised to correct a pronoun error?

E. sentence 1

F. sentence 2

G. sentence 3

H. sentence 4

Comparative/Superlative, Idioms, and Misused Words

Comparative/Superlative

When comparing like things, use adjectives that match the number of items being compared. When comparing two items or people, use the comparative form of the adjective. When comparing three or more items or people, use the superlative form.

Comparative (two items)	Superlative (three or more items)
better, more, newer, older, shorter, taller, worse, younger	best, most, newest, oldest, shortest, tallest, worst, youngest

Idioms

An idiom is a combination of words that must be used together to convey either a figurative or literal meaning. Idioms are tested in three ways on the SHSAT:

1. Proper Preposition Usage in Context: The preposition must reflect the writer's intended meaning.

   *She waits **on** customers.*

   *She waits **for** the bus.*

   *She waits **with** her friends.*

2. Idiomatic Expressions: Some words or phrases must be used together to be correct.

   *Simone will **either** bike **or** run to the park.*

   ***Neither** the principal **nor** the teachers will tolerate tardiness.*

   *This fall, Shari is playing **not only** soccer **but also** field hockey.*

3. Implicit Double Negatives: Some words imply a negative and therefore cannot be paired with an explicit negative.

   *Janie **can hardly** wait for vacation.*

Frequently Tested Prepositions	Idiomatic Expressions	Words That Can't Pair with Negative Words
at	as . . . as	barely
by	between . . . and	hardly
for	both . . . and	scarcely
from	either . . . or	
of	neither . . . nor	
on	just as . . . so too	
to	not only . . . but also	
with	prefer . . . to	

Misused Words

English contains many pairs of words that sound alike but are spelled differently and have different meanings.

Accept: to take or receive something that is offered	*My niece **accepts** her pile of birthday gifts with great enthusiasm.*
Except: with the exclusion of	*All of the presents are toys **except** for a box containing a popular book series.*

Affect: to act on, to have influence on something	*The dreary, rainy weather negatively **affected** Rahul's mood.*
Effect: something that is produced by a cause; a consequence	*A recent study explored the **effects** of weather on mental well-being.*

Whose: a possessive pronoun	***Whose** uniform shirt is this?*
Who's: a contraction meaning "who is"	***Who's** responsible for ordering new uniforms?*

Its: a possessive pronoun for a singular, gender-neutral noun or pronoun	*A sunflower is not just a pretty plant; **its** oil and seeds are quite useful.*
It's: a contraction of "it is"	***It's** common for some sunflower varieties to grow as tall as 12 feet.*

Their: a possessive pronoun for a plural noun or pronoun	*The college students plan to travel internationally after **their** graduation.*
They're: a contraction for "they are"	***They're** going to visit several countries in East Asia.*
There: at a certain point or place	*The students are excited to experience the foods and cultures **there**.*
There's: a contraction for "there is"	***There's** a tour of an ancient palace that they're looking forward to seeing.*

Try It Out

DIRECTIONS: Read and answer each of the following questions. You will be asked to recognize and correct errors in sentences or short paragraphs. Mark the **best** answer for each question.

3. Read this sentence.

> In the Middle Ages, when women were not hardly allowed to venture outside the domestic realm, Christine de Pisan became an acclaimed poet and is considered the first woman in France to have earned renown as a writer.

Which edit should be made to correct this sentence?

A. change ***when*** to **where**

B. change ***were not*** to **were**

C. change ***outside*** to **beyond**

D. change ***renown*** to **renowned**

4. Read this paragraph.

> (1) Translating any work is a much more complex process than simply exchanging one word for another, and the affect of a superbly translated play on an audience can be profound. (2) The script for a play is not a work to be appreciated on its own, but rather a map used to create such a work. (3) Since the audience for a play will rarely view the script itself, all of the plot points, emotions, subtleties—all of the meaning—must be transmitted simply through spoken dialogue. (4) Granted, when translating between languages that are closely related, a near word-for-word process can sometimes be sufficient.

Which sentence should be revised to correct a word choice issue?

E. sentence 1

F. sentence 2

G. sentence 3

H. sentence 4

The following practice sets provide an opportunity to apply the concepts and strategic thinking covered in this chapter. While many of the questions pertain to Punctuation and Usage, some touch on other English Language Arts concepts to ensure that your practice is test-like, with a variety of question types. To practice Test Day timing, follow the suggested timing guidelines for each section.

PRACTICE SET

Suggested Timing: 25 minutes

QUESTIONS 1–7: Revising/Editing in a Passage

DIRECTIONS: Read the passage below and answer the questions following it. You will be asked to improve the writing quality of the passage and to correct errors so that the passage follows the conventions of standard written English. You may reread the passage if you need to. Mark the **best** answer for each question.

Jean Piaget

(1) The study of mollusks and the formulation of a theory of the way children think may not seem like a rung of the same career ladder, but that's exactly what they were for Jean Piaget. (2) Piaget was born in Switzerland in 1896. (3) He studied at the University of Neuchatel. (4) He eventually received a doctorate in the natural sciences. (5) While observing the mollusks living in the region's many lakes, Piaget saw biological changes occurring in the creatures that could only be attributed to its environment.

(6) In 1918, Piaget moved to Zurich and switched his focus from natural science to psychology. (7) Eventually, he concluded that a person's mental development, like his or her physical growth, could be profoundly affected by the environment in which it took place. (8) He continued his studies at the Sorbonne in Paris. (9) Where he began focusing on the cognitive development of children. (10) B.F. Skinner and Albert Bandura also studied child development.

(11) Piaget's theory of cognitive development posited four stages. (12) He called the first phase, from birth to 24 months of age, the sensorimotor. (13) In this stage babies and very young children are driven primarily by basic actions such as sucking and looking at the world around them. (14) They also begin to realize that their actions, such as crying, can produce results, such as being fed or comforted.

(15) The second stage is from 24 months to seven years. (16) This is the preoperational stage in which children are learning to use symbols such as pictures and words. (17) From seven to 12 years is the concrete operational stage, when thinking, though still concrete, becomes more logical and organized.

(18) Finally, from adolescence through adulthood is the formal operational stage, characterized by the ability to think abstractly and the capability of hypothetical and theoretical reasoning. (19) Though it may seem that humans go through these stages instinctively, without their input, Piaget believed that children are active participants in each stage, observing, learning, experimenting, and changing. (20) Piaget died in 1980, after writing more than 50 books and receiving honorary degrees from 31 universities.

1. Which edit is needed to correct sentence 1?

   A. change ***mollusks*** to **mollusk**

   B. change ***a rung*** to **rungs**

   C. change ***career*** to **careers**

   D. change ***were*** to **are**

2. What is the best way to combine sentences 2, 3, and 4 to clarify the relationship among ideas?

   E. Born in Switzerland in 1896, Piaget studied at the University of Neuchatel, where he eventually received a doctorate in the natural sciences.

   F. Piaget was born in Switzerland in 1896 and studied at the University of Neuchatel and eventually received a doctorate in the natural sciences.

   G. Piaget was born in Switzerland in 1896; studied at the University of Neuchatel; eventually received a doctorate in the natural sciences.

   H. In 1896, Piaget was born in Switzerland, where he studied at the University of Neuchatel, eventually having received a doctorate in the natural sciences.

3. Which edit is needed to correct sentence 5?

   A. change ***saw*** to **seen**

   B. change ***biological changes occurring*** to **the occurrence of biological changes**

   C. change ***that*** to **who**

   D. change ***its*** to **their**

4. Where is the best place to insert the following sentence?

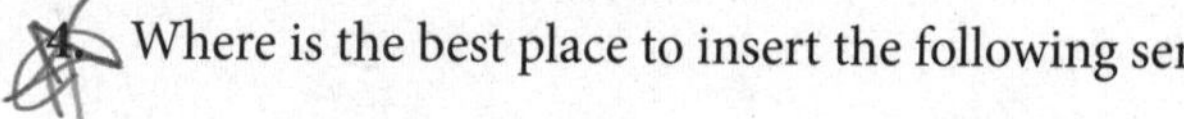

   There, he applied his knowledge of the environment's effect on biological change.

   E. after sentence 2

   F. after sentence 5

   G. after sentence 6

   H. after sentence 8

5. What is the best way to combine sentences 8 and 9?

   A. He continued his studies at the Sorbonne in Paris; where he began focusing on the cognitive development of children.

   B. He continued his studies at the Sorbonne in Paris, where he began focusing on the cognitive development of children.

   C. He continued his studies at the Sorbonne in Paris and he began focusing on the cognitive development of children.

   D. He continued his studies at the Sorbonne in Paris. He began focusing on the cognitive development of children.

6. Which sentence is irrelevant to the argument presented in the passage and should be deleted?

   E. sentence 7

   F. sentence 8

   G. sentence 9

   H. sentence 10

7. Which concluding sentence should be added after sentence 20 to support the argument presented in the passage?

   A. He also chaired many professional committees in several countries.

   B. He believed that growth was, in part, an adaptation to the environment.

   C. Alfred Binet also studied the cognitive development of children.

   D. His works, however, continue to form the core of many psychology courses around the world.

QUESTIONS 8–20: Revising/Editing Stand-Alone Items

DIRECTIONS: Read and answer each of the following questions. You will be asked to recognize and correct errors in sentences or short paragraphs. Mark the **best** answer for each question.

8. Read this sentence.

> Violet Palmer—professional basketball referee and one of the first women to officiate a National Basketball Association (NBA) game started her journey to forging her name in basketball's history in a typical way: she played the sport.

Which edit should be made to correct this sentence?

E. insert a dash after ***referee***

F. insert a dash after ***and***

G. insert a dash after ***game***

H. insert a dash after ***journey***

9. Read this paragraph.

> (1) Today the industries showing the most rapid growth are service and technology. (2) High-tech industries include computers, pharmaceuticals, and aerospace. (3) By the mid-1980s, three-quarters of workers in the United States had jobs in the service industry. (4) Service employees, who provide information or perform tasks for a customer, works in fields such as medicine, food service, and law.

Which sentence should be revised to correct a subject-verb agreement issue?

A. sentence 1

B. sentence 2

C. sentence 3

D. sentence 4

10. Read this paragraph.

> (1) Abraham Lincoln distinguished himself as a remarkable orator and was admired more for the Gettysburg Address and his two inaugural speeches. (2) His humble, patient, serious, and persuasive personality helped him gain attention. (3) When Lincoln ran for Senate reelection, he challenged Stephen A. Douglas to a discussion of issues; these became the Lincoln-Douglas debates. (4) Although Lincoln lost that election, he received countless invitations to speak all over the country.

Which sentence should be revised to correct an issue of comparatives and superlatives?

E. sentence 1
F. sentence 2
G. sentence 3
H. sentence 4

11. Read this paragraph.

> (1) The Liberty Bell, an enormous instrument that was eventually rang during the American Revolution, received its first small crack as it was being tested. (2) When the Declaration of Independence had its first public proclamation, the people of Philadelphia heard this bell ring out. (3) The Liberty Bell's crack grew much larger when it was rung on Washington's birthday in 1846, and the bell was rendered useless. (4) At its home in Independence Hall, the bell receives a tap each year on the Fourth of July.

Which sentence should be revised to correct a verb tense issue?

A. sentence 1
B. sentence 2
C. sentence 3
D. sentence 4

12. Read this paragraph.

> (1) Many adult readers of the Harry Potter series have celebrated its plots for the depth and intrigue they provide for readers of all ages. (2) J. K. Rowling's bestselling books have won a large number of awards for their clever use of mystery and suspense. (3) Adult readers appreciate the sophisticated portrayal of universal themes and magical adventures that transport them to a different world. (4) The books' mature heroes, creativity, and humor has made readers eager to know more about Harry Potter.

Which sentence should be revised to correct a subject-verb agreement issue?

E. sentence 1
F. sentence 2
G. sentence 3
H. sentence 4

13. Read this paragraph.

(1) Studies show that people who participate in competitive sports when they are in college tend toward remaining physically active throughout their lives. (2) Research shows that regular physical exercise keeps the brain strong, no matter how old someone is. (3) Competitive sports offer additional cognitive challenges, but any type of workout leads to resilience of the brain later in life. (4) Complex physical activities might require more communication between various parts of the brain, which could lead to brain preservation.

Which sentence should be revised to correct a verb tense issue?

A. sentence 1
B. sentence 2
C. sentence 3
D. sentence 4

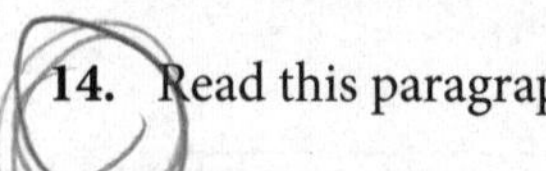

14. Read this paragraph.

(1) The winners of the "Best of Breed" cup and the "Best in Show" trophy are selected by a panel of breeders from the American Kennel Club. (2) Since 1884, this organization has promoted responsible dog ownership and has protected the rights of dog owners. (3) Each year, it hosts tens of thousands of events, including dog shows. (4) The American Kennel Club even reunites lost pets with their owners and offers scholarships to the brighter veterinary students.

Which sentence should be revised to correct a comparative/superlative issue?

E. sentence 1
F. sentence 2
G. sentence 3
H. sentence 4

15. Read this paragraph.

(1) Lacking sacred scriptures or codified dogma, Shinto is more properly regarded as a legacy of traditional religious practices and basic values than as a formal system of belief. (2) Although it has incorporated external influences from Confucianism, Taoism, and Buddhism, Shinto has stayed true to its own tradition. (3) Some shrines and works of art have officially became national treasures in Japan. (4) Japanese people observe ancient Shinto practices in modern social life.

Which sentence should be revised to correct a verb tense issue?

A. sentence 1
B. sentence 2
C. sentence 3
D. sentence 4

16. Read this paragraph.

> (1) As a playwright, Pinter is renowned for his mundane settings, his everyday yet poetic dialogue, and his aggressive, often mean-spirited characters. (2) He is one of the most important English playwrights of the twentieth century and has presented themes such as reality and human interaction. (3) His talent for accurately replicating ordinary speech through his plays might surprise the audience members, who may not associate the dialogue to the unexpected events occurring onstage. (4) In his dramas, Pinter demonstrates non-traditional styles and often uses a series of plays to explore a problem.

Which sentence should be revised to correct an idiom issue?

E. sentence 1
F. sentence 2
G. sentence 3
H. sentence 4

17. Read this paragraph.

> (1) Homeschooling programs, nearly unheard of twenty years ago, are now available through many public school systems. (2) Students of all ages enjoys the unlimited opportunities and variety of tailored options. (3) Many homeschool families choose an eclectic approach, which may combine the use of traditional textbooks, hands-on learning, online courses, and projects designed around a student's academic interests. (4) High-school students receive a transcript, which most universities accept.

Which sentence should be revised to correct an agreement issue?

A. sentence 1
B. sentence 2
C. sentence 3
D. sentence 4

18. Read this paragraph.

> (1) Attention span plays a role in many children's and teenagers' academic success. (2) Some students are unable to study for long, uninterrupted periods of time, but this does not mean they are incapable of getting good grades. (3) When families recognize a child's difficulty, they can view it of a treatable condition and attempt to adjust the study habits. (4) Countless resources offer academic advice about successfully addressing attention issues.

Which sentence should be revised to correct an idiom issue?

E. sentence 1
F. sentence 2
G. sentence 3
H. sentence 4

19. Read this paragraph.

> (1) Extensive study of atoms' movements have led scientists to theories of quantum mechanics, which hold that it is impossible to determine exactly how subatomic particles move and that the best we can do is make probable guesses. (2) Quantum mechanics represents a branch of physics that makes observations about atoms and the structure and behavior of matter. (3) For example, it explains processes such as how atoms form into molecules. (4) By applying quantum mechanics, scientists have developed CDs, barcode readers at stores, and nuclear energy.

Which sentence should be revised to correct a subject-verb agreement issue?

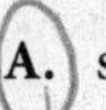

A. sentence 1

B. sentence 2

C. sentence 3

D. sentence 4

20. Read this sentence.

> The newly constructed athletic complex features a myriad of amenities multi-purpose gymnasiums, an elevated jogging track, squash courts, and exercise studios.

Which edit should be made to correct this sentence?

E. insert a colon after ***newly constructed***

F. insert a colon after ***complex***

G. insert a colon after ***amenities***

H. insert a colon after ***multi-purpose***

ANSWERS AND EXPLANATIONS

Punctuation

1. B

Category: Punctuation

Getting to the Answer: A comma is needed to properly combine an independent clause with a dependent clause. Inserting a comma after the last word in the independent clause, "medicine," **(B)**, is correct. **(A)**, **(C)**, and **(D)** do not address the error and place unnecessary commas within the sentence.

2. G

Category: Punctuation

Getting to the Answer: Sentence 3 is missing a necessary dash, so **(G)** is correct. The phrase "making sense out of technical political jargon" is a nonessential clause that must be set off from the rest of the sentence with either a pair of commas or a pair of dashes. Inserting a dash after "jargon" would fix the error.

3. B

Category: Punctuation

Getting to the Answer: A colon is used to introduce a list, so sentence 2 should use a colon instead of a comma after "bicycle"; **(B)** is correct. **(A)**, **(C)**, and **(D)** do not address the error.

4. G

Category: Punctuation

Getting to the Answer: The word "it's" means "it is," but the sentence requires the possessive "its"; **(G)** is correct. The other choices do not address this punctuation error and create new issues.

Usage

1. B

Category: Usage

Getting to the Answer: A verb must agree with its subject in number and tense. The singular verb "sees" does not match the plural subject "scientists." **(B)** fixes the error. The other answer choices do not fix the issue and introduce new errors.

2. E

Category: Usage

Getting to the Answer: A pronoun must agree with its antecedent in person and number. The singular pronoun "it" does not match the plural antecedent "Sandstone, limestone, and shale." **(E)** identifies the error. Sentences 2, 3, and 4 do not contain pronoun errors.

3. B

Category: Usage

Getting to the Answer: The word "hardly" is negative, so it cannot be paired with "not." Changing "were not" to "were" fixes the error, so **(B)** is correct. None of the other choices fixes the issue.

4. E

Category: Usage

Getting to the Answer: Although they sound the same, the noun *effect* and the verb *affect* are spelled differently. Sentence 1 requires the noun "effect," so **(E)** is correct. None of the other choices addresses the error.

PRACTICE SET

Jean Piaget

1. B

Category: Usage

Getting to the Answer: Verbs must agree with the subject to which they refer. "The study of mollusks and the formulation of a theory" create a plural subject, which does not match "a rung." **(B)** fixes this error. **(A)**, **(C)**, and **(D)** do not address the issue.

2. E

Category: Organization, Unity, and Cohesion

Getting to the Answer: (E) combines the three sentences clearly and concisely. **(F)** simply strings the three ideas together without relating them. **(G)** misuses the semicolon, since the second and third clauses are not independent. **(H)** is awkwardly worded and introduces an inconsistent verb tense.

3. D

Category: Usage

Getting to the Answer: Pronouns must agree in number with their antecedent nouns. Here, the "environment" under discussion is that of the "creatures"; since this noun is plural, the appropriate possessive pronoun is "their," so **(D)** is correct. **(A)** introduces an incorrect verb tense. **(B)** is unnecessarily wordy. **(C)** uses the relative pronoun "who" in reference to "changes"; "who" should only be used when referring to people.

4. G

Category: Organization

Getting to the Answer: "There" at the beginning of the sentence indicates that this sentence would follow one that references a location, which eliminates **(F)**. **(E)** is illogical. Of the remaining choices, **(G)** forms a logical connection between Piaget's switch to the study of psychology and his eventual conclusion that environment impacts mental development, so **(G)** is correct.

5. B

Category: Organization

Getting to the Answer: As written, sentence 9 is a fragment. Since it continues the idea of sentence 8, connecting the two sentences with a comma is the most logical way to fix the error, so **(B)** is correct. **(A)** misuses a semicolon. **(C)** is grammatically incorrect; a comma is needed before the coordinating conjunction "and." **(D)** does not connect the two ideas.

6. H

Category: Topic Development

Getting to the Answer: Every paragraph in a unified passage should stay on topic. The topic in this passage is Jean Piaget, so other psychologists—Skinner and Bandura—are off topic and jarring. Delete sentence 10, **(H)**, to keep the focus on Piaget, which all the other sentences in the paragraph do.

7. D

Category: Topic Development

Getting to the Answer: The final sentence in a passage should not introduce a topic not already mentioned. **(D)** is the logical sentence to end the passage since it concerns the use of Piaget's studies after his death. **(A)** would best be placed somewhere in paragraph 2. **(B)** is a rewording of some of the information in paragraph 1. **(C)** would incorrectly introduce topics not covered in the passage.

8. G

Category: Punctuation

Getting to the Answer: A dash is used either to indicate a break in thought or to separate a nonessential phrase from the rest of the sentence. The phrase "professional basketball referee and one of the first women to officiate a National Basketball Association (NBA) game" is a nonessential clause that must be properly set off with either two commas or two dashes. Inserting a dash after "game," **(G)**, properly punctuates the nonessential phrase. **(E)**, **(F)**, and **(H)** do not address the error and place unnecessary dashes within the sentence.

9. D

Category: Usage

Getting to the Answer: In sentence 4, the subject "employees" is plural, so a plural verb is needed to match. Keep in mind that a verb might not always appear close to its subject due to intervening phrases. The sentence could be revised to read, "work in fields." The correct choice is **(D)**. In choices **(A)**, **(B)**, and **(C)**, the sentences do not have errors.

10. E

Category: Usage

Getting to the Answer: Check to see that sentences have proper comparatives and superlatives. In sentence 1, the word "most" should replace "more," since Lincoln gave many speeches. The word "more" would compare only two things. The sentences in choices **(F)**, **(G)**, and **(H)** do not include errors, so the correct choice is **(E)**.

11. A

Category: Usage

Getting to the Answer: Be sure to use the past participle and not the simple past tense for this sentence. In sentence 1, the correct past participle would be "that was eventually rung." The correct choice is **(A)**; choices **(B)**, **(C)**, and **(D)** have grammatically correct sentences.

12. H

Category: Usage

Getting to the Answer: The last sentence presents a compound subject that is plural: "mature heroes, creativity, and humor." A verb needs to agree with its subject in number, so "has made" would need to be in the plural form, "have made." Choice **(H)** is correct; the sentences in choices **(E)**, **(F)**, and **(G)** do not have errors.

13. A

Category: Usage

Getting to the Answer: The first sentence includes the awkward and incorrect verb phrase "tend toward remaining." This could be revised to read, "are likely to remain." **(A)** is the correct choice. Choices **(B)**, **(C)**, and **(D)** do not have verb errors.

14. H

Category: Usage

Getting to the Answer: Check to see that sentences have proper comparatives and superlatives. In sentence 4, the word "brightest" should replace "brighter," since many veterinary students would apply for the scholarships. The word "brighter" would compare only two things. The sentences in choices **(E)**, **(F)**, and **(G)** do not include errors, so the correct choice is **(H)**.

15. C

Category: Usage

Getting to the Answer: Be sure to use the past participle and not the simple past tense for this sentence. In sentence 3, the correct past participle would be "have officially become." Choices **(A)**, **(B)**, and **(D)** do not have errors, so the correct choice is **(C)**.

16. G

Category: Usage

Getting to the Answer: Check to see that idioms are paired with the correct prepositions. Sentence 3 should include, "associate the dialogue with the." Choices **(E)**, **(F)**, and **(H)** use correct prepositions, so the correct choice is **(G)**.

17. B

Category: Usage

Getting to the Answer: In sentence 2, the subject "students" is plural, so a plural verb is needed. The revision could include, "students of all ages enjoy." The correct choice is **(B)**; in choices **(A)**, **(C)**, and **(D)**, the sentences do not have errors.

18. G

Category: Usage

Getting to the Answer: Check to see that idioms are matched with the correct prepositions. Sentence 3 should read, "view it as a treatable condition." Choice **(G)** is correct. Choices **(E)**, **(F)**, and **(H)** do not have errors.

19. A

Category: Usage

Getting to the Answer: A verb needs to agree with its subject in number, and the verb might not always appear close to its subject. In the first sentence, the subject "study" is singular, so the revision should include the verb phrase "has led." The correct choice is **(A)**; choices **(B)**, **(C)**, and **(D)** have grammatically correct sentences.

20. G

Category: Punctuation

Getting to the Answer: A colon is used to introduce an explanation, example, or list. Inserting a colon after "amenities," **(G)**, properly introduces the list that follows. **(E)**, **(F)**, and **(H)** do not address the error and place unnecessary colons within the sentence.

CHAPTER 6

Knowledge of Language

CHAPTER OBJECTIVES

By the end of this chapter, you will be able to:

- Apply the Kaplan Methods to answer Knowledge of Language questions
- Identify and correct Concision, Precision, and Ambiguity errors

KNOWLEDGE OF LANGUAGE

Good writing must be concise, precise, and consistent in tone. The SHSAT rewards your ability to identify and correct these Knowledge of Language issues.

Concision

A concise sentence includes no unnecessary words; avoid phrasing that is wordy or redundant. Each word must contribute to the meaning of the sentence; otherwise, it should be eliminated.

Wordy/Redundant Sentence	Concise Sentence
The superb musical score ***added enhancement to the experience of*** *the play's development.*	*The superb musical score* ***enhanced*** *the play's development.*
I ***did not anticipate*** *the* ***surprising, unexpected*** *plot twist.*	*I* ***did not anticipate*** *the plot twist.*
The students ***increased some of their knowledge of*** *Tuscan architecture.*	*The students* ***learned about*** *Tuscan architecture.*

Try It Out

DIRECTIONS: Read and answer each of the following questions. You will be asked to recognize and correct errors in sentences or short paragraphs. Mark the **best** answer for each question.

1. Read this sentence.

> My sister Mia and I spent all evening Saturday playing tennis at the park, and we only decided to stop when it became too hard and difficult to see the ball.

Which edit should be made to correct this sentence?

A. remove ***all***

B. remove ***decided to***

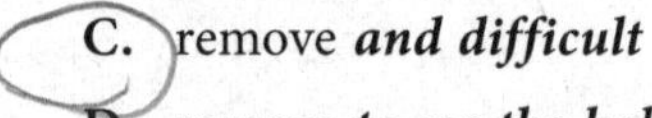
C. remove ***and difficult***

D. remove ***to see the ball***

2. Read this paragraph.

> (1) Before 1793, when Eli Whitney invented the cotton gin, cotton was not a profitable crop because the traditional method used in the separating of seeds from cotton fiber was enormously labor-intensive. (2) The cotton gin consisted of a rotating drum with wire spikes that caught the fibers and left behind the seeds. (3) Hodgen Holmes improved upon Whitney's cotton gin by removing the spikes and installing a circular saw. (4) Today's cotton gins make use of the same simple yet effective principles.

Which sentence should be revised to correct a wordiness issue?

E. sentence 1
F. sentence 2
G. sentence 3
H. sentence 4

Precision

Words should convey their meaning precisely, so be on the lookout for language that is vague or ambiguous. The SHSAT rewards your ability to distinguish between clear and unclear language.

Words within passages should be not only necessary but also relevant to the main point of the paragraph in which they occur. Make sure that no sentence includes phrases that detract from the main point.

Try It Out

> **DIRECTIONS:** Read and answer each of the following questions. You will be asked to recognize and correct errors in sentences or short paragraphs. Mark the **best** answer for each question.

3. Read this sentence.

> One way Cameron raised his math grade was through his doing of the extra-credit problems on his final exam.

Which edit should be made to correct this sentence?

A. change ***One way*** to **One of several ways**
B. change ***One way*** to **Only one way**
C. change ***through his doing of*** to **by doing**
D. change ***through his doing of*** to **because of doing**

4. Read this paragraph.

> (1) Although Jane Austen's novels are most often admired for their eloquence and imagery, they are also highly esteemed for their subtle, yet shrewd observations of nineteenth-century English society. (2) She drew from her experiences with family and acquaintances in various situations to do characters and settings for her novels. (3) In books such as *Sense and Sensibility*, she demonstrated her sophisticated literary technique even when portraying very ordinary events. (4) During her life, Austen received praise and positive reviews for her work.

Which sentence should be revised to correct a word choice issue?

E. sentence 1
F. sentence 2
G. sentence 3
H. sentence 4

Ambiguous Pronouns

A pronoun is ambiguous if its antecedent (the noun to which it refers) is either missing or unclear. The SHSAT tests your ability to identify and correct either of those issues. When you see a pronoun, make sure you can identify the noun to which it refers and check whether the pronoun clearly refers to that noun.

Ambiguous Pronoun Use	Clear Pronoun Use
*Anthony walked with Cody to the ice cream shop, and **he** bought a banana split.*	*Anthony walked with Cody to the ice cream shop, and **Cody** bought a banana split.*

Try It Out

DIRECTIONS: Read and answer each of the following questions. You will be asked to recognize and correct errors in sentences or short paragraphs. Mark the **best** answer for each question.

5. Read this sentence.

> The concessions made by the union were to increase wages and to give them more vacation time.

Which edit should be made to correct this sentence?

A. change ***concessions*** to **concession**

B. change ***were*** to **are**

C. change ***them*** to **workers**

D. change ***more*** to **most**

6. Read this paragraph.

> (1) Before tourism became a mainstay of the economy, the value of land in Mexico was defined by how well its soil could produce crops. (2) To many Americans, tropical tourist-oriented beach towns such as Acapulco and Puerto Vallarta characterize Mexico. (3) These may be the most common sorts of destinations for foreign travelers but certainly are not the most representative of itself. (4) These cities, and others like them, are set up to be attractive to the tourist trade, for better or worse.

Which sentence should be revised to correct an ambiguity issue?

E. sentence 1

F. sentence 2

G. sentence 3

H. sentence 4

The following practice sets provide an opportunity to apply the concepts and strategic thinking covered in this chapter. While many of the questions pertain to Knowledge of Language, some touch on other English Language Arts concepts to ensure that your practice is test-like, with a variety of question types. To practice Test Day timing, follow the suggested timing guidelines for each section.

PRACTICE SET

Suggested Timing: 25 minutes

QUESTIONS 1–14: Revising/Editing in a Passage

DIRECTIONS: Read the passage below and answer the questions following it. You will be asked to improve the writing quality of the passage and to correct errors so that the passage follows the conventions of standard written English. You may reread the passage if you need to. Mark the **best** answer for each question.

Questions 1–7 refer to the following passage.

Noctilucent Clouds

(1) Scientists generally agree that a change for atmospheric phenomena may signal pending changes to the Earth's climate. (2) Consequently, when NASA began to document increased sightings of noctilucent clouds in the latter half of the twentieth century, the agency institutes plans for a study to determine the cause and to learn what effect, if any, this may have on future weather patterns.

(3) Noctilucent, or night-shining, clouds are virtually unknown to most people, even those that stargaze on a regular basis. (4) This is because NLCs (as they are known in the scientific community) generally occur north of 50° latitude, above the polar region. (5) These clouds, however, are becoming increasingly visible in areas farther south. (6) In 1999, a dramatic display of NLCs appeared over Colorado and Utah, nearly 10° below the latitudes where scientists have come to expect them. (7) Seeing these things in Europe has also happened more and more in the past 50 years, for reasons that remain unsure.

(8) Ordinary clouds occur approximately 10 kilometers from the Earth's surface. (9) Noctilucent clouds are found at about 82 kilometers. (10) This is more than seven times higher than commercial airlines fly. (11) Cirrus clouds are about six kilometers high. (12) Although most scientists believe NLCs are formed of ice crystals, some are convinced that they are composed of cosmic or volcanic dust. (13) This theory is most likely attributable to the fact that the first NLC sightings were documented following a large volcanic explosion in Indonesia.

(14) What might be the connection between NLCs and changing weather patterns? (15) Atmospheric scientist Gary Thomas has studied the fact that early NCL sightings came about at the same time that the Indonesian volcano Krakatoa first erupted in 1883, sending a great deal of polluting ash into the air, and also during the early part of the Industrial Revolution, which resulted in air and water pollution. (16) Other scientists speculate that increased greenhouse gas makes the atmosphere cooler, which gives rise to more and wider-spread NCLs. (17) Though they think that there is some sort of relationship between the more NCLs and changing weather and climate patterns on earth, it remains very controversial.

1. Which edit is needed to correct sentence 1?

   A. change ***agree*** to **agrees**

   B. change ***for*** to **in**

   C. change ***changes*** to **changing**

   D. change ***climate*** to **climates**

2. Which edit is needed to correct sentence 2?

   E. change ***institutes*** to **instituted**

   F. change ***for a study*** to **for studying**

   G. change ***and*** to **but**

   H. change ***may have*** to **may have had**

3. Which edit is needed to correct sentence 3?

   A. change ***virtually*** to **virtual**

   B. change ***most*** to **few**

   C. change ***that*** to **who**

   D. change ***on*** to **for**

4. Which revision of sentence 7 uses the most precise language?

   E. Seeing these things in Europe has also become more frequent in the past 50 years, for reasons that remain unsure.

   F. Seeing these things in Europe has also become more frequent in the past 50 years, for reasons that remain unclear.

   G. Sightings in Europe have also happened more and more in the past 50 years, for reasons that remain unsure.

   H. Sightings in Europe have also become more frequent in the past 50 years, for reasons that remain unclear.

5. Which of the following is the best way to combine sentences 8, 9, and 10 to clarify the relationship among ideas?

   A. Ordinary clouds occur approximately 10 kilometers from the Earth's surface, noctilucent clouds are found at about 82 kilometers, and this is more than seven times higher than commercial airlines fly.

   B. Ordinary clouds occur approximately 10 kilometers from the Earth's surface; while noctilucent clouds, being found at about 82 kilometers, which is more than seven times higher than commercial airlines fly.

   C. Ordinary clouds occur approximately 10 kilometers from the Earth's surface, but noctilucent clouds are found at about 82 kilometers, which is more than seven times higher than commercial airlines fly.

   D. Ordinary clouds occur approximately 10 kilometers from the Earth's surface, so noctilucent clouds are found at about 82 kilometers, which is more than seven times higher than commercial airlines fly.

6. Which sentence is irrelevant to the argument presented in the passage and should be deleted?

   E. sentence 10

   F. sentence 11

   G. sentence 12

   H. sentence 13

7. Which revision of sentence 17 uses the most precise language?

   A. Though many scientists think that there is some sort of relationship between the more NCLs and changing weather and climate patterns on earth, it remains very controversial.

   B. Though many scientists think that there is some sort of relationship between the more NCLs and changing weather and climate patterns on earth, this possible connection remains very controversial.

   C. Though many scientists think that there is a connection between the increased appearance of NCLs and changing weather and climate patterns on earth, this possible connection remains very controversial.

   D. Though many scientists think that there is a connection between the increased appearance of NCLs and changing weather and climate patterns on earth, it remains very controversial.

Questions 8–14 refer to the following passage.

Icebreakers

(1) Scientists working in the Arctic and Antarctic have been investigating the effects of climate change. (2) However, research on climate change could not be accomplished without the aid of a tough and reliable icebreaker, a tool which has only been around for slightly more than a hundred years.

(3) Before that, when people needed to sail in ice-clogged waters, they adapted their traditional ship designs. (4) The indigenous Arctic people, who have been faced with ice for millennia, used their lightweight kayaks to skim over the ice rather than break through it. (5) In the eleventh century, Russians who lived by Arctic shores built *kochi*, traditional sailing ships with skin-reinforced areas at the water line. (6) The winter of 1880–1881 also froze the Elbe river in Germany. (7) Steam-powered ships, with their vastly increased propelling strength, ushered in the age of icebreaker shipbuilding. (8) City Iceboat No. 1, constructed in 1837, had wood paddles reinforced with iron and was powered by two 250-horsepower steam engines. (9) Over time, ship ice-breaking capability continued to improve.

(10) Though most people think that modern icebreakers literally break through ice, in reality icebreakers do not "push" the thick expanses of ice. (11) They are instead crushed under the weight of the ship's bow, which is pushed through by powerful engines. (12) The ship then reverses, powers ahead, and runs up onto the ice again. (13) So that the vessel clears a path for itself.

(14) This process is time-consuming because it can be up to 16 feet thick. (15) Rather, their ability to break through thick ice is due to several unique design features: the bow, the hull, and the propulsion system. (16) Since a typical icebreaker may only spend 25 percent of its time in ice, it must perform well in open water, too. (17) For example, the bow of an icebreaker does not go straight down, but rather slopes at a 30-degree angle.

(18) Aside from their role in helping scientists study climate change, icebreakers have other uses. (19) They are used to do helpful things about snow, ice, frozen ground, and other materials in cold places.

8. Which sentence from the second paragraph presents information that is irrelevant to the passage and should be deleted?

   E. sentence 4

   F. sentence 5

   G. sentence 6

   H. sentence 7

9. Which edit is needed to correct sentence 11?

   A. change ***They are*** to **The ice is**

   B. change ***which*** to **that**

   C. change ***is pushed*** to **are pushed**

   D. change ***through*** to **beyond**

10. What is the best way to combine sentences 12 and 13?

    E. The ship then reverses, powers ahead, and runs up onto the ice again, by which the vessel clears a path for itself.

    F. The ship then reverses, powers ahead, and runs up onto the ice again, because the vessel clears a path for itself.

    G. The ship then reverses, powers ahead, and runs up onto the ice again, and the vessel, clearing a path for itself.

    H. The ship then reverses, powers ahead, and runs up onto the ice again so that the vessel clears a path for itself.

11. Which edit is needed to correct sentence 14?

    A. change ***process*** to **lengthy process**

    B. change ***because*** to **due to**

    C. change ***it*** to **the ice**

    D. change ***thick*** to **high**

12. Which sentence would best follow sentence 14?

    E. Icebreakers do not have an immense weight that breaks the ice.

    F. It's cold on an icebreaker.

    G. Icebreakers may lead to decreased global warming.

    H. Icebreakers are also used by the army.

13. Which sentence is irrelevant to the argument presented in the passage and should be deleted?

    A. sentence 14

    B. sentence 15

    C. sentence 16

    D. sentence 17

14. Which revision of sentence 19 uses the most precise language?

    E. They are used to conduct fundamental research about snow, ice, frozen ground, and other materials in cold places.

    F. They are used to conduct fundamental research to understand stuff about snow, ice, frozen ground, and other materials in cold regions.

    G. They are used to conduct fundamental research to understand snow, ice, frozen ground, and other such cold things.

    H. They are used to conduct fundamental research to understand the nature and characteristics of snow, ice, frozen ground, and other materials in places such as Antarctica, the Arctic circle, and other cold areas.

QUESTIONS 15–20: Revising/Editing Stand-Alone Items

DIRECTIONS: Read and answer each of the following questions. You will be asked to recognize and correct errors in sentences or short paragraphs. Mark the **best** answer for each question.

15. Read this paragraph.

> (1) Babe Ruth started his career as a pitcher for the Boston Red Sox and then joined the New York Yankees. (2) In baseball's early days, hitting 20 home runs in a season was considered extraordinary, but that was drastically changed by Babe Ruth when he hit 54 home runs in 1920. (3) When he retired in 1935, he had made a total of 714 home runs. (4) Two movies about Babe Ruth feature his accomplishments, which include becoming the first player to hit three home runs in one game.

Which sentence should be revised to correct an ambiguity issue?

A. sentence 1

B. sentence 2

C. sentence 3

D. sentence 4

16. Read this paragraph.

> (1) The Northern Lights can awe many local residents, since they rarely appear in southern regions. (2) These shimmering lights occur most often near the Earth's north and south magnetic poles. (3) When the mysterious presentations occur far away from the poles, they light up the sky more frequently during periods of solar activity such as sunspots. (4) It is important to note that the Northern Lights can display not only rays of intense colors but also shimmering arcs and bright curtains.

Which sentence should be revised to correct an ambiguous pronoun issue?

E. sentence 1

F. sentence 2

G. sentence 3

H. sentence 4

17. Read this paragraph.

> (1) Recent fossil evidence suggests that carnivorous dinosaurs were accomplished swimmers. (2) The *Baptornis* looked liked a diving bird whose small wings could have helped it steer under water. (3) It probably had webbed feet and a torpedo-shaped body that would have allowed it to dive. (4) If this dinosaur was indeed a swimmer, it must have used its small, sharp teeth to locate fish in central North America's shallow seas.

Which sentence should be revised to correct a word choice issue?

A. sentence 1

B. sentence 2

C. sentence 3

D. sentence 4

18. Read this paragraph.

> (1) Although eventually embraced by mainstream media, the term *blogging,* which refers to online journaling, was initially utilized only by cutting-edge Internet users around the nation. (2) The term *blog* is short for "web log," and anyone can create or share a blog. (3) When people go online, their searches might lead them to blogs that offer various types of instructions or the latest entertaining anecdotes. (4) Blogs can stay up-to-date because the Internet is so flexible; unlike a book, which needs to be reprinted to correct mistakes, it can be corrected and relaunched in a matter of minutes.

Which sentence should be revised to correct an ambiguous pronoun issue?

E. sentence 1

F. sentence 2

G. sentence 3

H. sentence 4

19. Read this paragraph.

> (1) Recent experiments seem to indicate that the most effective defense against skin cancer is using sunscreen properly and consistently. (2) Today, 80 percent of Americans buy and purchase sunscreen, but they might need reminders to reapply it every two hours. (3) Melanoma and other types of skin cancer remain a problem, but careful sunscreen application minimizes the risk of skin damage. (4) In addition, people might consider switching to a more natural sunscreen, which is safer for human and marine life.

Which sentence should be revised to correct a wordiness issue?

A. sentence 1

B. sentence 2

C. sentence 3

D. sentence 4

20. Read this paragraph.

> (1) According to Howard Gardner, there are people that learn best when they hear information, but most learners benefit from having visual displays. (2) College students have adapted to traditional types of instruction, yet even auditory learners tend to have multiple learning styles. (3) University professors are, therefore, frequently encouraged to utilize multimedia materials in their class presentations. (4) With new advances each day, educational technology offers students and educators a wealth of options.

Which sentence should be revised to correct a word choice issue?

E. sentence 1

F. sentence 2

G. sentence 3

H. sentence 4

ANSWERS AND EXPLANATIONS

Knowledge of Language

1. C

Category: Knowledge of Language

Getting to the Answer: When you do not spot a grammatical error, check to see if the sentence is wordier than it needs to be. **(C)** is correct because "hard" and "difficult" have the same meaning in this sentence, so we can remove "and difficult." Removing "all" in **(A)** results in the illogical phrase "spent evening Saturday." Likewise, **(B)** and **(D)** eliminate phrases that are necessary to make the meaning clear.

2. E

Category: Knowledge of Language

Getting to the Answer: Sentences should convey their meaning concisely, and the first sentence is overly wordy. Choice **(E)** is correct; choices **(F)**, **(G)**, and **(H)** have concise sentences.

3. C

Category: Knowledge of Language

Getting to the Answer: Style errors may be difficult to spot; plug in each answer choice to see if a simpler choice is available. **(C)** is correct because "by doing" replaces the unnecessarily complicated phrase "through his doing of." **(A)** is incorrect because it is wordier than the original. **(B)** and **(D)** are both wordy and awkward.

4. F

Category: Knowledge of Language

Getting to the Answer: Accurate word choice is needed to clearly express an author's meaning. In the sentence for choice **(F)**, the clunky phrase "to do characters and settings" could be revised to read, "to create characters and settings." Choices **(E)**, **(G)**, and **(H)** do not have errors.

5. C

Category: Knowledge of Language

Getting to the Answer: The pronoun "them" is ambiguous. **(C)** fixes the error by changing the ambiguous pronoun to a specific noun, "workers." **(A)**, **(B)**, and **(D)** do not address the ambiguity issue and introduce new errors.

6. G

Category: Knowledge of Language

Getting to the Answer: The pronoun "itself" in sentence 3 does not have a clear antecedent, so **(G)** is correct. This sentence could be fixed by changing "itself" to "the country." **(E)**, **(F)**, and **(H)** do not address the error.

PRACTICE SET

Noctilucent Clouds

1. B

Category: Topic Development

Getting to the Answer: Based on context, the phrase "change for" is incorrect; the sentence requires "change in," so **(B)** is correct. None of the other answer choices addresses this idiomatic error.

2. E

Category: Usage

Getting to the Answer: In this sentence, "institutes" is incorrectly in the present tense, since the sentence is talking about something that happened in the latter half of the twentieth century. **(E)** corrects the error. **(F)** is not idiomatically correct English. **(G)** misrepresents the relationship between the two ideas. **(H)** introduces a verb tense that's incorrect in context.

3. C

Category: Usage

Getting to the Answer: The relative pronoun "who" is used when referring to people; "that" and "which" are used for things. Since "people" is the noun that the pronoun is referring to here, the pronoun "that" should be replaced with "who." **(C)** does this without introducing any additional errors. **(A)**, **(B)**, and **(D)** do not address the error.

4. H

Category: Knowledge of Language

Getting to the Answer: Sentence 7 uses vague and imprecise language and needs to be corrected. **(H)** is the only sentence that consistently uses precise and specific language.

5. C

Category: Topic Development

Getting to the Answer: **(C)** combines the sentences correctly using "but" to indicate the contrast between the first two clauses and "which" to make the third clause subordinate. **(A)** merely strings the sentences together without relating their ideas. **(B)** misuses the semicolon splice, since the second clause is not independent. In **(D)**, the transition word "so" indicates an inappropriate cause-and-effect relationship between the first and second clauses.

6. F

Category: Topic Development

Getting to the Answer: The focus of the passage is on what NCLs are and how they might affect earth's weather. Cirrus clouds, though high ones, are out of place in a discussion of NCLs. Sentence 11, **(F)**, therefore, should be deleted. All other sentences are in line with the focus of the passage.

7. C

Category: Knowledge of Language

Getting to the Answer: Sentence 17 uses vague and imprecise language and needs to be corrected. **(C)** is the only sentence that consistently uses precise and specific language.

Icebreakers

8. G

Category: Topic Development

Getting to the Answer: This paragraph is about the history of ice-breaking ships. The fact that the Elbe froze over with ice has nothing to do with the history of building these ships, so **(G)** is correct. All other sentences are focused on the topic of the history of icebreakers.

9. A

Category: Knowledge of Language

Getting to the Answer: A pronoun's antecedent may appear in an earlier passage, but it should still be unambiguous, and the noun and pronoun must agree in number. The possible plural antecedents for "They" are icebreakers, people, and expanses of ice. **(A)** eliminates the ambiguity and corrects the agreement error.

10. H

Category: Sentence Structure and Formation

Getting to the Answer: Here, sentence 13 is a fragment. Combining the two sentences, as in **(H)**, is the simplest way to correct this. Neither sentence contains a logical antecedent for the word "which" in **(E)**. **(F)** creates an illogical cause-and-effect relationship between the clauses. **(G)** leaves the meaning of the second clause incomplete.

11. C

Category: Knowledge of Language

Getting to the Answer: In context, the meaning of the pronoun "it" is unclear. **(C)** eliminates the ambiguity by specifying that "it" is "the ice." None of the other choices addresses the error.

12. E

Category: Topic Development

Getting to the Answer: Use context clues to determine the proper placement of new information. Since sentence 15 begins with "Rather," the sentence that comes before should provide a contrast to the idea that design features are what allow icebreakers to do their job. **(E)** does so. **(F)** is Out of Scope and also uses a pronoun without a clear antecedent. Global warming is discussed in paragraph 1 and other uses for icebreakers in paragraph 5, which eliminates **(G)** and **(H)**.

13. C

Category: Topic Development

Getting to the Answer: All of the answer choices but **(C)** provide information that is pertinent to the passage's topic.

14. H

Category: Knowledge of Language

Getting to the Answer: Sentence 19 uses vague and imprecise language and needs to be corrected. **(H)** is the only sentence that consistently uses precise and specific language.

15. B

Category: Knowledge of Language

Getting to the Answer: Sentence 2 makes an ambiguous reference to something that "was drastically changed." The sentence should instead include a specific subject, such as "that record" or "that idea." The correct choice is **(B)**; in choices **(A)**, **(C)**, and **(D)**, the sentences are clear.

16. E

Category: Knowledge of Language

Getting to the Answer: In sentence 1, the pronoun "they" is ambiguous, since it could refer to either of the sentence's plural nouns: "Northern Lights" or "residents." Choice **(E)** is correct. In choices **(F)**, **(G)**, and **(H)**, there are no pronoun errors.

17. D

Category: Knowledge of Language

Getting to the Answer: Accurate word choice is needed to clearly express an author's meaning. In **(D)**, the following could improve sentence 4: "teeth to *catch* fish." **(A)**, **(B)**, and **(C)** already use precise word choice.

18. H

Category: Knowledge of Language

Getting to the Answer: Sentence 4 makes an ambiguous reference to "it." Instead, the sentence could have a more specific subject such as "a web page." The correct choice is **(H)**. Choices **(E)**, **(F)**, and **(G)** do not have errors.

19. B

Category: Knowledge of Language

Getting to the Answer: Using two words with the same meaning in one sentence is redundant. "Buy" and "purchase" mean the same thing, so sentence 2 should be revised to fix the issue. Choice **(B)** is correct. Choices **(A)**, **(C)**, and **(D)** do not have wordiness issues.

20. E

Category: Knowledge of Language

Getting to the Answer: Use the relative pronouns "who" or "whom" to refer to people; use "that" or "which" to refer to any other kind of noun. Choices **(F)**, **(G)**, and **(H)** do not have errors, so the correct choice is **(E)**.

CHAPTER 7

Organization, Unity, and Cohesion & Topic Development

CHAPTER OBJECTIVES

By the end of this chapter, you will be able to:

- Apply the Kaplan Methods to answer Organization, Unity, and Cohesion questions
- Identify and correct Organization, Unity, and Cohesion errors
- Apply the Kaplan Methods to answer Topic Development questions
- Identify and correct Topic Development errors

ORGANIZATION, UNITY, AND COHESION & TOPIC DEVELOPMENT

Organization, Unity, and Cohesion

Organization, Unity, and Cohesion questions require you to assess the logic and coherence of an English passage. These questions differ in scope; you might be asked to organize the writing at the level of a sentence, a paragraph, or even an entire passage.

Transitions

If you are asked to insert a transition word or phrase, you must determine the writer's intended meaning and find the transition that best conveys this meaning. Writers use transitions to show relationships such as contrast, cause and effect, continuation, emphasis, and chronology. Knowing which types of words convey each type of transition will help you choose the correct word on Test Day.

Contrast Transitions	Cause-and-Effect Transitions	Sequential Transitions	Emphasis Transitions
although, but, despite, even though, however, in contrast, nonetheless, on the other hand, rather than, though, unlike, while, yet	as a result, because, consequently, since, so, therefore, thus	after, also, before, first (second, etc.), furthermore, in addition	certainly, in fact, indeed, that is

Passage Organization

Combining Sentences

Some Organization questions ask you to combine sentences. Your goal is to ensure that information and ideas are logically conveyed using correct grammar.

Opening, Transitional, and Closing Sentences

Some Organization questions task you with improving the beginning or ending of a paragraph or passage. The transition words, phrases, or sentences must be used effectively not only to connect information and ideas but also to maintain logical structure. To answer these questions effectively, determine the writer's intended purpose, eliminate answer choices that do not reflect this purpose, and choose the most correct and relevant option.

✔ Note

While concision is important, it should not be a primary goal when answering Organization questions. Instead, focus on picking answer choices that make the most sense logically, given your understanding of the writer's tone and purpose.

Topic Development

Topic Development questions test your ability to determine why a passage is written and whether particular information helps accomplish that purpose.

Adding Information

Some Topic Development questions ask you to insert new ideas into a passage. When inserting new information into a passage, begin by determining which paragraph of the passage most logically accompanies the new idea. If more than one answer choice includes the paragraph you have in mind, plug in each new idea to see how it fits within the context. Choose the answer that best reflects the writer's tone and purpose.

Deleting Information

When asked to delete information, determine which sentence does not specifically relate to the development of the passage. The passage should flow smoothly and logically when the irrelevant sentence is removed.

Try It Out

DIRECTIONS: Read the passage below and answer the questions following it. You will be asked to improve the writing quality of the passage and to correct errors so that the passage follows the conventions of standard written English. You may reread the passage if you need to. Mark the **best** answer for each question.

Questions 1–7 refer to the following passage.

Irrigation

(1) Irrigation waters plants, especially in areas where it doesn't rain very much. (2) The need for irrigation is a major reason why early settlements formed near rivers, the source of water not only for drinking and cooking, but also for crops. (3) There is considerable evidence that irrigation may have played a pivotal role in the foundation of the earliest civilizations, such as that of Sumer in the Tigris-Euphrates valley.

(4) The ancient Egyptians controlled water coming from the annual flooding of the Nile River to inundate the planting land. (5) Ancient Persians used a system of sloping wells and tunnels to direct water to their barley fields. (6) The Dujiangyan Irrigation System irrigated an enormous area of farmland, and even today provides water for over 5,300 square kilometers of agricultural land. (7) It was built in 256 b.c.e. in the Sichuan region of China. (8) In North America, the Hohokam people, a native culture living in what is now central Arizona, constructed canals and weirs (barriers across rivers, used to regulate the flow of water) to irrigate their crops of cotton, tobacco, and maize, among other crops. (9) The Hohokam are also known for their establishment of trading posts. (10) Modern irrigation systems, using powerful diesel and electric engines, have enormously increased the amount of both groundwater and either river or lake water that can be directed toward crops. (11) Such irrigation can have the negative effect of depleting water faster than it can be replenished.

(12) The reasons for the influence of irrigation are twofold. (13) The development of irrigation allowed for extremely efficient agricultural production, creating the surplus of food resources that must serve as the foundation for any civilization. (14) Furthermore, constructing the elaborate system of canals and drainage networks is a task of tremendous complexity.

1. Which revision of sentence 1 uses the most precise language?

   A. Irrigation waters plants, especially in areas with insufficient rainfall or during particularly dry seasons.

   B. Irrigation waters plants by controlled release of river or lake water, especially in areas where it doesn't rain very much.

   C. Irrigation is a process in which plants are watered by controlled release of river or lake water, especially in areas where it doesn't rain very much.

   D. Irrigation is a process in which plants are watered by controlled release of river or lake water, especially in areas with insufficient rainfall or during particularly dry seasons.

2. Which transition should be added to the beginning of sentence 3?

   E. However

   F. Not surprisingly

   G. Notwithstanding

   H. Later

3. What is the best way to combine sentences 6 and 7?

   A. The Dujiangyan Irrigation System, built in 256 b.c.e. in the Sichuan region of China, irrigated an enormous area of farmland, and even today provides water for over 5,300 square kilometers of agricultural land.

   B. The Dujiangyan Irrigation System irrigated an enormous area of farmland, and was built in 256 b.c.e. in the Sichuan region of China, and even today provides water for over 5,300 square kilometers of agricultural land.

   C. The Dujiangyan Irrigation System irrigated an enormous area of farmland, and even today provides water for over 5,300 square kilometers of agricultural land, it was built in 256 b.c.e. in the Sichuan region of China.

   D. The Dujiangyan Irrigation System, built in 256 b.c.e. in the Sichuan region of China, irrigated an enormous area of farmland, and even today provides water for over 5,300 square kilometers of agricultural land; the Dujiangyan Irrigation System was built in 256 b.c.e. in the Sichuan region of China.

4. Which sentence is irrelevant to the argument presented in the passage and should be deleted?

   E. sentence 7

   F. sentence 8

   G. sentence 9

   H. sentence 10

5. Which transition should be added to the beginning of sentence 11?

   A. In addition

   B. Furthermore

   C. However

   D. For example

6. Which sentence would best follow and support sentence 11?

   E. There are other irrigation problems, but irrigation has a long history.

   F. Despite some negative results of irrigation, it has been and remains integral to the development of communities.

   G. There are several reasons why irrigation is important.

   H. Ancient civilizations took the bad and the good of irrigation in stride.

7. Which concluding sentence should be added after sentence 14 to support the argument presented in the passage?

   A. The tough work that made irrigation possible was worth the effort because it led to important things.

   B. The centers of commerce, administration, and science that accomplished the task eventually blossomed into the cities that served as the cornerstones of Sumerian, and other, ancient civilizations.

   C. Irrigation was great in two ways: the building of it and the stuff that happened as a result.

   D. Between 550 and 200 b.c.e., there were noteworthy improvements in not only the irrigation-related features but also the entire canal systems throughout Mexico.

The following practice sets provide an opportunity to apply the concepts and strategic thinking covered in this chapter. While many of the questions pertain to Organization, Unity, and Cohesion & Topic Development, some touch on other English Language Arts concepts to ensure that your practice is test-like, with a variety of question types. To practice Test Day timing, follow the suggested timing guidelines for each section.

PRACTICE SET

Suggested Timing: 25 minutes

QUESTIONS 1–13: Revising/Editing in a Passage

DIRECTIONS: Read the passage below and answer the questions following it. You will be asked to improve the writing quality of the passage and to correct errors so that the passage follows the conventions of standard written English. You may reread the passage if you need to. Mark the **best** answer for each question.

QUESTIONS 1–7 refer to the following passage.

Vaccines

(1) Vaccination has become one of the most important and most widely used tools of modern medicine. (2) However, very few people know the history of vaccines and how they were developed. (3) Amazingly, the idea of vaccination goes back almost 300 years—a time when doctors still scoffed at the practice of washing their hands between patients—and found its inspiration in both traditional medicine and folklore. (4) The first vaccine was important in its own right, it also provided the foundation for the many vaccines that have been developed since.

(5) In the early eighteenth century, Lady Mary Wortley Montagu traveled to Turkey with her family. (6) She observed a traditional practice called "variolation," a process by which uninfected patients were exposed to smallpox to infect them with a mild form of the disease. (7) Variolation, however, still posed a risk of a potentially fatal, full-scale smallpox infection. (8) Later in the eighteenth century, Edward Jenner began to examine a local legend. (9) It held that milkmaids who were exposed to cowpox became immune to the more dangerous smallpox. (10) Administering a cowpox vaccine, by using a relatively safe, related virus, became the standard method of inoculating against smallpox.

(11) The cowpox vaccine developing from Jenner's work set the standard for vaccines—to find a "safe" virus that confers immunity without the risks of full-blown infection. (12) Later, the French scientist Louis Pasteur discovered that ineffective, outdated disease cultures could still confer immunity and could do so without causing infection. (13) He used this technique to develop a vaccine for rabies in 1885. (14) The technique of using "dead" viruses soon became an important method for developing new vaccines. (15) Vaccines using dead viruses include diphtheria, flu, and the injected polio vaccine. (16) Polio has been almost completely eliminated throughout the world by use of the Salk vaccine, an injection using a dead virus, as well as by the live but weakened Sabin vaccine given by mouth. (17) The Sabin vaccine substitutes 57 nucleotides and produces a mutation in the internal ribosome entry site. (18) Between the two, the World Health Organization reports that the worldwide incidence of polio went from 350,000 in 1988, to 74 in 2015.

Practice Set

1. Which edit is needed to correct sentence 4?

   A. change ***right, it*** to **right; and it**

   B. change ***right, it*** to **right, and it**

   C. change ***have been developed*** to **developed**

   D. change ***have been developed*** to **develops**

2. Which transition should be added to the beginning of sentence 6?

   E. Given that

   F. There

   G. Before

   H. Because

3. What is the best way to combine sentences 8 and 9?

   A. Later in the eighteenth century, Edward Jenner began to examine a local legend, milkmaids who were exposed to cowpox became immune to the more dangerous smallpox.

   B. Later in the eighteenth century, Edward Jenner began to examine a local legend and that milkmaids who were exposed to cowpox became immune to the more dangerous smallpox.

   C. Later in the eighteenth century, Edward Jenner began to examine a local legend that although milkmaids who were exposed to cowpox became immune to the more dangerous smallpox.

   D. Later in the eighteenth century, Edward Jenner began to examine a local legend that held that milkmaids who were exposed to cowpox became immune to the more dangerous smallpox.

4. Which transition should be added to the beginning of sentence 10?

   E. However

   F. Furthermore

   G. Thus

   H. For example

5. Which edit is needed to correct sentence 11?

   A. change ***developing*** to **developed**

   B. change ***Jenner's*** to **Edward Jenner's**

   C. change ***confers*** to **conferring**

   D. change ***full-blown*** to **full-blown, dangerous**

6. What is the best way to combine sentences 14 and 15 to clarify the relationship between ideas?

   E. However, the technique of using "dead" viruses soon became an important method for developing new vaccines using dead viruses, including diphtheria, flu, and the injected polio vaccine.

   F. Thus, an important method for developing new vaccines became the technique of using "dead" viruses, including diphtheria, flu, and the injected polio vaccine.

   G. By using "dead" viruses, the technique that became important for developing new vaccines including diphtheria, flu, and the injected polio vaccine.

   H. The technique of using "dead" viruses soon became an important method for developing new vaccines, including diphtheria, flu, and the injected polio vaccine.

7. Which sentence is irrelevant to the argument presented in the passage and should be deleted?

   A. sentence 14

   B. sentence 15

   C. sentence 16

   D. sentence 17

QUESTIONS 8–13 refer to the following passage.

Nizhny Novgorod

(1) The Russian city of Nizhny Novgorod has long been an important city in the Volga Vyatka economic region of the country. (2) Substantially contributing to the gross national product. (3) Founded in 1221, it stands at the meeting of two great rivers, the Volga and the Oka. (4) Its history was one of invasion and battle until 1612, when the Russian Romanov dynasty was established. (5) Nizhny Novgorod became a cultural center, with museums, art galleries, concert halls, and theaters.

(6) Perhaps its most famous museum is the Nizhny Novgorod State Art Museum, founded in 1896. (7) In that same year it was part of a grand exhibition of art and industry. (8) It featured industrial exhibits including the first Russian car, a radio receiver, oil products, and other examples of new Russian technology. (9) It was the art, however, which generate a storm of controversy in Russian newspapers. (10) The exhibit showcased two conflicting visions of Russian art, one of which was avant-garde. (11) There were numerous examples of various avant-garde art movements. (12) These included Cubo-Futurism, Neo-primitivism, Suprematism, and others. (13) The other art form was more academic, and according to some critics, very superficial. (14) Of the critics raising their voices on the matter, it is Maxim Gorky who is most remembered. (15) Gorky was a distinguished Russian author and activist. (16) Despite the fact that he was quite young at the time Gorky's opinions on the exhibit would prove to be remarkably in keeping with his political beliefs later in life.

(17) As Gorky saw it, the majority of the art on display had been generated by an economy of exploitation that only rewarded artists who created works inaccessible to the general population, such as those in the avant-garde styles. (18) Gorky took the side of those deriding the artwork as aimed only at the elite, and stated, "it is not artists, but the public who need art, and therefore the public should be given such paintings as it can understand." (19) This was an early manifestation of his later political activism as a supporter of the new Marxist-Socialist movement. (20) Nizhny Novgorod was renamed Gorky from 1932–1990.

8. What is the best way to combine sentences 1 and 2?

   E. The Russian city of Nizhny Novgorod has long been an important city in the Volga Vyatka economic region of the country; although substantially contributing to the gross national product.

   F. The Russian city of Nizhny Novgorod has long been an important city in the Volga Vyatka economic region of the country, however substantially contributing to the gross national product.

   G. The Russian city of Nizhny Novgorod has long been an important city in the Volga Vyatka economic region of the country, substantially contributing to the gross national product.

   H. The Russian city of Nizhny Novgorod, has long been an important city in the Volga Vyatka economic region of the country, whereas it substantially contributes to the gross national product.

9. Which transition should be added to the beginning of sentence 8?

   A. Despite this

   B. On the other hand

   C. Conversely

   D. Consequently

10. Which edit is needed to correct sentence 9?

    E. change ***It*** to **They**

    F. change ***however*** to **although**

    G. change ***generate*** to **generated**

    H. change ***newspapers*** to **newspaper**

11. What is the best way to combine sentences 11 and 12 to clarify the relationship between ideas?

    A. There were numerous examples of various avant-garde art movements, includes Cubo-Futurism, Neo-primitivism, Suprematism, and others.

    B. There were numerous examples of various avant-garde art movements; some of the examples of avant-garde art movements included Cubo-Futurism, Neo-primitivism, Suprematism, and others.

    C. There were numerous examples of various avant-garde art movements not excepting Cubo-Futurism, Neo-primitivism, Suprematism, and others.

    D. There were numerous examples of various avant-garde art movements, including Cubo-Futurism, Neo-primitivism, Suprematism, and others.

12. Which edit is needed to correct sentence 16?

    E. insert a comma after ***young***

    F. insert a comma after ***time***

    G. insert a comma after ***keeping***

    H. insert a comma after ***beliefs***

13. Which sentence is irrelevant to the argument presented in the passage and should be deleted?

    A. sentence 17

    B. sentence 18

    C. sentence 19

    D. sentence 20

QUESTIONS 14–20: Revising/Editing Stand-Alone Items

DIRECTIONS: Read and answer each of the following questions. You will be asked to recognize and correct errors in sentences or short paragraphs. Mark the **best** answer for each question.

14. Read this paragraph.

> (1) Engineered for speed, lighter bikes without brakes and gears are used by professional cyclists for time trials. (2) These bicycles have specialized racing tires with an inner tube made of thin rubber and an outer tire cover made of cotton or silk. (3) When purchasing a bicycle, consumers have options such as a weatherproof plastic saddle, blinking lights, and various other accessories. (4) Technology has greatly improved bicycles over the years; in 1868, the first known bike race featured bicycles that each weighed 160 pounds.

Which sentence should be removed to correct a topic development issue?

E. sentence 1

F. sentence 2

G. sentence 3

H. sentence 4

15. Read this paragraph.

> (1) Rosalind Franklin used the technique of X-ray crystallography to depict the structure of DNA by mapping the basic structure of the tiny molecules. (2) Because she has been celebrated by today's genetic researchers, Franklin was never recognized during her lifetime for her ground-breaking work. (3) Her valuable photos of a hydrated form of DNA greatly helped Watson and Crick portray the full structure of DNA. (4) As a result, these men received the Nobel Prize for their work.

Which sentence should be revised to correct a transition issue?

A. sentence 1

B. sentence 2

C. sentence 3

D. sentence 4

16. Read this paragraph.

> (1) Homeopathic remedies, though less widely prescribed than more traditional medications, are of interest to many consumers. (2) This alternative system of natural treatment began in the nineteenth century. (3) According to homeopathic theory, a disease can be treated with remedies having effects that mimic the ailment. (4) Patients often choose to make doctor's appointments in the morning, to lessen potential schedule conflict.

Which sentence should be removed to correct a topic development issue?

E. sentence 1
F. sentence 2
G. sentence 3
H. sentence 4

17. Read this paragraph.

> (1) The island continent of Australia consists of plateaus, ranges, plains, and coasts, which attract tourists and other people seeking adventure. (2) Most Australians live in the warm and sunny coastal cities, including Sydney. (3) Over the years, immigrants have arrived from places such as Europe and the United States for the gold rushes, among other reasons. (4) The unusual Australian wildlife includes primitive mammals, in addition to the wombat, koala bear, and emu.

Which sentence should be removed to correct a topic development issue?

A. sentence 1
B. sentence 2
C. sentence 3
D. sentence 4

18. Read this paragraph.

> (1) Dolores Huerta, one of the founders of the United Farm Workers union, has been a tireless advocate for California's field workers, sometimes traveling up to ten months of the year and sleeping as little as three hours each night. (2) The combined efforts of the United Farm Workers union included the work of Cesar Chavez, who organized the Chicano migrant farmers in California. (3) Agriculture has always faced challenges, due to factors such as unpredictable weather and pests. (4) After persevering through confrontations, strikes, and pickets, farm workers eventually received improved working conditions.

Which sentence should be removed to correct a topic development issue?

E. sentence 1
F. sentence 2
G. sentence 3
H. sentence 4

19. Read this paragraph.

> (1) Boxer Mike Tyson, the youngest heavyweight champion in history, showed a youthful predisposition toward fighting, perhaps because he grew up in a place where such aggression was often required to make it through the day. (2) Boxing has roots in ancient Greece's first Olympic games, and modern boxing comes from eighteenth-century England. (3) Beginning in the 1980s, Tyson earned championships in the World Boxing Association and World Boxing Council divisions. (4) Tyson earned some of his heavyweight titles by winning every round, knocking out his opponent almost every time.

Which sentence should be removed to correct a topic development issue?

A. sentence 1

B. sentence 2

C. sentence 3

D. sentence 4

20. Read this paragraph.

> (1) To dissect vital communications, the cryptologist, a specialist in the technology of deciphering messages, typically employs a host of complex mathematical formulas. (2) For example, the specialist unlocks codes and ciphers, which are devices that secretly send information. (3) Machines create complex messages consisting of letters, words, numbers, or symbols. (4) During wartime, international groups have attempted to monitor and solve systems even though having the opponent's information could provide a major advantage.

Which sentence should be revised to correct a transition issue?

E. sentence 1

F. sentence 2

G. sentence 3

H. sentence 4

ANSWERS AND EXPLANATIONS

Organization, Unity, and Cohesion & Topic Development

Irrigation

1. D

Category: Knowledge of Language

Getting to the Answer: Sentence 1 uses vague language. Only **(D)** consistently uses specific and precise language.

2. F

Category: Organization, Unity, and Cohesion

Getting to the Answer: Sentence 2 says settlements relied on rivers for drinking and cooking, and sentence 3 says irrigation played an important role in early civilizations. **(F)**, "Not surprisingly," is the only choice that logically connects the information. **(E)** and **(G)** are contrast transitions that do not make sense in context. **(H)**, "Later," creates an illogical sequence that the writer did not intend.

3. A

Category: Knowledge of Language

Getting to the Answer: The SHSAT testmakers prefer concise, clearly worded and organized sentences. **(A)**, creating an independent and dependent clause, makes the sentence clear and concise. **(B)** is poorly organized, putting the clause in the wrong place for the flow of the sentence and requiring an additional "and." **(C)** incorrectly joins two independent clauses with a comma, and **(D)** is unnecessarily wordy with the repetition of the irrigation system's location and year of construction.

4. G

Category: Topic Development

Getting to the Answer: The entire passage is about irrigation, so anything other than that topic is irrelevant. Though reference to the Hohokam tribe is relevant, the fact that they established trading posts is not, so sentence 9, **(G)**, should be deleted. All other sentences fit with the topic of the passage.

5. C

Category: Organization, Unity, and Cohesion

Getting to the Answer: Be sure to read this sentence in context. It is the last sentence in a paragraph devoted to irrigation systems throughout history, and the passage has already noted how important such systems were and still are. Sentence 11 is in contrast to this, introducing a negative result of modern irrigation. A contrast sentence needs a contrast word, which is what "however" is, **(C)**. All other choices incorrectly use continuation words.

6. F

Category: Topic Development

Getting to the Answer: Any sentence placed after sentence 11 will be a transition between paragraphs 2 and 3. Paragraph 1 introduces irrigation. Paragraph 2 describes irrigation methods and ends with a mention of one downside of irrigation. Paragraph 3 explains the reasons for the importance of irrigation, so a transition sentence must bridge the two ideas. **(F)** does this, alluding to the last sentence of paragraph 2 and introducing the topic of paragraph 3. **(E)** focuses on the problems of irrigation, which are irrelevant to paragraph 3. **(G)** is redundant, and **(H)**, like **(E)**, is off topic.

7. B

Category: Topic Development

Getting to the Answer: The passage discusses how irrigation benefited ancient civilizations in a variety of ways, which **(B)** reflects. **(A)** and **(C)** do not match the tone of the passage. **(D)** is appropriate in tone but outside the scope of the passage.

PRACTICE SET

Vaccines

1. B

Category: Sentence Structure and Formation

Getting to the Answer: Sentence 4 is a run-on because it joins two independent clauses with only a comma, creating a comma splice. **(B)** correctly inserts a FANBOYS conjunction after the comma to fix the error. **(A)** incorrectly combines a semicolon with a FANBOYS conjunction; semicolons are used without FANBOYS conjunctions.

2. F

Category: Organization, Unity, and Cohesion

Getting to the Answer: Sentence 5 says that Lady Montagu traveled to Turkey, and sentence 6 says she observed "variolation." **(F)**, "There" is the only choice that logically connects the information about where she traveled to what she saw while she was there. **(E)** and **(H)** are cause-and-effect transitions that not only do not make sense in context but also create a fragment. **(G)**, "Before," creates an illogical sequence that the writer did not intend.

3. D

Category: Topic Development

Getting to the Answer: **(D)** combines and relates the two sentences logically, without introducing any errors. **(A)** combines the sentences with just a comma, creating a run-on sentence. **(B)** has incorrect grammatical structure. **(C)** uses a contrast transition word ("although"), which is inappropriate in context.

4. G

Category: Organization, Unity, and Cohesion

Getting to the Answer: This question asks you to connect the final sentence of paragraph 2 to the rest of the paragraph. The only choice that effectively makes this connection is **(G)**. **(E)** indicates a contrast between ideas that is not present. **(F)** treats the sentence as if it were part of a progression. **(H)** incorrectly identifies the sentence as an illustration.

5. A

Category: Usage

Getting to the Answer: Paragraph 2 makes it clear that the development of the cowpox vaccine has already been completed, so "developing" is an inappropriate verb form. **(A)** corrects this. None of the other answer choices address the error.

6. H

Category: Topic Development

Getting to the Answer: Since both sentences deal with the use of dead viruses in vaccines, they can easily be combined. **(H)** does so without introducing any errors. **(E)** uses a transition word that is inappropriate in context. The wording of **(F)** alters the meaning of the sentences. **(G)** creates a sentence fragment.

7. D

Category: Topic Development

Getting to the Answer: Though sentence 17 is relevant to the information about vaccines, and the polio vaccine in particular, it is much too technical to fit the tone of the passage. Deleting this sentence, **(D)**, makes the passage more cohesive. The other sentences are a good fit with the overall topic of the history and development of vaccines.

Nizhny Novgorod

8. G

Category: Organization, Unity, and Cohesion

Getting to the Answer: As the two sentences stand now, sentence 2 is not a complete sentence, and therefore cannot stand on its own. Since it is further evidence of the importance of Nizhny Novgorod, it needs to be connected to sentence 1 with a continuation word. **(F)** uses the contrast word "however." Eliminate it. **(E)** joins the two with a semicolon, which is incorrect when joining a sentence and a dependent clause. **(H)** adds a contrast word, "whereas," and is also wordy. The best way to combine this complete sentence with an incomplete one is with a comma, **(G)**.

9. D

Category: Organization, Unity, and Cohesion

Getting to the Answer: Sentence 7 states that the museum was part of an art and industry exhibition, and sentence 8 lists the industrial exhibits. **(D)**, "Consequently," logically joins the two statements. **(A)**, **(B)**, and **(C)** are contrast transitions, which don't make sense in context.

10. G

Category: Usage

Getting to the Answer: Read the sentence in context; all verbs in the entire paragraph are in the simple past tense, so this sentence needs the simple past "generated," **(G)**. None of the other answer choices fix the error.

11. D

Category: Organization, Unity, and Cohesion

Getting to the Answer: Sentence 12 gives examples to support sentence 11, thus it makes sense to combine them. **(D)** does this in the most concise and clear way, making sentence 12 a dependent clause and adding it to sentence 11 with a comma. **(A)** uses the word "includes" when it should be "including." **(B)** properly joins two complete sentences with a semicolon but makes the resulting sentence wordy and redundant. The phrase "not excepting," **(C)**, implies that there was other avant-garde art in addition to these examples, which may be true but is awkward and unnecessary in the sentence.

12. F

Category: Punctuation

Getting to the Answer: A comma is used to separate an independent clause and a dependent clause. Placing the comma after "time" properly separates the two clauses, so **(F)** is correct. None of the other choices fixes the punctuation error.

13. D

Category: Topic Development

Getting to the Answer: All sentences in a paragraph should be on the same topic, though perhaps from different angles. A sentence which brings in new information irrelevant to the paragraph is out of place and should be deleted. The last sentence in this paragraph, sentence 20, introduces extraneous information about Gorky and renaming the city after him. This is not only out of keeping with the rest of the information in the paragraph but also a poor concluding sentence, so **(D)** is correct. All other sentences are relevant to paragraph 3.

14. G

Category: Topic Development

Getting to the Answer: Consider the paragraph's main idea and check to see if all four sentences connect to the same topic. Sentences 1, 2, and 4 provide information about lightweight racing bicycles, so choices **(E)**, **(F)**, and **(H)** belong in this paragraph. The correct choice is **(G)**.

15. B

Category: Organization, Unity, and Cohesion

Getting to the Answer: The transition "Because" in **(B)** should be "Although." This sentence has contrasting ideas, and keywords like "although" signal that contrast. Franklin did not get credit when she was alive but is now being celebrated by scientists in her field. The sentences in **(A)**, **(C)**, and **(D)** do not contain any errors.

16. H

Category: Topic Development

Getting to the Answer: Consider the paragraph's main idea and check to see if all four sentences connect to the same topic. Sentences 1, 2, and 3 provide information about homeopathic remedies, so the sentences in choices **(E)**, **(F)**, and **(G)** belong in this paragraph. The correct choice is **(H)**.

17. D

Category: Topic Development

Getting to the Answer: Consider the paragraph's main idea and check to see if all four sentences connect to the same topic. Sentences 1, 2, and 3 provide information about people who visit or live in Australia, so the sentences in choices **(A)**, **(B)**, and **(C)** belong in this paragraph. The correct choice is **(D)**.

18. G

Category: Topic Development

Getting to the Answer: Consider the paragraph's main idea and check to see if all four sentences connect to the same topic. Sentences 1, 2, and 4 provide information about advocating for the farmers. Since the sentences in choices **(E)**, **(F)**, and **(H)** provide support for the topic, the correct choice is **(G)**.

19. B

Category: Topic Development

Getting to the Answer: Consider the paragraph's main idea and check to see if all four sentences connect to the same topic. Sentences 1, 3, and 4 provide information about Tyson's athletic career. Since the sentences in choices **(A)**, **(C)**, and **(D)** provide support for the topic, the correct choice is **(B)**.

20. H

Category: Organization, Unity, and Cohesion

Getting to the Answer: Sentence 4 requires a cause-and-effect transition such as "because" rather than the contrast transition "even though." **(E)**, **(F)**, and **(G)** do not have errors.

CHAPTER 8

The Kaplan Method for Reading Comprehension

CHAPTER OBJECTIVES

By the end of this chapter, you will be able to:

- Apply Kaplan's 3-Step Method for Reading Comprehension
- Create Roadmaps for passages using the Kaplan Method for Reading Comprehension, identifying keywords and central ideas
- Predict an answer and find its match among the answer choices using a Roadmap

KAPLAN METHOD FOR READING COMPREHENSION

Kaplan has a method for all of the question types on the SHSAT because it is in your best interest to approach both the test as a whole and the individual sections systematically. If you approach every passage the same way, you will work your way through the Reading Comprehension passages and questions efficiently.

The Kaplan Method for Reading Comprehension has three steps:

Step 1: Read actively

Step 2: Examine the question stem

Step 3: Predict and answer

Let's take a closer look at Step 1: Read actively.

Step 1: Read Actively

Active reading means that as you read the passage, you are asking questions and taking notes.

You should ask questions such as:

- What do the keywords indicate?
- What is a good summary of each paragraph?
- What specific information is provided in the passage?
- What inferences can you make based on the information the author provides?
- What is the Main Idea of the passage?

Keywords

Use the keywords in the paragraph to answer the accompanying questions.

Some literary experts would say that writing in verse form cannot qualify as poetry unless it awakens the senses on a nonverbal level or elevates the emotions. However, the question of whether a verse fulfills these criteria may depend on the reader. Many haiku, for example, may awaken the senses on a nonverbal level in some readers but not in others. Thus, their classification as poems, according to these experts, may depend on what the haiku mean to readers, rather than on what they say.

1. What does the word "However" indicate about the second sentence?

2. What do the words "for example" indicate about the third sentence?

3. What does the word "Thus" indicate about the fourth sentence?

> ✔ **Remember**
>
> **Mark up the passage as you read!**
>
> **The first sentence or two of a paragraph will usually express the topic of the paragraph.**

Summarizing

Actively read the following paragraph. Then answer the accompanying questions that ask about summarizing the paragraph.

The four brightest moons of Jupiter were the first objects in the solar system discovered with the use of the telescope, and they played an important role in Galileo's famous argument supporting the Copernican model of the solar system. For several hundred years after the moons' discovery by Galileo in 1610, scientific understanding of these moons increased slowly but regularly. However, the spectacular close-up photographs sent back by the 1979 Voyager missions forever changed scientists' impressions of these bodies.

1. Why wouldn't "the early history of astronomy" be a good summary for this paragraph?

2. Why wouldn't "discoveries of the Voyager missions" be a good summary?

3. If you had to summarize this paragraph in just a few words, what would they be?

Specific Information

Use the details in the passage to answer the accompanying questions.

A human body can survive without water for several days and without food for as many as several weeks. If breathing stops for as little as 3–6 minutes, however, death is likely to occur. All animals require a constant supply of oxygen to the body tissues, especially to the heart and brain. In the human body, the respiratory system performs this function by delivering air, containing oxygen, to the blood.

But respiration in large animals possessing lungs involves more than just breathing. It is a complex process that delivers oxygen to internal tissues while eliminating carbon dioxide waste produced by cells. More specifically, respiration involves two processes known as bulk flow and diffusion. Oxygen and carbon dioxide are moved in bulk through the respiratory and circulatory systems; gaseous diffusion occurs at different points across thin tissue membranes.

1. What bodily function mentioned is the most critical to human survival? Least critical?
2. What need is shared by all animals?
3. What two processes are involved in respiration in large animals?
4. Where does gaseous diffusion occur?

Inference

Between the ages of 1 and 17, the average person learns the meaning of about 14 words per day. Dictionaries and traditional classroom vocabulary lessons account for only part of this spectacular growth. Far more influential is individuals' verbal interaction with people whose vocabularies are larger than their own. Conversation offers several benefits that make vocabulary learning interesting: it supplies visual information, offers frequent repetition of new words, and gives students the chance to ask questions.

1. The author would most likely recommend which method of increasing a student's vocabulary: classroom lessons or conversation?
2. How would the author most likely describe traditional classroom vocabulary lessons?

Taking Notes

Actively reading the passage includes taking notes to create a Roadmap of a passage, which should include the Main Idea of the passage and the Topic of each paragraph.

Create a Roadmap

The poems of the earliest Greeks, like those of other ancient societies, consisted of magical charms, mysterious predictions, prayers, and traditional songs of work and war. These poems were intended to be

sung or recited, not written down, because they were created before the Greeks began to use writing for literary purposes. All that remains of these poems are fragments mentioned by later Greek writers. Homer, for example, quoted an ancient work song for harvesters, and Simonides adapted the ancient poetry of ritual lamentation, songs of mourning for the dead, in his writing.

1. What words are mentioned repeatedly throughout paragraph 1?

2. What do the words "for example" tell us about the last sentence of paragraph 1?

3. ¶1 Topic ________________

The different forms of early Greek poetry all had something in common: they described the way of life of a whole people. Poetry expressed ideas and feelings that were shared by everyone in a community—their folktales, their memories of historical events, and their religious speculation. The poems were wholly impersonal, with little emphasis on individual achievement. It never occurred to the earliest Greek poets to tell us their names or to try to create anything completely new.

4. What is similar in paragraph 1 and paragraph 2?

5. How does paragraph 2 differ from paragraph 1?

6. ¶2 Topic ________________

In the "age of heroes," however, the content and purpose of Greek poetry changed. By this later period, Greek communities had become separated into classes of rulers and ruled. People living in the same community, therefore, had different, even opposing, interests; they shared fewer ideas and emotions. The particular outlook of the warlike upper class gave poetry a new content, one that focused on the lives of individuals. Poets were assigned a new task: to celebrate the accomplishments of outstanding characters, whether they were real or imaginary, rather than the activity and history of the community.

7. What word at the beginning of paragraph 3 indicates a change in the passage's focus?

8. How is the content of paragraph 3 different from that of paragraph 2?

9. How is later Greek poetry different from earlier Greek poetry?

10. ¶3 Topic ________________

In the Heroic Age, poets became singers of tales and performed long poems about the fates of warriors and kings. One need only study Homer's *Iliad* and *Odyssey,* which are recorded examples of the epic poetry that was sung in the Heroic Age, to understand the influence that the upper class had on the poet's performance. Thus, the poetry of the Heroic Age can no longer be called folk poetry. Nor was the poetry of the Heroic Age nameless, and in this period it lost much of its religious character.

11. How is the focus of paragraph 4 different from the focus of paragraph 3?

12. ¶4 Topic ________________

13. Passage Main Idea ________________

✔ Remember

Words that are repeated by the author are important and likely relate to a paragraph Topic or to the Main Idea.

✔ Remember

Strategies

Be a critical reader.
Make it simple.
Keep moving.
Don't sweat the details.

Roadmap

Look for the Main Idea.
Identify the paragraph Topics.

Now we're ready to tackle Steps 2 and 3.

Step 2: Examine the Question Stem

Five to seven questions will follow the passage. The first thing you'll need to do with each question is to determine exactly what is being asked before you can answer the question. Basically, you need to make the question make sense to you.

Step 3: Predict and Answer

This means you should:

- Predict, or **prephrase**, an answer before looking at the answer choices, also known as "predict before you peek"
- Select the best match

Predicting before you peek helps you:

- Know precisely what you are looking for in the answer choices
- Avoid weighing each answer choice equally, which saves time
- Eliminate the possibility of falling into wrong answer traps

Examine the Question Stem, Predict, and Answer

Answer the questions below using your researching skills, your Roadmap, and your general understanding of the passage.

1. Which of the following best tells what this passage is about?

   A. Where will you look for the answer to this question?

   ____

   B. **Prephrase** the answer:

   ____

   ____

2. The earliest Greek poems were probably written in order to

   A. What important phrase in the question stem tells you where to direct your research?

   ____

   B. What specific text is helpful?

   ____

   C. **Prephrase** the answer:

   ____

   ____

3. The phrase "folk poetry" (line 42) refers to poetry whose contents mainly depict

   A. What important element in the question stem tells you where to direct your research?

   B. What aspect of folk poetry is being questioned?

   C. **Prephrase** the answer:

4. Which of the following did poetry of the Heroic Age primarily celebrate?

   A. What important element in the question stem tells you where to direct your research?

   B. What aspect of this poetry is being questioned?

   C. What specific text from the passage is helpful in answering this question?

   D. **Prephrase** the answer:

5. The passage suggests that, compared to communities in an earlier period, Greek communities during the Heroic Age were probably

   A. What important elements in the question stem tell you where to direct your research?

   B. What specific text from the passage is helpful in answering this question?

   C. What can you infer about how Greek communities changed between these periods?

   D. **Prephrase** the answer:

6. Which of the following situations most closely parallels the one involving poets in the Heroic Age as it is presented in the passage?

   A. What was the focus of Greek poetry during the Heroic Age?

   B. **Prephrase** the answer:

1. Which of the following best tells what this passage is about?
   - A. how the role of early Greek poetry changed
   - B. how Greek communities became separated into classes
   - C. the superiority of early Greek poetry
   - D. the origin of the *Iliad* and the *Odyssey*

2. The earliest Greek poems were probably written in order to
   - E. bring fame to kings.
   - F. bring fame to poets.
   - G. express commonly held beliefs.
   - H. celebrate the lives of warriors.

3. The phrase "folk poetry" (line 42) refers to poetry whose contents mainly depict
   - A. the adventures of warriors.
   - B. the viewpoint of a ruling class.
   - C. the problems of a new lower class.
   - D. the concerns of a whole culture.

4. Which of the following did poetry of the Heroic Age primarily celebrate?
   - E. community life
   - F. individuals
   - G. religious beliefs
   - H. the value of work

5. The passage suggests that, compared to communities in an earlier period, Greek communities during the Heroic Age were probably
   - A. less prosperous.
   - B. less unified.
   - C. better organized.
   - D. more peaceful.

6. Which of the following situations most closely parallels the one involving poets in the Heroic Age as it is presented in the passage?
   - E. A school of artists abandons portrait painting in favor of abstract art.
   - F. A sports team begins to rely increasingly on the efforts of a star player.
   - G. A species of wolf is hunted to the verge of extinction.
   - H. A group of reporters publicize the influence of celebrities on historical events.

The following practice sets provide an opportunity to apply the concepts and strategic thinking covered in this chapter. To practice Test Day timing, follow the suggested timing guidelines for each section.

PRACTICE SET

Suggested Timing: 48 minutes

DIRECTIONS: Read each passage below and answer the questions following it. Base your answers **on information contained only in the passage.** You may reread a passage if you need to. Mark the **best** answer for each question.

Although the screen appeal of Humphrey DeForest Bogart has seemingly grown exponentially in the years following his death in 1957, the early stages of his career were not marked by success. When he finally made it onto the Broadway stage in the early 1920s after a series of struggles in the entertainment business, his performances were met with particularly poor reviews. In fact, when one considers Bogart's early academic pursuits and formative years, it is perhaps surprising that he even made it onto the stage at all.

Born in New York City in 1899 as the son of a prominent surgeon, young Humphrey was quickly put on the academic track to medical school. After finishing his early schooling, he was sent to the prestigious Phillips Academy in Andover, Massachusetts to prepare himself for eventual medical studies at Yale University. Bogart, however, was not inclined toward academics, and he was often described during his adolescent years as rather belligerent and a frequent instigator of trouble. Indeed, soon after he had arrived at Andover, he ran into disciplinary problems and was eventually expelled. In the spring of 1918, Bogart chose to enter the navy. It was in the service that he received an injury to his mouth that partially paralyzed his upper lip, creating a distinctive snarl that would come to be the signature of his eventual stardom.

When Bogart was released from the navy in 1920, he began to turn his attention toward the theater. He contacted a family friend in the business who hired him to work in a theater office in New York. Bogart eventually became a stage manager and finally worked himself into some minor roles on the stage. His inexperience showed, however, and he struggled to find any substantive parts. In the early 1930s, Bogart set out for Hollywood, and although he quickly signed a contract with Fox Pictures, he appeared, marginally, in only three films. Frustrated with his stagnant career, he returned to the Broadway stage and finally caught his break.

In the role of Duke Mantee in the play *The Petrified Forest*, Bogart found his calling. The play was a hit, and Bogart's performance as the quintessential tough guy soon catapulted his career. Whether it was as gumshoe Sam Spade in *The Maltese Falcon* or as café owner Rick Blaine in *Casablanca*, Bogart consistently created rich and complex screen images punctuated by his hangdog expressions, perennial five o'clock shadow, dangling cigarette, and world-weary attitude. From his early gangster roles to his consummate portrayal of the reluctant hero, Bogart's performances came to personify male elegance on the screen, and it is unlikely that his illustrious career will ever be forgotten.

1. Which of the following best tells what this passage is about?
   - **A.** why Bogart was able to overcome many challenges to eventually succeed as an actor
   - **B.** how Bogart's early life experiences shaped his portrayal of characters on the screen
   - **C.** how Bogart ignored his studies and his father's wishes to follow his dreams of acting
   - **D.** how Bogart's tremendous fame as an actor arose out of rather unsuccessful beginnings

2. Which of the following is **not** mentioned in the passage as an element of Bogart's formative years?
   - **E.** an injury that partially paralyzed his upper lip
   - **F.** the signature snarl of Bogart's stardom
   - **G.** a reputation as a troublemaker
   - **H.** the hope that Bogart would study medicine at Yale

3. According to the passage, which of the following statements about Bogart's acting career is accurate?
   - **A.** He was able to sign a lucrative contract with Fox Pictures.
   - **B.** He was often able to find substantive roles.
   - **C.** His early performances were not well received.
   - **D.** When he finally made it onto the Broadway stage, he caught his break.

4. From the comments of the author, what is the most likely reason Bogart never went to medical school?
   - **E.** A family friend in the theater guided Bogart toward acting instead of medicine.
   - **F.** While at Andover, Bogart got into too many fights.
   - **G.** Bogart was eventually expelled from Andover.
   - **H.** Bogart was uninterested in academics.

On October 29, 1929, the stock market crashed in one of the worst financial panics in American history. The ensuing economic meltdown, known as the Great Depression, left Americans thinking about what went wrong and how to ensure that it would never happen again. To this day, economists study the speculative boom of the Roaring '20s, the crash, and the Great Depression, trying to find patterns that can be applied to today's economy.

After World War I, America, having proven itself a world power, began to reap the benefits of new technologies and investments opening everywhere. Mass production made all types of new gadgets like vacuum cleaners and automobiles available to more Americans because of cheaper prices. The same was true of stocks and bonds. Throughout the 1920s, many Americans, not just the rich, played the stock market. Laws of the day made this investment possible by requiring only 10 percent, or a "margin," of an investment to be paid immediately, with the rest payable over time. If something went wrong, however, the investor would have to pay back the balance of the loan.

Economists of the time worried about how much investing was being done by people who could not afford the losses if the market crashed, but government policy of the day called for nonintervention into business matters. Economists, nonetheless, sought a way to wean the people away from margin investing, but no laws were implemented for fear of causing a panic. As long as the stock prices continued to go up and investors continued to benefit, no one was willing to take action. History has taught us, however, that markets are cyclic in nature, and eventually even the strongest bull market* will begin to fail.

In this case, the failure came in 1929. The year was filled with nervous tension as investors who had bought a great quantity of stock on credit sought a way out of a market that was declining. Finally, on October 29, the pressure of everyone trying to sell stock became too much, and the market began a downward spiral from which there would be no easy recovery.

The lessons of 1929 have taught investors that the stock market is no game. Laws have been passed that significantly reduce margin investing. In addition, many safeguards have been implemented to stem financial panic when the market starts to decline. Although the economy will always have high and low points, the hope is that by moderating people's behavior, the raw panic that allowed the crash of '29 and the Great Depression to occur can be prevented.

* bull market: a successful market with confident investors

5. Which of the following best summarizes the main focus of this passage?

   A. how panic affects investment in the stock market

   B. the causes that led up to the crash of 1929

   C. why economists were powerless to stop the crash of 1929

   D. the crash of 1929 and the lessons it has taught

6. Why does the author mention vacuum cleaners and automobiles in line 14 ?

   E. to give examples of new devices that were being invented during the 1920s

   F. to describe the types of companies that were making money during the 1920s

   G. to illustrate the types of things that were not available to Americans with lower incomes

   H. to demonstrate how many Americans could afford new items in the 1920s

7. According to the passage, why were more Americans able to invest in the stock market during the 1920s?
   - **A.** because they could buy large quantities of stock at only a fraction of the purchase price
   - **B.** because the economy at that time was booming
   - **C.** because of restrictions that prevented margin investing
   - **D.** because the government sought to encourage more investment

8. According to the passage, all of the following contributed to the crash of '29 **except**
   - **E.** the cyclic nature of economies.
   - **F.** lack of government intervention.
   - **G.** margin investing.
   - **H.** the people buying stocks on October 29th.

9. All of the following are stated as consequences of the crash of '29 **except**
   - **A.** safeguards reducing margin investing were implemented.
   - **B.** attempts were made to reduce panic when the stock market naturally declines.
   - **C.** the onset of the Great Depression.
   - **D.** the complete termination of irresponsible investment.

10. Which of the following situations is most similar to economists' studies of the crash of 1929?
    - **E.** scientists studying the bones of a dinosaur to find out how it lived
    - **F.** investigators studying the remains of a massive fire in order to prevent future fires
    - **G.** students studying the history of the civil war to learn more about their country
    - **H.** investors reading financial magazines to learn how to better invest their money

In 1895, after Wilhelm Conrad Röntgen discovered that X-rays had properties applicable to science and technology, many scientists in the fields of physics and chemistry sought to discover the origin of this phenomenon. In 1896, French physicist Antoine Henri Becquerel accidentally discovered that unexposed photographic plates left in a darkened drawer with uranium crystals became partially developed. Becquerel recognized that an invisible source of energy must be emitted from uranium in order to cause this phenomenon. Becquerel's discovery marked the beginning of scientific work with radioactivity, an exciting if somewhat disturbing new development in our understanding of the universe.

The source of the mysterious energy emanating from the uranium crystals lay at the atomic level. The atoms of all elements have heavy positively charged cores, or nuclei, made up of protons and neutrons. The bulk of an atom's mass lies in this nucleus. Some atoms are so big that their nuclei are unstable and unable to stay together. Within samples of radioactive elements, a process of radioactive decay breaks down these atoms and releases bursts of energy just as the uranium crystals did in Becquerel's drawer. After Becquerel made his discovery, it was left for other scientists to learn as much as possible about radioactivity.

In Becquerel's lab, other physicists and chemists went to work to explore the properties of radioactivity. The husband and wife team of Pierre and Marie Curie found that the radioactive decay of a sample of material happened at a predictable rate and could be measured. The half-life of a sample is the unit of measurement that the Curies developed to measure how long it takes for half of a sample of a radioactive substance to decay. The Curies also discovered that an ore of uranium pitchblende had more than 300 times the radioactive energy as a sample of the same amount of pure uranium. They reasoned that other radioactive elements present in pitchblende were responsible for this discrepancy, and through this knowledge, they were eventually able to isolate the previously undiscovered elements of radium and polonium. From this early work, modern nuclear science was born.

The discovery of radioactivity and the subsequent development of nuclear science have proved to be a double-edged sword for mankind. Although these discoveries have led to more precise models of the atom and more accurate information about the nature of matter and energy, nuclear science also has very harmful applications; using radioactive principles, for example, scientists were able to build the first nuclear weapons. Nonetheless, with the building of nuclear power stations, the use of carbon dating to authenticate archaeological finds, and the use of radioactive isotopes to treat cancer, it is clear that nuclear science is now a part of life.

11. Which of the following best describes what this passage is about?

A. how the hard work of the Curies contributed to the development of nuclear science

B. how the discovery of radioactivity has been very harmful to mankind

C. how the discovery of radioactivity has had significant consequences

D. the life and work of Antoine Henri Becquerel

12. According to the passage, how did Becquerel discover radioactivity?

E. He deliberately placed undeveloped photographic plates in a drawer with uranium.

F. He recognized that energy emitted from radioactive material could develop photographic plates.

G. He copied the experiments of Röntgen.

H. He isolated radium and polonium from pitchblende.

13. What is intended by the author's inclusion of the phrase "if somewhat disturbing" in line 13?

    A. The application of Becquerel's discovery has had destructive consequences.

    B. Others claim to have made the discovery before Becquerel.

    C. Nuclear science has not significantly impacted mankind since its discovery.

    D. Nuclear science has done nothing but harm since its discovery.

14. Why does the author mention "nuclear weapons" in line 54?

    E. to explain why the discovery of radioactivity has been a benefit to mankind

    F. to give an example of a potential destructive application of nuclear science

    G. to illustrate the potential of radium and polonium

    H. to refute the notion that the discovery of radioactivity has proved to be a mixed blessing

The cane toad, a large, brightly colored amphibian that can weigh more than a pound, was first introduced to the Australian continent by the sugarcane industry. The cane toad was a known predator of the cane beetle, which had been devouring the sugarcane crops since the early 1900s. The Australian farmers thought that by bringing these toads from their native habitats in the Americas, they could use the toads effectively to feast on these pests and eradicate the growing insect threat. So, in 1935, roughly 100 cane toads were carefully packed into crates and shipped to Australia; upon their arrival, the cane farmers eagerly brought them to a pond in the northeast province of Queensland.

Before long, the female cane toads had laid hundreds of thousands of eggs in elongated, gelatinous strings—and the farmers waited for their new predators to be born. As the eggs hatched, the pond became filled with great clouds of squirming, wriggling tadpoles that, upon reaching maturity, were taken to the sugarcane fields and turned loose. The situation that resulted from this fateful release, however, did not coincide with the farmers' plan. In fact, the introduction of cane toads into the wild in Australia has since been deemed nothing short of an ecological disaster.

Easily numbering well into the millions—an exact figure has been impossible to calculate—the cane toads dominated the landscape in Queensland. Following their release, some of the toads descended as planned on the sugarcane crops and began to eat the beetles; however, they soon lost interest in their new habitat. For one thing, the mature cane beetles could fly away from their predators, forcing these slow, fat toads to work very hard for their food. In addition, the fields were hot and dry and provided little sleeping shelter for the newcomers, who generally prefer wet shade. Yet these adverse conditions were not severe enough to kill off the toads; instead, the toads began to look elsewhere for food and shelter. The nearby towns, full of lush gardens and well-watered lawns, were extremely inviting, and soon the toads had overrun entire residential areas. They covered the lawns, filled the gardens, found shelter under flowerpots or on porches, and even began to eat bowls of food left outside for pets like cats and dogs.

Today, the people of Queensland hunt cane toads as if they were mosquitoes, but the toads continue to spread south and west through Australia in staggering numbers. As for the sugarcane industry, just five years after the release of the toads, an effective insecticide spray became available, and the cane beetles were easily exterminated. But scientists, as well as the Australian government, continue to grapple with the cane toad problem.

15. Which of the following best tells what this passage is about?

    A. why sugarcane farmers brought cane toads to Australia

    B. how the habits of the cane toad allowed for such rapid population expansion

    C. why the cane toads preferred residential areas to the sugarcane fields

    D. how the introduction of cane toads to Australia proved to be a disaster

16. Which of the following is **not** mentioned as a characteristic of the cane toad?

    E. It is brightly colored.

    F. It has a loud croak.

    G. It prefers shade.

    H. It can eat pet food.

17. According to the passage, why did the cane toads begin to migrate away from the sugarcane fields?

    A. The sugarcane fields did not provide enough beetles for the toad population.

    B. Residential areas provided greater shade and food that was easier to get.

    C. The sugarcane farmers grew impatient with the poor work of the toads.

    D. People in residential areas began to offer the toads food.

18. While describing the cane toad population growth, the author's inclusion of the fact that "an exact figure has been impossible to calculate" (lines 27–28) emphasizes

    E. the difficult task of finding the cane toads.

    F. the fact that different scientists have presented different population numbers.

    G. the incredible size of the cane toad population.

    H. the ineptitude of the sugarcane farmers in handling the problem.

19. The "farmers' plan" mentioned in line 23 of the passage refers to which of the following?

    A. the inability to grow as many toads as they thought they would need

    B. the plan to have the toads eat all the cane beetles

    C. the breeding instructions the farmers received with the toads

    D. the accidental introduction of millions of toads into Australia

20. According to the passage, how did the sugarcane industry resolve the cane beetle problem?

    E. They relied on the Australian government for help.

    F. They replanted the entire sugarcane crop.

    G. They called on the townspeople for assistance.

    H. They destroyed the beetles with chemicals.

For a jazz musician in New York City in the early 1940s, the most interesting place to spend the hours between midnight and dawn was probably a Harlem nightclub called Minton's. After finishing their jobs at other clubs, young musicians like Charlie Parker, Dizzy Gillespie, Kenny Clarke, and Thelonious Monk would gather at Minton's and have "jam" sessions, which were informal performances featuring lengthy group and solo improvisations. The all-night sessions resulted in the birth of modern jazz as these African American artists together forged a new sound, known as bebop.

Unlike "swing," the enormously popular jazz played in the 1930s, bebop was not dance music. It was often blindingly fast, incorporating tricky, irregular rhythms and discordant sounds that jazz audiences had never heard before. Earlier jazz, like practically all of Western music up to that time, used an eight-note scale. Bebop, in contrast, was based on a 12-note scale, thereby opening up vast new harmonic opportunities for musicians.

The musicians who pioneered bebop shared two common elements: a vision of the new music's possibilities and astonishing improvisational skill—the ability to play or compose a musical line on the spur of the moment. Improvisation within the context of a group setting is, after all, the essence of jazz, which has been described as the musical experience of the passing moment. Parker, perhaps the greatest instrumental genius jazz has known, was an especially brilliant improviser. He often played twice as fast as the rest of the band, but his solos were always in rhythm and exquisitely shaped, revealing a harmonic imagination that enthralled his listeners.

Like many revolutions, unfortunately, the bebop movement encountered heavy resistance. Opposition came from older jazz musicians initially, but also, later and more lastingly, from a general public alienated by the music's complexity and sophistication. Furthermore, due to the government ban on recording that was in effect during the early years of World War II (records were made of vinyl, a petroleum product that was essential to the war effort), the creative ferment that first produced bebop remains largely undocumented today.

21. Which of the following best tells what this passage is about?

A. a tribute to Charlie Parker's contribution to jazz

B. an account of informal jam sessions during the 1940s

C. a history of jazz music in the United States

D. the story of the birth of a modern jazz movement

22. In what way was bebop music different from the swing music of the 1930s?

E. It was enormously popular.

F. It was based on an eight-note scale.

G. It featured discordant sounds.

H. It was played at better dance tempos.

23. Why did bebop offer new harmonic opportunities for jazz musicians?

A. It was played twice as fast as other jazz styles.

B. It placed less emphasis on rhythm.

C. It was based on an unconventional new scale.

D. It replaced swing as the most popular form of jazz.

24. Which of the following is **not** mentioned as one of the reasons for Parker's success?

E. his musical vision

F. his improvisational ability

G. his harmonic imagination

H. his magnetic personality

25. The passage implies that the bebop movement was unpopular with the general public because

   A. the government banned all sales of bebop records.

   B. bebop was generally played at irregular hours.

   C. bebop was too difficult for many listeners to follow.

   D. many older jazz musicians were critical of bebop.

26. Which of the following best describes what is suggested by the statement that the bebop movement went "largely undocumented" (line 45)?

   E. Many bebop jazz recordings were made illegally.

   F. Historians have not fully researched the origins of bebop.

   G. A shortage of vinyl prevented bebop musicians from recording.

   H. Many musicians who would otherwise have recorded were enlisted in the U.S. Army.

ANSWERS AND EXPLANATIONS

Keywords

1. "However" indicates a contrast, or change in direction.
2. The words "for example" indicate that the author is providing an instance that will demonstrate something that was discussed in the preceding sentence.
3. "Thus" indicates a conclusion.

Summarizing

1. The paragraph focuses on four of Jupiter's moons, so "the early history of astronomy" isn't specific enough to be a good summary.
2. Only one sentence mentions the Voyager missions, so "discoveries of the Voyager missions" isn't broad enough to be a good summary.
3. Jupiter's four brightest moons

Specific Information

1. Breathing most critical: "If breathing stops for as little as 3–6 minutes, however, death is likely." Eating least critical: "A human body can survive...without food for as many as several weeks."
2. Oxygen is a need shared by all animals: "All animals require a constant supply of oxygen to the body tissues."
3. The two processes involved in respiration are bulk flow and diffusion: "respiration involves two processes known as bulk flow and diffusion."
4. Gaseous diffusion occurs across tissue membranes: "gaseous diffusion occurs at different points across thin tissue membranes."

Inference

1. The author would recommend conversation with people with larger vocabularies to increase a student's vocabulary because it is "Far more influential" (line 5) and "offers several benefits that make vocabulary learning interesting" (lines 7–8).
2. The author would describe traditional classroom vocabulary lessons as not as influential as conversations with people with larger vocabularies. In addition, traditional classroom vocabulary lessons do not offer benefits that make vocabulary learning interesting.

Create a Roadmap

1. Words repeated in paragraph 1 include "poetry" and "Greek."
2. The phrase "for example" tells you that this sentence provides an example of something that has already been mentioned.
3. ¶1 Topic: Early Greek poetry characteristics
4. Both paragraph 1 and paragraph 2 are about early Greek poetry.
5. Paragraph 2 elaborates on the topic of paragraph 1, focusing on a single common element of all early Greek poetry.
6. ¶2 Topic: Early Greek poetry focused on community
7. The word "however" indicates a change of direction in the passage.
8. Paragraph 2 discusses a common theme in early Greek poetry, while paragraph 3 introduces later Greek poetry.

9. Early Greek poetry focused on the community. Later poetry focused on individuals.

10. ¶3 Topic: Poetry changed as society changed, more focus on individuals

11. Paragraph 3 describes the purpose of later Greek poetry. Paragraph 4 describes the changed role of the poets who composed it.

12. ¶4 Topic: Heroic Age poetry influenced by upper class and individualism

13. Passage Main Idea: While early Greek poetry focused on the community as a whole, later Greek poetry was crafted by and about individuals.

Examine the Question Stem, Predict, and Answer

Passage Analysis: The purpose of the passage is to contrast the characteristics of two periods of Greek poetry. The Main Idea of the passage is that, although the earliest Greek poetry focused on the community as a whole, later Greek poetry of the Heroic Age celebrated individuals. Paragraph 1 describes general characteristics of the earliest Greek poetry. Paragraph 2 explains that the earliest Greek poetry focused on the community. Paragraph 3 explains that, after Greek society became separated into classes, poetry of the Heroic Age came to focus on accomplishments of individuals. Paragraph 4 explains that Heroic Age poets performed epic poems focused on the upper class.

1A. Look for the answer in the Roadmap notes.
1B. **Prephrase:** Early Greek poetry focused on community, later focused on individuals.

1. A

Category: Global

Getting to the Answer: Global questions such as this ask you for the Main Idea. Does the Main Idea from your Roadmap closely match one of the choices? Remember, the scope of the correct answer will incorporate everything discussed in the passage, but no more. In this case, the Main Idea involves the change in Greek poetry from the earliest poets focused on the community to Heroic Age poets focused on individuals. In other words, the passage is about how the role of early Greek poets changed—**(A)**. The author does not discuss how Greek communities became separated into classes or the superiority of early Greek poetry, making **(B)** and **(C)** Out of Scope. **(D)** is incorrect because it only mentions examples, which are not the focus of the entire passage.

2A. "The earliest Greek poems" indicates that the answer is in the first two paragraphs.
2B. Early Greek poems "described the way of life of a whole people" (lines 14–15) and "expressed ideas and feelings that were shared by everyone in a community" (lines 15–16).
2C. **Prephrase:** Early Greek poetry represented culture and society as a whole.

2. G

Category: Detail

Getting to the Answer: Use your Roadmap to navigate back to the section of the passage that discusses the purpose of the earliest Greek poetry—paragraph 2. You know from the paragraph topic in your Roadmap that the earliest poets focused on the community, so look for the choice that is consistent with that focus—**(G)**. **(E)** and **(H)** are both Distortions; celebrating kings and warriors is characteristic of later Heroic Age poetry. **(F)** is Out of Scope since the author never suggests that poets sought fame for themselves.

3A. The line reference provided indicates where to find the answer.

3B. The phrase "contents mainly depict" means that the question is asking about the general subject of this type of poetry.

3C. **Prephrase:** Folk poetry's general subject was the whole community.

3. D

Category: Detail

Getting to the Answer: Go back to the passage and study the context in which this phrase is used. Paragraph 4 says that poetry that celebrates individuals of the upper class can no longer be called "folk poetry." You can infer from "no longer" that earlier Greek poetry must have been folk poetry. Because the key difference discussed in the passage is that earlier poetry concerned the community as a whole, you can infer that this must be a characteristic of folk poetry. **(D)** reflects this best. Paragraph 4 says that folk poetry is not about warriors and the ruling class, making **(A)** and **(B)** incorrect. **(C)** is Out of Scope; the problems of the lower class are never discussed.

4A. The key phrase is "poetry of the Heroic Age."

4B. The phrase "primarily celebrate" means that the question is asking about the purpose of this type of poetry.

4C. Paragraph 4 states in lines 35–37, "In the Heroic Age, poets...performed long poems about the fates of warriors and kings."

4D. **Prephrase:** Later Greek poetry celebrated extraordinary individuals.

4. F

Category: Detail

Getting to the Answer: Use your Roadmap to find the answer. Paragraph 3 explains that Heroic Age poetry focused on individuals—**(F)**. **(E)** is incorrect because community life was a subject of earlier poetry. **(G)** is incorrect because paragraph 4 says that Heroic Age poetry wasn't very religious. **(H)** is Out of Scope; the passage did not address the value of work.

5A. Relevant phrases are "compared to communities in an earlier period" and "communities during the Heroic Age."

5B. Paragraph 2 states that "everyone in a community" shared "ideas and feelings," while paragraph 3 states that "By this later period, Greek communities had become separated into classes of rulers and ruled," and that they "shared fewer ideas and emotions."

5C. Later Greek communities became divided into different classes, so they were less unified than earlier ones.

5D. **Prephrase:** Greek communities during the Heroic Age were more diverse than during earlier periods.

5. B

Category: Inference

Getting to the Answer: What does the passage tell you about changes in Greek communities between the two periods? Paragraph 3, which provides the transition from the early period into the Heroic Age, tells you that "Greek communities had become separated into classes." If the communities were separated, the inference is that they were less unified—**(B)**. The passage does not compare the communities in terms of prosperity, organization, or peace, making **(A)**, **(C)**, and **(D)** Out of Scope.

6A. Greek poetry of the Heroic Age focused on the lives and deeds of extraordinary individuals.

6B. **Prephrase:** Heroic Age poets celebrated famous people.

6. H

Category: Inference

Getting to the Answer: You are asked here to find a situation that closely parallels that of the poets in the Heroic Age. Because the specifics of the choices will be different, break down what you know about poets in the Heroic Age to its basic, structural elements: writers celebrating important individuals. Which choice matches that basic structure? **(H)**. **(E)** is incorrect because style is not the issue of the passage—subject matter is. **(F)** might be tempting because it involves a celebrated individual, but the sports team does not parallel the role of the poet. **(G)** is Out of Scope; nothing in the passage involves hunting or eliminating anyone.

PRACTICE SET

Passage Analysis: The passage describes the early stages of Humphrey Bogart's career and his eventual and perhaps unlikely rise to fame. Paragraph 1 sets forth the idea that Bogart achieved great fame despite unsuccessful beginnings as an actor. Paragraph 2 describes Bogart's academic pursuits and service in the navy. Paragraph 3 describes Bogart's return to acting after the navy. Paragraph 4 describes his achievements and rise to fame.

1. D

Category: Global

Getting to the Answer: First, in order to find the best summary of the passage, make sure to identify a common theme running through every paragraph of the passage. In this case, every paragraph, in one way or another, focuses on how Bogart's eventual fame came from rather unlikely beginnings—his being a potential student of medicine and his enlistment in the navy, which matches **(D)**. **(A)** is Out of Scope; the passage never examines why Bogart was able to overcome early failures to succeed as an actor. **(B)** is also Out of Scope; the passage does explore a direct connection between Bogart's early life and his various screen portrayals, but this does not describe the passage as a whole. **(C)** is a Distortion; the passage never suggests that Bogart ignored his studies or that he defied his father's wishes.

2. F

Category: Detail

Getting to the Answer: As the question refers to Bogart's "formative years," first identify where in the passage these years are described. Paragraph 2 describes Bogart's academic pursuits and time in the navy; look for an answer choice that is not supported by the information in this paragraph—one that does not describe Bogart's early years. **(F)** is correct: while the injury that partially paralyzed his lip occurred during Bogart's "formative years," his "signature snarl" would be a characteristic of his later years and the fame he eventually enjoyed. **(E)**, **(G)**, and **(H)** are all mentioned in paragraph 2's description of Bogart's formative years.

3. C

Category: Detail

Getting to the Answer: Because the entire passage, with the exception of paragraph 2, describes Bogart's acting career, use the answer choices to direct your research of the passage's content. Be wary of answer choices that use wordings directly from the text but in fact misrepresent the information provided, as well as choices that seem to clearly run counter to the passage's purpose. Paragraph 1 describes Bogart's first performances as being "met with particularly poor reviews" (lines 7–8), so **(C)** is correct. **(A)** is a Distortion; the passage states in paragraph 3 that he signed a contract with Fox Pictures, but it never suggests that this was a "lucrative," or profitable, deal. **(B)** is Opposite; the passage states in paragraph 3 that he "struggled to find any substantive parts" (lines 35–36). **(D)** is a Distortion; Bogart did "catch his break" on the Broadway stage, but he had already performed there in the early 1920s with little success.

4. H

Category: Inference

Getting to the Answer: Although the author never explicitly states why Bogart never made it to medical school, reasons can be inferred from the information that the author does provide. In this case, although the author describes Bogart as a troublemaker and states that he was expelled from Andover, he also describes Bogart as "not inclined toward academics" (line 19). It is this latter piece of information that can be best connected with Bogart's decision to leave the path toward medical school. The correct choice is **(H)**. **(E)** is a Distortion; the passage mentions the help of a family friend but never suggests that this friend guided Bogart away from medicine. **(F)** is Out of Scope; the passage describes Bogart as a troublemaker and mentions disciplinary problems, but the nature of these problems is never described in any detail. **(G)** is a Distortion; although Bogart was indeed expelled, this fact alone would not have necessarily prevented him from reaching medical school.

Passage Analysis: The main focus of the passage is the stock market crash of 1929 and the lessons learned from it. Paragraph 1 introduces the crash of '29 and details its devastating effects. Paragraph 2 discusses the optimism of the 1920s and the speculative investing of many Americans. Paragraph 3 discusses how economists were concerned but essentially did nothing to prevent the crash. Paragraph 4 discusses how the crash actually happened. Paragraph 5 discusses steps taken by the government to try to prevent future crashes.

5. D

Category: Global

Getting to the Answer: Global questions ask you to summarize the Main Idea that runs throughout the passage. In this case, the passage discusses the stock market crash of '29 and the lessons learned from it. The correct answer will best summarize this focus. **(D)** is a great match for your prediction. **(A)** is a Misused Detail; although the passage does discuss panic in investment, the author's focus is specifically on the crash of '29. **(B)** is also a Misused Detail; the passage does discuss causes of the crash, but this is not the author's main focus. **(C)** is a Distortion; the passage does mention economists and how they were concerned about margin investing, but the passage does not state that they were powerless to stop the crash.

6. H

Category: Inference

Getting to the Answer: Vacuum cleaners and automobiles are mentioned in paragraph 2 to demonstrate how mass production made prices lower and products available to more Americans. Similarly, stocks were easy to purchase because only 10% of their price was required to buy them. This led to the speculative investment that preceded the crash. Therefore, **(H)** is correct. **(E)** and **(F)** are Out of Scope; the passage does not mention inventions of the 1920s nor does it mention which companies made money during the 1920s. **(G)** is Opposite; the passage indicates that such things were available to more Americans.

7. A

Category: Detail

Getting to the Answer: Paragraph 2 discusses the new financial power of Americans during the 1920s. Lines 18–21 state, "Laws of the day made this investment possible by requiring only 10 percent, or a 'margin,' of an investment to be paid immediately, with the rest payable over time." From this information, you can see that investors did not need to have the money all at once to buy stock. **(A)** matches this prediction. **(B)** is a Misused Detail; although the passage does state that the economy was booming, the passage does not connect the booming economy with stock investment by regular people. **(C)** is Opposite; the passage states that the laws allowed, rather than prevented, margin investing. **(D)** is a Distortion; the passage states that the government did not interfere in business affairs, so it is unlikely that the government would have encouraged investment.

8. H

Category: Detail

Getting to the Answer: Pay careful attention to the wording of the question. The question is asking for an answer choice that was not a contributing cause to the stock market crash of 1929. The correct choice is **(H)**—on October 29, panicky people were selling stocks, not buying them. **(E)** is mentioned in lines 33–35; when the economy started to fail as a result of this cyclical nature, investors panicked. **(F)** is mentioned in lines 26–28; because of a policy of nonintervention, the government did nothing to stop the crash. **(G)** is mentioned in lines 19–20; the passage states that a major cause of the crash was investors buying stock with money they essentially did not have.

9. D

Category: Detail

Getting to the Answer: For the most part, the consequences of the crash of '29 are listed in the concluding paragraph. Remember that you are looking for an answer choice that is not a stated consequence. While irresponsible investment may have been curbed as a consequence of the crash of '29, the passage does not state that it has ended entirely; therefore, **(D)** is correct. **(A)** is mentioned in lines 45–46, **(B)** is mentioned in lines 47–48, and **(C)** is mentioned in lines 3–4.

10. F

Category: Inference

Getting to the Answer: This question asks you to identify a particular pattern from the passage in an unrelated setting. After examining the passage, you should recognize that economists have studied the crash of '29 to learn how to prevent future crashes. The correct answer will contain this idea of studying a negative event to learn how to prevent a future occurrence. Choice **(F)** best matches your prediction; studying a fire to learn how to prevent such a fire in the future is a reasoning process quite similar to studying the crash of '29 in order to prevent future crashes. **(E)** and **(G)** are Distortions; **(E)** does not capture the idea of trying to prevent something, and **(G)** does not contain the idea of preventing future problems. **(H)** is also a Distortion; this choice might be tempting because it contains investment ideas from the passage, but it does not include the prevention of disaster.

Passage Analysis: The main focus of the passage is the discovery of radioactivity and the development and application of nuclear science. The focus of paragraph 1 is the discovery of radioactivity. Paragraph 2 discusses the science of radioactivity. Paragraph 3 details the work of the Curies in learning more about radioactivity. Paragraph 4 is about the positive and negative consequences of the discovery of radioactivity.

11. C

Category: Global

Getting to the Answer: In this passage, the idea that recurs throughout is the discovery of radioactivity and the subsequent development of nuclear science, so look for an answer choice that agrees with this focus. **(C)** best agrees with your prediction. **(A)** is a Misused Detail; the work of the Curies is discussed only in paragraph 3. **(B)** is Extreme; the passage does assert that nuclear science has negative applications, but the overall tone of the passage is mixed and does not support this statement. **(D)** is a Misused Detail; although Becquerel's discovery of radioactivity is discussed in the passage, the passage does not focus on his life and work.

12. F

Category: Detail

Getting to the Answer: When answering a Detail question, be wary of changes in wording between the passage and the answer choices. Often, correct answers will be worded differently from the passage, whereas incorrect answers may contain similar wordings to those found in the passage. In this case, the passage states that Becquerel made the discovery unknowingly when he placed photographic plates in a drawer with uranium and recognized that an energy source coming from the uranium must have developed the plates. **(F)** is correct; unintentionally, Becquerel was able to recognize that a previously unknown energy source developed the photographic plates, and you learn later that uranium is a radioactive substance. **(E)** is Opposite; the discovery of radioactivity was accidental, not deliberate. **(G)** is Out of Scope; the passage never states that Becquerel copied Röntgen. **(H)** is a Distortion; the Curies, not Becquerel, isolated radium and polonium.

13. A

Category: Inference

Getting to the Answer: This question is asking you for an interpretation of the cited phrase based on the information in the passage. The phrase "if somewhat disturbing" indicates a contrast to the positives associated with the discovery of radioactivity. Because you know from later in the passage that nuclear weapons are one aspect of the discovery of radioactivity, you can predict that the cited phrase means that not all applications of Becquerel's discovery were good. **(A)** is correct. **(B)** is Out of Scope; the passage does not mention anyone trying to make this claim. **(C)** is Opposite; the entire passage states that the impact of nuclear science has been significant, just not always good. **(D)** is Extreme; the author does mention positive applications of nuclear science; therefore, this answer choice cannot be correct.

14. F

Category: Inference

Getting to the Answer: The author mentions nuclear weapons immediately after describing the discovery of radioactivity as a mixed blessing. Because weapons are used to destroy, you can infer from the context that nuclear weapons are an example of a destructive application of nuclear science: **(F)**. **(E)** is Opposite; the mention of nuclear weapons is given as a negative, not a positive, consequence of the development of nuclear science. **(G)** is a Misused Detail; the author never makes a connection between radium and polonium and the invention of nuclear weapons. **(H)** is Opposite; the context of the passage indicates that the mention of nuclear weapons reinforces, rather than refutes, the assertion that nuclear science is a mixed blessing.

Passage Analysis: The purpose of this passage is to describe the unfortunate introduction of cane toads into Australia. The purpose of paragraph 1 is to introduce the history of and reasons behind the cane toad's arrival in Australia. The purpose of paragraph 2 is to describe the breeding and subsequent disastrous release of the toads into the wild. The purpose of paragraph 3 is to describe the disaster that developed and the reasons behind the cane toad population explosion. The purpose of paragraph 4 is to describe the current cane toad situation in Australia.

15. D

Category: Global

Getting to the Answer: Because you are looking for a statement that summarizes the entire passage, the correct answer must capture the focus of all four paragraphs. In this case, every paragraph of the passage focuses on the introduction of the cane toad into Australia and the resulting, rather disastrous consequences, so look for an answer choice that best represents this overall focus. The answer is **(D)**. **(A)** is a Misused Detail; the passage states that the farmers brought the toads to Australia to eradicate the cane beetle, but this fact is not the focus of the passage. **(B)** is another Misused Detail; the passage only briefly mentions cane toad habits, falling far short of focusing the entire passage on these details. **(C)** is also a Misused Detail; the passage mentions the reasons why the toads moved away from the sugarcane fields, but this information is not the focus of the passage.

16. F

Category: Detail

Getting to the Answer: Because the characteristics of the cane toad are listed throughout the passage, begin with the answer choices, identifying and eliminating those you know to be true from your first reading and checking those you are unsure of with the text of the passage. The one characteristic not mentioned is likely one not associated with the purpose of the passage; be wary of choices that may apply to toads in general but are not referenced by the passage. The passage never mentions the croak of the cane toad, nor would this characteristic be connected with the purpose of the passage; therefore, **(F)** is correct. **(E)** is mentioned in the first sentence, and **(G)** and **(H)** are mentioned in paragraph 3.

17. B

Category: Detail

Getting to the Answer: First, identify the place in the passage the question stem is referring to, as you may not immediately remember from your first reading all of the reasons given for the toad migration. Paragraph 3 gives two major reasons that the toads left the fields: the beetles could fly, and there was not enough damp shade. Look for an answer choice that takes into account at least one of these reasons. The answer is **(B)**. **(A)** is a Distortion; the passage never suggests that there were not enough beetles to eat. **(C)** is Out of Scope; the passage never mentions the patience of the farmers. **(D)** is a Distortion; the passage describes the toads eating food put out for pets but never suggests that people purposely fed the toads.

18. G

Category: Inference

Getting to the Answer: First, examine the context of the cited phrase, noticing that here the author is describing the now enormous size of the population, "easily" numbering in the millions. Look for an answer choice that takes this remarkable population explosion into account. The answer is **(G)**. **(E)** is Opposite; the information is supporting the fact that cane toads are so numerous that they have overrun the Queensland area and are certainly not hard to find. **(F)** is Out of Scope; the passage never discusses research conducted by scientists. **(H)** is Extreme; the passage never describes ineptitude on the part of the farmers.

19. B

Category: Function

Getting to the Answer: Often a passage will use a variety of wordings to refer to a single recurring idea or concept. In this case, the quoted words are found within the context of the farmers' intentional release of the toads; answer choice **(B)** best represents this context. **(A)** is Opposite; the passage never suggests that the farmers did not have enough toads; in fact, the passage focuses on a population explosion. **(C)** is Out of Scope; the passage never discusses any breeding instructions. **(D)** is a Distortion; the introduction of the toads was planned, not accidental.

20. H

Category: Detail

Getting to the Answer: As the passage largely follows the cane toad story chronologically, look for a resolution in the final paragraph. Indeed, in the second to last sentence, the author notes that the sugarcane industry found an insecticide with which they combated the cane beetle; answer choice **(H)** best captures this detail. **(E)**, **(F)**, and **(G)** are not mentioned in the passage and are thus Out of Scope.

Passage Analysis: The main focus of this passage is on bebop jazz, its characteristics, and its history. Paragraph 1 discusses the origins of bebop jazz. Paragraph 2 compares bebop to previous jazz movements, and paragraph 3 discusses its principal characteristics. Paragraph 4 discusses reasons for the unpopularity and lack of documentation of bebop jazz.

21. D

Category: Global

Getting to the Answer: Global questions test your comprehension of the passage as a logical whole. In order to correctly answer Global questions, you must be able to correctly synthesize information from each paragraph. In this case, each paragraph in the passage discusses bebop jazz, its characteristics, and its development. The correct answer is **(D)**. **(A)** is a Misused Detail; Charlie Parker is mentioned more than once for his contribution to bebop jazz, but this is not the primary focus of the passage. **(B)** is also a Misused Detail; these sessions, while important to the development of bebop jazz, are not the main focus of the passage. **(C)** is Out of Scope; the passage is concerned with bebop jazz, not jazz in general.

22. G

Category: Detail

Getting to the Answer: Research the part of the passage that the question is referring to and form your prediction based on this reexamination of the text. In this case, the question refers to the comparison between bebop and swing jazz addressed in paragraph 2. After researching paragraph 2, you should note that the fast speed and discordant sounds of bebop jazz were the elements that jazz audiences had never heard before. The correct answer is **(G)**. **(E)** is Opposite; the passage states that swing jazz was more popular than bebop jazz. **(F)** is also Opposite; the passage states that swing jazz was played on an 8-note scale, whereas bebop was played on a 12-note scale. **(H)** is another Opposite answer; the passage states that swing was better dance music.

23. C

Category: Detail

Getting to the Answer: Lines 19–21 of the passage directly state that "Bebop, in contrast, was based on a 12-note scale, thereby opening up vast new harmonic opportunities for musicians." According to this information, the 12-note scale created the new opportunities. The answer is **(C)**. **(A)** is a Distortion; the passage does state that Charlie Parker played twice as fast as other musicians but does not directly state that this speed was what opened up new opportunities for jazz musicians. **(B)** is Out of Scope; the passage never states that bebop jazz placed less emphasis on rhythm. **(D)** is Opposite; the passage states that bebop failed to gain the acceptance of swing jazz.

24. H

Category: Detail

Getting to the Answer: The end of paragraph 3 discusses Charlie Parker's success as a jazz musician. You should research this portion of the passage and eliminate answer choices that are stated as being responsible for Charlie Parker's success. Nothing in the passage mentions

Charlie Parker having a "magnetic personality"; therefore, answer **(H)** is correct. **(E)** is mentioned in lines 23–24, **(F)** is mentioned in line 31, and **(G)** is mentioned in line 34.

25. C

Category: Inference

Getting to the Answer: Paragraph 4 discusses the resistance encountered by the bebop jazz movement. The passage states that older musicians resisted bebop, the general public disliked its complexity, and because of the rationing of petroleum, it was poorly documented. The correct answer, **(C)**, contains one of these elements. **(A)** is a Distortion; bebop records could not be made due to a rationing of vinyl, not because bebop records were banned. **(B)** is a Misused Detail; the passage does discuss the irregular hours at which bebop was played but never relates this to bebop's unpopularity. **(D)** is also a Misused Detail; although the passage indeed indicates that older musicians opposed the music, this does not explain the general public's distaste for bebop.

26. G

Category: Detail

Getting to the Answer: The passage states in paragraph 4 that bebop went largely undocumented partly because it was unpopular and partly because of a shortage of vinyl used to make records. These reasons will suffice as a prediction. The correct answer is **(G)**. The topics mentioned in **(E)**, **(F)**, and **(H)** are not mentioned in the passage and are therefore Out of Scope.

CHAPTER 9

SHSAT Reading Question Types

CHAPTER OBJECTIVES

By the end of this chapter, you will be able to:

- Identify Reading Comprehension question types
- Apply the appropriate strategies to answer questions correctly

SHSAT READING QUESTION TYPES

As you already know, Reading points come from answering the questions, not simply reading the passages. This doesn't mean that it is not important to approach the passage strategically—it is. However, if you do not answer the questions correctly, the passage hasn't done you much good.

There are four basic question types in the Reading section: Global, Detail, Function, and Inference questions.

Global Questions

Global questions either ask you to choose a correct summary of the passage as a whole or to identify key information and ideas within the passage.

To answer Global questions successfully:

- Identify the central idea or theme of the passage
- Do not reread the entire passage
- Use your Roadmap as a brief summary

Avoid these major wrong answer traps when answering Global questions:

- Out of Scope—the answer includes information that is not in the passage
- Misused Detail—the answer is a true statement from the passage, but it doesn't answer the question
- Extreme—the answer takes a stronger position (often more positive or more negative) than the passage takes

✓ Summarizing Sentences

A key strategy for Global questions is to look for a choice that summarizes the entire passage—not just a detail that's mentioned once or discussed in a single paragraph, but information that's present throughout the whole passage.

Detail Questions

Detail questions ask you to track down a piece of information directly stated in the passage, so you will not have to make any inferences as you answer these. Remember that you will not (and should not!) remember every detail from your reading of the passage. Your Roadmap can help you find the *location* of the detail in question; then, you should research the passage text to answer Detail questions.

You can recognize Detail questions because they will often use wording like "According to the passage/author," "The author states," or "The passage makes clear." These questions will almost never have phrases such as "The author suggests" or "The author implies," which indicate an Inference question.

To answer Detail questions successfully:

- Use line references or specific phrasing in the question to find the relevant section of the passage
- Quickly skim through the relevant section to find specific evidence for your prediction; you should be able to put your finger on the exact information required to answer the question
- Rephrase the evidence in the passage in your own words to make a prediction and find a match among the answer choices

Avoid these major wrong answer traps when answering Detail questions:

- Misused Detail—the answer includes details that are directly from the passage but are unrelated to or do not answer the question
- Distortions—the answer includes details from the passage that are altered to be partially incorrect

Function Questions

Function questions ask about the purpose of a particular part of the passage. They can ask about the purpose of any of the following:

- a word
- a sentence
- a paragraph
- a detail
- a quote
- punctuation

To answer Function questions successfully:

- Focus on the author's reason for including the cited feature
- Take note of any transition words, and read around the cited text to get context and an understanding of the author's reasoning

Avoid these major wrong answer traps when answering Function questions:

- Distortions—the answer includes details from the passage that are altered to be partially incorrect
- Out of Scope—the answer includes information that is not in the passage

Inference Questions

An Inference question, like a Detail question, asks you to find relevant information in the passage. But once you've located the details, you've got to go one step further: to figure out the underlying point of a particular phrase or example.

To answer Inference questions successfully:

- Look for clues that show how the author connects relevant details within the passage
- Consider how the author's point of view limits the range of what could be true

Avoid these major wrong answer traps when answering Inference questions:

- Out of Scope—the answer includes information that is not in the passage
- Extreme—the answer is too extreme to reflect the author's purpose
- Misused Detail—the answer is a true statement from the passage, but it doesn't answer the question

Create a Roadmap

Is industrial progress a mixed blessing? A hundred years ago, this question was seldom asked. Science and industry were flooding the world with products that made life easier. But today we know that many industrial processes create pollution that can destroy our environment. Industries produce toxic waste, discharging harmful chemicals directly into lakes, rivers, and the air. One of the results of this pollution that must be managed in order to protect our ecosystems is acid rain.

1. In paragraph 1, what contrasts are introduced? What Keyword signifies this?

2. ¶ 1 Topic ________________

Air, clouds, and rain containing acids caused by industrial pollution can have terrible effects. Acid droplets in the air can be inhaled, causing illness. From clouds, these acid droplets fall as rain. If natural chemical processes in soils do not deactivate the acids, these acids can accumulate and kill plant life. In some parts of the Northeast and Midwest, 10 percent of all lakes show dangerous acid levels. In eastern mountains, large forest tracts have been lost at elevations where trees are regularly bathed in acidic clouds.

3. ¶ 2 Topic ________________

Acid rain is caused by industrial processes that release compounds of nitrogen and sulfur. When these

pollutants combine with clean air, the results are nitric and sulfuric acids. The main components of acid rain are oxides of nitrogen and sulfur dioxide, exhausted from oil- and coal-burning power plants. To reduce acid rain, emissions from these plants, particularly sulfur dioxide, must be restrained. One way is to install machines that remove sulfur dioxide from a plant's exhausts. Another is to build new plants, modeled on experimental designs that produce less sulfur dioxide.

4. ¶ 3 Topic ______________

5. Passage Main Idea ______________

✓ Remember

Consider all Paragraph Topics when prephrasing your Main Idea.

Global

Refer back to the passage and your Roadmap in answering the following questions:

1. What is the author's Main Idea?

2. What do you think would be a good title for this passage?

3. How well do the following words describe the tone of the passage?

A. Argument

B. Defense

C. Description

Now, using your prephrasing and Roadmapping skills, answer the following test-like Global question:

1. Which of the following best tells what this passage is about?

A. drawbacks to industrial progress

B. a description of a dangerous kind of pollution

C. an attack on the irresponsibility of industrial leaders

D. a comparison between industry in the nineteenth century and industry today

Detail

1. What skill is required when answering Detail questions?
2. How does your Roadmap help you answer Detail questions?

Now, referring to the passage, research the answers to the following questions:

3. What can happen when acids are not deactivated in soils?
4. Acid rain is caused by the release of compounds of which two chemicals?
5. What, in particular, must be restrained in order to reduce acid rain?

Now, using your researching skills, answer the following test-like Detail question:

2. Which of the following is mentioned in the passage as a harmful effect of acid rain?

   E. destroying the fertility of the soil

   F. lowering sulfur levels in the air

   G. damaging high-altitude woodlands

   H. corroding steel structures

Function

1. What do Function questions ask you to do?
2. What is the function of the first paragraph?

Now, using your researching skills, answer the following test-like Function question:

3. The author asks a question at the beginning of the passage in order to

   A. outline why acid rain is so harmful to humans and plants.

   B. introduce a discussion about the benefits and detriments of industrial progress.

   C. explain the causes of acid rain as well as potential methods for its reduction.

   D. point out that the effect of industrial progress on the environment is a puzzling phenomenon.

Inference

1. What is an inference?
2. Where do I get the information I need to make an inference?
3. Is an inference the same thing as an opinion?
4. The first sentence of the passage asks, "Is industrial progress a mixed blessing?" Do you think the author would answer that it is or is not? Why?
5. Based on the passage, how have opinions regarding industrial progress changed since 100 years ago?
6. Would the author agree that industrial progress should be stopped in order to reduce acid rain?

Now, using your researching and inference skills, answer the following test-like Inference question:

4. The experimental designs mentioned in the passage would most likely

   E. devastate forest and lake ecosystems.
   F. reduce the pollution-driven deforestation.
   G. deactivate sulfuric acid that falls in rain.
   H. neutralize the acidity of contaminated lakes.

The following practice sets provide an opportunity to apply the concepts and strategic thinking covered in this chapter. To practice Test Day timing, follow the suggested timing guidelines for each section.

PRACTICE SET

Suggested Timing: 12 minutes

Practice using your Roadmapping skills on the following passage:

The first truly American art movement, the Hudson River School, was formed by a group of landscape painters who emerged in the early nineteenth century. The first works in this style were created by Thomas Cole, Thomas Doughty, and Asher Durand, a trio of painters who worked during the 1820s in the Hudson River Valley and surrounding locations. Heavily influenced by European romanticism, these painters set out to convey the remoteness and splendor of the American wilderness. The strongly nationalistic tone of their paintings caught the spirit of the times, and within a generation, the movement had mushroomed to include landscape painters from all over the United States. Canvases celebrating such typically American scenes as Niagara Falls, Boston Harbor, and the expansion of the railroad into rural Pennsylvania were greeted with enormous popular acclaim.

One factor contributing to the success of the Hudson River School was the rapid growth of American nationalism in the early nineteenth century. The War of 1812 had given the United States a new sense of pride in its identity, and as the nation continued to grow, there was a desire to compete with Europe on both economic and cultural grounds. The vast panoramas of the Hudson River School fit the bill perfectly by providing a new movement in art that was unmistakably American in origin. The Hudson River School also arrived at a time when writers in the United States were turning their attention to the wilderness as a unique aspect of their nationality. The Hudson River School painters profited from this nostalgia because they effectively represented the continent the way it used to be. The view that the American character was formed by the frontier experience was widely held, and many writers were concerned about the future of a country that was becoming increasingly urbanized.

In keeping with this nationalistic spirit, even the painting style of the Hudson River School exhibited a strong sense of American identity. Although many of the artists studied in Europe, their paintings show a desire to be free of European artistic rules. Regarding the natural landscape as a direct manifestation of God, the Hudson River School painters attempted to record what they saw as accurately as possible. Unlike European painters, who brought to their canvases the styles and techniques of centuries, the Hudson River School painters sought neither to embellish nor to idealize their scenes, portraying nature with the objectivity and attention to detail of naturalists.

1. ¶ 1 Topic ________________
2. ¶ 2 Topic ________________
3. ¶ 3 Topic ________________
4. Passage Main Idea ________________

✔ Remember

As you read, underline or circle Keywords, important words, and words that are repeated.

5. Which of the following best describes what this passage is about?

   A. the history of American landscape painting

   B. why an art movement caught the public imagination

   C. how European painters influenced the Hudson River School

   D. why writers began to romanticize the American wilderness

6. What does the passage suggest the Hudson River School painters were primarily famous for painting?

   E. the War of 1812

   F. the development of the American railroad

   G. themes of European romanticism

   H. American landscapes

7. Which of the following is **not** mentioned as one of the reasons for the success of the Hudson River School?

   A. Painters wanted to break with established conventions.

   B. Americans were nostalgic about the frontier.

   C. Writers began to focus on the wilderness.

   D. City dwellers became concerned about environmental pollution.

8. Which of the following statements about the popularity of Hudson River School paintings would the author most likely agree with?

   E. They conformed to the accepted rules of painting.

   F. They appealed to widespread nationalistic sentiments.

   G. They were fine imitations of European paintings.

   H. They portrayed the dangers of urban development.

9. Which of the following best describes what is suggested by the statement that the Hudson River School paintings "fit the bill perfectly" (lines 25–26)?

   A. The paintings depicted famous battle scenes.

   B. The paintings were very successful commercially.

   C. The paintings reflected a new pride in the United States.

   D. The paintings were favorably received in Europe.

10. The attitude of the Hudson River School painters toward European artistic traditions is most similar to which of the following?

    E. a successful businessman who changes careers and becomes a teacher

    F. a sculptor who imitates the technique of a more famous sculptor

    G. a soldier who always obeys her officers' orders

    H. a trained surgeon who rejects existing methods of brain surgery and develops a new technique

ANSWERS AND EXPLANATIONS

Create a Roadmap

1. The keyword "But" signifies contrast. The contrast here is between our views of science and industry today versus 100 years ago.
2. ¶1 Topic: Acid rain
3. ¶2 Topic: Why acid rain is so harmful
4. ¶3 Topic: Causes of acid rain and potential methods for its reduction
5. Passage Main Idea: Acid rain, a result of industrial progress, is harmful to the environment.

Passage Analysis: The purpose of the passage is to inform the reader about acid rain. The Main Idea is that acid rain, a result of industrial progress, is harmful to the environment. Paragraph 1 says that industrial progress is a mixed blessing because it gives us both helpful products and harmful pollution, like acid rain. The topic of paragraph 2 is the effects of acid rain. Paragraph 3 discusses the causes of acid rain and potential methods of reducing it.

Global

1. Acid rain, a result of industrial progress, is harmful to the environment.
2. The Causes and Effects of Acid Rain, or something similar
3. A. Not well; the author does not present two sides of an issue. B. Not well; the author does not include any challenge against which he or she is defending. C. Very well; the author states a topic (drawbacks of industrial progress) and scope (acid rain), then goes on to describe the causes and effects of acid rain.

1. B

Category: Global

Getting to the Answer: If you have already identified the Main Idea on your own, you will have a much easier time finding the correct answer choice. Remember, the correct choice will match both the tone and the scope of the passage. **(B)** does this best. **(A)** is a Misused Detail; the passage focuses on only one drawback, not many. Since the author is not openly critical of anyone, **(C)** doesn't match the tone of the passage. **(D)** is Out of Scope since the nineteenth century is never discussed.

Detail

1. Research! Finding and understanding cited details.
2. Paragraph topics (and underlined/circled words and phrases) will help you locate details efficiently.
3. They "can accumulate and kill plant life" (line 16).
4. Nitrogen and sulfur (line 23).
5. Emissions from these power plants, specifically sulfur dioxide (lines 27–29).

2. G

Category: Detail

Getting to the Answer: Use your Roadmap to find your way back to the paragraph that discusses the effect of acid rain. Paragraph 2 tells you that "large forest tracts have been lost at elevations where trees are regularly bathed in acidic clouds." At what elevation are clouds regularly found? High. So trees at high altitudes are being harmed, which matches **(G)**. **(E)** is a Distortion; paragraph 2 mentions that acids can kill life, but it does not say that they destroy the fertility of the soil itself. **(F)** is also a Distortion since reducing sulfur dioxide is mentioned in paragraph 3 as a means of reducing acid rain, but it is not itself an effect of acid rain. Steel structures are never mentioned, making **(H)** Out of Scope.

Function

1. Function questions ask you to determine the purpose of a particular part of the passage.
2. The first paragraph introduces the idea that our views of industrial progress have changed over time.

3. B

Category: Function

Getting to the Answer: The question at the beginning of the passage includes the phrase "mixed blessings," which indicates that industrial progress has created both good and bad results, which matches **(B)**. **(A)** and **(C)** are incorrect because **(A)** describes the function of paragraph 2 and **(C)** describes the function of paragraph 3. **(D)** is a Distortion; the author is not puzzled or confused by the effects of industrial progress.

Inference

1. An inference is something that is true based on the information in the passage, though not directly stated.
2. The information you need is in the passage; a correct inference will not go beyond it.
3. No! The correct answer comes straight from the passage.
4. The author would say that it is; you may infer this because the author provides examples of benefits and drawbacks.
5. People are probably more skeptical, or guarded, about it now because "we know that many industrial processes create pollution that can destroy our environment."
6. No. Nothing in the passage suggests that the author would endorse so drastic a measure as stopping industrial progress because of acid rain.

4. F

Category: Inference

Getting to the Answer: Experimental plant designs are mentioned in paragraph 3. The purpose of such designs is to reduce pollution. One of the effects of pollution described in paragraph 2 is loss of forests. You can deduce, therefore, that by reducing pollution, the experimental designs would reduce pollution-driven deforestation—**(F)**. **(E)** is Opposite since experimental designs would reduce the pollution. **(G)** and **(H)** are both Distortions; the experimental designs would not deactivate the acid that falls as rain and would not clean up the existing pollution.

PRACTICE SET

Create a Roadmap

1. ¶1 Topic: The Hudson River School was the first truly American art movement.
2. ¶2 Topic: The contribution of nationalism to the popular success of the Hudson River School
3. ¶3 Topic: The influence of nationalism on the style of the Hudson River School painters
4. Passage Main Idea: The Hudson River School, influenced by nationalism in both subject and style, was the first truly American art movement.

Passage Analysis: The author's purpose is to inform the reader about the Hudson River School. The Main Idea is that the Hudson River School, influenced by nationalism in both subject and style, was the first truly American art movement. Paragraph 1 describes the emergence of the Hudson River School as the first truly American art movement. Paragraph 2 describes the nationalistic motivations and subject matter of the Hudson River School. Paragraph 3 describes the influence of nationalism on the style of the Hudson River School.

5. B

Category: Global

Getting to the Answer: The correct choice will agree with the passage in subject, scope, and tone. This passage is about a popular art movement; the answer is **(B)**. **(A)** is Out of Scope since the passage is concerned with only one specific movement, not the entire history of American landscape painting. **(C)** is a Misused Detail; such influence is mentioned in paragraph 1, but it is not the focus of the whole passage. **(D)** is only mentioned in paragraph 2, making it a Misused Detail.

6. H

Category: Detail

Getting to the Answer: Even though this is a Detail question, you should still pay attention to the scope. Which choice accurately describes the works of the Hudson River School collectively, rather than individual examples? The very first sentence of the passage tells you that the members of the Hudson River School were "landscape painters," which matches **(H)**. **(E)** and **(G)** are both Distortions; while the passage mentions the War of 1812 and European romanticism, neither are described as the subjects of paintings. **(F)** is a Distortion since railroad expansion is only one example of Hudson River School subject matter.

7. D

Category: Detail

Getting to the Answer: Be careful! You are looking for the choice that is not mentioned. Use the specific answer choices to research the passage and eliminate any that are mentioned. The only one you won't find is **(D)**. While concerns about urbanization are mentioned, nothing is ever said about pollution. **(A)** is found in paragraph 3. **(B)** and **(C)** are found in paragraph 2.

8. F

Category: Inference

Getting to the Answer: Even though you are not asked about the Main Idea directly, remember that anything the author is likely to agree with is never going to stray far from the Main Idea of the passage itself. Keep the Main Idea in mind for any type of question. A central part of the Main Idea for this passage is nationalism—**(F)**. **(E)** and **(G)** are incorrect since these painters sought "to be free of European artistic rules." They did not seek to imitate anyone. **(H)** is incorrect because paragraph 2 says that they depicted wilderness and frontiers.

9. C

Category: Inference

Getting to the Answer: The cited phrase is used in the discussion of growing national pride. Only **(C)** is consistent with this context. **(A)** is a Distortion; the War of 1812 is mentioned, but the passage never says that these artists ever painted battle scenes. **(B)** and **(D)** are never mentioned in the passage.

10. H

Category: Inference

Getting to the Answer: You are asked to identify a parallel structure, but the answer choices use specifics unrelated to the passage. So look beyond the specifics. Start by stripping the given situation from the passage down to its basic, non-specific elements: someone rejects something old and develops something new. Which choice has that same basic structure? **(H)**. **(E)** is Out of Scope since the painters do not change to a different profession. **(F)** and **(G)** are both Opposite; the painters did not imitate others or follow accepted rules.

CHAPTER 10

SHSAT Science Passages & Elimination Strategies

CHAPTER OBJECTIVES

By the end of this chapter, you will be able to:

- Identify key information and ideas within a science passage
- Identify the five SHSAT Reading wrong answer traps

SHSAT SCIENCE PASSAGES

A Word about Science Passages

You can expect to see at least one passage in the Reading section that deals with a science or technical topic. There is one thing to keep in mind here—you are *not* being tested on any outside science knowledge. Do not answer the questions based on anything other than the information contained in the passage.

A Reminder about Timing

Plan to spend approximately three minutes reading the passage and roughly a minute to a minute and a half on each question. When you first start practicing, you'll probably find yourself spending more time on the passages. That's okay. However, you need to pay attention to your timing and cut the time down to around three minutes. If you do not, it will hurt you on Test Day.

Create a Roadmap

Green sea turtles, shelled reptiles that plowed the oceans eons before mammals evolved, are known for their prodigious migrations. One group of green sea turtles makes a regular journey from feeding grounds near the Brazilian coast to breeding beaches on Ascension Island, a barren, relatively predator-free island in the central equatorial Atlantic. Unfailingly slow on land, these turtles cover the distance of more than 2,000 kilometers in as little as two weeks. But how is this navigation of deep, featureless ocean accomplished? The sun's movements seem to provide the turtles with a navigational aid, but this is only part of the answer.

1. What's the passage about?

2. What will the next paragraph likely talk about?

3. ¶ 1 Topic _______________

In addition to possessing good eyesight, green turtles appear to have an excellent sense of smell. In fact, the turtles may orient themselves by detecting traces of substances released from Ascension Island itself. Because Ascension Island lies in the midst of a major west-flowing ocean current, scientists

believe that chemical substances picked up from the islands would tend to flow westward toward the feeding grounds of the turtle. As a result, these substances may provide a scented chemical trail that the turtles are able to follow. A mathematical model has been used to show that a concentration of substances delivered from Ascension to the turtles' feeding grounds, though diluted, would probably be sufficient to be sensed by the turtles.

4. Did this paragraph match your prediction from paragraph 1?

5. ¶ 2 Topic ________________

The turtles' eyesight, meanwhile, may help direct the turtles from their feeding grounds into the path of this chemical trail. It is an established fact that turtles are capable of distinguishing between different light densities. Turtles recognize at least four colors and are especially attuned to the color red because it often appears in their shell coloration. Researchers believe that these turtles swim east toward the rising sun at the beginning of their migration, changing course toward Ascension's beaches as soon as their route intersects with the scented path.

6. What new topic is discussed in detail here?

7. How does the paragraph change focus from the beginning to the end?

8. ¶ 3 Topic ________________

9. Passage Main Idea ________________

✓ Remember

Don't get bogged down with scientific jargon like "mathematical model" and "light densities." Just focus on what the passage is saying overall.

Science Passage Questions

Refer to the Roadmap and passage to research and prephrase answers to the following questions.

1. Which of the following best tells what the passage is about?

   1A. Prephrase the Main Idea of the passage:

   1B. Which choice is a Misused Detail?

   1C. Which choice is Out of Scope?

   A. how green sea turtles swim in the ocean
   B. the outstanding eyesight and sense of smell that the green turtle has
   C. the importance of ocean currents in the South Atlantic
   D. the migratory behavior of some green sea turtles

2. Why do green sea turtles most likely breed on Ascension Island?

   2A. What does the phrase "most likely" tell you about this question?

   2B. Which paragraph describes Ascension Island?

   E. There is an abundance of food there.
   F. It has a cooler climate than Brazil.
   G. The turtles have fewer natural enemies there.
   H. Its beaches are cleaner than Brazil's beaches.

3. Which of the following best describes the intended meaning of the author's statement that the sun's movements are "only part of the answer" (line 13)?

   3A. What's the author's point in the lines surrounding the quote?

   3B. The quote suggests that there is a question. What question is being asked?

   A. Scientists don't yet fully understand the migration patterns of green sea turtles.
   B. Green sea turtles use their sense of smell to compensate for their poor eyesight.
   C. Knowledge about green sea turtles is limited by a lack of scientific evidence.
   D. Green sea turtles use more than one sense to navigate toward their breeding grounds.

4. What do turtles seem to use to locate the trail of chemical substances released from Ascension Island?

   4A. Where are the Keywords "chemical trail" mentioned in the passage?

   E. the position of the rising sun
   F. an instinctive sense of direction
   G. the path of underwater ocean currents
   H. a mathematical model

5. The passage implies that turtles are especially sensitive to the color red because

   5A. Where does the passage mention red?

   5B. What does the author imply about the color?

   A. it helps them identify other turtles.
   B. it is the most intense of the primary colors.
   C. it matches the colors of the rising sun.
   D. it seems more attractive than other colors.

6. Which of the following situations is most like the journey of the green sea turtles as it is presented in the passage?

   6A. How do the turtles migrate? What helps them?

   6B. Which choice is most similar to the way sea turtles migrate?

   E. A group of cyclists wins a mountain race through determination and teamwork.
   F. A pair of detectives track down a criminal by uncovering a series of clues.
   G. A truck driver delivers his consignment of goods by following clearly marked road signs.
   H. A pilot discovers an uncharted island when his ship is blown off course.

SHSAT READING ELIMINATION STRATEGIES

Elimination Strategies: Global Questions

Global questions ask you to summarize the topic of the passage. The correct answer choice should correspond to the topic in your Roadmap.

One key strategy for determining the correct answer choice is to eliminate the wrong choices. The wrong choices most often fall into specific categories. Once you know the categories, elimination is easy!

Wrong Answer Trap	Description
Distortion	The answer slightly alters details from a passage so they are no longer correct.
Extreme	The answer takes a stronger position (often more positive or more negative) than the passage takes.
Misused Detail	The answer is a true statement from the passage, but it doesn't answer the question.
Opposite	The answer contradicts the information in the passage.
Out of Scope	The answer includes information that is not in the passage.

Extreme, Misused Detail, and Out of Scope are the most common wrong answer traps for Global questions.

Test Day Tip

Knowing common wrong answer traps will help you avoid them on Test Day.

Create a Roadmap

What do paper airplanes and large commercial airliners such as the Boeing 747 have in common? Plenty. Despite differences in size and weight, both must make use of the same physical forces in order to fly. The flight of any airplane results from the interaction of four different forces: thrust, drag, gravity, and lift.

1. Based only on the last sentence of this paragraph, what will the entire passage most likely discuss?

2. What two things does the paragraph compare?

3. ¶ 1 Topic ________________

All of the forces acting on the airplane must balance each other in order for the plane to travel along in steady horizontal flight. Thrust supplied by jet engines or propellers (or by a person's hand for a paper airplane) is the force that drives the airplane forward. The airplane cannot actually move any distance forward, however, unless the amount of thrust is enough to overcome the force of drag. Drag is the air resistance that the plane encounters in flight. Just as the name indicates, air resistance has the effect of dragging the airplane backward as it moves through the air. Jet engines are designed so that the airplane has the necessary thrust to overcome air resistance. Drag can be reduced if the airplane is streamlined—that is, constructed in such a way that air flows smoothly around it so that there is little friction at the airplane's surface.

4. How does the term "air resistance" help you understand what "drag" means?

5. ¶ 2 Topic ________________

To rise into the air, an airplane has to overcome the force of gravity, the downward pull that the Earth exerts on everything on or near its surface. The airplane accomplishes this feat with lift force, which acts in an upward direction opposite to gravity. Lift is provided by the airplane's wings. The wings and wing flaps are shaped and angled so that air will flow more rapidly over them than under them.

When air flows more rapidly over the wing tops, air pressure above the wings drops in comparison with the air pressure below the wings. (This phenomenon is known to engineers as Bernoulli's principle.) When an airplane taxis down the runway (or when a paper airplane is released from a person's hand), the greater air pressure below the wings pushes the wings upward, allowing the airplane to rise despite the pull of gravity. Once the plane is safely in the air, all four of the basic aerodynamic forces figure into the flight as well, whether it is the flight of a big jet or a paper airplane.

6. ¶ 3 Topic ________________

7. Passage Main Idea ________________

1. Which of the following best tells what this passage is about?

1A. How can you find the Main Idea?

1B. Is there a choice that seems Out of Scope?

1C. Is there a choice that looks like a Misused Detail?

1D. Is there a choice that seems Extreme?

A. how a commercial airliner moves forward

B. why jet airplanes can fly but paper airplanes cannot

C. the practical application of physics

D. how all airplanes are able to fly

✔ Remember

The three most common wrong answer types for Global questions are Out of Scope, Misused Detail, and Extreme.

Elimination Strategies: Detail Questions

Detail questions ask you to research information that is directly stated in the passage.

There are five common types of wrong answer choices for Detail questions:

- Out of Scope
- Misused Detail
- Extreme
- Opposite
- Distortion

Let's look at two Detail questions relating to the passage you just read.

2. Which of the following plays the most direct part in the creation of lift force?

   2A. Where is "lift force" discussed in the passage?

   E. the pull exerted by the Earth's gravity
   F. drag caused by air resistance
   G. weather conditions surrounding the airplane
   H. the angling of an airplane's wing flaps

3. Which of the following do paper airplanes and Boeing 747s have in common?

   3A. Where are Boeing 747s mentioned in the passage?

   A. They are hardly affected by the force of gravity.
   B. They fly like no other airplanes.
   C. They obey the same scientific principles.
   D. They are constructed from lightweight materials.

> ✔ **Remember**
>
> **The answer must not only be accurate for the passage, but also answer the specific question that's asked.**

Elimination Strategies: Inference Questions

Inference questions ask you to figure out the underlying point of a particular phrase or example. They often use the words "imply" and "suggest." To answer this type of question, you should figure out which answer choice is most consistent with what happens in the passage.

There are three common types of wrong answer choices for Inference questions. Can you think of examples of each type?

- Out of Scope
- Misused Detail
- Extreme

Let's look at two examples of Inference questions relating to the passage you just read.

4. The passage implies that the forces of thrust and drag are

   4A. How do you recognize that this is an Inference question?

   4B. Where would you look to find the answer?

   4C. What wrong answer types do you notice in the answer choices?

   E. complementary forces.
   F. opposing forces.
   G. responsible for lift.
   H. stronger than the force of gravity.

5. Why is a fast-moving plane on an airport runway able to rise into the air?

   5A. What wrong answer types do you notice in the answer choices?

   A. The air pressure above its wings decreases.
   B. The force of gravity decreases as the plane gathers speed.
   C. Its wings are able to negate the drag force.
   D. Increased pressure under the wing overcomes gravity.

✔ Remember

Answering questions too quickly, without researching the appropriate place in the passage, makes it more likely that you will fall for a classic wrong answer trap.

REVIEW

Suggested Timing: 12 minutes

There are thousands of species of birds in the natural world, and nearly every species has its own special courtship procedures and "identification checks." Courtship procedures enable birds to find suitable mates of the opposite sex. Identification checks perform a slightly more basic function—they allow birds to ensure that they are mating with members of their own species. Identification checks are important because if members of different species mate, the offspring are usually sterile or badly adapted to their surroundings.

For many bird species, plumage plays a key role in both identification and courtship. In breeding season, male birds acquire distinctive plumage that they use to attract females, and the females respond only to males with the correct markings. The most striking example of such plumage is the magnificently colored head, chest, and tail feathers of the male bird of paradise. When attempting to attract a mate, the male perches on a branch and then gradually leans forward until he is hanging upside down, covered with his own brilliant feathers. A female bird of paradise will watch the display and then respond. Scientists refer to the bird displaying the plumage as the "actor," while the bird that observes is the "reactor." Although the male is the actor and the female is the reactor in the case of birds of paradise, the females of some species are more brightly colored than the males, and the courtship roles are reversed.

Distinctive behavioral changes can also be important aspects of courtship and breeding activity. Aggressiveness among males, and sometimes among females, is quite common. Some birds, such as whooping cranes and trumpeter swans, perform wonderfully elaborate courtship dances in which both sexes are enthusiastic participants. The purpose of the dances is to establish and maintain a "pair bond" that will last between the male and female through the period of the reproductive season, or at least until the nesting has been completed. Each species has its own set of inherited courtship behaviors, which helps prevent mating between birds of different species.

Bird sounds are also a central part of identification between individuals in a given species. When a female migrates to her breeding region in the spring, she often encounters numerous birds of different species. The males of her species identify themselves by their singing and communicate to her that they are in breeding condition. This information allows the female to predict the response of a male to her approach. Later, after mating has taken place, the note patterns of a particular male's song enable the nesting female to continue to identify her partner.

1. Which of the following best tells what this passage is about?
   - **A.** how birds raise their offspring
   - **B.** key aspects of the mating activities of birds
   - **C.** the beauty of some male bird songs
   - **D.** how a pair bond is formed between male and female birds

2. Why does a bird engage in identification and courtship procedures?
   - **E.** to find a better nesting spot
   - **F.** to find the most colorful partner it can
   - **G.** to attract a mate of its own species
   - **H.** to increase its control over its nesting partner

3. What is the most likely reason that the male bird of paradise hangs upside down when attempting to court a mate?

   A. to observe the actor in the ritual

   B. to perform an identification check

   C. to establish a pair bond

   D. to better display his plumage

4. Which of the following is mentioned in the passage as a function of male bird songs?

   E. to communicate information to a potential nesting partner

   F. to warn rival birds away from the nest

   G. to distract predators

   H. to inform females that it is time to begin spring migration

5. Why does the author most likely mention the example of the whooping crane (lines 34–37)?

   A. It seldom participates in courtship procedures.

   B. It acquires a distinctive breeding plumage.

   C. It behaves in an unusual way during courtship.

   D. It reverses the normal male and female courtship roles.

6. The passage implies that, in bird species in which sounds are a crucial form of identification check, the female bird

   E. is unable to sing.

   F. is not aggressive.

   G. chooses the mate.

   H. must be in breeding condition.

✔ Remember

Build your Roadmap in the margins and don't get bogged down in the scientific details.

The following practice sets provide an opportunity to apply the concepts and strategic thinking covered in this chapter. To practice Test Day timing, follow the suggested timing guidelines for each section.

PRACTICE SET

Suggested Timing: 55 minutes

DIRECTIONS: Read each passage below and answer the questions following it. Base your answers **on information contained only in the passage.** You may reread a passage if you need to. Mark the **best** answer for each question.

What do samurai,[1] cowboys, shogun,[2] gangsters, peasants, and William Shakespeare all have in common? These are just some of the varied influences on the work of Akira Kurosawa (1910–1998), a Japanese film director considered by movie critic Leonard Maltin to be "one of the undisputed giants of cinema." Over his career, Kurosawa's unique blend of Western themes and Eastern settings has made him arguably the most important Japanese filmmaker in history.

Kurosawa's style reflects his own experiences. As a young man, he studied Western art and literature, deciding to be a painter. However, World War II led Kurosawa to film; he acted as an assistant director of wartime propaganda films in Tokyo. After Japan's surrender in 1945, he took the lessons he learned in Tokyo and began making his own films—works that took the values and traditions of the West and reinterpreted them with a Japanese sensibility, using distinctly Japanese settings and characters.

The most famous example of Kurosawa's style is his 1954 film *Seven Samurai*. Although the setting is medieval Japan, with peasants and samurai, its story is influenced by Western films: a group of villagers, terrorized by local bandits, turns to a down-on-his-luck, yet good-hearted, samurai for their protection. Like the movie cowboy, the samurai is a lonely hero, sure of his morals and battling clear forces of evil. This contrasts with the traditional Japanese version of a samurai as a noble, often distant, symbol of Japan's imperial heritage. To Kurosawa, the samurai was a distinctly human character, with a conscience and the willful action to correct the wrongs around him.

Although Kurosawa's films enjoyed—and still enjoy—a lofty reputation in the West, Japanese audiences have regarded his work with suspicion. By using Western ideals and themes—even reinterpreting Western authors such as William Shakespeare and Fyodor Dostoyevsky—Kurosawa is regarded by many critics and moviegoers in his home country as not being particularly Japanese. They see him using Japanese culture as mere "window dressing" to what were essentially foreign stories. Ironically, it was Kurosawa's success that opened the door for other, "more Japanese" directors, such as Yasujiro Ozu and Kenji Mizoguchi, to gain a wider audience.

Regardless of the criticism, Kurosawa's effect on Western filmmaking is beyond dispute. Ironically, his films have influenced the very same American movie genres that Kurosawa admired so much. *Seven Samurai* became the basis for the American Western epic *The Magnificent Seven*. *Yojimbo*, another story of a samurai for hire, strongly influenced the film *A Fistful of Dollars*. Other genres benefited from Kurosawa's work as well; *Rashomon*, a crime story told from different points of view, has influenced almost every crime movie since. Finally, *The Hidden Fortress*, about two peasants escorting a princess during a war, became George Lucas's expressed basis for the science fiction masterpiece *Star Wars*.

[1] samurai: noble warriors of medieval Japan, similar to European knights
[2] shogun: military dictators of Japan from 1603 to 1868

1. The author's main purpose in writing this passage is to
   - **A.** describe how the American Western film gained popularity in Japan.
   - **B.** illustrate how Akira Kurosawa was the most important filmmaker in history.
   - **C.** compare Kurosawa to other Japanese directors like Ozu and Mizoguchi.
   - **D.** describe Kurosawa's controversial style and its influence on filmmaking.

2. According to the passage, what was one experience in Kurosawa's life that affected his films?
   - **E.** studying Western literature
   - **F.** working as an assistant director on American Western films in Tokyo
   - **G.** collaborating with Ozu and Mizoguchi
   - **H.** seeing and admiring the film *A Fistful of Dollars*

3. What is one reason that the Japanese regarded Kurosawa's films with suspicion?
   - **A.** His films used samurai as noble symbols of Japan's imperial past.
   - **B.** Kurosawa did not film his movies in Japanese, but rather in English.
   - **C.** The Japanese disliked the cowboy movies that influenced Kurosawa.
   - **D.** Kurosawa used influences and stories that were not Japanese.

4. The author uses the phrase "window dressing" (line 42) in order to
   - **E.** describe the superior directing abilities of Ozu and Mizoguchi.
   - **F.** show how the Japanese view Kurosawa's use of Japanese culture in his films.
   - **G.** illustrate the limited influence of Western films in Kurosawa's work.
   - **H.** explain the concepts of Japanese interior design.

5. In light of the passage, which of the following might be viewed as ironic?
   - **A.** George Lucas became more successful than Kurosawa using the same story.
   - **B.** Lack of copyright laws made copies of Kurosawa's work inevitable.
   - **C.** Westerns, crime stories, and science fiction have all benefited from Japanese directors.
   - **D.** Kurosawa influenced the same types of films that gave him inspiration.

6. Kurosawa's style in filming *Seven Samurai* (lines 21–28) can best be compared to
   - **E.** a cowboy movie set on a ranch.
   - **F.** a cooking show that is filmed in a firehouse.
   - **G.** a play that is set in the future.
   - **H.** a Greek tragedy set in Iowa featuring corn farmers.

The Galápagos Islands, located 600 miles off the Pacific coast of Ecuador, were made famous by the naturalist Charles Darwin, who visited the 13 islands during a voyage in the 1830s. This small, isolated archipelago,[1] administered as a province of Ecuador, is home to a number of unique species of plant and animal life. In fact, some of these species are so unique that they can be found only in the Galápagos. One of the most fascinating of these species is the cormorant, a bird whose rather ordinary-looking brown feathers might not cause one to immediately place it in the same category as some of the islands' more spectacular creatures. Yet the cormorants that live on these volcanic islands are unlike any other species of cormorant in the world because they have lost the ability to fly.

The Galápagos Islands' flightless cormorant species is distinguished by an abnormally small breastbone that supports two scruffy, stunted wings. These undersized wings are so disproportionate to the rest of the cormorant's body that the bird appears almost comical. These flightless cormorants, though somewhat less than impressive, do have some advantages over their flying relatives. Instead of strong wings, the flightless cormorant has heavier and more powerful legs that it uses to propel its sleek body quickly through the water after various prey. In addition, although the common cormorant must hold out its sizeable wings to dry in the sun upon emerging from an underwater hunting session, the flightless cormorant need not wait so long to dry out.

Most naturalists attribute these significant differences to the unique environment of the Galápagos. Like many of the Islands' creatures, the flightless cormorant has no known natural predators. Despite this evolutionary advantage, these birds are among the rarest of the Galápagos seabirds, with a population size of only about 800 pairs. Scientists, however, do not consider the flightless cormorant an endangered species, partly because of the female's ability to breed as many as three times a year and the independent nature of newly born chicks. For these reasons, the flightless cormorant population has been able to recover relatively quickly from the various environmental disasters that have struck the Galápagos over the years—a resiliency that bodes well for the survival of these distinctive birds well into the future.

[1]archipelago: chain of islands

7. The main purpose of this passage is to
   - **A.** explain why the world's seabirds are so incredibly varied.
   - **B.** describe how the Galápagos Islands are administered by Ecuador.
   - **C.** discuss why the flightless cormorant is considered so unique.
   - **D.** reveal how seabirds have a difficult time keeping their wings dry.

8. Which of the following is **not** mentioned as a characteristic of the flightless cormorant?
   - **E.** undersized breastbone
   - **F.** stunted wings
   - **G.** brown feathers
   - **H.** weak legs

9. Which of the following is given as a difference between flightless cormorants and other species of cormorants?
   - **A.** ordinary-looking brown feathers
   - **B.** attraction to the sun
   - **C.** scruffy, stunted wings
   - **D.** webbed feet

10. What is the "evolutionary advantage" that the author refers to in lines 35–36 of the passage?
    - **E.** the flightless cormorant's small breastbone
    - **F.** the isolation of the Galápagos Islands
    - **G.** the brilliant studies made by Charles Darwin in the 1830s
    - **H.** the lack of known natural predators for the flightless cormorant

11. Which of the following is suggested by the phrase "somewhat less than impressive" in line 23 of the passage?
    - A. The flightless cormorant may be funny-looking but is actually quite vicious.
    - B. The small wings of the flightless cormorant give the bird an unintimidating appearance.
    - C. The Galápagos Islands are so small that most naturalists consider them insignificant.
    - D. The legs of the flightless cormorant are surprisingly powerful.

12. Which of the following best summarizes the author's opinion on the chances for survival of the flightless cormorant population?
    - E. The Galápagos Islands are too environmentally damaged for these birds to survive.
    - F. The flightless cormorant population size of 800 pairs is too small for these birds to survive.
    - G. The many natural predators of the flightless cormorant will soon wipe out their population.
    - H. The flightless cormorant is very resilient and has a good chance of survival.

Many modern forms of music can trace their lineage to earlier styles often forgotten. Rock and roll, for example, owes much of its power to the obscure "blues" sounds of the Mississippi Delta. Likewise, jazz can be directly traced to the earlier jaunty rhythms of ragtime and Tin Pan Alley. The most representative sound of Jamaica, reggae, also has an obscure grandparent—ska. Though largely hidden by more popular music, ska has had an influence far greater than the confines of its small Caribbean birthplace.

Ska developed in the 1950s as urban dance music for young Jamaicans. Although Jamaicans recognize ska as indigenous to their island, it is in fact a derivative style like rock and jazz. Ska has elements of "rhythm and blues," a predecessor of rock and roll, as well as American "boogie-woogie" jazz and several Caribbean rhythms, notably the mambo from Cuba and the native mento from Jamaica. The blending together of such disparate elements created ska's distinctive beat: a pulsating, multilayered rhythm driven by horns, saxophones, trumpets, trombones, pianos, and guitars.

Because of the layered nature of the music, ska was primarily an instrumental genre, and groups such as Toots and the Maytals and the Skatalites gained prominence. Most ska bands backed a select number of vocalists, most important among them Derrick Morgan, Prince Buster, and Desmond Dekker. Ska lyrics, like its music, drew much from outside influences but with a distinctive native flair; besides widely popular themes of love and heartbreak, many songs took on political issues such as poverty, police brutality, and Jamaica's growing cry for independence from Great Britain. When Jamaica finally gained independence in 1962, ska achieved its high point as it celebrated the country's new autonomy.

In the subsequent decades, ska evolved into different styles, including rocksteady and reggae. The connections between these styles and ska were glaringly apparent. Reggae, for example, the sound most closely associated with Jamaica today, is actually just an extremely slow version of ska, with varying instruments and lyrical themes. This similarity helped ska groups like Toots and the Maytals easily adapt to changing tastes. Even Bob Marley, reggae's most famous artist, began his career as a ska performer.

The genre also influenced many musicians outside of Jamaica. In the 1970s, British rock bands such as the Clash, the Specials, Madness, and the Police further developed and adapted ska, using their own styles like punk and new wave. American groups like No Doubt, Sublime, and the Mighty Mighty Bosstones also made use of ska rhythms in their own way in the 1990s, though they have not necessarily billed their music as ska. Although largely masked by the din of mainstream music, ska has played a prominent—if quiet—role in the development of popular music worldwide.

13. Which statement best describes what this passage is about?

- **A.** the influence of foreign musical styles on Jamaican music
- **B.** the development and influence of ska
- **C.** the evolution of ska into reggae and rocksteady
- **D.** the influence of ska beyond its small Caribbean birthplace

14. The author lists jazz and rock and roll in the first paragraph in order to

- **E.** show how ska is more influential than either of these styles.
- **F.** show the different sounds that influenced the development of ska.
- **G.** contrast the development of jazz and rock to the development of ska.
- **H.** provide examples of other genres that were derived from earlier styles.

15. Which of the following was **not** mentioned as an influence on the development of ska?

    A. mento

    B. rock and roll

    C. jazz

    D. mambo

16. In lines 34–35, what does the author suggest by including the phrase "Jamaica's growing cry for independence"?

    E. Great Britain was dominating the reggae musical landscape.

    F. The Jamaicans' desire for freedom was one theme expressed in ska music.

    G. Ska singers often sounded like they were weeping.

    H. When Jamaica gained independence in 1962, ska became even more popular.

17. What could be a reason that ska has had a "quiet" influence on worldwide popular music?

    A. American ska groups find it unprofitable to label their sound that way.

    B. Outside of Jamaica, reggae became more important than ska.

    C. Ska became adapted to and infused with punk music in the 1970s.

    D. Despite using ska rhythms, some American popular groups have not specifically identified their music with this genre.

18. The themes of ska vocalists would most closely resemble those of

    E. a popular singer of love songs on the radio.

    F. a political protest against a repressive government.

    G. Caribbean singers and their concerns for the region.

    H. a popular singer who also sings about his country's struggles.

James Knox Polk, for much of his distinguished career, followed in the footsteps of Andrew Jackson.[1] Like the fiery Jackson, Polk was born in North Carolina and moved to Tennessee to begin a political career. In fact, "Young Hickory's" policies were very similar to Jackson's: both men favored lower taxes, championed the frontiersmen, farmers, and workers, and opposed the controversial Bank of the United States. Polk, however, did not share Jackson's rather fierce temperament, but was instead known for remaining soft-spoken even as he worked energetically toward his goals. Although history will likely always remember the frontier persona of Andrew Jackson, it was Polk who did much more to shape the course of American history.

Polk was born in Mecklenburg, North Carolina, in 1795, as the oldest of 10 children. From an early age, Polk suffered ill health that would turn out to be a lifelong affliction. Despite his physical shortcomings, he was an able student and graduated from the University of North Carolina with honors in 1818. Two years later, Polk was admitted to the bar, and in 1823, he was elected to the Tennessee House of Representatives. From there, he was elected to the U.S. House of Representatives in 1825, serving until 1839. Polk was also Speaker of the House from 1835 to 1839, a post that catapulted him to a position of prominence in politics.

After he left Congress to serve as governor of Tennessee in 1839, it became clear that Polk's political aspirations were high indeed. During the 1844 presidential campaign, the leading Democratic candidate was ex-President Martin van Buren, and the Whig candidate was Henry Clay. Both men, as part of their platforms, opposed expansionist policies, and neither intended to annex the independent state of Texas or the Oregon Territory. Polk, spurred on by Jackson's advice, recognized that neither candidate had correctly surmised the feelings of the people, so he publicly announced that, as president, he would do his utmost to acquire Texas and Oregon. Polk was the first political "dark horse" in American politics, coming out of nowhere to win the Democratic nomination and the election.

As the eleventh president of the United States, Polk worked tirelessly to expand the borders of the nation. First, he reached an agreement with England that divided the Oregon Territory, carving out the present-day states of Washington and Oregon. Polk also quickly annexed Texas and provoked war with Mexico to acquire California and the New Mexico territory. While these triumphs were somewhat diminished by controversy from abolitionists who opposed the spread of slavery into new territories, under Polk's leadership the dream of "manifest destiny" became a reality and the United States fully extended its borders from the Atlantic to the Pacific.

[1] Seventh U.S. President from 1829 to 1837 and War of 1812 hero, often referred to as "Old Hickory"

19. Which of the following best describes the main idea of this passage?

A. to demonstrate how Polk had a greater impact on American history than Andrew Jackson

B. to discuss how Polk's decisions as president led to the Mexican War

C. to illustrate how Polk's ill health affected his ability to be an effective politician

D. to detail the life and political achievements of James Polk

20. The words "Polk, however, did not share Jackson's rather fierce temperament" in lines 9–10 suggest that

E. Polk was less courageous than Jackson.

F. Jackson was not a man who worked toward his goals.

G. Polk was soft-spoken, whereas Jackson was not.

H. Polk and Jackson differed in their policies.

21. The author included the phrase "catapulted him to a position of prominence" in lines 27–28 in order to point out that
    - A. Polk quickly gained political power from this new role.
    - B. Polk rapidly took control of the Democratic Party.
    - C. Polk suddenly became known throughout the country.
    - D. Polk became the leading Democratic candidate for president.

22. All of the following are true of Polk's election as president **except**
    - E. Polk was elected president as the Democratic candidate.
    - F. Polk did not run as an expansionist.
    - G. most Americans in 1844 favored expansion.
    - H. Jackson supported Polk's candidacy.

23. Which of the following occurred during Polk's presidency?
    - A. Slavery was outlawed in the territories acquired during the Mexican War.
    - B. Texas officially became a state.
    - C. Polk recognized that most Americans favored expansion.
    - D. Polk negotiated with England regarding the boundaries of the Oregon Territory.

24. How does the author's mention of abolitionist controversy in line 53 support the passage overall?
    - E. It asserts that Polk's presidency was marred by criticism.
    - F. It explains why Polk narrowly lost his bid for reelection.
    - G. It suggests that the Polk administration, although successful, was not without criticism.
    - H. It demonstrates Polk's ability to defuse a diplomatic crisis.

As the fifth planet from the Sun, and by far the most massive in our solar system at 318 times the mass of Earth, Jupiter has fascinated scientists for centuries. In fact, it was the initial discovery of this massive, gaseous planet that marked the first time astronomers considered the existence of planetary centers of motion not revolving around Earth. More specifically, when Jupiter was first viewed from Earth by the Italian astronomer Galileo in 1610, four large moons were also spotted in orbit around this enormous planet. It was these moons, now known as the Galilean moons, that provided important evidence for Galileo's outspoken support of Copernicus's heliocentric theory of planetary movement, because these moons seemed to revolve around a planet other than Earth.

The first close look at Jupiter came in 1973, when the unmanned NASA probe Pioneer 10 completed a successful flyby and collected important data regarding the planet's chemical composition and interior structure. Designated as one of the gas planets—along with Saturn, Uranus, and Neptune—Jupiter is composed of about 90 percent hydrogen and 10 percent helium and has no solid surface, only varying densities of gas. In fact, very little is known about the interior of Jupiter. What is visible when looking at a gas planet like Jupiter is really only the tops of clouds making up the outermost atmosphere, and probes have been able to penetrate only about 90 miles below this layer. Scientists, however, believe it is likely, largely due to the traces of water and minerals that have been collected from Jupiter's atmospheres, that the planet has a core of rocky material amounting to a mass perhaps as much as 15 times that of Earth.

Like other gaseous planets, Jupiter has high-velocity winds that blow in wide bands of latitude, each moving in an alternate direction. Slight chemical and temperature changes between these bands, and the resulting chemical reactions, are probably responsible for the array of vibrant colors that dominate the planet's appearance. Measurements taken by a number of probes indicate that the powerful winds moving these bands can reach speeds exceeding 400 miles per hour and likely extend thousands of miles below Jupiter's outer atmosphere.

Yet perhaps the most fascinating characteristic of this planet is the rotational speed of the entire globe of gas itself. While Earth takes 24 hours to make a full revolution, Jupiter completes a full revolution in less than half that time, an amazingly short period of time for a planet with a diameter roughly 11 times that of our own planet. How Jupiter is able to rotate so fast is just one of many mysteries that scientists continue to explore in their efforts to understand our largest neighbor.

25. Which of the following best tells what this passage is about?

A. how scientists determined the chemical composition of Jupiter

B. why the discovery of Jupiter led to the popular acceptance of Copernicus's heliocentric theory

C. how probes have been unable to gather definitive information about Jupiter

D. how scientists have long studied Jupiter but have determined only some of its characteristics

26. According to the passage, which of the following is **not** given as a characteristic of Jupiter?

E. considered nearly identical to other gaseous planets

F. orbited by four large moons

G. composed mostly of hydrogen

H. features wide bands of color pushed by violent winds

27. Given the context of the passage, Copernicus's "heliocentric theory of planetary movement" (lines 13–14) most likely incorporates which of the following?

    A. the enormous mass of the planet Jupiter

    B. Galileo's initial discovery of Jupiter in 1610

    C. the idea that planets do not necessarily revolve around the Earth

    D. the concept that it is Jupiter that orbits the Galilean moons

28. The passage suggests that water and minerals are indicators of which of the following?

    E. the chemical makeup of an entire planet

    F. the possible presence of rocky material

    G. the existence of hydrogen and helium in gaseous planets

    H. the fact that Jupiter has a solid core

29. According to the author, which of the following is unusual, given Jupiter's relatively large size?

    A. its similarity to Saturn, Uranus, and Neptune

    B. its lack of a solid surface

    C. the fact that it is a gaseous planet

    D. the time it takes to make one full revolution

30. According to the details of the passage, probes can be used to

    E. measure rotational speed.

    F. separate chemicals like hydrogen and helium.

    G. identify bands of latitude.

    H. determine wind speed.

ANSWERS AND EXPLANATIONS

Create a Roadmap

1. Green sea turtles and their migrations—specifically, one group that goes from Brazil to Ascension Island to breed.
2. How sea turtles accomplish long migrations quickly
3. ¶1 Topic: Green sea turtles make great migrations in short time spans.
4. Yes, if your prediction had to do with turtles migrating.
5. ¶2 Topic: Green turtles' strong sense of smell helps them detect a scented chemical trail.
6. The green sea turtles' eyesight
7. The passage shifts from talking generally about green sea turtles and their migrations to talking about specific attributes of turtles that assist in those migrations.
8. ¶3 Topic: The turtles' eyesight helps them find the path of the chemical trail.
9. Passage Main Idea: Green sea turtles and their migrations

Science Passage Questions

Passage Analysis: This passage describes how one group of green sea turtles makes its regular 2,000-kilometer ocean migration from the Brazilian coast to Ascension Island. The passage argues that the turtles use their exceptional sense of smell and eyesight to lead them to a chemical trail that they follow to Ascension Island.

1A. Green sea turtles and their migrations
1B. **(B)**
1C. **(A)** and **(C)**

1. D

Category: Global

Getting to the Answer: The point of the passage is to describe how green sea turtles make their "prodigious migrations." This matches **(D)**. The passage doesn't discuss the importance of ocean currents or how the turtles swim, making both **(A)** and **(C)** Out of Scope. **(B)** is a Misused Detail since it does not include anything about migration.

2A. It is an Inference question.
2B. Paragraph 1

2. G

Category: Inference

Getting to the Answer: Ascension Island is described in the paragraph 1 as "relatively predator-free," which supports **(G)**. The turtles leave their feeding grounds to go to Ascension Island, making **(E)** incorrect. The passage does not compare Brazil and Ascension Island in terms of climate or cleanliness, making both **(F)** and **(H)** Out of Scope.

3A. The previous sentence asks how the turtles accomplish their migration. The subsequent paragraph discusses how smell helps turtles find Ascension Island.
3B. How do the turtles accomplish such a long migration in a relatively short time?

3. D

Category: Function

Getting to the Answer: "Part of the answer" refers back to the question of how green sea turtles navigate the ocean. The passage states that the turtles use their eyesight to track the sun and their sense of smell to follow a chemical trail to Ascension Island. The phrase "part of the answer" suggests that green sea turtles use more than just their eyesight to navigate, which matches **(D)**. **(A)** is incorrect because the phrase "part of the answer" isn't referring to scientists' understanding. **(B)** is Opposite since the turtles have good eyesight. **(C)** is Out of Scope; the passage doesn't discuss the limitations of scientific evidence concerning green sea turtles.

4A. Paragraphs 2 and 3 and lines 29–31 mention the chemical trail.

4. E

Category: Detail

Getting to the Answer: According to paragraph 3, researchers think that the turtles swim toward the rising sun until they come across the chemical trail. Thus, the position of the sun leads turtles to the chemical trail, **(E)**. Paragraph 3 doesn't mention the turtles' sense of direction, making **(F)** incorrect **(G)** and **(H)** are both Distortions of information provided in the passage.

5A. Paragraph 3, lines 33–35.

5B. The author mentions that red is common in the turtles' shell coloration, so it must aid them in recognizing each other.

5. A

Category: Inference

Getting to the Answer: The last paragraph states that the turtles are especially sensitive to red because it "appears in their shell coloration." This suggests that seeing red helps them to see other turtles' shells. This supports **(A)**. The passage doesn't compare the "intensity" of the primary colors or address the "attractiveness" of the color red, making **(B)** and **(D)** Out of Scope. **(C)** is incorrect because the passage doesn't make a connection between the color red and the sun.

6A. Green sea turtles go to Ascension Island to breed, and they use their senses to help them find their way.

6B. **(F)** is the best match. The turtles use their senses of sight and smell to locate and follow a chemical trail, which is closest to the example of the detectives uncovering a series of clues.

6. F

Category: Inference

Getting to the Answer: The sea turtles get from their feeding grounds to their breeding grounds by first using their eyesight to locate a chemical trail and then using their sense of smell to follow that trail. In other words, they follow subtle clues to get from point A to point B. **(F)** most closely matches this idea. **(E)** is incorrect because the cyclists are not using their senses. **(G)** is incorrect because the road signs the truck driver follows are not as subtle as the clues detected by the turtles. **(H)** is incorrect because the turtles do not get to their destination by accident.

Create a Roadmap

1. The four forces involved in flight
2. Paper airplanes and large commercial jets
3. ¶1 Topic: Paper airplanes vs. jets; Four forces involved in flight
4. It provides a definition.
5. ¶2 Topic: Thrust and drag
6. ¶3 Topic: Gravity and lift
7. Passage Main Idea: There are four forces involved in flight, whether for big jets or paper airplanes.

Passage Analysis: The Main Idea of this passage is that even though paper airplanes and real commercial airliners seem to be completely different, they actually use the exact same four physical principles in order to achieve flight: thrust, drag, gravity, and lift. Paragraph 1 simply states the Main Idea. Paragraph 2 explains how thrust and drag work and how a plane's jet engines help it balance these two forces; thrust is the force that propels the plane forward, and drag is the air resistance in the opposite direction. Paragraph 3 explains gravity, which pulls objects toward the ground, and lift, which is what planes use to defy gravity.

Questions

1A. Find a topic that is dealt with in every paragraph.
1B. **(C)** is Out of Scope.
1C. **(A)** is a Misused Detail.
1D. No. **(D)** uses the word "all," but the passage does deal with the principles of physics that allow "all planes to fly."

1. D

Category: Global

Getting to the Answer: (D) is correct because the Main Idea of the passage is summed up in paragraph 1. All airplanes fly by the balanced interaction of four physical forces: thrust, drag, gravity, and lift. **(A)** is a Misused Detail; the passage concerns all types of planes. **(B)** is incorrect because both types of planes can fly. **(C)** is Out of Scope; the passage is concerned only with the physics of airplanes.

2A. Paragraph 3

2. H

Category: Detail

Getting to the Answer: (H) is correct because paragraph 3 states that lift is created by the design of an airplane's wings and wing flaps. **(E)** is Opposite; gravity does not create lift—it works against lift. **(F)** is a Distortion; the opposing force to drag is thrust. The passage never mentions any direct relationship between drag and lift. **(G)** is Out of Scope since weather conditions are not mentioned in the passage.

3A. Paragraph 1

3. C

Category: Detail

Getting to the Answer: (C) is correct because it is directly related to the Main Idea. The very first sentence says that paper airplanes and Boeings have a lot in common. The second sentence states that both types of planes make use of the same physical forces in order to fly. The third sentence says that any airplane makes use of these same forces. **(A)** is incorrect since the passage says that gravity is one of the forces that affects airplanes. **(B)** is incorrect because the passage says that all planes use the same principles to fly. The construction materials are not discussed, making **(D)** Out of Scope.

4A. From the word "implies"
4B. Paragraph 2
4C. **(E)** is Opposite. **(G)** and **(H)** are Misused Details.

4. F

Category: Inference

Getting to the Answer: **(F)** is correct because in paragraph 2, lines 14–15 say that thrust must overcome drag. Therefore, thrust and drag are opposing forces. **(E)** is Opposite since this contradicts paragraph 2. **(G)** and **(H)** are both Misused Details; lift and gravity are not directly related to thrust and drag.

5A. **(A)**, **(B)**, and **(C)** are all Misused Details.

5. D

Category: Inference

Getting to the Answer: **(D)** is correct because lines 39–41 state, "the greater air pressure below the wings pushes the wings upward, allowing the airplane to rise despite the pull of gravity." **(A)** is a Misused Detail; the air pressure above the wings does drop when the air pressure under the wings increases, but it is the air pressure under the wings, or lift, that actually gets the plane off the ground. **(B)** is also a Misused Detail because the paragraph never states that the force of gravity changes. **(C)** is another Misused Detail; the drag force is negated mostly by thrust and the streamlined design, which could involve the wings.

Review

Passage Analysis: This science passage talks about some important aspects of bird courtship and breeding behavior. Paragraph 1 states that, during courtship, identification is especially important among individual birds within each species because healthy offspring are produced only by two individuals of the same species. Paragraph 2 explains that bright plumage is used by some birds to attract mates, especially birds of paradise, which go so far as to hang upside down from branches in order to better show off their plumage. Paragraph 3 explains behavioral changes that some birds undergo, such as courtship dances, which help to establish and maintain "pair bonds." Finally, paragraph 4 explains how bird sounds can help birds find others of their species and help females determine a male's level of interest.

1. B

Category: Global

Getting to the Answer: **(B)** is correct because it states the basic theme that runs through all four paragraphs—key aspects of birds' mating activities. **(A)** and **(C)** are Out of Scope; how birds raise offspring and whether or not male birds' songs are beautiful are not mentioned. **(D)** is a Misused Detail since pair bonds are only mentioned in paragraph 3.

2. G

Category: Detail

Getting to the Answer: Paragraph 1 explains that courtship procedures enable birds to find mates and that identification checks allow birds to make sure they are mating with the same species. This matches choice **(G)**. Finding nesting spots and increasing control over nesting partners are not mentioned, making **(E)** and **(H)** incorrect. **(F)** is a Misused Detail; plumage is mentioned in paragraph 2, but it's never suggested that birds search for mates with only the brightest colors.

3. D

Category: Inference

Getting to the Answer: **(D)** is correct because paragraph 2 says that the male bird of paradise hangs upside down so far that he is "covered with his own brilliant feathers." You can infer that he takes this position in order to better display his plumage. **(A)** is incorrect because the male bird of paradise is the actor in the ritual. **(B)** is Opposite; the female performs the identification check. **(C)** is a Misused Detail since the pair bonding is mentioned in regard to swans in paragraph 3, not to birds of paradise.

4. E

Category: Detail

Getting to the Answer: **(E)** is correct because it is explained in paragraph 4 that male birds use their songs to identify themselves as potential mates of the same species and to give females a way of determining the male's level of interest. The ideas of warning rivals or distracting predators are never mentioned in the passage, making **(F)** and **(G)** Out of Scope. **(H)** is incorrect because it's never stated that females migrate when males tell them it's time.

5. C

Category: Inference

Getting to the Answer: **(C)** is correct because whooping cranes are mentioned in paragraph 3 as an example of birds with unique courtship procedures. **(A)** is incorrect because it is Opposite: the whooping crane *does* participate in courtship procedures. **(B)** is Out of Scope because the whooping crane's plumage is never discussed. **(D)** is a Distortion; the passage mentions that roles are reversed in different species, but it never establishes that there are "normal" male and female courtship roles.

6. G

Category: Inference

Getting to the Answer: **(G)** is correct because in the final paragraph, it is stated that males identify themselves by their singing and that the female interprets their singing in order to predict "the response of a male to her approach." Since the female makes the approach, it's implied that she chooses the male. **(E)** is Extreme; just because the female's singing ability is never mentioned does not mean that it doesn't exist. Aggression is not mentioned in regard to bird sounds, making **(F)** Out of Scope. The breeding condition of the females is never mentioned, making **(H)** also Out of Scope.

PRACTICE SET

Passage Analysis: This passage sets out to explain the films of director Akira Kurosawa and their importance. Paragraph 1 establishes the high stature of Kurosawa. Paragraph 2 details some of Kurosawa's experiences and the impact they had on his filmmaking. Paragraph 3 talks about *Seven Samurai* and how it is emblematic of Kurosawa. Paragraph 4 details some controversy that Kurosawa's films have inflamed within Japan. Finally, paragraph 5 reiterates Kurosawa's stature and the many films he influenced.

1. D

Category: Global

Getting to the Answer: To answer Global questions, use your Roadmap to locate the Main Idea present throughout the passage. According to your Roadmap, the Main Idea is Kurosawa—his unique style, its controversy, and his influence on films. Make sure that your answer takes this information into account. The only answer that does this is **(D)**. **(A)** is Out of Scope; the popularity of American Westerns in Japan is never discussed in the passage. **(B)** is Extreme; Kurosawa is referred to as the most important Japanese filmmaker in cinema history, not the most important filmmaker of any nationality. **(C)** is a Misused Detail; Ozu and Mizoguchi are mentioned late in the passage but are not directly compared with Kurosawa.

2. E

Category: Detail

Getting to the Answer: Always note where important details are in the passage and understand how they fit into the structure of the text. In this case, the second paragraph discusses Kurosawa's life experiences—specifically his study of Western art and literature and his work on Japanese propaganda films. **(E)** refers to studying Western literature, which matches the details in paragraph 2. **(F)**, **(G)**, and **(H)** are all Distortions: Kurosawa worked on Japanese wartime propaganda films in Tokyo, not Westerns; Ozu and Mizoguchi are mentioned, but their collaboration with Kurosawa is not; and *A Fistful of Dollars* is mentioned as a film influenced by Kurosawa, not one that affected his films.

3. D

Category: Detail

Getting to the Answer: Sometimes details are phrased in the passage in a different way from the question stem. Be aware of the ideas of the passage, but don't try to memorize each word. This means that you should understand what to look for and where to look for it. In this case, paragraph 4 explains the Japanese suspicion about Kurosawa—that his films are not really Japanese and are overly influenced by the West. **(D)** fits this detail. **(A)** is Opposite; Kurosawa portrays samurai as human characters, not as noble symbols. **(B)** and **(C)** are Out of Scope; Kurosawa's choice of language is never discussed in the passage, and Japanese attitudes toward cowboy movies are never mentioned.

4. F

Category: Function

Getting to the Answer: Look for context clues in the cited lines to figure out how the phrase is used. Read the phrase in context—it states how the Japanese viewed the use of their culture in Kurosawa's work. Use this detail to find the correct answer choice, **(F)**. **(E)** is a Distortion; Ozu and Mizoguchi are "more Japanese," but they are not discussed as superior directors. **(G)** is Opposite; Western films greatly influenced Kurosawa's work. **(H)** is Out of Scope; interior design is never discussed in the passage.

5. D

Category: Detail

Getting to the Answer: Irony is when something happens that is contrary to the normal order of things. Because Kurosawa was influenced by Westerns at first, it is ironic that his films ended up influencing later Westerns. Choice **(D)** reflects that irony. **(A)** is a Distortion; it is never discussed that George Lucas was more successful than Kurosawa. **(B)** is Out of Scope; copyright laws are never discussed in the passage. **(C)** is also a Distortion; these genres have benefited from Kurosawa, not Japanese directors in general.

6. H

Category: Inference

Getting to the Answer: This question asks you to apply the themes explored in the passage to different settings and concepts. To have the best understanding of what the cited lines mean, you must read above and below the sentence and then apply your knowledge of the author's purpose to the answer choices. In this case, the cited lines talk about *Seven Samurai*, a Western story with Japanese setting and characters. Kurosawa has merged two different cultures, as choice **(H)** also does. **(E)** is Opposite; a cowboy movie set on a ranch is an expected relationship. **(F)** is Out of Scope; there is no real relationship between a cooking show and a firehouse. **(G)** is a Distortion; a play can be set in the future without expressing differences in cultures.

Passage Analysis: This passage describes the flightless cormorant, which is native to the Galápagos Islands. Paragraph 1 describes the Galápagos Islands and introduces the cormorant as one of the unusual species that lives on them. Paragraph 2 details the physical characteristics of the cormorant. Paragraph 3 explains the uniqueness of the cormorant and discusses its survival chances.

7. C

Category: Global

Getting to the Answer: When trying to determine how to best paraphrase the purpose of a passage, look for a common theme that runs through every paragraph. In this case, all three of the passage's paragraphs focus on the distinctive characteristics of the flightless cormorant, so look for an answer choice that reflects this. **(C)** matches what you're looking for. **(A)** is Out of Scope; the passage never discusses the variety of all the world's seabirds. **(B)** is a Misused Detail; although the passage does mention that Ecuador administers the Galápagos Islands as a province, this is not the focus of the passage. **(D)** is a Distortion; the passage never states that all seabirds have difficulty keeping their wings dry.

8. H

Category: Detail

Getting to the Answer: Because Detail questions are aimed at determining if you carefully read the passage, the one untrue answer choice that you are looking for may be close to, or even the opposite of, the facts given in the passage. In this case, the passage mentions the cormorant's brown feathers, small breastbone, stunted wings, strong legs, and sleek body. See which of the answer choices does not fit with this list. Choice **(H)** is correct: the legs of the flightless cormorant are mentioned in the passage but are described as heavy and powerful, not weak. **(E)** and **(F)** are mentioned in paragraph 2; **(G)** is mentioned in paragraph 1.

9. C

Category: Detail

Getting to the Answer: Research the passage to distinguish between characteristics that are differences and those that are shared between the two types of birds. It is the flightless cormorants' wings that make them so different from other cormorants, so **(C)** is correct. **(A)** is a Misused Detail; the passage does not compare the feather color of various cormorant species. **(B)** is also a Misused Detail; the passage states that cormorants dry their wings in the sun but does not present this fact as a difference. **(D)** is Out of Scope; the passage never mentions webbed feet.

10. H

Category: Detail

Getting to the Answer: By rereading the line in question and its context, you'll notice that the previous sentence focuses on the lack of natural predators for the flightless cormorant. Since this is the evolutionary advantage, the correct answer is **(H)**. **(E)**, **(F)**, and **(G)** are Misused Details. The details in **(E)** and **(F)** are mentioned in the passage but never described as advantages. Regarding **(G)**, the studies of Darwin are never associated with the flightless cormorant's "evolutionary advantage."

11. B

Category: Inference

Getting to the Answer: The word "suggested" in the question stem should indicate to you that the quoted words imply a meaning rather than explicitly stating that meaning. In this question, the referenced sentence describes the physical appearance of the flightless cormorant, a description that highlights the rather "comical" proportions of the bird. Look for an answer choice that accurately reflects this. In **(B)**, the word "unintimidating" is similar to the phrase in the question stem. **(A)** is a Distortion; although this answer choice contains the tempting word "funny-looking," the word "vicious" distorts the passage's description of these birds. **(C)** is also a Distortion; the passage never states that the islands themselves are "insignificant." **(D)** is Opposite; a feature that is considered powerful is not synonymous with "unimpressive."

12. H

Category: Detail

Getting to the Answer: First, locate where in the passage the author makes the statement to which the question refers. In the last sentence of the passage, the author writes, "a resiliency that bodes well for the survival of these distinctive birds well into the future." The words "bodes well" indicate the author's optimistic opinion about the survival of the flightless cormorant, which matches **(H)**. **(E)** is Out of Scope; the passage never suggests that the islands are too damaged to support these birds. **(F)** is a Distortion; the passage actually mentions that this small population size is not a threat to the flightless cormorant's survival. **(G)** is Opposite; the passage clearly states that these cormorants lack natural predators.

Passage Analysis: The Main Idea of this passage is to discuss the characteristics and influence of ska music. Paragraph 1 tells of genres that have borrowed from earlier styles and introduces ska as an example of this trend. Paragraph 2 details the influences that created ska's unique sound. Paragraph 3 highlights selected ska artists and discusses the themes in ska lyrics. Paragraph 4 tells of ska's rather seamless evolution into reggae. Paragraph 5 discusses ska's influence outside of Jamaica.

13. B

Category: Global

Getting to the Answer: A good answer to a Global question should capture an idea that runs through each paragraph of the passage. According to your Roadmap, the correct answer should involve the development and influence of ska music, as this idea is prominent throughout the passage. Since these themes are present in all paragraphs, **(B)** is the correct answer. **(A)** is a Distortion; the passage only discusses the influence of foreign musical styles on one style of Jamaican music, ska. **(C)** is a Misused Detail; ska's evolution into reggae and rocksteady is mentioned in paragraph 4, but this is not the Main Idea of the passage. **(D)** is another Misused Detail; this answer choice captures only part of the Main Idea, the influence of ska, but does not take into account ska's development.

14. H

Category: Inference

Getting to the Answer: In paragraph 1, the author mentions a list of comparisons, all related by a common theme: music styles that evolved from obscure earlier forms, including reggae. The author states that ska derived from both American and Caribbean music, as **(H)** reflects. **(E)** is a Distortion; the author is not listing other styles to make a comparison with ska. **(F)** is also a Distortion; although these sounds are listed later on in the passage, their purpose in paragraph 1 is not to detail ska's influences. **(G)** is Out of Scope; ska's development is never mentioned in the paragraph; rather, reggae is mentioned as evolving from ska.

15. B

Category: Detail

Getting to the Answer: Be careful—you're looking for the one wrong answer. First, identify the answer choices that are supported by information in the passage. Paragraph 2 describes ska's influences. See which answer choice is not listed. **(B)** is not mentioned, so it is correct. **(A)**, **(C)**, and **(D)** are all mentioned in paragraph 2.

16. F

Category: Inference

Getting to the Answer: When you're asked about a phrase in context, reread a little before and a little after the quoted phrase. Here, it says that "many songs took on political issues such as...Jamaica's growing cry for independence from Great Britain," so the best answer will match this idea. **(F)** is about a political issue—independence—so it matches what you're looking for. **(E)** and **(G)** are Distortions; Great Britain dominated Jamaica politically, not musically, and "growing cry" is a figure of speech that expresses the general feeling of the people of Jamaica. **(H)** is a Misused Detail; though this is suggested by the passage, it is not what was meant by this cited phrase.

17. D

Category: Detail

Getting to the Answer: Here, the last paragraph tells how American ska bands use ska rhythms in their own way, without necessarily calling their music ska, thus making its influence "quiet" or hidden. It is this refusal to identify the bands with ska which makes **(D)** the best answer. **(A)** and **(B)** are Out of Scope; the profitability of ska groups is never discussed in the passage, and reggae's worldwide importance is never mentioned. **(C)** is a Distortion; while this is true according to the passage, the fact that ska influenced punk music does not mean that it had an influence on all popular music.

18. H

Category: Inference

Getting to the Answer: This question asks you to take the ideas expressed in the passage and apply them to a different setting. The third paragraph discusses the themes of ska lyrics, particularly two important aspects: the popular mainstream styles and an emphasis on Jamaican issues and problems. **(H)**, a popular singer who also sings about struggles in his country, matches this nicely. **(E)** is a Distortion; this situation takes in only half the answer and does not address the aspect dealing with local issues and problems. **(F)** is a Distortion that reflects only one aspect of the correct answer; popular themes are not addressed. **(G)** is Out of Scope; the passage discusses only Jamaican singers, not Caribbean singers in general.

Passage Analysis: The primary focus of the passage is the life and presidency of James K. Polk. Paragraph 1 compares Polk with his political role model, Andrew Jackson. Paragraph 2 discusses Polk's early life and the beginning of his political career. Paragraph 3 discusses the 1844 presidential campaign and Polk's election as a "dark horse" candidate. Lastly, paragraph 4 details the triumphs and shortcomings of the Polk administration.

19. D

Category: Global

Getting to the Answer: Global questions require a proper understanding of the passage as a whole to identify the unifying idea that connects all the content together. In this case, the passage discusses the life and successes of James K. Polk. The correct answer will take all of this information into account. **(D)** takes into account the entire passage. **(A)** is a Misused Detail; the passage does state that Polk had a greater impact on history, but this was not the prime focus of the passage. **(B)** is also a Misused Detail; the passage mentions the United States provoking war with Mexico, but the entire passage does not focus on this. **(C)** is Out of Scope; the passage mentions Polk's ill health but does not describe its impact on his political effectiveness.

20. G

Category: Inference

Getting to the Answer: Inference questions ask you to make a connection between two pieces of information. In this case, the passage tells you that Jackson was "fiery" and had a "frontier persona," whereas Polk was "soft-spoken." From this information, you can infer that Jackson was most assuredly not soft-spoken. The correct answer is **(G)**. **(E)** is Extreme; the passage never makes this assertion. **(F)** is a Distortion; although the passage does state that Polk was determined and worked toward his goals, there is nothing in the passage to suggest that Jackson did not. **(H)** is Opposite; the passage states that Polk and Jackson did not differ in their policies.

21. A

Category: Function

Getting to the Answer: The passage tells you that Polk became Speaker of the House of Representatives and was catapulted "to a position of prominence in politics." Because you know that not long after this, Polk became president as a "dark horse" candidate, you can infer that becoming Speaker made Polk powerful but not necessarily famous. **(A)** fits this meaning. **(B)** is Extreme; Polk may have become more powerful, but nothing in the passage states that he took control of the Democratic Party. **(C)** is a Distortion; this choice does not fit the information that Polk was a "dark horse" candidate later in his career. **(D)** is Opposite; the passage states that Polk came out of nowhere to win the Democratic nomination for president and that Van Buren was initially the leading Democratic candidate.

22. F

Category: Detail

Getting to the Answer: Be wary of the wording in Detail questions; often the question will insert words like "not" and "except" that will completely alter the meaning of the question. In this case, you are looking for something that is not true according to the description of the 1844 election in paragraph 3. According to the passage, Polk made it clear to voters that he did favor expansion; therefore, **(F)** is correct. **(E)** is mentioned in lines 43–44; Polk won the Democratic nomination. **(G)** is mentioned in lines 38–39; the passage states that the anti-expansionist views of the other candidates were not popular. **(H)** is mentioned in lines 37–38; the passage states that Polk was "spurred on" by Jackson's advice.

23. D

Category: Detail

Getting to the Answer: The events of the Polk administration are mentioned in the last paragraph. The United States negotiated the Oregon border with England, won California and New Mexico from Mexico, and annexed Texas. Any of these details will serve as a correct answer. **(D)**, the agreement with England, includes one of those details. **(A)** is Out of Scope; the passage never states whether slavery was outlawed. **(B)** is a Distortion; the passage states that Texas was annexed, but you do not know if this means Texas became a state. **(C)** is a Misused Detail; Polk recognized the feelings of Americans toward expansion before his election.

24. G

Category: Inference

Getting to the Answer: The last paragraph states that Polk's achievements were "somewhat diminished" by the growing slavery controversy, but the overall tone of the paragraph is positive. In this case, the author is merely drawing attention to the fact that the Polk administration, although successful, was not perfect; this matches **(G)**. **(E)** is Extreme; the passage states that Polk's presidency did face criticism from abolitionists, but the overall tone of the passage is positive and suggests that Polk's presidency was actually successful. **(F)** is Out of Scope; the passage does not state why Polk was not reelected. **(H)** is a Distortion; although the passage does suggest that Polk was an able president, there is no mention of how Polk dealt with the abolitionist controversy.

Passage Analysis: The purpose of the passage is to describe the planet Jupiter, its discovery, and the subsequent explorations of its chemical composition, interior structure, and other characteristics. Paragraph 1 describes the history and implications of Jupiter's discovery. Paragraph 2 describes Jupiter's chemical composition and interior structure. Paragraph 3 describes Jupiter's winds. Paragraph 4 describes Jupiter's amazing rotational speed.

25. D

Category: Global

Getting to the Answer: First, identify the Main Idea; in this case, the entire passage focuses on what is known about Jupiter from the hundreds of years that scientists have been studying the planet and what is still not completely understood. Look for an answer choice that takes this focus into account. Since **(D)** includes the scientific study of Jupiter and what scientists do and do not know about the planet, this is the correct answer. **(A)** is Out of Scope; the passage mentions probes but never describes exactly how Jupiter's chemical composition was determined. **(B)** is a Distortion; the passage merely states that

Galileo's observance of Jupiter's moons provided evidence for his support of Copernicus's theory, not "popular acceptance." **(C)** is also a Distortion; the passage states that much is still unknown about Jupiter, but this statement is never suggested by the content of the passage.

26. E

Category: Detail

Getting to the Answer: Because nearly the entire passage is devoted to describing the known characteristics of Jupiter, use the answer choices to direct your reexamination of the text. Also, be wary of answer choices that tempt you with wordings drawn directly, yet inaccurately, from the text. The passage groups Jupiter among the other gaseous planets and uses wording "like other gaseous planets" to open paragraph 3, but nowhere in the passage is it stated that Jupiter is "considered nearly identical" to these planets. **(E)** is correct. **(F)** is mentioned in paragraph 1, **(G)** is mentioned in paragraph 2, and **(H)** is mentioned in paragraph 3.

27. C

Category: Detail

Getting to the Answer: Although you may not be able to precisely define the word "heliocentric" on your own, context provides some important clues as to its meaning. For example, the words immediately preceding the phrase "because these moons seemed to revolve around a planet other than Earth" indicate, at the very least, that a heliocentric theory suggests the idea that planets do not necessarily revolve around the Earth. **(C)** makes that connection. **(A)** is a Misused Detail; although the enormous mass of Jupiter is mentioned, this information is not connected in the passage to the cited words. **(B)** is also a Misused Detail; although this discovery is mentioned, it is not directly connected to the meaning of a heliocentric theory. **(D)** is a Distortion; the passage never suggests it was believed that Jupiter orbits its own moons.

28. F

Category: Inference

Getting to the Answer: Although the passage may not directly state what can be indicated by the presence of water and minerals, look to the context to establish a connection. In this case, the words "largely due to" (line 31) suggest that water and minerals have led scientists to believe that Jupiter "has a core of rocky material" (lines 33–34). **(F)** makes the correct inference. **(E)** is a Distortion; the passage never suggests that water and minerals are an indicator of the "entire" chemical makeup of a planet. **(G)** is also a Distortion; the passage never connects the presence of hydrogen and helium on Jupiter with the discovery of water and minerals. **(H)** is another Distortion; the passage never states that it is a fact that Jupiter has a solid core.

29. D

Category: Detail

Getting to the Answer: First, identify where in the passage the author discusses an unlikely characteristic of Jupiter's large size; in this case, paragraph 4 uses the words "amazingly short" (line 51) to refer to the amount of time Jupiter takes to complete one full revolution. **(D)** says the same thing in different words. **(A)** is a Misused Detail; the fact that Jupiter could be considered similar to these planets is not described as unlikely in the passage. **(B)** is also a Misused Detail; Jupiter's lack of a solid surface is never connected to its large mass. **(C)** is another Misused Detail; Jupiter's classification as a gaseous planet is not connected to its mass.

30. H

Category: Detail

Getting to the Answer: As probes are mentioned a number of times throughout the passage, use the answer choices to direct your research of the text. In this case, the relevant information can be found in paragraph 3, where it is mentioned that "measurements taken by a number of probes" have indicated the wind speeds on Jupiter, as choice **(H)** states. **(E)** is a Distortion; although rotational speed is mentioned in the passage, it is never suggested that that is consistent with the use of probes. **(F)** and **(G)** are Out of Scope; the separation of hydrogen and helium is never mentioned in the passage, nor is the identification of the bands.

CHAPTER 11

SHSAT Fiction & Poetry

CHAPTER OBJECTIVES

By the end of this chapter, you will be able to:

- Actively read fiction and poetry passages
- Apply the appropriate strategies to answer fiction and poetry questions correctly

SHSAT FICTION PASSAGES

Fiction Passages

Fiction passages are different from the other passages because:

- There are often multiple characters and, therefore, multiple opinions.
- The tone will be nuanced and emotion-based, rather than informative or explanatory.

As you read a fiction passage, you should:

1. Identify the narrator, if there is one. The narrator is likely the most important character.
    - Who is the narrator?
    - Age?
    - Gender?
    - Background?
    - How does the passage describe the narrator?
2. Identify the characters, evaluate how the author describes them, and determine the relationships among the characters.
    - What do the characters want?
    - What are the characters doing?
    - What adjectives describe each character?
    - How do the characters know one another?
3. Assess the characters' opinions of each other and themselves.
    - Do they like each other? Do they dislike each other?
    - Why does each character make particular decisions or take particular courses of action?
    - What do these decisions or actions tell you about the character?
4. Identify the tone and themes within the story.
    - What is the overall tone of the passage?
    - What are the "turning points" in the passage?
    - Is there a moral to the story?

✔ Remember

Because fiction passages often have multiple characters with multiple opinions, remember to keep straight who said what.

Fiction Questions

Fiction passages will be accompanied by Global, Detail, and Function questions.

Global questions ask about the theme or central idea of the passage.

- Identify the main idea or theme of the passage and match it to the correct answer choice.
- Avoid answer choices that are too narrow (Misused Details) or that are not discussed in the passage (Out of Scope).

Detail questions ask about specific information from the passage. They may ask about a word, a phrase, or an idea.

- Use the clues in the question, reread that specific section of the passage, put your finger on the answer in the passage, and compare the choices to that information in the passage.
- Common incorrect choices will misstate the information in the passage (Distortions), include details that are directly from the passage but are unrelated to the question (Misused Details), or not be mentioned in the passage (Out of Scope).

Function questions identify a feature of the passage—a line, a paragraph, an example, or an opinion—and ask you to consider either why or how the poet uses the feature.

- Think of the tone and the main idea, or the theme, of the passage, reread the part of the passage the question asks about, predict an answer, and match your prediction to the correct answer.
- Common incorrect choices will describe the purpose of another part of the passage (Misused Detail), will not be mentioned in the passage (Out of Scope), or will not match the tone of the passage (Distortion).

To answer fiction questions successfully:

1. Read each question carefully and thoroughly. Determine exactly what the question is asking.
2. Go back to the lines mentioned in the question or to the section of the passage where the idea in the question is discussed, and research the answer in the passage.
    - Find support for your answer using information from the passage before you pick it from among the other choices.
    - Don't rely on your memory. It's an open-book test, so use the passage!
3. If a question is difficult, circle it, guess, and move to the next one. You'll maximize your score by finding and answering every question you *can* get correct. You can go back and spend time on difficult questions at the end if time remains.

Try It Out

The following is an excerpt from "The Shinansha," from *Japanese Fairy Tales*, compiled by Yei Theodora Ozaki.

The compass, with its needle always pointing to the North, is quite a common thing, and no one thinks that it is remarkable now, though when it was first invented it must have been a wonder.

Now long ago in China, there was a still more wonderful invention called the shinansha. This was a kind of chariot with the figure of a man on it always pointing to the South. No matter how the chariot was placed the figure always wheeled about and pointed to the South.

This curious instrument was invented by Kotei, one of the three Chinese Emperors of the Mythological age. Kotei was the son of the Emperor Yuhi. Before he was born his mother had a vision which foretold that her son would be a great man.

One summer evening she went out to walk in the meadows to seek the cool breezes which blow at the end of the day and to gaze with pleasure at the star-lit heavens above her. As she looked at the North Star, strange to relate, it shot forth vivid flashes of lightning in every direction. Soon after this her son Kotei came into the world.

Kotei in time grew to manhood and succeeded his father the Emperor Yuhi. His early reign was greatly troubled by the rebel Shiyu. This rebel wanted to make himself King, and many were the battles which he fought to this end. Shiyu was a wicked magician, his head was made of iron, and there was no man that could conquer him.

At last Kotei declared war against the rebel and led his army to battle, and the two armies met on a plain called Takuroku. The Emperor boldly attacked the enemy, but the magician brought down a dense fog upon the battlefield, and while the royal army were wandering about in confusion, trying to find their way, Shiyu retreated with his troops, laughing at having fooled the royal army.

No matter however strong and brave the Emperor's soldiers were, the rebel with his magic could always escape in the end.

Kotei returned to his Palace, and thought and pondered deeply as to how he should conquer the magician, for he was determined not to give up yet. After a long time he invented the shinansha with the figure of a man always pointing South, for there were no compasses in those days. With this instrument to show him the way he need not fear the dense fogs raised up by the magician to confound his men.

1. Read this sentence from paragraph 1.

   The compass, with its needle always pointing to the North, is quite a common thing, and no one thinks that it is remarkable now, though when it was first invented it must have been a wonder.

   How does the sentence contribute to the development of the plot?

   A. It defines what a compass is so that the reader better appreciates Kotei's invention of it.

   B. It explains the background of Kotei leading up to his birth.

   C. It suggests that the shinansha is a marvel on par with Shiyu's magical fog.

   D. It explains that 'shinansha' is just a synonym for a north-pointing compass.

2. In paragraph 3, how does the phrase "of the Mythological age" affect the tone of the excerpt?

   E. It establishes the excerpt's factual tone, which matches the fact that events from recorded history are recounted.

   F. It highlights the excerpt's comedic tone, which highlights that magical events are presented as historical fact.

   G. It illustrates the excerpt's heroic tone about events that took place before China had any emperors.

   H. It establishes the excerpt's epic tone, which suggests to the reader that events are set in an era of heroes and magic.

3. Which of the following best explains why Kotei's mother thought her son would be great?

   A. "This curious instrument was invented by Kotei, one of the three Chinese Emperors of the Mythological age." (paragraph 3)

   B. "Kotei was the son of the Emperor Yuhi." (paragraph 3)

   C. "As she looked at the North Star... it shot forth vivid flashes of lightning in every direction." (paragraph 4)

   D. "...his head was made of iron, and there was no man that could conquer him." (paragraph 5)

4. The phrase "strange to relate" in paragraph 4 shows that the author

   E. knows that the event he is about to describe is difficult to put into words.

   F. believes that the event he is about to describe was hard for Kotei's mother to understand.

   G. acknowledges that the event he is about to describe is surprising and curious.

   H. believes that the event Kotei's mother witnessed meant nothing important.

5. How does paragraph 5 contribute to the plot of the excerpt?

   A. It suggests that the failures of Kotei's father, Emperor Yuhi, led to the rebellion by Shiyu.

   B. It explains that every newly crowned Chinese emperor must fight off a rival to his throne.

   C. It pivots from the story of Kotei's origin to the story of why Kotei came to invent the shinansha.

   D. It shows that Kotei and Shiyu each wanted the best for China, even if circumstances made them enemies.

6. How does the presence of the dense fog in paragraph 6 influence the Emperor's army?

   E. The fog causes the Emperor's army to use shinanshas as a defensive measure.

   F. The fog causes the Emperor's army to fall into disarray as the soldiers find themselves lost.

   G. The fog causes the Emperor's army to quickly retreat in a panic.

   H. The fog causes the Emperor's army to be left open to an enemy attack.

7. Which of the following best explains the shinansha's military importance?

   A. "One summer evening she went out to walk in the meadows to seek the cool breezes which blow at the end of the day and to gaze with pleasure at the star-lit heavens above her." (paragraph 4)

   B. "His early reign was greatly troubled by the rebel Shiyu." (paragraph 5)

   C. "Shiyu was a wicked magician, his head was made of iron, and there was no man that could conquer him." (paragraph 5)

   D. "No matter however strong and brave the Emperor's soldiers were, the rebel with his magic could always escape in the end." (paragraph 7)

8. Read this sentence from paragraph 8.

   Kotei returned to his Palace, and thought and pondered deeply as to how he should conquer the magician, for he was determined not to give up yet.

Which statement best describes how the sentence fits into the overall structure of the excerpt?

   E. It provides a reason why the shinansha's creation is rooted in Kotei's personal greatness.

   F. It introduces the concept of the shinansha to the story as a means to defeat Shiyu's army.

   G. It emphasizes a shift from the fairy-tale nature of the story to the factual basis of compasses.

   H. It indicates a shift away from a war that Kotei is in danger of losing to one that he will win.

SHSAT POETRY PASSAGES

Poetry Passages

Poetry passages are different from the other passages because:

- Poems express thoughts in verse.
- Poetry is written in stanzas and uses line breaks.

As you read a poetry passage, you should:

1. Identify the topic and the narrator (when applicable).

   - Start by identifying the topic; a poem will use imagery and symbolism, but it will feature a specific topic.
   - If the poem is a narrative, look for context clues that help to identify the narrator.
   - Don't worry about difficult words; you will likely be able to figure them out from the context. In addition, the questions may not directly ask about them.

2. Identify the theme or main idea.

   - Focus on understanding the main idea or theme of the poem.
   - You do not need to memorize or remember small details. If a detail is required to answer a question, you can reread that part of the passage.

3. Identify the mood.

   - What adjectives are included in the poem?
   - What feelings does the poem create in the reader?
   - What words would you use to describe the mood?

4. Paraphrase the poet's words.

   - What does the poem mean in your own words?
   - What information is the poet trying to convey?

Poetry Questions

Poetry passages will be accompanied by Global, Detail, Inference, and Function questions.

Global questions ask about the theme or central idea of the poem.

- Identify the main idea or theme of the poem and match it to the correct answer choice.
- Common incorrect choices will be too narrow or will not be discussed in the poem.

Detail questions ask about specific information in the poem. They may ask about a word, a phrase, or specific language the poet includes.

- Research the answer in the poem and compare the answer choices to that section of the poem.
- Avoid answer choices that misstate an idea presented in the poem.

Inference questions ask you to support an idea from the poem with specific lines from the poem or to explain the meaning of imagery in the poem.

- Review the section of the poem the question is asking about and then compare the answer choices to that idea.
- Common incorrect choices will not match the poem's ideas exactly or will not be mentioned in the poem.

Function questions identify a feature of the poem—a line, a stanza, or imagery—and ask you to consider either why or how the poet uses the feature.

- Identify the main idea or the theme of the poem, read the part of the poem the question asks about, predict an answer, and then find the choice that matches your prediction.
- Avoid answer choices that describe the purpose of an unrelated part of the poem or an idea that is not featured in the poem.

To answer poetry questions successfully:

1. Read the question carefully and thoroughly. Determine exactly what the question is asking.
2. Go back to the lines or stanza mentioned in the question to look up the answer in the poem.
    - Find support for your answer using information from the poem before you pick it from among the other choices.
    - Do not rely on your memory.
3. If a question is difficult, circle it, guess, and move to the next one. You'll maximize your score by finding and answering every question you *can* get correct. You can go back and spend time on difficult questions at the end if time remains.

Try It Out

The following poem, "Storm," was written by Hilda Doolittle, who lived from 1886 to 1961.

You crash over the trees,
you crack the live branch—
the branch is white,
the green crushed,
each leaf is rent like split wood.

You burden the trees
with black drops,
you swirl and crash—
you have broken off a weighted leaf
in the wind,
it is hurled out,
whirls up and sinks,
a green stone.

1. The description in the first stanza (lines 1–5) helps establish a central idea of the poem by
   - **A.** depicting the dramatic way a leaf falls in a storm.
   - **B.** mimicking the sound of a raging wind.
   - **C.** using colors to evoke the devastation of the storm.
   - **D.** describing the effect of a powerful storm on a tree.

2. What impact do the words "crash," "crack," and "crushed" have on the meaning of the poem?
   - **E.** Their similar sounds unite the first and second stanzas.
   - **F.** Their harsh sounds emphasize the fury of the storm.
   - **G.** Their rhythmic, repeated beginnings imitate the sound of the rain.
   - **H.** They provide a dramatic contrast to the quiet peace that follows the storm.

3. Read lines 1–2 and 6–8 that begin the two stanzas.

   You crash over the trees,
   you crack the live branch—

   You burden the trees
   with black drops,
   you swirl and crash—

The parallel structure of the two stanzas

   - **A.** serves to contrast the effects at the start of the storm with those at the end of the storm.
   - **B.** indicates that wind mentioned in the first stanza is less important than the rain.
   - **C.** emphasizes that the second stanza will be a continuation of the first.
   - **D.** shows that the first stanza was more important than the second.

4. Read lines 6–7.

You burden the trees
with black drops,

The lines help develop the theme of the poem by suggesting that the rain

E. is so heavy it may damage the trees.
F. will harm the trees because it is black from pollution.
G. is necessary for the growth of the trees.
H. will cause widespread flooding.

5. Read lines 11–13.

it is hurled out,
whirls up and sinks,
a green stone.

How do the lines contribute to the development of ideas in the stanza?

A. They indicate the start of new life after the destruction of the storm.
B. They explain what the storm did to the branch.
C. They show the power and intensity of the storm.
D. They describe the flood water left behind from the storm.

6. The personification in the poem suggests that the storm is

E. an angry warrior fighting to right a wrong.
F. an impersonal act of nature without reason or motive.
G. ready to pass by the tree as it moves through the countryside.
H. intentional in its assault on the tree and the leaves.

The following practice sets provide an opportunity to apply the concepts and strategic thinking covered in this chapter. To practice Test Day timing, follow the suggested timing guidelines for each section.

FICTION PRACTICE SET

Suggested Timing: 12 minutes

The following is an excerpt from *Three Men and a Maid* by P. G. Wodehouse, originally published in 1922.

Through the curtained windows of the furnished apartment which Mrs. Horace Hignett had rented for her stay in New York rays of golden sunlight peeped in like the foremost spies of some advancing army. It was a fine summer morning. The hands of the Dutch clock in the hall pointed to thirteen minutes past nine; those of the ormolu clock in the sitting-room to eleven minutes past ten; those of the carriage clock on the bookshelf to fourteen minutes to six. In other words, it was exactly eight; and Mrs. Hignett acknowledged the fact by moving her head on the pillow, opening her eyes, and sitting up in bed. She always woke at eight precisely.

Was this Mrs. Hignett the Mrs. Hignett, the world-famous writer on Theosophy, the author of "The Spreading Light," "What of the Morrow," and all the rest of that well-known series? I'm glad you asked me. Yes, she was. She had come over to America on a lecturing tour.

The year 1921, it will be remembered, was a trying one for the inhabitants of the United States. Every boat that arrived from England brought a fresh swarm of British lecturers to the country. Novelists, poets, scientists, philosophers, and plain, ordinary bores; some herd instinct seemed to affect them all simultaneously. It was like one of those great race movements of the Middle Ages. Men and women of widely differing views on religion, art, politics, and almost every other subject; on this one point the intellectuals of Great Britain were single-minded, that there was easy money to be picked up on the lecture platforms of America and that they might just as well grab it as the next person.

Mrs. Hignett had come over with the first batch of immigrants; for, spiritual as her writings were, there was a solid streak of business sense in this woman and she meant to get hers while the getting was good. She was half way across the Atlantic with a complete itinerary booked before 90 per cent of the poets and philosophers had finished sorting out their clean collars and getting their photographs taken for the passport.

She had not left England without a pang, for departure had involved sacrifices. More than anything else in the world she loved her charming home, Windles, in the county of Hampshire, for so many years the seat of the Hignett family. Windles was as the breath of life to her. Its shady walks, its silver lake, its noble elms, the old grey stone of its walls—these were bound up with her very being. She felt that she belonged to Windles, and Windles to her. Unfortunately, as a matter of cold, legal accuracy, it did not. She did but hold it in trust for her son, Eustace, until such time as he should marry and take possession of it himself. There were times when the thought of Eustace marrying and bringing a strange woman to Windles chilled Mrs. Hignett to her very marrow. Happily, her firm policy of keeping her son permanently under her eye at home and never permitting him to have speech with a female below the age of fifty had averted the peril up till now.

Eustace had accompanied his mother to America. It was his faint snores which she could hear in the adjoining room, as, having bathed and dressed, she went down the hall to where breakfast awaited her. She smiled tolerantly. She had never desired to convert her son to her own early rising habits, for, apart from not allowing him to call his soul his own, she was an indulgent mother. Eustace would get up at half-past nine, long after she had finished breakfast, read her mail, and started her duties for the day.

Breakfast was on the table in the sitting-room, a modest meal of rolls, cereal, and imitation coffee. Beside the pot containing this hell-brew was a little pile of letters. Mrs. Hignett opened them as she ate. The majority were from disciples and dealt with matters of purely theosophical interest. There was an invitation from the Butterfly Club asking her to be the guest of honour at their weekly dinner. There was a letter from her brother Mallaby—Sir Mallaby Marlowe, the eminent London lawyer—saying that his son Sam, of whom she had never approved, would be in New York shortly, passing through on his way back to England, and hoping that she would see something of him. Altogether a dull mail. Mrs. Hignett skimmed through it without interest, setting aside one or two of the letters for Eustace, who acted as her unpaid secretary, to answer later in the day.

1. In paragraph 1, how does the phrase "sunlight peeped in like the foremost spies of some advancing army" affect the tone in the excerpt?

   A. It creates the martial tone that runs through Mrs. Hignett's first-person narration.

   B. It sets the dry, humorous tone of the third-person narration.

   C. It establishes the sullen tone of Mrs. Hignett's first-person perspective.

   D. It introduces the factual tone of the third-person narration.

2. Read these sentences from paragraph 1.

   The hands of the Dutch clock in the hall pointed to thirteen minutes past nine; those of the ormolu clock in the sitting-room to eleven minutes past ten; those of the carriage clock on the bookshelf to fourteen minutes to six. In other words, it was exactly eight; and Mrs. Hignett.... always woke at eight precisely.

   How do these sentences contribute to the development of the plot?

   E. They show that Mrs. Hignett is rooming with other people working on different schedules.

   F. They show that Mrs. Hignett needs repeated reminders by multiple alarm clocks to wake up.

   G. They illustrate Mrs. Hignett's homesickness, as the clocks are still set to her native time zone.

   H. They illustrate Mrs. Hignett's willpower, as she does not need clocks to wake on schedule.

3. Read these sentences from paragraph 2.

   Was this Mrs. Hignett the Mrs. Hignett, the world-famous writer on Theosophy, the author of "The Spreading Light," "What of the Morrow," and all the rest of that well-known series? I'm glad you asked me. Yes, she was.

   How do these sentences affect the tone of the excerpt?

   A. They create a formal, ponderous impression of the lecture circuit's role in American culture.

   B. They establish the informal, chatty nature of the narrator when relaying the story.

   C. They suggest that the narration will be an erudite, professional overview of famous writers.

   D. They introduce a serious and deep author of profound philosophical books.

4. Which of the following best explains why so many English lecturers were coming to the United States in 1921?

   E. The history of the Middle Ages was a topic of interest to Americans.

   F. Americans needed a great deal of education on numerous topics.

   G. There were no Americans who spoke on lecture tours.

   H. Americans were willing to pay money to attend lectures.

5. Read this sentence from paragraph 4.

   She was half way across the Atlantic with a complete itinerary booked before 90 per cent of the poets and philosophers had finished sorting out their clean collars and getting their photographs taken for the passport.

How does the sentence contribute to the development of the central idea of the excerpt?

   A. It emphasizes that Mrs. Hignett acts decisively.

   B. It illustrates how desperate Mrs. Hignett is for lecture circuit money.

   C. It shows how Mrs. Hignett has traveled to America several times in the past.

   D. It illustrates that Mrs. Hignett is willing to sabotage her rivals to secure her fame.

6. Read this sentence from paragraph 5.

   Unfortunately, as a matter of cold, legal accuracy, it did not.

What statement best describes how the sentence fits into the overall structure of the excerpt?

   E. It signals a shift from the perspective of Mrs. Hignett to the perspective of her son.

   F. It signals a shift from the description of Mrs. Hignett's family home to the means by which she has held onto that home.

   G. It provides the reason that Mrs. Hignett is traveling the lecture circuit by herself despite having living family members.

   H. It provides the reason that the Hignett's family home has been lost to them.

7. How does Windles being held in a legal trust influence Mrs. Hignett's behavior?

   A. She has grown to dislike her family's home because it no longer belongs to her.

   B. She goes on the lecture circuit in order to make enough money to save her family's home.

   C. She has tried to buy her son's affection so that he won't throw her out.

   D. She closely monitors her son and steers him away from young, single women.

POETRY PRACTICE SET

Suggested Timing: 10 minutes

The following poem, "Ozymandias," written by Percy Shelley, was first published in 1818.

I met a traveller from an antique land
Who said: Two vast and trunkless legs of stone
Stand in the desert. Near them on the sand,
Half sunk, a shatter'd visage lies, whose frown
And wrinkled lip and sneer of cold command
Tell that its sculptor well those passions read
Which yet survive, stamp'd on these lifeless things,
The hand that mock'd them and the heart that fed.
And on the pedestal these words appear:
"My name is Ozymandias, king of kings:
Look on my works, ye Mighty, and despair!"
Nothing beside remains: round the decay
Of that colossal wreck, boundless and bare,
The lone and level sands stretch far away.

1. Read lines 10–13 from the poem.

   "My name is Ozymandias, king of kings:
   Look on my works, ye Mighty, and despair!"
   Nothing beside remains: round the decay
   Of that colossal wreck, boundless and bare,

   How do the lines develop the central theme of the poem?

   A. They suggest that all objects will deteriorate over time.
   B. They paint a picture of the vast size and desolation of the desert.
   C. They suggest that Ozymandias has continued to be a powerful and glorious figure.
   D. They highlight the impermanence of power and glory.

2. How does the author's use of words like "half sunk," "shatter'd," "wrinkled," and "sneer" contribute to the meaning of the poem?

   E. They evoke a sense of desolation and loss of a powerful figure.
   F. They imply that the statue was marred and unpleasant to look at.
   G. They suggest that the statue was of someone old and decrepit.
   H. They highlight the unhappiness of the figure depicted in the statue.

3. It can be inferred that Ozymandias cautions those who see the statue to "despair" (line 11) because

   A. they will never be able to match his power.

   B. they will surely be defeated in war.

   C. the face is sad and inspires despair.

   D. Ozymandias knows his reign will soon end.

4. Which detail from the poem best suggests that the statue lies in ruins?

   E. "whose frown And wrinkled lip and sneer of cold command" (lines 4–5)

   F. "The hand that mock'd them and the heart that fed." (line 8)

   G. "And on the pedestal these words appear: 'My name is Ozymandias, king of kings:'" (lines 9–10)

   H. "Nothing beside remains: round the decay Of that colossal wreck, boundless and bare," (lines 12–13)

5. Which of the following lines from the poem best supports the idea that a skillful sculptor crafted a true likeness of Ozymandias?

   A. "Two vast and trunkless legs of stone Stand in the desert. Near them on the sand, Half sunk, a shatter'd visage lies," (lines 2–4)

   B. "Tell that its sculptor well those passions read. Which yet survive, stamp'd on these lifeless things" (lines 6–7)

   C. "My name is Ozymandias, king of kings: Look on my works, ye Mighty, and despair!" (lines 10–11)

   D. "Of that colossal wreck, boundless and bare, The lone and level sands stretch far away." (lines 13–14)

6. How does the phrase "colossal wreck" (line 13) serve the meaning of the poem?

   E. It symbolizes the power and might of King Ozymandias by suggesting that the statue was enormous.

   F. It contributes to the poem's irony to reveal that a significant tribute to a powerful ruler now stands in ruins.

   G. The phrase evokes a sense of the magnitude of the archeological find that the traveler stumbled upon.

   H. It is meant to stir disgust and anger over the fact that the statue has been broken.

ANSWERS AND EXPLANATIONS

Fiction Passages

Passage Analysis: The folktale from China describes the invention of the shinansha, a directional instrument that always points south. The first paragraph notes how common a compass is today, while the second introduces an instrument invented even before the compass—the shinansha. The next paragraph describes Emperor Kotei, the inventor, while the fourth paragraph tells of the strange event Kotei's mother witnessed while pregnant with Kotei, which seemed to be an omen of greatness. As the story continues, Kotei grows up, becomes Emperor, and is faced with the rebel magician Shiyu, who wants to be king. In paragraph 6, Kotei and Shiyu go to war, but Kotei's forces are rendered helpless and confused by a magic fog that Shiyu spreads over the battlefield. It seems as if the Emperor's forces could never defeat Shiyu, until, in paragraph 8, Kotei ponders how to overcome this fog and develops the shinansha, which always points south—thus, always showing his soldiers the way, even in the densest magical fog.

1. C

Category: Global

Getting to the Answer: Because a compass is a commonplace tool in the modern world, the author makes an effort to explain how wondrous it must have seemed when first invented. The author then uses the discussion of the compass as a springboard to talk about a similar invention, the mythic shinansha. This functions as a way to make Emperor Kotei appear as impressive as the mage Shiyu with his fog magic. Thus, **(C)** is correct. Kotei does not invent the compass, which points north, but the shinansha, which points south; **(A)** is incorrect. While the excerpt goes on to talk about omens that heralded Kotei's greatness ahead of his birth, this happens in paragraphs 3 and 4, not paragraph 1; **(B)** is incorrect. A shinansha, which points south, is not a compass, which points north; **(D)** is incorrect.

2. H

Category: Function

Getting to the Answer: As with so many folktales from around the world, this one pits good against evil. The magician rebel, with his iron head and magic fog, represents evil, while the Emperor, destined to be "a great man" (line 15) with determination and intelligence, creates the shinansha, which overcomes the evil magician. This is a story out of mythology; **(H)** is correct. As mythological events are ones that did not actually occur, **(E)** is incorrect. Although events involving magic happen in the story, the tone throughout is not comedic; **(F)** is incorrect. The excerpt defines Kotei as one of the three Chinese Emperors of the Mythological age; **(G)** is incorrect.

3. C

Category: Detail

Getting to the Answer: Kotei's mother was gazing at the night sky and saw "vivid flashes of lightning in every direction" (lines 20–21). This omen foreshadowed the greatness of her son; **(C)** is correct. Although **(A)** is tempting because Kotei did invent the shinansha, it is incorrect because Kotei's mother had no way of knowing that her son would create this specific invention many years later. While Kotei was the son of the Emperor, **(B)** is incorrect because that does not explain why his mother thought he would be especially great when he took the throne from his father. **(D)** is incorrect because it describes the rebel Shiyu rather than Kotei.

4. G

Category: Function

Getting to the Answer: Lightning shooting out from the North Star is not an everyday occurrence; it would have been odd and surprising to Kotei's mother. Thus, **(G)** is correct. Because the author managed to put the event into words, it could not have been too difficult to express; **(E)** is incorrect. The mother knew that the lightning signaled that her son would be a "great man" (line 15). So she did understand the strange omen, and there is no suggestion that she scoffed at the omen and considered it false; **(F)** and **(H)** are incorrect.

5. C

Category: Global

Getting to the Answer: Paragraph 5 functions as a pivot in the story. After establishing the setting and Kotei's origin, it now transitions to a specific incident to explain his greatness: how he invented the shinansha. The war against the evil mage Shiyu gives him the motivation to create his invention. Thus, **(C)** is correct. There is nothing to suggest that Emperor Yuhi caused the rebellion to occur; **(A)** is incorrect. Likewise, **(B)** is incorrect because we only know that Kotei had to fight off a rebellion. We know nothing about other Chinese emperors. **(D)** is incorrect because Shiyu is presented as an evil enemy, not a sympathetic character.

6. F

Category: Detail

Getting to the Answer: The fog unleashed in paragraph 6 caused the Emperor's army to fall into disarray as the soldiers found themselves lost in it, unable to see or tell which direction they were facing. Thus, **(F)** is correct. Although the shinanshas would be used as a countermeasure to the fog, this does not come until later. The shinanshas had not been invented yet at this point in the story; **(E)** is incorrect. Paragraph 8 describes the Emperor's soldiers as "strong and brave" even in the dense fog; **(G)** is incorrect. Shiyu's army is described as retreating under the cover of the magic fog, not attacking; **(H)** is incorrect.

7. D

Category: Detail

Getting to the Answer: The shinansha's military importance was that it allowed the royal army to orient themselves in a dense fog. That way, they would not get turned around and lose track of their enemy, which is described as happening in paragraph 7. Thus, **(D)** is correct. **(A)** is discussing Kotei's mother, not the shinansha, and is therefore incorrect. While Shiyu was a major rebel and was personally very tough, that is not why the shinansha was important; **(B)** and **(C)** are incorrect.

8. E

Category: Function

Getting to the Answer: Because the royal army is foiled by the fog of the evil mage Shiyu, the rebel army cannot be defeated. Kotei has to single-handedly invent a kind of compass through sheer personal effort, and then presumably lead his army to victory using it. This signals his personal greatness; **(E)** is correct. Although this is the point where the shinansha is invented, it is introduced much earlier in the excerpt, in paragraph 2. So, **(F)** is incorrect. The story never shifts away from its mythic, fairy-tale nature; **(G)** is incorrect. While **(H)** is tempting because Kotei will now be able to lead his army to victory, it is incorrect because the royal army is not in danger of losing the war. Shiyu always retreats under the cover of fog, and he would not need to resort to a retreat if he were in a position to defeat the royal army and win the war.

Poetry Passages

Poem Analysis: This short poem by Hilda Doolittle, who wrote under the pen name H. D., displays her powerful imagery conveyed with an economy of words. There are two stanzas, together describing a raging storm and its effect on the trees. The first stanza tells of how the wind roars and, perhaps, of how lightning breaks a branch and rends leaves. The second stanza describes how a leaf breaks off, is flung wildly around, and finally falls to the ground.

1. D

Category: Global

Getting to the Answer: The entire poem describes how a storm wreaks havoc on a tree and its leaves. The first stanza shows that the storm "crashes" in, breaks off a branch, and tears the leaves of a tree; **(D)** is correct. **(A)** is incorrect because it describes the falling leaf of the second stanza. **(B)** is incorrect because the wind is merely an aspect of the poem, not a central idea. **(C)** is incorrect because the author uses colors to describe the tree branch, not the storm, and the branch is merely one aspect of the storm's effects on the tree.

2. F

Category: Detail

Getting to the Answer: The poem describes a violent storm, and the author's use of "crash," "crack," and "crushed" almost sound like thunder. The author uses these short, harsh words to emphasize how strong the storm is; **(F)** is correct. While "crash" is repeated in the second stanza, the word doesn't appear until the end of the third line. The word is not being used to unite the stanzas; **(E)** is incorrect. **(G)** is incorrect because the author is not describing the sound of the rain, but rather the violent effects of the wind and the rain. **(H)** is incorrect because the poem does not close with a description of the calm that followed the storm.

3. C

Category: Function

Getting to the Answer: The two stanzas of the poem both describe the storm's fury, and the poet's repetition of the "You..." structure indicates that the second stanza will continue to discuss the topic introduced in the first stanza; **(C)** is correct. **(A)** is incorrect because there is no language in the poem to indicate that the storm is ending. **(B)** is incorrect because the second stanza discusses the violence of the wind, not the rain. Also, there is no comparison made between the wind and the rain. **(D)** is incorrect because the similar structure indicates the stanzas are basically similar. While parallel structure can be used to contrast two ideas, this poem does not contrast the two stanzas.

4. E

Category: Global

Getting to the Answer: These lines are describing the heavy rain that accompanies the storm. Rain is usually helpful for trees, but in this storm, it is a "burden." The poet describes the drops as "black," a dark, heavy color that is usually a symbol for death or sadness. So, **(E)** is correct. **(F)** is incorrect because "black" is a symbolic color, evoking a very heavy rain where the sun is darkened. There is no mention of pollution turning the rain black. **(G)** is incorrect because while water is certainly needed for the growth of trees, this rain is described as a "burden." **(H)** is incorrect because there is no mention in the poem of flooding.

5. C

Category: Function

Getting to the Answer: When you see the pronoun "it," always look back in the poem to find out what "it" is. In this case, it is the leaf broken off the tree in line 9. Leaves usually float or drift, not "whirl" and "sink" like "a green stone," so the wind of the storm must be making it behave strangely. Thus, **(C)** is correct. **(A)** is incorrect because there is no mention of the end of the storm, much less new life coming up as a result of the storm. **(B)** is incorrect because the description is of the leaf, not the branch. **(D)** is incorrect because the water that may have accumulated because of the storm is not mentioned.

6. H

Category: Inference

Getting to the Answer: Replace the "You" in the poem with "the storm" to get an idea of the effect that the author's use of personification has on the poem. For example, the storm "crashes" and the storm "cracks." In doing so, the poem begins to sound like a factual weather report. By using personification, the author is able to nearly accuse the storm of intentionally damaging the tree and the leaves; **(H)** is correct. **(E)** is incorrect because although the poet depicts an "angry" storm, the tree committed no apparent wrong for the storm to avenge. **(F)** is incorrect because it describes how the storm would be perceived by the reader if it were not personified. **(G)** is incorrect because the motion of the storm through the countryside is not mentioned.

Fiction Practice Set

Passage Analysis: This excerpt from a story by noted British humorist P. G. Wodehouse introduces the somewhat eccentric writer and lecturer, Mrs. Horace Hignett. The first moment of the passage describes three clocks that all tell different times; however, Mrs. Hignett knew it was exactly 8:00. From this point onwards, we are drawn into the life of this rather odd woman. The first paragraph introduces Mrs. Hignett, and the second notes that she is a famous writer of Theosophy (a philosophy based on mysticism). Paragraph 3 explains that 1921 was witness to a vast influx of English lecturers to the United States, all determined to earn "easy" money on the lecturing

circuit. Paragraph 4 explains that Mrs. Hignett was one of the first lecturers to come, eager to earn that "easy" money, and the last paragraph relates her reason for leaving England and her emotions about it. Paragraphs 5 and 6 describe Mrs. Hignett's thoughts and actions as she began her daily tasks while her son still slept.

1. B

Category: Function

Getting to the Answer: The phrase "sunlight peeped in like the foremost spies of some advancing army" affects the tone of the excerpt by setting the dry, humorous tone of the third-person narration. **(B)** is correct; this tone is later fully established when the narrator directly addresses the reader in the second paragraph. While Mrs. Hignett does display a certain martial vigor in how she wakes and how she tackles both problems and opportunities, that is not the tone of voice of the excerpt; **(A)** is incorrect. It is also never Mrs. Hignett's first-person narration, although the narrator does slip into it in paragraph 2. **(C)** is incorrect because the tone is not sullen, but humorous. Likewise, **(D)** is incorrect because the tone is humorous, not strictly factual.

2. H

Category: Global

Getting to the Answer: Those sentences from paragraph 1 contribute to the development of the plot by illustrating Mrs. Hignett's willpower. She does not need any of the clocks to wake on schedule, but instead wakes precisely at eight. Thus, **(H)** is correct. There is nothing to suggest that Mrs. Hignett is rooming with other people; **(E)** is incorrect. Likewise, there is no indication that Mrs. Hignett struggles to wake up and needs multiple alarms; **(F)** is incorrect. Although **(G)** is tempting because Mrs. Hignett does display homesickness later in the excerpt, **(G)** is incorrect because the three clocks are described as being set to wildly different times, not one time zone.

3. B

Category: Function

Getting to the Answer: Think about the words Wodehouse uses in the passage. He addresses the reader as "you" and says, "I'm glad you asked me" (line 16), giving the impression that the author is having a conversation with someone he knows. He also indicates that the reader knows about Mrs. Hignett and the events of 1921, assuming that he and the reader know the same things; in other words, he implies that he and the reader are two (or more) of a kind. His tone is therefore informal and chatty; he is relating a story to a friend, as **(B)** states. **(A)**, **(C)**, and **(D)** are incorrect because they refer to a passage which would be formal and stilted in language, creating distance between the reader and the author.

4. H

Category: Detail

Getting to the Answer: As the passage states, English lecturers expect to make "easy money" (line 30) on the American lecture tour. That money would have come from people paying to attend those lectures, so **(H)** is correct. The Middle Ages are mentioned in the passage, but only as a point of comparison; the passage does not state that Americans were interested in the history of the Middle Ages, so **(E)** is incorrect. It can't be inferred that Americans needed to be educated on these topics; perhaps they attended lectures because they already knew a great deal about the topics and were especially interested in them. So, eliminate **(F)**. **(G)** is likewise Extreme; there may have been many Americans who also lectured.

5. A

Category: Global

Getting to the Answer: That sentence from paragraph 4 contributes to the development of the central idea of the excerpt by emphasizing that Mrs. Hignett acts decisively. It contrasts her with the slower pace of 90 percent of the other English people on the American lecture circuit. Thus, **(A)** is correct. There is nothing in the excerpt to suggest that Mrs. Hignett is desperate for money; **(B)** is incorrect. Likewise, there is nothing to suggest that she has visited America in the past, nor that she took steps to sabotage her rivals on the lecture circuit. Given how she wakes precisely at eight in the morning without the aid of a clock, the implication is that she is merely a determined person; **(C)** and **(D)** are incorrect.

6. F

Category: Function

Getting to the Answer: That statement from paragraph 5 signals a shift from the fond, loving description of Mrs. Hignett's family home to the means by which she has held onto that home. Namely, she made sure that her son never married and would not kick her out of the house in favor of his wife and possible children. Thus, **(F)** is correct. **(E)** is incorrect because the excerpt is always told in third-person narration, and it stays focused on Mrs. Hignett. Although **(G)** discusses Mrs. Hignett's history with her son, there is no indication or motive given for why she is traveling without him. **(H)** is incorrect because their family home has not been lost.

7. D

Category: Detail

Getting to the Answer: Recall that in paragraph 5, Windles is described as Mrs. Hignett's long-time family home in the county of Hampshire. She is very attached to it and feels as if she belongs to it. As the paragraph states, Mrs. Hignett is holding it "in trust" (line 50), and she is "chilled" (line 54) to think of her son marrying and owning it with a strange woman. Consequently, Mrs. Hignett has tried to keep her son away from marriageable women, as the house would then leave her trust. Thus, **(D)** is correct. There is no suggestion that her son or anyone else had already taken possession of it, **(A)**, that she could not afford the house, **(B)**, or that she needed money to keep her in the good graces of her son, **(C)**.

Poetry Practice Set

Poem Analysis: The sonnet "Ozymandias," written by Percy Bysshe Shelley and published in 1818, may have been inspired by the imminent arrival of a part of a statue of Egyptian Pharaoh Ramses II, also known as Ozymandias, to the British Museum. The poem tells of the speaker meeting a traveler who described seeing the stark remains of what once was a great statue in an "antique" land—probably Egypt. On the pedestal, the statue is identified as that of Ozymandias, the mightiest of kings. Yet the statue is now a ruin, alone and insignificant in the sands of the desert. The contrast between a great tribute to a once-mighty king and the present ruined sculpture is a powerful literary device.

1. D

Category: Global

Getting to the Answer: This question asks for something that contributes to the poem's central theme. It is therefore a Global question. Look for an answer that speaks to the main idea expressed in the poem—that the statue of Ozymandias, the "king of kings," is now just a crumbling, fragmentary statue in the desert sands. Shelley is saying that all things that may have once been great and mighty inevitably crumble into nothingness; match this with answer choice **(D)**. **(A)** is too broad; the poem is specifically about the statue, not about all things deteriorating. **(B)** is incorrect because the desolation of the desert is not related to the poem's central theme. **(C)** is incorrect because this is the opposite of the poem's meaning.

2. E

Category: Function

Getting to the Answer: The question asks how certain words are used to highlight the poem's meaning; thus, it is a Function question. Consider how and why the author chose these terms. They are bold, negative ideas that collectively present a picture of something impressive, even intimidating, that has now sunk. Answer choice **(E)** is a good match to this idea. Whether the statue was aesthetically pleasing (ugly or beautiful) is never discussed, which eliminates **(F)**. **(G)** is incorrect; the statue's features do not suggest old age or decrepitude. **(H)** is incorrect because the author never states or suggests that Ozymandias was sad; though the word "despair" appears later in the poem, it is in another context.

3. A

Category: Inference

Getting to the Answer: The answer to an Inference question may not be found directly in the text cited, but it is implied in its meaning. This portion of the poem tells us that the sculpture was of a man named Ozymandias and that he is "king of kings." That alone suggests that

he is the most powerful of all, but the statue's inscription cements that idea further by declaring that others should look at the things he (Ozymandias) has done and, even though these others might be "mighty," they will never match his power and glory, so they should "despair"; **(A)** is correct. No place in the poem hints at a war, making **(B)** incorrect. **(C)** is incorrect because it is a distortion of the idea of "despair." The term is used as described above, not to suggest a sad face. **(D)** is incorrect because it is unsupported by anything in the poem and cannot be inferred. If anything, Ozymandias's statue celebrates his power, not the end of his reign.

4. H

Category: Detail

Getting to the Answer: The question asks for a line from the poem that tells the reader that the statue lies in ruins. It is a Detail question. The ruined state of the statue is mentioned in several places in the poem, including in lines 12–13 cited in **(H)**: "Nothing beside remains: round the decay Of that colossal wreck, boundless and bare." Eliminate **(E)**, **(F)**, and **(G)** because these have nothing to do with the state of the statue.

5. B

Category: Inference

Getting to the Answer: The question asks the reader to glean meaning from the poem based on the author's statements. Where in the poem do we get the suggestion that the statue was crafted by a talented artist? Where do we learn anything about who made the statue? In lines 6–7, the author tells us about the sculptor. The poem states that the person depicted in the statue has certain particular features (a frown, a wrinkled lip, and a sneer of command), and the fact that the sculptor included them in the statue shows that this artisan was able to "read" these qualities "well." **(B)** is correct. Eliminate **(A)** and **(D)** because each suggests the setting the sculpture is found in but nothing about the artist who made it. Finally, **(C)** is incorrect because it gives a detail about the inscription but does not suggest that it took talent to craft that label.

6. F

Category: Function

Getting to the Answer: This Function question asks how a phrase serves the meaning of the poem. The idea of a "colossal wreck" is an interesting one. "Colossal" means huge, impressive, significant. "Wreck" means pretty much the opposite—conjuring ideas of devastation and destruction. This phrase is a condensed expression of the central irony of the poem: that a magnificent tribute to a great leader now stands in ruins. **(F)** is correct. **(E)** is incorrect because its suggestion that the statue was large misses the point. The size of the statue is not addressed and is not part of the author's purpose. Regarding **(G)**, while it might be true that this would be a great archaeological find, nothing in the poem addresses that, so this is incorrect. Although line 13 focuses on destruction, nothing in the poem suggests that the reader is meant to feel disgusted or angry over that; **(H)** is incorrect.

PART 3

SHSAT Math

CHAPTER 12

Introducing SHSAT Math

CHAPTER OBJECTIVES

By the end of this chapter, you will be able to:

- Identify key components of the SHSAT Math section
- Apply useful strategies to SHSAT Math questions

MATH OVERVIEW

There's a lot of math out there. Someday you may need or may choose to immerse yourself in the intricacies of number theory or multivariable calculus. However, for the purposes of the SHSAT, you need to know a relatively small subset of all of the math out there. You are not permitted to use a calculator, but the most commonly tested math concepts fall within the areas of arithmetic, algebra, and geometry. It is also not uncommon to see simple probability and statistics. As you read earlier, you will see some math with which you are unfamiliar because the Department of Education deliberately tests unfamiliar math.

How SHSAT Math Is Set Up

There are 57 Math questions; 5 are grid-in and 52 are multiple-choice questions.

Know What to Expect

The beginning of the Math section will look like this:

PART 2—MATHEMATICS

Suggested Time—90 Minutes

57 QUESTIONS

IMPORTANT NOTES

1. Formulas and definitions of mathematical terms and symbols are **not** provided.
2. Diagrams other than graphs are **not** necessarily drawn to scale. Do not assume any relationship in a diagram unless it is specifically stated or can be figured out from the information given.
3. Assume that a diagram is in one plane unless the problem specifically states that it is not.
4. Graphs are drawn to scale. Unless stated otherwise, you can assume relationships according to appearance. For example, (on a graph) lines that appear to be parallel can be assumed to be parallel; likewise for concurrent lines, straight lines, collinear points, right angles, etc.
5. Reduce all fractions to lowest terms.

GRID-IN PROBLEMS

QUESTIONS 58–62

DIRECTIONS: Solve each problem. On the answer sheet, write your answer in the boxes at the top of the grid. Start on the left side of each grid. Print only one number or symbol in each box. **DO NOT LEAVE A BOX BLANK IN THE MIDDLE OF AN ANSWER.** Under each box, fill in the circle that matches the number or symbol you wrote above. **DO NOT FILL IN A CIRCLE UNDER AN UNUSED BOX.**

Multiple-Choice Instructions

MULTIPLE CHOICE PROBLEMS

QUESTIONS 63–114

DIRECTIONS: Solve each problem. Select the best answer from the choices given. Mark the letter of your answer on the answer sheet. You can do your figuring in the test booklet or on paper provided by the proctor. **DO NOT MAKE ANY MARKS ON YOUR ANSWER SHEET OTHER THAN FILLING IN YOUR ANSWER CHOICES.**

The directions are pretty straightforward on the Math section. Essentially, they tell you to answer the questions and mark the answers on your answer sheet. However, the directions do include a few notes that can help with your preparation and save you time on Test Day. Here are a few things you should know:

Math formulas and definitions are NOT provided.

What this means: The Department of Education is not going to provide the shortcuts, so memorize those math formulas. Of course, you don't have to know very many, but make certain you know the basics.

Diagrams other than graphs are NOT drawn to scale unless otherwise noted.

What this means: You cannot take much for granted about diagrams unless you are specifically told that they are drawn to scale. For example, lines that look parallel may, in fact, not be parallel. Figures that look like squares may not be square. Lines that look like the diameter of a circle may not be the diameter. You get the picture.

Diagrams are in one plane, unless otherwise stated.

What this means: One thing that you can assume is that diagrams are in one plane. In other words, assume that figures are flat unless you are told otherwise.

Graphs are drawn to scale, unless otherwise stated.

What this means: You can eyeball graphs and take what you see for granted. For example, if lines look parallel, you can assume that they are. You can also estimate and label coordinates of points on graphs.

Fractions should be reduced to their lowest terms.

What this means: If you solve a problem that has a fraction for its answer and you do not reduce the fraction to its lowest terms, you will not find your answer among the answer choices.

✔ Don't Waste Time Reading Directions!

Know what to expect on Test Day. The directions are not going to change, so learn them now and save yourself time later.

HOW TO APPROACH SHSAT MATH

You've done math before. You've most likely been exposed to the majority of the math concepts you'll see on the SHSAT. This raises the question as to why you would need to approach SHSAT math differently than you would approach any other math.

The answer to this question is that it's not that you necessarily have to do the math *differently*, it's just that you have to do it very deliberately. What this means is that you'll be under a lot of time pressure when you take the test, so you'll want to use your time well. You may not want to answer every SHSAT math problem the way that you would approach the same problem in math class.

✔ The SHSAT Is Not Math Class

No one is going to check your work. Choose the *fastest* method to solve the problem, even if your math teacher would not approve.

Ultimately, the best way to take control of your testing experience is to approach every SHSAT math problem the same way. This doesn't mean that you will solve every problem the same way. Rather, it means that you'll use the same process to decide how to solve—or whether to solve—each problem.

Read Through the Question

Okay, this may seem a little too obvious. Of course you're going to read the question. How else can you solve the problem? In reality, this is not quite as obvious as it seems. The point here is that you need to read the entire question carefully before you start solving the problem. When you do not read the question carefully, it's incredibly easy to make careless mistakes. Consider the following problem:

1. For what positive value of x does

$\frac{6}{5} = \frac{x^2}{30}$?

A. 5
B. 6
C. 10
D. 12

It's crucial that you pay close attention to precisely what the question is asking. Question 1 contains a classic trap that's very easy to fall into if you don't read the question carefully. Did you notice how easy it would be to solve for x^2 instead of x? Yes, this would be careless, but it's easy to be careless when you're working quickly. By the way, the answer is **(B)**, 6.

There are other reasons to read the whole question before you start solving the problem. One is that you may save yourself some work. If you start to answer too quickly, you may assume that a problem is more difficult than it actually is. Similarly, you might assume that the problem is less difficult than it actually is and skip a necessary step or two.

Another reason to read carefully before answering is that you probably shouldn't solve every problem on your first pass. A big part of taking control of your SHSAT experience is deciding which problems to answer and which to save for later.

Decide Whether to Do the Problem or Skip It for Now

Every time you approach a new math problem, you have the option of whether or not to answer the question. Therefore, you have to make a decision each time about how to best use your time. You have three options.

1. If you can solve the problem relatively quickly and efficiently, do it. This is the best option.
2. If you think you can solve it but it will take you a long time, circle the number in your test booklet and go back to it later.
3. If you have no idea what to do, skip the problem and circle it. Save your time for the problems you can do.

Remember that when you go back to the problems you skip, you want to fill in an answer even if it's a random guess. You'll see more about this later, but do not underestimate your ability to eliminate wrong answers even when you do not know how to solve a problem. Every time you eliminate a wrong answer, you increase your chances of guessing correctly.

2. Tamika, Becky, and Kym were investors in a new restaurant. Tamika and Becky each invested one-half as much as Kym invested. If the total investment made by these three was $5,200, how much did Kym invest?

E. $900
F. $1,300
G. $1,800
H. $2,600

Different test takers are going to have different reactions to question 2. Some test takers may quickly see the algebra—or the backdoor method for solving this problem—and do the math. Others may see a word problem and run screaming from the room. This approach is not recommended. However, if despite practice, you know that you habitually have difficulty with algebra word problems, you may choose to save this problem for later or make an educated guess.

Here's the algebra, by the way. Kym, Tamika, and Becky contributed a total of \$5,200. You can represent this algebraically as $K + T + B = \$5{,}200$. Since Tamika and Becky each contributed $\frac{1}{2}$ as much as Kym, you can represent these relationships as follows:

$$T = \frac{1}{2}K$$

$$B = \frac{1}{2}K$$

Now, substitute variables so that you can solve the equation.

$$K + T + B = K + \frac{1}{2}K + \frac{1}{2}K$$

$$K + \frac{1}{2}K + \frac{1}{2}K = \$5{,}200$$

$$2K = \$5{,}200$$

$K = \$2{,}600$ Choice **(H)** is correct.

If you choose to tackle the problem, look for the fastest method.

3. Jenna is now x years old, and Amy is 3 years younger than Jenna. In terms of x, how old will Amy be in 4 years?

A. $x - 1$

B. x

C. $x + 1$

D. $x + 4$

Imagine a dialogue between Jenna and Amy:

Jenna: This is an easy problem. If my age is x, then your age, Amy, is $x - 3$ because you're three years younger than me. Therefore, in four years, you'll be $(x - 3) + 4$ or $x + 1$.

Amy: You may be right, but there's a much easier way to figure it out. Let's say you're 10 years old now. That makes me 7 because I'm three years younger. In four years, I'll be 11. Now let's just substitute your age, 10, for x in all the answer choices and see which answer gives us 11. Once you try all the answers, you see that only choice **(C)**, $x + 1$, works.

Jenna: That's so much extra work. Why not just do the algebra?

Amy: You can do the algebra, but I'll do it my own way.

Here's the point: Know your strengths and make decisions about how to approach math problems accordingly!

Some people "get" algebra. Some people have a harder time with it. The same is true for geometry, word problems, and so on. There is often more than one way to do a particular problem. The "best" method is the method that will get you the correct answer accurately and quickly.

Again, know your strengths and use them to your advantage.

Make an Educated Guess

Don't leave any answers blank on the SHSAT. Since there's no penalty for wrong answers, there is no harm in guessing when you don't know the answer.

> ✔ **Don't Underestimate the Value of Guessing**
>
> **Remember, there's no penalty for wrong answers. Even if you guess randomly, you have a 1 in 4 chance of guessing correctly.**

Of course, you should still guess strategically whenever possible. Remember, every answer choice you eliminate increases your odds of guessing correctly.

4. What is the greatest common factor of 95 and 114?

E. 1
F. 5
G. 6
H. 19

If you looked at this problem and either could not remember how to find the greatest common factor or were running out of time and wanted to save your time for other questions, you should be able to eliminate at least one answer choice pretty easily. Do you see which one?

> ✔ **Note What You Skip**
>
> **When you skip a question, circle it so that it will be easy to spot if you have time to go back.**

Since all multiples of 5 end in either 5 or 0, 5 cannot be a factor of 114, and so choice **(F)** must be incorrect.

CHAPTER 13

Math Foundations

CHAPTER OBJECTIVES

By the end of this chapter, you will be able to:

- Apply the Kaplan Method for SHSAT Math
- Use properties of real numbers to answer questions and perform basic operations

MATH FOUNDATIONS

The Kaplan Method for SHSAT Math

Step 1: What is the question?

Step 2: What information is provided in the question?
In what format do the answers appear?

Step 3: What can I do with the information?

- Picking Numbers
- Backsolving
- Straightforward Math

Step 4: Am I finished?

Applying the Kaplan Strategy for Math Grid-In Questions

The Kaplan Strategy for Math Grid-In Questions is a strategy you apply as you answer questions using the Kaplan Method for Math.

Once you've determined what the question is asking in **Step 1** and identified the information provided in **Step 2**, you're ready to apply the Kaplan Strategy for Math Grid-In Questions in **Step 3**.

The Kaplan Strategy for Math Grid-In Questions

The Kaplan Strategy for Math Grid-In Questions helps you stay organized as you answer the five grid-in questions you are guaranteed to see on Test Day.

- Define any variables, choosing letters that make sense.
- Break sentences into short phrases.
- Translate each phrase into a mathematical expression.
- Use the information in the question stem to logically organize the expressions and solve.

Try It Out

DIRECTIONS: Solve each problem. Write your answer in the boxes at the top of each grid. Print only one number or symbol in each box. **DO NOT LEAVE A BOX BLANK IN THE MIDDLE OF AN ANSWER.** Under each box, fill in the circle that matches the number or symbol you wrote above. **DO NOT FILL IN A CIRCLE UNDER AN UNUSED BOX.**

1. $(8 \div 2 + 3) - (4 - 2)^2 = ?$

Picking Numbers

This strategy relates to questions that contain variables. You can Pick Numbers to make abstract problems—ones that insist on dealing with variables rather than numbers—more concrete. **Use this strategy when there are variables in the answer choices.** You may not even need to solve for the variables, but rather just determine how they would behave if they were real numbers. Thus, don't assume—pick a real number and see for yourself. Follow these guidelines:

> **Step 1:** Pick a simple number to stand in for the variables, making sure it follows the criteria stated in the question stem. Does the number have to be even or odd? Positive or negative? Be careful when using 0 and 1, as they behave differently than most other numbers, but always pick easy-to-use numbers.
>
> **Step 2:** Solve the *question* using the number(s) you picked.
>
> **Step 3:** Test each of the *answer choices* using the number(s) you picked, eliminating those that give you a result that is different from the one you're looking for.
>
> **Step 4:** If more than one choice remains, pick a different set of numbers and repeat steps 1–3.

Picking Numbers is the perfect strategy to apply to story problems that ask for an expression that represents a given scenario. This is called *modeling*. Let's use this strategy to answer the modeling question that follows.

Money collected by c charities is to be divided equally among those charities. A trust fund has been set up to collect and distribute the money. According to donation records, p people gave d dollars each. Which expression represents the amount of money each charity will receive?

A. $\frac{c}{pd}$

B. $\frac{pd}{c}$

C. $pd + c$

D. $\frac{dc}{p}$

Getting to the Answer: If the mere thought of this question gives you a headache, Picking Numbers can provide you with a safe way to quickly get to the answer. The key is to choose numbers that make the math easy for you. Because the money will be divided evenly among the charities, pick numbers that relate easily to each other to make the math go smoothly. Try 2 for p, 4 for c, and 8 for d. Now the question asks: If 2 people each donated $8 to a trust fund that will distribute the money equally among 4 charities, how much money, in dollars, did each charity receive? So, this becomes $16 divided by 4. The answer to this question would be $4. Now replace p with 2, d with 8, and c with 4 in each of the answer choices and see which one comes out to 4.

Choice **(A)**: $\frac{c}{pd} = \frac{4}{2 \times 8} = \frac{4}{16} = \frac{1}{4}$ Eliminate.

Choice **(B)**: $\frac{pd}{c} = \frac{2 \times 8}{4} = \frac{16}{4} = 4$ Keep.

Choice **(C)**: $pd + c = 2 \times 8 + 4 = 16 + 4 = 20$ Eliminate.

Choice **(D)**: $\frac{dc}{p} = \frac{8 \times 4}{2} = \frac{32}{2} = 16$ Eliminate.

Only **(B)** works, so it must be correct.

Questions that involve properties of numbers (even/odd, prime/composite, rational/ irrational, etc.) are another example where Picking Numbers can make your life easier. Let's give the next question a try.

If a is an odd integer and b is an even integer, which of the following must be odd?

E. $2a + b$

F. $a + 2b$

G. ab

H. a^2b

Getting to the Answer: Rather than trying to think this one through abstractly, it may be easier to Pick Numbers for a and b. There are rules that predict the evenness or oddness of sums, differences, and products, but there's no need to memorize those rules.

The question states that a is odd and b is even, so let $a = 3$ (remember, 1 can be used but is not typically helpful) and $b = 2$. Plug those values into the answer choices, and you'll find that only one choice will be odd:

Choice **(E):** $2a + b = 2(3) + 2 = 8$ Eliminate.

Choice **(F):** $a + 2b = 3 + 2(2) = 7$ Keep.

Choice **(G):** $ab = (3)(2) = 6$ Eliminate.

Choice **(H):** $a^2b = (3)^2(2) = 18$ Eliminate.

Choice **(F)** is the only odd result when $a = 3$ and $b = 2$, so it *must* be the one that's odd no matter *what* odd number a and even number b actually stand for. Even if you're not positive **(F)** will always be right, you know for a fact that all the others are definitely wrong, which is just as good!

> ✔ **Note**
>
> **Had more than one of the answer choices returned an odd value, you would simply try another pair of numbers, such as $a = 5$ and $b = 8$. Very rarely would you need to pick more than two sets of numbers before you find the correct answer.**

Backsolving

On the SHSAT, you know for certain that one of the answer choices is correct (as opposed to a fill-in-the-blank test). Therefore, with some SHSAT Math problems, it may actually be easier to try out each answer choice until you find the one that works, rather than attempt to solve the problem and then look among the choices for the answer. This approach is called Backsolving. Let's try it out.

Suppose 200 tickets were sold for a particular concert. Some tickets cost \$10 each, and the others cost \$5 each. If total ticket sales were \$1,750, how many of the more expensive tickets were sold?

- **A.** 20
- **B.** 75
- **C.** 100
- **D.** 150

There are ways to solve this problem by setting up an equation or two, but if you're not comfortable with the algebraic approach to this one, why not just try out each answer choice? You know one of them will work.

Here's the next part you need to know: **When Backsolving, always start with a middle answer choice (B/F** or **C/G).** The numerical answer choices on the SHSAT are always either in ascending or descending order. If you solve for the one in the middle and it comes out too big, you can eliminate it *and the two larger numbers*, and the same if it's too small. So trying *one* answer choice can eliminate up to three options.

Getting to the Answer: Start with **(C)**. If 100 tickets were sold for $10 each, then the other 100 have to have been sold for $5 each: 100 at $10 is $1,000, and 100 at $5 is $500, for a total of $1,500—too small. There *must* have been more than 100 tickets sold at the higher price point ($10).

This is great news! If you know it's not **(C)**, and you know **(C)** is too small, you can eliminate **(A)** and **(B)** as well. By solving for one value, you've eliminated up to three answer choices.

If 150 tickets went for $10, then the other 50 went for $5. Do the math: 150 tickets at $10 is $1,500, and 50 tickets at $5 is $250, for a total of $1,750—that's it! The answer is **(D)**, no need to go any further.

✔ Expert Tip

Backsolving your way to the answer may not be a method you'd show your algebra teacher, but your algebra teacher won't be watching on Test Day. Remember, all that matters is correct answers—it doesn't matter how you get them.

PEMDAS

PEMDAS is an acronym for the order in which you must do mathematical calculations. It stands for

P: Parentheses

E: Exponents

MD: Multiplication and Division (from left to right)

AS: Addition and Subtraction (from left to right)

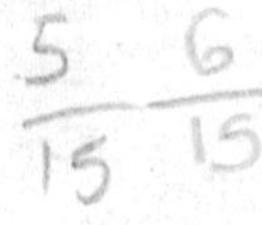

A. $(3 + 2)^2 - 6 \times 2^2 =$

B. $3 + (2^2 - 6) \times 2^2 =$

2. $\left(\frac{1}{3} + \frac{2}{5}\right) \div \frac{3}{4} =$

E. $\frac{9}{32}$

F. $\frac{1}{2}$

G. $\frac{11}{20}$

H. $\frac{44}{45}$

✔ Remember

PEMDAS can be remembered using the expression "Please Excuse My Dear Aunt Sally."

Although the SHSAT will seldom test PEMDAS directly, you will need to remember the order of operations for every calculation.

Basic Terms

SHSAT math questions test your knowledge of fundamental math concepts and operations. Being comfortable with how numbers look and work can make your life easier on all sorts of math question types on the SHSAT.

Here are some essential rules and definitions to know:

- **Integers** include 0 and negative whole numbers. If a question says "*x* and *y* are integers," it's not ruling out numbers like 0 and −1.
- A **fraction** represents part of a whole. The bottom number (the denominator) indicates how many parts the whole is divided into, and the top number (the numerator) shows how many parts are present.
- The **reciprocal** of a fraction is the inverse of that fraction. To find the reciprocal of a fraction, switch the numerator and the denominator. The reciprocal of $\frac{3}{7}$ is $\frac{7}{3}$. The reciprocal of 5 (or $\frac{5}{1}$ because all whole numbers can be written over 1) is $\frac{1}{5}$. The product of two reciprocals is always 1.
- **Evens and odds** include 0 and negative whole numbers. Zero and −2 are even numbers; −1 is an odd number.

Evens and Odds

A. Odd +/− Odd = ____________

B. Odd × Odd = ____________

C. Positive + Negative = ____________

D. Positive ×/÷ Positive = ____________

E. Odd +/− Even = ____________

F. Odd × Even = ____________

G. Negative − Positive ____________

H. Positive ×/÷ Negative = ____________

I. Even +/− Even = ____________

J. Even × Even = ____________

K. Negative + Negative = ____________

L. Negative ×/÷ Negative = ____________

✓ Remember

Positive and negative number properties are always the same in multiplication, but not always in addition and subtraction.

Even and odd number properties are always the same for addition, subtraction, and multiplication. Picking any two numbers proves the rule. There are no rules for evens and odds in division.

Zero is an even number.

Prime Numbers and Prime Factorization

A **factor** of an integer is any number that divides precisely into that integer (with no remainder).

A **multiple** of an integer is that integer times any number. In other words, factor × factor = multiple.

A **prime number** is a positive integer that is divisible without a remainder by only 1 and itself. The number 2 is the smallest prime number and the only even prime number; 1 is not considered prime.

To find the **prime factorization** of an integer, use a factor tree to keep breaking the integer up into factors until all the factors are prime numbers. To find the prime factorization of 36, for example, you could begin by breaking it into 4 × 9. Then break 4 into 2 × 2 and break 9 into 3 × 3. The prime factorization of 36 is 2 × 2 × 3 × 3.

The **greatest common factor (GCF)** of two numbers is the highest number that divides precisely into each of them without a remainder. To find the greatest common factor, break down both numbers into their prime factorizations and take all the prime factors they have in common. For example, try 36 and 48: 36 = 2 × 2 × 3 × 3 and 48 = 2 × 2 × 2 × 2 × 3. What they have in common is two 2s and one 3, so the GCF is 2 × 2 × 3 = 12.

The **least common multiple (LCM)** of two numbers is the smallest multiple both of those numbers divide into. To find the LCM of two or more numbers, check out the multiples of the larger number until you find one that's also a multiple of the smaller. For example, to find the LCM of 12 and 15, begin by taking the multiples of 15: 1 × 15 = 15, which is not divisible by 12; 2 × 15 = 30, not divisible by 12; nor is 45, which is 3 × 15. But the next multiple of 15, 4 × 15 = 60, is divisible by 12, so it's the LCM.

3. What is the greatest prime number less than 35?

A. 29
B. 31
C. 33
D. 34

4. 9 × 14 is equal to which of the following?

E. 3 × 3 × 4
F. 3 × 4 × 7
G. 6 × 21
H. 7 × 12

✔ Remember

2 is the only even prime, and 1 is not a prime number.

There are only a few factors of a number but many multiples.

When a question seems to involve a lot of complex multiplication or division, consider looking at the prime factors to break it down.

Adding and Subtracting Variables

A **variable** is a letter that represents an unknown value. For example, x is a variable in the expression $x + 3$.

To **add** or **subtract** variables, **combine like terms**.

$x + x = 2x$
$2x + x = 3x$
$6x - 2x = 4x$

$3 + 3 = 2(3)$
$2(3) + 3 = 3(3)$
$6(3) - 2(3) = 4(3)$

A. $4n + 5n =$
B. $4x + x + 6x =$

C. $6g + 5g =$
D. $d + n + d + 2n =$

E. $8y + 7y =$
F. $5x - 3y + 2x - y =$

5. $5a + a =$

A. 6
B. $4a$
C. $5 + 2a$
D. $6a$

6. $xy + 2xy =$

E. xy
F. $2xy$
G. $3xy$
H. $2x^2y$

7. $(3d - 7) - (5 - 2d) =$

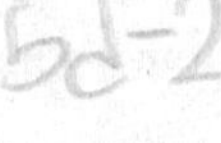

A. $d - 12$

B. $5d - 2$

C. $5d + 12$

D. $5d - 12$

8. If $x = 11$ and $y = 13$, which of the following is equivalent to $15x - 3y - 7x + 4y - 8x + x$?

E. 2

F. 24

G. 169

H. 180

✔ Remember

You should collect like terms whenever you are asked to add or subtract variables.

Multiplying and Dividing Variables

To **multiply** variables, multiply the numbers and the variables separately: $2a \times 3a = (2 \times 3)(a \times a) = 6a^2$.

$x \times y = xy$

$2x \times 3y = 2 \times x \times 3 \times y = 6xy$

$x \times x = x^2$

A. $4g \times 6h =$

B. $2(5x \times 3y) =$

C. $\frac{1}{2}x(3y)(4z) =$

To **divide** variables with coefficients, simplify expressions and cancel like terms.

$x \div y = \frac{x}{y}$

$\frac{6x}{3y} = \frac{2x}{y}$

D. $\frac{12r}{4s} =$ __________

E. $\frac{15j}{3k} =$ __________

F. $\frac{21wx}{7} =$ __________

9. $5r(3s) + 6r - 2rs =$

A. $9rs$

B. $11r + s - 2rs$

C. $13rs + 6r$

D. $19rs$

10. $2x(3x) + y^2 =$

E. $5x + y^2$

F. $5x^2 + y^2$

G. $6x + y^2$

H. $6x^2 + y^2$

11. $\frac{25xyz}{5z} =$

A. xy

B. $5x$

C. $5xy$

D. Cannot be determined from the information given.

12. $a(3b) + b(-3a) =$

E. 0

F. $-ab$

G. $6ab$

H. $a + b - 3$

Distributive Property with Variables

Multiplying

Variables or numbers just outside of parentheses are multiplied by each term inside the parentheses.

$4(2x + y) = 8x + 4y$

A. $3(5s - 3r) =$ ______________

B. $-b(4 - 3a) =$ ______________

C. $-2(3a - 2b) =$ ______________

D. $x(x + y - z) =$ ______________

13. $3(x + y) - 3(-x - y) =$

A. 0

B. $3x + y$

C. $6x + 6y$

D. $3xy$

14. $-5n(3m - 2) =$

E. $-15mn + 10n$

F. $15mn - 10n$

G. $-8mn + 7n$

H. $8mn + 7n$

Factoring

The same number or variable can be divided out from every term and placed outside parentheses.

$8x + 4y = 4(2x + y)$

A. $12x + 9y =$ ______

B. $8ab - 6b + 2bc =$ ______

C. $25g + 15h =$ ______

D. $xy + 3x =$ ______

15. $12cd + 6c =$

A. $3d(4c + 2)$

B. $3c(4d + 2c)$

C. $6c(2d + 1)$

D. $6d(2c + 1)$

16. $3(x + 2) - (x - 4) =$

E. $2x - 2$

F. $2x + 2$

G. $2(x + 5)$

H. $3x + 10$

✔ Remember

Work carefully when you distribute negative signs! One of the answer choices will trap test takers who neglect the signs.

Always look for common factors and variables to factor out of expressions.

WORD PROBLEMS/VARIABLES IN ANSWER CHOICES

Variables in the Answer Choices

17. If x people working together make a total of y dollars after an hour of work, how much money will z people make if they work 4 hours at the same rate per person?

A. $4xyz$

B. $xy + 4z$

C. $\frac{4yz}{x}$

D. $\frac{4xy}{z}$

18. Each of the n members of an organization may invite up to 3 guests to a conference. What is the maximum number of members and guests who might attend the conference?

E. $n + 3$

F. $3n$

G. $3n + 4$

H. $4n$

19. Paolo sold x tickets, and Gina sold y tickets. The number that Gina sold is 10 less than 3 times as many tickets as Paolo sold. What is the value of y in terms of x?

A. $10x - 3$

B. $10 - 3x$

C. $3x - 10$

D. $3(x - 10)$

Percentage Increase/Decrease

20. Mandy buys a sweater that is on sale for 20% less than the original price, and then she uses a coupon worth an additional 15% off of the sale price. What percentage of the original price has she saved?

E. 32%

F. 34%

G. 35%

H. 38%

> **✔ Remember**
>
> When Picking Numbers, avoid picking fractions, 0, and 1.

> **✔ Remember**
>
> When Picking Numbers, always pick 100 for questions involving percentages of unknown numbers.

The following practice sets provide an opportunity to apply the concepts and strategic thinking covered in this chapter. To practice Test Day timing, follow the suggested timing guidelines for each section.

MATH FOUNDATIONS PRACTICE SET

Suggested Timing: 60 minutes

Integers and Fractions

Which of the following is an integer?

1. A. 0.112
   B. 1.12
   C. $\frac{11}{2}$
   D. 1,120

Improper/Mixed Fractions

Convert mixed fractions to improper fractions:

2. $8\frac{1}{5} =$

Convert improper fractions to mixed fractions:

3. $\frac{7}{5}$

Reciprocals

Find the reciprocal of each of the following:

4. $1\frac{1}{100}$
5. $4\frac{9}{10}$
6. $7\frac{1}{8}$

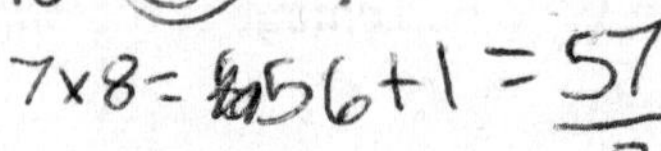

Prime Numbers

Which of the following are prime?

7. A. 9
   B. 10
   C. 11

What is the prime factorization of each number?

8. 99
9. 64
10. 49

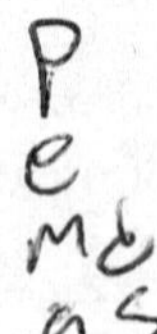

Odd/Even

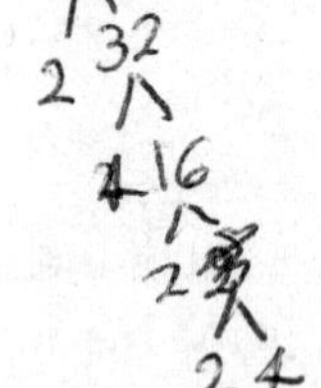

11. The number of dollars John is paid for each hour that he works is an odd integer. If he is paid $50, what is a possible number of hours he worked?
    A. 7
    B. 9
    C. 10
    D. 28

Positive/Negative

12. What is the value of $\left(\frac{-3(6-2)}{-2}\right)-\left(\frac{-6(2-4)}{-3}\right)$?
    E. −10
    F. −2
    G. 2
    H. 10

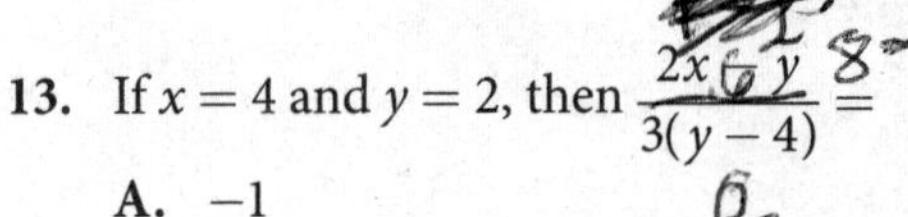

13. If $x = 4$ and $y = 2$, then $\frac{2xy}{3(y-4)} =$
    A. −1
    B. $-\frac{2}{3}$
    C. $\frac{2}{3}$
    D. 1

PEMDAS

14. $6 \div 10 \cdot 5 \div 3 =$

E. $\frac{1}{25}$

F. $\frac{3}{5}$

G. 1

H. $\frac{5}{3}$

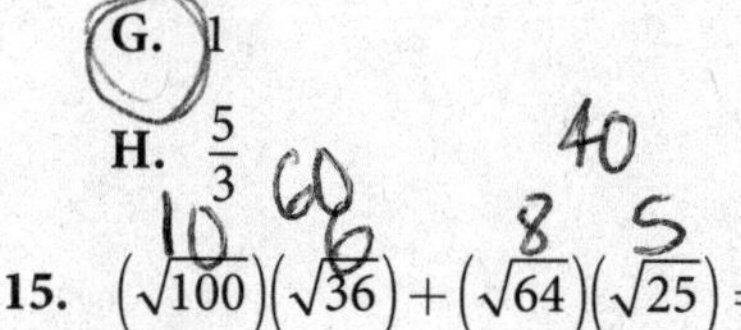

15. $(\sqrt{100})(\sqrt{36}) + (\sqrt{64})(\sqrt{25}) =$

A. 29

B. 100

C. 340

D. $80\sqrt{150}$

16. What is the value of $x + y(x + y)$ if $x = 4$ and $y = \frac{1}{2}$?

E. 2

F. $6\frac{1}{4}$

G. $6\frac{1}{2}$

H. 18

17. If $x = 1$ and $y = 2$, what is the value of $x^y y^x$?

A. 2

B. 4

C. 8

D. 9

18. $2x \cdot 7 + 2 - 4x =$

E. $9 - 2x$

F. $9 - 8x^2$

G. $10x + 2$

H. $16x$

19. $10^2 \cdot 3^2 =$

A. 30

B. 90

C. 900

D. 90,000

20. $\frac{1}{3} - \frac{1}{4} - \frac{1}{9} =$

E. $-\frac{3}{16}$

F. $-\frac{1}{10}$

G. $-\frac{1}{36}$

H. $\frac{7}{36}$

21. If $\frac{x}{10 + 2 \cdot 7} = 6$, what does x equal?

A. 4

B. 24

C. 144

D. 504

22. $x + x \cdot y + y =$

E. xy

F. $2xy + y$

G. $4xy$

H. $x + xy + y$

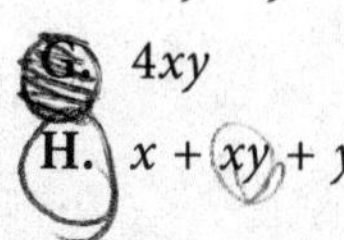

23. $7 + 5 \cdot 3^2 =$

A. 37

B. 52

C. 108

D. 1,296

Combining Like Terms

24. $-3x + 6y + 4x - 7y =$

25. $5x + 4x + 3x + 2x + x =$

26. $6y - 8y + y =$

27. $9n - 3p - 3n + 3p =$

28. $2y + 3x - 4x + 2y =$

Multiplying and Dividing Monomials

29. $\dfrac{3x \times 4y}{3y}$

30. $\dfrac{2n \times p \times 3n}{4n}$

Factoring and the Distributive Property with Monomials

Distribute the following to eliminate the parentheses:

31. $4n(5p + 2) =$

32. $2x(2y + 3) =$

33. $-3x(y - 4z) =$

Factor the following:

34. $-6x - 9y =$

35. $24xy - 8x =$

PEMDAS Combinations

36. $2a(3a - 5a^2) =$

E. $-4a^3$

F. $6a - 10a^2$

G. $6a^2 - 10a^3$

H. $6a^2 + 10a^3$

37. $4xy\left(\dfrac{1}{2y} + \dfrac{3}{2x}\right) =$

A. $2x + 6y$

B. $2x + 12y$

C. $4x + 6y$

D. $4x + 12y$

38. $3x(y + 4) =$

E. $3x + 12$

F. $3xy + 4x$

G. $3xy + 12x$

H. $15x + y$

39. $3x(2y - 3x - 2) =$

A. $3xy - 9x^2 - 6x$

B. $3xy - 15x$

C. $6xy - 9x^2 - 6x$

D. $6xy + 9x^2 - 6x$

40. $4x(4x - 4 - 4x) =$

E. $-16x$

F. $16x$

G. $16x^2 - 16x$

H. $32x^2 - 16x$

Word Problems and Picking Numbers

41. Susan mailed y letters in January. She mailed 3 times as many letters in February. In March, she mailed 10 letters more than half of what she mailed in January and February together. If a letter costs \$0.37 to mail, which expression represents the amount of money Susan spent mailing letters in March?

A. $1.48y$

B. $0.74y + 3.7$

C. $1.48y + 3.7$

D. $2y + 10$

42. Mary is twice as likely to randomly pick a blue marble from a bag as she is to pick a red marble. If there are x red marbles and the bag contains 40 marbles, what is the probability that Mary will pick a blue marble from the bag?

E. $\dfrac{16}{40}$

F. $\dfrac{x}{10}$

G. $\dfrac{x}{20}$

H. $\dfrac{x}{40}$

43. A pizza is cut into x pieces. Kevin takes $\frac{1}{4}$ of the total pieces. Keith takes one piece less than twice the number of pieces Kevin took. How many pieces of pizza are left?

A. $\frac{1}{4}x$

B. $\frac{1}{4}x+1$

C. $\frac{1}{2}x+1$

D. $\frac{3}{4}x-1$

44. Jamie is n years old. Brian is twice as old as Jamie. In 8 years, Morgan will be 2 years more than half of Brian and Jamie's combined present age. How old is Morgan today?

E. $\frac{1}{2}n-8$

F. $\frac{3}{2}n-8$

G. $\frac{3}{2}n-6$

H. $\frac{3}{2}n+2$

45. Thermometer A reads $x°$. Thermometer B reads 2° below the reading on thermometer A. Thermometers C and D each read 4° less than twice the reading on thermometer B. What is the average temperature, in degrees, of the 4 thermometers?

A. $\frac{x-4}{2}$

B. $x-4$

C. $\frac{3x-9}{4}$

D. $\frac{3x-9}{2}$

Grid-Ins

46. What value of g makes the equation $3(2+g)=23.5$ true?

47. In the equation $5f-45=115$, what is the value of f?

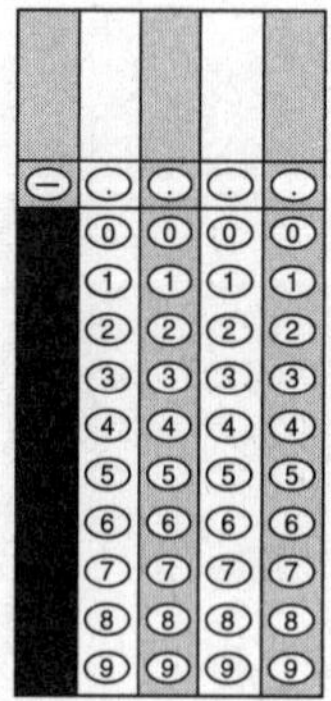

48. If $\frac{c}{6}+8=14$, what is the value of c?

49. If $4b - 12 = 92$, what is the value of b?

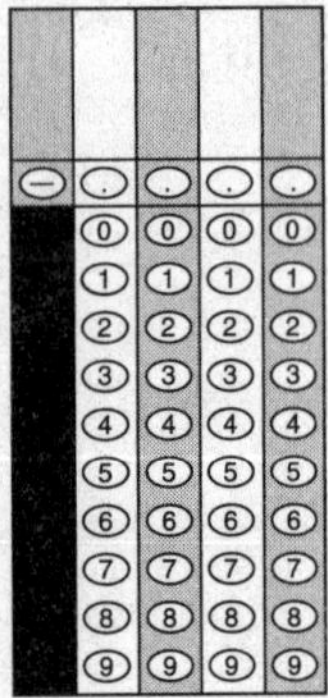

50. If $3.45x + 2.1 = 9$, what is the value of x?

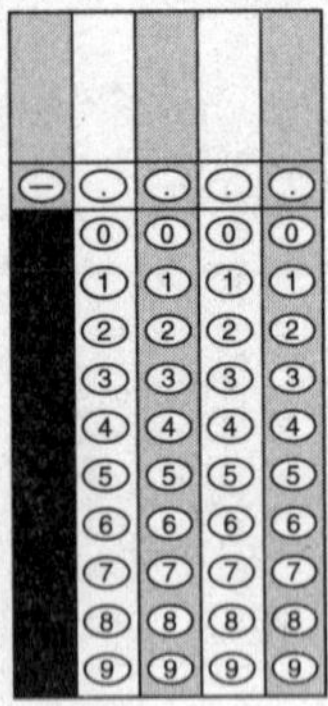

51. $(3 + |4 - 12| \times 8)^2 = ?$

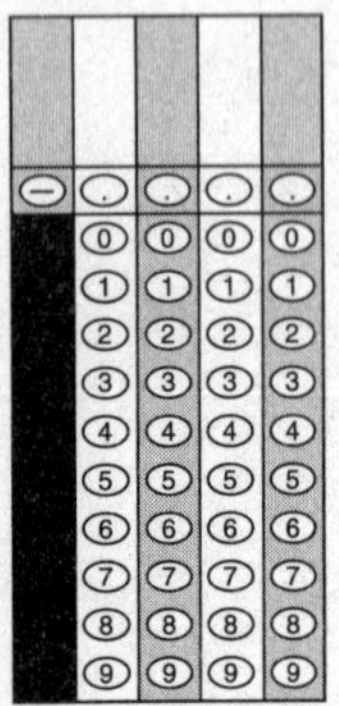

52. What value of m satisfies the equation $m - 2 = 2 - m$?

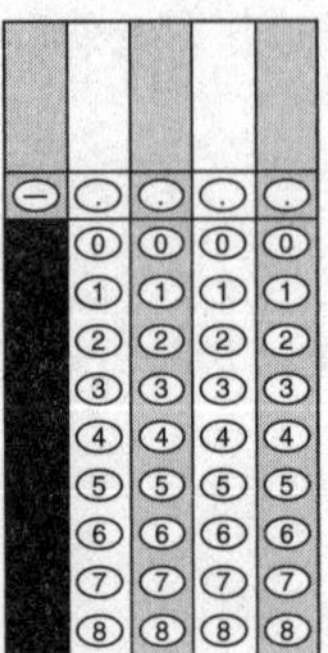

53. $\left(\frac{1}{2}\right)^3 = ?$

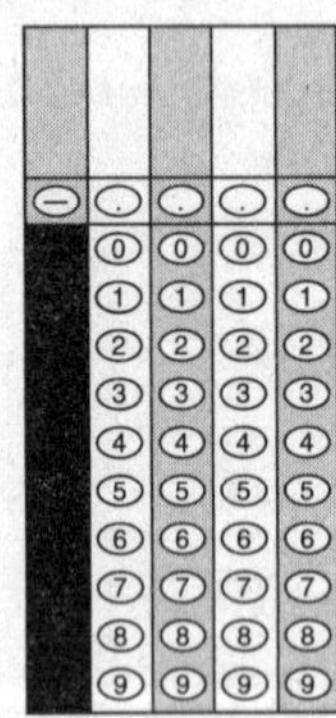

54. $14 - 25 \div 5^2 = ?$

55. If $12\left(2^2 - 3\right)^2 = x$, what is the value of x?

ANSWERS AND EXPLANATIONS

Kaplan Strategy for Math Grid-In Questions

1. 3

Getting to the Answer: Remembering the order of operations is crucial to getting a question like this correct! If you remember PEMDAS, then you should have no problem answering this question correctly:

$$(8 \div 2 + 3) - (4 - 2)^2$$
$$(4 + 3) - (2)^2$$
$$7 - 4 = 3$$

PEMDAS

A. $(3 + 2)^2 - 6 \times 2^2 = 1$

B. $3 + (2^2 - 6) \times 2^2 = -5$

2. H

Subject: Algebra

Getting to the Answer: Follow PEMDAS one step at a time.

$\left(\frac{1}{3} + \frac{2}{5}\right) \div \frac{3}{4} =$

$\left(\frac{5}{15} + \frac{6}{15}\right) \div \frac{3}{4}$ Add the fractions in parentheses.

$\frac{11}{15} \times \frac{4}{3} = \frac{44}{45}$ To divide fractions, multiply by the reciprocal of the divisor.

Basic Terms: Evens and Odds

A. Even

B. Odd

C. Positive

D. Positive

E. Odd

F. Even

G. Negative

H. Negative

I. Even

J. Even

K. Negative

L. Positive

Prime Numbers and Prime Factorization

3. B

Subject: Prime Numbers

Getting to the Answer: Because you are looking for the greatest qualifying number, start with **(D)**, the largest. You know that it is not prime because all even numbers are multiples of 2, so eliminate **(D)**. Eliminate **(C)** because 33 is a multiple of 3 and 11 and is therefore not prime. **(B)** is prime, so there's your answer.

4. G

Subject: Prime Factorization

Getting to the Answer: Compare the prime factorization of the operation in the question stem to the prime factorization of the answer choices. Equal operations will have identical prime factors.

$$9 \times 14 = 3 \times 3 \times 2 \times 7$$
$$6 \times 21 = 2 \times 3 \times 3 \times 7$$

Adding and Subtracting Variables

A. $9n$

B. $11x$

C. $11g$

D. $2d + 3n$

E. $15y$

F. $7x - 4y$

5. D

Subject: Algebra

Getting to the Answer: Simply add the number of a terms you have in the operation. $5a + a = 6a$

6. G

Subject: Algebra

Getting to the Answer: Add like terms; in this case, add up the xy terms.

$$xy + 2xy = 3xy$$

7. **D**

Subject: Algebra

Getting to the Answer:

$(3d - 7) - (5 - 2d) =$	Get rid of the parentheses.
$3d - 7 - 5 + 2d =$	Combine like terms.
$5d - 12$	

8. **F**

Subject: Algebra

Getting to the Answer: Simplify the equation before you substitute for the variables.

$15x - 3y - 7x + 4y - 8x + x =$	Combine like terms.
$x + y =$	Substitute values for variables.
$11 + 13 =$	24

Multiplying and Dividing Variables

A. $24gh$

B. $30xy$

C. $6xyz$

D. $\frac{3r}{s}$

E. $\frac{5j}{k}$

F. $3wx$

9. **C**

Subject: Algebra

Getting to the Answer:

$5r(3s) + 6r - 2rs =$	Do the multiplication first.
$15rs + 6r - 2rs =$	Now, combine like terms.
$13rs + 6r$	

10. **H**

Subject: Algebra

Getting to the Answer:

$$2x(3x) + y^2 = 6x^2 + y^2$$

11. **C**

Subject: Algebra

Getting to the Answer:

$\frac{25xyz}{5z}$	Cancel common factors in the numerator and the denominator.
$5xy$	

12. **E**

Subject: Algebra

Getting to the Answer:

$a(3b) + b(-3a) =$	Do the multiplication operations first.
$3ab - 3ab = 0$	Combine like terms.

Distributive Property with Variables: Multiplying

A. $15s - 9r$

B. $-4b + 3ab$

C. $-6a + 4b$

D. $x^2 + xy - xz$

13. **C**

Subject: Algebra

Getting to the Answer:

$3(x + y) - 3(-x - y) =$	Multiply; distribute across parentheses.
$3x + 3y + 3x + 3y =$	Combine like terms.
$6x + 6y$	

14. **E**

Subject: Algebra

Getting to the Answer:

$-5n(3m - 2) =$	Distribute the $5n$ across the parentheses.
$-15nm + 10n$	

Distributive Property with Variables: Factoring

A. $3(4x + 3y)$

B. $2b(4a - 3 + c)$

C. $5(5g + 3h)$

D. $x(y + 3)$

15. C

Subject: Algebra

Getting to the Answer: Pull out the common factors in each side of the expression.

$12cd + 6c =$

$6c(2d + 1)$

16. G

Subject: Algebra

Getting to the Answer:

$3(x + 2) - (x - 4) =$	Get rid of the parentheses first.
$3x + 6 - x + 4 =$	Combine like terms.
$2x + 10 =$	Pull out the common factor.

$2(x + 5)$

Variables in the Answer Choices

17. C

Subject: Algebra

Getting to the Answer: With variables in the answer choices, pick easy numbers to work with: $x = 2$, $y = 6$ and $z = 3$.

If 2 people work 1 hour, they make 6 dollars, so each person makes \$3 an hour. This means that 3 people working 4 hours at that rate will make $3 \times 4 \times \$3 = \$36$.

Now check each answer choice to see which one works out to \$36.

(A) $4xyz = 144$

(B) $xy + 4z = 12 + 12 = 24$

(C) $\frac{4yz}{x} = \frac{72}{2} = 36$

(C) is your answer. You can always check the other answers, but be aware of time constraints.

18. H

Subject: Algebra

Getting to the Answer: With variables in the question and the answer choices, you can Pick Numbers: $n = 5$; if 5 members each brought 3 guests, there are 15 guest attendees plus the original 5 members = 20. Check the answer choices:

(E) $n + 3 = 8$, which is incorrect.

(F) $3n = 15$, which is also incorrect.

(G) $3n + 4 = 19$, which is also incorrect.

(H) $4n = 20$, which matches your answer above.

19. C

Subject: Algebra

Getting to the Answer: Pick $x = 4$ for Paolo. To find out how many tickets Gina sold, follow the math in the question stem:

$$4 \times 3 = 12 \text{ and } 12 - 10 = 2, \text{ so } y = 2.$$

Now, check the answer choices, looking for a value for y:

(A) $10x - 3 = 37$, which does not work.

(B) $10 - 3x = -2$, which is incorrect.

(C) $3x - 10 = 2$, which matches your choice of $y = 2$.

Percentage Increase/Decrease

20. E

Subject: Algebra

Getting to the Answer: If the original price was 100, then:

$\$100 \times 20\% = \$20$

$\$100 - \$20 = \$80$

$\$80 \times 15\% = \$12$ and $\$12 + \$20 = \$32$ less than the original price.

$\frac{32}{100} = 32\%$

ANSWERS AND EXPLANATIONS

Math Foundations Practice Set

Integers and Fractions

1. D

Improper/Mixed Fractions

2. $\frac{41}{5}$

3. $1\frac{2}{5}$

Reciprocals

4. $\frac{100}{101}$

5. $\frac{10}{49}$

6. $\frac{8}{57}$

Prime Numbers

7. C

8. $3 \cdot 3 \cdot 11$

9. $2 \cdot 2 \cdot 2 \cdot 2 \cdot 2 \cdot 2$

10. $7 \cdot 7$

Odd/Even

11. C

Subject: Arithmetic

Getting to the Answer: John's total pay is the product of his number of hours and his rate. Because his hourly rate is odd and his total pay is an even number, he must have worked for an even number of hours. The only possible answers are **(C)** and **(D)**. Because 50 ÷ 28 is not an odd integer, **(C)** must be the answer.

Positive/Negative

12. H

Subject: Arithmetic

Getting to the Answer:

$$\left(\frac{-3(6-2)}{-2}\right)-\left(\frac{-6(2-4)}{-3}\right)=$$ Work inside the parentheses first.

$$\left(\frac{-3(4)}{-2}\right)-\left(\frac{-6(-2)}{-3}\right)=$$ Remember your rules for multiplying positive and negative numbers.

$$\left(\frac{-12}{-2}\right)-\left(\frac{12}{-3}\right)=$$ Remember your rules for dividing positive and negative numbers.

$$6-(-4)=$$ Add the positive.

$$6+4=10$$

13. A

Subject: Algebra

Getting to the Answer:

$$\frac{2x-y}{3(y-4)}=$$

$$\frac{2(4)-(2)}{3(2-4)}=$$ Substitute the given values.

$$\frac{8-2}{3(-2)}=$$

$$\frac{6}{-6}=-1$$ A positive divided by a negative always equals a negative.

PEMDAS

14. G

Subject: Arithmetic

Getting to the Answer:

$$6 \div 10 \cdot 5 \div 3 = \frac{6}{10} \times 5 \div 3$$
$$= 3 \div 3$$
$$= 1$$

15. B

Subject: Arithmetic

Getting to the Answer:

$$(\sqrt{100})(\sqrt{36})+(\sqrt{64})(\sqrt{25}) = (10)(6)+(8)(5) = 60+40 = 100$$

16. F

Subject: Algebra

Getting to the Answer:

$$x+y(x+y) = 4+\left(\frac{1}{2}\right)\left(4+\frac{1}{2}\right) = 4+\left(\frac{1}{2}\right)\left(4\frac{1}{2}\right) = 4+2\frac{1}{4} = 6\frac{1}{4}$$

17. A

Subject: Algebra

Getting to the Answer:

$1^2 2^1 = (1)(2) = 2$

18. G

Subject: Algebra

Getting to the Answer:

$$2x \cdot 7 + 2 - 4x = 14x + 2 - 4x = 10x + 2$$

Now you can combine like terms.

19. C

Subject: Arithmetic

Getting to the Answer:

$$10^2 \cdot 3^2 = 100 \times 9 = 900$$

20. G

Subject: Arithmetic

Getting to the Answer:

The least common multiple (LCM) of 3, 4, and 9 is 36, so:

$$\frac{1}{3}-\frac{1}{4}-\frac{1}{9} = \frac{12}{36}-\frac{9}{36}-\frac{4}{36} = \frac{3}{36}-\frac{4}{36} = -\frac{1}{36}$$

Go from left to right when there is only one operation!

21. C

Subject: Algebra

Getting to the Answer:

$$\frac{x}{10+2\cdot 7} = 6$$
$$\frac{x}{24} = 6$$
$$x = 6\cdot 24 = 144$$

22. H

Subject: Algebra

Getting to the Answer:

$x+x\cdot y+y = x+xy+y$

23. B

Subject: Arithmetic

Getting to the Answer:

$$7+5\cdot 3^2 = 7+5\times 9 = 7+45 = 52$$

Combining Like Terms

24. $x-y$

25. $15x$

26. $-y$

27. $6n$

28. $4y-x$

Multiplying and Dividing Monomials

29. $4x$

30. $\frac{3}{2}np$

Factoring and the Distributive Property with Monomials

31. $20np + 8n$

32. $4xy + 6x$

33. $-3xy + 12xz$

34. $-3(2x + 3y)$ or $3(-2x - 3y)$

35. $8x(3y - 1)$

PEMDAS Combinations

36. G

Subject: Algebra

Getting to the Answer: Distribute:

$2a(3a - 5a^2) = 6a^2 - 10a^3$

37. A

Subject: Algebra

Getting to the Answer: Distribute:

$$4xy\left(\frac{1}{2y} + \frac{3}{2x}\right) =$$
$$\frac{4xy}{2y} + \frac{12xy}{2x}$$
$$2x + 6y$$

38. G

Subject: Algebra

Getting to the Answer: Distribute:

$3x(y + 4) = 3xy + 12x$

39. C

Subject: Algebra

Getting to the Answer: Distribute:

$3x(2y - 3x - 2) = 6xy - 9x^2 - 6x$

40. E

Subject: Algebra

Getting to the Answer:

$4x(4x - 4 - 4x) = 4x(-4) = -16x$

Word Problems and Picking Numbers

41. B

Subject: Algebra

Getting to the Answer:

$y = 10$	Pick a number for January's letters, y.
$3y = 3(10) = 30$	Compute the number of February's letters.
$\frac{1}{2}(y + 3y) + 10 =$ $\frac{1}{2}(10 + 30) + 10 =$ $\frac{1}{2}(40) + 10 = 30$	Compute the number of March's letters.
$0.37(30) = 11.10$	Calculate the price for March's letters.
$0.74y + 3.7 =$ $0.74(10) + 3.7 =$ $7.40 + 3.7 = 11.10$	Find the answer choice that matches, **(B)**.

42. G

Subject: Algebra

Getting to the Answer:

x	This is the number of red marbles.
$2x$	Figure out the number of blue marbles.
$\frac{2x}{40} = \frac{x}{20}$	Compute the probability of picking blue.

43. B

Subject: Algebra

Getting to the Answer:

$x = 12$	Pick a number for the total pieces, x.
$\frac{1}{4}(12) = 3$	Figure out Kevin's pieces.
$2(3) - 1 = 5$	Figure out Keith's pieces.
$3 + 5 = 8$	Add the two together.
$12 - 8 = 4$	Calculate how many were left.
$\frac{1}{4}x + 1 =$ $\frac{1}{4}(12) + 1 =$ $3 + 1 = 4$	Find the answer choice that matches, **(B)**.

44. G

Subject: Algebra

Getting to the Answer:

$n = 10$	Pick a number for Jamie's age today.
$2(10) = 20$	Find Brian's age today.
$\frac{1}{2}(20+10)+2=$	Find Morgan's age in 8 years.
$\frac{1}{2}(30)+2=$	
$15 + 2 = 17$	
$17 - 8 = 9$	Find Morgan's age today.
$\frac{3}{2}n-6=$	Find the answer choice that matches, **(G)**.
$\frac{3}{2}(10)-6=9$	

45. D

Subject: Algebra

Getting to the Answer:

$x = 30$	Pick a value for x.
$30 - 2 = 28$	Find the temperature on thermometer B.
$2(28) - 4 = 56 - 4 = 52$	Find the temperature for thermometers C and D.
$30 + 28 + 52 + 52 = 162$	Remember to add the C and D temperature twice.
$\frac{162}{4} = 40.5$	Calculate the average.
$\frac{3x-9}{2} =$	Find the answer choice that matches, **(D)**.
$\frac{3(30)-9}{2} = \frac{81}{2} = 40.5$	

Grid-Ins

46. 5.83

Subject: Algebra

Getting to the Answer: Start by distributing the 3 on the left side of the equation. From there, isolate g like you would in any other equation:

$$3(2 + g) = 23.5$$
$$(2 + g) = 7.83$$
$$g = 7.83 - 2$$
$$g = 5.83$$

Grid in 5.83 and move to the next question.

47. 32

Subject: Algebra

Getting to the Answer: Solve this equation like you would any other two-step equation. Add 45 to both sides, then divide by 5:

$$5f - 45 = 115$$
$$5f = 160$$
$$f = 32$$

Grid in 32.

48. 36

Subject: Algebra

Getting to the Answer: Isolate the variable here like you would in any other two-step equation:

$$\frac{c}{6}+8=14$$
$$\frac{c}{6}=6$$
$$c = 36$$

Grid in 36.

49. 26

Subject: Algebra

Getting to the Answer: Solve this equation like you would any other equation. Add 12 to both sides and divide by 4 to get b by itself:

$$4b - 12 = 92$$
$$4b = 104$$
$$b = 26$$

Grid in 26.

50. 2

Subject: Algebra

Getting to the Answer: Don't let the decimals change your approach! Isolate x as you would in any other equation by subtracting 2.1 from both sides and then dividing by 3.45:

$$3.45x + 2.1 = 9$$
$$3.45x = 6.9$$
$$x = 2$$

Grid in 2.

51. 4489

Subject: Arithmetic

Getting to the Answer: Knowledge of the order of operations will help you answer this question correctly. Start with the subtraction within the absolute value brackets. Proceed to multiplication, then addition, and then finally apply the exponent outside the parentheses.

$$(3 + |4 - 12| \times 8)^2$$
$$(3 + 8 \times 8)^2$$
$$(3 + 64)^2 = 67^2 = 4{,}489$$

Grid in 4489.

52. 2

Subject: Algebra

Getting to the Answer: Don't try to take any shortcuts with this equation! Just solve as you would any other equation:

$$m - 2 = 2 - m$$
$$2m = 4$$
$$m = 2$$

Grid in 2.

53. .125

Subject: Arithmetic

Getting to the Answer: Taking a number to the third power simply means to multiply a number by itself 3 times. Don't let the fraction throw you off:

$$\left(\frac{1}{2}\right)^3 = \frac{1}{2} \times \frac{1}{2} \times \frac{1}{2} = \frac{1}{8}$$

Grid in .125, which is equivalent to 1/8.

54. 13

Subject: Arithmetic

Getting to the Answer: Remembering the order of operations is the key to answering this question correctly. Address the exponent first, then do division, and finish with subtraction:

$$14 - 25 \div 5^2$$
$$14 - 25 \div 25$$
$$14 - 1 = 13$$

Grid in 13.

55. 12

Subject: Algebra

Getting to the Answer: Even though this question may look like an equation, the order of operations and basic computational skills are all that is necessary to answer this question correctly. Remember to start inside the parentheses, and then follow the order of operations accordingly:

$$12(2^2 - 3)^2$$
$$12(4 - 3)^2$$
$$12(1)^2 = 12$$

Grid in 12.

CHAPTER 14

Arithmetic

CHAPTER OBJECTIVES

By the end of this chapter, you will be able to:

- Answer questions involving number properties
- Apply rules of exponents to simplify expressions and to manipulate numbers written in scientific notation
- Simplify numerical expressions that contain square roots and cube roots

ARITHMETIC I

Fraction Operations

Any number that can be expressed as a fraction or a repeating decimal is a **rational number**. This includes numbers like 3, $\frac{2}{5}$, -0.1666, or $0.\overline{3}$.

- Generally speaking, when you work with fractions on the SHSAT, you'll need to put them in **lowest terms**. This means the numerator and the denominator are not divisible by any common integer greater than 1. The fraction $\frac{1}{2}$ is in lowest terms, but the fraction $\frac{3}{6}$ is not, because 3 and 6 are both divisible by 3. The process used to write a fraction in lowest terms is called **reducing**, which simply means dividing out any common multiples from both the numerator and denominator. This process is also commonly called **canceling.**
- To add or subtract fractions, first find a **common denominator**, and then add or subtract the numerators. Finding a common denominator often involves multiplying one or more of the fractions by a number so that the denominators will be the same: $\frac{2}{15}+\frac{3}{10}=\frac{4}{30}+\frac{9}{30}=\frac{4+9}{30}=\frac{13}{30}$.
- To **multiply fractions**, multiply straight across—numerator times numerator and denominator times denominator: $\frac{5}{7}\times\frac{3}{4}=\frac{5\times3}{7\times4}=\frac{15}{28}$.
- To **divide fractions**, invert the fraction in the denominator and multiply: $\frac{1}{2}\div\frac{3}{5}=\frac{1}{2}\times\frac{5}{3}=\frac{1\times5}{2\times3}=\frac{5}{6}$.
- To **convert a mixed number**, which is a whole number with a fraction, to an improper fraction, which is a fraction where the numerator is bigger than the denominator, multiply the whole number part by the denominator, then add the numerator. The result is the new numerator (over the same denominator). To convert $7\frac{1}{3}$, first multiply 7 by 3, then add 1 to get the new numerator of 22. Put that over the same denominator, 3, to get $\frac{22}{3}$.
- To **convert an improper fraction** to a mixed number, divide the denominator into the numerator, and the remainder will be the numerator of the fraction part, with the same denominator. For example, to convert $\frac{108}{5}$, first divide 5 into 108, which yields 21 with a remainder of 3. Therefore, $\frac{108}{5}=21\frac{3}{5}$.
- The **reciprocal** of a fraction is the inverse of that fraction. To find the reciprocal of a fraction, switch the numerator and the denominator. The reciprocal of $\frac{3}{7}$ is $\frac{7}{3}$. The reciprocal of 5 (or $\frac{5}{1}$ because all whole numbers can be written over 1) is $\frac{1}{5}$. The product of two reciprocals is always 1.

- One way to **compare fractions** is to manipulate them so they have a common denominator. For instance, compare $\frac{3}{4}$ and $\frac{5}{7}$:

  $\frac{3}{4} = \frac{21}{28}$ and $\frac{5}{7} = \frac{20}{28}$; $\frac{21}{28}$ is greater than $\frac{20}{28}$, so $\frac{3}{4}$ is greater than $\frac{5}{7}$.

  Another way to compare fractions is to convert them both to decimals: $\frac{3}{4}$ converts to 0.75, and $\frac{5}{7}$ converts to approximately 0.714, and 0.75 is greater than 0.714.

- To **convert a fraction to a decimal**, divide the numerator by the denominator. To convert $\frac{5}{8}$, divide 5 by 8, yielding 0.625. Often, these numbers will start repeating, such as with $\frac{1}{6}$. When 1 is divided by 6, the decimal starts repeating almost right away, 0.16666666..., so it can be written as $0.1\overline{66}$ (the line over the 66 means "repeating") To find a particular digit in a repeating decimal, note the number of digits in the cluster that repeats. If there are two digits in that cluster, then every second digit is the same. If there are three digits in that cluster, then every third digit is the same. And so on.

Reduce

A. Cancel out common factors on top and bottom.

$\frac{39}{72} = \underline{\qquad\qquad} = \underline{\qquad\qquad}$

Divide

B. To divide by a fraction, simply multiply by the reciprocal.

$\frac{1}{4} \div \frac{1}{3} = \frac{1}{4} \times \underline{\qquad\qquad} = \underline{\qquad\qquad}$

Multiply

C. Multiply the numerators to get the new numerator, and multiply the denominators to get the new denominator.

$\frac{1}{3} \times \frac{2}{5} = \underline{\qquad\qquad}$

Add and Subtract

D. Get a common denominator. Add the numerators.

$\frac{5}{9} + \frac{2}{6} = \underline{\qquad\qquad} + \underline{\qquad\qquad} = \underline{\qquad\qquad} = \underline{\qquad\qquad}$

E. Get a common denominator. Subtract the numerators.

$$\frac{1}{2}-\frac{3}{7}=\_\_\_\_\_\_\_\_-\_\_\_\_\_\_\_\_=\_\_\_\_\_\_\_\_$$

1. $\frac{1}{2}\left(\frac{3}{5}-\frac{3}{10}\right)\div\frac{2}{3}=$

A. 0

B. $\frac{9}{40}$

C. $\frac{2}{5}$

D. $\frac{9}{20}$

✓ Remember

Squaring a fraction is the same as multiplying the fraction by itself.

Using the correct order of operations will help you avoid traps on Test Day. Don't fall into any traps here—following PEMDAS means easy points!

Divisibility Rules

Divisible by:	Rule:	Example:
2	The last digit must be even.	2002
3	The sum of the digits is a multiple of 3.	813
4	The last two digits comprise a multiple of 4.	456
5	The last digit must be 5 or 0.	705
6	The rules for both 2 and 3 must apply.	924
9	The sum of the digits is a multiple of 9.	891

2. Which of the following is a multiple of 3?

E. 115

F. 370

G. 465

H. 890

3. Which of the following is **not** a multiple of 6?

A. 10,224

B. 12,024

C. 12,420

D. 20,242

Factors/Multiples

A **factor** of an integer is any number that divides precisely into that integer (with no remainder).

A **multiple** of an integer is that integer times any number. In other words, factor $\times$ factor $=$ multiple.

A. 4 is a factor/multiple of 24.

B. 49 is a factor/multiple of 7.

C. 8 is a factor/multiple of 8.

4. What is the sum of the odd factors of 21?

E. 10

F. 11

G. 28

H. 32

✔ Remember

Knowing these rules cold will save you time on Test Day. The SHSAT will never explicitly ask you for these definitions, but you are expected to know them.

Greatest Common Factor (GCF)

The **greatest common factor (GCF)** of two numbers is the highest number that divides precisely into each of them without a remainder. To find the greatest common factor, break down both numbers into their prime factorizations and take all the prime factors they have in common. For example, try 36 and 48: $36 = 2 \times 2 \times 3 \times 3$ and $48 = 2 \times 2 \times 2 \times 2 \times 3$. What they have in common is two 2s and one 3, so the GCF is $2 \times 2 \times 3 = 12$.

For a GCF problem, simply check the largest answer choice to see if it divides evenly into both numbers. If not, proceed to the second-largest answer choice. Keep going until you've found the greatest factor of both numbers!

5. What is the greatest common factor of 48 and 180?

A. 4

B. 12

C. 16

D. 18

Least Common Multiple (LCM)

The **least common multiple (LCM)** of two numbers is the smallest multiple both of those numbers divide into. To find the LCM of two or more numbers, check out the multiples of the larger number until you find one that's also a multiple of the smaller. For example, to find the LCM of 12 and 15, begin by taking the multiples of 15: $1 \times 15 = 15$, which is not divisible by 12; $2 \times 15 = 30$, not divisible by 12; nor is 45, which is 3×15. But the next multiple of 15, $4 \times 15 = 60$, is divisible by 12, so it's the LCM.

To find the LCM, begin with the smallest answer choice. Check to see if it is a multiple of both numbers. If not, proceed to the second-smallest answer choice. Keep going until you've found the smallest multiple of both numbers!

6. What is the least common multiple of 12 and 32?

E. 64

F. 72

G. 96

H. 384

✔ Remember

Knowing your divisibility rules could save you time on LCM and GCF questions.

You're given the answer choices—use them!

Greatest Common Factor with Prime Factorization

A **prime number** is a positive integer that is divisible without a remainder by only 1 and itself. The number 2 is the smallest prime number and the only even prime number; 1 is not considered prime.

Let's say you are given a problem that looks like this:

$$A = 2 \cdot 2 \cdot 2 \cdot 2 \cdot 3 \cdot 5$$

$$B = 2 \cdot 2 \cdot 5 \cdot 7 \cdot 7$$

To find the greatest common factor of A and B, identify all of the prime factors the two have in common.

A. They share a _____, another _____, and a _____.

B. The answer is _________.

C. Should you multiply the numbers together to find out what A and B each are? Yes / No

✓ Remember

For a GCF or LCM problem with prime factorization, all of the answer choices are presented in prime factorization. This means there is no need to multiply any of the numbers out!

Least Common Multiple with Prime Factorization

To find the **prime factorization** of an integer, use a factor tree to keep breaking the integer up into factors until all the factors are prime numbers. To find the prime factorization of 36, for example, you could begin by breaking it into 4×9. Then break 4 into 2×2 and break 9 into 3×3. The prime factorization of 36 is $2 \times 2 \times 3 \times 3$.

Take each factor (not just factors common to both numbers) and raise it to the highest power with which it appears.

$$A = 2 \cdot 2 \cdot 2 \cdot 2 \cdot 3 \cdot 5$$

$$B = 2 \cdot 2 \cdot 5 \cdot 7 \cdot 7$$

Even though A and B are the same here and above, the LCM will be quite different from the GCF.

What is the least common multiple of A and B?

A. First of all, what are the distinct factors? ______, ______, ______, and ______

B. Now raise them to the highest power with which they appear: __________

That's all there is to it! Now, try another:

$$A = 2 \cdot 2 \cdot 2 \cdot 5 \cdot 7 \cdot 7$$

$$B = 3 \cdot 3 \cdot 5 \cdot 5 \cdot 7$$

7. What is the least common multiple of A and B?

A. $3 \cdot 5 \cdot 7$

B. $2 \cdot 3 \cdot 5 \cdot 7$

C. $2 \cdot 2 \cdot 2 \cdot 3 \cdot 3 \cdot 5 \cdot 5 \cdot 7 \cdot 7$

D. $2 \cdot 2 \cdot 2 \cdot 3 \cdot 3 \cdot 5 \cdot 5 \cdot 5 \cdot 7 \cdot 7 \cdot 7$

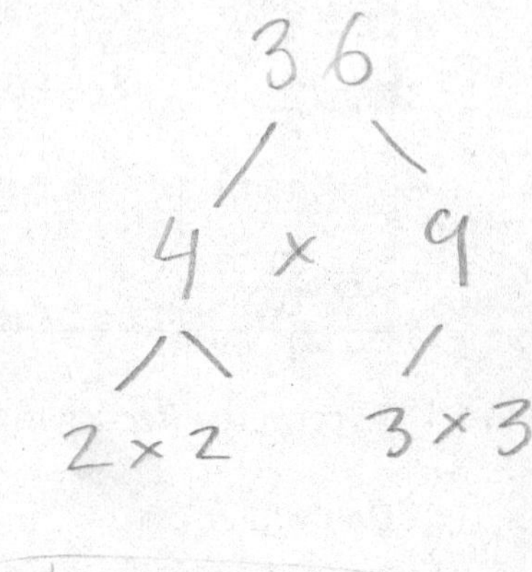

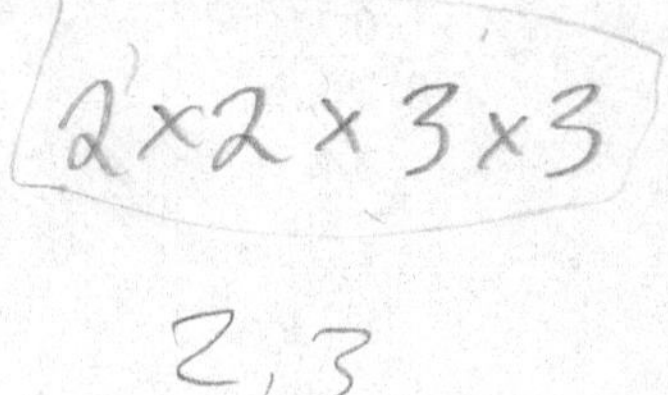

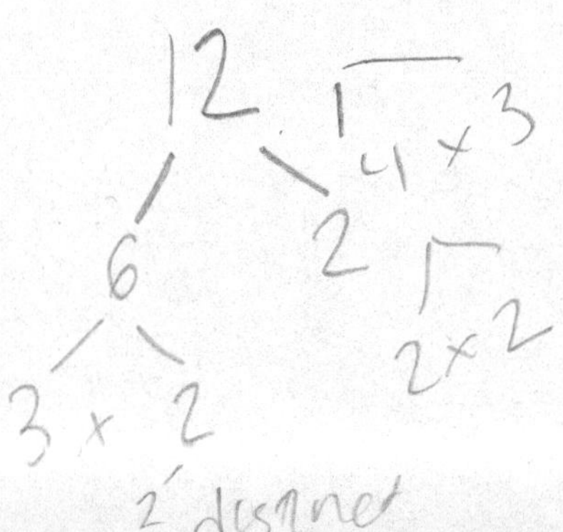

Decimals, Fractions, and Percents

$$\text{Percent} = \frac{\text{Part}}{\text{Whole}} \times 100 \text{ or Percent} = \text{Decimal} \times 100$$

To convert a decimal to a fraction:

The number to the left of the decimal is an integer and thus does not need to be converted into a fraction.

Put each number to the right of the decimal over the power of 10 that corresponds to that number's digit.

3 .2 (tenths) 4 (hundredths) 6 (thousandths)

$$3 + \frac{2}{10} + \frac{4}{100} + \frac{6}{1000} = 3\frac{246}{1000}$$

Then reduce $3\frac{246}{1000} = 3\frac{123}{500}$

	Fraction	Decimal	Percent
A.	$\frac{1}{4}$		
B.	$\frac{1}{6}$		
C.			99%
D.		0.35	

To convert a fraction to a decimal:

Do the division.

$$\frac{3}{8} = 8\overline{)3.000} = 0.375$$

$$\begin{array}{r} 3.000 \\ -2.4 \\ \hline 60 \\ -56 \\ \hline 40 \\ -40 \\ \hline 0 \end{array}$$

8. Express the sum of $\frac{1}{5}$ and $\frac{3}{4}$ as a decimal.

E. 0.19
F. 0.49
G. 0.95
H. 4.9

✔ Remember

The SHSAT will reward you not only for knowing some common equivalences but also for being able to work with them.

To remember how to convert a fraction to a decimal, think of a fraction as an unfinished division problem.

Rounding

Look at the number to the right of the digit in question. If the number is 4 or lower, round down. If the number is 5 or greater, round up.

9. Which of the following represents 357.428 rounded to the nearest tenth?

A. 357.43
B. 357.4
C. 357
D. 360

Remainder, Quotient, and Divisor

A **divisor** is the number by which you divide a given number, and a **quotient** is the number that results from the division. For example, when you divide 50 by 5 (which equals 10), 5 is the divisor and 10 is the quotient.

Remainders are integers left over when dividing. If a question asks for the remainder when 15 is divided by 2, don't say "15 divided by 2 is 7.5, so the remainder is 0.5." What you should say is: "15 divided by 2 is 7 with a remainder of 1."

$$8\overline{)60}\quad 7\text{R}4$$

A. In the example above, which number is the divisor? ____________

B. Which is the quotient? ____________

C. Which is the remainder? ____________

One common way that division/remainder problems appear on the SHSAT is in word problems. Here's an example of what you may see on Test Day:

Joe has 57 candies, and he wants to fill as many 10-candy boxes as possible. How many candies will end up in the last box?

D. What is this problem really asking you to find?

____

E. What if it asked how many boxes are completely filled?

____

F. What if it asked how many total boxes are used?

____

✔ Remember

Know your definitions. Even though the test doesn't explicitly ask for them, you can't get a good score without knowing them.

10. In a certain movie theater, each row has 15 seats. If there are 218 people in the theater and all the rows are filled except one, how many people sit in the unfilled row?

E. 15
F. 14
G. 8
H. 7

11. There are 587 people traveling by bus for a field trip. If each bus seats 48 people and all the buses are filled to capacity except one, how many people sit in the unfilled bus?

A. 37
B. 36
C. 12
D. 11

Multiplying and Dividing with Decimals

Multiplying decimals is also a lot like multiplying whole numbers. Multiply each digit in the first number by each digit in the second number. The number of decimal places in the product will equal the total number of decimal places in the original numbers.

For example: 9.76×0.4.

First, multiply the digits as whole numbers.

$$\begin{array}{r} 976 \\ \times\ 04 \\ \hline 3904 \end{array}$$

Then, find the total number of decimal places.

- There are 2 decimal places in 9.76.
- There is 1 decimal place in 0.4.
- The product must have $2 + 1 = 3$ decimal places. Write 3.904.

$$9.76 \times 0.4 = 3.904$$

Dividing decimals is similar to dividing whole numbers.

First, make the divisor a whole number by multiplying the dividend and the divisor by the same power of 10. For example, to divide $18.93 \div 1.5$:

1. Change the divisor to a whole number by multiplying by a power of 10. So, $1.5 \times 10 = 15$.
2. Multiply the dividend by the same power of 10. $18.93 \times 10 = 189.3$.
3. Divide. Line up the decimal point in the quotient.
4. Continue dividing until there is no amount left over or you see a repeating pattern. You can add 0s to the end of the dividend.

Scientific Notation

Scientific notation is used to express very large or very small numbers. A number written in scientific notation is a number that is greater than or equal to 1, but less than 10, raised to a power of 10. For example, 3.64×10^8 is written in scientific notation, while 36.4×10^7 is not. The two numbers are equivalent, but the second doesn't meet the definition of scientific notation because 36.4 is not between 1 and 10.

To write a number in scientific notation, move the decimal point (to the right or to the left) until the number is between 1 and 10. Count the number of places you moved the decimal point—this tells you the power of 10 that you'll need. If the original number was a tiny decimal number (which means you had to move the decimal to the right), the exponent will be negative; if the original number was a large number (which means you had to move the decimal point to the left), the exponent will be positive.

Examples: $0.000000819 = 8.19 \times 10^{-7}$

$14{,}250{,}000{,}000 = 1.425 \times 10^{10}$

You can **add and subtract** numbers written in scientific notation as long as the power of 10 in each term is the same. Simply add (or subtract) the numbers and keep the same power of 10. Be careful—you may have to adjust the final answer if it is no longer written in scientific notation.

Example: $(4.3 \times 10^5) + (8.2 \times 10^5) = (4.3 + 8.2) \times 10^5 = 12.5 \times 10^5$
Because 12.5 is not between 1 and 10, move the decimal one place to the left and adjust the power of 10 to get 1.25×10^6.

You can **multiply and divide** numbers written in scientific notation using rules of exponents. Simply multiply (or divide) the numbers and add (or subtract) the powers of 10. As before, you may have to adjust the final answer if it is no longer written in scientific notation.

Example: $(12 \times 10^9) \div (3 \times 10^2) = (12 \div 3) \times 10^{9-2} = 4 \times 10^7$

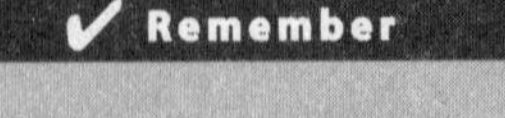

Remember

$$x^{-1} = \frac{1}{x}$$

Think of scientific notation as a kind of shorthand for really big or really small numbers. The exponent of the power of 10 tells you how many places to move the decimal point. For example:

A. $2.038 \times 10^2 =$ ____________

We started with 2.038. The 10 was raised to the power of 2, so we move the decimal point two places to the right. But what if we have a negative exponent?

B. $1.86 \times 10^{-4} =$ ____________

Even if you feel rusty on the rules for exponents, scientific notation is nothing to freak out about.

C. As we saw, a negative exponent simply means we move the decimal point to the left, adding zeros as necessary. Note that multiplying by 10^{-4} is the same as dividing by what? ____________

12. Which of the following is equal to 5.3079×10^3?

E. 53,079

F. 5,307.9

G. 5.3079

H. 0.53079

13. 8.34×10^3 is equal to which of the following numbers?

A. 0.834

B. 834

C. 834×100

D. $83,400 \times 0.10$

✔ Remember

In correct scientific notation, there is exactly one nonzero digit to the left of the decimal point.

Absolute Value

The **absolute value** of a number (integers, fractions, and decimals alike) is its distance from zero on the number line, which is why absolute value is always positive. Treat absolute value signs a lot like parentheses. Do what's inside them first and then take the absolute value of the result. Don't take the absolute value of each piece between the bars before calculating. In order to calculate $|(-12) + 5 - (-4)| - |5 + (-10)|$, first do what's inside the bars to arrive at $|-3| - |-5|$, which is $3 - 5$, or -2.

A. What is $|3|$? ___________

B. What is $|-3|$? ___________

✔ Remember

For the sake of PEMDAS, absolute variable signs should be treated as parentheses.

14. $|9| + |-3| - |-4|$

E. -7
F. 2
G. 8
H. 16

✔ Remember

Absolute value represents the distance from zero—it does not make everything positive!

15. When $x = -2$, what is the value of $|2x^2| + 4x - (3 + |-2x|)$?

A. -7
B. -3
C. 1
D. 9

ARITHMETIC II

Exponents

An **exponent** refers to the number of times a base is multiplied by itself. For example, $4^3 = 4 \times 4 \times 4$. An integer times itself is the **square** of that integer (5×5 is 5^2), and an integer times itself twice is the **cube** of that integer ($4 \times 4 \times 4$ is 4^3).

- To **multiply** two terms with the same base, keep the base and add the exponents.

  Write it out: $2^2 \times 2^3 = (2 \times 2)(2 \times 2 \times 2) = 2 \times 2 \times 2 \times 2 \times 2 = 2^5$
  Use the rule: $2^2 \times 2^3 = 2^{2+3} = 2^5$

- To **divide** two terms with the same base, keep the base and subtract the exponent of the denominator from the exponent of the numerator.

  Write it out: $5^4 \div 5^2 = \frac{5 \times 5 \times \cancel{5 \times 5}}{\cancel{5 \times 5}} = \frac{5 \times 5}{1} = 5^2$
  Use the rule: $5^4 \div 5^2 = 5^{4-2} = 5^2$

- To raise a **power to another power**, multiply the exponents.

  Write it out: $(3^2)^4 = (3 \times 3)^4 = (3 \times 3)(3 \times 3)(3 \times 3)(3 \times 3) = 3^8$
  Use the rule: $(3^2)^4 = 3^{2 \times 4} = 3^8$

- To evaluate a **negative exponent**, take the reciprocal of the base and change the sign of the exponent: $2^{-3} = \left(\frac{1}{2}\right)^3 = \frac{1}{2^3} = \frac{1}{8}$.
- Any nonzero number raised to the zero power is equal to 1. For example, $7^0 = 1$.

A. $3^2 =$ ________ $=$ ________

B. $2^4 =$ ________ $=$ ________

C. $3^2 \times 3 =$ ________ $=$ ________

D. $(-3)^2 =$ ________ $=$ ________

E. $\frac{3^2}{3} =$ ________ $=$ ________

F. $(2^2)^2 =$ ________ $=$ ________

G. $\left(\frac{4}{5}\right)^2 =$ ________ $=$ ________

H. $(-3)^3 =$ ________ $=$ ________

1. What is the value of $a^b - b^a$ if $a = 2$ and $b = 5$?

   A. −27

   B. −21

   C. 3

   D. 7

2. $(-1)^3 \times (-1)^3 + (-1)^7 =$

   E. −2

   F. −1

   G. 0

   H. 1

3. $2^5 \times 2^2 =$

   A. 2^3

   B. 2^7

   C. 2^{10}

   D. 2^{12}

4. If x lies between 6 and 7, which of the following could be the value of x^2?

   E. 27

   F. 36

   G. 41

   H. 49

> ✔ **Remember**
>
> **A negative raised to an odd power is always negative. A negative raised to an even power is always positive.**

Radicals

A **radical** expression is any expression that contains a radical ($\sqrt{\ }$) symbol. This is often referred to as a *square root* symbol, but keep in mind that it can also be used to describe a cube root ($\sqrt[3]{\ }$), a fourth root ($\sqrt[4]{\ }$), or higher. The little number outside the radical is called the **index**.

You already know that addition and subtraction (and multiplication and division) are inverse operations; similarly, raising a number to a power and taking the root of the number are inverse operations. Specifically, when you raise a term to the *n*th power, taking the *n*th root will return the original term. Consider for example $3^4 = 3 \times 3 \times 3 \times 3 = 81$. If you take the fourth root of 81 (that is, determine the number that can be multiplied by itself four times to get 81), you will arrive at the original term: $\sqrt[4]{81} = \sqrt[4]{3 \times 3 \times 3 \times 3} = 3$.

Radicals can be intimidating at first, but remembering the basic rules for radicals can make them much easier. The following table contains all the formulas you'll need to know to achieve "radical" success on the SHSAT.

Rule	Example
When a fraction is under a radical, you can rewrite it using two radicals.	$\sqrt{\frac{a}{b}} = \frac{\sqrt{a}}{\sqrt{b}}$ $\sqrt{\frac{4}{9}} = \frac{\sqrt{4}}{\sqrt{9}} = \frac{2}{3}$
Two factors under a single radical can be rewritten as separate radicals multiplied together.	$\sqrt{ab} = \sqrt{a} \times \sqrt{b}$ $\sqrt{75} = \sqrt{25} \times \sqrt{3} = 5\sqrt{3}$
A radical can be written using a fractional exponent.	$\sqrt{a} = a^{\frac{1}{2}}, \sqrt[3]{a} = a^{\frac{1}{3}}$ $\sqrt{225} = 225^{\frac{1}{2}} = 15$
When you have a fractional exponent, the numerator is the power to which the base is raised, and the denominator is the root to be taken (power over root).	$a^{\frac{b}{c}} = \sqrt[c]{a^b}$ $8^{\frac{2}{3}} = \sqrt[3]{8^2} = \sqrt[3]{64} = 4$

✔ **Note**

Note this difference: By definition, the square root of a number is positive. However, when you take the square root to solve for a variable, you get two solutions, one that is positive and one that is negative. For instance, by definition $\sqrt{4} = 2$. However, if you are solving $x^2 = 4$, x will have two solutions: $x = \pm 2$.

To **simplify a square root**, factor out the perfect squares under the radical, take their square roots, and put the result in front of whatever is left under the square root symbol (the non-perfect-square factors):

$$\sqrt{12} = \sqrt{4 \times 3} = \sqrt{4} \times \sqrt{3} = 2\sqrt{3}$$

You can **add or subtract radicals** only if the part under the radicals is the same. In other words, treat terms with radicals like terms with variables. Just as $2x + 3x = 5x$ (where you add the coefficients of x):

$$2\sqrt{3} + 3\sqrt{3} = 5\sqrt{3}$$

In other words, you add or subtract the numbers in front of the square root symbol—the numbers under the radical stay the same.

A. $\sqrt{2} + 4\sqrt{2} =$ ________

B. $\sqrt{2} + 4\sqrt{3} =$ ________

C. $\sqrt{20} =$ ________ $=$ ________

D. $2\sqrt{3} \times 3\sqrt{5} =$ ________

E. $\sqrt{\frac{9}{4}} =$ ________ $=$ ________

F. $4\sqrt{6} \div 2\sqrt{3} =$ ________ $=$ ________ $=$

5. $\frac{\sqrt{81}}{\sqrt{36}} =$

A. $1\frac{1}{2}$

B. $2\frac{1}{4}$

C. 3

D. 9

6. $3\sqrt{41}$ is between

E. 6 and 7

F. 15 and 18

G. 18 and 21

H. 21 and 24

7. $\sqrt{64} =$

A. 2^3

B. 4^2

C. 4^3

D. 8^2

✔ Remember

The SHSAT rewards you for being able to blend two concepts together. Here, you must use both exponent and radical rules.

Use this number line to help you approximate square roots.

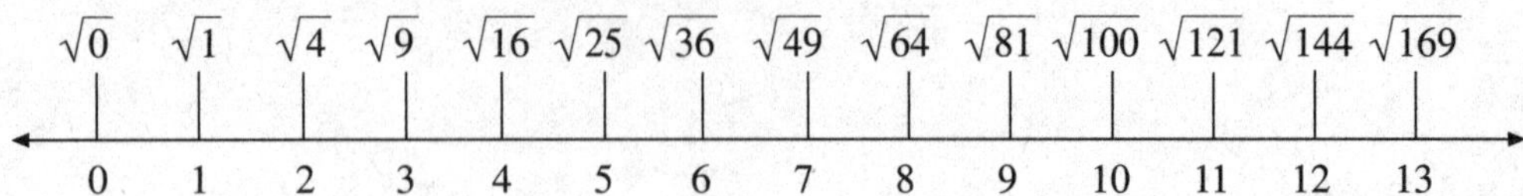

Percents

Percents are one of the most commonly used mathematical relationships and are quite popular on the SHSAT. *Percent* is just another word for *hundredth*. For example, 27% (27 percent) means:

27 hundredths

$\frac{27}{100}$

0.27

27 out of every 100 things

27 parts out of a whole of 100 parts

✔ Note

In percent questions, whether you need to find the part, the whole, or the percent, use the same three-part percent formula: Part = percent × whole.

When you work with a percent in a formula, be sure to convert the percent into decimal form:

Example: What is 12% of 25?

Setup: Part $= 0.12 \times 25$

Example: 15 is 3% of what number?

Setup: $15 = 0.03 \times$ whole

Example: 45 is what percent of 9?

Setup: $45 =$ percent $\times 9$

Here are some other types of questions that may involve percents:

- To **increase a number by a percent**, add the percent to 100%, convert to a decimal, and multiply. For example, to increase 40 by 25%, add 25% to 100%, convert 125% to 1.25, and multiply by 40. The result is $1.25 \times 40 = 50$. To decrease, just subtract the percent from 100%, convert to a decimal, and multiply.

- To calculate a **percent increase** (or decrease), use the formula:

$$\text{Percent change} = \frac{\text{amount of change}}{\text{original amount}} \times 100\%$$

- When there are **multiple percent increases** and/or decreases, and the question asks for the combined percent increase or decrease, the easiest and most effective strategy is to pick 100 for the original value and see what happens.

Example: A price went up 10% one year, and the new price went up 20% the next year. What was the combined percent increase over the two-year period?

Setup: First year: $100 + (10\% \text{ of } 100) = 110$. Second year: $110 + (20\% \text{ of } 110) = 132$. That's a combined 32% increase.

- To find the **original whole before a percent increase or decrease**, set up an equation with a variable in place of the original number. Suppose you have a 15% increase over an unknown original amount, say *x*. You would follow the same steps as always: 100% plus 15% is 115%, which is 1.15 when converted to a decimal. Then multiply by the number, which in this case is *x*, and you get $1.15x$. Finally, set that equal to the new amount.

Example: After a 5% increase, the population was 59,346. What was the population *before* the increase?

Setup: $1.05x = 59{,}346 \rightarrow x = 56{,}520$

✔ Remember

Questions may ask for part, whole, or percent. No matter which of them the question asks for, the question will give you the other two pieces of information you need to find the missing one.

A. Regina wants to donate 15% of her paycheck to charity. If she receives a paycheck of $300, how much money will she donate?

____

____

B. Andrew has a coupon for 20% off of the price of any CD. If he purchases a CD originally priced at $16, what will the discounted price be?

Solve the above problem by using decimals.

____

____

8. In a certain class, 35 out of 50 students are female. What percentage of the students are not female?

   E. $\frac{3}{10}\%$
   F. 15%
   G. 30%
   H. 70%

9. How much greater is 70% of 5 than 5% of 70?

   A. 0
   B. 3.5
   C. 7
   D. 31.4

10. Julie buys a sweater that is on sale for 20% less than the original price. If she pays $40, what was the original price?

   E. $30
   F. $45
   G. $48
   H. $50

✔ Remember

For any percent problem, you can use the formula, set up two proportions, or use decimals. On Test Day, use the method with which you are most comfortable.

Mean, Median, and Mode

Suppose you took five quizzes in an algebra class and earned scores of 85, 92, 85, 80, and 96. Descriptions of three fundamental statistical measures you can find for this data set follow:

- **Mean (also called average):** The sum of the values divided by the number of values. For your algebra class, the mean of your quiz scores is

$$\frac{85+92+85+80+96}{5}=\frac{438}{5}=87.6.$$

- **Median:** The value that is in the middle of the set *when the values are arranged in order (ascending or descending).* The test scores in ascending order are 80, 85, 85, 92, and 96, making the median 85. Be careful: The SHSAT could give you a set of numbers that is not in order. Make sure you properly arrange them before determining the median.
- **Mode:** The value that occurs most frequently. The score that appears more than any other is 85 (twice vs. once), so it is the mode. If more than one value appears the most often, that's okay: A set of data can have multiple modes.

✔ Note

To find the median of a data set that contains an even number of terms, arrange the terms in ascending order, then find the average of the two middle terms.

✔ Remember

The SHSAT won't ask you for these definitions, but you will be expected to know them.

As with percent, if you have two components of the average formula, you can find the missing piece.

A. Juan went to the bookstore 3 times. The first time, he bought 3 books. On both of the other trips, he bought 6 books. What is the average number of books he bought per trip?

____

B. Alyssa has an average of 90 in English class after taking 4 tests. What is the sum of her scores?

____

C. Muriel makes an average of $30 a day babysitting. If she made $270 in one month, how many days did she work?

____

11. There are 5 children whose ages are 11, 5, 8, 5, and 6. What is the average age of the children?

A. 5
B. 6
C. 7
D. 8

12. A certain item is available in 7 stores. Three stores sell it for $20, 2 stores sell it for $15, one store sells it for $13, and one store sells it for $16. What is the average (or mean) of the median and mode price?

E. $16
F. $17
G. $18
H. $20

13. After taking 9 tests, Carol's average grade in her Italian class is 90. Her teacher drops the lowest of the 9 test scores to determine the final grade. If Carol's final grade is 91, what was her lowest test score?

    A. 70

    B. 77

    C. 82

    D. 90

> ✔ **Remember**
>
> **Don't be intimidated by complex problems. Break them down into manageable pieces.**

Rates

Rate Formula: $\text{Rate} = \dfrac{\text{Distance}}{\text{Time}}$

Of course, this formula can be modified to $\text{Rate} = \dfrac{\text{Dollars}}{\text{Hour}}$ or $\text{Rate} = \dfrac{\text{Pages}}{\text{Minute}}$, as needed.

Speed is a measure of distance/time, such as miles per hour or meters per second.

When two objects are moving, their average speed is the total distance traveled divided by the total time.

> ✔ **Remember**
>
> **As you saw with percent and average, if you have two components of the formula, you can find the third.**

A. Regina drove 325 miles in 5 hours. What was her average speed?

____

B. Bob produces 70 widgets every hour. If he worked 3.5 hours, how many widgets did he make?

____

C. A grocery store has salmon on sale for $5.50 per pound. If Andres spent $13.75 on salmon, how many pounds did he buy?

____

D. A car travels at 20 mph for 1 hour, then at 40 mph for 2 hours. What is the average speed for the entire trip?

____

14. If Jordan took 3 hours to bike 48 miles, what was his average speed in miles per hour?

E. 3

F. 8

G. 16

H. 48

15. If Henry traveled 225 miles at 45 miles per hour, how many hours did his trip take him?

A. 3

B. $4\frac{1}{2}$

C. 4

D. 5

16. Last week, Jennifer babysat on 4 different days for the Fosters. She babysat for $3\frac{1}{2}$ hours each day. If her total pay for the week was $77.00, how much was she paid per hour?

E. $4.75

F. $5.50

G. $6.20

H. $22.00

✔ Remember

The SHSAT rewards you for being able to manipulate a formula. Be flexible on Test Day!

Ratios and Proportions

A **ratio** expresses the **relationship** between two numbers.

A **ratio** is a comparison of one quantity to another. In a ratio of two numbers, the numerator is often associated with the word *of*, and the denominator with the word *to*. For example, the ratio *of* 3 *to* 4 is $\frac{of\ 3}{to\ 4} = \frac{3}{4}$.

A **part-to-part ratio** can be turned into two **part-to-whole ratios** by putting each number in the original ratio over the sum of the parts. If the ratio of males to females is 1 to 2, then the males-to-people ratio is $\frac{1}{1+2} = \frac{1}{3}$ and the females-to-people ratio is $\frac{2}{1+2} = \frac{2}{3}$. This is the same as saying $\frac{1}{3}$ of all the people are male and $\frac{2}{3}$ are female.

A **proportion** is two ratios set equal to each other. Proportions are an efficient way to solve certain problems, but you must exercise caution when setting them up. Watching the units of each piece of the proportion will help you with this. To solve a proportion, cross multiply:

$$\frac{x}{5} = \frac{3}{4}$$

$$4x = 5(3)$$

$$x = \frac{15}{4} = 3.75$$

✔ Remember

Ratios get reduced to the simplest form the same way that fractions do. In fact, fractions are really part-to-whole ratios.

17. $\frac{36}{x} = \frac{9}{y}$. If $x = 8$, what is the value of y?

A. 2

B. 4

C. 8

D. 32

18. There are 60 people in a movie theater. If 36 of those people have seen the movie before, what is the ratio of people who haven't seen the movie before to those who have?

E. 2:5

F. 2:3

G. 3:5

H. 3:2

19. Kate began a novel on Monday and read $\frac{1}{4}$ of it. If she read an additional $\frac{1}{6}$ of the novel on Tuesday, what is the ratio of the amount of the novel she has read to the amount of the novel she has not read?

A. 1:6

B. 1:4

C. 5:12

D. 5:7

✔ Remember

On Test Day, a question may ask for a part-to-part, part-to-whole, or whole-to-part ratio. Pay careful attention to exactly what the question is asking for.

If you are given a proportion with one missing value, you can cross multiply to solve it.

Probability

Probability measures the likelihood of an event taking place. It can be expressed as a fraction ("The probability of snow tomorrow is $\frac{1}{2}$"), a decimal ("There is a 0.5 chance of snow tomorrow"), or a percent ("The probability of snow tomorrow is 50%").

To compute a probability, divide the number of desired outcomes by the number of possible outcomes.

$$\text{Probability} = \frac{\text{number of desired outcomes}}{\text{number of possible outcomes}}$$

Example: If you have 12 shirts in a drawer and 9 of them are white, what is the probability of picking a white shirt at random?

Setup: When picking a shirt in this situation, there are 12 possible outcomes, 1 for each shirt. Of these 12, 9 of them are white, so there are 9 desired outcomes. Therefore, the probability of picking a white shirt at random is $\frac{9}{12} = \frac{3}{4}$. The probability can also be expressed as 0.75 or 75%.

A **probability of 0** means that the event has no chance of happening. A **probability of 1** means that the event will always happen.

Thus, probability is just another ratio, specifically a part-to-whole ratio. How many parts desired? How many total parts? Finding the probability that something *won't* happen is simply a matter of taking the other piece of the pie.

If the probability of picking a white shirt is $\frac{3}{4}$, the probability of not picking a white shirt is $\frac{1}{4}$, or 1 minus the probability that it will happen. These two events are called **complementary events.**

To find the probability that **two separate events** will both occur, *multiply* the probabilities.

A. There are 24 marbles in a bag: 6 green, 8 red, and 10 white. If one marble is chosen at random, what is the probability that it will be green?

____

What is the probability that it will **not** be red?

____

B. Express the probabilities in the above questions as decimals.

Will be green: ____________________

Will **not** be red: ____________________

C. The probability that a single cookie taken from a jar will be chocolate chip is $\frac{1}{5}$. If there are 6 chocolate chip cookies in the jar, how many are **not** chocolate chip?

✓ Remember

Probability can also be expressed as a fraction or a decimal. Convert probability fractions and decimals as you would any other fractions and decimals.

20. In a drawer, there are 6 white socks, 5 blue socks, and 4 black socks. If one sock is pulled out at random, what is the probability that it will not be white?

E. $\frac{4}{15}$

F. $\frac{1}{3}$

G. $\frac{2}{5}$

H. $\frac{3}{5}$

21. There are 9 blue marbles, 4 black marbles, 5 white marbles, and 6 red marbles in a box. Six marbles are drawn at random. If the probability of drawing a blue marble is now $\frac{1}{3}$, how many of the 6 marbles removed were blue?

A. 0

B. 1

C. 3

D. 6

✓ Remember

Probability falls between 0 and 1, inclusive. Something with a probability of 0 will *never* happen, and something with a probability of 1 will *always* happen.

Combinations

Combination questions ask "how many ways" might elements of a set be arranged or "how many arrangements" are possible.

A. Amy has brought 3 shirts and 4 pairs of pants on vacation. Assuming that an outfit consists of one shirt and one pair of pants, how many different outfits are possible?

____

B. Miguel has 4 cans of soda and 6 pieces of fruit. He plans to make himself a snack consisting of one can of soda and one piece of fruit. How many snack possibilities does he have?

____

The previous two problems deal with combinations of multiple objects. But the SHSAT is also known to test combinations of a single type of object.

C. Anita owns 4 different books and will place one book on her top shelf and one book on her bottom shelf. How many different arrangements are possible?

____

> **✓ Remember**
>
> **If the same object cannot be used twice, there are fewer possibilities for the second item than there are for the first.**

22. A scientist is trying to breed plants. He has 5 of plant *A* and 6 of plant *B*. If he breeds only combinations of *A* and *B*, how many different breeding pairs are possible?

E. 5

F. 6

G. 10

H. 30

23. Jennifer has 9 cookie cutters but only enough dough left for 2 cookies. How many different arrangements of cookies are possible, assuming she uses each cookie cutter no more than once?

A. 2

B. 9

C. 72

D. 81

> **✓ Remember**
>
> **On the SHSAT, there's almost always at least one alternative, more efficient approach to any Math question.**

The following practice sets provide an opportunity to apply the concepts and strategic thinking covered in this chapter. To practice Test Day timing, follow the suggested timing guidelines for each section.

ARITHMETIC I PRACTICE SET

Suggested Timing: 15 minutes

1. $\frac{3\times7\times1}{3\times1\times2}=$

   A. $\frac{2}{7}$

   B. $\frac{3}{5}$

   C. $3\frac{1}{2}$

   D. $7\frac{1}{2}$

2. Which of the following is a multiple of 3?

   E. 121

   F. 385

   G. 468

   H. 589

3. $\frac{7}{8}\div3\frac{1}{2}=$

   A. $\frac{2}{24}$

   B. $\frac{1}{4}$

   C. $1\frac{1}{48}$

   D. $3\frac{1}{16}$

4. Which of the following is a multiple of both 6 and 8?

   E. 18

   F. 32

   G. 48

   H. 64

5. Express the sum of $\frac{1}{8}$ and $\frac{2}{5}$ in decimal form.

   A. 0.4125

   B. 0.525

   C. 4.125

   D. 5.25

6. If the value of $\frac{154}{361}$ is estimated by rounding the numerator to the nearest 10 and the denominator to the nearest 100, what is the result?

   E. $\frac{3}{8}$

   F. $\frac{2}{5}$

   G. $\frac{5}{12}$

   H. $\frac{1}{2}$

7. Lydia is filling soda machines with soda. Each machine should get 25 cans. If she has 140 sodas and fills all but the last machine to capacity, how many sodas will go into the last machine?

   A. 5

   B. 10

   C. 15

   D. 25

8. What is the least common multiple of 8 and 9?

   E. 16

   F. 17

   G. 18

   H. 72

9. What is the greatest common factor of:

$2 \cdot 2 \cdot 2 \cdot 2 \cdot 3 \cdot 3 \cdot 5$

$2 \cdot 2 \cdot 3 \cdot 3 \cdot 3 \cdot 7$

A. 2

B. $2 \cdot 3$

C. $2 \cdot 2 \cdot 3 \cdot 3$

D. $2 \cdot 3 \cdot 5 \cdot 7$

10. 5.5555×10^5 is equal to which of the following numbers?

E. 55,555

F. $55{,}555 \times 100$

G. 555×55

H. 555,550

ARITHMETIC II PRACTICE SET

Suggested Timing: 15 minutes

1. $-2^3(1-2)^3+(-2)^3=$

   A. -12

   B. -4

   C. 0

   D. 4

2. $\sqrt{49}-\sqrt{16}=$

   E. $\sqrt{33}$

   F. $\sqrt{3}$

   G. 3

   H. 9

3. If 35 percent of x is 7, what is x percent of 35?

   A. $1\frac{3}{4}$

   B. $3\frac{1}{2}$

   C. 5

   D. 7

4. A museum records 16 visitors to an exhibit on Monday, 21 on Tuesday, 20 on Wednesday, 17 on Thursday, 19 on Friday, 21 on Saturday, and 17 on Sunday. What is the median number of visitors for the week?

   E. 18.5

   F. 18.75

   G. 19

   H. 19.5

5. If Matthew scored an average of 15 points per basketball game and played 24 games in one season, how many points did he score in the season?

   A. 15

   B. 180

   C. 240

   D. 360

6. Adam runs for 10 minutes at 30 miles per hour. How far does he run?

   E. $\frac{1}{30}$ mile

   F. $\frac{1}{3}$ mile

   G. 5 miles

   H. 300 miles

7. A bag contains 8 white, 4 red, 7 green, and 5 blue marbles. Eight marbles are withdrawn randomly. How many of the withdrawn marbles were white if the chance of withdrawing a white marble is now $\frac{1}{4}$?

   A. 0

   B. 3

   C. 4

   D. 6

8. A motorist travels 90 miles at a rate of 20 miles per hour. If he returns the same distance at a rate of 40 miles per hour, what is the average speed for the entire trip, in miles per hour?

E. 20

F. $\frac{65}{3}$

G. $\frac{80}{3}$

H. 30

9. A car travels 60 kilometers in one hour before a piston breaks, then travels at 30 kilometers per hour for the remaining 60 kilometers to its destination. What is its average speed in kilometers per hour for the entire trip?

A. 20

B. 40

C. 45

D. 50

10. When $x = 2$, which is the value of $(|x^2 - 2x| - 3)^2 - 4x$?

E. 1

F. 5

G. 9

H. 17

ARITHMETIC GRID-IN PRACTICE SET

Suggested Timing: 15 minutes

1. $(6 \div 2 + 3)^2 + (6 \times 2 - 3) = ?$

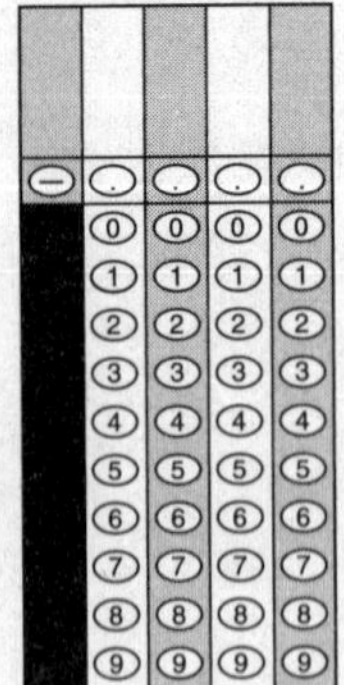

2. $\frac{5}{6} - \frac{4}{9} = ?$

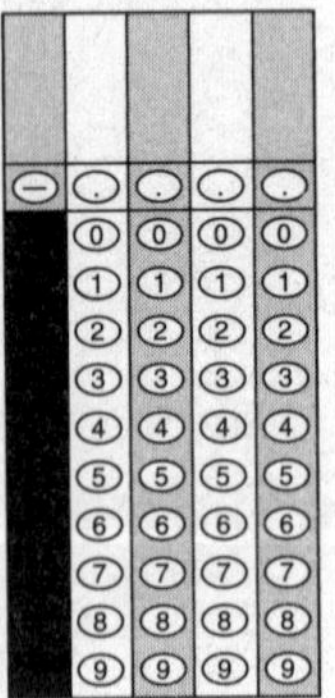

3. What is the remainder when 215 is divided by 18?

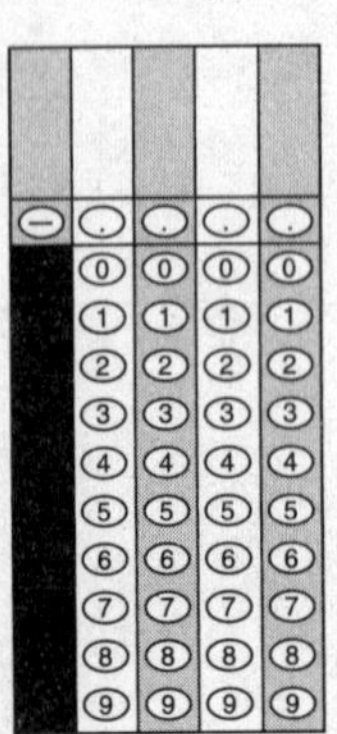

4. What number is halfway between 33 and 111?

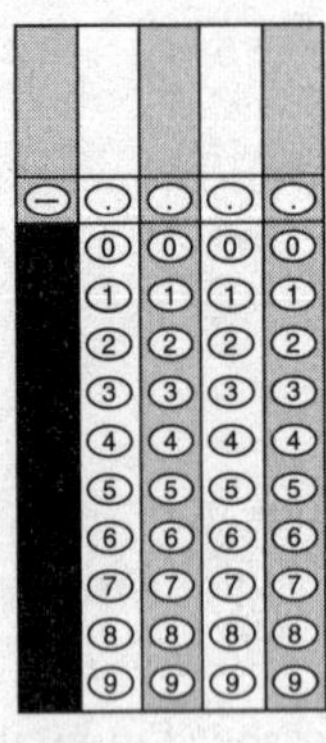

5. $\frac{1}{5} \times \frac{3}{12} = ?$

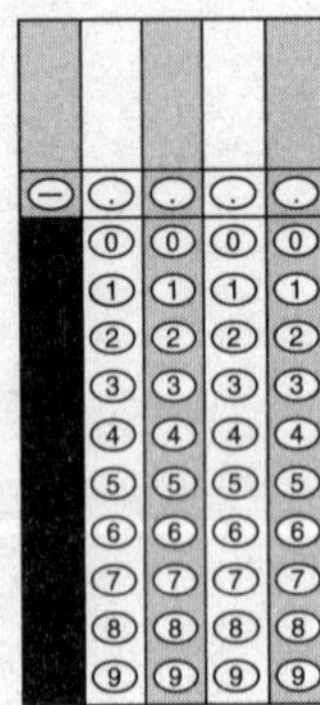

6. $5^{-2} = ?$

7. $\frac{1}{2} \times 2\frac{1}{2} = ?$

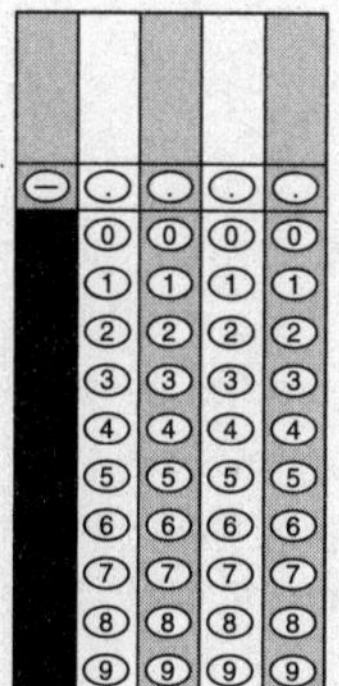

8. $4\left(\frac{1}{2}\right)^4 = ?$

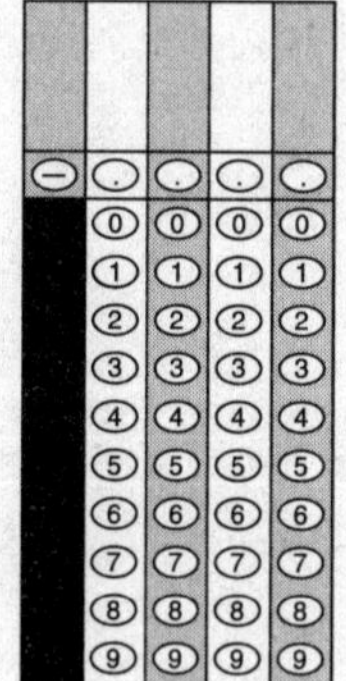

9. $2.7 \div 0.3 = ?$

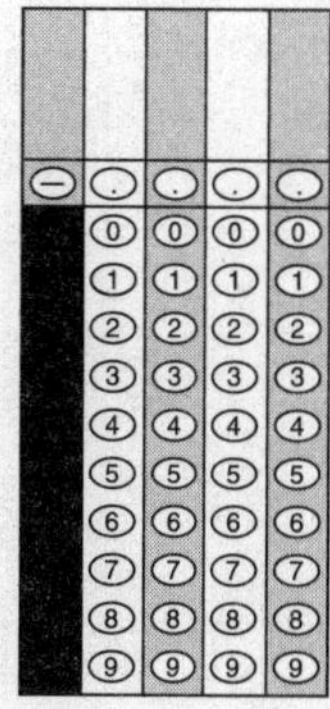

10. $\frac{3}{5} + 4\frac{1}{2} = ?$

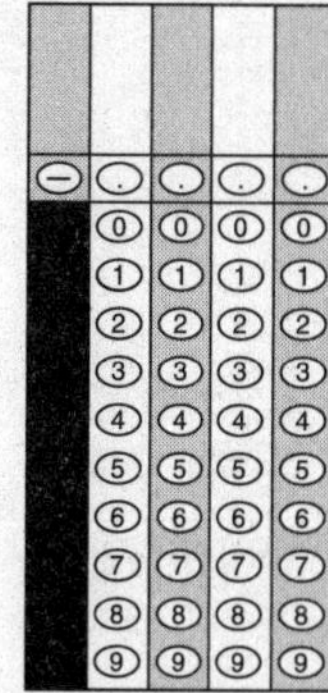

ANSWERS AND EXPLANATIONS

Arithmetic I

Fraction Operations

A. $\frac{39}{72}=\frac{3\times13}{3\times24}=\frac{13}{24}$

B. $\frac{1}{4}\div\frac{1}{3}=\frac{1}{4}\times\frac{3}{1}=\frac{3}{4}$

C. $\frac{1}{3}\times\frac{2}{5}=\frac{2}{15}$

D. $\frac{5}{9}+\frac{2}{6}=\frac{10}{18}+\frac{6}{18}=\frac{16}{18}=\frac{8}{9}$

E. $\frac{1}{2}-\frac{3}{7}=\frac{7}{14}-\frac{6}{14}=\frac{1}{14}$

1. B

Subject: Arithmetic

Getting to the Answer: Follow PEMDAS:

$\frac{1}{2}\left(\frac{3}{5}-\frac{3}{10}\right)\div\frac{2}{3}=$ Find a common denominator.

$\frac{1}{2}\left(\frac{6}{10}-\frac{3}{10}\right)\div\frac{2}{3}=$ Subtract the fractions inside the parentheses.

$\frac{1}{2}\left(\frac{3}{10}\right)\div\frac{2}{3}=$ Multiply the first two fractions.

$\frac{3}{20}\times\frac{3}{2}=\frac{9}{40}$ Take the reciprocal and multiply.

2. G

Subject: Arithmetic

Getting to the Answer: To find the correct answer, you must find the choice that fits the divisibility rules.

(E) $1+1+5=7$, which is not divisible by 3.

(F) $3+7+0=10$, which is not divisible by 3.

(G) $4+6+5=15$, which is divisible by 3, is the right answer.

3. D

Subject: Arithmetic

Getting to the Answer: You have to find the answer choice that does not fit the criteria for a multiple of 6. If you notice, all the answers are even, and three of the four answers all have the same digits; therefore start with choice **(D)** which has different digits than the others. $2+0+2+4+2=10$, which is not divisible by 3, and therefore cannot be a multiple of 6.

Factors/Multiples

A. Factor

B. Multiple

C. Both a factor and multiple

4. H

Subject: Arithmetic

Getting to the Answer: First you need to figure out the factors for 21: 1 and 21 and 3 and 7; that's it. $1+3+7+21=32$.

5. B

Subject: Arithmetic

Getting to the Answer: Start with the largest answer choice and work your way down.

(D) This is a factor of 180, but not of 48.

(C) This is a factor of 48, but not of 180.

(B) This is a factor of both and therefore the answer.

6. G

Subject: Arithmetic

Getting to the Answer: In this case, begin with the smallest number and work your way higher.

(E) This is a multiple of 32, but not of 12.

(F) This is a multiple of 12, but not of 32.

(G) This is a multiple of both numbers and therefore your answer.

Greatest Common Factor with Prime Factorization

A. 2, 2, 5

B. 20

C. No

Least Common Multiple with Prime Factorization

A. 2, 3, 5, 7

B. $2^4 \times 3 \times 5 \times 7^2$

7. C

Subject: Arithmetic

Getting to the Answer: The question gives you the factors already. You need to raise each factor to the highest power with which it appears:

$2 \times 2 \times 2 \times 3 \times 3 \times 5 \times 5 \times 7 \times 7$

Decimals, Fractions, and Percents

	Fraction	Decimal	Percent
A.	$\frac{1}{4}$	.25	25%
B.	$\frac{1}{6}$	$.1\overline{6}$	$16.\overline{6}\%$
C.	$\frac{99}{100}$	.99	99%
D.	$\frac{7}{20}$	0.35	35%

8. G

Subject: Arithmetic

Getting to the Answer: Change the fractions to decimals and add:

$\frac{1}{5} = 0.20$ and $\frac{3}{4} = 0.75$

$0.20 + 0.75 = 0.95$

Rounding

9. B

Subject: Arithmetic

Getting to the Answer: For 357.428, the number to the right of the digit in the tenths position is a 2, so we must round down to 357.4.

Remainder, Quotient, and Divisor

A. Divisor = 8

B. Quotient = 7

C. Remainder = 4

D. What is the remainder?

E. Quotient, which is 5 boxes

F. Quotient + 1, which is 6 boxes

10. G

Subject: Arithmetic

Getting to the Answer: There are 218 people in total and 15 people in each row:

$218 \div 15 = 14$ remainder 8. Therefore, 14 rows are completely filled, and 8 people are in the unfilled row.

11. D

Subject: Arithmetic

Getting to the Answer: There are 587 people who are going to be on the buses, with each bus seating 48 people:

$587 \div 48 = 12$ remainder 11. Therefore, 12 buses are completely filled and 11 people are on the unfilled bus.

Scientific Notation

A. 203.8

B. 0.000186

C. 10,000

12. F

Subject: Arithmetic

Getting to the Answer: The exponent tells you to move the decimal that many places to the right: 5.3079 moved 3 places ⇒ 5,307.9.

13. D

Subject: Arithmetic

Getting to the Answer:

$$8.34 \times 10^3 = 8{,}340 = 83{,}400 \times 0.10$$

Absolute Value

A. 3

B. 3

14. G

Subject: Arithmetic

Getting to the Answer: Keep in mind what the absolute value symbol affects:

$|9| + |-3| - |-4| = 9 + 3 - 4 = 8$

15. A

Subject: Arithmetic

Getting to the Answer:

$$|2x^2| + 4x - (3 + |-2x|) =$$
$$|2 \times (-2)^2| + 4(-2) - (3 + |-2 \times -2|)$$
$$= |2 \times 4| - 8 - 7$$
$$= 8 - 8 - 7$$
$$= -7$$

ANSWERS AND EXPLANATIONS

Arithmetic II

Exponents

A. $3^2 = 3 \times 3 = 9$

B. $2^4 = 2 \times 2 \times 2 \times 2 = 16$

C. $3^2 \times 3 = 3 \times 3 \times 3 = 27$

D. $(-3)^2 = -3 \times -3 = 9$

E. $\frac{3^2}{3} = \frac{3 \times 3}{3} = 3$

F. $(2^2)^2 = (2 \times 2) \times (2 \times 2) = 16$

G. $\left(\frac{4}{5}\right)^2 = \frac{4}{5} \times \frac{4}{5} = \frac{16}{25}$

H. $(-3)^3 = (-3)(-3)(-3) = -27$

1. D

Subject: Exponents

Getting to the Answer: Plug in the given value and solve.

$2^5 - 5^2 = 32 - 25 = 7$

2. G

Subject: Exponents

Getting to the Answer: Remember, a negative raised to an odd power will always be negative.

$(-1)^3 \times (-1)^3 + (-1)^7 =$	Following PEMDAS, work out the exponents.
$(-1) \times (-1) + (-1) =$	Then do the multiplication operation.
$1 + (-1) = 0$	Then do the addition.

3. B

Subject: Exponents

Getting to the Answer: To multiply exponents with the same base, simply add the exponents and keep the same base.

$2^5 \times 2^2 = 2^7$

4. G

Subject: Exponents

Getting to the Answer: If x is between 6 and 7, then x^2 must be between the squares of 6 and 7.

$6 < x < 7$

$6^2 < x^2 < 7^2$

$36 < x^2 < 49$

So x^2 is greater than 36 but less than 49. **(G)**, 41, is your answer.

Radicals

A. $\sqrt{2} + 4\sqrt{2} = 5\sqrt{2}$

B. $\sqrt{2} + 4\sqrt{3}$ cannot be combined into one term

C. $\sqrt{20} = \sqrt{4 \times 5} = \sqrt{4}\sqrt{5} = 2\sqrt{5}$

D. $2\sqrt{3} \times 3\sqrt{5} = 6\sqrt{15}$

E. $\sqrt{\frac{9}{4}} = \frac{\sqrt{9}}{\sqrt{4}} = \frac{3}{2}$

F. $\frac{4\sqrt{6}}{2\sqrt{3}} = 2\frac{\sqrt{6}}{\sqrt{3}} = 2\sqrt{\frac{6}{3}} = 2\sqrt{2}$

5. A

Subject: Radicals

Getting to the Answer: Work out the radicals first, then simplify the resulting fraction.

$\frac{\sqrt{81}}{\sqrt{36}} = \frac{9}{6} = 1\frac{1}{2}$

6. G

Subject: Radicals

Getting to the Answer: Because 41 falls between 36 and 49, the square root of 41 must be between the square roots of 36 and 49, so set up an inequality, multiplying each part by 3 like the question stem.

$\left(3\sqrt{36}\right) < \left(3\sqrt{41}\right) < \left(3\sqrt{49}\right)$

$18 < 3\sqrt{41} < 21$

7. A

Subject: Radicals

Getting to the Answer: Undo the radical, then find the equivalent exponent in the answer choices.

$\sqrt{64} = 8 = 2 \times 2 \times 2 = 2^3$

Percents

A. $\$300 \times 15\% = \$300 \times 0.15 = \$45$

B. $\$16 - \$16(.20) = \$16 - \$3.20 = \$12.80$

8. G

Subject: Percent

Getting to the Answer: Find the number who are not female:

50 total − 35 female = 15 not female

Compare that to the total to calculate percent:

$\frac{15}{50} = 30\%$

9. A

Subject: Percent

Getting to the Answer:

70% of 5 = 0.70(5) = 3.5

5% of 70 = 0.05(70) = 3.5

The two percentages are equal!

10. H

Subject: Percent

Getting to the Answer:

P = Original Price

$P - 20\%P = 40$	Translate the situation in the question stem into an equation.
$P - 0.2P = 40$	Convert the percentage to a decimal.
$0.8P = 40$	Combine like terms.
$P = 50$	Divide both sides by 0.8 to solve for P.

Mean, Median, and Mode

A. $\frac{\text{sum of terms}}{\text{number of terms}} = \frac{3+6+6}{3} = \frac{15}{3} = 5$

B. sum = (# of terms)(average) = $4 \times 90 = 360$

C. # of days = $\frac{\text{total earnings}}{\text{average earnings}} = \frac{\$270}{\$30} = 9$

11. C

Subject: Average

Getting to the Answer:

$\frac{\text{Sum of the Ages}}{\text{Number of Children}} = \text{Average Age}$

$\frac{11+5+8+5+6}{5} = \frac{35}{5} = 7$

12. G

Subject: Average

Getting to the Answer: The question asks for the average of the median and mode prices. The median price is the one in the middle of the list when the prices from each of the 7 stores are listed in order: $16. The mode is the price that occurs most frequently: $20.

Find the average (mean) of these two numbers.

$\text{Average} = \frac{\$16+\$20}{2} = \frac{\$36}{2} = \$18$

13. C

Subject: Average

Getting to the Answer: Plug the information you have for each scenario into the different averages equations and solve for the sum of test scores for each scenario. The difference between the two test score sums will be the lowest test score that was dropped.

$\frac{\text{Sum of 9}}{\text{9 tests}} = 90$	Multiply each side by 9.
Sum of 9 = 810	
$\frac{\text{Sum of 8}}{\text{8 tests}} = 91$	Multiply each side by 8.
Sum of 8 = 728	

810 − 728 = 82

Rates

A. $r = \frac{d}{t} = \frac{325}{5} = 65$ mph

B. # of widgets = (rate)(time) = $70 \times 3.5 = 245$ widgets

C. # of pounds = $\frac{\text{total price}}{\text{price per pound}} \frac{\$13.75}{\$5.50} = 2.5$ pounds

D. $\frac{\text{total number of miles}}{\text{total number of hours}} = \frac{20+40+40}{3} = \frac{100}{3} = 33.\bar{3}$ mph

14. G

Subject: Rates

Getting to the Answer: The rate you are looking for is miles per hour, so use the information you have about distance (miles) and time (hours) to set up this ratio.

$\frac{\text{48 miles}}{\text{3 hours}}$ or 16 miles per hour

15. D

Subject: Rates

Getting to the Answer:

Rate $= \frac{\text{Distance}}{\text{Time}}$	Rearrange the equation so that time is on its own.
Time $= \frac{\text{Distance}}{\text{Rate}}$	Plug in the given values for distance and rate.
Time $= \frac{\text{225 miles}}{\text{45 miles per hour}}$	Solve for time.
Time = 5 hours	

16. F

Subject: Rates

Getting to the Answer:

Rate $= \frac{\text{Total Pay}}{\text{Total Hours}}$

Rate $= \frac{\$77}{4 \times 3\frac{1}{2}\text{ Hours}} = \frac{\$77}{\text{14 Hours}}$

Rate = \$5.50/hour

Ratios and Proportions

17. A

Subject: Ratios and Proportions

Getting to the Answer: Plug in the given value for *x*.

$\frac{36}{8} = \frac{9}{y}$	
$36y = 72$	Cross multiply.
$y = 2$	Divide both sides by 36 to solve for *y*.

18. F

Subject: Ratios and Proportions

Getting to the Answer: The question asks for a ratio that compares the number of people who have not seen the movie to the number of people who have seen it.

60 total − 36 who have seen = 24 who have not seen

Have Not/Have = 24:36 or 2:3

19. D

Subject: Ratios and Proportions

Getting to the Answer:

$\frac{1}{4}+\frac{1}{6}=\frac{3}{12}+\frac{2}{12}=\frac{5}{12}$	Calculate how much of the book Kate has read—5 parts.
$1-\frac{5}{12}=\frac{7}{12}$	Calculate the amount of the book she has not read—7 parts.
Read:Unread = 5:7	Compare parts read to parts unread in a ratio.

Probability

A. The probability of picking a green marble is $\frac{6}{24} = \frac{1}{4}$. There are 8 red out of 24 total marbles, so 16 are not red. The probability of picking a marble that is not red is $\frac{16}{24} = \frac{2}{3}$.

B. Probability that it is green = 0.25

Probability that it is not red = 0.67

C. $\frac{1}{5}$ of the cookies are chocolate chip. 6 is $\frac{1}{5}$ of 30, so there must be 30 total cookies and, therefore, 24 are not chocolate chip.

20. H

Subject: Probability

Getting to the Answer: The non-white socks are all of the blue and black socks, so there are nine socks that are not white out of a total of 15 socks.

Probability $= \frac{9}{15} = \frac{3}{5}$

21. C

Subject: Probability

Getting to the Answer: If six marbles are removed, then 18 are left in the bag. Because you know that the probability of pulling out a blue marble is now $\frac{1}{3}$, set up a proportion with remaining blue marbles as an unknown, and then solve for the blue marbles.

$24 - 6 = 18$	Marbles remaining.
$\frac{x}{18} = \frac{1}{3}$	Let $x =$ remaining blue marbles.
$3x = 18$	Cross multiply.
$x = 6$	Divide both sides by 3 to solve for number of blue marbles remaining.
$9 - 6 = 3$	Subtract remaining blue from original blue to find number of blue removed.

Combinations

A. For each of the 3 shirts, 4 pairs of pants are possible. That makes 12 total combinations (the product of 3 and 4).

B. For each of the 4 cans of soda, 6 pieces of fruit are possible. That makes 24 total combinations (the product of 4 and 6).

C. For the first shelf there are 4 books available, and for the second shelf there are 3 books available; $4 \times 3 = 12$ arrangements.

22. H

Subject: Combinations

Getting to the Answer: Each *A* plant has six possible *B* plants to breed with. There are five *A* plants, each with six breeding options, so the total number of possible pair combinations is $5 \times 6 = 30$.

23. C

Subject: Combinations

Getting to the Answer: For each of the 9 cookie cutters you could make the first cookie with, you have eight others left to make the second cookie with. So the total number of cookie arrangements possible is $9 \times 8 = 72$.

ANSWERS AND EXPLANATIONS

Arithmetic I Practice Set

1. C

Subject: Arithmetic

Getting to the Answer: Multiply and reduce:

$$\frac{3\times7\times1}{3\times1\times2}=\frac{21}{6}=\frac{7}{2}=3\frac{1}{2}$$

2. G

Subject: Arithmetic

Getting to the Answer: Go down the list and add up the digits of each answer choice. Whichever sum is divisible by three is the answer.

(E) $1+2+1=5$, which is not divisible by 3.

(F) $3+8+5=16$, which is not divisible by 3.

(G) $4+6+8=18$, which is divisible by 3 and is the right answer.

3. B

Subject: Arithmetic

Getting to the Answer:

$\frac{7}{8}\div3\frac{1}{2}=$

$\frac{7}{8}\div\frac{7}{2}=$ Convert the mixed number to an improper fraction.

$\frac{7}{8}\times\frac{2}{7}=\frac{14}{56}=\frac{1}{4}$ To divide fractions, multiply by the reciprocal of the divisor.

4. G

Subject: Arithmetic

Getting to the Answer: A number is a multiple of 6 if it is even and the sum of its digits is a multiple of 3. Use this rule to narrow down your choices to multiples of 6: **(E)** and **(G)**. Only **(G)** is also a multiple of 8.

5. B

Subject: Arithmetic

Getting to the Answer: First, add the two fractions.

$$\frac{1}{8}+\frac{2}{5}=\frac{5}{40}+\frac{16}{40}=\frac{21}{40}$$

Before you start dividing 21 by 40 to convert to a decimal, compare the fraction to the answer choices. The sum of the fractions is less than 1, so you can eliminate **(C)** and **(D)**. The sum of the fractions is also slightly more than one-half, so you can eliminate **(A)**, which is less than half. So you've already got the correct answer, **(B)**, without spending valuable time with tough division to convert the fraction to a decimal.

6. E

Subject: Arithmetic

Getting to the Answer: Simply round as instructed and reduce.

$$\frac{154}{361}\rightarrow\frac{150}{400}=\frac{3}{8}$$

7. C

Subject: Algebra

Getting to the Answer: 140 sodas $\div$ 25 = 5 remainder 15

8. H

Subject: Arithmetic

Getting to the Answer: Use Backsolving, starting with **(E)**:

(E) 16 is only divisible by 8.

(F) 17 is prime. It is not divisible by any numbers, other than itself and 1.

(G) 18 is only divisible by 9.

(H) 72 is divisible by 8 and 9. It is their product.

72 is the LCM of 8 and 9.

9. C

Subject: Arithmetic

Getting to the Answer: Compare the factorizations of the two numbers. The GCF will have all the common primes.

$$GCF=2\times2\times3\times3$$

10. H

Subject: Arithmetic

Getting to the Answer: Move the decimal 5 places to the right, which means you have to add a zero.

$$5.5555 \times 10^5 = 555{,}550$$

Arithmetic II Practice Set

1. C

Subject: Exponents

Getting to the Answer:

$-2^3(1-2)^3 + (-2)^3 =$	Do the operations in parentheses first.
$-2^3(-1)^3 + (-2)^3 =$	Then take care of the exponents.
$-8(-1) + (-8) =$	Then multiply.
$8 + (-8) = 0$	Then add.

2. G

Subject: Radicals

Getting to the Answer:

$$\sqrt{49} - \sqrt{16} =$$
$$7 - 4 = 3$$

3. D

Subject: Percentage

Getting to the Answer: First, solve for x:

$$35\% \text{ of } x = 7 \text{ or } .35x = 7$$
$$x = 20$$

$$\text{Then, } x\% \text{ of } 35 =$$
$$.20 \times 35 = 7$$

4. G

Subject: Arithmetic

Getting to the Answer: You need to put the numbers in sequential order and determine which is the middle number:

16 17 17 19 20 21 21

The middle number is 19.

5. D

Subject: Rates

Getting to the Answer:

$$\text{Rate} = \frac{\text{Points}}{\text{Games}}$$

$\text{Points} = \text{Rate} \times \text{Games}$	Rearrange the equation to solve for total points.
$\text{Points} = 15 \times 24$	Plug in the given rate and number of games.
$\text{Points} = 360$	Multiply to solve for total points.

6. G

Subject: Rates

Getting to the Answer: Because your rate is in hours, first convert the time in minutes to hours. Then plug the value in to the rate formula and solve for distance.

$10 \text{ min} \times \frac{1 \text{ hour}}{60 \text{ min}} = \frac{1}{6} \text{ hours}$	Convert minutes to hours.
$\text{Rate} = \frac{\text{Distance}}{\text{Time}}$	
$\text{Distance} = \text{Rate} \times \text{Time}$	Rearrange the equation to solve for distance.
$\text{Distance} = 30 \times \frac{1}{6}$	Plug in the values for rate and time.
$\text{Distance} = \frac{30}{6} = 5 \text{ miles}$	Man, that guy is fast!

7. C

Subject: Probability

Getting to the Answer: If 8 marbles are removed, then 16 are left in the bag. Because you know that the probability of pulling out a white marble is now $\frac{1}{4}$, set up a proportion with remaining white marbles as an unknown, then solve for the remaining white marbles. But you're not done there—subtract the remaining white marbles from the original number of white marbles to determine how many were removed.

$\frac{x}{16} = \frac{1}{4}$	Cross multiply.
$4x = 16$	Divide both sides by 4 to solve for the white marbles remaining.
$x = 4$	Subtract the number left from the original to get the number removed.
$8 - 4 = 4$	

8. G

Subject: Algebra

Getting to the Answer: During the first part of the trip, the motorist traveled at 20 miles per hour for 90 miles. This took him $\frac{90 \text{ miles}}{20 \text{ mph}} = \frac{9}{2}$ hours.

On the way back, he traveled the same distance at 40 miles per hour, so it took him $\frac{90 \text{ miles}}{40 \text{ mph}} = \frac{9}{4}$ hours.

Total distance: 90 miles + 90 miles = 180 miles

Total time: $\frac{9}{2}$ hours $+ \frac{9}{4}$ hours $= \frac{18}{4} + \frac{9}{4} = \frac{27}{4}$ hours

Average speed: $\frac{180 \text{ miles}}{\frac{27}{4} \text{ hours}} = 180 \times \frac{4}{27} = \frac{720}{27} = \frac{80}{3}$ miles per hour, **(G)**. **(H)**, the average of the two speeds, is a trap.

9. B

Subject: Algebra

Getting to the Answer: Before the piston broke, the car took one hour to travel 60 kilometers. Afterwards, it traveled another 60 kilometers at a speed of 30 kilometers per hour, so it took 2 hours to travel the second 60 kilometers.

Total distance: 60 km + 60 km = 120 km

Total time: 1 hr + 2 hr = 3 hr

Average speed: $\frac{120 \text{ km}}{3 \text{ hr}} = \frac{40 \text{ km}}{\text{hr}}$, choice **(B)**. Notice that **(C)** is a trap—it is the average of the two speeds.

10. E

Subject: Arithmetic

Getting to the Answer:

$$\begin{aligned}(|x^2 - 2x| - 3)^2 - 4x &= (|4 - 4| - 3)^2 - 8 \\ &= 9 - 8 \\ &= 1\end{aligned}$$

Arithmetic Grid-In Practice Set

1. 45

Subject: Arithmetic

Getting to the Answer: The order of operations is the key to answering this question. Remember to do operations within parentheses first. Within the parentheses, multiplication and division should be performed before addition and subtraction:

$$(6 \div 2 + 3)^2 + (6 \times 2 - 3)$$
$$(3 + 3)^2 + (12 - 3)$$
$$(6)^2 + 9 = 36 + 9 = 45$$

Grid in 45.

2. .389

Subject: Arithmetic

Getting to the Answer: To add or subtract fractions, you need to have a common denominator. The common denominator of $\frac{5}{6}$ and $\frac{4}{9}$ is 18, so convert both fractions to have denominators of 18, then subtract:

$$\frac{5}{6} - \frac{4}{9}$$
$$\frac{15}{18} - \frac{8}{18} = \frac{7}{18}$$

Grid in the decimal equivalent of 7/18, which is .389.

3. 17

Subject: Arithmetic

Getting to the Answer: Consider the multiples of 18. 18 × 10 = 180, and 18 × 11 = 198. 215 − 198 = 17, so the remainder when 215 is divided by 18 is 17. Grid in 17.

4. 72

Subject: Arithmetic

Getting to the Answer: To find the halfway point between two numbers, simply add the two numbers together and divide by 2. In this questions, 33 + 111 = 144, and 144 divided by 2 is 72. Grid in 72. You can confirm this by checking the distance between 72 and 33 and 111. 72 is 39 away from both numbers.

5. .05

Subject: Arithmetic

Getting to the Answer: To multiply two fractions together, simply multiply across. Before you multiply, see if you can simplify either of the fractions:

$$\frac{3}{12} = \frac{1}{4}$$

$$\frac{1}{5} \times \frac{3}{12} \Rightarrow \frac{1}{5} \times \frac{1}{4} = \frac{1}{20} = .05$$

Grid in .05.

6. .04

Subject: Arithmetic

Getting to the Answer: Remember the definition of a negative exponent to answer this question correctly:

$$5^{-2} \Rightarrow \frac{1}{5^2} = \frac{1}{25} = .04$$

Because you can't grid in a fraction, grid in .04.

7. 1.25

Subject: Arithmetic

Getting to the Answer: Start by converting the mixed number to an improper fraction. From there, multiply across and simplify:

$$\frac{1}{2} \times 2\frac{1}{2} \Rightarrow \frac{1}{2} \times \frac{5}{2} = \frac{5}{4} = 1.25$$

Grid in 1.25.

8. .25

Subject: Arithmetic

Getting to the Answer: Be careful with the order of operations! Apply the exponent to the 1/2 before multiplying:

$$4\left(\frac{1}{2}\right)^4 \Rightarrow 4\left(\frac{1}{16}\right) = \frac{4}{16} = \frac{1}{4}$$

Grid in .25.

9. 9

Subject: Arithmetic

Getting to the Answer: Don't let the decimals distract you! You know that 27 divided by 3 is 9; notice that each number is just divided by 10 (2.7 and .3). Thus 2.7 divided by .3 is 9, so grid in 9.

10. 5.1

Subject: Arithmetic

Getting to the Answer: You may want to find a common denominator to add these fractions, but converting to decimals is probably easier. When converted to fractions, this question becomes .6 + 4.5, which is 5.1.

CHAPTER 15

Algebra

CHAPTER OBJECTIVES

By the end of this chapter, you will be able to:

- Evaluate an algebraic expression
- Solve algebraic equations
- Solve an equation in terms of a specified variable
- Solve inequalities

ALGEBRA I

Evaluate an Algebraic Expression

Evaluating an expression typically involves substituting a given value (or values) for the variables into the expression and then simplifying. For example, the value of $3x + 4y$ when $x = 5$ and $y = -2$ is $3(5) + 4(-2) = 15 - 8 = 7$.

A. If $a = 3$, then $a(5 - a) =$

B. If $a = 3$, then $a(5) - a =$

C. If $b = -7$, then $4 - b =$

D. If $b = 7$, then $4 - b =$

E. When $c = 3$ and $d = 2$, what is the value of $c^d - d^c$?

F. If $n = 4$, then $2\left(\frac{n}{n+1}\right) =$

G. If $x = 2$, then $x(3^x) =$

1. What is the value of $x(y - 2) + xz$, if $x = 2$, $y = 5$, and $z = 7$?

A. 12
B. 20
C. 22
D. 28

2. If $x = \sqrt{3}$, $y = 2$, and $z = \frac{1}{2}$, then $x^2 - 5yz + y^2 =$

E. 1
F. 2
G. 4
H. 12

3. If $a + b = 17$ and $c = 2$, then $ac + bc =$

A. 17
B. 18
C. 34
D. Cannot be determined from the information given.

✓ Remember

You must always follow the order of operations when solving algebraic equations. PEMDAS = Parentheses, Exponents, Multiplication/Division, Addition/Subtraction.

Solve Equations with One Variable

To **solve an equation**, isolate the variable. As long as you do the same thing to both sides of the equation, the equation is still balanced. To solve $5x - 12 = -2x + 9$, first get all the x terms on one side by adding $2x$ to both sides: $7x - 12 = 9$. Then add 12 to both sides: $7x = 21$. Finally, divide both sides by 7 to get $x = 3$.

A. $2x + 4 = 8$
B. $\frac{x}{3} + 1 = 5$
C. $x - 5 = 3x - 10$
D. If $\left(\frac{1}{3}\right) x = 8$, then $\left(\frac{1}{4}\right) x =$
E. For what value of d would the following expression equal an even integer?
$(3d - 7) - (5 - 2d)$

4. If $0.5n + 2 = 3$, what is the value of n?

E. 0.5
F. 1
G. 2
H. 2.5

5. For what value of x is $2x - 13 = 25$ true?

A. 6
B. 6.5
C. 19
D. 38

6. If $q \neq 0$, for what value of p is $p(12q) = 6q$?

E. 0.5
F. 2
G. 4
H. 8

✓ Remember

When manipulating an equation, always perform the same operation on both sides of the equal sign.

Solve Equations with Two Variables

Equations often contain more than one variable. When two variables are present, solve the equation piece by piece. If you are given a value, substitute the value for its variable. Then isolate the remaining variable and solve.

A. What is the value of a in the equation $3a - 6 = b$, if $b = 18$?

B. If $k = \frac{1}{3}$ in the equation $2m + \frac{1}{3}k = \frac{1}{3}k^2$, then $m =$

C. If $\frac{4a+b}{b} = 7$ and $b = 2$, $a =$

D. If x is a positive odd number less than 10, list all of the potential solutions for y in the following equation:
$x^2 + 2x + 1 = y$

x	y

7. What is the value of x in the equation $5x - 7 = y$, if $y = 8$?

A. -1

B. 1

C. 3

D. 33

8. If $\frac{x}{y} = \frac{2}{5}$ and $x = 10$, $y =$

E. 4

F. 10

G. 15

H. 25

9. If $m = 2$ and $2m(2m - 3n) = 34$, what is the value of n?

A. -6

B. $-\frac{3}{2}$

C. -1

D. $\frac{3}{2}$

✔ Remember

Perform only one step at a time. First substitute and simplify the resulting equation, then isolate the remaining variable.

Solve for One Variable in Terms of the Other

Even if you aren't given numerical values to substitute, you can still solve for one variable in an equation in terms of the other variable(s).

A. If $2r + 8s = 24$, then $r =$

B. Solve for c in the equation $b(a - 1) = \frac{bc}{2}$

C. $3x + 2y + 4z = 12$

Solve for each of the variables.

$x =$

$y =$

$z =$

10. If $\frac{(a+b)}{2} = 8$, then $a =$

E. $b + 4$

F. $4 - b$

G. $16 - b$

H. $\frac{16}{b}$

11. If $3(2t + 6) = 12s$, then $t = ?$

A. $2s + 3$

B. $2s - 3$

C. $4s$

D. $3s - 8$

12. If $3(a - 2) = 5m - 6 + 2a$, what is the value of a, in terms of m?

E. $\frac{3m}{2}$

F. 3

G. $5m$

H. $3m - 3$

✔ Remember

When you perform the same operation to both sides of an equation, you are not altering the equation—merely rearranging it.

Consecutive Multiples

To calculate **multiples** of a given number, multiply the number by positive integers. To calculate consecutive multiples, multiply that number by positive integers that increase by 1 each time.

A. List the three smallest multiples of both 6 and 8.

____

B. Four consecutive multiples of 6 yield a sum of 156. What are these multiples?

____

C. Five consecutive multiples of 3 yield a sum that is equal to the product of 7 and 15. What are these multiples?

____

13. Three consecutive multiples of 7 have a sum of 84. What is the greatest of these numbers?

A. 7
B. 21
C. 35
D. 42

14. Three consecutive multiples of 4 have a sum of 60. What is the greatest of these numbers?

E. 8
F. 12
G. 16
H. 24

15. Five consecutive multiples of 11 have a sum of 220. What is the greatest of these numbers?

A. 33
B. 44
C. 55
D. 66

> ✔ **Remember**
>
> **Always set up an equation and write it down rather than trying to work it out in your head.**

ALGEBRA II

Review of Expressions and Equations

PEMDAS:

A. Solve $2(3 + 1)^2 + 5 - 6 \div 3 =$

Substitution:

B. When $x = 2$, $2x + 3 =$

C. When $x = \frac{1}{4}$, $y = \frac{1}{5}$, and $z = \frac{1}{6}$, what is the value of $\frac{x}{15} + \frac{y}{6} + \frac{z}{5}$?

Isolation:

D. What is x when $4x + 3 = 19$?

E. Solve for x in terms of y: $7xy = 3y^2$.

1. If $3x + 7 = 14$, then $x =$

A. -14

B. 0

C. $\frac{7}{3}$

D. 7

2. If $4z - 3 = -19$, then $z =$

E. -16

F. -5

G. -4

H. 4

3. For what value of y is $4(y - 1) = 2(y + 2)$?

A. 0

B. 2

C. 4

D. 6

4. If $5p + 12 = 17 - 4\left(\frac{p}{2} + 1\right)$, what is the value of p?

E. $\frac{1}{7}$

F. $\frac{1}{3}$

G. $\frac{6}{7}$

H. $1\frac{2}{7}$

5. If $-2x + xy = 30$ and $y = 8$, then what is the value of x?

A. $-\frac{15}{4}$

B. $-\frac{15}{16}$

C. 3

D. 5

6. $15 + xy \div 3 = 35$ and $x = 5$. What is the value of y?

E. $-\frac{2}{3}$

F. $5\frac{1}{4}$

G. 12

H. 18

7. If $\frac{2x}{5y} = 6$, what is the value of y, in terms of x?

A. $\frac{x}{15}$

B. $\frac{x}{2}$

C. $\frac{15}{x}$

D. $15x$

8. If $3ab = 6$, what is the value of a in terms of b?

E. 2

F. $\frac{2}{b}$

G. $2b^2$

H. $2b$

9. If $2(a + m) = 5m - 3 + a$, what is the value of a, in terms of m?

A. $\frac{3m}{2}$

B. 3

C. $m - 1$

D. $3m - 3$

✔ Remember

Always perform the same mathematical operation on both sides of an equation.

✔ Remember

Questions that ask for one variable "in terms of" another can also be answered effectively by Picking Numbers for the variables. Always pick numbers that fit the rules, and be sure to check every answer choice.

Symbolism Equations

In symbolism problems, a symbol stands in for an operation or set of operations. To solve these problems, you must focus on substitution and PEMDAS.

If $x \bigstar y = \sqrt{x+y}$,

A. What is $36 \bigstar 64$?

B. What is $43 \bigstar 6$?

C. If $a \bigstar 4 = 5$, what is the value of a?

If $a \varphi b = a - b(a - 2b)$,

D. What is $4 \varphi 3$?

E. What is $3 \varphi 4$?

F. What is $-5 \varphi -2$?

G. What is $x \varphi 3$?

10. $a \blacksquare b = (a \times b) \div 2$. What is $\frac{24}{45} \blacksquare \frac{90}{240}$?

E. $\frac{1}{10}$

F. $\frac{1}{9}$

G. $\frac{1}{5}$

H. $\frac{2}{3}$

11. $a \square b = \frac{3a}{b}$. What is $\frac{14}{32} \square 1\frac{3}{4}$?

A. $\frac{1}{4}$

B. $\frac{1}{3}$

C. $\frac{3}{4}$

D. $\frac{49}{64}$

✔ **Remember**

Haven't seen the symbol before? Don't worry—the question will tell you what it means.

Translated Symbolism

Sometimes a symbol stands for an operation you must translate before you can solve the problem.

Translating from English into Math	
English	**Math**
equals, is, equivalent to, was, will be, has, costs, adds up to, the same as, as much as	=
times, of, multiplied by, product of, twice, double, by	×
divided by, per, out of, each, ratio	÷
plus, added to, and, sum, combined, total, increased by	+
minus, subtracted from, smaller than, less than, fewer, decreased by, difference between	−
a number, how much, how many, what	*x*, *n*, etc.

Use the table above to translate the following statements into mathematical operations:

A. Two less than twice the sum of x and 5.

____

B. Five more than the product of 9 times y.

____

C. Three times the positive difference of 6 and z.

____

D. Solve each of the above statements if $x = 3$, $y = 2$, and $z = 4$.

____

____

____

12. Assume that the notation $(r, s, t) means "Divide the product of *r* and *s* by the sum of *s* and *t*." What is the value of $(8, 3, 1)?

E. 3

F. 4

G. 6

H. 24

13. The notation ##(a, b, c) produces a number that is a less than the product of b and c raised to the a power. When ##(2, 5, x) = 23, what is the value of x?

A. 0

B. $\frac{1}{2}$

C. 1

D. 5

✓ Remember

Set up the equation before you plug in the numbers. This will help you to avoid careless mistakes.

Standard Inequalities

Solving an inequality means finding the set of all values that satisfy the given statement. They work just like equations: Your task is to isolate the variable on one side of the inequality symbol. The only significant difference is that if you multiply or divide by a negative number, you must reverse the direction of the inequality symbol.

A. Solve for a: $4a + 5 > 9a + 15$

B. Solve for y: $2y - 3 < 9 + y$

C. Solve for y: $3y - 10 > 11$

D. Solve for x: $7 - 2x > 3y$

14. Which of the following is equivalent to the inequality $9 > 5x - 6$?

E. $x < 3$

F. $x > 3$

G. $x > -3$

H. $x > 5$

15. Which of the following is equivalent to $13 - 2y < 7$?

A. $y < -\frac{7}{13}$

B. $y < 3$

C. $y > 3$

D. $y < 10$

16. What is the range of possible values of y when $2y - 3 < 6$?

E. $y > \frac{2}{9}$

F. $y > \frac{3}{2}$

G. $y < \frac{9}{2}$

H. $y < 6$

> **✓ Remember**
>
> **Always perform the same operation on both sides of the inequality.**

Ranges

Ranges are inequalities with three parts. When you perform a mathematical operation on one part, you have to do the same thing to all three parts.

Find the range of values for each of these variables:

A. y when $(y - 2)$ is greater than 3 and less than 10

B. z when $(2z)$ is less than 6 and greater than -2

C. x^2 when x lies between 8 and 9

D. a when $-a$ lies between -4 and 7

17. Which of the following is equivalent to the inequality $7 > -3x > -12$?

A. $-7 < x < 12$

B. $\frac{7}{3} < x < 4$

C. $-\frac{7}{3} < x < 4$

D. $-4 < x < -\frac{7}{3}$

18. Which of the following is equivalent to the inequality $-8 < -2x < 12$?

E. $-3 < x < 2$

F. $-4 < x < 6$

G. $-6 < x < 4$

H. $-12 < x < 8$

19. The number a is a number less than -3. What is the range of possible values of $\frac{1}{a^2}$?

A. $\frac{1}{a^2} < -9$

B. $\frac{1}{a^2} < -3$

C. $-\frac{1}{9} < \frac{1}{a^2} < \frac{1}{9}$

D. $0 < \frac{1}{a^2} < \frac{1}{9}$

✓ Remember

When you divide or multiply the parts of a range by a negative number, you must change the direction of the inequality signs.

Number Lines

The solution to an inequality can be represented on a number line. For example, $x > 4$ could be graphed like this:

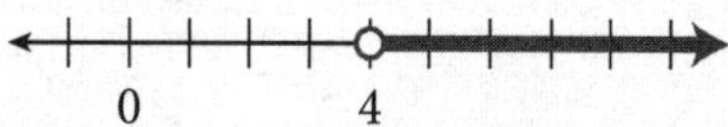

Notice the open dot at 4, indicating that 4 is not a solution to the inequality. This is called a **strict** inequality. By contrast, the graph of $x \leq 4$ looks like this:

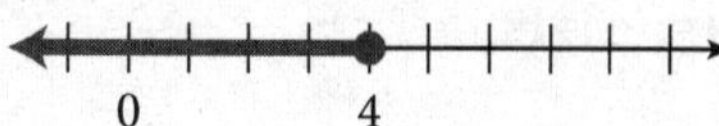

Notice the closed (solid) dot, indicating that 4 should be included in the solution set for the inequality.

Draw the following ranges onto the number lines provided:

A. $-6 < x < 4$

B. $4 > -2y > -2$

C. $3 \leq |z| \leq 5$

20. A B C

−3 −2 −1 0 1 2 3 4 5 6 7 8 9

The value x^2 is greater than 4 and less than 9. Which region or regions above represent the range of values for x?

E. A

F. B

G. C

H. A and B

21.

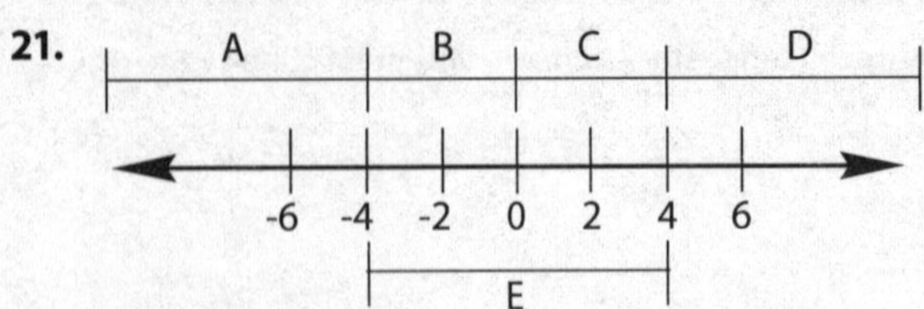

Which region(s) above is the set of all possible values of $-4x$, where $x > 1$?

A. A

B. B

C. C

D. D and E

Algebraic Division with Remainders

Some questions will require you to solve long division problems with variables instead of numbers. Picking Numbers is a fantastic approach to use when answering these questions.

What is the remainder in the following equations?

A. $\begin{array}{r} y \\ x\overline{)xy+a} \end{array}$

where a is less than x

B. $\begin{array}{r} x \\ x\overline{)n+x^2} \end{array}$

where n is less than x

22. $x\overline{)2xy+1}$ with quotient $2y$ rem n

If $1 < x$, what is the value of n?

E. 1

F. 2

G. $y + 1$

H. 3

23. $x\overline{)xy-2}$ with quotient $y - 1$ rem n

If $2 < x$, what is the value of n?

A. 1

B. 2

C. $x - 1$

D. $x - 2$

✔ Remember

When Picking Numbers, be sure to write down what numbers you picked and for which variables. This makes it less likely that you will make a mistake when checking the answer choices.

Be sure to check every answer choice. If the number you picked works for more than one choice, you'll need to pick another number.

The following practice sets provide an opportunity to apply the concepts and strategic thinking covered in this chapter. To practice Test Day timing, follow the suggested timing guidelines for each section.

ALGEBRA I PRACTICE SET

Suggested Timing: 15 minutes

1. What is the value of $3x(9 - 9x)$ when $x = \frac{4}{3}$?

A. -12

B. -9

C. 4

D. 12

2. $\frac{11}{4} - a = 3$

What is the value of a in the equation above?

E. $-\frac{23}{4}$

F. $-\frac{11}{4}$

G. $-\frac{1}{4}$

H. $\frac{1}{4}$

3. What is the value of x in the equation $10 = 5x - 5$?

A. 2

B. 3

C. 5

D. 7

4. Rachel is now 11 years old. Five years ago, Lily was twice as old as Rachel. How old is Lily now?

E. 12

F. 13

G. 16

H. 17

5. If n is an integer, which of the following **must** be odd?

A. $3n - 5$

B. $3n + 4$

C. $4n + 10$

D. $4n - 5$

6. When z is divided by 8, the remainder is 5. What is the remainder when $4z$ is divided by 8?

E. 1

F. 3

G. 4

H. 5

7. If the price of a stock increases by 40% and then by an additional 25%, by what percentage has the price increased from its original value?

A. 60%

B. 62%

C. 65%

D. 75%

8. If $a + 2b + 2c = 5$ and $a + 2b + 3c = 5$, what is the value of $a + 2b + 4c$?

E. 0

F. 5

G. 10

H. 15

9. If $a^5 - 25 = a^5 - b$, then what is the value of b?

   A. −25

   B. 0

   C. 5

   D. 25

10. A computer programmer receives \$100 a day, plus \$0.05 for each line of code that she writes. If this is her entire salary, which of the following expressions represents the number of dollars she would make in a day that she wrote n lines of code?

    E. $100 + n$

    F. $(100 + 0.05)n$

    G. $0.05 + 100n$

    H. $100 + 0.05n$

ALGEBRA II PRACTICE SET

Suggested Timing: 15 minutes

1. If $6z - 1 = -37$, then $z =$

A. -6

B. -5

C. 5

D. 6

2. If $m \ddagger = \frac{m}{m^2 - m}$, what is the value of $6\ddagger - [(-5)\ddagger]$?

E. $\frac{1}{30}$

F. $\frac{1}{20}$

G. $\frac{1}{4}$

H. $\frac{11}{30}$

3. Which of the following indicates that n is less than double the value of m and that n is greater than 1?

A. $1 < n < 2m$

B. $1 > n > \frac{m}{2}$

C. $\frac{1}{2} < 2n < m$

D. $1 < 2n < m$

4. If $50 - xy = 75$ and $y = -5$, what does x equal?

E. -25

F. -5

G. 5

H. 25

5. Simplify the following inequality: $x - 20 > 20 - x$

A. $x > -20$

B. $x > 10$

C. $x > 20$

D. $x < 20$

6. If $\varphi\ (a, b, c, d)$ means you subtract the absolute value of d from the sum of a, b, and c, then $\varphi\ (2, 5, 6, -10) + \varphi\ (1, 2, 3, 7) =$

E. 2

F. 4

G. 16

H. 22

7. 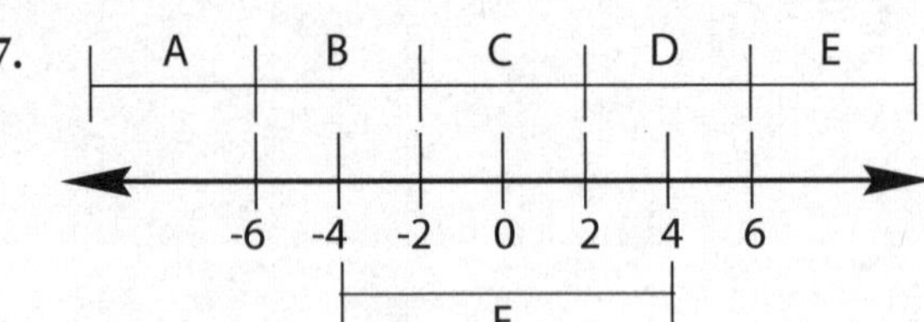

Which region above is the set of all values of $-\frac{x}{3}$, where $-6 < x < 6$?

A. B

B. C

C. D

D. F

8. $y\overline{)xy - 3}$ with quotient $x - 1$ rem n

If $y > 3$, what is the value of n?

E. 2

F. 3

G. $y - 2$

H. $y - 3$

9. If $a < b < c < 0$, then which of the following must be true?

I. $a + b < b + c$

II. $c - a > 0$

III. $a < b + c$

A. I only
B. II only
C. I and II only
D. I and III only

10. For every positive integer x, let $(x\varphi) = (x - 1) + (x - 2) + (x - 3) + ... + (x - x)$. For example, $(4\varphi) = 3 + 2 + 1 + 0$. What is the value of $(500\varphi) - (497\varphi)$?

E. 997
F. 1,490
G. 1,494
H. 1,497

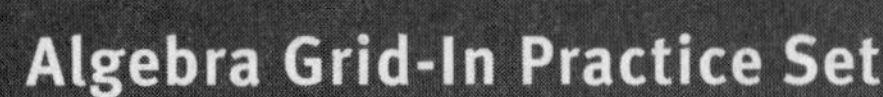

ALGEBRA GRID-IN PRACTICE SET

Suggested Timing: 15 minutes

1. What is the value of b in the equation $3b - 14 = -5$?

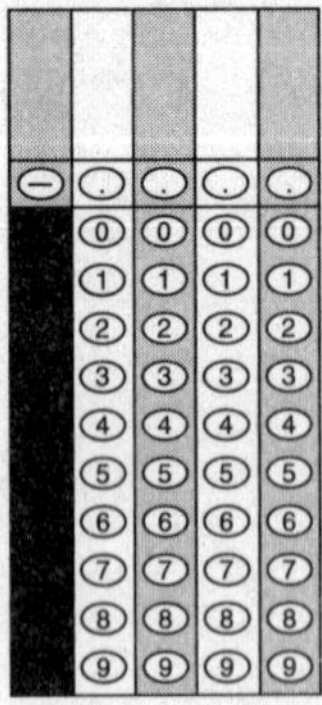

2. If $x < 24$ and $2y + 3 < 17$, and x and y are both positive integers, what is the largest possible value of $x + y$?

3. If $0.02a = 2$, what is the value of a?

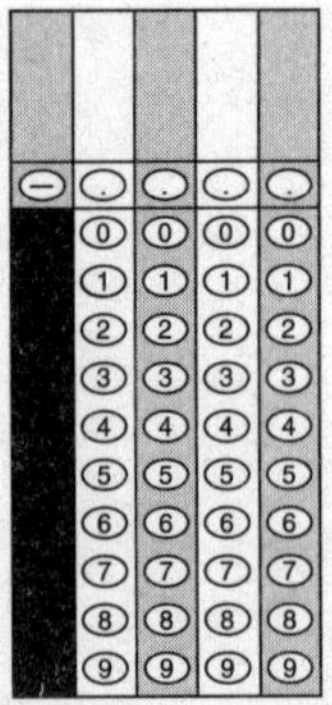

4. What is the value of b in the equation $4b = 8b - 88$?

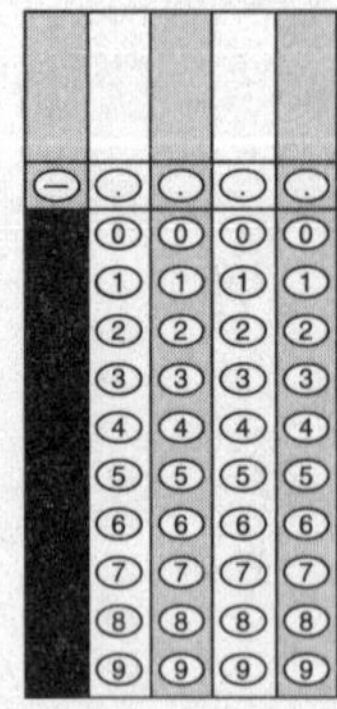

5. If $x - 4 \leq 10$ and $x + 2 \geq 6$, and x is an integer, how many possible values of x are there?

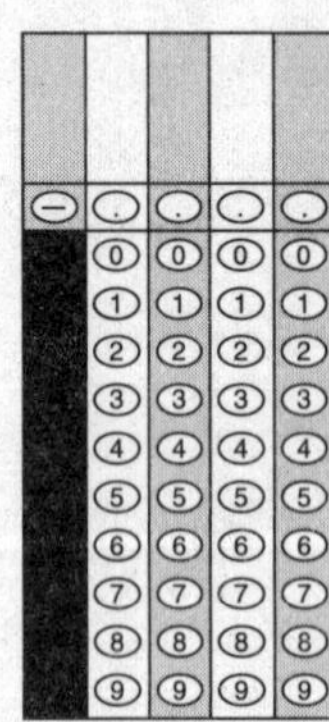

6. If $\frac{1}{3}(6z + 18) = 3z - 9$, what is the value of z?

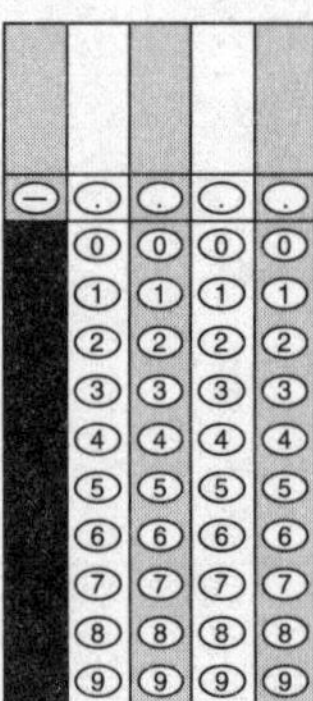

7. What is the value of the expression $a^2 - 4a + 12$ if $a = -6$?

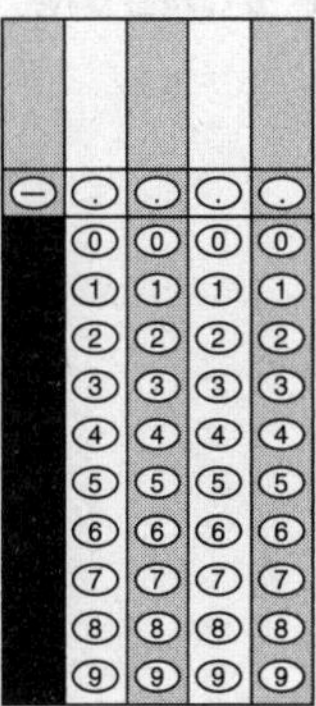

8. What is the value of z in the equation $4\left(\frac{1}{2}z - 10\right) = 10z + 4$?

9. If $\sqrt{h} = 21$, what is the value of h?

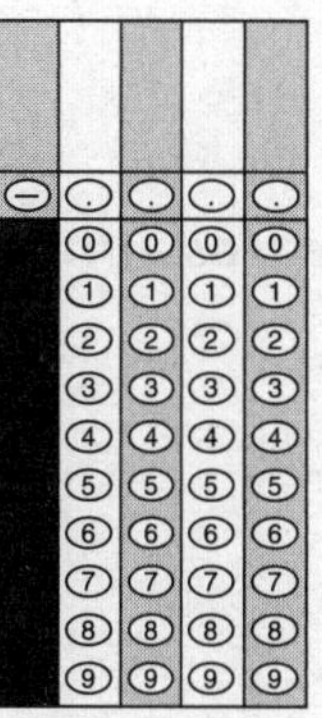

10. What is the value of the expression $\sqrt{x - y} + x^2 - y^2$ if $x = 9$ and $y = 5$?

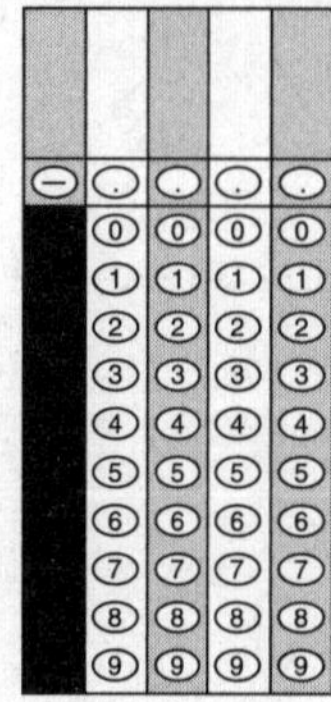

ANSWERS AND EXPLANATIONS

Algebra I

Evaluate an Algebraic Expression

A. $a(5-a)=3(5-3)=3(2)=6$

B. $a(5)-a=3(5)-3=15-3=12$

C. $4-b=4-(-7)=4+7=11$

D. $4-b=4-7=-3$

E. $c^d-d^c=3^2-2^3=9-8=1$

F. $2\left(\frac{n}{n+1}\right)=2\left(\frac{4}{4+1}\right)=2\left(\frac{4}{5}\right)=\frac{8}{5}$

G. $x(3^x)=2(3^2)=2(9)=18$

1. B

Subject: Algebra

Getting to the Answer: The equation is ready for substitution as it stands. Just substitute:

$x(y-2)+xz=$
$2(5-2)+2\times 7=6+14=20$

2. F

Subject: Algebra

Getting to the Answer: Substitute carefully:

$x^2-5yz+y^2=$

$\sqrt{3}^2-5\times 2\times\frac{1}{2}+2^2=$

$3-5+4=2$

3. C

Subject: Algebra

Getting to the Answer: Given that you are looking for $ac+bc$, you can look to simplify:

$ac+bc=c(a+b)$

You know that $c=2$ and $a+b=17$, therefore $c(a+b)=2\,(17)=34$.

Solve Equations with One Variable

A. $2x+4=8$
$2x=4$
$x=2$

B. $\frac{x}{3}+1=5$
$\frac{x}{3}=4$
$x=12$

C. $x-5=3x-10$
$-5=2x-10$
$5=2x$
$\frac{5}{2}=x$

D. $\left(\frac{1}{3}\right)x=8$
$x=24$
$\left(\frac{1}{4}\right)x=\left(\frac{1}{4}\right)(24)=6$

E. $(3d-7)-(5-2d)$
$3d-7-5+2d$
$5d-12$
Try a value for d such as $d=2$.
$5(2)-12=10-12=-2$
Therefore, $d=2$ produces an even integer (-2).
Any other even value for d will also work.

4. G

Subject: Algebra

Getting to the Answer: You need to isolate the variable:

$0.5n+2=3$

$0.5n=1$ or $\frac{1}{2}n=1$ Multiply by 2.

$n=2$

5. C

Subject: Algebra

Getting to the Answer: Isolate the x:

$2x=13+25$
$2x=38$ Divide by 2.
$x=19$

6. E

Subject: Algebra

Getting to the Answer: Solve for p:

$p(12q) = 6q$ Divide by $6q$.

$p(2) = 1$

$p = \frac{1}{2}$ or 0.5

Solve Equations with Two Variables

A. $3a - 6 = b$

$3a - 6 = 18$

$3a = 24$

$a = 8$

B. $2m + \frac{1}{3}k = \frac{1}{3}k^2$; plug in $k = \frac{1}{3}$

$2m + \frac{1}{3}\left(\frac{1}{3}\right) = \frac{1}{3}\left(\frac{1}{3}\right)^2$

$2m + \frac{1}{9} = \frac{1}{27}$

$2m = -\frac{2}{27}$

$m = -\frac{1}{27}$

C. $\frac{4a + b}{b} = 7$; plug in $b = 2$

$\frac{4a + 2}{2} = 7$

$4a + 2 = 14$

$4a = 12$

$a = 3$

D.

x	y
1	4
3	16
5	36
7	64
9	100

7. C

Subject: Algebra

Getting to the Answer: Plug the 8 in for y and isolate the x:

$5x - 7 = y$

$5x - 7 = 8$

$5x = 15$ Substitute, isolate, and reduce.

$x = 3$

8. H

Subject: Algebra

Getting to the Answer: Cross multiply and then substitute the value given for x.

$\frac{x}{y} = \frac{2}{5}$

$5x = 2y$

$5(10) = 2y$

$50 = 2y$

$25 = y$

9. B

Subject: Algebra

Getting to the Answer: Substitute:

$2m(2m - 3n) = 34$

$2(2)[2(2) - 3n] = 34$

$4(4 - 3n) = 34$

$16 - 12n = 34$

$-12n = 18$ Divide by -12.

$n = -\frac{18}{12} = -\frac{3}{2}$

Solve for One Variable in Terms of the Other

A. $2r + 8s = 24$

$2r = 24 - 8s$

$r = 12 - 4s$

B. $b(a - 1) = \frac{bc}{2}$

$2b(a - 1) = bc$

$2(a - 1) = c$

$2a - 2 = c$

C. $3x + 2y + 4z = 12$

Solving for x:

$3x = 12 - 2y - 4z$

$x = 4 - \frac{2}{3}y - \frac{4}{3}z$

Solving for y:

$2y = 12 - 3x - 4z$

$y = 6 - \frac{3}{2}x - 2z$

Solving for z:

$4z = 12 - 3x - 2y$

$z = 3 - \frac{3}{4}x - \frac{1}{2}y$

10. G

Subject: Algebra

Getting to the Answer: Keep in mind what question you are answering:

$\frac{(a+b)}{2} = 8$

$(a+b) = 16$ — After you have eliminated the fraction, isolate a.

$a = 16 - b$

11. B

Subject: Algebra

Getting to the Answer: In this case, you have to distribute through and then isolate:

$3(2t + 6) = 12s$

$6t + 18 = 12s$ — Divide each side by 6 to reduce.

$t + 3 = 2s$

$t = 2s - 3$

12. G

Subject: Algebra

Getting to the Answer: Simplify and work to isolate a.

$3(a - 2) = 5m - 6 + 2a$

$3a - 6 = 5m - 6 + 2a$ — Subtract $2a$.

$a - 6 = 5m - 6$ — Add 6.

$a = 5m$

Consecutive Multiples

A. First three multiples of both 6 and 8 are 24, 48, 72.

B. Four multiples of 6 can be expressed as $6x, 6(x+1), 6(x+2)$, and $6(x+3)$.

Adding the multiples and setting equal to 156:

$6x + 6(x+1) + 6(x+2) + 6(x+3) = 156$

$6x + 6x + 6 + 6x + 12 + 6x + 18 = 156$

$24x + 36 = 156$

$24x = 120$

$x = 5$

Therefore, the multiples are $6(5), 6(5+1), 6(5+2), 6(5+3)$, *or* 30, 36, 42, 48.

C. Five multiples of 3 can be expressed as:

$3x, 3(x + 1), 3(x + 2), 3(x + 3)$, and $3(x + 4)$

The product of 15 and 7 is 105.

Adding the multiples and setting equal to 105:

$3x + 3(x+1) + 3(x+2) + 3(x+3) + 3(x+4) = 105$

$3x + 3x + 3 + 3x + 6 + 3x + 9 + 3x + 12 = 105$

$15x + 30 = 105$

$15x = 75$

$x = 5$

The multiples are $3(5), 3(5+1), 3(5+2), 3(5+3), 3(5+4)$, *or* 15, 18, 21, 24, and 27.

13. C

Subject: Algebra

Getting to the Answer: Since you're asked for three consecutive multiples of 7, the second would be 7 more than the first, and the third 14 more than the first. Put these expressions into an equation:

$$x + (x + 7) + (x + 14) = 84$$
$$3x + 21 = 84$$
$$3x = 63$$
$$x = 21$$

However, the question asks for the *greatest* number, so:

$x + 14 = 21 + 14 = 35$

14. H

Subject: Algebra

Getting to the Answer: Set up an equation that translates what is stated in the question:

$$x + (x + 4) + (x + 8) = 60$$
$$3x + 12 = 60$$
$$3x = 48$$
$$x = 16$$

However, the question asks for the *greatest* number, so

$x + 8 = 16 + 8 = 24$

15. D

Subject: Arithmetic

Getting to the Answer: $x + (x + 11) + (x + 22) + (x + 33) + (x + 44) = 220$

$$5x + 110 = 220$$
$$5x = 110$$
$$x = 22$$

However, the question asks for the *greatest* number, so

$x + 44 = 22 + 44 = 66.$

ANSWERS AND EXPLANATIONS

Algebra II

Review of Expressions and Equations

A. $2(3+1)^2+5-6\div3=$

$2(4)^2+5-6\div3=$

$2(16)+5-6\div3=$

$32+5-6\div3=$

$32+5-2=$

$37-2=$

35

B. When $x=2$, $2x+3=2(2)+3=4+3=7$

C. When $x=\frac{1}{4}$, $y=\frac{1}{5}$, and $z=\frac{1}{6}$,

$$\frac{x}{15}+\frac{y}{6}+\frac{z}{5}=$$

$$\frac{\frac{1}{4}}{15}+\frac{\frac{1}{5}}{6}+\frac{\frac{1}{6}}{5}=$$

$$\frac{1}{60}+\frac{1}{30}+\frac{1}{30}=$$

$$\frac{1}{60}+\frac{2}{60}+\frac{2}{60}=$$

$$\frac{5}{60}=\frac{1}{12}$$

D. $4x+3=19$

$4x=16$

$x=4$

E. $7xy=3y^2$

$$x=\frac{3y^2}{7y}$$

$$x=\frac{3y}{7}$$

1. C

Subject: Algebra

Getting to the Answer: You need to isolate the terms with x in them and then solve:

$$3x+7=14$$
$$3x=7$$
$$x=\frac{7}{3}$$

2. G

Subject: Algebra

Getting to the Answer: Solve for z:

$4z-3=-19$

$4z=-16$

$\frac{4z}{4}=\frac{-16}{4}$ Once you have the z terms on one side, reduce.

$z=-4$

3. C

Subject: Algebra

Getting to the Answer: The problem is straightforward; distribute and solve:

$$4(y-1)=2(y+2)$$
$$4y-4=2y+4$$
$$2y=8$$
$$\frac{2y}{2}=\frac{8}{2}$$
$$y=4$$

4. E

Subject: Algebra

Getting to the Answer: Combine like terms:

$5p+12=17-4\left(\frac{p}{2}+1\right)$

$5p+12=17-2p-4$

$5p+12=13-2p$ Combine like terms, and then solve for p.

$7p=1$

$p=\frac{1}{7}$

5. D

Subject: Algebra

Getting to the Answer: Substitute 8 for y:

$-2x+xy=30\rightarrow-2x+(8)x=30$

$-2x+(8)x=30\rightarrow6x=30$

$6x=30\rightarrow x=5$ Combine variable terms. Divide by 6 to solve for x.

6. G

Subject: Algebra

Getting to the Answer: Substitute 5 for x:

$15 + xy \div 3 = 35 \rightarrow 15 + 5y \div 3 = 35$
$15 + 5y \div 3 = 35 \rightarrow 5y \div 3 = 20$

Subtract 15 from both sides.

$5y \div 3 = 20 \rightarrow 5y = 20 \cdot 3$	Now, multiply by 3 to isolate the variable term.
$5y = 60 \rightarrow y = 12$	Divide by 5 to solve for x.

7. A

Subject: Algebra

Getting to the Answer:

$\frac{2x}{5y} = 6$

$2x = 30y$

$\frac{2x}{30} = \frac{30y}{30}$ After cross multiplying, just reduce the terms.

$\frac{x}{15} = y$

8. F

Subject: Algebra

Getting to the Answer: Isolate the a:

$a = \frac{6}{3b}$ Divide by $3b$.

$a = \frac{2}{b}$

9. D

Subject: Algebra

Getting to the Answer: You'll need to get the a on one side of the equation:

$2(a + m) = 5m - 3 + a$
$2a + 2m = 5m - 3 + a$ Distribute the 2, and then combine like terms.
$a = 3m - 3$

Symbolism Equations

A. $36 \bigstar 64 = \sqrt{36+64} = \sqrt{100} = 10$

B. $43 \bigstar 6 = \sqrt{43+6} = \sqrt{49} = 7$

C. $a \bigstar 4 = 5; \sqrt{a+4} = 5; a+4 = 25; a = 21$

D. $4 \varphi 3 = 4 - 3[4-(2)(3)] = 4 - 3[4-6]$
$= 4 - 3(-2) = 10$

E. $3 \varphi 4 = 3 - 4(3-8) = 3 - 4(-5) = 3 + 20 = 23$

F. $-5 \ \varphi \ -2 = -5 - (-2)[-5-(2)(-2)] =$
$-5 + 2(-5+4) = -5 + 2(-1) = -5 - 2 =$
-7

G. $x \varphi 3 = x - 3[x - 2(3)] = x - 3(x-6) =$
$x - 3x + 18 = -2x + 18$

10. E

Subject: Algebra

Getting to the Answer: With symbolism, just substitute:

$a = \frac{24}{45}$ and $b = \frac{90}{240}$

$\left(\frac{24}{45} \times \frac{90}{240}\right) \div 2 =$

$\left(\frac{1}{1} \times \frac{2}{10}\right) \div 2 =$

$\frac{2}{10} \div 2 = \frac{1}{5} \div 2 =$

$\frac{1}{5} \times \frac{1}{2} = \frac{1}{10}$

11. C

Subject: Algebra

Getting to the Answer: You have to substitute here:

$a = \frac{14}{32}, b = 1\frac{3}{4}$ or $\frac{7}{4}$

$\frac{3 \times \frac{14}{32}}{\frac{7}{4}} = \frac{42}{32} \times \frac{4}{7} =$ Plug in a and b, and invert the denominator; then reduce.

$\frac{6}{8} \times \frac{1}{1} = \frac{6}{8}$ or $\frac{3}{4}$

Translated Symbolism

A. $2(x + 5) - 2$

B. $9y + 5$

C. $3|6 - z|$

D. $2(3 + 5) - 2 = 2(8) - 2 = 14$; $9(2) + 5 = 18 + 5 = 23$; $3|6 - 4| = 3(2) = 6$

12. G

Subject: Algebra

Getting to the Answer: You have been given a symbol in the problem, for which you must follow the directions:

$$\$(r,s,t) = \frac{r \times s}{s+t}$$

$$\$(8,3,1) = \frac{8 \times 3}{3+1} = \frac{24}{4} = 6$$

13. C

Subject: Algebra

Getting to the Answer: Just create the equation, and then substitute:

$$\#\#(a, b, c) = (b \times c)^a - a$$
$$\#\#(2, 5, x) = (5 \times x)^2 - 2 = 23$$
$$25x^2 - 2 = 23$$
$$25x^2 = 23 + 2$$
$$x^2 = 1$$
$$x = 1$$

Standard Inequalities

A. $4a + 5 > 9a + 15$

$-10 > 5a$

$-2 > a$

B. $2y - 3 < 9 + y$

$y < 12$

C. $3y - 10 > 11$

$3y > 21$

$y > 7$

D. $7 - 2x > 3y$

$-2x > 3y - 7$

$x < \frac{-3y + 7}{2}$

14. E

Subject: Algebra

Getting to the Answer: Go about it like a regular equation:

$$9 > 5x - 6$$
$$9 + 6 > 5x$$
$$15 > 5x$$
$$3 > x$$
$$x < 3$$

15. C

Subject: Algebra

Getting to the Answer: Solve for y:

$13 - 2y < 7$

$-2y < -6$ Divide by 2, and then switch the sign

$-y < -3$ when you divide by -1.

$y > 3$

16. G

Subject: Algebra

Getting to the Answer: Solve for y:

$$2y - 3 < 6$$
$$2y < 9$$
$$y < \frac{9}{2}$$

Ranges

A. $3 < y - 2 < 10$

$5 < y < 12$

B. $-2 < 2z < 6$

$-1 < z < 3$

C. $8 < x < 9$

$64 < x^2 < 81$

D. $-4 < -a < 7$

$4 > a > -7$

$-7 < a < 4$

17. C

Subject: Algebra

Getting to the Answer: Solve for the range of x:

$7 > -3x > -12$	Divide through by 3, and then reverse the signs.
$-\frac{7}{3} > -x > -4$	
$-\frac{7}{3} < x < 4$	

18. G

Subject: Algebra

Getting to the Answer: Solve for the range of x:

$$-8 < -2x < 12$$
$$-4 < -x < 6$$
$$4 > x > -6 \text{ or}$$
$$-6 < x < 4$$

19. D

Subject: Algebra

Getting to the Answer: If a is a number less than −3, to find the range of values for $\frac{1}{a^2}$, you have to plug in values for a starting with −3 and working downward (−4, −5, etc.).

if $a = -3$, then $\frac{1}{a^2} = \frac{1}{9}$

if $a = -4$, then $\frac{1}{a^2} = \frac{1}{16}$

As a gets smaller, the value gets closer to zero but never reaches zero:

$$0 < \frac{1}{a^2} < \frac{1}{9}$$

Number Lines

A. Put open dots at −6 and 4, and shade between −6 and 4.

B. Simplify the range first by dividing all sides by −2, so that $-2 < y < 1$. Put open dots at −2 and 1, then shade between −2 and 1.

C. Sometimes a range will require two brackets, particularly with absolute value and squaring questions. In this case, put closed dots at −3 and −5, then shade between. Next, put closed dots at 3 and 5, then shade between.

20. H

Subject: Algebra

Getting to the Answer: First, set up the inequality described in the question stem: x is the square root of x^2, so the parameters of x will be the square roots of the given parameters of x^2.

$$4 < x^2 < 9$$
$$\sqrt{4} < \sqrt{x^2} < \sqrt{9}$$
$$2 < x < 3 \text{ or } -2 > x > -3$$

21. A

Subject: Algebra

Getting to the Answer:

$x > 1$	Consider the original inequality.
$-4x$	Consider what you must do to x to produce the new situation
$(-4)\,x > 1\,(-4)$	Do that to both sides of the inequality. Remember to change the sign.
$-4x < -4$	Look for the values that are less than −4.

Algebraic Division with Remainders

A. Remainder $= a$

Pick Numbers: $x = 4$, $y = 3$, $a = 2$

$$x\overline{)xy+a}^{\;y} \qquad 4\overline{)4(3)+2}^{\;3} \qquad 4\overline{)14}^{\;3\text{ R2}} \qquad a = 2$$

B. Remainder $= n$

Pick Numbers: $x = 4$, $n = 3$

$$x\overline{)n+x^2}^{\;x} \qquad 4\overline{)3+4^2}^{\;4} \qquad 4\overline{)19}^{\;4\text{ R3}} \qquad n = 3$$

22. E

Subject: Algebra

Getting to the Answer:

$\frac{2xy+1}{x} = 2y + \frac{n}{x}$	Convert the division problem into a fraction equation.
$2xy+1 = x\left(2y+\frac{n}{x}\right)$	Remember, the remainder is a fraction of the divisor *x*, so *rem* $= \frac{n}{x}$.
$2xy + 1 = 2xy + n$	Multiply both sides by *x*.
$1 = n$	Distribute the *x* on the right side of the equation.

23. D

Subject: Algebra

Getting to the Answer: Remember, the remainder is a fraction of the divisor *x*, so the value of the remainder is $\frac{n}{x}$.

$\frac{xy-2}{x} = y-1+\frac{n}{x}$	Convert the division problem to a fractional equation.
$xy-2 = x\left(y-1+\frac{n}{x}\right)$	Multiply both sides by *x*.
$xy - 2 = xy - x + n$	Distribute the *x* in the parentheses on the right.
$-2 = -x + n$	Subtract *xy* from both sides.
$x - 2 = n$	Add *x* to both sides to solve for *n*.

ANSWERS AND EXPLANATIONS

Algebra I Practice Set

1. A

Subject: Algebra

Getting to the Answer: Substitute:

$$3\times\frac{4}{3}\left(9-9\times\frac{4}{3}\right)=$$
$$4(9-12)=$$
$$4(-3)=$$
$$-12$$

2. G

Subject: Algebra

Getting to the Answer: Isolate the *a*:

$$\frac{11}{4}-a=3$$
$$-a=3-\frac{11}{4}$$
$$-a=\frac{12}{4}-\frac{11}{4}$$ Combine the fractions, reduce, and divide by -1.
$$-a=\frac{1}{4}$$
$$a=-\frac{1}{4}$$

3. B

Subject: Algebra

Getting to the Answer:

$$10=5x-5$$
$$10+5=(5x-5)+5$$ Isolate the variable by adding 5 to both sides.
$$15=5x$$
$$\frac{15}{5}=\frac{5x}{5}$$ Divide both sides by 5.
$$3=x$$

4. H

Subject: Algebra

Getting to the Answer: Take the problem step by step. If Rachel is now 11 years old, then 5 years ago she was $11-5=6$ years old. If Lily was twice as old then as Rachel was, then Lily was $2\times6=12$ years old, and therefore *now*, 5 years later, she is $12+5=17$ years old.

5. D

Subject: Algebra

Getting to the Answer: Pick Numbers to elicit the answer you are looking for. In this case, choosing an odd and an even number makes sense. Try 1 and 2:

(A) If $n=1$, then $3n-5=-2$. If $n=2$, then $3n-5=6$.

(B) If $n=1$, then $3n+4=7$. If $n=2$, then $3n+4=10$.

(C) If $n=1$, then $4n+10=14$. If $n=2$, then $4n+10=14$.

(D) If $n=1$, then $4n-5=-1$. If $n=2$, then $4n-5=3$.

Therefore, the answer is **(D)**, which will always be an odd integer.

6. G

Subject: Algebra

Getting to the Answer: Because you always want to pick the easiest numbers to work with, using the divisor $8\left(\frac{8}{8}=1\right)$ plus the remainder 5 works best. $z=8+5=13$. Therefore, $4z=52$, and $\frac{4z}{8}=\frac{52}{8}=6$ remainder 4.

7. D

Subject: Algebra

Getting to the Answer: Use \$100 as the original price of the stock. If the stock increases by 40%, then \$100 × 40% = \$40 increase. \$100 + \$40 = \$140 new price. If the stock then increases 25%, \$140 × 25% = \$35 increase. \$140 + \$35 = \$175 new price. The change in price is \$175 − \$100 = \$75. The percent increase is $\frac{\$75}{\$100}=75\%$.

8. F

Subject: Algebra

Getting to the Answer: Ordinarily you would not be able to solve for three variables with only two equations. In this case however, what can you deduce from the fact that both equations are identical except for the coefficient of *c*? By subtracting the first equation from the second you will see that $c=0$. This is the only way that both $a+2b+2c$ and $a+2b+3c$ can equal 5. Therefore, $a+2b=5$ and $a+2b+4c=a+2b+0=5$.

9. D

Subject: Algebra

Getting to the Answer:

$$\begin{aligned} a^5 - 25 &= a^5 - b \\ -25 &= -b \\ 25 &= b \end{aligned}$$

10. H

Subject: Algebra

Getting to the Answer: Think about each part of the programmer's salary, then put it together. She gets \$100 a day for showing up. She gets \$0.05 per line of code, so if she writes n lines, she earns \$0.05n. So her total salary is $100 + 0.05n$ dollars.

Algebra II Practice Set

1. A

Subject: Algebra

Getting to the Answer: You're given the equation, so just solve for z.

$6z - 1 = -37$

$6z = -36$ Add 1 to both sides.

$z = -6$ Divide both sides by 6 to solve for z.

2. H

Subject: Algebra

Getting to the Answer: Translate the expression into basic arithmetic by plugging the values into the defined form. Then solve.

$$\frac{6}{6^2-6} - \left(\frac{-5}{-5^2-(-5)}\right) =$$

$$\frac{6}{36-6} - \left(\frac{-5}{25+5}\right) =$$

$$\frac{6}{30} - \left(-\frac{5}{30}\right) =$$

$$\frac{6}{30} + \frac{5}{30} = \frac{11}{30}$$

3. A

Subject: Algebra

Getting to the Answer: Carefully translate the words into math.

"n is less than double the value of m" → $n < 2m$

"n is greater than 1" → $1 < n$

combined → $1 < n < 2m$

4. G

Subject: Algebra

Getting to the Answer:

Substitute -5 for y:

$50 - xy = 75 \rightarrow 50 - (-5)x = 75$

$50 - (-5)x = 75 \rightarrow 50 + 5x = 75$ Cancel out the negative signs.

$50 + 5x = 75 \rightarrow 5x = 25$ Subtract 50 from both sides to simplify.

$5x = 25 \rightarrow x = 5$ Divide by 5 to solve for x.

5. C

Subject: Algebra

Getting to the Answer:

$x - 20 > 20 - x \rightarrow 2x > 40$ Add x and 20 to both sides to isolate the x term.

$2x > 40 \rightarrow x > 20$ Divide both sides by 2 to solve for x.

6. E

Subject: Algebra

Getting to the Answer: If $\varphi(a, b, c, d)$ means you subtract the absolute value of d from the sum of a, b, and c, then:

$$\begin{aligned} \varphi(2,5,6,-10) &= (2+5+6) - |-10| \\ &= 13 - 10 \\ &= 3 \\ \varphi(1,2,3,7) &= (1+2+3) - |7| \\ &= 6 - 7 \\ &= -1 \\ \varphi(2,5,6,-10) + \varphi(1,2,3,7) &= 3 + (-1) \\ &= 2 \end{aligned}$$

7. B

Subject: Algebra

Getting to the Answer:

$-6 < x < 6$	Consider the original inequality.
$-6 < x \quad x < 6$	Split the inequality into separate parts.
$-\frac{x}{3}$	Consider what you must do to x to produce the new situation (multiply by $-\frac{1}{3}$).
$\left(-\frac{1}{3}\right)(-6) > \left(-\frac{1}{3}\right)x \quad \left(-\frac{1}{3}\right)x > 6\left(-\frac{1}{3}\right)$	Do that to both sides of both inequalities. Remember to change the signs.
$2 > -\frac{x}{3} \quad -\frac{x}{3} > -2$	Now merge the two back together.
$2 > -\frac{x}{3} > -2$	Look for values between −2 and 2.

8. H

Subject: Algebra

Getting to the Answer: Pick Numbers ($x = 7, y = 4$)

$$4\overline{)(7 \cdot 4) - 3}\quad = 7 - 1$$

$$4\overline{)\ 25}\quad = 6 \text{ rem } 1$$

$$y - 3 = 4 - 3 = 1$$

Pick different numbers ($x = 8, y = 10$)

$$10\overline{)(8 \cdot 10) - 3}$$

$$10\overline{)\ 77}\quad = 7 \text{ rem } 7$$

$$y - 3 = 10 - 3 = 7$$

The remainder each time is different, so you must consider which variable answer fits the remainder each time. Just plug the value into each to find the answer as done above.

9. C

Subject: Algebra

Getting to the Answer: Pick Numbers: a = −3, b = −2, c = −1

Substitute:

I. $-3 + (-2) < -2 + (-1)$
$-5 < -3$ Correct.

II. $-1 - (-3) > 0$
$2 > 0$ Correct.

III. $-3 < -2 + (-1)$
$-3 \nless -3$ Incorrect.

I and II are true, so **(C)** is correct.

10. G

Subject: Algebra

Getting to the Answer:

(500φ) − (497φ)
= [(500 − 1) + (500 − 2) + (500 − 3) + (500 − 4). . .]
− [(497 − 1) + (497 − 2). . .]
= [499 + 498 + 497 + 496. . .] − [496 + 495. . .]

Everything cancels except for:
(500 − 1) + (500 − 2) + (500 − 3)
= 499 + 498 + 497 = 1,494

Note that the sequences begin with $n - 1$, so they start with 499 and 496 respectively. Incorrectly starting with 500 and 497 leads to trap answer **(H)**.

Algebra Grid-In Practice Set

1. 3

Subject: Algebra

Getting to the Answer: Solve this equation as you would any other equation: Add 14 to both sides and divide by 3 to isolate the variable:

$$\begin{aligned} 3b - 14 &= -5 \\ 3b &= 9 \\ b &= 3 \end{aligned}$$

Grid in 3.

2. 29

Subject: Algebra

Getting to the Answer: Begin by simplifying the second inequality. The second inequality simplifies to $y < 7$. You know that $x < 24$ and $y < 7$, and both numbers are integers. To maximize $x + y$, you want the largest possible values of the two numbers. The largest possible values of x and y are 23 and 6, respectively, and $23 + 6 = 29$. Grid in 29.

3. 100

Subject: Algebra

Getting to the Answer: Simply divide both sides by 0.02 to get a by itself. Dividing by 0.02 is like multiplying by 50, so you should end up with $a = 100$. Grid in 100.

4. 22

Subject: Algebra

Getting to the Answer: Start by subtracting the $8b$, then divide both sides by -4:

$$\begin{aligned} 4b &= 8b - 88 \\ -4b &= -88 \\ b &= 22 \end{aligned}$$

Grid in 22.

5. 11

Subject: Algebra

Getting to the Answer: Start by solving both inequalities. Doing this tells you that x must be greater than or equal to 4 and less than or equal to 14. There are 11 integers between 4 and 14, so grid in 11.

6. 15

Subject: Algebra

Getting to the Answer: Start by distributing the fraction on the left side of the equation. From there, combine like terms and solve for z:

$$\begin{aligned} \frac{1}{3}(6z + 18) &= 3z - 9 \\ 2z + 6 &= 3z - 9 \\ 15 &= z \end{aligned}$$

Grid in 15.

7. 72

Subject: Algebra

Getting to the Answer: Simply substitute -6 in for a in the given expression and simplify. Don't forget what happens to negative numbers multiplied by other negative numbers:

$$\begin{gathered} a^2 - 4a + 12 \\ (-6)^2 - 4(-6) + 12 \\ 36 + 24 + 12 = 72 \end{gathered}$$

Grid in 72.

8. −5.5

Subject: Algebra

Getting to the Answer: Start by distributing the 4 on the left side of the equation. From there, solve as you would any other equation:

$$\begin{aligned} 4\left(\frac{1}{2}z - 10\right) &= 10z + 4 \\ 2z - 40 &= 10z + 4 \\ -8z &= 44 \\ z &= -5.5 \end{aligned}$$

Don't forget the negative sign! Grid in −5.5.

9. 441

Subject: Algebra

Getting to the Answer: Simply square both sides of the equation to solve for h. $21 \times 21 = 441$, so grid in 441.

10. 58

Subject: Algebra

Getting to the Answer: Begin by substituting 9 and 5 for x and y, respectively. Do the subtraction under the radical first, followed by the exponents, then the addition and subtraction:

$$\begin{gathered} \sqrt{x - y} + x^2 - y^2 \\ \sqrt{9 - 5} + 9^2 - 5^2 \\ \sqrt{4} + 81 - 25 \\ 2 + 81 - 25 = 58 \end{gathered}$$

Grid in 58.

CHAPTER 16

Word Problems

CHAPTER OBJECTIVES

By the end of this chapter, you will be able to:

- Translate word problems into mathematical terms
- Solve SHSAT word problems

WORD PROBLEMS

Translation

Basic Translation

Translating from English into Math	
English	**Math**
equals, is, equivalent to, was, will be, has, costs, adds up to, the same as, as much as	=
times, of, multiplied by, product of, twice, double, by	×
divided by, per, out of, each, ratio	÷
plus, added to, and, sum, combined, total, increased by	+
minus, subtracted from, smaller than, less than, fewer, decreased by, difference between	−
a number, how much, how many, what	*x*, *n*, etc.

Use the table above to translate the following expressions into mathematical operations or equations:

<u>Statement:</u> <u>Translation:</u>

A. 2 more than z is twice the value of z ________________

B. 5 fewer than x equals y ________________

C. The product of 3 and x subtracted from 3 ________________

D. What fraction of x is y? ________________

E. One-fourth of the sum of 4 and x ________________

Translate the following equations or operations into words:

<u>Equation or Operation:</u> <u>Translation:</u>

F. $3z$ ________________

G. b^2 ________________

H. $\frac{a}{b-c}$ ________________

I. $8x = \frac{x^3}{2}$ ________________

J. $\frac{h}{g} = 4h$ ________________

Advanced Translation

Translate the following statements into mathematical operations or equations:

Statement: Translation:

K. An integer greater than 0, when divided by the square of itself equals 2. ________________

L. The product of two distinct real numbers is 2 greater than the sum of the numbers. ________________

✔ Keys to Translation Success

1. Learn the common terms for all major operations.

2. Pay close attention to PEMDAS when translating.

Translation Questions

1. "Seven less than 4 times x is equal to twice x plus 9." Which of the following equations is a mathematical translation of the previous statement?

A. $4x - 7 = 2 + 9x$

B. $4x - 7 = 2x + 9$

C. $7 - 4x = 2 + 9x$

D. $7 - 4x = 2x + 9$

2. Moira had D dollars in her wallet. She withdrew B dollars from the bank. Then she spent S dollars at the store. How many dollars does Moira have now?

E. $D + B + S$

F. $D + B - S$

G. $D - B + S$

H. $D - B - S$

Typical Word Problems

3. Anna is now y years old, and Marco is 3 years younger. In terms of y, how old was Marco 5 years ago?

   A. $y - 2$
   B. $y - 3$
   C. $y - 5$
   D. $y - 8$

4. Matt has c baseball cards, and Jen has d baseball cards. Jen has 9 fewer than 5 times as many cards as Matt. What is the value of d in terms of c?

   E. $5c - 9$
   F. $5c$
   G. $5c + 9$
   H. $9c - 5$

5. Anne has n pairs of shoes, and Fiona has 3 times as many pairs of shoes. If Fiona gives Anne 6 pairs of shoes, the girls will have an equal number of shoes. How many pairs of shoes did Anne have originally?

   A. 3
   B. 6
   C. 9
   D. 15

6. Frank has x stamps, and Chris has 8 more than 7 times the number of stamps Frank has. How many stamps do Frank and Chris have in total?

   E. $8x$
   F. $7x + 8$
   G. $8x + 7$
   H. $8x + 8$

✔ Common Subjects for Word Problems

translations, age, money, collections, percentages, and time

✔ Remember

Picking Numbers often works well when you're faced with variables in the answer choices, percentages, number properties, or unknown values.

Translation with Formulas

Ratios

The ratio of a to b can be written as $a{:}b$ or as $\frac{a}{b}$.

A. A grocery store stocks 6 apples for every 8 oranges. What is the ratio of apples to oranges?

B. If there are 28 pieces of fruit on the shelf and they are all either apples or oranges, how many apples are there?

Percentages

Percentage $= \frac{\text{Part}}{\text{Whole}}$ Percentage change $= \frac{\text{Change}}{\text{Original}}$

C. What percentage of 50 is 35?

D. 12 is 20% of what number?

Rates

Common rate equations: $r = \frac{d}{t}$, $d = tr$, $t = \frac{d}{r}$

E. John travels 80 miles in 2 hours. What is his average speed?

F. Mary makes $72 on Friday. If she works for 8 hours, how much does she make per hour?

> ✔ **Remember**
>
> **As with all translation questions, first translate the English into equations. Only when you are sure you have the translation correct should you begin on the actual math.**

7. If the price of a stock decreases by 20%, and then by an additional 25%, by what percentage has the price decreased from its original value?

A. 40
B. 45
C. 50
D. 55

8. Alicia has to take $\frac{3}{4}$ ounces of a liquid vitamin supplement daily. If her bottle contains 15 ounces, how many days will it last?

E. 10
F. 12
G. 15
H. 20

Word Problems with No Variable

Label your own variables to translate problems in which the variables you're trying to solve for aren't explicitly labeled.

Identify the variable(s) in each of the phrases below, and translate the statements into appropriate equations:

Statement:	Translation:
A. Martha is 3 times as old as Ann.	______
B. There are 5 more orange marbles than blue marbles in a bag.	______
C. There are 3 empty boxes for every full box.	______

✔ Remember

When translating, try to avoid using *o, l, s,* and *z* if you can. These letters can be easily confused with numbers. If the variables are included in a question, keep your numbers and letters straight.

Problems with numbers in the answer choices are often solved quickly with Kaplan's Backsolving strategy.

9. Five less than 3 times a certain number is equal to twice the original number plus 7. What is the original number?

A. 2
B. $2\frac{2}{5}$
C. 6
D. 12

10. A class of 30 is divided into 2 groups such that the size of the smaller group is $\frac{2}{3}$ the size of the larger group. How large is the smaller group?

E. 10
F. 12
G. 16
H. 20

11. Paul developed a roll of film containing 36 pictures. If he made 2 prints each of half of the pictures and 1 print of each of the rest, how many prints did he make in all?

A. 27
B. 36
C. 54
D. 72

12. The average weight of Jake, Ken, and Larry is 60 kilograms. If Jake and Ken each weigh 50 kilograms, how much does Larry weigh, in kilograms?

E. 40

F. 50

G. 60

H. 80

Word Problems with Geometry

Translation of geometry problems typically involves putting information from the question directly into the given diagram or, occasionally, drawing a brand new figure.

A. If the width of a rectangle is 4 and the length is twice the width, what is the area?

____

B. *ABC* is an isosceles triangle. Sides *AB* and *AC* are 7 units each and side *BC* is 3 units. The measure of angle *ABC* is 78°. What is the measure of angle *CAB*? ______________

____

C. Six bridges are connected at points *A*, *B*, *C*, *D*, *E*, and *F*, in a hexagon. The points appear clockwise when viewed from above, from *A* to *F*. If Jenny starts at point *A* and walks 725 bridges in a clockwise direction, at what point will she be when she has stopped?

____

13.

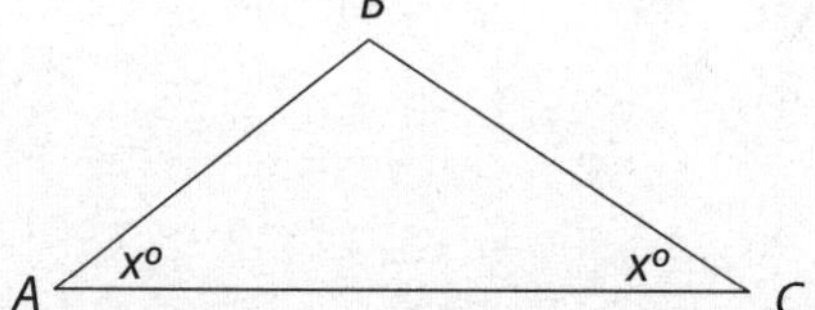

The perimeter of triangle *ABC* is 18. If $AC = 4$, then $BC =$

A. 4

B. 7

C. 10

D. 14

14. 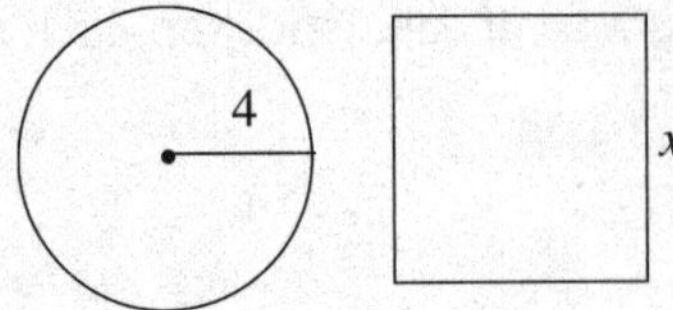

If the area of the circle is equal to the area of the square, which of the following is closest to the value of x?

E. 3

F. 4

G. 5

H. 7

15. If the circumference of a circle is 100π, what is its area?

A. 20π

B. 50π

C. $1{,}000\pi$

D. $2{,}500\pi$

16. A rectangular plot of land measuring 18 acres by 48 acres is to be divided into square lots of equal size. What is the smallest possible number of square lots if all of the lots are to be equal, without any waste?

E. 4

F. 6

G. 24

H. 54

New Terminology

Learn to look past confusing terminology to determine what a question is really asking and then solve accordingly.

Translate the following statements into equations you can solve:

Statement:	Translation and solution:
A. There are 7 filberts in a quoodle. If John travels 8 quoodles, how many filberts has he traveled?	______
B. A perfectly circular track is 8π karbles long all the way around. How many square karbles is its interior area?	______
C. In order to "mangle" a number, you must perform the following three steps: Step 1: Multiply the number by 5. Step 2: Add 11 to the result. Step 3: Add the result of Step 2 to the original number.	Translate the steps of "mangling" into Math: Step 1: ______ Step 2: ______ Step 3: ______

17. Using the above definition of "mangle," when you "mangle" the number 3, you get

A. 14
B. 18
C. 26
D. 29

18. A number is considered "blue" if the sum of its digits is equal to the product of its digits. Which of the following numbers is "blue"?

E. 111
F. 220
G. 321
H. 422

✔ Remember

You are not expected to know these terms. The test maker makes these terms up but always defines them in the question.

Unusual Word Problems

Some problems can't be easily classified. Your approach should be the same as it is for all word problems: straightforward translation.

Translate the following statements into equations:

Statement:	Translation:
A. John has 4 coins that add up to \$0.46.	______________
If 1 coin is a quarter, what are the other 3 coins?	______________
B. The high temperature on Monday,	______________
measured in degrees Fahrenheit, was 2°	______________
above freezing. If the low temperature	______________
was 3° below zero, what was the range	______________
of temperatures on Monday?	______________

19. A cable television station runs a marathon, broadcasting 11 hours of program *A*, immediately followed by 11 hours of program *B*, immediately followed by 11 hours of program *C*. If the first episode of program *A* begins at 8 p.m., what time does the last episode of program *C* end?

A. 7 a.m.
B. 7 p.m.
C. 5 a.m.
D. 5 p.m.

20. Rishi has a jar containing dimes, nickels, and pennies. There are 29 coins totaling \$1.46 in the jar. If Rishi then removes 8 dimes, 8 nickels, and 10 pennies from the jar, which coins remain?

E. 2 dimes, 1 nickel
F. 2 nickels, 1 penny
G. 3 nickels
H. 1 dime, 1 nickel, 1 penny

✓ Remember

When faced with unusual questions, look for standard units, like 24-hour blocks of time, and convert quarters to \$0.25.

Sequences and Sets

Sequences and sets require you to detect patterns in problems and then extrapolate answers.

Predict the next item in each of the following sequences:

A. 15, 12, 9, … __________

B. 1, 3, 4, 6, 7, 9, 10, … __________

C. 2, 3, 5, 9, 17, … __________

Answer the following questions about sets:

D. How many odd numbers are there between 1 and 99? __________

E. How many multiples of 6 are there in the following set: {2, 4, 6, …, 34, 36, 38}?

____

✔ Remember

Sequences are often generated by equations but can also be based on number properties.

✔ Remember

In most cases, you won't have to count out every item in a set. Look for a pattern instead.

21. Which of the following sets contains multiples of 3 but not of 9?

A. {120, 126, 135, 138, 141}

B. {141, 144, 147, 150, 156}

C. {183, 186, 192, 201, 204}

D. {12, 13, 14, …, 22, 23, 24}

22. The set Q is defined as {1.2, 6.5, 4.0, 3.3, 9.0}. If x belongs to set Q and $10x - 5$ is prime, what is x?

E. 1.2

F. 3.3

G. 5.0

H. 6.5

23. The first number in a sequence is 8. If each number in the sequence is 10 less than three times the previous number, then what will the fourth term be?

A. 32

B. 60

C. 86

D. 248

24. {1, 2, 3, …, 200}

How many numbers in the above set are divisible by 11 but not by 22?

E. 21

F. 18

G. 15

H. 9

The following practice sets provide an opportunity to apply the concepts and strategic thinking covered in this chapter. To practice Test Day timing, follow the suggested timing guidelines for each section.

WORD PROBLEMS PRACTICE SET

Suggested Timing: 15 minutes

1. Meghan has 100 dollars more than Andrew. After Meghan spends 20 dollars on groceries, she will have 5 times as much money as Andrew. How much money does Andrew have?

   A. \$20

   B. \$30

   C. \$40

   D. \$50

2. The original price of an item is reduced by 40% for a sale. After two weeks, the sale price is reduced by an additional 25%. The final price is what percentage less than the original price?

   E. 45%

   F. 50%

   G. 55%

   H. 60%

3. If a car travels at 60 miles per hour for 8 hours, how far will the car travel?

   A. 360 miles

   B. 400 miles

   C. 420 miles

   D. 480 miles

4. A number p is equal to 3 times a number q plus 7. What is the value of q if $p = 19$?

   E. -4

   F. -2

   G. 1

   H. 4

5. Four more than 3 times a number x is equal to 5 less than 6 times a number y. Which of the following expresses this relationship?

   A. $x + 3 = 2y$

   B. $3x + 4 = 6y + 5$

   C. $3x - 1 = 6y$

   D. $4x - 3 = 6y + 5$

6. If the average height of a group of 5 people is 67 inches, what is the total height, in inches, of the people?

   E. 305

   F. 320

   G. 335

   H. 365

7. Ron is 3 years older than Sherry, who is 4 years less than twice as old as John. Which of the following represents Ron's age, if J = John's age?

   A. $J - 1$

   B. $J + 3$

   C. $2J - 1$

   D. $2J - 4$

8. The width of a rectangle is one-half of its length. If the area of the rectangle is 18, what is its length?

   E. 3

   F. 4

   G. 5

   H. 6

9. Thirty percent of high school senior boys play in the school band. If a certain high school has 60 senior boys, how many boys play in the school band?

   A. 12
   B. 18
   C. 22
   D. 30

10. {1, 2, 3, …, 167, 168, 169}

    How many numbers in the set above have 8 as a factor but do not have 16 as a factor?

    E. 21
    F. 18
    G. 15
    H. 11

WORD PROBLEMS GRID-IN PRACTICE SET

Suggested Timing: 15 minutes

1. A trail mix contains nuts, granola, and fruits in the ratio 2:3:5. If there are 27 ounces of granola in the mix, how many ounces of fruit are in the mix?

2. Mark is 5 years less than 3 times Jessica's age. If Mark is 25 years old, what is Jessica's age?

3. Alex, Brian, Chandler, Doug, and Eve all ate pizza at a pizza party. Alex ate 3 slices of pizza, Brian and Chandler each ate 4 pieces of pizza, Doug ate 5 pieces of pizza, and Eve ate 2 pieces of pizza. If a pizza contains 8 slices, how many pizzas did they eat?

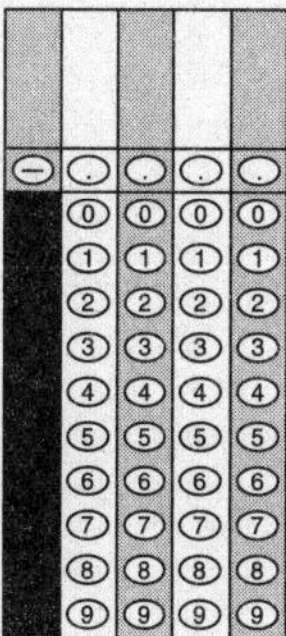

4. Bruce and Robin went trick or treating this Halloween and collected pieces of candy. Bruce collected 10 less than four times the number of pieces of candy that Robin collected. If Bruce and Robin collected a combined 50 pieces of candy, how many pieces of candy did Bruce collect?

5. Frances and Gloria enjoy knitting. They both like to use many different types of yarn. Frances has 81 different types of yarn. Gloria has 15 more than one-third the number of types of yarn that Frances has. How many different types of yarn does Gloria have?

6. A bag of gummy worms contains red gummy worms and blue gummy worms in the ratio of 4:7. If there are 42 blue gummy worms in a bag, how many total gummy worms are in the bag, assuming red and blue are the only two colors of candy?

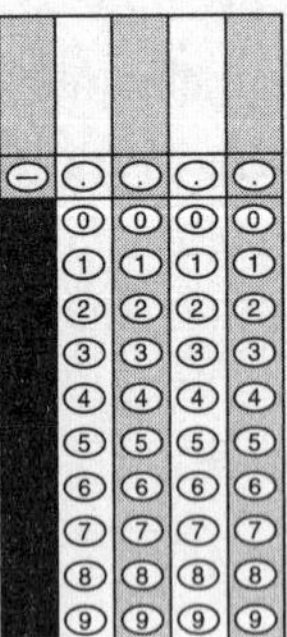

7. A grocery store sells cartons of orange juice. Each carton contains 40 ounces of juice. If Roberta pays \$15 for three cartons of orange juice, what is the cost of orange juice per ounce? Express your answer in cents.

8. A department store sells white and red candles. On Friday, there were *w* white candles, and there were 10 more than 3 times this number of red candles. If there were 110 candles in the store on Friday and all of the candles were either red or white, how many white candles were in the store on Friday?

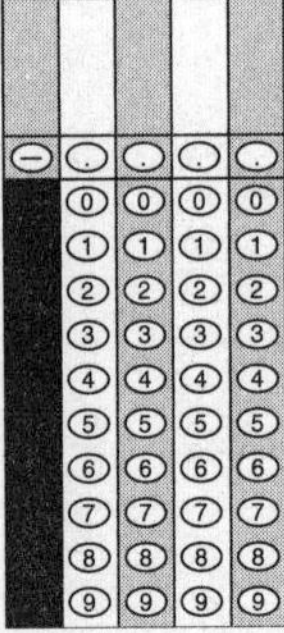

9. Samantha has two sizes of paper cups. She has small cups, which hold 8 ounces of liquid, and large cups, which hold 12 ounces of liquid. If Samantha has 100 ounces of water and fills an assortment of the two sizes of cups fully with water, what is the largest number of large cups she could have filled if she had no water left over?

10. Tennis balls are usually packed in vacuum-sealed tubes that contain 3 tennis balls. If Pam has 77 tennis balls, how many full containers of tennis balls can she pack?

ANSWERS AND EXPLANATIONS

Translation

A. $z + 2 = 2z$

B. $x - 5 = y$

C. $3 - 3x$

D. $\frac{y}{x}$

E. $\frac{1}{4}(4 + x)$

F. The product of 3 and *z*

G. The square of *b*

H. *a* divided by the quantity of *b* minus *c*

I. 8 times *x* is half as large as *x* cubed

J. The quotient of *h* and *g* is equivalent to 4 times the value of *h*

K. $\frac{x}{x^2} = 2$

L. $xy = 2 + x + y$

1. B

Subject: Algebra

Getting to the Answer:

Seven less than 4 times *x*	$4x - 7$
Is equal to	$4x - 7 =$
Twice *x* plus 9	$4x - 7 = 2x + 9$

2. F

Subject: Algebra

Getting to the Answer:

D Dollars	in Moira's wallet
+ *B* Dollars	withdrawn from bank (added to Moira's wallet)
− *S* Dollars	spent (subtracted from Moira's wallet)
$D + B - S$	

3. D

Subject: Algebra

Getting to the Answer:

Anna's age $= y$
Marco's age $= y - 3$
Let $y = 20$
Marco's age $= 20 - 3 = 17$
Marco's age 5 years ago $= 17 - 5 = 12$

Find the answer choice that matches.

(A) $y - 2 = 20 - 2 = 18$. Eliminate it.

(B) $y - 3 = 20 - 3 = 17$. Eliminate it.

(C) $y - 5 = 20 - 5 = 15$. Eliminate it.

(D) $y - 8 = 20 - 8 = 12$. This is the answer.

4. E

Subject: Algebra

Getting to the Answer:

Matt $= c$
Jen $= d$
9 fewer than 5 times as many cards as Matt
Jen $= 5c - 9$

5. B

Subject: Algebra

Getting to the Answer:

Anne $= n$
Fiona $= 3n$

If Fiona gives Anne 6 pairs of shoes, then they are equal, so

$$3n - 6 = n + 6$$
$$3n = n + 12$$
$$2n = 12$$
$$n = 6$$

6. H

Subject: Algebra

Getting to the Answer:

$$\text{Frank} = x$$
$$\text{Chris} = 7x + 8$$
$$x + 7x + 8 = 8x + 8$$

Translation with Formulas

A. 6 apples:8 oranges

B. 3 apples:7 fruits = 12 apples:28 fruits

C. $\frac{35}{50} = \frac{70}{100} = 70\%$

D. $12 = 20\%(x)$; $12 = 0.20x$; $60 = x$

E. $s = \frac{d}{t} = \frac{80 \text{ miles}}{2 \text{ hours}} = 40$ miles per hour

F. $\text{rate} = \frac{\text{total}}{\text{time}} = \frac{\$72}{8 \text{ hours}} = \$9$ per hour

7. A

Subject: Algebra

Getting to the Answer:

Price of the stock = 100

$100 - 20\% = 100 - (100 \times 0.20) = 100 - 20 = 80$

$80 - 25\% = 80 - (80 \times 0.25) = 80 - 20 = 60$

$100 - 60 = 40$

$\frac{40}{100} = 40\%$ Always divide the difference by the original number to find the percent change.

8. H

Subject: Algebra

Getting to the Answer:

$$15 \div \frac{3}{4} =$$
$$15 \times \frac{4}{3} = 20$$

Word Problems with No Variable

A. $m = 3a$

B. $r = b + 5$

C. $e = 3f$

9. D

Subject: Algebra

Getting to the Answer:

$$3x - 5 = 2x + 7$$
$$x - 5 = 7$$
$$x = 12$$

Backsolve:

(C) $6: 3(6) - 5 = 2(6) + 7$

$18 - 5 = 12 + 7$

$13 = 19$ The number must be higher.

Through the process of Backsolving, you know that **(D)** is the answer, but let's check anyway.

(D) $12: 3(12) - 5 = 2(12) + 7$

$36 - 5 = 24 + 7$

$31 = 31$

10. F

Subject: Algebra

Getting to the Answer:

$$a + \frac{2}{3}a = 30$$
$$\frac{3}{3}a + \frac{2}{3}a = 30$$
$$\frac{5}{3}a = 30$$
$$a = 30\left(\frac{3}{5}\right)$$
$$a = 18$$

Since the larger group is a, the smaller group is $\frac{2}{3}(18) = 12$

11. C

Subject: Algebra

Getting to the Answer:

$$\frac{36}{2} = 18$$

one-half has 2 prints each $18 \times 2 = 36$

one-half has 1 print each $18 \times 1 = 18$

$36 + 18 = 54$

12. H

Subject: Algebra

Getting to the Answer:

$$\frac{(\text{Jake} + \text{Ken} + \text{Larry})}{3} = 60$$
$$\text{Jake} + \text{Ken} + \text{Larry} = 180$$

If Jake and Ken each are 50, then

$$50 + 50 + \text{Larry} = 180$$
$$100 + \text{Larry} = 180$$
$$\text{Larry} = 80$$

Word Problems with Geometry

A. $w = 4$, $l = 8$, $Area = 4 \times 8 = 32$

B. Draw an isosceles triangle with A at the apex. Side AB = side $AC = 7$, and base $BC = 3$. $\angle ACB$ must be equal to $\angle CBA$ (78°), since they are opposite equal sides. $\angle CAB = 180° - 78° - 78° = 24°$

C. Draw a regular hexagon. Label the points *A*... *F*. Since she walks over 725 bridges, divide by 6 to find how many times she goes all the way around the hexagon.

$$\frac{725}{6} = 120 \text{ remainder } 5$$

Her final trip around will take her over 5 bridges. Jenny stops at bridge *F*.

13. B

Subject: Geometry

Getting to the Answer: The perimeter is given as 18, and $AC = 4$. Since angles BAC and ACB are equal, AB and BC are also equal. Therefore, $AB + BC + AC = 18$.

Substitute x for both AB and BC.

$$x + x + 4 = 18$$
$$2x = 14$$

$x = 7$, which is side AB and side BC.

14. H

Subject: Geometry

Getting to the Answer:

$$\text{Circle Area} = \pi r^2$$
$$\text{Area} = \pi(4^2)$$
$$\text{Area} = 16\pi$$
$$\text{Area} = 16(3.14)$$
$$\text{Area} = 50.24$$
$$\text{Square Area} = \text{side}^2$$
$$50.24 = x^2$$
$$7.09 = x$$

The answer is 7.

15. D

Subject: Geometry

Getting to the Answer:

$$\text{Circumference} = 2\pi r$$
$$100\pi = 2\pi r$$
$$50\pi = \pi r$$
$$50 = r$$
$$\text{Area} = \pi r^2$$
$$\text{Area} = \pi(50^2)$$
$$\text{Area} = 2{,}500\pi$$

16. G

Subject: Geometry

Getting to the Answer: You need to find the largest number that divides evenly into both 18 and 48.

This number is 6.

$$\frac{18}{6} = 3$$
$$\frac{48}{6} = 8$$

You will have 6×6 squares in 3 rows of 8 columns each; therefore, you will have 3×8, or 24 squares.

New Terminology

A. $7f = q$; therefore, 7 times 8 equals the total number of filberts in 8 quoodles: 56.

B. The length given is a circumference, so $2\pi r = 8\pi$ karbles. This means that the radius of the track is 4 karbles. The area is then π (4 karbles)^2 or 16π karbles^2.

C. Step 1: $5x$
Step 2: $5x + 11$
Step 3: $5x + 11 + x$, or $6x + 11$

17. D

Subject: Algebra

Getting to the Answer:

Step 1: $3 \times 5 = 15$
Step 2: $15 + 11 = 26$
Step 3: $26 + 3 = 29$

18. G

Subject: Algebra

Getting to the Answer:

Backsolve beginning with **(E)**:

(E) 111 $1 + 1 + 1 = 3$ $(1)(1)(1) = 1$ Eliminate it.

(F) 220 $2 + 2 + 0 = 4$ $(2)(2)(0) = 0$ Eliminate it.

(G) 321 $3 + 2 + 1 = 6$ $(3)(2)(1) = 6$ This is your answer.

Unusual Word Problems

A. A penny and 2 dimes

B. Since freezing is 32 degrees, the high was 34 and the low was -3. $34 - (-3) = 37$.

19. C

Subject: Algebra

Getting to the Answer: If each show is 11 hours and there are 3 complete shows to run, there will be 3×11 or 33 hours of programming.

This is 1 complete day with 9 hours remaining. One complete day will take you back to 8 p.m., then just add the 9 hours to that, taking the end of show C to 5 a.m.

20. H

Subject: Algebra

Getting to the Answer: Rishi removes 26 coins with a total value of $8 \times \$0.10 + 8 \times \$0.05 + 10 \times \$0.01 = \$1.30$. This means that there are three coins left in the jar, and they have a value of 16 cents. Therefore, the three remaining coins must be a dime, a nickel, and a penny.

Sequences and Sets

A. 6

B. 12

C. 33

D. Between 1 and 100, there are 50 even numbers and 50 odd numbers. Since 100 is even, between 1 and 99 there are 50 odd numbers.

E. There are 6 multiples of 6, which are 6, 12, 18, 24, 30, and 36.

21. C

Subject: Arithmetic

Getting to the Answer: Starting with **(A)**, look for a number divisible by 9. When you can't find one, you have found the answer.

(A) $\frac{135}{9} = 15$

(B) $\frac{144}{9} = 16$

(C) There is no multiple of 9; therefore, this is your answer.

22. E

Subject: Arithmetic

(E) 1.2: $10(1.2) - 5 = 12 - 5 = 7$ This is prime, and the answer.

23. C

Subject: Algebra

Getting to the Answer: The second term will be $(3 \times 8) - 10 = 14$. The third term will be $(3 \times 14) - 10 = 32$. The fourth term will be $(3 \times 32) - 10 = 86$.

24. H

Subject: Algebra

Getting to the Answer: First, list all the multiples of 11 in the above set. This list will include 11, 22, 33, 44, 55, 66, 77, 88, 99, 110, 121, 132, 143, 154, 165, 176, 187, and 198. Of these 18 numbers, every other one is a multiple of 22, so only 9 numbers are divisible by 11 but not by 22.

ANSWERS AND EXPLANATIONS

Word Problems Practice Set

1. A

Subject: Algebra

Getting to the Answer: Translate the given information into math. Meghan has $100 more than Andrew, so $m = a + 100$. After spending $20, Meghan has five times as much money as Andrew, so $m - 20 = 5a$. The problem is asking you to find a, so substitute $a + 100$ into the second equation for m, and solve for a.

$$\begin{aligned} m - 20 &= 5a \\ a + 100 - 20 &= 5a \\ 80 &= 4a \\ a &= 20 \end{aligned}$$

Andrew has $20, so **(A)** is correct.

2. G

Subject: Algebra

Getting to the Answer: Let 100 be the original price.

$$100 - 40\% = 100 - (100 \times 0.40) = 100 - 40 = 60$$
$$60 - 25\% = 60 - (60 \times 0.25) = 60 - 15 = 45$$

$$\frac{(100 - 45)}{100} = \frac{55}{100} = 55\%$$

3. D

Subject: Algebra

Getting to the Answer: Simply multiply the mph by the hours traveled. $60 \times 8 = 480$ miles.

4. H

Subject: Algebra

Getting to the Answer:

p	A number p is equal to 3 times a
$p =$	number q plus 7.
$p = 3q + 7$	
$p = 19$	
$19 = 3q + 7$	
$12 = 3q$	
$4 = q$	

5. A

Subject: Algebra

Getting to the Answer:

$3x + 4$	Four more than 3 times a number x
$3x + 4 =$	is equal to
$3x + 4 = 6y - 5$	5 less than 6 times a number y.

Since this is not an answer choice, you must manipulate the equation.

$3x + 9 = 6y$	Factor out the 3 on the left.
$3(x + 3) = 6y$	Divide both sides by 3.
$x + 3 = 2y$	This is an answer choice.

6. G

Subject: Arithmetic

Getting to the Answer:

$$\text{Average} = \frac{(\text{total height of the group})}{5}$$

$$67 = \frac{(\text{total height of the group})}{5}$$

$$335 = \text{total height of the group}$$

7. C

Subject: Algebra

Getting to the Answer:

John's age $= J$
Sherry's age $= 2J - 4$
Ron $= (2J - 4) + 3$
$2J - 1$

8. H

Subject: Geometry

Getting to the Answer:

$$\text{Area} = \text{length} \times \text{width}$$
$$\text{Width} = \frac{1}{2}\ \text{length}$$
$$\text{Area} = \text{length} \times \frac{1}{2}\ \text{length}$$
$$18 = \frac{1}{2}\ \text{length} \times \text{length}$$
$$36 = \text{length}^2$$
$$6 = \text{length}$$

9. B

Subject: Algebra

Getting to the Answer:

Set up a ratio:

$$\frac{30}{100} = \frac{x}{60}$$
$$100x = 1800$$
$$x = 18$$

10. H

Subject: Arithmetic

Getting to the Answer: To find how many are multiples of 8, divide the highest member of the group (since these are consecutive integers) by 8.

$\frac{169}{8} = 21\text{ r }1$ There are 21 numbers that are a multiple of 8.

Since 16 is a multiple of 8, you must reduce the figure by the number in the set that are multiples of 16.

$\frac{169}{16} = 10\text{ r }9$ There are 10 numbers that are multiples of 16.

$21 - 10 = 11$ that are multiples of 8 but not 16.

Word Problems Grid-In Practice Set

1. 45

Subject: Arithmetic

Getting to the Answer: Only use the information that is relevant to the question! You are asked how many ounces of fruit are needed for the trail mix, and you are given an amount of granola. The amount of nuts is not needed, so don't use it: The ratio of granola to fruits is 3:5 and there are 27 ounces of granola, so the following proportion can be written:

$$\frac{3}{5} = \frac{27}{x}$$

Cross multiplication gives $3x = 135$, so $x = 45$. Grid in 45.

2. 10

Subject: Arithmetic

Getting to the Answer: Start with Mark's age. He is 25, so Mark is 5 years less than 3 times Jessica's age. 3 times Jessica's age must be 30. Thus, Jessica's age is 10, so grid in 10.

3. 2.25

Subject: Arithmetic

Getting to the Answer: Start by computing the number of pieces that the five of them ate total: $3 + 4 + 4 + 5 + 2 = 18$ slices. There are 8 slices in an entire pizza, so they ate 2 pizzas, with 2 slices left over. 2 slices is one quarter of a pizza, so they ate $2\frac{1}{4}$ pizzas, or 2.25 pizzas. Grid in 2.25.

4. 38

Subject: Algebra

Getting to the Answer: Begin by translating the question to algebra. Let r represent the number of pieces of candy that Robin collected. If Bruce collected 10 less than four times this number, Bruce collected 4r − 10 pieces of candy. Since together they collected 50 pieces of candy, we can create the equation $r + (4r - 10) = 50 \Rightarrow 5r - 10 = 50$. Adding 10 to both sides and dividing by 5 gives $r = 12$. However, you aren't done yet! The question asks you for the number of pieces of candy that Bruce collected, which is $4(12) - 10 = 48 - 10 = 38$. Grid in 38.

5. 42

Subject: Arithmetic

Getting to the Answer: Start with the fact that Frances has 81 different types of yarn. You know that Gloria has 15 more than $\frac{1}{3}$ this amount, so perform the necessary calculations. $\frac{1}{3}$ of 81 is 27, and 15 more than 27 is 42 $(27 + 15 = 42)$. Gloria has 42 different types of yarn, so grid in 42.

6. 66

Subject: Algebra

Getting to the Answer: Use the information given in the question to form a proportion. You know that the ratio of red to blue gummy worms is 4:7 and there are 42 blue gummy worms. This gives a proportion that can be used to solve for the number of red gummy worms:

$$\begin{aligned} \frac{4}{7} &= \frac{x}{42} \\ 7x &= 168 \\ x &= 24 \end{aligned}$$

There are 24 red gummy worms, but don't grid in 24! The question asks you for the number of total gummy worms, which is $42 + 24 = 66$. Grid in 66.

7. 12.5

Subject: Arithmetic

Getting to the Answer: You know that 3 cartons of orange juice cost \$15. That means that one carton of orange juice costs \$5. If there are 40 ounces of orange juice in a carton, then the cost per ounce would be \$5 divided by 40. This operation yields 0.125. Since the question asks for the cost per ounce in cents, convert this value to cents by multiplying by 100. This gives 12.5, so grid in 12.5.

8. 25

Subject: Algebra

Getting to the Answer: Start by constructing an equation from the information given in the question. There are w white candles. There are 10 more than 3 times w red candles, which can be represented as $3w + 10$. Put this together to form an equation, then solve for w:

$$\begin{aligned} w + 3w + 10 &= 110 \\ 4w + 10 &= 110 \\ 4w &= 100 \\ w &= 25 \end{aligned}$$

The question asks you to solve for the number of white candles, so you are done. Grid in 25.

9. 7

Subject: Arithmetic

Getting to the Answer: Just think about possible combinations of large and small cups. The largest number of large cups that could be filled is 8 $(8 \times 12 = 96)$. If 8 large cups were filled, that would only leave 4 ounces of water, so that doesn't work. If 7 large cups were filled, that would be $7 \times 12 = 84$ ounces of water in large cups. That leaves 16 ounces of water, which would completely fill 2 small cups. Thus, the largest number of large cups that could be filled is 7, so grid in 7.

10. 25

Subject: Arithmetic

Getting to the Answer: At first, this question appears to be a straightfoward division question. There are 77 tennis balls that are being packed into containers of three, so 77 divided by 3 should get you to the answer. However, when you divide, you will get 25 with a remainder of 2. This means there are 25 full containers of tennis balls with 2 leftover. Thus, you should grid in 25.

CHAPTER 17

Geometry

CHAPTER OBJECTIVES

By the end of this chapter, you will be able to:

- Solve geometry questions involving lines, angles, triangles, and other complex shapes
- Solve for unknown parts of circles

GEOMETRY I

Angle Addition

When two angles share a line or segment, you can add the two angles to form one bigger angle.

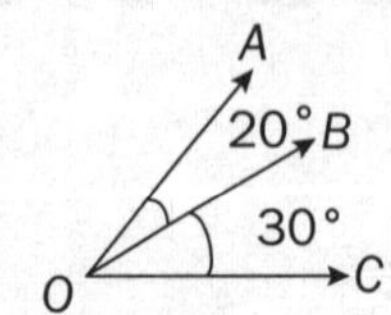

A. $\angle AOC =$ ______________

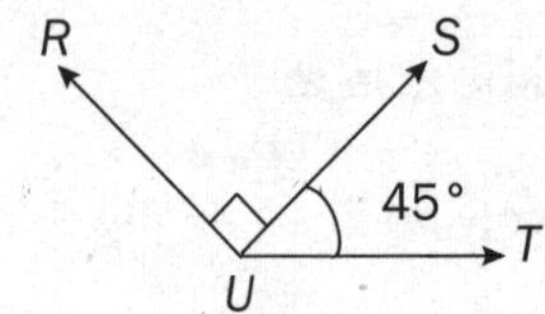

B. $\angle RUT =$ ______________

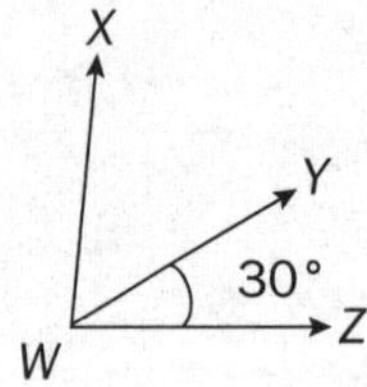

$\angle XWZ = 70°$

C. $\angle XWY =$ ______________

Straight Line Angles

There are 180 degrees in a straight line.

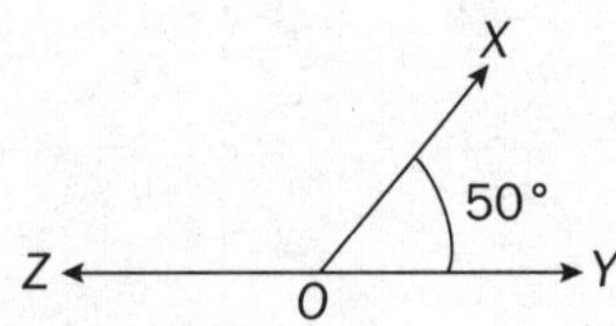

D. $\angle XOZ =$ ______________

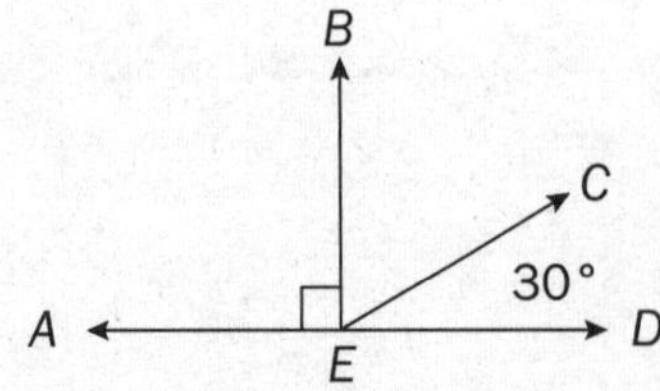

E. $\angle BEC =$ ______________

✓ Remember

Figures on the SHSAT may not necessarily be drawn to scale. Don't guess solely based on how a figure looks.

1.

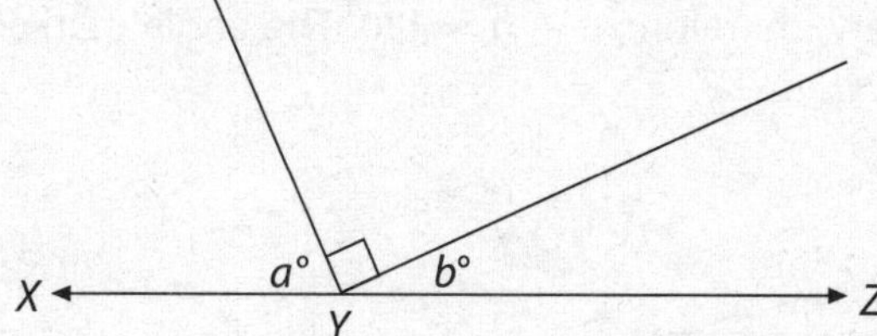

In the figure above, Y is a point on line XZ. What is the value of $a + b$?

A. 0

B. 45

C. 90

D. Cannot be determined from the information given.

2.

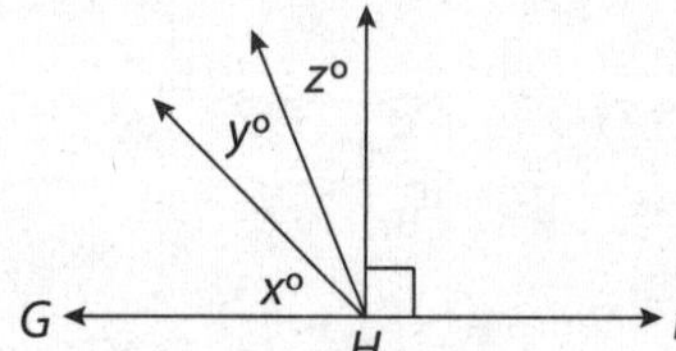

In the figure above, H is a point on line GI. If $x = 40$ and $z = 20$, what is the value of y?

E. 10

F. 20

G. 30

H. 50

Full Circle Angles

Intersecting lines create angles with special relationships you'll need to know. When two lines intersect, adjacent angles are supplementary because they add up to 180 degrees, and **vertical** angles (two angles opposite a vertex) are equal, or **congruent**.

The angles marked $a°$ and $b°$ are supplementary; therefore, $a + b = 180$. The angle marked $a°$ is vertical (and thus equal) to the one marked $c°$, so $a = c$.

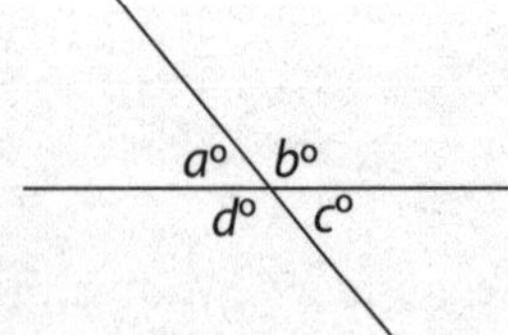

Use the information provided to solve for the missing angle measures.

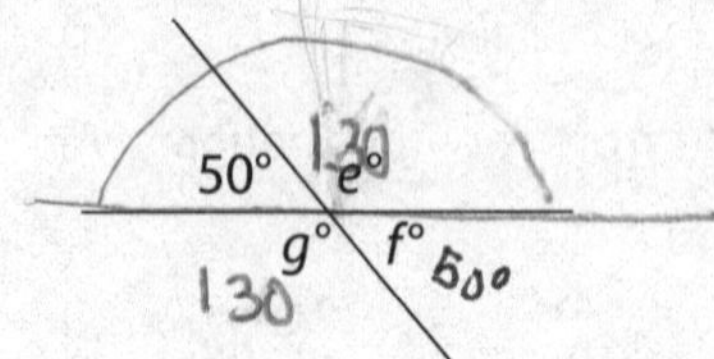

A. $e =$ 130°

B. $f =$ 50°

C. $g =$ 130°

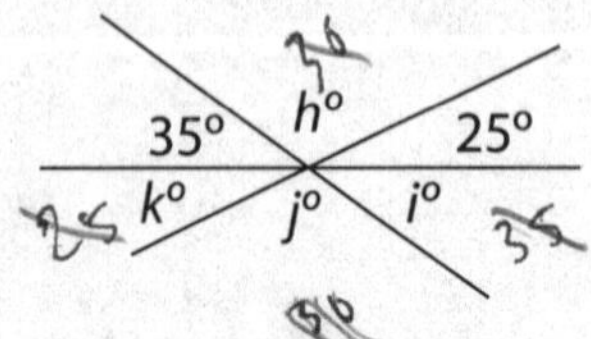

D. $h =$ __________

E. $i =$ __________

F. $j =$ __________

G. $k =$ __________

3. 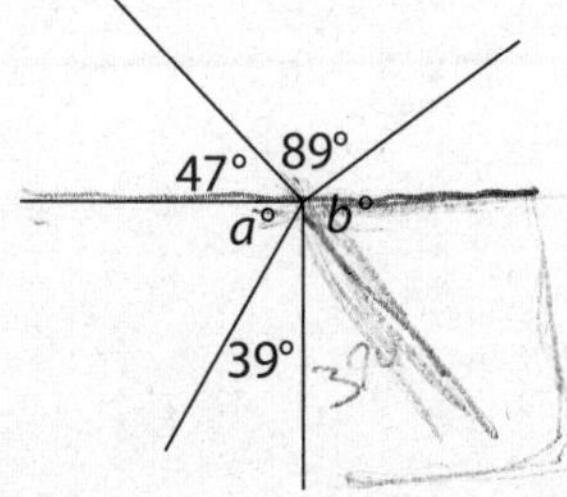

In the figure above, what is the value of $a + b$?

A. 145°

B. 175°

C. 185°

D. Cannot be determined from the information given.

4. 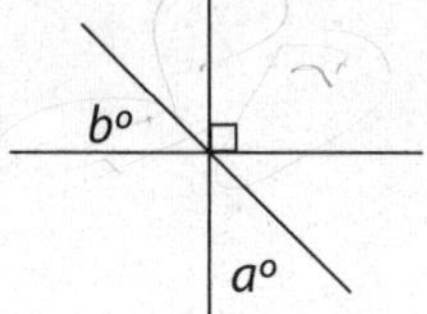

In the figure above, $a + b =$

E. 30°

F. 45°

G. 90°

H. Cannot be determined from the information given.

✔ Remember

Two intersecting lines create two sets of congruent angles called vertical angles.

If two lines intersect at a 90° angle, they are perpendicular. If one intersection is 90°, then all four angles are 90°.

If a question asks for the value of $a + b$, see if you can find the answer without solving for a and b separately.

Line Segments

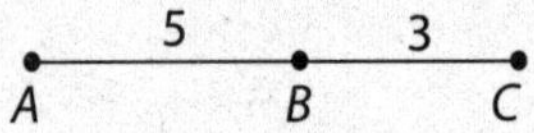

5 3
A B C

A. $AC =$ ______________

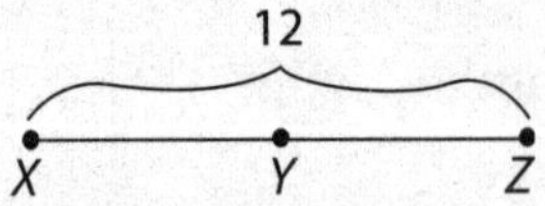

12
X Y Z

Point Y is the midpoint of segment XZ.

B. $YZ =$ ______________

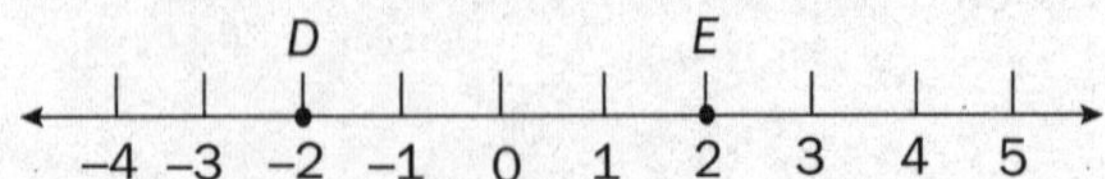

Point F (not shown) is the midpoint of line segment DE.

C. What is the location of point F? ______________

5. A B
–2 –1 0 1 2 3 4 5 6 7 8 9

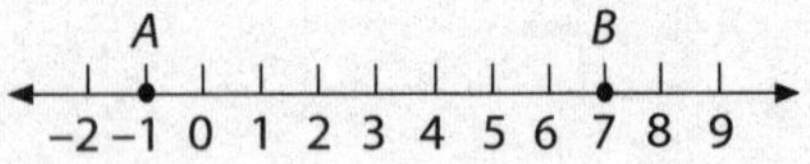

Point M (not shown) is the midpoint of line segment AB. What is the location of point M?

A. 2
B. 3
C. 4
D. 5

6. A B C D

In the figure above, $AD = 35$ and $BD = 21$. If $AB = BC$, what is the length of CD?

E. 4
F. 7
G. 14
H. 21

7. D E F G

In the figure above, if $DF = 5$ and $EG = 6$, what is the length of EF?

A. 1

B. 3

C. 5

D. Cannot be determined from the information given.

✔ **Remember**

A midpoint is a point that is the same distance from both ends of a line segment.

Label the diagram in the test booklet whenever possible. You can and should write in the test booklet.

Perimeter and Area of Quadrilaterals

Perimeter and area are basic properties that all two-dimensional shapes have. The **perimeter** of a quadrilateral can be calculated by adding the lengths of all its sides. **Area** is the amount of two-dimensional space a shape occupies. The most common shapes for which you'll need these two properties on Test Day are squares, rectangles, parallelograms, and trapezoids.

The area (A) of a **square** is given by $A = s^2$, where s is the side of the square.
To find the area of a **rectangle**, multiply the length by the width.

Parallelograms are quadrilaterals with two pairs of parallel sides. Rectangles and squares are subsets of parallelograms. You can find the area of a parallelogram using $A = bh$. As with triangles, you can use any side of a parallelogram as the base; in addition, the height is still perpendicular to the base. Use the side perpendicular to the base as the height for a rectangle or square; for any other parallelogram, the height (or enough information to find it) will be given.

A **trapezoid** is a quadrilateral with only one set of parallel sides. Those parallel sides form the two bases. To find the area, average those bases and multiply by the height.

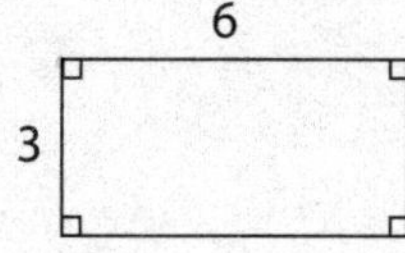

A. Perimeter = ______________

B. Area = ______________

8

4 $\sqrt{15}$ 4

6

C. Perimeter = ______________

D. Area = ______________

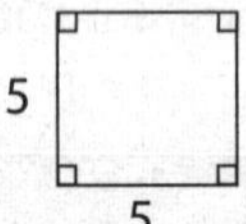

E. Perimeter = ______________

F. Area = ______________

G. Draw a rectangle with an area of 40, labeling the sides. What is the perimeter?

____

8.

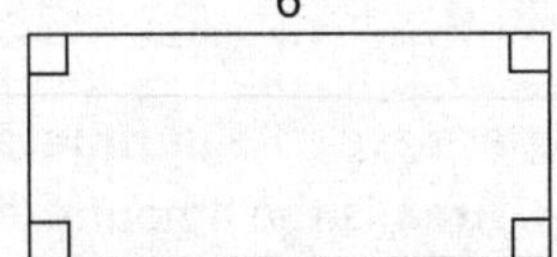

If the perimeter of the rectangle above is 20, what is its area?

E. 4
F. 8
G. 12
H. 24

9. The length of a rectangle is three times its width. If the area of the rectangle is 48, what is its length?

A. 4
B. 8
C. 12
D. 16

10.

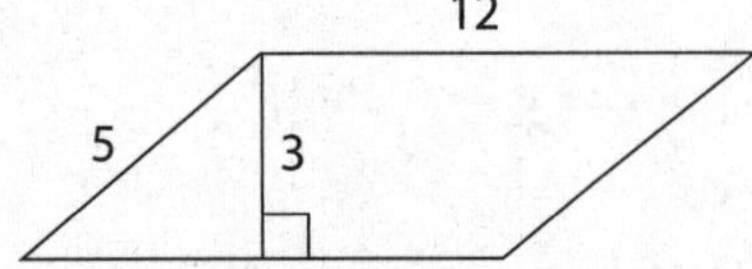

What is the area of the parallelogram above?

E. 15
F. 18
G. 36
H. 60

✔ Remember

Be careful to answer exactly what the question asks. If a question asks for area, the perimeter is often among the wrong answers, and vice versa.

Circumference and Area of Circles

A circle's **perimeter** is known as its **circumference** (C) and is found using $C = 2\pi r$, where r is the radius (distance from the center of the circle to its edge). **Area** is given by $A = \pi r^2$. The strange symbol is the lowercase Greek letter pi (π, pronounced "pie"), which is approximately 3.14.

Find the missing measurement for each circle.

A. Radius = 8
Circumference = ________________

B. Radius = 5
Area = ________________

C. Area = 16π
Radius = ________________

D. Circumference = 6π
Area = ________________

11.

5

If the radius of the circle above is 5, what is its circumference?

A. 5π
B. 10π
C. 15π
D. 25π

12.

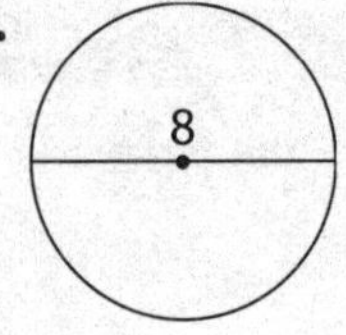

What is the area of the circle above?

E. 4π

F. 8π

G. 16π

H. 64π

13. If the circumference of a circle is 16π, what is its diameter?

A. 4

B. 8

C. 16

D. 4π

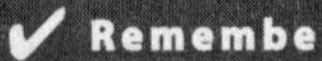
Remember

You will rarely be asked to calculate the actual area or circumference. Answers will almost always be in terms of π.

Perimeter and Area of Triangles

Perimeter of a triangle: The perimeter of a triangle is the distance around the triangle. In other words, the perimeter is equal to the sum of the lengths of the sides.

Area of a triangle: The area of a triangle refers to the space it takes up. The area of a triangle is $\frac{1}{2} \times$ base $\times$ height.

Formulas:

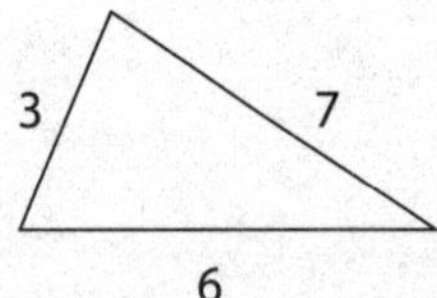

A. Perimeter = ______________

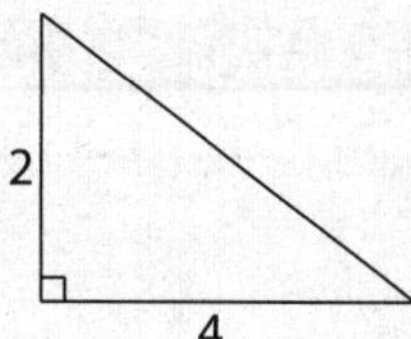

B. Area = ______________

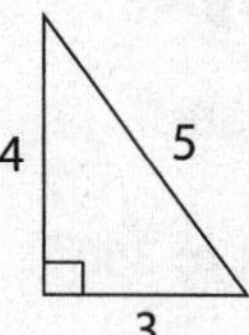

C. Area = ______________

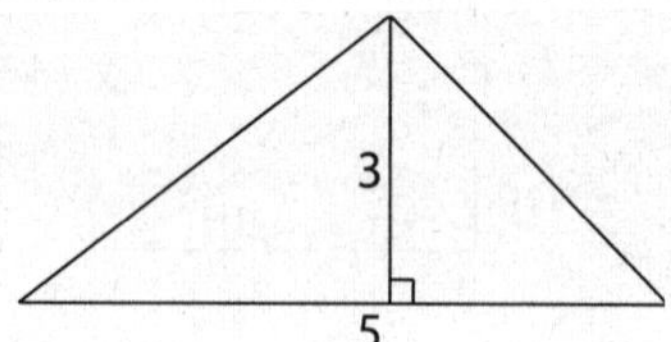

D. Area = ______________

14.

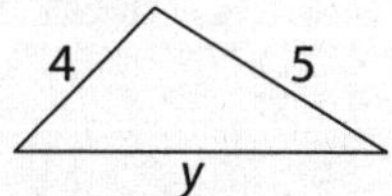

If the perimeter of the triangle above is 16, what is the value of y?

E. 5

F. 6

G. 7

H. 9

15.

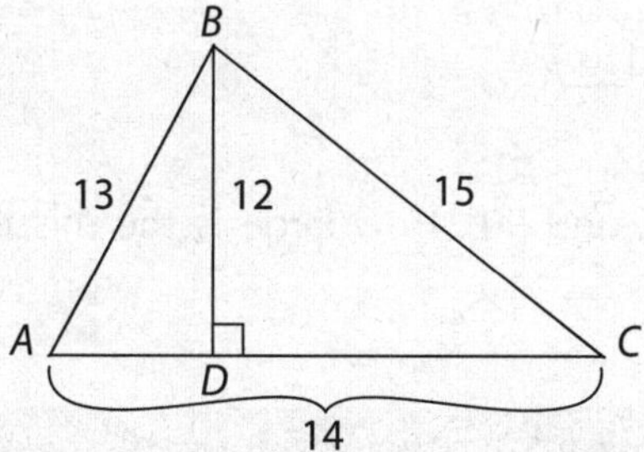

What is the area of triangle ABC?

A. 60

B. 78

C. 84

D. 90

✓ Remember

The height of a triangle is the perpendicular distance from any side chosen as the base to the opposite vertex.

Degrees of Quadrilaterals and Triangles

The interior angles of any triangle sum to 180°.

The interior angles of any quadrilateral sum to 360°.

For any polygon, the total degrees of the interior angles = 180°(n − 2), where n is the number of sides.

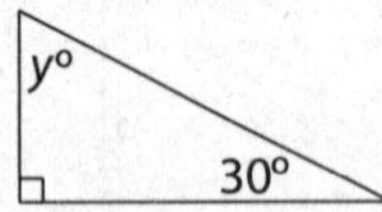

A. $y° =$ ____________

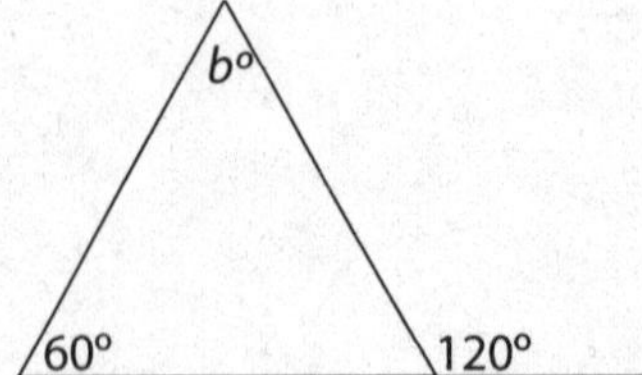

B. $b° =$ ____________

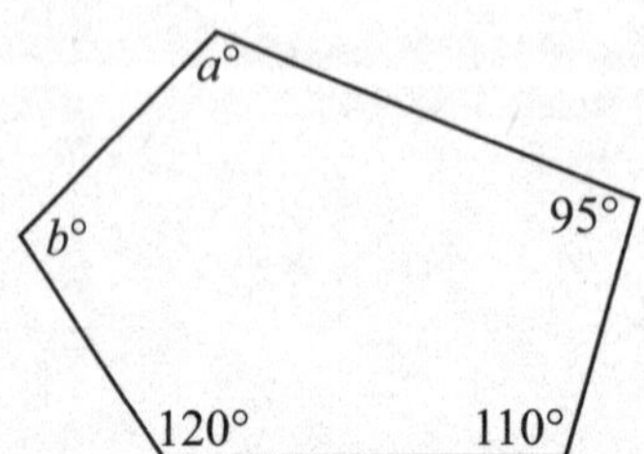

C. $a° + b° =$ ____________

D. A quadrilateral has angles measuring 56°, 78°, and 90°. How large is the missing angle? ____________

✓ Remember

For Test Day, you must know that the interior angles of a triangle sum to 180° and the interior angles of a quadrilateral sum to 360°.

16. In triangle XYZ, the measure of angle Y is twice the measure of angle X, and the measure of angle Z is three times the measure of angle X. What is the measure of angle Y?

E. 15°

F. 30°

G. 45°

H. 60°

17.

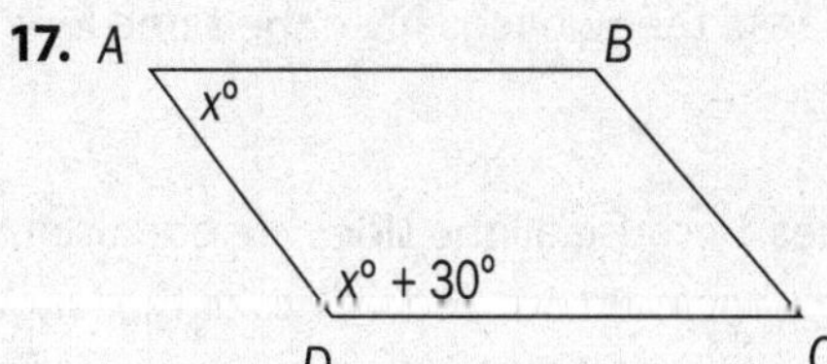

In the parallelogram $ABCD$ above, what is the measure of angle ADC?

A. 60°

B. 75°

C. 105°

D. 150°

Triangle Inequality Theorem

Triangle Inequality Theorem: The length of any side of a triangle is less than the sum of the lengths of the other two sides and greater than their positive difference. For example, if two sides of a triangle are 8 and 5, the third side has to be greater than the difference, 3, and less than the sum, 13. The third side must fall between those two values in order to form a triangle.

A. If you were presented with a triangle that had side lengths of 18 and 23, could the third side have a length of 30? ________________

B. Could it have a length of 5? ________________

C. If two sides of a triangle are 5 and 8, which of the following could be the length of the triangle's third side?

(Circle all that are possible.)

3 5 9 12 15

D. If two sides of a triangle are 2 and 6, which of the following could be the length of the triangle's third side?

(Circle all that are possible.)

3 5 6 8 12

✔ Remember

The third side of a triangle must always have a length greater than the difference between and less than the sum of the other two side lengths.

Isosceles, Equilateral, and Right Triangles

An **isosceles** triangle is a triangle that has at least two sides of equal length. The two equal sides are called the legs, and the third side is called the base. Because the two legs have the same length, the two angles opposite the legs must have the same measure.

An **equilateral triangle** is a triangle that has three equal sides. Because all the sides are equal, all the angles are also equal. All three angles in an equilateral triangle measure 60°, regardless of the lengths of the sides. All equilateral triangles are also isosceles, but not all isosceles triangles are equilateral.

A **right triangle** has one interior angle of 90°. The longest side, which lies opposite the right angle, is called the **hypotenuse**. The other two sides are called the **legs**.

✔ Remember

Be on the lookout for special triangles on Test Day.

18.

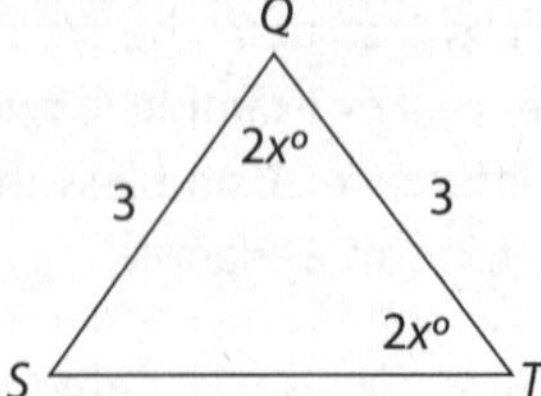

In the figure above, what is the length of ST?

E. $1\frac{1}{2}$

F. 3

G. $4\frac{1}{2}$

H. Cannot be determined from the information given.

Similar Quadrilaterals and Triangles

Similarity between shapes indicates that they have identical angles and proportional sides. Think of taking a shape and stretching or shrinking each side by the same ratio. The resulting shape will have the same angles as the original. While the sides will not be identical, they will be proportional.

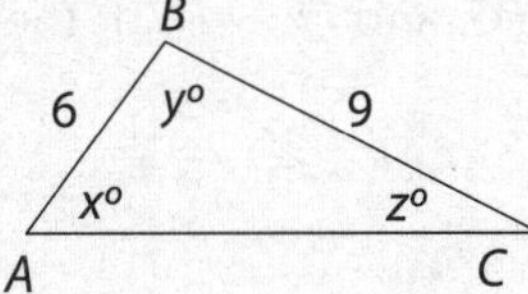

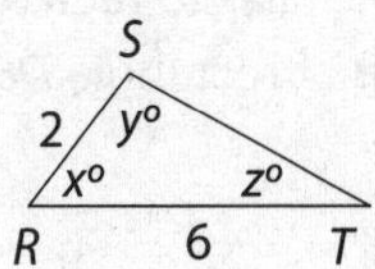

Triangle *ABC* is similar to triangle *RST.*

A. What is the length of *AC*? ________________

B. What is the length of *ST*? ________________

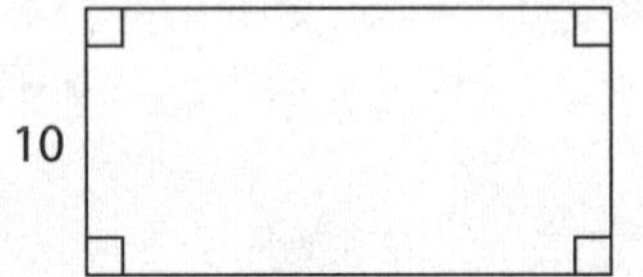

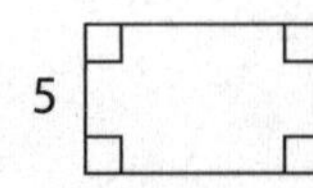

C. The rectangles above are similar. If the area of the larger rectangle is 250, what is the length of the smaller rectangle? ________________

19.

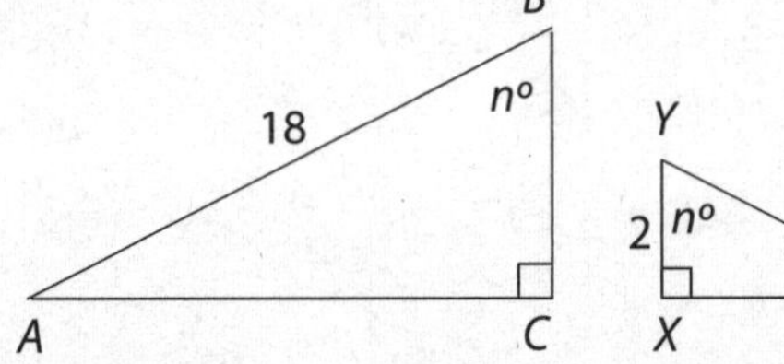

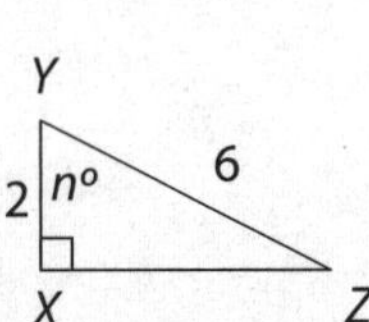

Triangle *ABC* is similar to triangle *XYZ.* What is the length of *BC*?

A. 6

B. 9

C. 12

D. 14

20.

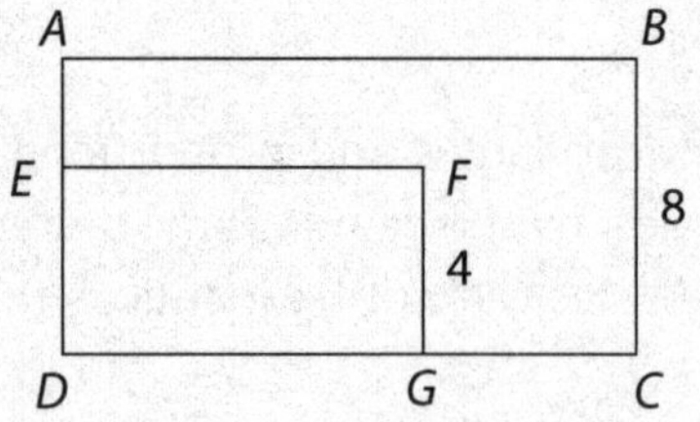

A B
E F
8
4
D G C

Rectangle *ABCD* is similar to rectangle *DEFG*, and $EF > FG$. If the area of rectangle *ABCD* is 96, what is the area of rectangle *DEFG*?

E. 6

F. 12

G. 24

H. 32

GEOMETRY II

Coordinate Plane

Understanding how to read and use the coordinate plane.

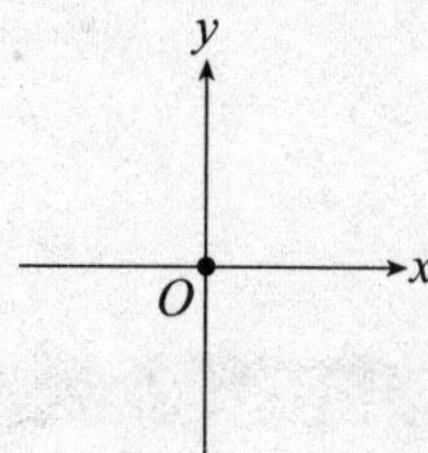

The horizontal line is the *x*-axis.
The vertical line is the *y*-axis.
The two lines meet at the origin.
A location is given by two numbers in parentheses.

The first is the *x*-coordinate.
The second is the *y*-coordinate.

If you start at the origin and move:

to the right, *x* is positive.
to the left, *x* is negative.
up, *y* is positive.
down, *y* is negative.

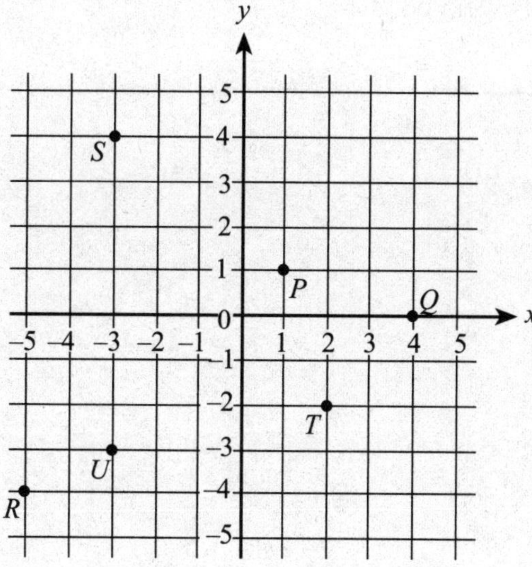

Write the coordinates of the following points:

A. *P:* ______________

B. *Q:* ______________

C. *R:* ______________

D. *S:* ______________

E. *T:* ______________

F. *U:* ______________

✔ Remember

Understanding the basics of the coordinate grid will help you unlock more difficult problems and get more points on Test Day!

Slope

The **slope** of a line is the ratio of the change in *y*-values over the change in *x*-values (rise over run, or the slant of the line). To find the slope of a line from its graph, identify two points that lie on the line and use the slope formula: $m = \frac{y_2 - y_1}{x_2 - x_1}$. You can also count the "rise" and the "run" if the line intersects the grid lines in convenient places.

The slope of a horizontal line is 0. The slope of a vertical line is undefined.

Find the slopes of the lines that contain the following points:

A. (0, 3) and (4, 5); slope = ______________

B. (–1, 2) and (9, 8); slope = ______________

Find the slopes of the following lines:

C. $y = 2x - 3$

D. $y = -\frac{1}{5}x + 2$

1.

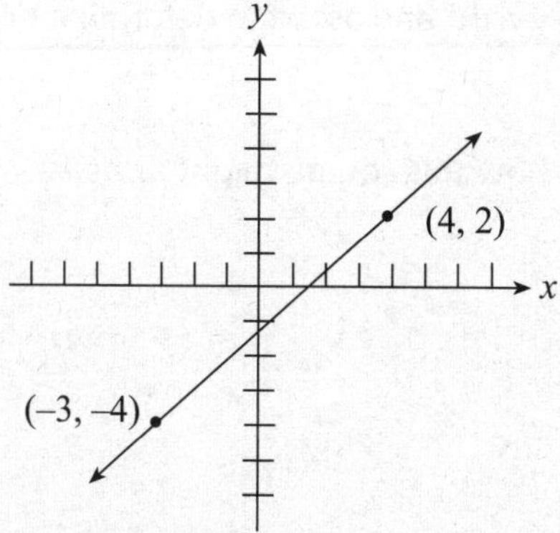

What is the slope of the line above?

A. $-\frac{3}{4}$

B. 0

C. $\frac{6}{7}$

D. $\frac{7}{6}$

✔ Remember

Don't let slope intimidate you. Remember, it's just a number describing how "tilted" a line is.

Figures in the Coordinate Plane

For some questions, you'll have to combine what you know about different geometric figures with what you know about the coordinate plane.

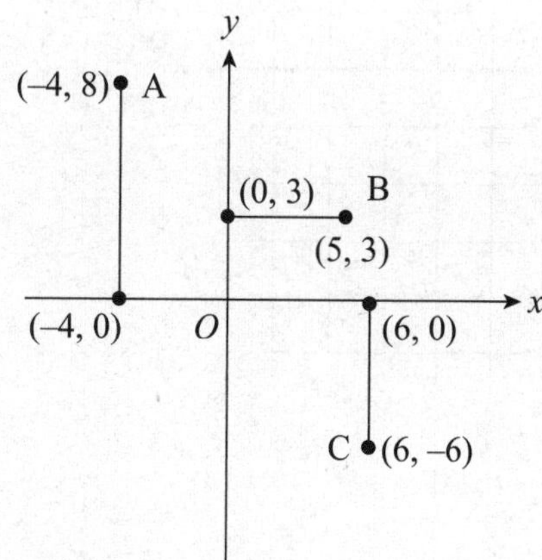

Find the lengths of the lines graphed above:

A. $\ell_1 =$ ______________

B. $\ell_2 =$ ______________

C. $\ell_3 =$ ______________

You may be told that a figure lies "on the *x*-axis" or "on the *y*-axis" and asked to determine information about the figure. Let's take a look at such situations.

A square lies on the *x*-axis. Draw different possibilities for how this square might appear.

D.

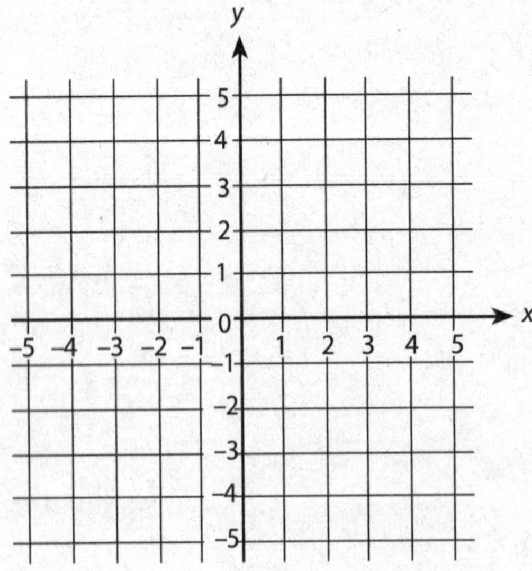

E.

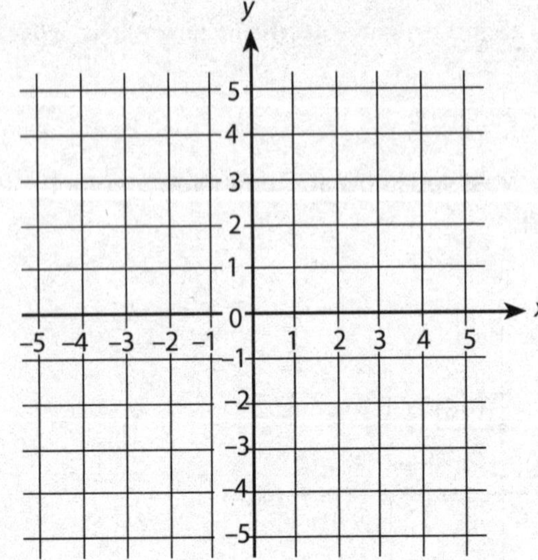

F.

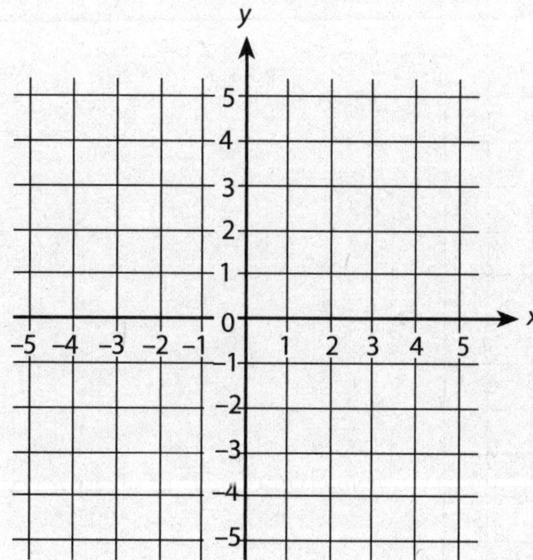

The diagonal of a square lies on the *y*-axis. Draw the possibilities.

G.

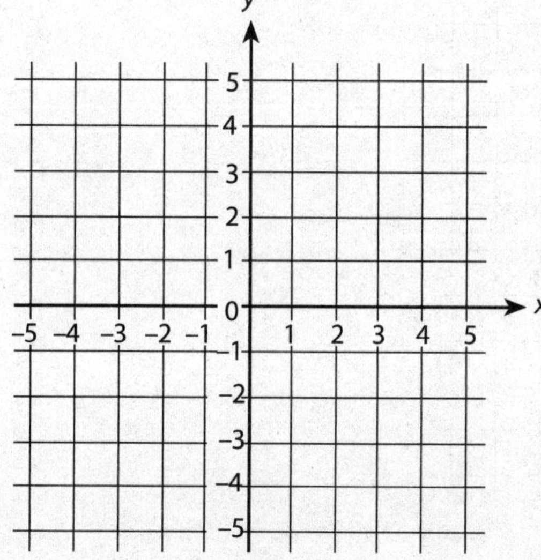

H.

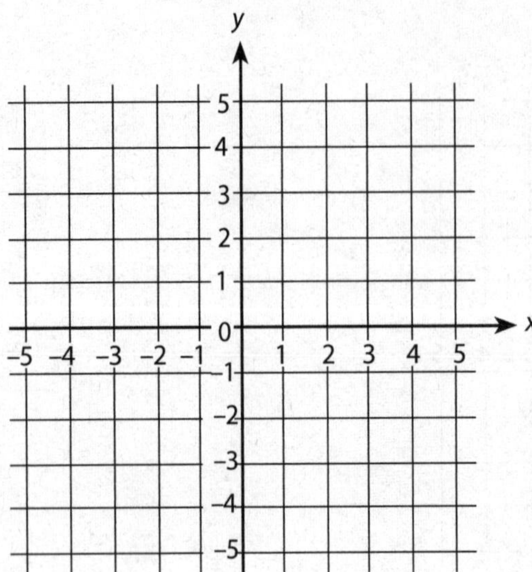

I.

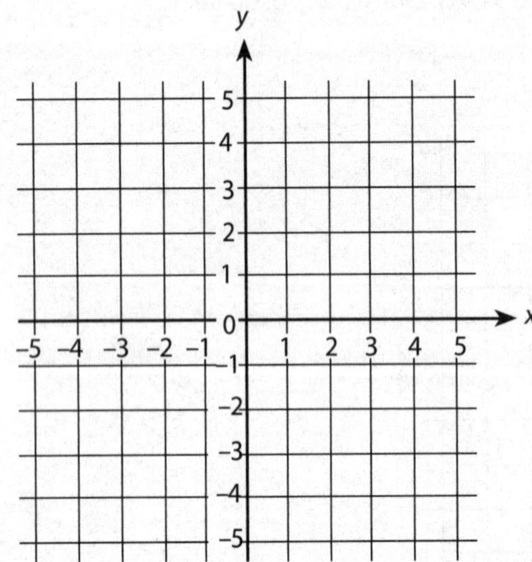

2.

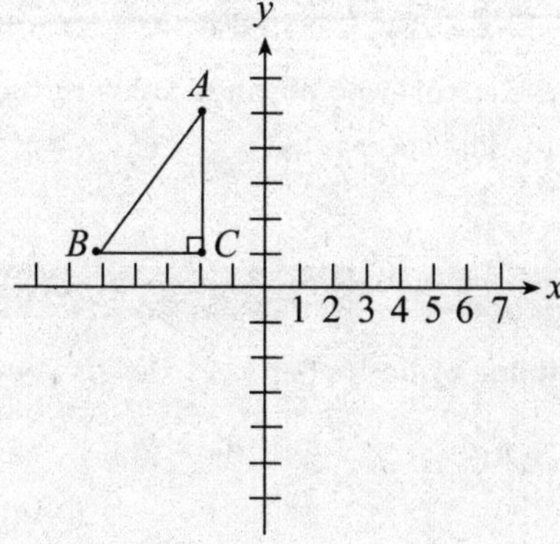

What is the area of right triangle *ABC* above?

E. −12

F. 6

G. 7.5

H. Cannot be determined from the information given.

3.

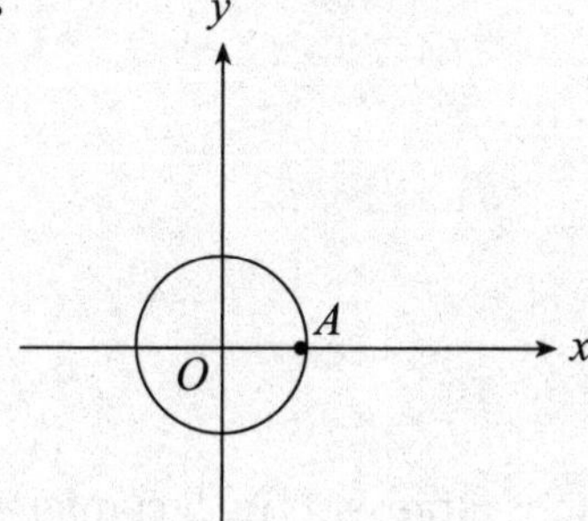

The center of circle *O* is at the origin. If the circle's area is 4π, what are the coordinates of point *A*?

A. (2, 0)

B. (4, 0)

C. (16, 0)

D. (0, 2)

4. What is the distance from the point (0, 6) to the point (0, 8) in a standard coordinate plane?

E. 2

F. 7

G. 10

H. 14

✓ Remember

To find the length of a line segment that is parallel to either axis, take the absolute value of the difference between the coordinates that are at either end of the line segment.

✓ Remember

Often, coordinate plane questions ask you to use your knowledge of basic shapes as well as your understanding of the coordinate plane.

Questions without Diagrams

The SHSAT will test your ability to handle geometry problems that do not have a diagram. What should you do when the question does not have a diagram?

Drawing your own diagram may seem like it will take up valuable time, but it will actually prevent you from making careless errors on Test Day.

5. The perimeter of a rectangular field is 40. If the length is 8, what is the area?

Draw your diagram for question 5 here:

A. 5

B. 26

C. 96

D. Cannot be determined from the information given.

6. If the radius of circle *A* is $3x$, which of the following expressions represents its circumference?

Draw your diagram for question 6 here:

E. 3π

F. 6π

G. $3x\pi$

H. $6x\pi$

7. What is the maximum number of points of intersection between a circle and a square?

Draw your diagram for question 7 here:

A. 4

B. 5

C. 8

D. Cannot be determined from the information given.

8. If the area of a rectangle is 40, what is its perimeter?

   Draw your diagram for question 8 here:

   E. 26
   F. 28
   G. 44
   H. Cannot be determined from the information given.

✔ **Remember**

Be sure to draw your own diagram if none is provided on Test Day.

Sometimes one diagram isn't enough. Some questions require you to consider a situation that might have several potential diagrams. Never jump to the most obvious conclusion; consider the different possibilities.

Multiple Figures

Many geometry questions combine two or more common shapes. You must understand the relationships between the shapes to answer the questions correctly.

9.

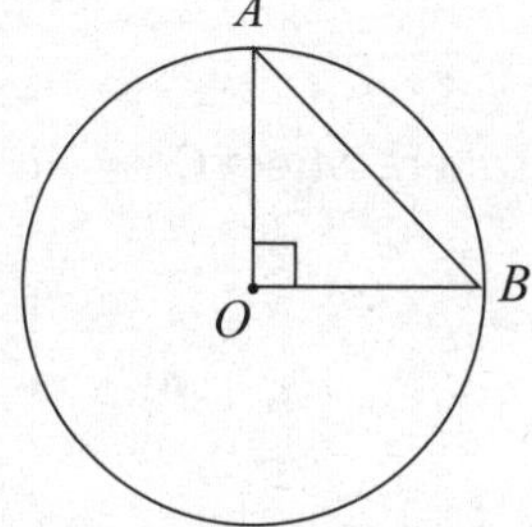

If the area of circle O is 64π, what is the area of right triangle AOB?

A. 16
B. 32
C. 64
D. Cannot be determined from the information given.

10. 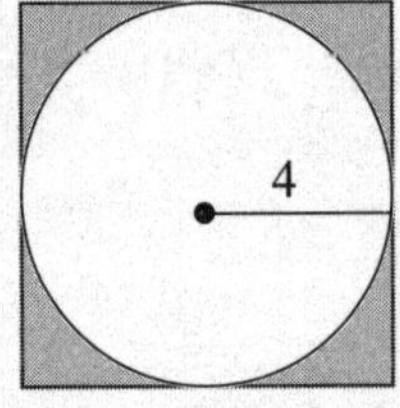

The diagram above represents a circle inscribed within a square. If the radius of the circle is 4, what is the area of the shaded region?

E. $64 - 4\pi$

F. $64 - 8\pi$

G. $64 - 16\pi$

H. $16 - 8\pi$

11. 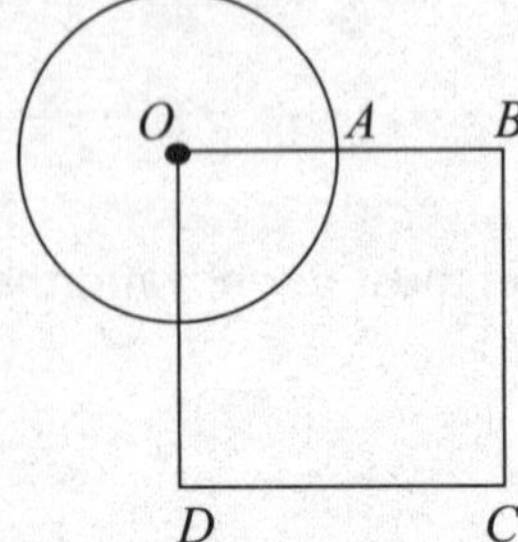

In the figure above, *O* is the center of the circle, and *OBCD* is a square where $OA = AB$. If the area of the square is 64, what is the area of the circle?

A. 4π

B. 8π

C. 16π

D. 64π

12. 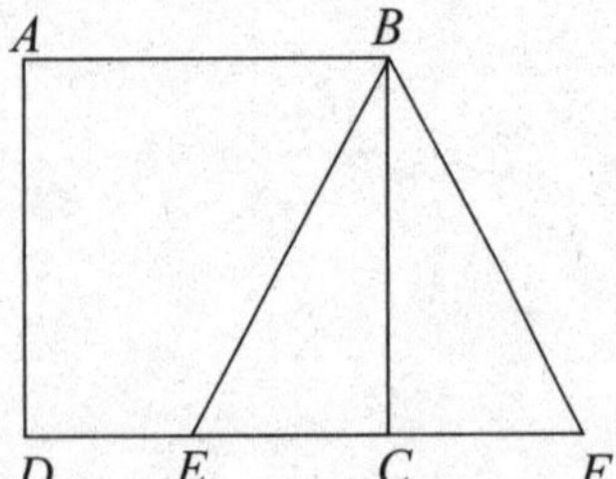

A square and a triangle are drawn together as shown above. The area of the square is 64, and $DC = EF$. What is the area of triangle *BEF*?

E. 32

F. 64

G. 128

H. Cannot be determined from the information given.

✓ Remember

We have no new rules to memorize for multiple figure problems. Just take them step by step, using a bit of information from one figure and plugging it into the equation for another figure.

Multiple Figures: Variations

13.

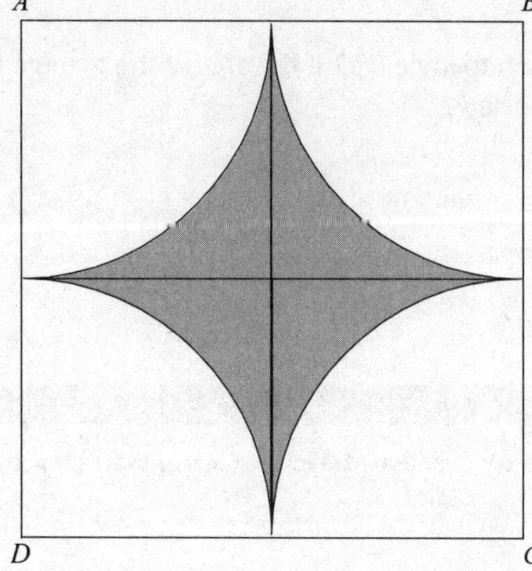

In the figure above, *ABCD* is a square that has been divided into four smaller squares, each of which has had a quarter circle cut out of it. If the perimeter of square *ABCD* is 24 centimeters, what is the area of the shaded region?

A. $(36 - 36\pi)$ sq cm

B. $\left(9 - \frac{9}{4}\pi\right)$ sq cm

C. $(36 - 9\pi)$ sq cm

D. 9π sq cm

14.

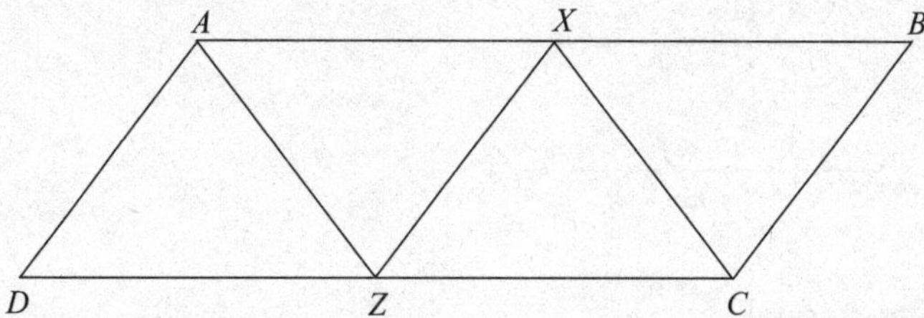

In the figure above, *ABCD* is a parallelogram with $m\angle B = 60°$, $BC = XC = AZ = 4$, and $\overleftrightarrow{XZ} \parallel \overleftrightarrow{BC}$. What is the perimeter of parallelogram *ABCD*?

E. 16

F. 24

G. 32

H. Cannot be determined from the information given.

15.

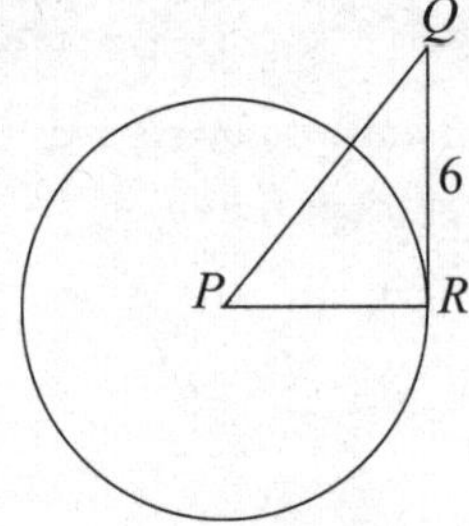

P is the center of circle P and is one point on triangle PRQ. If the area of the triangle PRQ is 12 and its height is 6, what is the area of circle P?

A. 35π

B. 16π

C. 12π

D. 6π

✓ Remember

Each step of the math is standard geometry. It is the combination of steps that makes these problems challenging.

Parallel Lines

When two parallel lines are intersected by another line (called a **transversal**), all acute angles are equal, and all obtuse angles are equal. Additionally, **corresponding angles** are angles that are in the same position but on different parallel lines/transversal intersections; they are also equal. Furthermore, **alternate interior angles** and **alternate exterior angles** are equal. Alternate interior angles are angles that are positioned between the two parallel lines on opposite sides of the transversal, whereas alternate exterior angles are positioned on the outside of the parallel lines on opposite sides of the transversal. Consider the following figure:

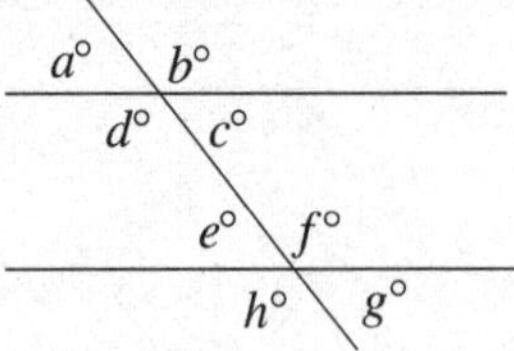

- Angles *a*, *c*, *e*, and *g* are acute and equal.
- Angles *b*, *d*, *f*, and *h* are obtuse and equal.
- Angle pairs (*b* and *f*), (*c* and *g*), (*a* and *e*), and (*d* and *h*) are corresponding angles.

- Angle pairs (*a* and *g*) and (*b* and *h*) are alternate exterior angles.
- Angle pairs (*d* and *f*) and (*c* and *e*) are alternate interior angles.

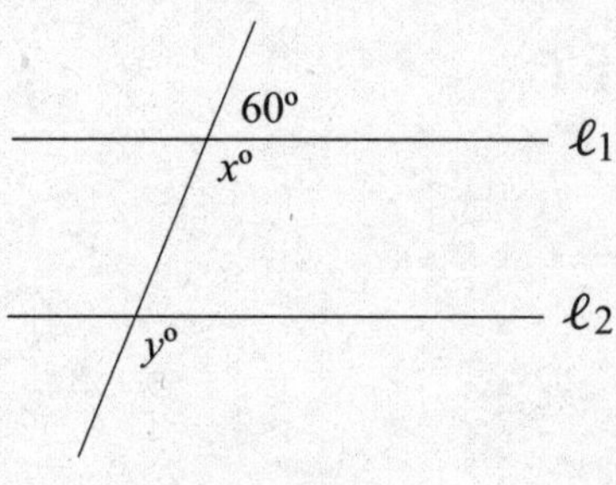

A. $x =$

B. $y =$

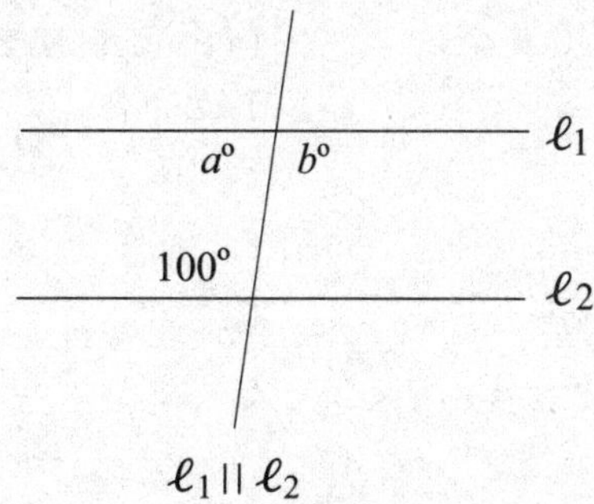

C. $a =$

D. $b =$

16.

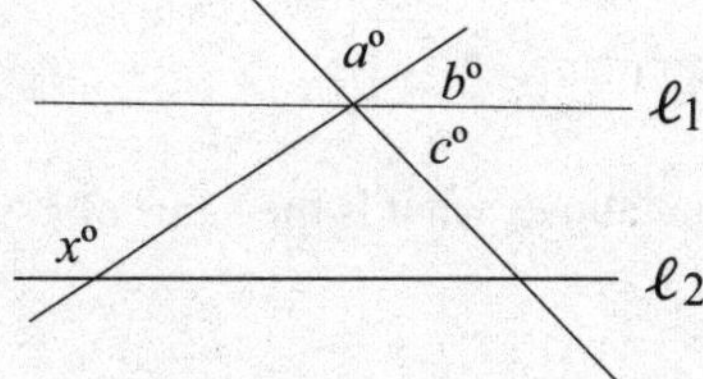

If ℓ_1 is parallel to ℓ_2 in the figure above, which of the following must be equal to x?

E. $a + b$

F. $c + a$

G. $b + c$

H. $90 + a$

✔ Remember

Having the rules for parallel lines memorized for Test Day translates to easy points!

The following practice sets provide an opportunity to apply the concepts and strategic thinking covered in this chapter. To practice Test Day timing, follow the suggested timing guidelines for each section.

GEOMETRY I PRACTICE SET

Suggested Timing: 10 minutes

1.

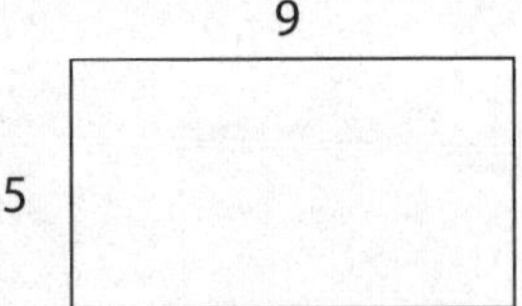

What is the area, in square units, of a square that has the same perimeter as the rectangle above?

A. 25 square units

B. 45 square units

C. 49 square units

D. 64 square units

2. If the circumference of a circle is 16π, what is its area?

E. 16π

F. 32π

G. 64π

H. 256π

3.

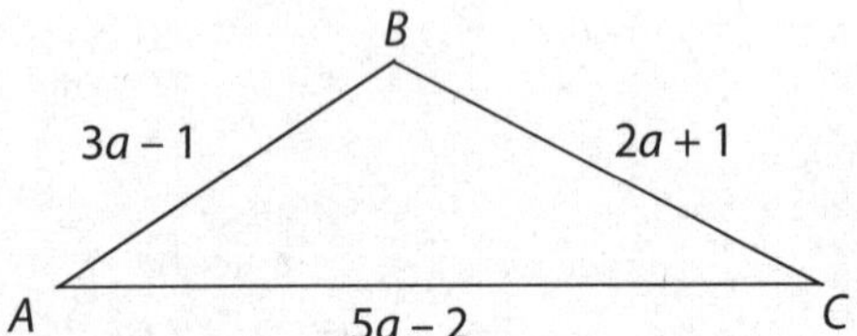

If the perimeter of triangle ABC is 18, what is the length of AC?

A. 2

B. 4

C. 5

D. 8

4.

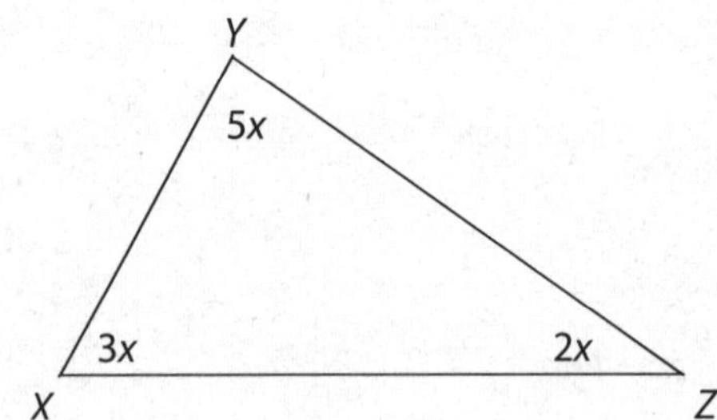

In triangle XYZ, what is the measure of angle YXZ?

E. 18°

F. 36°

G. 54°

H. 72°

5.

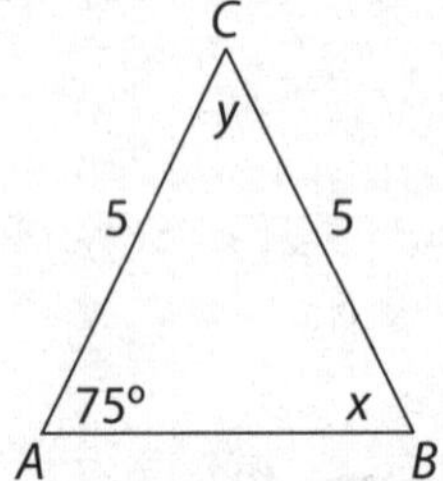

In the figure above, what is the value of $x - y$?

A. 30

B. 45

C. 75

D. 105

6. 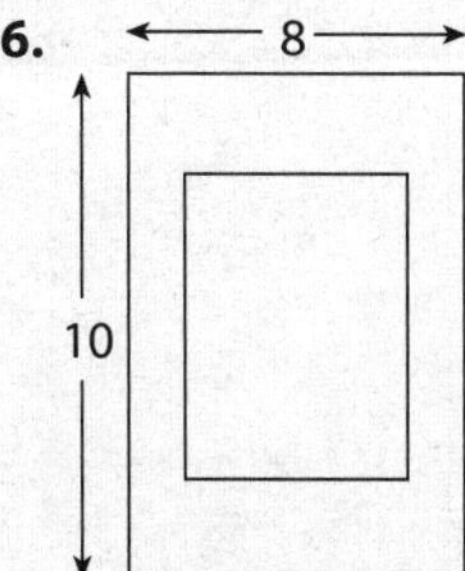

What is the area of the frame in the diagram above if the inside picture has a length of 8 and a width of 4?

E. 8

F. 16

G. 32

H. 48

GEOMETRY II PRACTICE SET

Suggested Timing: 10 minutes

1. 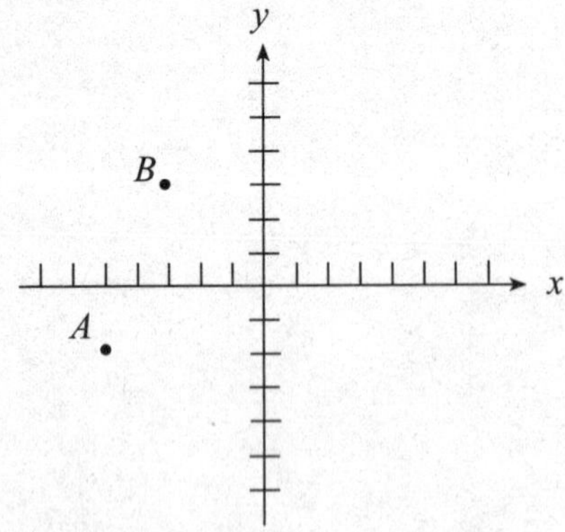

Which of the following correctly identifies the coordinates of points A and B shown graphed above?

A. A (−5, −2) and B (−3, −3)

B. A (−5, 2) and B (−3, 3)

C. A (5, −2) and B (−3, −3)

D. A (−5, −2) and B (−3, 3)

2. What is the slope of the line that contains points (3, −5) and (−1, 7)?

E. −3

F. $-\frac{1}{3}$

G. $-\frac{1}{4}$

H. $\frac{1}{3}$

3. 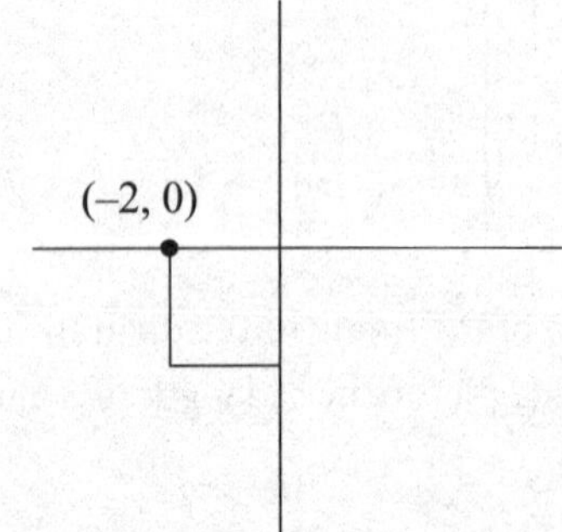

In the figure above, a square is graphed on the coordinate plane. If the coordinates of one corner are (−2, 0), what is the area of the square?

A. −4

B. 0

C. 2

D. 4

4. Two distinct lines and a circle lie in a plane. If both lines intersect the circle, what is the least possible number of points of intersection the three objects can have?

E. 1

F. 2

G. 3

H. 4

5. 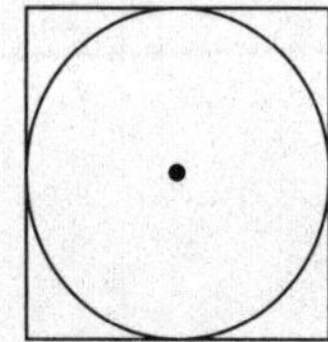

If the area of the square is 36, what is the circumference of the circle?

A. 6π

B. 9π

C. 12π

D. 15π

6. 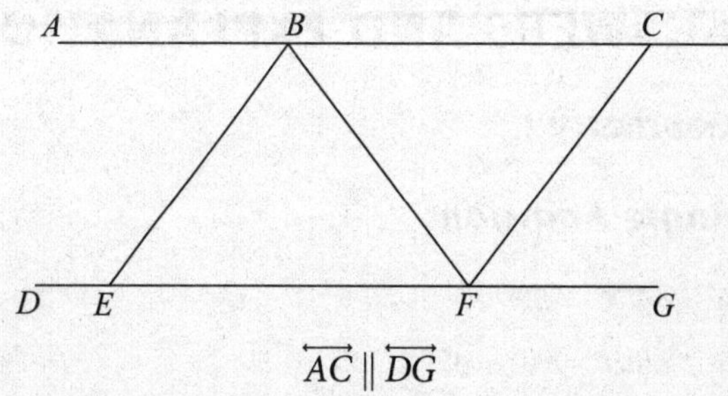

$\overleftrightarrow{AC} \parallel \overleftrightarrow{DG}$

In the figure above, $m\angle DEB = 110°$, $m\angle EBF = 80°$, and $m\angle BCF = 50°$. What is $m\angle BFC$?

E. 80°

F. 90°

G. 100°

H. 110°

ANSWERS AND EXPLANATIONS

Geometry I

Angle Addition

A. $\angle AOC = 50°$

B. $\angle RUT = 90° + 45° = 135°$

C. $\angle XWY = 70° - 30° = 40°$

D. $\angle XOZ = 180° - 50° = 130°$

E. $\angle BEC = 180° - 120° = 60°$

1. C

Subject: Geometry

Getting to the Answer: Because a line is 180° and the angle between $a°$ and $b°$ is 90°, the sum of $a°$ and $b°$ must be $180° - 90° = 90°$.

2. G

Subject: Geometry

Getting to the Answer: Because a line has 180° and the figure shows one right angle on the right side, the sum of $x°$, $y°$, and $z°$ must be 90°. Plug in the given values for x and z, and solve for y.

$$x + y + z = 90 \quad \text{Substitute values.}$$
$$40 + y + 20 = 90 \quad \text{Isolate the variable.}$$
$$y = 30$$

Full Circle Angles

A. $e = 180° - 50° = 130°$

B. $f = 50°$

C. $g = 130°$

D. $h = 180° - 60° = 120°$

E. $i = 35°$

F. $j = 120°$

G. $k = 25°$

3. C

Subject: Geometry

Getting to the Answer: Angles around a single point total 360°, so set up an equation with what you know.

$$\begin{aligned} a° + 47° + 89° + b° + 39° &= 360° \\ a° + b° + 175 &= 360° \\ a° + b° &= 185° \end{aligned}$$

4. G

Subject: Geometry

Getting to the Answer: Because vertical angles are equal, the angle to the right of b must have a value of $a°$. Since the angle in the upper right is 90°, all four angles created by the vertical and horizontal lines must be 90°. Therefore:

$$a° + b° = 90°$$

Line Segments

A. $AC = 5 + 3 = 8$

B. $YZ = \frac{1}{2}(12) = 6$

C. The midpoint F is at 0

5. B

Subject: Geometry

Getting to the Answer: The difference in value between the two endpoints is 8. So, since the midpoint is halfway between the endpoints, it must be four units from each end. Four units to the right of -1 and to the left of 7 puts the midpoint at 3.

6. F

Subject: Geometry

Getting to the Answer: Since you know the values of *AD* and *BD*, you can easily find the difference between the two to determine *AB*, which is equal to *BC*. Then subtract the values of *AB* and *BC* from *AD* to determine *CD*.

$AD - BD = AB = BC$	Solve for *AB* and *BC*.
$AB = BC = 35 - 21 = 14$	
$AB + BC + CD = AD$	Plug in your new values for *AB* and *BC*.
$14 + 14 + CD = 35$	Solve for *CD*.
$CD = 7$	

7. D

Subject: Geometry

Getting to the Answer: In order to determine the length of *EF* you would also need to know the length of either *DE* or *FG*. Since you don't have that information, it is impossible to find the length of *EF*.

Perimeter and Area of Quadrilaterals

A. $2(6+3)=2(9)=18$

B. $6\times3=18$

C. 22

D. $\frac{1}{2}\sqrt{15}(8+6)=7\sqrt{15}$

E. 20

F. 25

G. The perimeter depends on knowing the side lengths of the rectangle. Since we only know the area is 40, we do not know the exact dimensions. To see that we get different perimeters, let's pick values based on having an area of 40. If we pick sides 4 and 10, the perimeter is 2(4 + 10) = 28. If we pick sides 20 and 2, the perimeter is 2(20 + 2) = 44.

8. H

Subject: Geometry

Getting to the Answer: To determine the area of the rectangle, you need to know the length and the width. You can use the information you are given about the length and perimeter to figure out the width, then you can multiply length times width to determine area.

$P = 2\ell+2w$	Use what you know to find the width.
$20 = 12+2w$	
$2w = 8$	Then use the width to find the area.
$w = 4$	
$A = \ell\times W = 6\times4 = 24$	

9. C

Subject: Geometry

Getting to the Answer: Set up an area equation expressing length as three times width.

$\ell = 3w$	
$3w\times w = A = 48$	
$3w^2 = 48$	
$w^2 = 16$	Solve for width.
$w = 4$	Then use width to solve
$\ell = 3(4) = 12$	for length.

10. G

Subject: Geometry

Getting to the Answer: The area of a parallelogram is base times height, where height is the measure from the perpendicular base to the top side of the figure, in this case 3. Because opposite sides of a parallelogram are equal, the base is 12 just like the top.

$$A = B\times H$$
$$A = 12\times3 = 36$$

Circumference and Area of Circles

A. Circumference $= 16\pi$

B. Area $= 25\pi$

C. Radius $= 4$

D. Area $= 9\pi$

11. B

Subject: Geometry

Getting to the Answer:

$$C = 2\pi r$$
$$C = 2(5)\pi = 10\pi$$

12. G

Subject: Geometry

Getting to the Answer: Divide the diameter in half to find the radius, then plug the radius into the area formula and solve.

$$d = 2r$$
$$d = 8$$
$$r = 4$$
$$a = \pi r^2$$
$$a = \pi 4^2 = 16\pi$$

13. C

Subject: Geometry

Getting to the Answer: Because the formula for circumference is πd, d in this case must be 16.

$c = \pi d$	
$16\pi = \pi d$	Plug in the given value for circumference.
$16 = d$	Divide both sides by π, and there's the diameter.

Perimeter and Area of Triangles

A. Perimeter = 16

B. Area = 4

C. Area = 6

D. Area = 7.5

14. G

Subject: Geometry

Getting to the Answer:

$P = s1 + s2 + s3$	Set up an equation for perimeter.
$16 = 4 + 5 + y$ $y = 7$	Plug in what you know and solve for y.

15. C

Subject: Geometry

Getting to the Answer: Base (b) is AC and height (h) is BD.

$$a = \frac{1}{2}bh$$
$$a = \frac{1}{2}(14)(12) = 84$$

Degrees of Quadrilaterals and Triangles

A. $y° = 60°$

B. $b° = 60°$

C. Total degrees in polygon = $(n - 2)(180°)$
For 5 sides: $(5 - 2)(180°) = 540°$
$95 + 110 + 120 + a° + b° = 540°$
$a° + b° = 215°$

D. Quadrilaterals have 360° inside
$56° + 78° + 90° = 224°$
Missing angle $= 360° - 224° = 136°$

16. H

Subject: Geometry

Getting to the Answer: Remember, the sum of the interior angles of a triangle is 180°. You are given the measure of all three angles in terms of X, so set up an equation setting the sum of the three angles equal to 180°, solve for X, and then use X to calculate Y.

$$Y = 2X$$
$$Z = 3X$$
$$X + 2X + 3X = 180$$
$$6X = 180$$
$$X = 30$$
$$Y = 2X = 60$$

17. C

Subject: Geometry

Getting to the Answer: In the parallelogram $ABCD$, angles BAD and ADC have to equal 180°; therefore

$x + (x + 30)$ must equal 180°.

$$x + (x + 30°) = 180°$$
$$2x + 30° = 180°$$
$$2x = 150°$$
$$x = 75°$$
$$x + 30° = 105°$$

Triangle Inequality Theorem

A. The third side is between 5 and 41, so yes, the third side could be 30.

B. The third side cannot be 5 since the third side must be strictly greater than 5.

C. 5, 9, and 12

D. 5 and 6

18. F

Subject: Geometry

Getting to the Answer: Because angle *SQT* is equal to angle *STQ*, then *ST* must equal *SQ*, which is 3.

$$ST = SQ = 3$$

Similar Quadrilaterals and Triangles

A. $AC = 18$

B. $ST = 3$

C. Length of smaller rectangle $= 12.5$

19. A

Subject: Geometry

Getting to the Answer: Because *AB* is three times the corresponding side *YZ*, then *BC* must be three times corresponding side *XY*.

$$XY = 2$$
$$BC = 3(XY)$$
$$BC = 3(2) = 6$$

20. G

Subject: Geometry

Getting to the Answer: Plug what you know about *ABCD*—area and width—into the area formula and solve for length.

$$96 = \ell \times 8 \quad \text{Calculate the length of } ABCD.$$
$$\ell = 12$$

Because the measure of a side of *ABCD* is two times the measure of a corresponding side of *DEFG*, the length of *DEFG* must be 6. Now that you have both its length and width, you can calculate the area of *DEFG*.

$$A = \ell \times w$$
$$A = 6 \times 4 = 24$$

ANSWERS AND EXPLANATIONS

Geometry II

Coordinate Plane

A. $P(1, 1)$

B. $Q(4, 0)$

C. $R(-5, -4)$

D. $S(-3, 4)$

E. $T(2, -2)$

F. $U(-3, -3)$

Slope

A. $m = \frac{5-3}{4-0} = \frac{2}{4} = \frac{1}{2}$

B. $m = \frac{8-2}{9-(-1)} = \frac{6}{10} = \frac{3}{5}$

C. $m = 2$

D. $m = -\frac{1}{5}$

1. C

Subject: Geometry

Getting to the Answer: You are given two points, so you have the necessary information to calculate the slope:

$$\frac{\text{rise}}{\text{run}} = \frac{2-(-4)}{4-(-3)} = \frac{6}{7}$$

Figures in the Coordinate Plane

A. $\ell_1 = 8$

B. $\ell_2 = 5$

C. $\ell_3 = 6$

D. The possibilities here include the square appearing solely in quadrant one, straddling quadrants one and two, in quadrant two, in quadrant three, straddling quadrants three and four, and in quadrant four.

E. Same answer as (D).

F. Same answer as (D).

G. The possibilities include a square bisected by quadrants one and two, a square bisected by quadrants three and four, and a square straddling all four quadrants.

H. Same answer as (G).

I. Same answer as (G).

2. F

Subject: Geometry

Getting to the Answer: Even though the triangle is on a coordinate plane, you still need to have the base and the height to calculate the area. The height would be *AC*, or the change in the *y*-coordinates from *A* to *C*: $5 - 1 = 4$. The base would be *BC*, or the change in *x*-coordinates: $-5 - (-2) = 3$

$$\text{Area} = \frac{1}{2} b \times h$$

$$A = \frac{1}{2} \times 3 \times 4 = 6$$

3. A

Subject: Geometry

Getting to the Answer: The approach is exactly the same: the area of the circle is 4π. Using the formula for the area: $A = \pi r^2$, then $4\pi = \pi r^2$ or $r = 2$.

The radius of the circle is 2. Point A lies on the *x*-axis, so the *y*-coordinate has to be zero. Because the distance from the center of a circle to any point on its circumference is the radius, the *x*-coordinate $= 2$. The coordinates are (2, 0).

4. E

Subject: Geometry

Getting to the Answer: You need to calculate the difference between the points. The only difference is between the *y*-coordinates, as the *x*-coordinates remain constant, so $8 - 6 = 2$.

Questions without Diagrams

5. C

Subject: Geometry

Getting to the Answer: The perimeter of the field is 40, and the length is 8. You know that the perimeter is twice (length plus width): $40 = 2(8 + x) = 16 + 2x$ and $x = 12$, which is the width. The area is length $\times$ width or $8 \times 12 = 96$.

6. H

Subject: Geometry

Getting to the Answer: This problem is very straightforward. $C = 2r\pi$, and if $r = 3x$, then $C = (2)(3x\pi) = 6x\pi$.

7. C

Subject: Geometry

Getting to the Answer: Assume the center of the square and the center of the circle are the same. If the diameter of the circle equals the length of the side of the square, the figures meet at four points. If the circle gets slightly larger, the circle will intersect each side of the square twice, so they will meet at eight points. If the diameter of the circle equals the diagonal of the square, the figures meet at four points. Thus, the maximum number of points of intersection is 8.

8. H

Subject: Geometry

Getting to the Answer: To determine the perimeter of a rectangle you must have the length and width of the rectangle or its area and either the length or width. This is not the case here.

Multiple Figures

9. B

Subject: Geometry

Getting to the Answer: The area of the circle is 64π, therefore $r = 8$.

The radius is 8, and therefore *AO* and *BO* are both equal to the radius and represent the base and the height. Therefore, $\frac{1}{2} \times 8 \times 8 = 32$.

10. G

Subject: Geometry

Getting to the Answer: If the radius is 4, then the diameter is 8, which is the side of the square. The area of the square is then $8 \times 8 = 64$. If the radius is 4, the area of the circle is πr^2 or 16π. The area of the shaded region would be the area of the square less the area of the circle: $64 - 16\pi$.

11. C

Subject: Geometry

Getting to the Answer: This answer takes two separate calculations. If the area of the square is 64, then the sides have to be 8. Therefore $OB = 8$, and *OA* and *AB* both must equal half of 8, or 4. *OA* is the radius of the circle, and the formula for the area of the circle is $A = \pi r^2 = \pi 4^2 = 16\pi$.

12. E

Subject: Geometry

Getting to the Answer: The area of the square is 64; therefore the sides of the square are 8. Therefore, *DC* and *BC* are 8 because they are sides of the square. You are given that $DC = EF$, so $EF = 8$, and it is the base of the triangle. $BC = 8$ and is the height.

$$\frac{1}{2} \times 8 \times 8 = 32$$

Multiple Figures: Variations

13. C

Subject: Geometry

Getting to the Answer: This problem is simplified greatly if you realize that the four quarter circles together form a complete circle whose radius is equal to the length of a side on one of the smaller squares. If the big square has a perimeter of 24 centimeters, each side must have a length of 6 centimeters (one-fourth the perimeter). So the lengths of the sides of the smaller squares and the radius of the circle are both 3 centimeters. The area of the shaded region is really the area of the big square (36 square cm) minus the area of the circle (9π square cm), or $(36 - 9\pi)$ square centimeters.

14. F

Subject: Geometry

Getting to the Answer: Since $m\angle B = 60°$ and $BC = XC$, you can deduce that triangle *XBC* is equilateral. (Any isosceles triangle with a 60 degree angle is.) So $XB = 4$. Also, since $\overleftrightarrow{XB} \parallel \overleftrightarrow{CZ}$, *XBCZ* must be a parallelogram (more specifically a rhombus) with opposite sides congruent, so $XZ = ZC = 4$. Now looking at the opposite end of the big parallelogram, $AD = 4$ and $m\angle D = 60°$, since opposite sides and angles of a parallelogram are congruent. So you can conclude using the same logic that triangle *ADZ* is equilateral (it is isosceles with $AD = AZ = 4$ and has a 60 degree angle) and $DZ = 4$. Finally, $AX = DZ = 4$, since they are opposite sides of parallelogram *AXZD*. Therefore, the perimeter of parallelogram *ABCD* really consists of 6 segments of length 4, so the perimeter is 24.

15. B

Subject: Geometry

Getting to the Answer:

Area of triangle $PRQ = \frac{1}{2}bh$

$$12 = \frac{1}{2}x(6)$$
$$24 = 6x$$
$$x = 4$$

Area of circle $P = \pi r^2$

$$A = \pi(4)^2$$
$$A = 16\pi$$

Parallel Lines

A. $x = 120°$

B. $y = 120°$

C. $a = 80°$

D. $b = 100°$

16. F

Subject: Geometry

Getting to the Answer: The angle opposite angle *c* is equal to angle *c*. That opposite angle plus angle *a* together form a corresponding angle to angle *x*. Therefore angles $a + c =$ angle *x*.

ANSWERS AND EXPLANATIONS

Geometry I Practice Set

1. C

Subject: Geometry

Getting to the Answer: Determine the perimeter of the rectangle and divide by four to determine the length of a side of a square with the same perimeter. Square the measure of the side to find the area of the square.

$P = 2(\ell + w)$ Find the perimeter.
$P = 2(9 + 5)$
$p = 2(14) = 28$

$s = p \div 4$ Find the side of the square.
$s = 28 \div 4 = 7$

$a = s^2$ Find the area of the square.
$a = 7^2 = 49$

2. G

Subject: Geometry

Getting to the Answer: You need the radius to find the area, so use what you know about circumference to determine the radius.

$C = 2\pi r$ Use the circumference formula to solve for radius.

$2\pi r = 16\pi$
$r = 8$
$A = \pi r^2$ Then use the radius to solve for area.

$A = \pi 8^2 = 64\pi$

3. D

Subject: Geometry

Getting to the Answer: To determine the length of *AC* you need to know *a*. Perimeter is the sum of the sides, so set up a perimeter equation using the given algebraic expressions—all in terms of *a*—to represent the sides. Solve for *a*, then plug *a* back into the expression for *AC* to determine the length of *AC*.

$P = s1 + s2 + s3$ Use the perimeter equation to solve for *a*.

$18 = 3a - 1 + 2a + 1 + 5a - 2$
$18 = 10a - 2$ Combine like terms.
$20 = 10a$
$a = 2$ Plug the value for *a* into the expression for *AC*.
$AC = 5a - 2$
$AC = 5(2) - 2$

$AC = 8$ Solve for *AC*.

4. G

Subject: Geometry

Getting to the Answer: Because the sum of the interior angles of a triangle is always 180°, set up an equation setting the sum of the three angles, in terms of *x*, equal to 180°. Solve for *x*, then plug the value for *x* into the expression for angle *YXZ*.

$$3x + 5x + 2x = 180$$
$$10x = 180$$
$$x = 18$$

$$\angle YXZ = 3x$$
$$\angle YXZ = 3(18) = 54$$

5. B

Subject: Geometry

Getting to the Answer: Because sides *AC* and *BC* are equal, angles *CAB* and *CBA* are also equal, and *x* must be 75°. Because you know that the sum of interior angles of a triangle is always 180°, you can calculate *y*. Then subtract *y* from *x* to find the answer.

$$x = 75$$
$$y = 180 - 75 - 75 = 30$$
$$x - y = 75 - 30 = 45$$

6. H

Subject: Geometry

Getting to the Answer: The area of the frame is the area between the two rectangles, so find the difference between the areas of the two rectangles to determine the area of the frame.

$$A_{outer} = \ell \times w = 10 \times 8 = 80$$
$$A_{inner} = \ell \times w = 8 \times 4 = 32$$
$$A_{frame} = A_{outer} - A_{inner} = 80 - 32 = 48$$

ANSWERS AND EXPLANATIONS

Geometry II Practice Set

1. D

Subject: Geometry

Getting to the Answer: Point *A* is 5 places left (negative) on the *x*-axis and 2 places down (negative) on the *y*-axis: (–5, –2). Point *B* is 3 places left (negative) on the *x*-axis and 3 places up (positive) on the *y*-axis: (–3, 3).

2. E

Subject: Geometry

Getting to the Answer: You are given two points, so you have the necessary figures to calculate the slope:

$$\frac{rise}{run} = \frac{7-(-5)}{(-1)-3} = -3$$

3. D

Subject: Geometry

Getting to the Answer: The area of the square is the length of one of the sides squared. One side of the square goes from (0, 0) to (–2, 0), which creates a side equal to 2; this makes the area 4.

4. G

Subject: Geometry

Getting to the Answer: Regardless of the size of the circle, to create the fewest points of intersection, the two lines should intersect the circle at one common point and then intersect the circle separately at two different points. Therefore, the lines and circle would intersect 3 times.

5. A

Subject: Geometry

Getting to the Answer: The square has an area of 36; therefore it has sides of 6. This is the diameter of the circle. The circumference is the diameter $\times$ π. Therefore, the circumference is 6π.

6. G

Subject: Geometry

Getting to the Answer: Since $\overleftrightarrow{AC} \parallel \overleftrightarrow{DG}$, $\angle DEB \cong \angle EBC$ because the two angles are corresponding. Therefore, both angles have a measure of 110°. But $\angle EBC$ is composed of two angles, one of which you know the measure of ($m\angle EBF = 80°$). The other angle must make up the difference between the two measures, so $m\angle CBF = 110° - 80° = 30°$. Finally, you have the measure of two of the angles in triangle *BCF* and can solve for the third by setting the sum of all three measures equal to 180°: $30° + 50° + m\angle BFC = 180°$.

CHAPTER 18

Advanced Math

CHAPTER OBJECTIVES

By the end of this chapter, you will be able to:

- Answer questions that accompany charts and graphs
- Use the Pythagorean theorem to answer questions involving triangles
- Solve complex geometric word problems

ADVANCED MATH

Charts/Data Interpretation

To excel at data interpretation, you must recognize the many ways that charts communicate information. The most common types of charts and graphs include pie charts, line graphs, bar graphs, and pictographs.

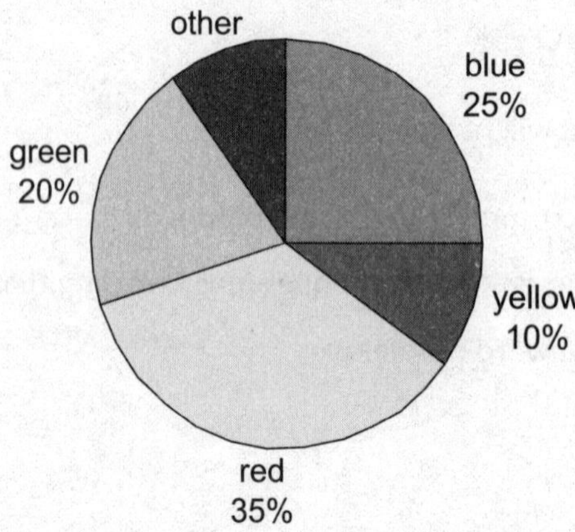

A. What conclusions can you draw from the circle graph?

____

B. What's missing from the circle graph?

____

C. If 200 people were surveyed, how many more people picked red than picked yellow as their favorite color?

____

✔ Remember

Before working on data interpretation questions, briefly study the chart and determine what it represents and what patterns are apparent in the data.

Questions 1 and 2 refer to the graph below.

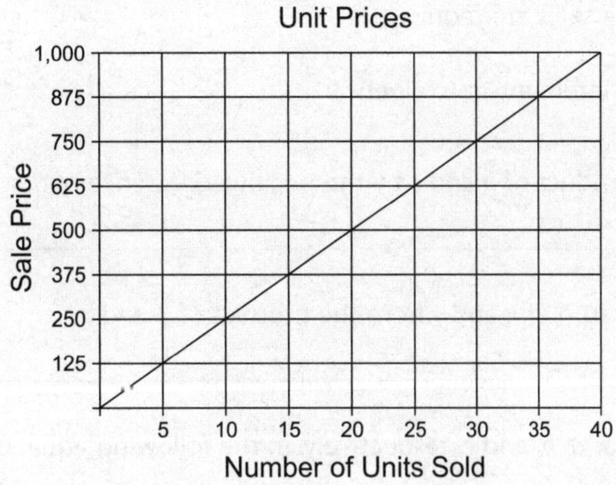

1. What is the sale price of a single unit?

A. $25

B. $50

C. $100

D. $125

2. How many units can be sold for $150?

E. 2

F. 3

G. 4

H. 6

✓ Remember

When tackling charts and graphs, first identify the title and what the chart represents. Next, determine what the *x*-axis represents and what the *y*-axis represents. Your success will be determined by your ability to keep track of different pieces of information.

Symbolism

Harder symbolism problems require you to do more substitution and deal with more complex operations, but the same skills are required.

Translate the following statements into algebra:

A. Divide the product of *a* and *c* by the positive difference of *d* and *b*.

____

B. Subtract the sum of *x* and *y* from the product of 3 and *z*.

____

Substitute 3, 7, and $-x$ for *a*, *b*, and *c*, respectively, in the following equations:

C. $a\,(b - c) - cb =$

D. $a \div c - b \times c =$

3. The symbol ♣ between two numbers means "multiply the sum of the two numbers by the difference of the two numbers." What is the value of 7 ♣ 5?

A. 2
B. 12
C. 24
D. 70

4. Assume that the notation ♦ (*a*, *b*, *c*) means "add the sum of *a*, *b*, and *c* to the product of *a*, *b*, and *c*." If ♦ (*x*, 2, 3) = 12, what is the value of *x*?

E. 1
F. 2
G. 7
H. 12

5. Assume that $r \blacksquare s$ means $rs - s$. What is the value of $2 \blacksquare 3 + 4 \blacksquare 5$?

A. 3
B. 9
C. 18
D. 20

✓ Remember

Symbolism problems require translation, substitution, and PEMDAS.

Right Triangles

Know the Pythagorean theorem and how to work with right triangles.

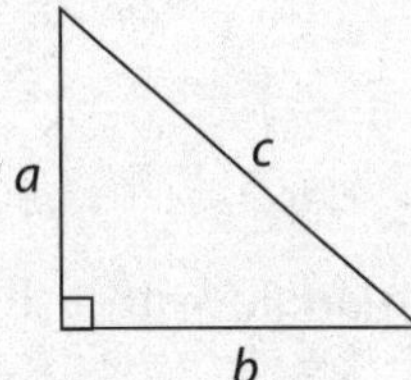

The Pythagorean theorem states that $a^2 + b^2 = c^2$ where a and b are the lengths of the legs of a right triangle, and c is the length of the hypotenuse.

Solve for each of the unknown variables in the triangles below:

A.

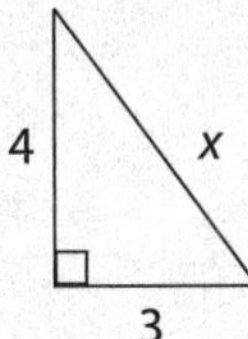

B.

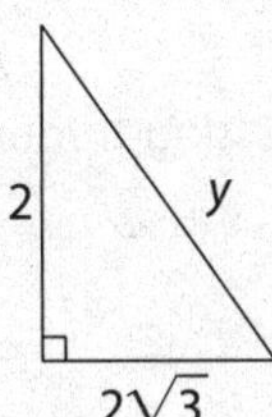

C.

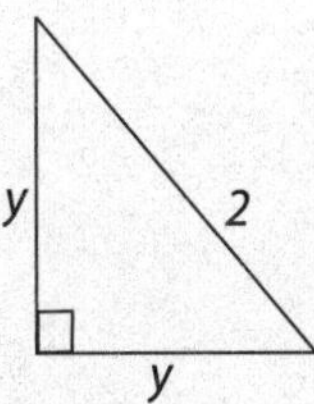

D.

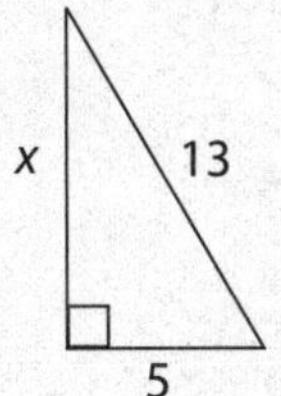

✓ Remember

If you know two sides of a right triangle, you can always solve for the third.

6. What is the area of a square with diagonals of length 6?

E. 9

F. 12

G. $9\sqrt{2}$

H. 18

7. What is the perimeter of a right triangle with a hypotenuse of length 15 and a leg of length 12?

A. 9

B. 25

C. 36

D. 54

8.

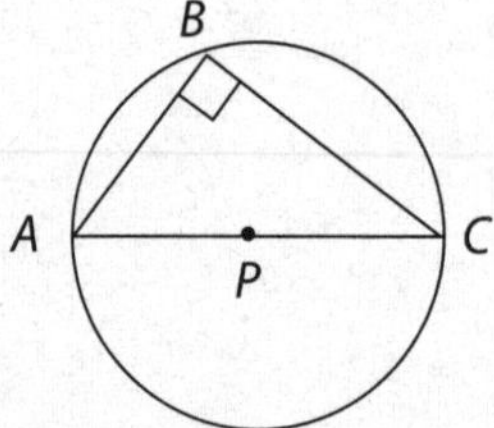

In the figure above, right triangle *ABC* is inscribed in circle *P*, with *AC* passing through center *P*. If $AB = 6$ and $BC = 8$, what is the area of the circle?

E. 10π

F. 14π

G. 25π

H. 100π

Complex Geometric Word Problems

9. A circle of area 25π is graphed on the coordinate plane. If its center has coordinates (8, 0), which of the following points **must** lie on the circumference of the circle?

A. (0, 0)

B. (0, 5)

C. (16, 0)

D. (3, 0)

10. A triangle and a square have equal areas. If the base of the triangle and the side of the square each have a length of 6, what is the height of the triangle?

E. 3

F. 6

G. 12

H. Cannot be determined from the information given.

11. The diameter of a circle is 3 times the side length of a square. If the square has an area of 144, what is the length of the radius of the circle?

A. 3

D. 9

C. 18

D. 36

> ✔ **Remember**
>
> **If you ever have to plot a circle on a coordinate plane, use the radius to find the four points that are directly above, below, to the right, and to the left of the center. Then sketch in the rest.**

Scaling

Scaling involves changing the size of one or more sides of a shape and then evaluating the difference in the new shape's area or perimeter.

Determine how much the area of the given shapes will change when they are transformed in the following ways:

A. Triple the radius of a circle with an original radius of 5.

____

B. Double the side lengths of a square with an area of 16.

____

C. Quadruple the base of a triangle with an area of 8 and a height of 4.

____

12. The circumference of a certain circle is doubled. By what factor is its area increased?

E. 2

F. 3

G. 4

H. 6

13. If you double the length and triple the width of a rectangle with an area of 20 cm^2, what will the area of the new rectangle be?

A. 60 cm^2

B. 100 cm^2

C. 120 cm^2

D. Cannot be determined from the information given.

14. The area of a certain square is 64. What would be the area of a second square whose perimeter was half as large as that of the first?

E. 8

F. 16

G. 25

H. 32

✔ **Remember**

You can always draw figures when you are dealing with scaling Geometry questions. These figures can be useful for comparison.

Unusual Diagrams

Unusual diagrams will typically include more than four sides and will showcase unconventional shapes.

Find the area of each of the shapes below:

A. Area: ______________________________

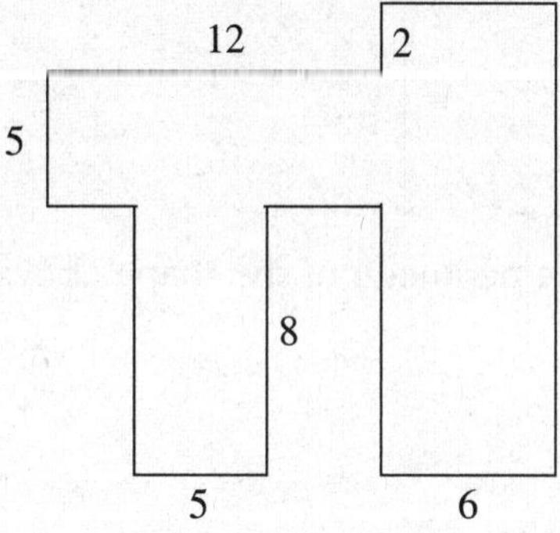

B. Area: ______________________________

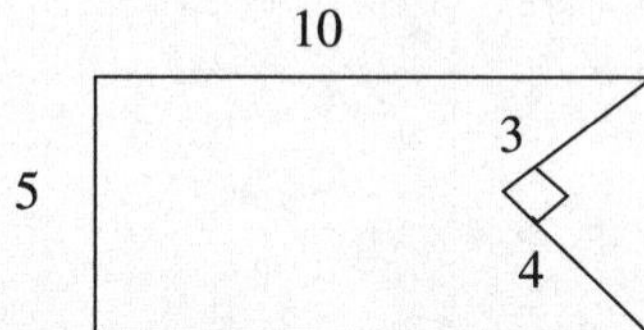

C. Area: ______________________________

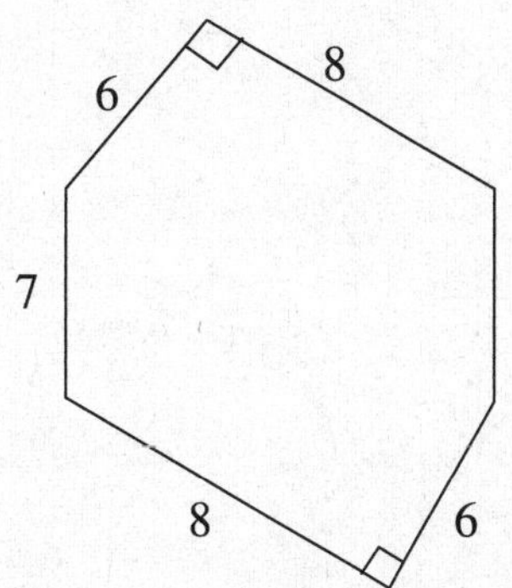

✔ Remember

Most complex shapes can be broken down into common shapes that are much easier to work with.

✔ Remember

Use what you know about common shapes and right triangles to get the information you need.

15.

10

4

What is the approximate perimeter of the shape above?

A. 20

B. 22

C. 25

D. 28

16.

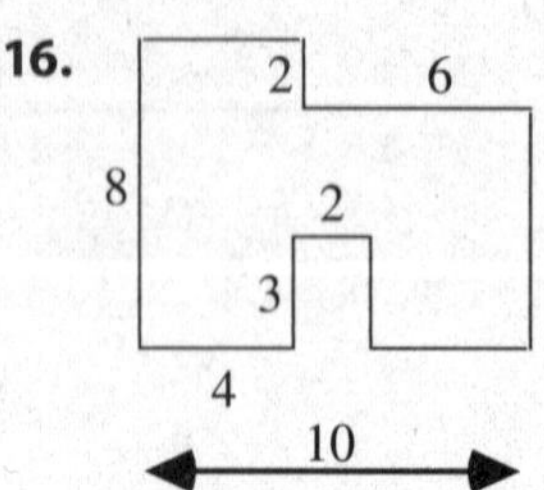

What is the area of the polygon above if each corner of the polygon is a right angle?

E. 40

F. 62

G. 68

H. 80

17.

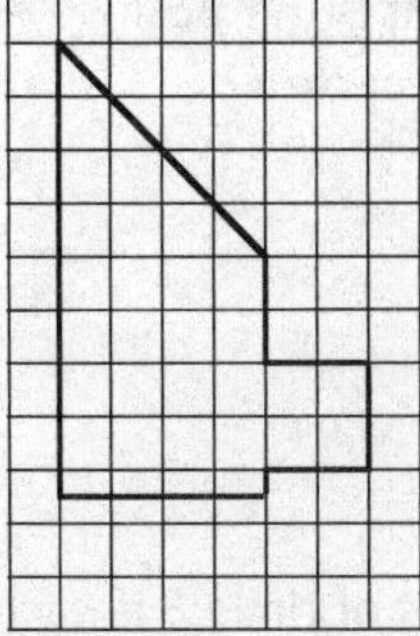

Scale: 1 inch = 6 feet

The grid above is made up of 1-inch squares. Approximately how many square **yards** are contained in the figure above?

A. 30

B. 60

C. 120

D. 180

Remember

Challenging questions often don't include extremely difficult math. Instead, they usually test many different concepts at the same time, making the problem more complex.

Complex Algebra in Geometric Figures

A few questions on the test will challenge you to use high-level algebra and high-level geometry skills in tandem.

Solve the following problem:

A fence surrounds a rectangular field whose length is 3 times its width. If the fence is 240 meters long, what is the width of the field?

A. 30 meters

B. 40 meters

C. 60 meters

D. 80 meters

A. First, draw a picture: ____________________

B. Next, translate the question into an algebraic equation: ____________________

C. Finally, solve for the width: ____________________

18. Circle A has a radius of $r + 1$. Circle B has a radius of $r + 2$. What is the positive difference between the circumference of circle B and the circumference of circle A?

E. 1

F. 2π

G. $2\pi + 3$

H. $2\pi r + 3$

19. The area of circle B is one-fourth the area of circle A. If the radius of circle B is r, what is the radius of circle A, in terms of r?

A. $\frac{r}{2}$

B. $r + 4$

C. $2r$

D. $4r$

20.

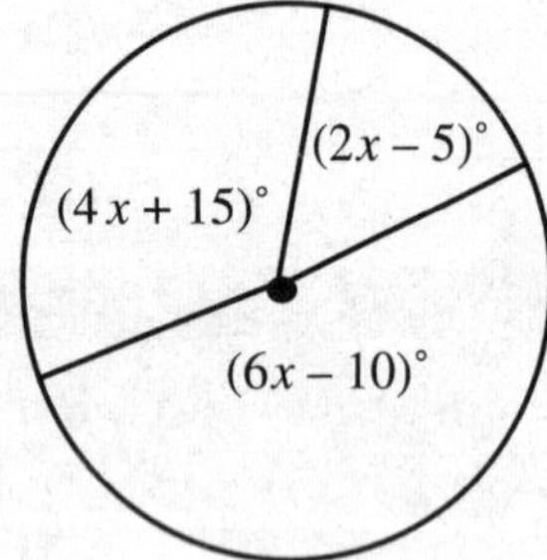

In the figure above, what is the value of x?

E. 15

F. 30

G. 55

H. 70

21. The number of square units in the area of circle O is equal to the number of units in the circumference of circle O. Assuming that the diameter of the circle must be greater than zero, what is the radius of circle O?

A. 2

B. 2π

C. 4

D. Cannot be determined from the information given.

> ✓ **Remember**
>
> **You can Pick Numbers when you have variables in the answer choices.**

> ✓ **Remember**
>
> **You can use Backsolving if you have trouble setting up a problem.**

Multiple Figures

When you encounter questions with multiple figures, look for the connections between the figures.

Solve the following test like problem.

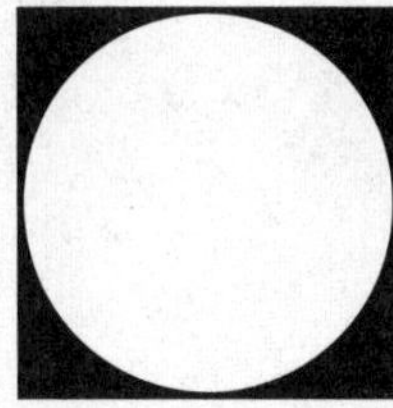

In the figure above, a circle is inscribed within a square. If the area of the circle is 25π, what is the perimeter of the shaded region?

A. $40 + 5\pi$

B. $40 + 10\pi$

C. $100 + 10\pi$

D. $100 + 25\pi$

A. First, determine the connection between the shapes: ______________________

B. Next, decide what information you need to find, and solve for unknown variables: ___

C. Finally, solve the question: ______________________________________

22. 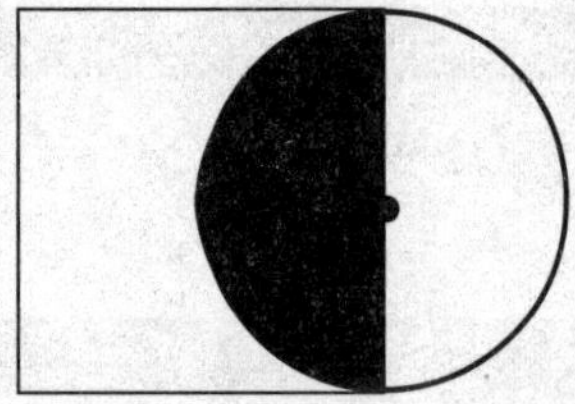

A square and a circle are drawn as shown above. The area of the square is 64. What is the area of the shaded region?

E. 4π

F. 8π

G. 16π

H. Cannot be determined from the information given.

23. 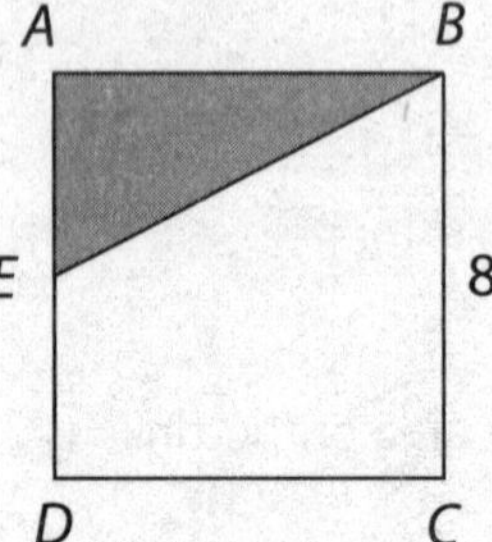

ABCD is a square. If *E* is the midpoint of *AD,* what is the area of the shaded region?

A. 8

B. 12

C. 16

D. 24

24. 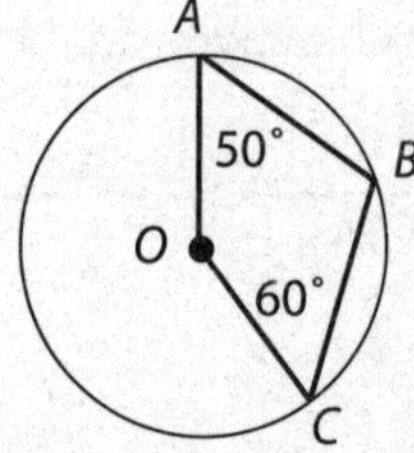

In the figure above, points *A, B,* and *C* lie on the circumference of the circle centered at *O.* If $\angle OAB$ measures 50° and $\angle BCO$ measures 60°, what is the measure of $\angle AOC$?

E. 110°

F. 125°

G. 140°

H. Cannot be determined from the information given.

✔ Remember

Draw information into the figure.

Break up unusual figures into common shapes.

Use what you know about common shapes to determine the missing information.

Surface Area and Volume of Solids

Because formulas are not given on the SHSAT, you will need to memorize the ones that will help you most. Be smart when you memorize—sometimes you can break up a solid into polygons with area formulas you already know.

Shape	Surface Area	Volume
Cube	$6s^2$	s^3
Rectangular Prism	$2\ell w + 2hw + 2\ell h$ Think: find the area of each rectangle, then add.	ℓwh Think: area of the base times the height.
Cylinder	$2\pi r^2 + 2\pi rh$ Think: twice the area of the base, plus the area of the side rolled out as a rectangle—the width is the circumference of the circle.	$\pi r^2 h$ Think: area of the base times the height.

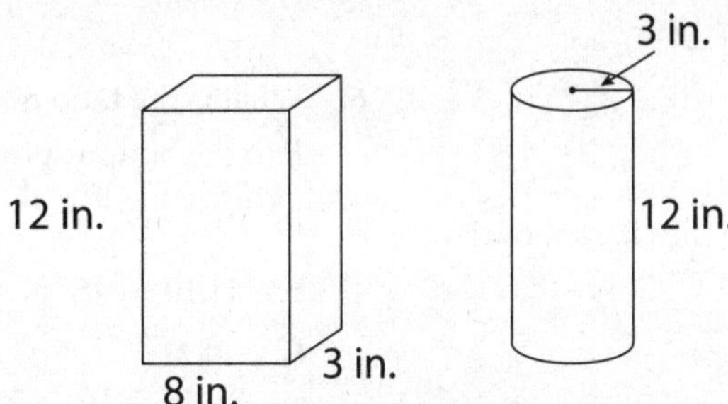

[not drawn to scale]

A. In terms of π, how much larger is the larger container than the smaller container?.

______________________________ cubic inches

B. A cube has a surface area of 294 square centimeters. What is the length of each edge of the cube?

______________________________ centimeters

The following practice sets provide an opportunity to apply the concepts and strategic thinking covered in this chapter. To practice Test Day timing, follow the suggested timing guidelines for each section.

ADVANCED MATH PRACTICE SET

Suggested Timing: 45 minutes

Charts/Data Interpretation

Questions 1–6 refer to the chart below.

Factory	Number of Buttons
A	6,200
B	6,300
C	6,000
D	6,200
E	6,100
F	6,500

1. Which of the following is closest to the mean number of buttons produced in the six factories?

   A. 6,000

   B. 6,117

   C. 6,200

   D. 6,217

2. What is the mode according to the chart above?

   E. 6,000

   F. 6,200

   G. 6,216.67

   H. 6,400

3. What is the median number of buttons produced in the six factories?

   A. 6,000

   B. 6,200

   C. 6,216.67

   D. 6,416.67

4. If the two factories with the highest number of buttons produced are removed from the data, what is the new median?

   E. 6,000

   F. 6,100

   G. 6,125

   H. 6,150

5. If the number of buttons produced by Factory *A* is increased by 100, what is the new mode?

   A. 6,200

   B. 6,216.67

   C. 6,233.33

   D. 6,300

6. What is the ratio of buttons produced by Factory *B* to the buttons produced by Factory *C*?

   E. 2:1

   F. 11:10

   G. 20:21

   H. 21:20

Right Triangles/Pythagorean Theorem

Questions 7–10 refer to the figure below.

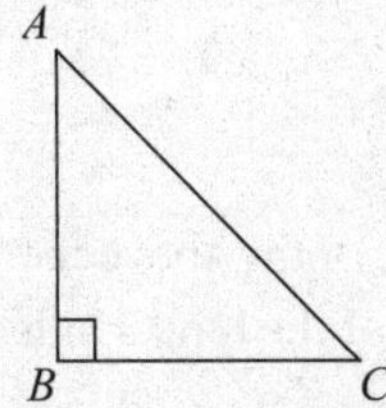

7. If $AB = 5$ and $BC = 12$, what is the length of AC?

   A. 7
   B. 13
   C. 15
   D. 17

8. If $AC = 25$ and $BC = 15$, what is the length of AB?

   E. 10
   F. 12
   G. 15
   H. 20

9. If $AB = 6$ inches and the area of triangle ABC is 18 square inches, what is the length of AC?

   A. 3 inches
   B. $3\sqrt{2}$ inches
   C. 6 inches
   D. $6\sqrt{2}$ inches

10. If $AB = 2$ yards and $BC = 6$ yards, what is the perimeter of triangle ABC?

    E. $4\sqrt{2}$ yards
    F. 8 yards
    G. $8 + 2\sqrt{10}$ yards
    H. $8 + 2\sqrt{14}$ yards

Complex Geometric Word Problems

11. A circle has an area of 25π cm^2. If a circle is drawn within that circle with a diameter equal to the radius of the first circle, what is the area of the second circle?

    A. $2\frac{1}{2}\pi\,\text{cm}^2$
    B. $4\frac{1}{4}\pi\,\text{cm}^2$
    C. $5\frac{1}{4}\pi\,\text{cm}^2$
    D. $6\frac{1}{4}\pi\,\text{cm}^2$

12. A square has an area of 64 cm^2. If a rectangle with the same area has a length twice that of a side of the square, what is its width?

    E. 4 cm
    F. 6 cm
    G. 8 cm
    H. 12 cm

13. A triangle has an area of 15 cm^2 and a base of 5 cm. If a circle is drawn with a diameter equal to the length of the triangle's height, what is the area of the circle?

    A. 6π cm^2
    B. 9π cm^2
    C. 12π cm^2
    D. 36π cm^2

14. A rectangle has a length of 6 inches and an area of 18 inches. If the radius of a circle is equal to the width of the rectangle, what is the area of the circle?

    E. $2\frac{1}{4}\pi$ square inches
    F. $4\frac{1}{4}\pi$ square inches
    G. 6π square inches
    H. 9π square inches

15. A square measures 12 cm × 12 cm and is divided into four equal squares. If equal circles are inscribed within each of the four squares, what is the circumference of each circle?

A. 4π cm

B. 6π cm

C. 8π cm

D. 12π cm

16. A circle has a circumference of 24π cm. If one side of a square is the same length as the diameter of the circle, what is the area of the square?

E. 96 cm^2

F. 256 cm^2

G. 480 cm^2

H. 576 cm^2

Algebra in Geometry

17. A nine-sided polygon has two sides that each have a length of x, three sides that each have a length of $x + 1$, one side with a length of $x + 3$, and three sides that each have a length of $x + 4$. What is the value of x if the perimeter is 108?

A. 9

B. 10

C. 11

D. 12

18. A circle is divided into three sectors with angle measures of x°, $2x$° and $(2x + 10)$°. What is the value of the largest sector's angle?

E. 70°

F. 100°

G. 120°

H. 150°

19.

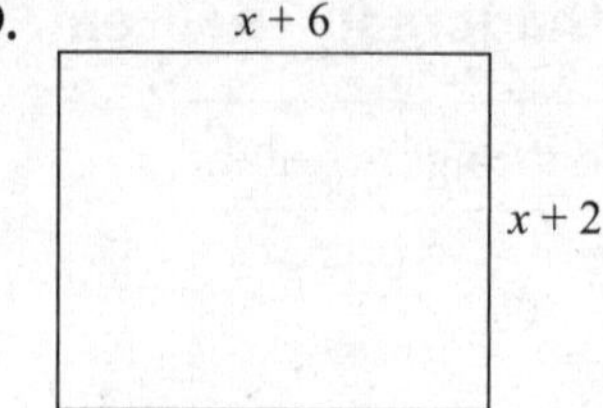

The perimeter of the above rectangle is 64. How long are each of the longer sides?

A. 8

B. 12

C. 14

D. 18

20.

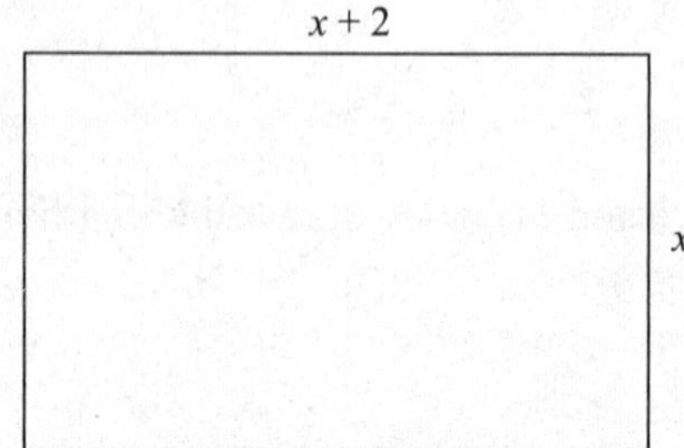

The perimeter of the above rectangle is 24 cm. If a new rectangle is created by doubling the lengths of the original rectangle's longer sides, what would the new rectangle's perimeter be?

E. 17 cm

F. 24 cm

G. 31 cm

H. 38 cm

Unusual Diagrams

21. 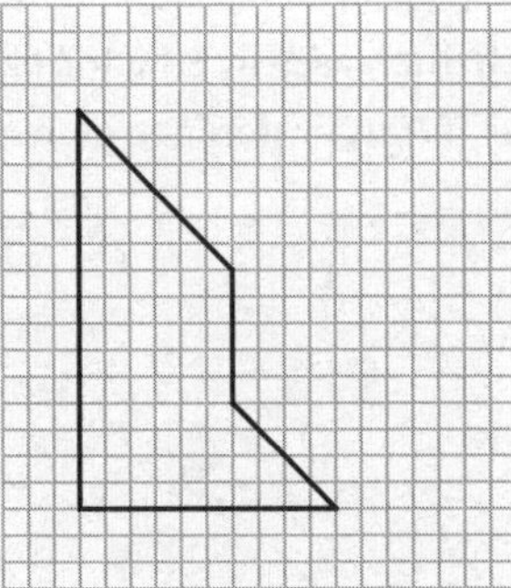

If each of the small squares in the figure above has an area of 1 sq inch, what is the area of the shape above?

A. 54 sq inches
B. 62 sq inches
C. 80 sq inches
D. 106 sq inches

22. 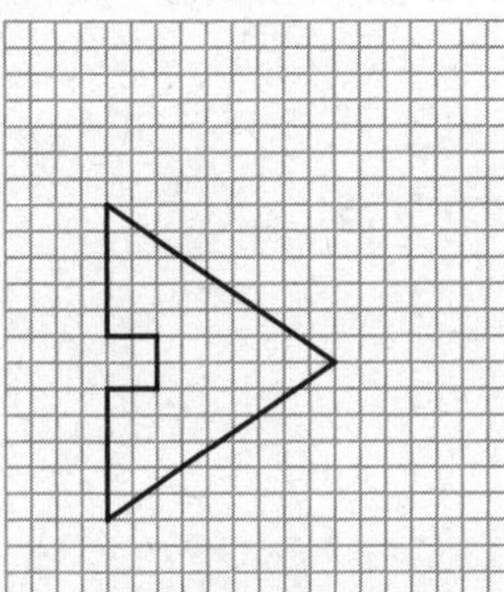

If each of the small squares in the figure above has an area of 1 sq cm, what is the area of the shape above?

E. 108 sq centimeters
F. 104 sq centimeters
G. 54 sq centimeters
H. 50 sq centimeters

23. 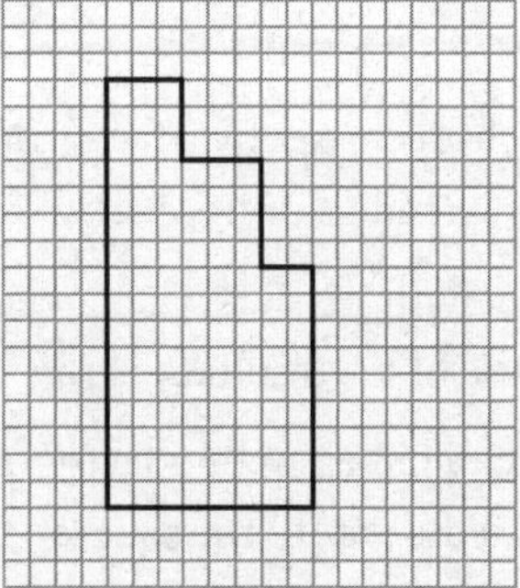

If each of the small squares in the figure above has an area of 1 sq inch, what is the area of the shape above?

A. 64 sq inches
B. 88 sq inches
C. 97 sq inches
D. 105 sq inches

Questions 4 and 5 refer to the figure below.

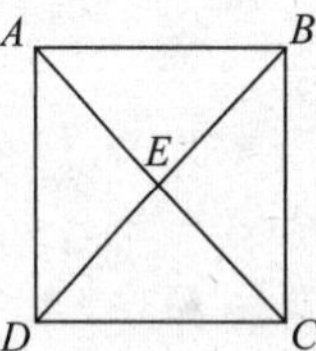

24. Quadrilateral *ABCD* is a square. If the area of triangle *CDE* is 14 sq cm, what is the area of square *ABCD*?

E. 32 sq cm
F. 42 sq cm
G. 56 sq cm
H. 62 sq cm

25. If the area of square *ABCD* is 36 sq inches, what is the area of triangle *ABE*?

A. 18 sq inches
B. 12 sq inches
C. 10 sq inches
D. 9 sq inches

Scaling

26. If the area of a circle decreases by a factor of 4, by what factor has its radius decreased?
27. If a square of side length x is cut in half, what is the perimeter of one of the resultant halves?
28. If the side of a square increases by a factor of 3, by what factor does the area of the square increase?
29. If the radius of a circle is doubled, by what factor does the circumference increase?
30. If the area of a circle increases by a factor of 9, by what factor does its circumference increase?

ANSWERS AND EXPLANATIONS

Advanced Math

Charts/Data Interpretation

A. The largest number of people chose red, then blue, then green.

B. No percentage given for "other."

C. First, find how many people picked red and yellow if 200 people were surveyed. $200 \times 0.35 = 70$ picked red; $200 \times 0.10 = 20$ picked yellow. Then subtract $70 - 20 = 50$ more picked red.

1. A

Subject: Data Interpretation

Getting to the Answer:

5 units at \$125, so

$$\frac{\$125}{5} = \$25 \text{ per unit}$$

2. H

Subject: Data Interpretation

Getting to the Answer: According to the chart, 5 are sold at \$125, so

$$\frac{\$125}{5} = \$25 \text{ per unit}$$

$$\frac{\$150}{\$25} \text{ per unit} = 6 \text{ units}$$

Symbolism

A. $\frac{ac}{|d-b|}$

B. $3z-(x+y)$

C. $a(b-c)-cb$

$3[7-(-x)]-(-x)(7)$

$3(7+x)+7x$

$21+3x+7x$

$21+10x$

D. $a \div c - b \times c$

$3 \div (-x) - 7(-x)$

$-\frac{3}{x}+7x$

3. C

Subject: Symbolism

Getting to the Answer: The operation described in the question stem translates as $(x+y)(x-y)$. Plug in the given numbers for the variables, just like the example in the question stem, and solve.

$(x+y)(x-y) = (7+5)(7-5) = (12)(2) = 24$

4. E

Subject: Symbolism

Getting to the Answer: Translate the defined operation into an algebraic expression, and then plug the given values into that expression, substituting the variable x for a, and set it equal to 12.

$(a+b+c)+(a \cdot b \cdot c)$	Translate the expression.
$(x+2+3)+(x \cdot 2 \cdot 3) = 12$	Plug in values.
$x+5+6x = 12$	Solve for x.
$7x+5 = 12$	
$7x = 7$	
$x = 1$	

5. C

Subject: Symbolism

Getting to the Answer: The question asks you to simplify the sum of two of the defined *rs* expressions. To keep it simple, translate and simplify each *rs* expression on its own, and then add those values together to get your answer.

$rs \blacksquare s \rightarrow rs - s$	
$2 \blacksquare 3 \rightarrow (2)(3)-3 = 3$	Translate each *rs* expression and simplify.
$4 \blacksquare 5 \rightarrow (4)(5)-5 = 15$	
$3+15=18$	Add the two resulting values.

Right Triangles

A. $3^2 + 4^2 = x^2$

$9 + 16 = x^2$

$25 = x^2$

$5 = x$

B. $2^2 + (2\sqrt{3})^2 = y^2$

$4 + 4(3) = y^2$

$16 = y^2$

$4 = y$

C. $y^2 + y^2 = 2^2$

$2y^2 = 4$

$y^2 = 2$

$y = \sqrt{2}$

D. $x^2 + 5^2 = 13^2$

$x^2 + 25 = 169$

$x^2 = 144$

$x = 12$

6. H

Subject: Geometry

Getting to the Answer: Set up the Pythagorean theorem with the information given. The diagonal of the square forms the hypotenuse of the resulting triangle. The two sides of the triangle are equal, so use the same variable to represent each in the equation. Remember, you are looking for the area of the square, which is side squared, or s^2.

$$
\begin{aligned}
a^2 + b^2 &= c^2 \\
s^2 + s^2 &= 6^2 \\
2s^2 &= 36 \\
s^2 &= 18 = \text{area}
\end{aligned}
$$

7. C

Subject: Geometry

Getting to the Answer:

$a^2 + b^2 = c^2$	Use the Pythagorean theorem. Solve for the third side.
$a^2 + 12^2 = 15^2$	
$a^2 + 144 = 225$	
$a^2 = 81$	
$a = 9$	
$p = 9 + 12 + 15 = 36$	Add the lengths of the three sides to get the perimeter.

8. G

Subject: Geometry

Getting to the Answer: Use the Pythagorean theorem to find side *AC*, which is the diameter of the circle. Divide the diameter in half to find the radius, and then solve for area.

$a^2 + b^2 = c^2$	Use the Pythagorean theorem to find the diameter.
$6^2 + 8^2 = AC^2$	
$36 + 64 = AC^2$	
$100 = AC^2$	
$AC = 10 = d$	
$r = \frac{d}{2} = 5$	Half of the diameter is the radius.
$A = \pi r^2$	Solve for the area.
$A = \pi 5^2$	
$A = 25\pi$	

Complex Geometric Word Problems

9. D

Subject: Geometry

Getting to the Answer: The coordinates put the center of the circle at 8 on the *x*-axis. From the area, you can figure out that the radius of the circle is 5. So the circumference of the circle must pass through coordinates five away from the center: therefore, to find the coordinates, add and subtract 5: $8 - 5 = 3$ and $8 + 5 = 13$, so the coordinates are (3, 0), (D), and (13, 0).

10. G

Subject: Geometry

Getting to the Answer:

Area of a triangle $= \frac{1}{2}bh$

Area of a square $= s^2$

$\frac{1}{2}bh = s^2$ Set the two area formulas equal to each other.

$\frac{1}{2}(6)h = 6^2$ Plug in known values.

$3h = 36$

$h = 12$ Solve for height.

11. C

Subject: Geometry

Getting to the Answer: Find the square root of the area of the square to get the length of a side. Calculate the diameter of the circle, which is given in terms of a side of the square. Divide the diameter in half to determine the radius.

$$A_{square} = s^2 = 144$$
$$s = 12$$
$$d = 3s = 3(12) = 36$$
$$r = \frac{1}{2}d = \frac{1}{2}(36) = 18$$

Scaling

A. $r = 5 \rightarrow A = 25\pi$

$r = 3(5) = 15 \rightarrow A = 225\pi$

$\frac{225\pi}{25\pi} = 9$

Therefore, the area is 9 times larger.

B. $A = 16 \rightarrow side = 4$

Then, double the side length to get the new side length, 8.

$A = 8^2 = 64$

$\frac{64}{16} = 4$

Therefore, the new area is 4 times larger.

C. Area $= \frac{1}{2}bh$

$8 = \frac{1}{2}(b)(4) \rightarrow b = 4$

New base is $4(4) = 16$

Area $= \frac{1}{2}(16)(4) = 32$

$\frac{32}{8} = 4$

Therefore, the new area is 4 times larger.

12. G

Subject: Geometry

Getting to the Answer: Pick Numbers. Pick two circumference values, one twice the other. Solve for radius and then area for each case. Then calculate how many more times one area is than the other.

circumference$_1 = 2\pi r = 10\pi$
radius$_1 = 5$
area$_1 = \pi r^2 = 25\pi$
circumference$_2 = 2\pi r = 20\pi$
radius$_2 = 10$
area$_2 = \pi r^2 = 100\pi$
area$_2 = 4 \times$ area$_1$

13. C

Subject: Geometry

Getting to the Answer: Doubling length and tripling width is the same as multiplying the area by 6.

$(\ell \times 2)(w \times 3) = \ell \times 2 \times w \times 3 = (\ell \times w)(2 \times 3) =$ (area)(6) $=$ (20)(6) $= 120$

14. F

Subject: Geometry

Getting to the Answer:

area$_1 = 64 =$ side$_1{}^2$
side$_1 = 8$
perimeter$_1 = 4 \times$ side$_1 = 32$
perimeter$_2 = \frac{1}{2}$ perimeter$_1 = 16$
side$_2 = \frac{1}{4}$ perimeter$_2 = 4$
area$_2 =$ side$_2{}^2 = 16$

Unusual Diagrams

A. Start by dividing each shape into individual parts, and then solve for areas of each part and add the results. Find the missing side by adding together the given lengths: $2 + 5 + 8 = 15$

Find the areas for each rectangle:

$5 \times 12 = 60$; $8 \times 5 = 40$; $15 \times 6 = 90$

Add them together: $60 + 40 + 90 = 190$

B. Find the area of the rectangle: $10 \times 5 = 50$

Find the area of the triangle: $\frac{1}{2}(3)(4) = 6$

Subtract: $50 - 6 = 44$

C. Use the Pythagorean theorem to find the width of the rectangle, which is the hypotenuse of each of the triangles. Find the areas of each of the individual shapes and add them:

$7 \times 10 = 70$; $\frac{1}{2}(6)(8) = 24$;

$70 + 24 + 24 = 118$

15. C

Subject: Geometry

Getting to the Answer: Imagine a rectangle circumscribing the rounded shape that has a length of 10 and a width of 4. The rectangle's perimeter would be 28. Since the figure shown essentially takes little short cuts at the corner, its perimeter would be slightly less than that of the rectangle. 25, choice **(C)**, is a good approximation.

16. F

Subject: Geometry

Getting to the Answer: The shape is essentially an 8×10 rectangle that is missing a 2×6 rectangle and a 2×3 rectangle.

$a = (8 \times 10) - (2 \times 6) - (2 \times 3)$
$a = 80 - 12 - 6 = 62$

17. C

Subject: Geometry

Getting to the Answer: The side of each square in the grid is equivalent to 6 feet, or 2 yards. Remember, calculate everything in yards from the beginning. Break up the complex shape into three simple shapes: a triangle on top with a base of 8 yards and height of 8 yards, a 9×8 yard rectangle below, and a 4×4 yard square on the right. Calculate the areas of these simple shapes individually. Then add them up, and you've got the area of the complex shape.

$$\left(\frac{1}{2}bh\right) + (\ell \times w) + (s^2) =$$

$$\left(\frac{1}{2} \times 8 \times 8\right) + (9 \times 8) + (4^2) =$$

$$32 + 72 + 16 = 120 \text{ square yards}$$

Complex Algebra in Geometric Figures

A. Draw a picture of a rectangle that is taller than it is wide. Label the width x and the length $3x$.

B. The problem provides the length of the fence, so use the perimeter equation:

$x + 3x + x + 3x = 240$

C. Simplify: $8x = 240$, so $x = 30$

18. F

Subject: Geometry

Getting to the Answer: Radius *B* is one greater than radius *A*. Circumference is $2\pi r$, or r times 2π, so an increase of 1 in radius means an increase of 2π in circumference. Alternatively, you could Pick Numbers here.

19. C

Subject: Geometry

Getting to the Answer: Set the area of *B* equal to one quarter the area of *A*. Use r to represent radius *B* and x to represent radius *A*. Then solve for x.

$\text{area}\,B = \frac{1}{4}\,\text{area}\,A$	
$\pi r^2 = \frac{1}{4}\pi x^2$	Multiply each side by 4.
$4\pi r^2 = \pi x^2$	Divide each side by π.
$4r^2 = x^2$	Take the square root of each side.
$2r = x$	Solve for radius $A(x)$.

20. F

Subject: Geometry

Getting to the Answer: You are given the measures, in terms of x, of three angles which comprise a circle. Since a circle contains 360°, set the sum of the angles equal to 360° and solve for x.

$$(4x+15)+(2x-5)+(6x-10) = 360 \quad \text{Get rid of the parentheses.}$$
$$4x+15+2x-5+6x-10 = 360 \quad \text{Combine like terms.}$$
$$12x = 360 \quad \text{Solve for } x.$$
$$x = 30$$

21. A

Subject: Geometry

Getting to the Answer: You know the formulas for area and circumference, so set up an equation with one equal to the other, and solve for radius.

$$2\pi r = \pi r^2 \quad \text{Circumference} = \text{area.}$$
$$2 = r \quad \text{Divide both sides by } \pi r \text{ to solve for } r.$$

Multiple Figures

A. Since the circle is inscribed in the square, the circle's diameter is equal to the length of a side of the square.

B. In this case, the perimeter of the square provides the outside perimeter of the shaded shape, while the circumference of the circle will be the inside perimeter. Add them together to find the total. Since the area of the circle is 25π, the radius of the circle is 5. That makes the diameter and the lengths of the sides of the square all equal to 10.

C. The circumference of the circle is πd or 10π.

The perimeter of the square is $4 \times 10 = 40$.

Add these quantities together: $40 + 10\pi$.

22. F

Subject: Geometry

Getting to the Answer: If the area of the square is 64, then its side must be 8. The side of the square is also the diameter of the circle, so the radius is 4. The shaded region is half of the circle, so calculate half of the circle's area.

$$a_{square} = s^2 = 64$$
$$s = d = 8$$
$$r = \frac{1}{2}d = 4$$
$$a_{shade} = \frac{1}{2}\pi r^2$$
$$a_{shade} = \frac{1}{2}\pi 4^2 = \frac{1}{2}\pi 16 = 8\pi$$

23. C

Subject: Geometry

Getting to the Answer: Because *ABCD* is a square, *AB* is 8 and *AE*, which is half of *AD*, is 4. Now just calculate the area of triangle *AEB*.

$$a = \frac{1}{2}bh$$
$$a = \frac{1}{2}(8)(4) = 16$$

24. G

Subject: Geometry

Getting to the Answer: Draw an additional radius from *O* to *B*. Since radii *OA*, *OB*, and *OC* are all equal, you now have two isosceles triangles. Since the angles opposite the equal sides of an isosceles triangle are also equal, then angle *OBC* and angle *OCB* are both 60°. Since the sum of the interior angle of any triangle is 180°, then angle *BOC* is 60°. Likewise, angle *OAB* and angle *OBA* are both 50°, so angle *BOA* is 80°. The sum of angles *BOC* and *BOA* equal angle *AOC*, so the measure of angle *AOC* is 140°.

Surface Area and Volume of Solids

A. Volume of the prism $= \ell wh = 12 \times 3 \times 8 = 288$ inches^3

Volume of cylinder $= \pi r^2 h = \pi(3)^2 \times 12 = 108\pi$ inches^3

The cylinder is $108\pi - 288$ cubic inches larger.

B. Surface area of a cube $= 6s^2 = 294$

$s^2 = 49$

$s = 7$

ANSWERS AND EXPLANATIONS

Advanced Math Practice Set

Charts/Data Interpretation

1. D

Subject: Arithmetic

Getting to the Answer: Mean = total of all values/number of values.

$6{,}200 + 6{,}300 + 6{,}000 + 6{,}200 + 6{,}100 + 6{,}500 = 37{,}300$

$$\text{Mean} = \frac{37{,}300}{6}$$

Mean = 6,216 or 6,217 when rounded.

2. F

Subject: Arithmetic

Getting to the Answer: The mode is the most frequent value. In this case, the mode is 6,200.

3. B

Subject: Arithmetic

Getting to the Answer: Put the values in order.

6,000 6,100 6,200 6,200 6,300 6500

The median is the middle value. As there are 6 values, the median is halfway between value 3 and 4. As values 3 and 4 are both 6,200, the median is 6,200.

4. H

Subject: Arithmetic

Getting to the Answer: List the values in order and then remove the two highest (6,300 and 6,500).

6,000 6,100 6,200 6,200

The median is the middle value. Because there are four values, the median will be halfway between the second and third value. Here, the second value is 6,100 and the third is 6,200. The average of these two numbers is:

$$\frac{(6{,}100 + 6{,}200)}{2}$$

$$\frac{12{,}300}{2}$$

$$6{,}150$$

5. D

Subject: Arithmetic

Getting to the Answer: The mode is the most frequent value. If the value for Factory *A*, which was 6,200, is increased by 100 to 6,300, 6,300 becomes the new mode.

6. H

Subject: Arithmetic

Getting to the Answer:

6,300:6,000

63:60

21:20

Right Triangles/Pythagorean Theorem

7. B

Subject: Geometry

Getting to the Answer: By the Pythagorean theorem you know that $AB^2 + BC^2 = AC^2$. Because you know the lengths of the legs, you can solve for *AC* as follows:

$$5^2 + 12^2 = AC^2$$
$$169 = AC^2$$
$$AC = 13$$

The 5-12-13 right triangle is a very common one that is useful to memorize.

8. H

Subject: Geometry

Getting to the Answer: Thanks to the Pythagorean theorem, you know that if you know the length of a leg and the length of the hypotenuse, you can solve for the length of the other leg as follows:

$$AB^2 + 15^2 = 25^2$$
$$AB^2 = 25^2 - 15^2 = 400$$
$$AB = 20$$

Note that this is just a 3-4-5 right triangle with all the sides multiplied by 5.

9. D

Subject: Geometry

Getting to the Answer: In a right triangle, you can find area by taking half the product of the lengths of the legs. You know one of the legs, *AB*, has a length of 6 inches, so you can figure out the length of the other leg as follows:

$$A = \frac{1}{2}(AB)(BC)$$
$$18 = \frac{1}{2}(6)(BC) = 3BC$$
$$6 = BC$$

Now you know that *BC* is the same length as *AB*. When the legs of a right triangle are congruent, you have a 45-45-90 triangle and you know that the hypotenuse equals the length of one leg times $\sqrt{2}$, which in this case means $6\sqrt{2}$ inches, **(D)**.

10. G

Subject: Geometry

Getting to the Answer: In order to find the perimeter of this triangle, you must find the length of the hypotenuse. This is easily done using the Pythagorean theorem.

$$AB^2 + BC^2 = AC^2$$
$$2^2 + 6^2 = AC^2$$
$$40 = AC^2$$
$$2\sqrt{10} = AC$$

The perimeter is just the sum of the three lengths, or $8 + 2\sqrt{10}$ yards, **(G)**.

Complex Geometric Word Problems

11. D

Subject: Geometry

Getting to the Answer: The area is 25π, so the radius must be 5. If the diameter of the second circle is 5, then its radius is 2.5. The area is then 6.25π or 6 ¼π.

12. E

Subject: Geometry

Getting to the Answer: The square has an area of 64, so its sides are each 8 ($8 \times 8 = 64$). Therefore, the length of the rectangle is $2 \times 8 = 16$. If the area is 64, the width is $16 \times \text{width} = 64$; width = 4.

13. B

Subject: Geometry

Getting to the Answer: Because the triangle has an area of 15, $15 = \frac{1}{2} \times 5 \times \text{height}$. Therefore, height = 6. Because the diameter is equal to the height of the triangle, the radius is equal to half of that.

$\left[\left(\frac{1}{2}(6) = 3\right)\right]$ and its area is $\pi r^2 = \pi 3^2 = 9\pi$.

14. H

Subject: Geometry

Getting to the Answer: A rectangle with an area of 18 and a length of 6 has a width $= \frac{18}{6} = 3$. A circle with a radius of 3 has an area $= \pi r^2 = \pi 3^2 = 9\pi$.

15. B

Subject: Geometry

Getting to the Answer: The square is divided into four equal squares, which will all measure 6 × 6. Therefore, the radius of each circle is 3. The circumference would be $2\pi r = 2\pi(3) = 6\pi$.

16. H

Subject: Geometry

Getting to the Answer: If the circumference is 24π, then the radius, using $C = 2\pi r$, is 12, and the diameter and the length of the side of the square are 24. Therefore, the area is $24 \times 24 = 576$.

Algebra in Geometry

17. B

Subject: Algebra

Getting to the Answer: Calculate x using the perimeter given. The perimeter is

$108 = 2x + 3(x + 1) + (x + 3) + 3(x + 4)$

$$\begin{aligned} 9x + 18 &= 108 \\ 9x &= 90 \\ x &= 10 \end{aligned}$$

18. H

Subject: Algebra

Getting to the Answer: A circle is 360°, and therefore the angles of the three sectors have to add up to that. So $x + 2x + (2x + 10) = 360°$ and $5x + 10 = 360°$, and $x = 70°$, and the largest sector is $2x + 10 = 2 \times 70 + 10 = 150°$.

19. D

Subject: Algebra

Getting to the Answer: Because you are given that the perimeter is 64, $(x + 2) + (x + 2) + (x + 6) + (x + 6) = 64$. Just solve for x and put it back into the values given for the lengths. $4x + 16 = 64$, and therefore $x = 12$. The length is $x + 6$, or 18.

20. H

Subject: Algebra

Getting to the Answer: The rectangle has sides of $x + 2$ and x; therefore, the perimeter is $(x + 2) + (x + 2) + x + x = 24$, or $4x + 4 = 24$, or $4x = 20$, and $x = 5$. The length is $x + 2 = 7$. Doubling the length gives you a rectangle that is 14 by 5. The new perimeter is $14 + 14 + 5 + 5 = 38$.

Unusual Diagrams

21. C

Subject: Geometry

Getting to the Answer: You could simply count the squares, but it is much quicker to use area formulas. This shape consists of a rectangle and two right triangles. The rectangle is 6 inches by 9 inches, so it has an area of 54 square inches. The triangle on the top has a base and a height both of 6 inches, and the one on the bottom right has a base and a height of 4 inches. So their areas are 18 square inches and 8 square inches, respectively, and the total area is 80 square inches.

22. H

Subject: Geometry

Getting to the Answer: You could determine the area of the shape by counting squares; however, it will be easier if you realize that it is a triangle with a square removed from it. The triangle has a base of 12 centimeters and a height of 9 centimeters, so its area is $\frac{1}{2}(12)(9) = 54$ square centimeters. The square is 2 centimeters by 2 centimeters, so its area is 4 square centimeters. Therefore, the area of the shape is 50 square centimeters.

23. D

Subject: Geometry

Getting to the Answer: This complex shape can be broken into a 3-inch by 3-inch square, a 6-inch by 4-inch rectangle, and a 9-inch by 8-inch rectangle. The total area of the shape, therefore, is

$(3 \times 3) + (6 \times 4) + (8 \times 9) = 105$ square inches.

24. G

Subject: Geometry

Getting to the Answer: The diagonals of a square intersect to form four congruent triangles. Therefore, the area of the square is four times the area of any of the triangles, or $4 \cdot 14 = 56$ square centimeters.

25. D

Subject: Geometry

Getting to the Answer: Each of the four triangles is congruent and has one-fourth of the area of the square. Therefore, the area of triangle *ABE* is one-fourth of 36 square inches, or 9 square inches.

Scaling

26. 2

27. 3*x*

28. 9

29. 2

30. 3

PART 4

Ready, Set, Go!

CHAPTER 19

Countdown to the Test

CHAPTER OBJECTIVES

By the end of this chapter, you will be able to:

- Recall important test information that will help you avoid surprises on Test Day
- Identify what to do the week before the test, the night before the test, and the morning of the test

STRATEGIC REVIEW: READING

The Kaplan Method for Reading Comprehension

Step 1: Read actively

Step 2: Examine the question stem

Step 3: Predict and answer

Try It Out: Reading Review

Despite growing up in poverty and suffering from a debilitating fear of public speaking, Daniel Webster (1782–1852) matured to become one of his era's most outspoken statesmen. Webster's initial exposure to serious education, as a student at the prestigious Phillips Exeter Academy, was traumatic. His enrollment lasted only nine months, and he displayed a seemingly unconquerable aversion to public debate; unfortunately for Webster, a significant curriculum requirement for students of the Academy was "public declamation." In fact, historical records indicate that Webster became so petrified when asked to speak in front of an audience that he simply refused to stand up, usually returning to his room in shame and in tears.

Webster's aversion to oration, however, proved to be short-lived. While enrolled as an undergraduate at Dartmouth College in the late 1790s, Webster finally laid his powerful phobia to rest by plunging himself into activities that demanded he speak before an audience. As a member of the United Fraternity, for example, Webster soon found that he could put his phenomenal memory and skills as a writer to use in public debate. Indeed, by the time he graduated in 1801, Webster had so thoroughly overcome his childhood fears that he was invited to deliver the Independence Day oration on campus.

But Webster, known for his relentless determination and lofty aspirations, was not satisfied with merely giving holiday speeches. He opened his own law practice in Portsmouth in 1807, and his reputation as a

particularly effective lawyer grew rapidly. In 1812, he officially entered politics with election to the U.S. House of Representatives—an achievement that historians attribute to his fervently articulated opposition to the War of 1812. In fact, as a politician, Webster soon became known as a passionate American nationalist, championing the importance of a unified nation independent of international influences and entanglements. After being elected to the U.S. Senate in 1827, Webster joined the National Republican Party and quickly became a leader, largely due to his skills as an orator.

Although his several attempts at gaining the presidency were thwarted, Webster remained a debater to be reckoned with throughout his political career. Given the political positions he eventually held, including a stint as U.S. Secretary of State under President William Harrison, it is certainly surprising that, as a young student, Webster struggled so mightily with public speaking. Numerous times, Webster successfully defended controversial political stances on the floor of the Senate, and he even gained several legal victories arguing before the U.S. Supreme Court. If nothing else, Webster's accomplishments powerfully demonstrate that even the most intense fears can be overcome.

GLOBAL

Refer back to the passage and your Roadmap in answering the following questions:

1. What is the subject of the passage?
2. What does the author say about that subject?

Now, using your prephrasing and Roadmapping skills, answer the following test-like Global question:

1. Which of the following best tells what this passage is about?

    A. why Webster was so scared of speaking before a large audience

    B. how Webster laid his phobias to rest and became the most effective politician of his time

    C. how Webster's lofty aspirations for the presidency were never fulfilled

    D. how Webster overcame his aversion to public speaking to become a successful politician

DETAIL

1. Where in the passage are Webster's skills as a public speaker addressed?
2. Based on the information in the passage, prephrase an answer for the question below.
3. Based on your prephrase, which choices can you eliminate?

Now, using your researching skills, answer the following test-like Detail question:

2. According to the passage, why was Webster able to become such an effective public speaker?

   E. He was a graduate of the prestigious Dartmouth College.
   F. He plunged himself into activities that required him to speak before an audience.
   G. He was a strong writer with a good memory.
   H. He developed a successful law practice and entered politics.

FUNCTION

1. Why does the author begin the passage with a discussion of Webster's fear of public speaking?
2. Why does the author characterize Webster's phobia as "powerful" in line 19?

Now, using your researching skills, answer the following test-like Function question:

3. The author uses the word "powerful" in line 19 in order to

   A. highlight that Webster's ability to overcome such an all-consuming fear was impressive.
   B. foreshadow Webster's eventual failure within the political sphere.
   C. assert that Webster was regarded as a particularly effective lawyer.
   D. introduce the idea that Webster's efforts to overcome his considerable fear were ineffective.

INFERENCE

1. Which paragraph mentions holiday speeches?
2. What does the passage say about "giving holiday speeches" specifically?

Now, using your researching and inference skills, answer the following test-like Inference question:

4. It can be inferred that the author's use of the phrase "merely giving holiday speeches" (lines 29–30)

   E. supports the author's statement that Webster was famous for his determination.
   F. suggests that Webster refused the invitation to speak on Independence Day.
   G. hints at Webster's passionate nationalism.
   H. previews Webster's rise as a prominent statesman.

ANSWERS AND EXPLANATIONS

Reading

Global

1. Daniel Webster was one of the most outspoken politicians of his time.
2. Webster overcame a big fear of public speaking in order to achieve his goals.

1. D

Category: Global

Getting to the Answer: If you have already identified the Main Idea on your own, you will have a much easier time finding the correct answer choice. Remember, the correct choice will match both the tone and the scope of the passage. **(D)** does this best. **(A)** is a Misused Detail; the passage discusses Webster's fear, but it is how he overcomes his fear that is the focus. **(B)** is Extreme; the passage does not say that Webster was the "most effective" politician of his time. **(C)** is a Misused Detail; the author mentions that Webster did not become president, but it is not the primary idea of the passage.

Detail

1. Paragraph 2, lines 22–24.
2. Webster soon found that he could put his phenomenal memory and skills as a writer to use in public debate.
3. Any answer that doesn't match the prediction, and any wrong answer traps.

2. G

Category: Detail

Getting to the Answer: Paragraph 2 tells you that "Webster soon found that he could put his phenomenal memory and skills as a writer to use in public debate," which matches **(G)**. **(E)**, **(F)**, and **(H)** are Misused Details; they are mentioned in the passage, but they do not specifically answer the question.

Function

1. To provide information about a fear that Webster was eventually able to overcome.
2. To show that Webster's fear was considerable, which makes it all the more admirable that he was able to move past it.

3. A

Category: Function

Getting to the Answer: The author describes Webster's fear of public speaking as greatly affecting his life before he courageously overcame it, which matches **(A)**. **(B)** is a Distortion. While Webster did not become president, the author does not characterize his political career as a failure. **(C)** is incorrect because Webster's success as a lawyer is mentioned in paragraph 3, not paragraph 2. **(D)** is Opposite; Webster did overcome his fear.

Inference

1. Paragraph 3.
2. Webster did more than give holiday speeches; he became a lawyer and politician.

4. H

Category: Inference

Getting to the Answer: Paragraph 3 discusses Webster's pursuit of political esteem. The phrase "merely giving holiday speeches" introduces the idea that Webster wished to fulfill greater goals, in this case a political career, which matches **(H)**.

STRATEGIC REVIEW: REVISING/EDITING TEXT

The Kaplan Method for Revising/Editing Paragraphs

Step 1: Read the text and identify the issue

Step 2: Select the sentence that should be revised

The Kaplan Method for Revising/Editing Passages and Sentences

Step 1: Read the text and identify the issue

Step 2: Eliminate answer choices that do not address the issue

Step 3: Select the choice that creates the most correct, concise, and relevant text

QUESTIONS 1–14: Revising/Editing in a Passage

DIRECTIONS: Read the passage below and answer the questions following it. You will be asked to improve the writing quality of the passage and to correct errors so that the passage follows the conventions of standard written English. You may reread the passage if you need to. Mark the **best** answer for each question.

Questions 1–7 refer to the following passage.

Milton Hershey

(1) Who has not enjoyed a Hershey Bar or Kiss? (2) Both were created by master confectioner Milton Hershey, born into a Pennsylvania farm family in 1857. (3) His education was limited—he went only as far as the fourth grade—and after a disastrous first apprenticeship to a printer, his mother than arranged for his training with a local caramel candy maker. (4) Here Hershey learned his craft and began a lifelong dedication to quality ingredients. (5) In 1883, Hershey opened the highly successful Lancaster Caramel Company, packaging caramels in bulk. (6) This was a new and profitable innovation.

1. Which edit is needed to correct sentence 3?

A. change ***than*** to **then**

B. change ***arranged*** to **had arranged**

C. change ***his training*** to **him to be trained**

D. change ***local*** to **nearby**

(7) Hershey's interest in chocolate was sparked by his 1893 visit to the World's Columbian Exposition. (8) In 1900 he sold the caramel company and used the money to open the Hershey Chocolate company. (9) Because of its location near the farmland of Lancaster, Pennsylvania, Hershey was able to buy fresh milk and incorporate it into his own milk chocolate recipe. (10) At the time, it was considered a luxury product, but the mass production of the Hershey Bar, introduced in 1903, and Hershey's Kisses, first sold in 1907, made chocolate widely available and affordable.

2. Which is the best way to combine sentences 5 and 6 to clarify the relationship between ideas?

E. In 1883, Hershey opened the highly successful Lancaster Caramel Company, packaging caramels in bulk, this was a new and profitable innovation.

F. In 1883, Hershey opened the highly successful Lancaster Caramel Company, packaging caramels in bulk, however this was a new and profitable innovation.

G. In 1883, Hershey opened the highly successful Lancaster Caramel Company, packaging caramels in bulk, a new and profitable innovation.

H. In 1883, Hershey opened the highly successful Lancaster Caramel Company, packaging caramels in bulk, starting a new and profitable innovation.

3. Which transition should be added to the beginning of sentence 8?

A. Nonetheless

B. Even so

C. Unfortunately

D. Afterward

(11) In 1905, Hershey's huge new factory opened and becomes the center of a town that grew up around it. (12) With his workers in mind, Hershey oversaw the construction of houses, schools, churches, public transportation, and even a zoo. (13) Today the town is a tourist attraction, popularly called Chocolatetown, USA; Hershey called it "the sweetest place on earth." (14) It is one of several locations named after their founders, such as Disneyland.

4. Which revision of sentence 10 uses the most precise language?

E. At the time, chocolate was considered a luxury product, but the mass production of the Hershey Bar, introduced in 1903, and Hershey's Kisses, first sold in 1907, made chocolate widely available and affordable.

F. During that period in the United States, milk was considered a luxury product, but the mass production of the Hershey Bar, introduced in 1903, and Hershey's Kisses, first sold in 1907, made chocolate widely available and affordable.

G. At the time, chocolate was considered a product, but the mass production of the Hershey Bar, introduced in 1903, and Hershey's Kisses, first sold in 1907, made chocolate widely available and affordable.

H. Milk, being a luxury product, was first introduced in 1903, and Hershey's Kisses, first sold in 1907, made chocolate widely available and affordable.

5. Which edit is necessary to correct sentence 11?

A. change ***In 1905*** to **After 1905**

B. change ***becomes*** to **became**

C. change ***center*** to **focal point**

D. change ***that*** to **who**

6. Which sentence is irrelevant to the argument presented in the passage and should be deleted?

E. sentence 11

F. sentence 12

G. sentence 13

H. sentence 14

(15) Hershey and his wife Catherine had no children, so they funneled a great deal of their attention to philanthropic projects. (16) Their best known was an orphanage, called the Hershey Industrial School (later renamed the Milton Hershey School). (17) In 1918 he put all his shares of the Hershey's Chocolate Company into a trust for the school, which today provides an excellent education for children from troubled backgrounds. (18) Milton Hershey died in 1945, having happily given away most of his money in his lifetime.

7. Which sentence would best follow and support sentence 15?

   A. Indeed, Milton Hershey is in the Philanthropy Hall of Fame.

   B. The two were equal partners in philanthropic contributions.

   C. Not every married couple without children gives to charity, though.

   D. Their contributions went to all manner of charitable organizations.

Questions 8–14 refer to the following passage.

Three-toed Sloth

(1) The rarely sighted three-toed sloth is one of the most unusual animal's on earth. (2) In fact, many characteristics of this tree-dwelling mammal seem to run counter to the instincts displayed by almost all wild animals.

(3) All sloths are descended from the extinct giant ground sloth. (4) The four living species of three-toed sloths are found in South and Central America, and though similar to the more common two-toed sloths, they are identified scientifically as a separate family. (5) Three-toed sloths grow to approximately 18 inches long and weigh 8–10 pounds. (6) They also live to be 25–30 years of age. (7) While two-toed sloths tend to be active during the night, the three-toed variety is a daytime creature. (8) Both sloths are incredibly slow, tending to move no faster than six feet per minute, even when confronted by a predator. (9) Tortoises are also slow-moving, going about 0.17 miles per hour on land. (10) Unlike them, three-toed sloths are excellent swimmers. (11) They will sometimes even drop from a tree directly into a body of water, where there long, strong arms easily propel them.

8. Which edit is needed to correct sentence 1?

E. change ***rarely sighted*** to **hard to see**

F. change ***most*** to **more**

G. change ***animal's*** to **animals**

H. change ***on earth*** to **in earth**

9. Which is the best way to combine sentences 5 and 6 to clarify the relationship between ideas?

A. Three-toed sloths grow to approximately 18 inches long, weigh 8–10 pounds, and live to be 25–30 years of age.

B. Three-toed sloths grow to approximately 18 inches long and weigh 8–10 pounds though they also live to be 25–30 years of age.

C. Three-toed sloths grow to approximately 18 inches long and weighing 8–10 pounds and living to be 25–30 years of age.

D. Three-toed sloths grow to approximately 18 inches long and weigh 8–10 pounds, they also live to be 25–30 years of age.

10. Which revision of sentence 10 uses the most precise language?

E. Like them, three-toed sloths are excellent swimmers.

F. Unlike the two-toed variety, three-toed sloths are excellent swimmers.

G. Unlike tortoises, three-toed sloths are excellent swimmers.

H. Unlike slow-moving sloths, three-toed sloths are excellent swimmers.

11. Which sentence is irrelevant to the argument presented in the passage and should be deleted?

A. sentence 7

B. sentence 8

C. sentence 9

D. sentence 10

(12) Three-toed sloths have long fur that often looks green due to an accumulation of algae on the fur. (13) Like all sloths, three-toed sloths are adapted to tree living (they spend almost their entire lives hanging upside down from tree limbs, even when eating and sleeping) and are clumsy on the ground. (14) Their weak hind legs and long claws make it difficult for them to walk, so they drag their bodies, using their front legs to move themselves. (15) On the ground, they are vulnerable to attacks by predators, including jaguars, eagles, and human hunters, and if attacked by a predator while on the ground, the sloth has no defense other than biting and clawing. (16) They have the advantage of seven cervical vertebrae bones, two more than most mammals, enabling them to turn their heads a full 270 degrees.

(17) As a testament to our fascination with sloths, October 20th has unofficially been declared National Sloth Day. (18) During National Sloth Day, people are encouraged to learn more about sloths.

12. Which edit is necessary to correct sentence 11?

E. change ***they*** to **them**

F. change ***sometimes*** to **always**

G. change ***there*** to **they're**

H. change ***there*** to **their**

13. Which transition should be added to the beginning of sentence 16?

A. On the other hand

B. Consequently

C. Even though two-toed sloths are clumsy when not in trees

D. Furthermore

14. Which is the best way to combine sentences 17 and 18 to clarify the relationship between ideas?

E. As a testament to our fascination with sloths, October 20th has unofficially been declared National Sloth Day, during which people are encouraged to learn more about sloths.

F. As a testament to our fascination with sloths, October 20th has unofficially been declared National Sloth Day, a day in which people are encouraged to learn more about sloths.

G. As a testament to our fascination with sloths, October 20th has unofficially been declared National Sloth Day which is a good time to encourage people to learn more about sloths.

H. As a testament to our fascination with sloths, October 20th has unofficially been declared National Sloth Day, people are encouraged to learn more about sloths.

QUESTIONS 15–20: Revising/Editing Stand-Alone Items

DIRECTIONS: Read and answer each of the following questions. You will be asked to recognize and correct errors in sentences or short paragraphs. Mark the **best** answer for each question.

15. Read this paragraph.

(1) The new music class, eagerly anticipated by the students, includes exercises for developing vocal range and for making musical notation understandable to new musicians. (2) The course provides instruction in a variety of topics, such as tonality and harmony, as well as formal and modern styles of music. (3) Young musicians often plan to audition for talent shows on television, although they need to fully prepare due to the serious competition on the shows. (4) While learning about music, students notice the interaction of theory and technique as these features apply to rhythm, scales, improvisation, and creative expression.

Which sentence should be revised to correct a topic development issue?

A. sentence 1

B. sentence 2

C. sentence 3

D. sentence 4

16. Read this paragraph.

(1) Built in 1889 for the World's Fair, the Eiffel Tower was almost destroyed due to Parisians' dislike of this architectural wonder. (2) Fortunately, the tower became home to a radio antenna in 1909 and has since had over 200 million visitors who have taken the elevator to the top level. (3) Visitors might notice that every seven years, the tower receives a new coat of paint, which takes 15 months to apply to its network of beams. (4) While taking a sightseeing tour of Paris, the Eiffel Tower is a tourist's first stop.

Which sentence should be revised to correct a misplaced modifier issue?

E. sentence 1

F. sentence 2

G. sentence 3

H. sentence 4

17. Read this paragraph.

> (1) Canada's ten provinces and two territories cover an extremely large portion of North America. (2) The country includes forests, mountains, rivers, and grasslands, which can be influenced by extreme seasonal temperatures. (3) Canadians speak English and French and tend to live in the southern part of the country, where they generally inhabiting urban locations. (4) Since it shares a long border with America, Canada has developed trading arrangements and various shared interests with the United States.

Which sentence should be revised to correct a parallelism issue?

A. sentence 1

B. sentence 2

C. sentence 3

D. sentence 4

18. Read this sentence.

> To prepare for their event, the competitive swimmers dedicated and devoted many hours to practicing the various swimming strokes.

Which edit should be made to correct this sentence?

E. remove ***for their event***

F. remove ***the competitive***

G. remove ***competitive***

H. remove ***and devoted***

19. Read this sentence.

> When washing a car, rinse it to remove excess dirt, wipe it with a soapy sponge, and then the car is dried with a clean cloth.

Which edit should be made to correct this sentence?

A. change ***washing*** to **washed**

B. change ***to remove*** to **removing**

C. change ***then the car is dried with*** to **dry it with**

D. change ***is dried with*** to **has dried with**

20. Read this sentence.

Aretha Franklin, one of the most honored musicians in Grammy Award history, the first woman to be inducted into the Rock and Roll Hall of Fame.

Which edit should be made to correct this sentence?

E. insert ***became*** after **Franklin,**

F. insert ***became*** after **history,**

G. remove ***to be inducted***

H. remove ***into***

ANSWERS AND EXPLANATIONS

Milton Hershey

1. A

Category: Usage

Getting to the Answer: In context, the word in question is meant to show time—after Hershey was fired, his mother arranged another job. The proper word for this is "then," which makes **(A)** correct. "Than" is a comparative word, as in "chocolate tastes better than vanilla." **(B)** puts the word into the incorrect past perfect tense. **(C)** is unnecessarily wordy, and **(D)** changes the meaning of the sentence.

2. G

Category: Organization, Unity, and Cohesion

Getting to the Answer: Since both sentences are about packaging in bulk, the two can logically be joined by making the second one dependent and adding it to the first with a comma. **(G)** is correct. **(E)** incorrectly joins two independent clauses with a comma, and **(F)** contrasts the two whereas one is a continuation of the other. **(H)** is redundant; both "new" and "innovation" imply "starting."

3. D

Category: Organization, Unity, and Cohesion

Getting to the Answer: In context, it can be inferred that after visiting the exposition and becoming interested in chocolate, Hershey sold the caramel company to make chocolate candies instead. The best word to describe this change of events is **(D)**, "afterward." **(A)** and **(B)** are contrast words, and **(C)** adds a point of view that the author doesn't state. As a matter of fact, in the context of the entire passage, the switch from caramels to chocolate was very fortunate.

4. E

Category: Knowledge of Language

Getting to the Answer: "It" is a vague word, but **(E)** makes the sentence clear: it was chocolate that was considered a luxury product until Hershey began to mass produce it. **(F)** and **(H)** refer to the wrong product—milk instead of chocolate—and **(G)** omits the important word "luxury."

5. B

Category: Usage

Getting to the Answer: The sentence is in the past tense (note the words "opened" and "grew," not to mention 1905), so the verb "become" also has to be in the past tense. This makes **(B)** correct. **(A)** changes the meaning of the sentence, and **(C)** is an unnecessary change; center and focal point mean essentially the same thing. **(D)** creates a new error; "who" is used to refer to people, not places.

6. H

Category: Topic Development

Getting to the Answer: The entire passage is about Milton Hershey, including the fact that the town he built is named after him. It's true that this is just one example of towns or other locations named after their founders, but that is irrelevant in a passage about a specific person. **(H)** is correct; all other sentences make sense in the passage.

7. D

Category: Knowledge of Language

Getting to the Answer: The previous sentence introduces the Hersheys' philanthropy, and **(D)** provides a logical transition from the introduction of philanthropy to the example provided in sentence 16. None of the other answers provides a supporting example of sentence 15.

Three-toed Sloth

8. G

Category: Punctuation

Getting to the Answer: The problem with this sentence is the possessive of the word "animal." In context, the word should be plural, not possessive, making **(G)** the correct answer. **(E)** changes the meaning; it is not that it's hard to see three-toed sloths but that they are so rare that they're seldom seen. **(F)** also changes the meaning; "more" and "most" don't mean the same thing. **(H)** incorrectly states that sloths are within the earth, not on it.

9. A

Category: Organization, Unity, and Cohesion

Getting to the Answer: Both sentences describe sloth characteristics and can logically be combined. The best way to do this is to create a list using two commas and a conjunction. This is exactly what **(A)** does. **(B)** joins the two with a contrast word, but nothing is in contrast here. **(C)** changes the present tense verbs into present participles, and **(D)** incorrectly joins two independent clauses with a comma.

10. F

Category: Knowledge of Language

Getting to the Answer: "Them" is a vague word which could refer to either of the sloths or even to the tortoise. The writer means to contrast the two kinds of sloths, not sloths and tortoises. **(F)** makes this very clear. **(E)** changes "unlike" to "like" and retains the word "them." **(G)** makes an incorrect comparison, and **(H)** doesn't make sense since all sloths are slow moving.

11. C

Category: Topic Development

Getting to the Answer: Because the entire paragraph—indeed, the entire passage—is about the three-toed sloth, any reference to another animal is irrelevant. Sentence 9, **(C)**, is about the tortoise, so it should be deleted. All other sentences are relevant to the topic.

12. H

Category: Usage

Getting to the Answer: Be careful not to confuse "they're" (the contraction of "there is"), "there" (a place), and "their" (the possessive). Because the long arms belong to the sloths, "there" has to be in the possessive, making **(H)** the necessary revision and eliminating **(G)**. **(E)** turns the subjective into the objective case, and **(F)** changes the meaning of the sentence.

13. A

Category: Organization, Unity, and Cohesion

Getting to the Answer: Sentence 16 is in contrast to sentence 15, so a contrast word or phrase is needed, which matches **(A)**. **(B)** and **(D)** are continuation words. Though **(C)** is a contrast phrase, it is redundant (you already know they are clumsy on the ground) and wordy.

14. E

Category: Organization, Unity, and Cohesion

Getting to the Answer: Sentence 18 tells more about sentence 17, so they can be combined by making sentence 18 a dependent clause and joining it to sentence 17 with a comma, as **(E)** does. **(F)** unnecessarily repeats the word "day." **(G)** is very wordy, and **(H)** incorrectly joins two independent clauses with a comma.

15. C

Category: Topic Development

Getting to the Answer: Consider the paragraph's main idea, and check to see if all four sentences connect to the same topic. Sentences 1, 2, and 4 provide information about studying music, so **(A)**, **(B)**, and **(D)** develop the topic. The sentence that needs revision is **(C)**.

16. H

Category: Sentence Structure and Formation

Getting to the Answer: Be sure that any modifying words and phrases are properly placed for the words they are intended to modify. As written in sentence 4, it is "the Eiffel Tower" that is "taking a . . . tour of Paris." The revision could contain "tourists first stop at the Eiffel Tower." This places the correct noun, "tourists," after the modifying phrase. The correct choice is **(H)**; **(E)**, **(F)**, and **(G)** are clear sentences.

17. C

Category: Sentence Structure and Formation

Getting to the Answer: When a sentence presents a series of verbs, check to see that they follow the rules of parallel structure. In sentence 3, "inhabiting" should be "inhabit," keeping it consistent with the verbs "speak" and "tend." **(A)**, **(B)**, and **(D)** have correct structure, so **(C)** is correct.

18. H

Category: Knowledge of Language

Getting to the Answer: Using two words with the same meaning in one sentence is redundant. "Dedicated" and "devoted" mean the same thing, so the sentence should be revised to fix the issue. The revision in **(H)** corrects the sentence. The sentences in **(E)**, **(F)**, and **(G)** do not correct the issue and would remove words that provide necessary details.

19. C

Category: Sentence Structure and Formation

Getting to the Answer: When a sentence presents a series of verbs, check to see that they follow the rules of parallel structure. In the sentence, the word "dry" would be consistent with the rest of the verbs. The revision in **(C)** is correct. **(A)** makes the verb tense inconsistent. **(B)** uses the incorrect tense. **(D)** does not correct the sentence.

20. F

Category: Sentence Structure and Formation

Getting to the Answer: A complete sentence should have a subject and a predicate verb and should express a complete thought. As written, the sentence is a fragment, so **(F)** correctly includes a predicate verb to form a complete sentence. **(E)** places the verb in the incorrect location because "one of the most honored musicians in Grammy Award history" is nonessential information. **(G)** creates an error by deleting a necessary verb phrase. **(H)** incorrectly removes the word "into" and is still a fragment.

STRATEGIC REVIEW: MATH

The Kaplan Method for SHSAT Math

Step 1 What is the question?

Step 2 What information is provided in the question? In what format do the answers appear?

Step 3 What can I do with the information?

- Picking Numbers
- Backsolving
- Straightforward Math

Step 4 Am I finished?

Arithmetic

Greatest Common Factor

1. A plank of wood measuring 14 inches by 63 inches is to be cut into equal squares. What are the largest squares that can be cut if the squares are all equal, and no waste remains?

A. 3 inches × 3 inches
B. 5 inches × 5 inches
C. 7 inches × 7 inches
D. 9 inches × 9 inches

Average/Mean

2. The average amount of money held by each child in a group of 5 is $0.50. If one of the children loses a quarter, what is the new average amount of money held by each child?

E. $0
F. $0.25
G. $0.45
H. $0.56

Probability

3. There are 2,000 horses on a ranch in random pens. In one pen there are 25 brown horses, 20 black horses, and 15 white horses. If there are only black, brown, and white horses, what is the best estimate of the number of white horses on the ranch?

A. 50
B. 75
C. 500
D. 600

Algebra

Distance, Speed, and Time

4. A man is walking 4 miles per hour toward point *B* from point *A*. At the same time, a woman is running 8 miles per hour toward point *A* from point *B*. If point *A* and point *B* are 15 miles apart, how far from point *B* will they meet?

E. 5 miles

F. 6 miles

G. 9 miles

H. 10 miles

Inequalities

5. *x* is an integer less than –5. What is the range of possible values of $\frac{1}{x^3}$?

A. $\frac{1}{x^3} > -\frac{1}{5}$

B. $\frac{1}{x^3} < -\frac{1}{5}$

C. $0 > \frac{1}{x^3} > -\frac{1}{125}$

D. $\frac{1}{x^3} < \frac{1}{125}$

6. This week, Jenna earned twice as much as Keegan earned. Riley earned $250 more than twice what Keegan earned. If Riley earned $500, how much did Jenna earn?

E. $200

F. $250

G. $400

H. $500

Symbolism

7. If $\hat{x} = \frac{1}{x^2}$, what is the value of $2 \cdot \hat{2}$?

A. $\frac{1}{16}$

B. $\frac{1}{4}$

C. $\frac{1}{2}$

D. 1

Remainder

8. When $x + 3$ is divided by 8, the remainder is 2. What will the remainder be if $x + 5$ is divided by 4?

E. 0

F. 2

G. 3

H. 5

Geometry

Angles

9.

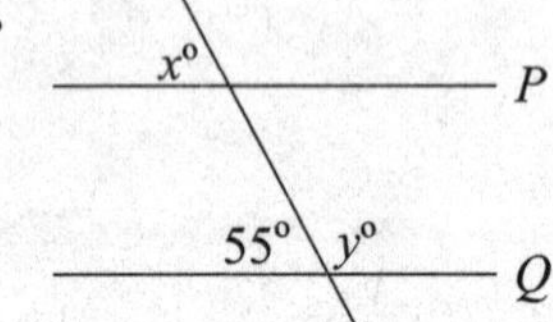

If line P is parallel to line Q, what is the value of $x + y$?

A. 110°

B. 125°

C. 180°

D. 250°

Circles

10.

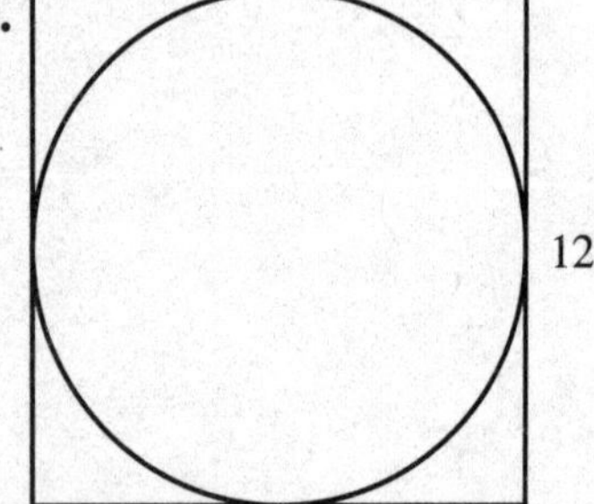

What is the circumference of the circle inscribed in the square above?

E. 2π

F. 6π

G. 9π

H. 12π

Triangles

11.

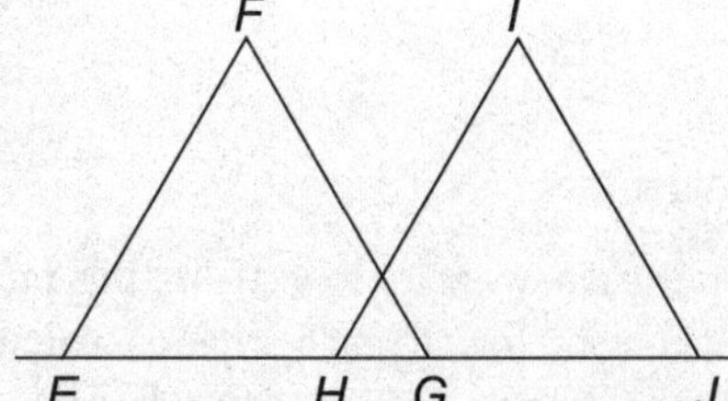

In the figure above, the two triangles have the same base. In addition, angles *FGJ* and *IHE* are equal. What can you conclude about angles *HGF* and *GHI*?

A. They are equal.
B. They add up to 90°.
C. *HGF* is larger than *GHI*.
D. *GHI* is larger than *HGF*.

Coordinate Plane

12. One diagonal of a square lies on the *x*-axis of a coordinate system. The coordinates of one corner of the square are (–2, 2). What are the coordinates of the opposite corner?

E. (–2, –2)
F. (2, –2)
G. (2, 2)
H. (–2, 4)

ANSWERS AND EXPLANATIONS

1. C

Subject: Arithmetic

Getting to the Answer: Backsolve to find the largest possible factor of the sides.

Start with **(D)**.

$\frac{14}{9} = 1$ remainder 5; $\frac{63}{9} = 7$

This will leave waste. Eliminate it.

Move to **(C)**.

$\frac{14}{7} = 2$; $\frac{63}{7} = 9$

This will not leave waste. **(C)** is your answer.

2. G

Subject: Arithmetic

Getting to the Answer: Even though one child loses a quarter, the number of children you are taking the average of stays the same.

To find the average, you need to find the total sum of the money after one quarter is lost.

(5)(0.50) is the original total sum

New total sum = (5)(0.50) − (0.25) = (2.50) − (0.25) = 2.25

$$\text{New average} = \frac{2.25}{5} = 0.45$$

3. C

Subject: Arithmetic

Getting to the Answer: You are given that the horses are penned randomly, and therefore, each pen would represent a random sample. Of the 60 total horses in the pen, 15 horses, or 25 percent, are white. Therefore, 25% of 2,000, or 500, is the best estimate of the number of white horses; the answer is **(C)**.

4. H

Subject: Algebra

Getting to the Answer: Try to visualize this problem as two people moving toward each other on a number line. Each hour, these two people move 12 miles closer to each other, so if you divide the total distance of 15 miles by 12, you get the time it takes for them to meet.

$$\frac{15}{12} = 1\frac{1}{4} \text{ hours}$$

This is how long it takes the two people to cover the 15 miles when they meet.

To determine the distance from point B, see how far the person beginning at point B travels. This is your answer, **(H)**.

$$8\left(1\frac{1}{4}\right) = 10$$

5. C

Subject: Algebra

Getting to the Answer: Make sure you pay close attention to the parameters for x. In order to find the range for $\frac{1}{x^3}$, you must do the same thing as the parameter guideline.

$$\frac{1}{(-5)^3} = \frac{1}{-125}$$

$$\frac{1}{-6^3} = \frac{1}{-216}$$

As x gets smaller, the fraction gets bigger $\left(\text{as } \frac{1}{-125} \text{ is less than } \frac{1}{-216}\right)$. Taking the reciprocal flips the sign of the inequality. The values will continue to increase, approaching zero, but will never actually get to zero. Therefore,

$$0 > \frac{1}{x^3} > -\frac{1}{125}$$

6. F

Subject: Algebra

Getting to the Answer: Make sure that you read the question carefully and understand what is being asked. Take it step by step.

Jenna = 2 (Keegan)
Riley = 2 (Keegan) + $250
$500 = 2 (Keegan) + $250
$250 = 2 (Keegan)
$125 = Keegan

Jenna = 2 ($125)
Jenna = $250. **(F)**

7. C

Subject: Algebra

Getting to the Answer: Substitute the values given for your symbol immediately to avoid confusion. The question tells you that $\hat{x} = \frac{1}{x^2}$, so plug the numbers into the equation.

$$2 \cdot \hat{2}$$

$$2 \cdot \frac{1}{2^2}$$

$$2 \cdot \frac{1}{4} = \frac{1}{2}$$

8. E

Subject: Algebra

Getting to the Answer:

$2 + 8 = 10 = x + 3$

$x = 7$ You can get a value for x by adding the remainder to the divisor and setting it equal to the original expression.

$7 + 5 = 12$

$\frac{12}{4} = 3$ remainder 0

9. C

Subject: Geometry

Getting to the Answer: Angle x is equal to 55°, because along the parallel line it is a corresponding angle to the angle labeled as 55°. Angle y and 55° add up to 180° because they form a straight line, and therefore angles $x + y = 180°$.

10. H

Subject: Geometry

Getting to the Answer: To solve this problem, you must know the formula for the circumference of a circle (π times diameter). You must also recognize that a circle inscribed in a square with a side of length 12 has a diameter of 12. Therefore, the circle has a circumference of 12π, **(H)**.

11. A

Subject: Geometry

Getting to the Answer: Patiently go through the question and indicate what you know and also what you can infer. If angles *FGJ* and *IHE* are equal, then the supplements must be equal. The supplements of *FGJ* and *IHE* are angles *HGF* and *GHI*, respectively. They must be equal. The answer is **(A)**.

12. E

Subject: Geometry

Getting to the Answer:

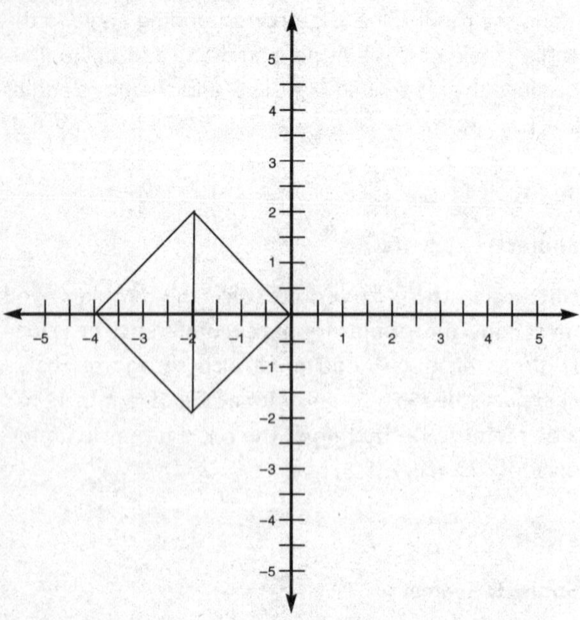

Because the diagonal is on the *x*-axis, the opposite of the given point must be the same distance from the *x*-axis in the opposite direction. The answer is **(E)**.

STRATEGIC REVIEW: MATH GRID-IN QUESTIONS

The Kaplan Strategy for Math Grid-In Questions

The Kaplan Strategy for Math Grid-In Questions is a strategy you apply as you answer questions using the Kaplan Method for Math.

Once you've determined what the question is asking in **Step 1** and identified the information provided in **Step 2**, you're ready to apply the Kaplan Strategy for Math Grid-In Questions in **Step 3**.

- Define any variables, choosing letters that make sense.
- Break sentences into short phrases.
- Translate each phrase into a mathematical expression.
- Use the information in the question stem to logically organize the expressions and solve.

1. $(12 + 4 \times 3) + 10 \div 2 = ?$

2. If $2x - 5 > -3$ and $x + 5 < 7$, what is one possible value of x?

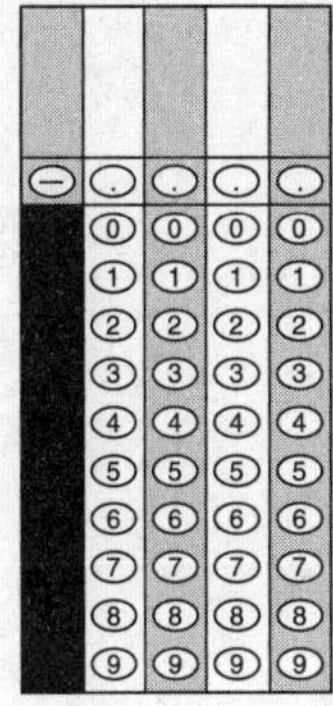

3. In the equation $3a + 13 = 9a + 4$, what is the value of a?

4. What value of x makes the equation $5(3x - 20) + 10 = 12x + 9$ true?

5. $2\frac{2}{3} - 1\frac{5}{6} = ?$

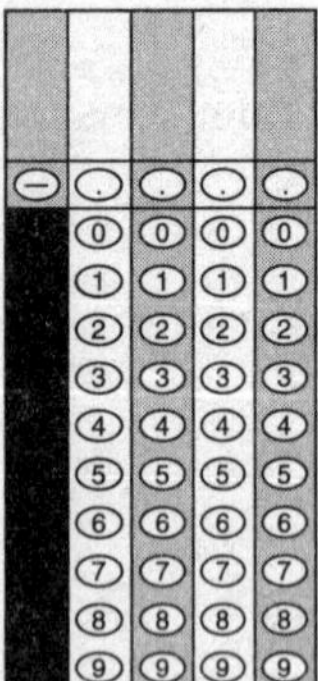

6. If the expression $1\frac{2}{5} + 3\frac{3}{4} = x$ is true, what is the value of x?

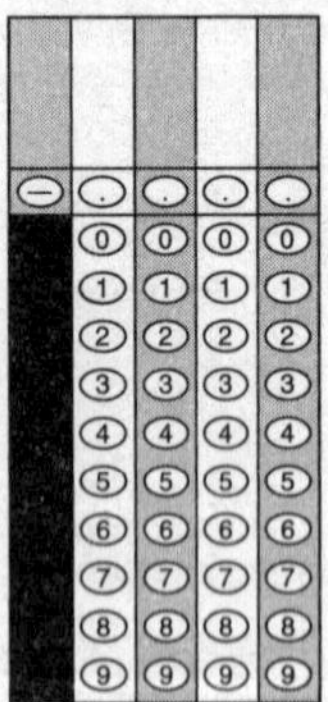

7. If $\frac{2x+1}{4} = \frac{12}{20}$, what is the value of x?

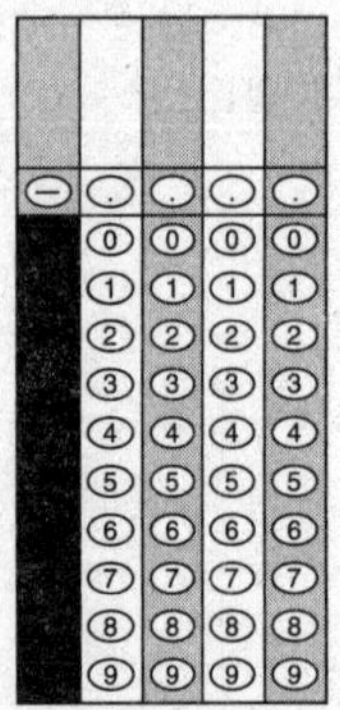

8. What is the value of y in the equation $7.5 + 1.4y = 19.4$?

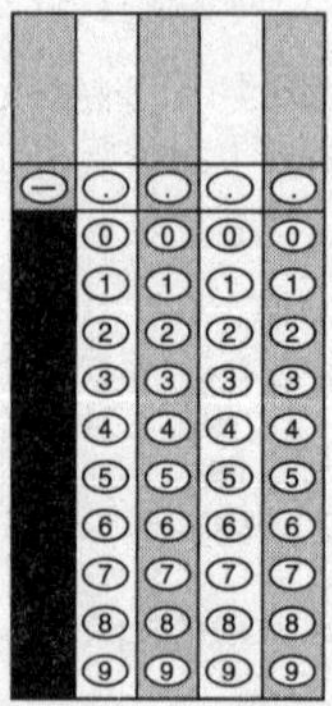

9. If $\frac{2a}{4} = \frac{6a+4}{16}$, what is the value of a?

10. If $c + 5 < 16$ and $2c + 3 > 9$, and c is an integer, then how many possible values can c take?

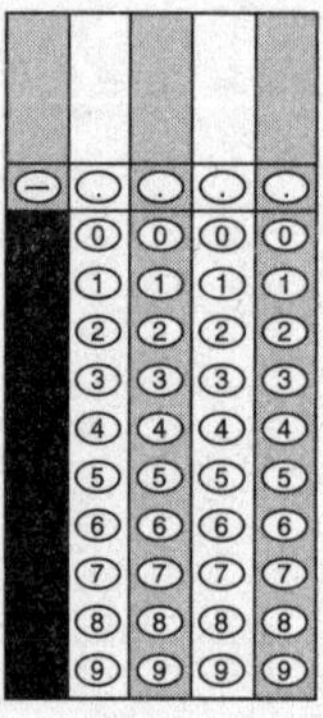

11. In the equation $\frac{c}{2}+13=-20$, what is the value of c?

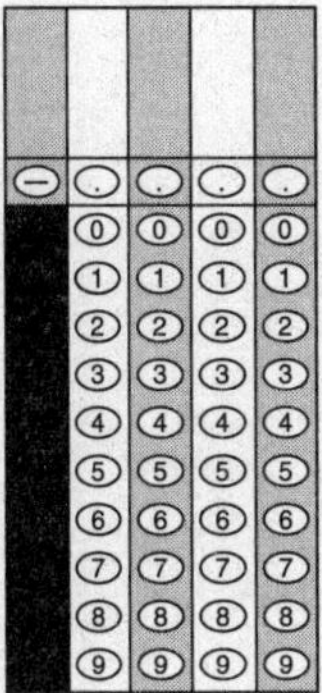

12. What is the value of m in the equation $0.4m + 4.8 = 33.8$?

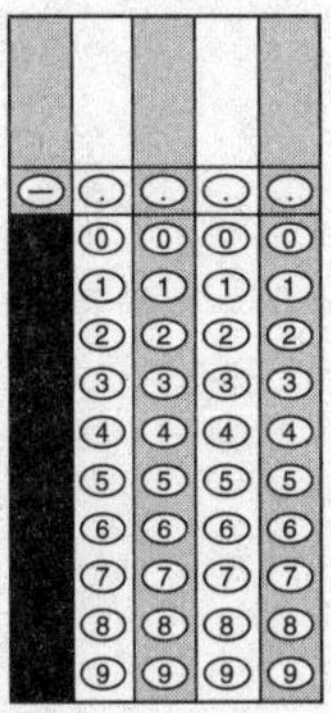

13. In the equation $\sqrt[3]{x}=5$, what is the value of x?

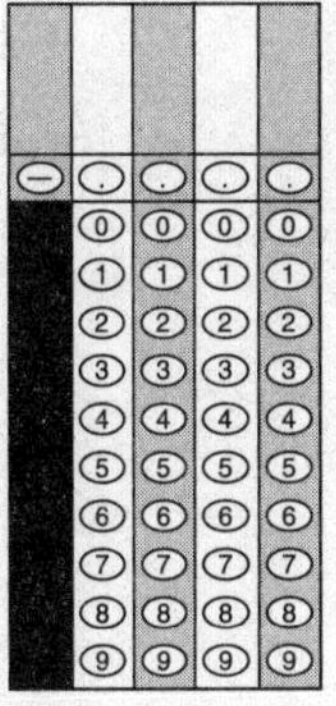

14. If x^2+5x+6, what is the value of this expression when $x = 3$?

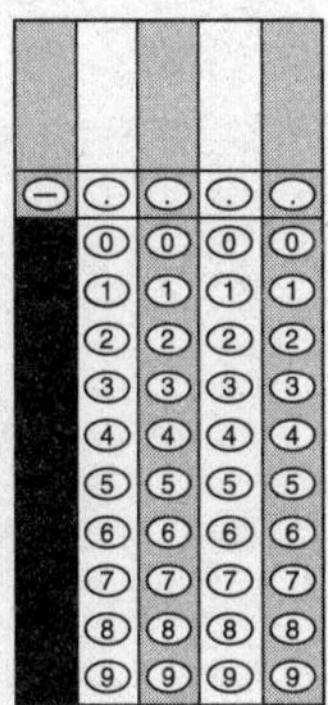

15. What is the value of the expression $2z^2-5z-4$ when $z=-4$?

16. What value of x satisfies the equation $x^3 = -64$?

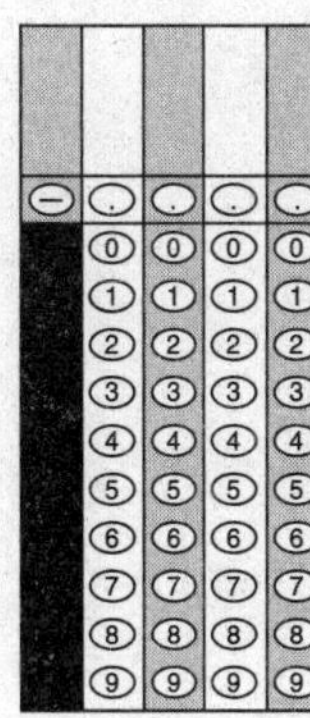

17. If $\frac{b}{12} = \frac{48}{b}$ and $b > 0$, what is the value of b?

18. In the equation $2n^2 = 242$, what is the value of n if n is positive?

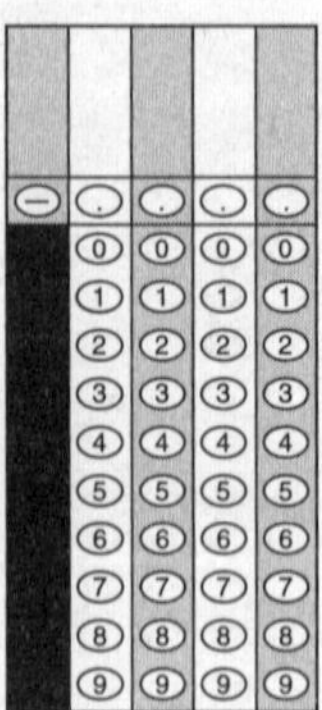

19. If $-4x + 16 = 4$, what is the value of x?

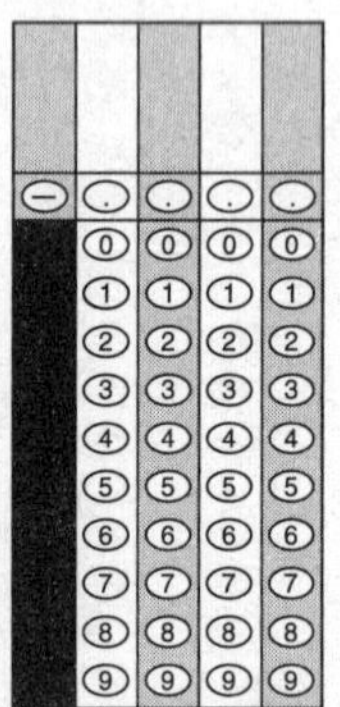

20. What is the value of t in the equation $t^2 - 12 = 24$ if $t > 0$?

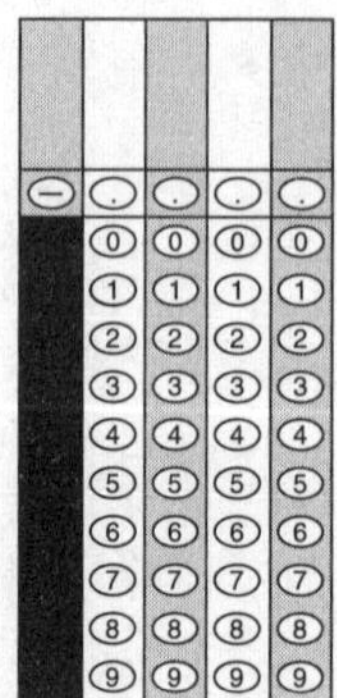

21. If $8x < 6$ and $x > 0$, then what is one possible value of x?

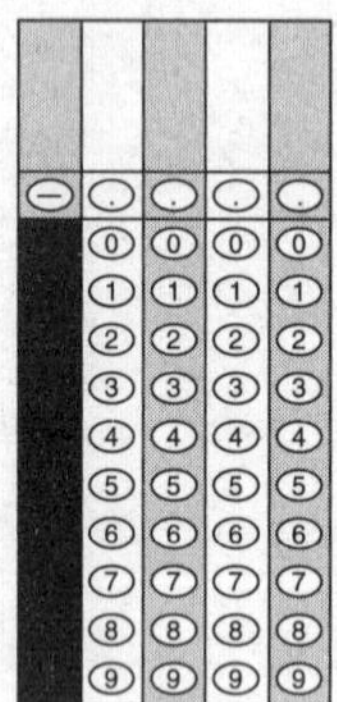

22. What value of b makes the equation $7b + 12 = 96$ true?

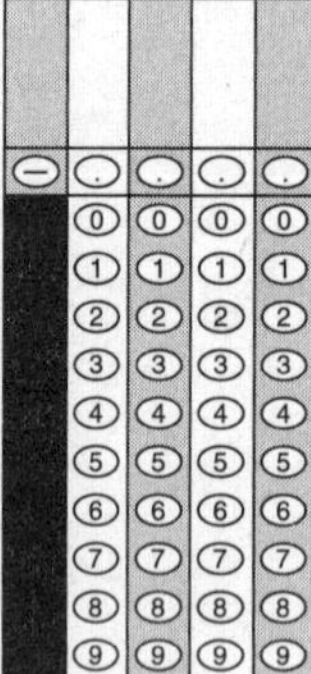

23. If $\frac{8}{11} = \frac{56}{g}$, what is the value of g?

24. If $\sqrt{h} = 21$, what is the value of h?

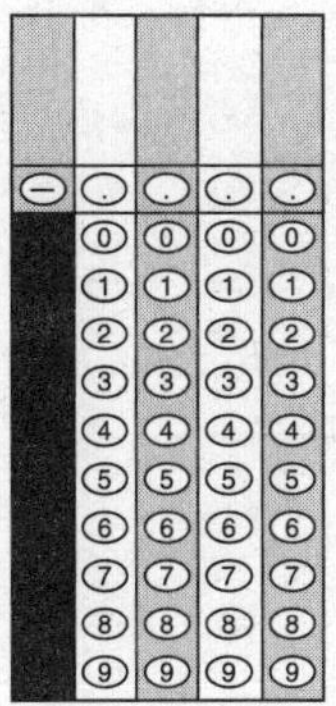

25. What is the value of z in the equation $\frac{4}{9} = \frac{z+8}{27}$?

26. If $3c + 10 = -2(c - 13)$, what is the value of c?

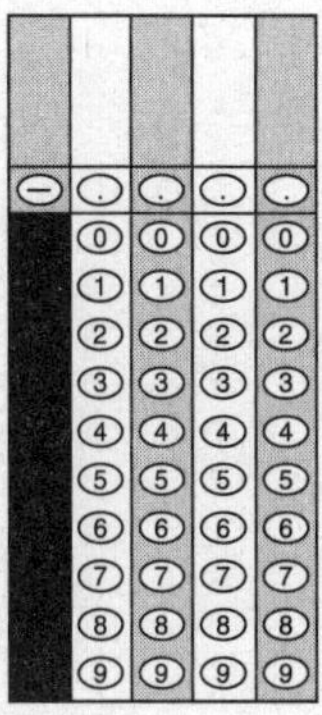

27. If $\sqrt{g} + 4 = 13$, what is the value of g?

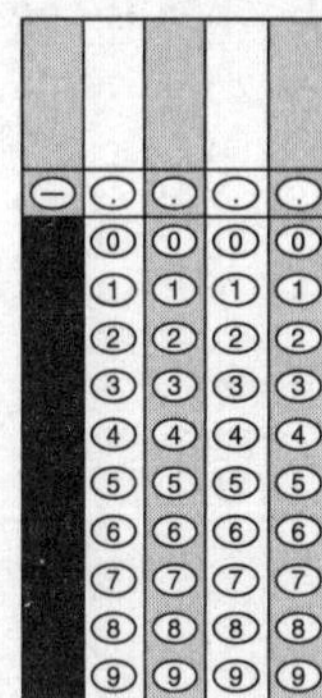

28. In the equation $\frac{h}{12} - 10 = -6$, what is the value of h?

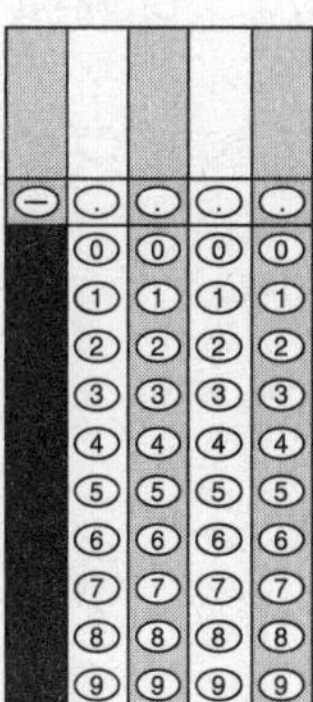

29. What value of b makes the equation $\frac{b}{12} - 23 = 36$ true?

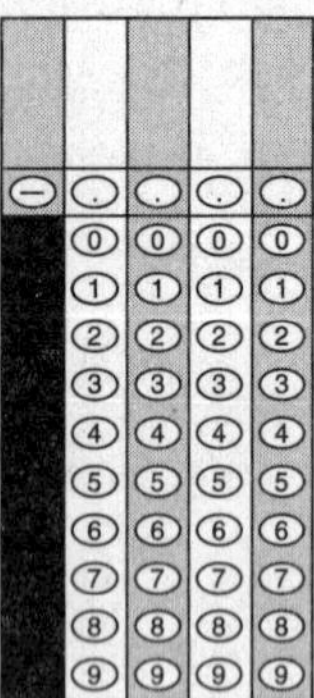

30. If $m^2 = 2.25$ and $m > 0$, what is the value of m?

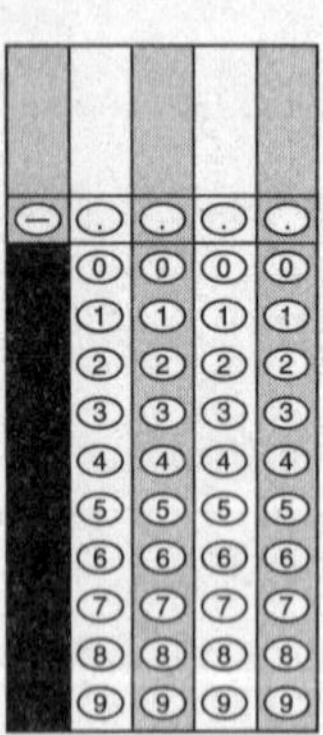

31. If $3t + 10 > 5t + 8$ and $t > 0$, what is one possible value of t?

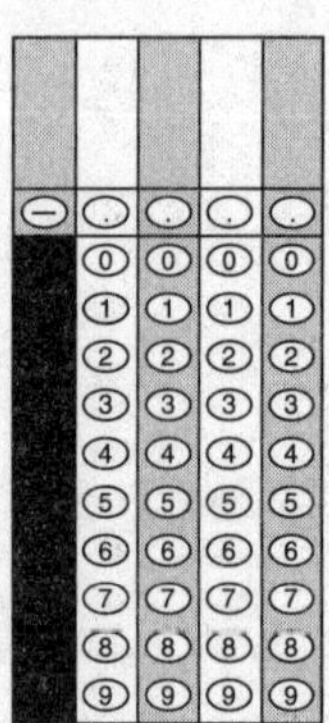

32. What is the value of the expression $2(a - 5)^2 + 3a \div 4$ if $a = 8$?

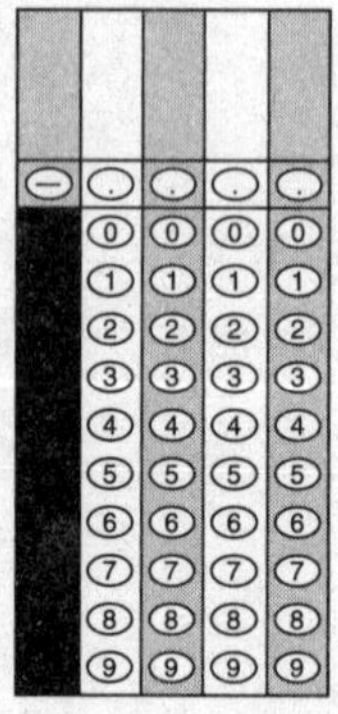

33. $144^{\frac{1}{2}} = ?$

34. $36 \div 4 + 9 \times 2 + 3 = ?$

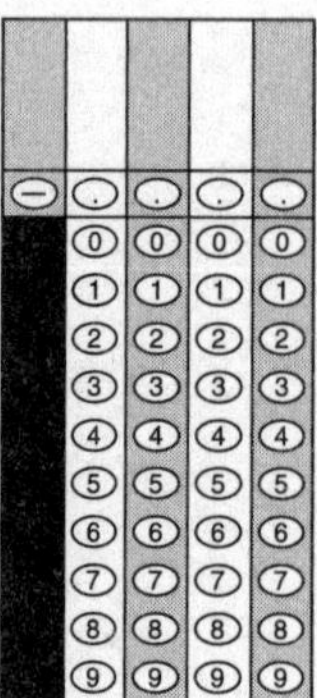

35. $\left(\frac{1}{4}\right)^{-3} = ?$

36. $\frac{2}{3} \times 1\frac{1}{6} = ?$

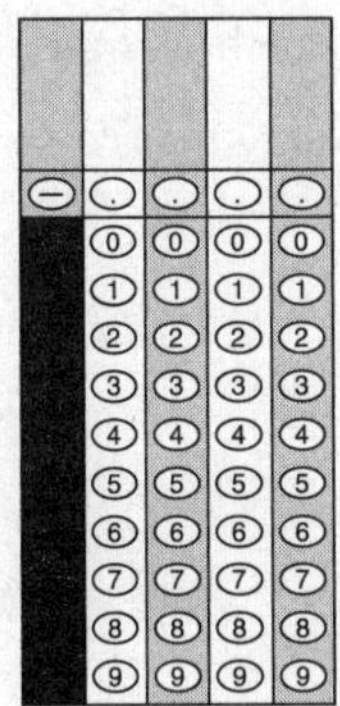

37. In a chocolate chip cookie recipe, 2 cups of chocolate chips are used to make 35 cookies. How many cookies can be made using 24 cups of chocolate chips?

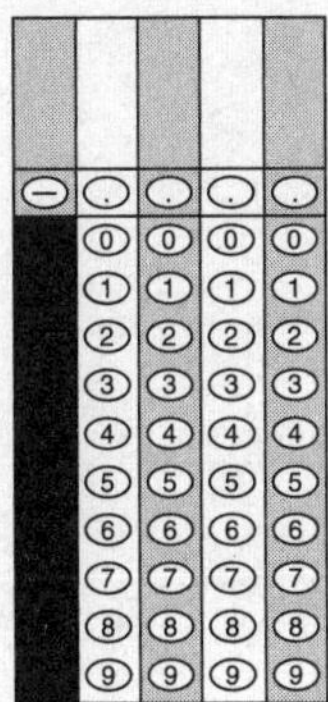

38. Crystal is filling cartons of eggs. Each carton contains one dozen (12) eggs. If she starts with 500 eggs, how many complete cartons of eggs can she fill?

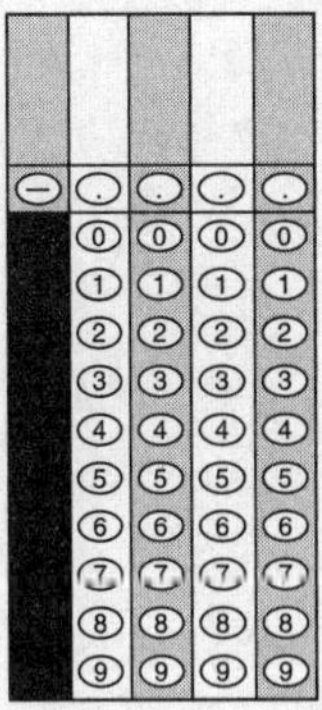

39. Peter is 42 years old. In 8 years, Peter will be twice as old as Chris. How old is Chris now?

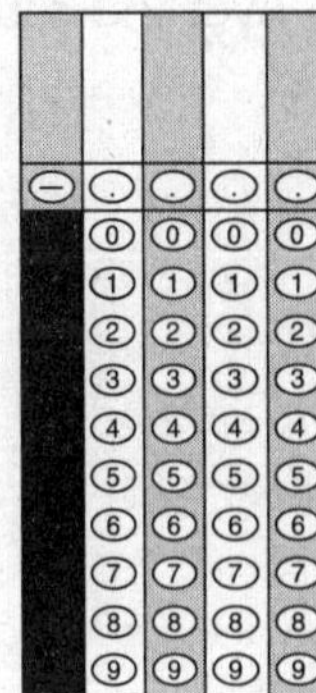

40. If a skirt that is marked down at a 20% discount costs $20, how much does the skirt cost at full price?

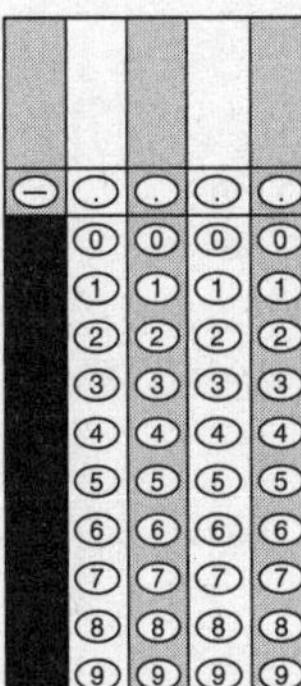

41. If Michael is m years old, Chris is 8 years less than twice Michael's age, and the sum of Michael's and Chris's ages is 46, how old is Michael?

42. If Maria ran 2.3 miles on Monday, 3.9 miles on Tuesday, and 5 miles on Wednesday, how many miles did she run over the course of three days?

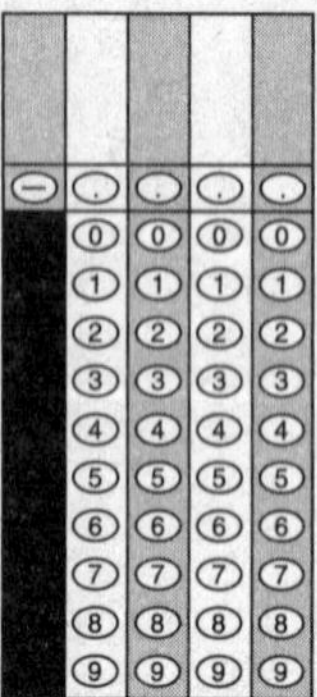

43. In a certain school, the ratio of males to females is 3:4. If there are 48 males in the school, how many students are in the school?

44. If Alfred ate $\frac{2}{3}$ of a pizza, Brad ate $\frac{3}{5}$ of a pizza, and Charlie ate $\frac{5}{6}$ of a pizza, how many pizzas did the three of them eat total?

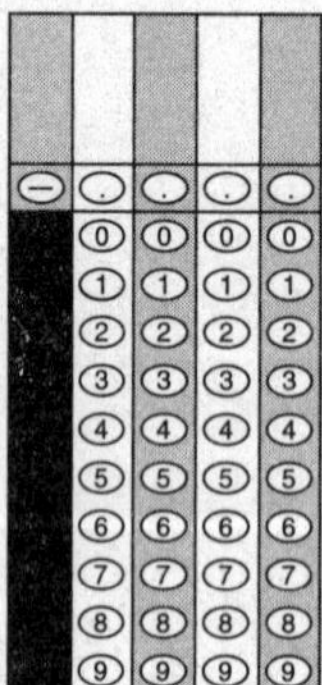

45. Mark paints houses as part of his job. In a given week, he has 28 houses to paint. If he paints $\frac{1}{4}$ of these houses on Monday and $\frac{1}{7}$ of the remaining houses on Tuesday, how many houses does Mark still have to paint after Tuesday?

46. A magazine pays authors by the word for essays that are submitted. Authors are paid \$0.10 per word for the first 250 words, and \$0.05 per word for every word after 250 words. Sam submitted three essays: a 300-word essay, a 400-word essay, and a 500-word essay. How much did the magazine pay Sam for his three essays?

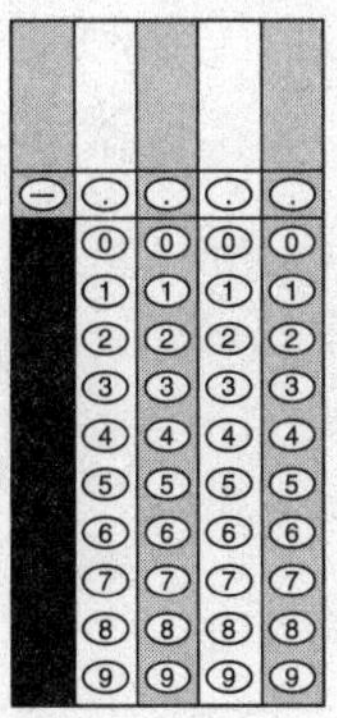

47. What value of z makes the equation $2z + 3(z + 8) = \frac{1}{2}(12z + 22)$ true?

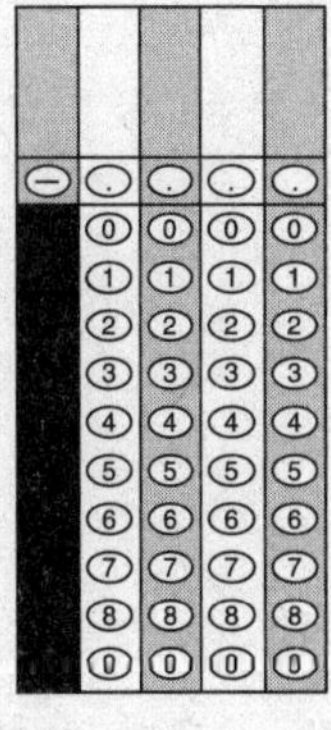

48. $\frac{7}{8} \times \frac{2}{5} = ?$

49. What number is halfway between -5 and 23?

50. If $f + 2 > 5$ and $f + 4 < 9$, and f is an integer, how many possible values can f take?

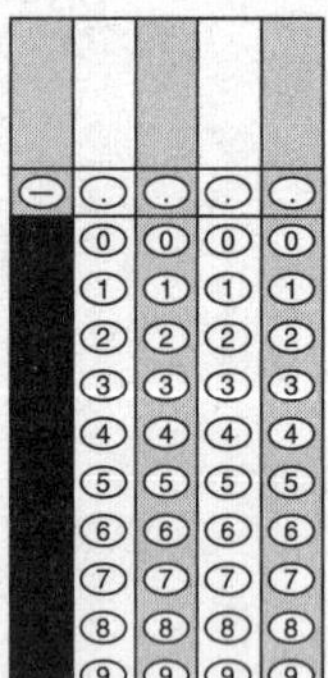

51. In the equation $20c + 36 = 24c - 8$, what is the value of c?

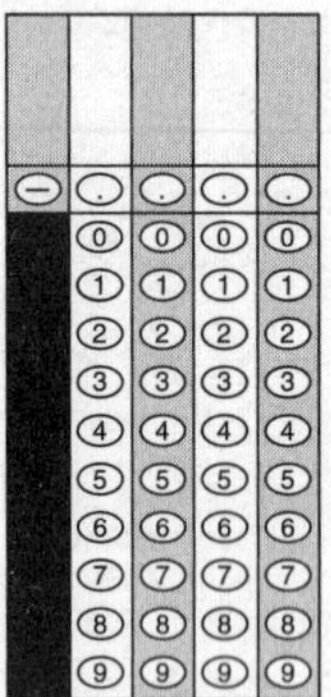

52. If $a > 0$, what is the value of a in the expression $\frac{a}{6} = \frac{24}{a}$?

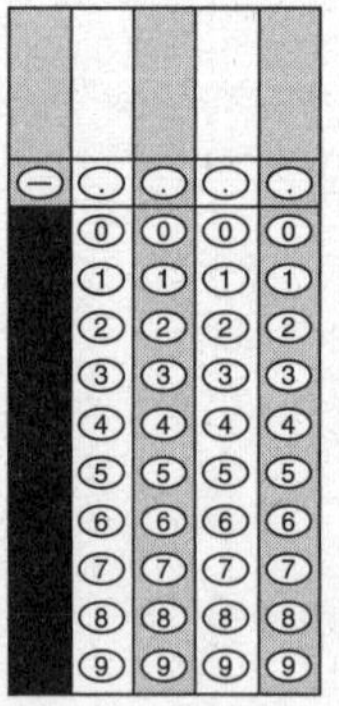

53. $\frac{3}{5} - \frac{1}{4} = ?$

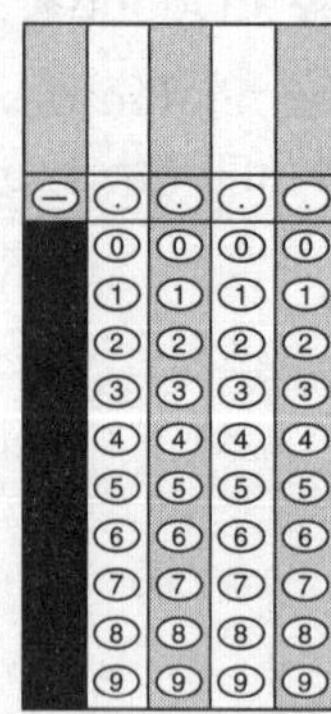

54. $\frac{2}{3} \div \frac{1}{2} = ?$

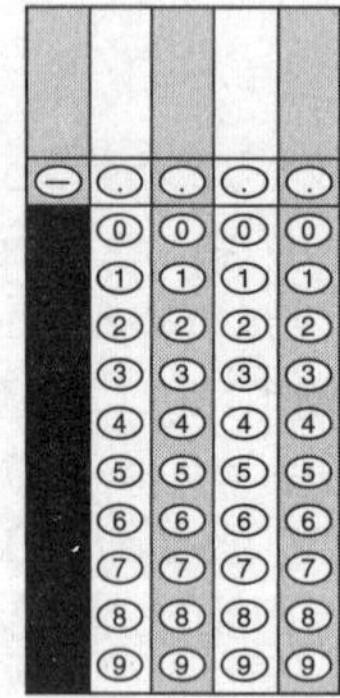

55. $\frac{5}{6} - \frac{1}{2} \times \frac{1}{3} = ?$

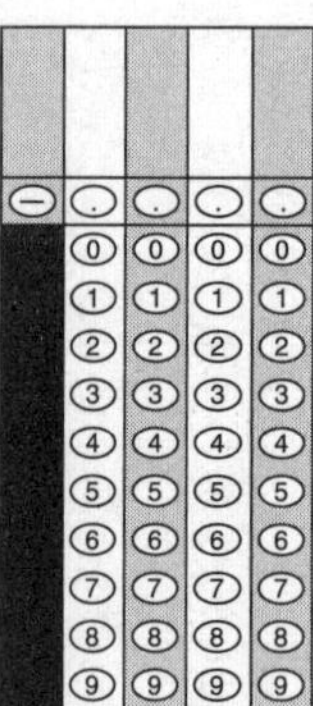

56. If $m + 8 < 22$ and $n - 4 < 13$, and m and n are both integers, what is the largest possible value of $m + n$?

57. What value of x makes $3(2x + 5) = -2(x - 8)$ true?

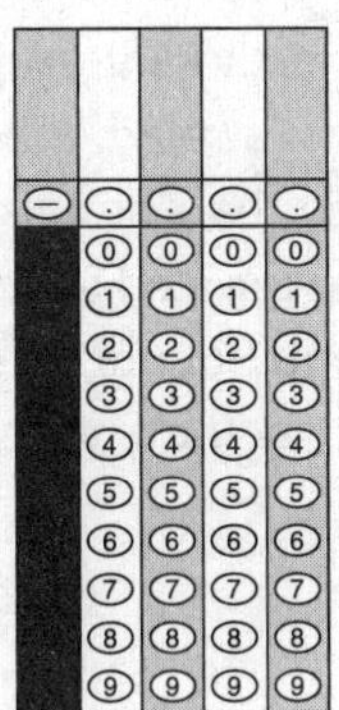

58. Bob is an art instructor and is buying tubes of paint and paintbrushes for his class. If a tube of paint costs \$5 and a paintbrush costs \$1.50, how much does Bob spend if his class has 8 students and each student needs 5 tubes of paint and a paintbrush?

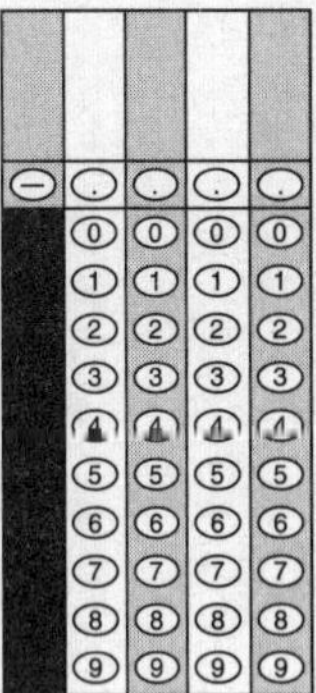

59. Maria recently took a nonstop flight from Miami to Quito, Ecuador. If the airplane flew at a constant speed of 436 miles per hour and the flight took 4.5 hours, what is the distance from Miami to Quito?

60. William is enrolled in a book-of-the-month club. This club sends members leather-bound editions of classic books the same day each month. As a reward for loyalty, William receives a free book at the end of each year. If William pays $468 per year for the club, what is the average price he pays for each book?

61. Tammy has a drawer full of socks that contains only blue socks and yellow socks. If 4 of every 7 socks are blue, and there are 28 blue socks, how many yellow socks are in Tammy's drawer?

62. Danielle and Emma participated in a book reading contest over the summer. Danielle read 13 books, and Emma read 15 less than 3 times the number of books that Danielle read. How many books did Danielle and Emma read over the summer?

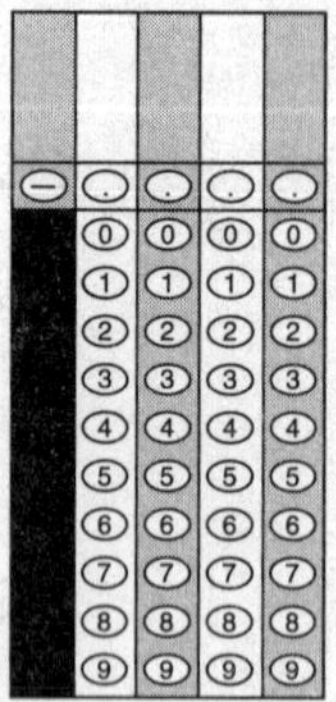

63. Patricia ate lunch at a restaurant yesterday. She ordered three items: a salad, a bowl of soup, and a glass of iced tea. The salad cost $3, the soup cost $4, and the iced tea cost $1. If there is a 6% tax on food but not on drinks, how much did Patricia pay for lunch?

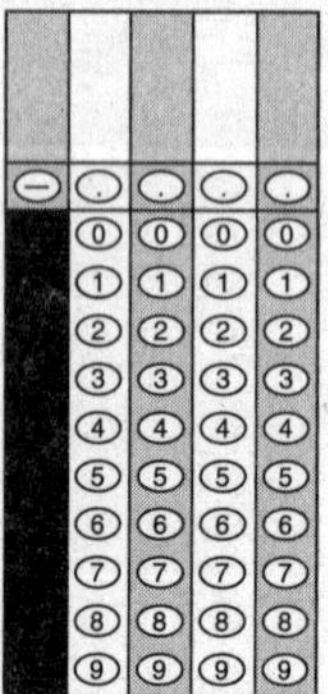

64. Wally's World of Wheels sells both cars and trucks. The ratio of cars to trucks is always 7:3 at any given time. If there are 56 cars on the lot at Wally's, how many total vehicles are at Wally's (assuming cars and trucks are the only two types of vehicles he sells)?

65. A certain cake recipe calls for $1\frac{2}{3}$ cups of water, $\frac{1}{2}$ cup of oil, and $\frac{5}{6}$ cup of milk. If these are the only three liquids used in the recipe, then how much total liquid is used to make this cake?

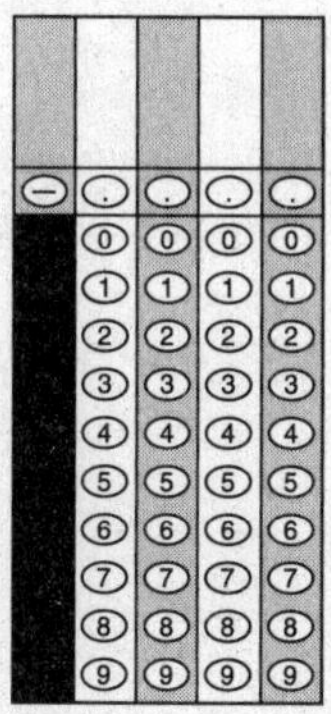

66. Christine and Diane are both avid coffee drinkers and have many different coffee mugs. Diane has 4 more than half the number of mugs that Christine has, and together they have 19 coffee mugs. How many coffee mugs does Christine have?

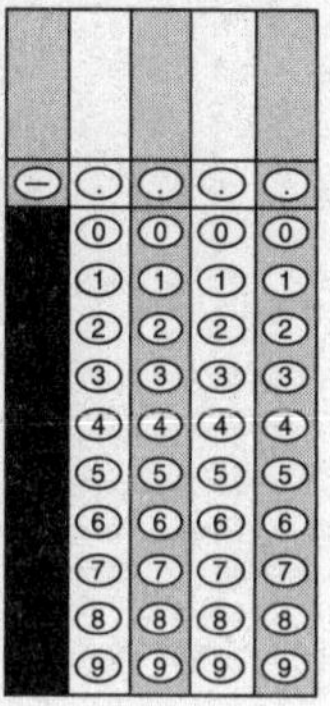

67. A baseball team uses 5 bats, 9 gloves, and 15 baseballs over the course of a typical game. How many pieces of equipment would be needed for 4 teams to play games (assuming none of the teams are playing each other and sharing equipment)?

68. Barney's bookstore has 125 books for sale. Adam's bookstore has 50 less than three times this number of books for sale. How many books does Adam's store have for sale?

69. Plow trucks are used to clear snow off of highways after snowstorms, as well as to spread anti-skid material on the road to help snow melt and give drivers more traction. A certain anti-skid material is 3 parts gravel to 2 parts salt. If 300 tons of salt were used in this material last year, how much total anti-skid material was used?

70. Sally's supermarket sells cases of water. A case of 35 bottles costs $3.99. To the nearest cent, what is the price per bottle of water from a case of water at Sally's? (Express your answer in cents, not dollars.)

ANSWERS AND EXPLANATIONS

1. 29

Subject: Arithmetic

Getting to the Answer: As long as you remember the order of operations, the calculations should be fairly straightforward:

$$(12 + 4 \times 3) + 10 \div 2$$
$$(12 + 12) + 5$$
$$24 + 5 = 29$$

Grid in 29.

2. Any value between 1 and 2

Subject: Algebra

Getting to the Answer: Start by simplifying each of the two inequalities. The first inequality simplifies to $x > 1$ and the second inequality simplifies to $x < 2$. Thus, x must be between 1 and 2 (not including 1 or 2), so grid in any value between 1 and 2, such as 1.5.

3. 1.5

Subject: Algebra

Getting to the Answer: Be sure you move all variable terms to one side and all numerical terms to the other side:

$$\begin{aligned} 3a + 13 &= 9a + 4 \\ 9 &= 6a \\ \frac{3}{2} &= a \end{aligned}$$

Grid in 1.5.

4. 33

Subject: Algebra

Getting to the Answer: Start by distributing the 5 on the left side of the equation. From there, combine like terms and isolate x:

$$\begin{aligned} 5(3x - 20) + 10 &= 12x + 9 \\ 15x - 100 + 10 &= 12x + 9 \\ 15x - 90 &= 12x + 9 \\ 3x &= 99 \\ x &= 33 \end{aligned}$$

Grid in 33.

5. .833

Subject: Arithmetic

Getting to the Answer: Convert both mixed numbers to improper fractions. Then, find a common denominator and subtract the two fractions:

$$2\frac{2}{3} - 1\frac{5}{6}$$
$$\frac{8}{3} - \frac{11}{6}$$
$$\frac{16}{6} - \frac{11}{6} = \frac{5}{6}$$

Grid in .833, which is the decimal equivalent of 5/6.

6. 5.15

Subject: Algebra

Getting to the Answer: At first glance, you may think that converting each mixed number to an improper fraction and finding common denominators is the way to go. However, this will result in large fractions that may be difficult to work with. Notice that each mixed number can easily be converted to a decimal. The original expression simplifies to 1.4 + 3.75, which is 5.15.

7. .7

Subject: Algebra

Getting to the Answer: As with any proportion, start by cross multiplying (keeping in mind that simplifying/reducing fractions first can make calculations easier), then perform the necessary algebra to isolate x:

$$\begin{aligned} \frac{2x + 1}{4} &= \frac{12}{20} \\ 40x + 20 &= 48 \\ 40x &= 28 \\ x &= \frac{28}{40} = \frac{7}{10} \end{aligned}$$

Grid in .7.

8. 8.5

Subject: Algebra

Getting to the Answer: Don't let the decimals affect your approach: solve this equation like you would any other equation:

$$\begin{aligned} 7.5 + 1.4y &= 19.4 \\ 1.4y &= 11.9 \\ y &= 8.5 \end{aligned}$$

After subtracting 7.5 from both sides and dividing by 1.4, you will end up with $y = 8.5$. Grid in 8.5 and move to the next question.

9. 2

Subject: Algebra

Getting to the Answer: When you see a proportion, start by cross multiplying (keeping in mind that simplifying/reducing fractions first can make calculations easier). From there, do the necessary algebra to isolate the variable; in this case, *a*:

$$\begin{aligned} \frac{2a}{4} &= \frac{6a+4}{16} \\ 24a + 16 &= 32a \\ 16 &= 8a \\ 2 &= a \end{aligned}$$

Grid in 2.

10. 7

Subject: Algebra

Getting to the Answer: Start by simplifying both inequalities. Doing this yields $c < 11$ and $c > 3$. Thus, *c* can be any number between 3 and 11. Since *c* must be an integer, *c* can be 4, 5, 6, 7, 8, 9, or 10. There are seven possible values, so grid in 7.

11. −66

Subject: Algebra

Getting to the Answer: This equation can be solved by subtracting 13 from both sides, then multiplying by 2:

$$\begin{aligned} \frac{c}{2} + 13 &= -20 \\ \frac{c}{2} &= -33 \\ c &= -66 \end{aligned}$$

Grid in −66. Don't forget to include the negative sign!

12. 72.5

Subject: Algebra

Getting to the Answer: Solve this equation like you would any other two-step equation: subtract 4.8 from both sides, then divide by .4:

$$\begin{aligned} .4m + 4.8 &= 33.8 \\ .4m &= 29 \\ m &= 72.5 \end{aligned}$$

Remember that when you divide by a fraction or decimal less than one, the result should be larger than what you started with. Grid in 72.5 and move to the next question.

13. 125

Subject: Algebra

Getting to the Answer: To solve for *x*, you must do the opposite of taking the third root of a number, which is cubing the number. Cube both sides to get $x = (5)(5)(5) = 125$. Grid in 125.

14. 30

Subject: Algebra

Getting to the Answer: Substitute 3 in for *x* in the given expression. Be sure to remember the order of operations when doing computations:

$$x^2 + 5x + 6$$
$$(3)^2 + 5(3) + 6$$
$$9 + 15 + 6 = 30$$

Grid in 30.

15. 48

Subject: Algebra

Getting to the Answer: Substitute −4 for *z* in the given expression and simplify, being sure to use the order of operations correctly:

$$2z^2 - 5z - 4$$
$$2(-4)^2 - 5(-4) - 4$$
$$2(16) + 20 - 4$$
$$32 + 20 - 4 = 48$$

Grid in 48.

16. −4

Subject: Algebra

Getting to the Answer: Remember that a number to the third power can be negative! You are looking for a number that, when multiplied by itself 3 times, gives you −64. $(-4)(-4)(-4) = -64$, so grid in −4.

17. 24

Subject: Algebra

Getting to the Answer: Begin by cross-multiplying the proportion. To solve for *b*, take the square root of both sides. Remember that the question states that *b* is positive, so don't grid in the negative solution.

$$\frac{b}{12} = \frac{48}{b}$$
$$b^2 = 576$$
$$b = \pm 24$$

Remember, *b* is positive, so grid in 24.

18. 11

Subject: Algebra

Getting to the Answer: The first step should be to divide both sides by 2. This should be followed by taking the square root of both sides to solve for *n*:

$$2n^2 = 242$$
$$n^2 = 121$$
$$n = \pm 11$$

Because *n* is positive, grid in 11.

19. 3

Subject: Algebra

Getting to the Answer: Solve this question as you would any other equation. Isolate the variable by subtracting 16 from both sides, then dividing by −4:

$$-4x + 16 = 4$$
$$-4x = -12$$
$$x = 3$$

Grid in 3.

20. 6

Getting to the Answer: Solve this equation by adding 12 to both sides and then taking the square root of both sides:

$$t^2 - 12 = 24$$
$$t^2 = 36$$
$$t = \pm 6$$

Since *t* is positive, grid in 6.

21. Any value between 0 and 0.75 ($0 < x < 0.75$)

Subject: Algebra

Getting to the Answer: Start by simplifying the inequality: dividing both sides by 8 will yield $x < 0.75$. You are also given that $x > 0$, so grid in any value greater than 0 and less than 0.75. 0.5 would be one example of an acceptable answer.

22. 12

Subject: Algebra

Getting to the Answer: Solve this equation like you would any other equation. Subtract 12 from both sides, then divide by 7:

$$7b + 12 = 96$$
$$7b = 84$$
$$b = 12$$

Grid in 12.

23. 77

Getting to the Answer: Begin by cross-multiplying this proportion, as you would any other proportion. From there, solve for *g*:

$$\frac{8}{11} = \frac{56}{g}$$
$$8g = 616$$
$$g = 77$$

Grid in 77.

24. 441

Getting to the answer: Simply square both sides of the equation to solve for *h*. $21 \times 21 = 441$, so grid in 441.

25. 4

Subject: Algebra

Getting to the Answer: Start by cross-multiplying the proportion. You will need to distribute the 9 over the $z + 8$ term. From there, solve like you would any other equation:

$$\begin{aligned} \frac{4}{9} &= \frac{z+8}{27} \\ 9(z+8) &= 108 \\ 9z + 72 &= 108 \\ 9z &= 36 \\ z &= 4 \end{aligned}$$

Grid in 4.

26. 3.2

Subject: Algebra

Getting to the Answer: Begin by distributing the -2 on the right side of the equation. Combine like terms and solve for c:

$$\begin{aligned} 3c + 10 &= -2(c - 13) \\ 3c + 10 &= -2c + 26 \\ 5c &= 16 \\ c &= 3.2 \end{aligned}$$

16 divided by 5 is 3.2, so grid in 3.2.

27. 81

Subject: Algebra

Getting to the Answer: To solve an equation with a radical, start by isolating the term with the radical. In this question, this means subtracting 4 from both sides. After that, undo the radical by squaring both sides:

$$\begin{aligned} \sqrt{g} + 4 &= 13 \\ \sqrt{g} &= 9 \\ g &= 81 \end{aligned}$$

Grid in 81.

28. 48

Subject: Algebra

Getting to the Answer: To solve this equation, begin by adding 10 to both sides. The final step is to multiply both sides by 12 to undo the fraction.

$$\begin{aligned} \frac{h}{12} - 10 &= -6 \\ \frac{h}{12} &= 4 \\ h &= 48 \end{aligned}$$

Grid in 48.

29. 708

Subject: Algebra

Getting to the Answer: This equation can be solved by first adding 23 to both sides, then multiplying both sides by 12:

$$\begin{aligned} \frac{b}{12} - 23 &= 36 \\ \frac{b}{12} &= 59 \\ b &= 708 \end{aligned}$$

Grid in 708.

30. 1.5

Subject: Algebra

Getting to the Answer: Recall that the square root of 225 is 15, so the square root of 2.25 is 1.5. Either positive or negative 1.5 satisfies the equation, but the question also states that m is positive, so grid in 1.5

31. $0 < t < 1$

Subject: Algebra

Getting to the Answer: Solve this inequality like you would a similar equation. Move all of the t terms to one side and the constants to the other side:

$$\begin{aligned} 3t + 10 &> 5t + 8 \\ -2t &> -2 \\ t &< 1 \end{aligned}$$

Because you divided both sides by -2, don't forget to flip the direction of the inequality. We know that $t < 1$, and we also know from the question that $t > 0$. Grid in any value that is between 0 and 1, such as .6.

32. 24

Subject: Algebra

Getting to the Answer: Substitute 8 in for *a* everywhere it appears in the given expression. Compute and simplify, keeping in mind the correct rules for the order of operations:

$$2(a-5)^2+3a\div 4$$
$$2(8-5)^2+3(8)\div 4$$
$$2(3)^2+24\div 4$$
$$18+6=24$$

Grid in 24.

33. 12

Subject: Arithmetic

Getting to the Answer: Remember that the $\frac{1}{2}$ power means to take the square root of a number.

$$144^{\frac{1}{2}} \Rightarrow \sqrt{144}=12$$

Grid in 12.

34. 30

Subject: Arithmetic

Getting to the Answer: Remembering the rules for the order of operations is the key to answering this question correctly. Start with multiplication and division before moving to the addition:

$$36\div 4+9\times 2+3$$
$$9+18+3=30$$

Grid in 30.

35. 64

Subject: Arithmetic

Getting to the Answer: Be sure that you remember the rule for negative exponents in this question. Also be sure that you don't get confused with fractions within fractions:

$$\left(\frac{1}{4}\right)^{-3}=\frac{1}{\left(\frac{1}{4}\right)^3}=4^3=64$$

Grid in 64.

36. .778

Subject: Arithmetic

Getting to the Answer: Start by converting the mixed number to an improper fraction. After the conversion, multiply across and simplify:

$$\frac{2}{3}\times 1\frac{1}{6}\Rightarrow \frac{2}{3}\times\frac{7}{6}=\frac{14}{18}=\frac{7}{9}\approx .778$$

7/9 rounds to the decimal .778, so grid this value in.

37. 420

Subject: Arithmetic

Getting to the Answer: Set up a proportion to solve this question. Since you know 2 cups of chocolate chips are used to make 35 cookies, and you are given that 24 cups of chocolate chips are used, you can set up the following proportion:

$$\frac{2}{35}=\frac{24}{x}$$
$$2x=840$$
$$x=420$$

Grid in 420.

38. 41

Subject: Arithmetic

Getting to the Answer: If Crystal has 500 eggs and is filling cartons that contain 12 eggs, then division will tell you how many cartons of eggs she can fill completely. 500 divided by 12 is 41 with a remainder of 8. That means she can fill 41 cartons completely (with 8 eggs left over), so grid in 41.

39. 17

Subject: Arithmetic

Getting to the Answer: If Peter is 42 years old now, then he will be 50 years old in 8 years. This means that, when Peter is 50 years old, Chris will be 25 years old. Thus, Chris must be 8 years less than 25 years old now, or 17 years old. Grid in 17.

40. 25

Subject: Arithmetic

Getting to the Answer: If a skirt is discounted 20%, that means that the skirt's price is 80% of the full price. Algebraically, this translates to $0.8x = 20$. Divide both sides by 0.8 to get $x = 25$. Grid in 25.

41. 18

Subject: Algebra

Getting to the Answer: Begin by translating the information in the question to an equation. Chris's age is 8 less than twice Michael's age; this translates to $2m - 8$. The sum of both ages is 46, so $m + (2m - 8) = 46$. Combine like terms and solve:

$$\begin{aligned} 3m - 8 &= 46 \\ 3m &= 54 \\ m &= 18 \end{aligned}$$

Michael's age is 18, so grid in 18.

42. 11.2

Subject: Arithmetic

Getting to the Answer: To find the distance that Maria ran over the three days, simply add the three distances together: $2.3 + 3.9 + 5 = 11.2$ miles. Grid in 11.2.

43. 112

Subject: Algebra

Getting to the Answer: First, create a proportion that expresses the given information. You know that the ratio of males to females is 3:4, and there are 48 males:

$$\begin{aligned} \frac{3}{4} &= \frac{48}{x} \\ 3x &= 192 \\ x &= 64 \end{aligned}$$

Don't grid in 64, though! You are asked how many total students there are, so add 48 and 64 together to get 112. Grid in 112.

44. 2.1

Subject: Arithmetic

Getting to the Answer: To get to the answer, simply add the three fractions. Remember that you will need a common denominator to add these fractions together. In this case, the common denominator will be 30:

$$\frac{2}{3} + \frac{3}{5} + \frac{5}{6}$$

$$\frac{20}{30} + \frac{18}{30} + \frac{25}{30} = \frac{63}{30} = 2\frac{3}{30} = 2\frac{1}{10}$$

Since mixed numbers cannot be gridded in, convert the fraction to a decimal and grid in 2.1.

45. 18

Subject: Arithmetic

Getting to the Answer: On Monday, Mark paints one-fourth of the 28 houses, or 7 houses. On Tuesday, he paints one-seventh of the remaining 21 (not 28!) houses, which is 3 houses. This means that he paints $7 + 3 = 10$ houses on Monday and Tuesday, leaving 18 houses for the rest of the week. Grid in 18.

46. 97.5

Subject: Arithmetic

Getting to the Answer: Start by calculating how much Sam was paid for each essay. Essay 1 was 300 words, so he received 250($0.10) + 50($0.05) = $25 + $2.50 = $27.50. Essay 2 was 400 words, so he received 250($0.10) + 150($0.05) = $25 + $7.50 = $32.50. Essay 3 was 500 words, so he received 250($0.10) + 250($0.05) = $25 + $12.50 = $37.50. Together, Sam was paid $27.50 + $32.50 + $37.50 = $97.50. Grid in 97.5.

47. 13

Subject: Algebra

Getting to the Answer: Start by distributing over the two sets of parentheses. From there, combine like terms and perform the necessary algebra to isolate z:

$$\begin{aligned} 2z + 3(z + 8) &= \frac{1}{2}(12z + 22) \\ 2z + 3z + 24 &= 6z + 11 \\ 5z + 24 &= 6z + 11 \\ 13 &= z \end{aligned}$$

Grid in 13.

48. .35

Subject: Arithmetic

Getting to the Answer: To multiply fractions, simply multiply across the numerators and denominators, and then simplify, if possible:

$$\frac{7}{8} \times \frac{2}{5} = \frac{14}{40} = \frac{7}{20}$$

Grid in 0.35, which is the decimal equivalent of $\frac{7}{20}$.

49. 9

Subject: Arithmetic

Getting to the Answer: Finding the halfway point between two numbers is the same as finding the midpoint of two numbers. To find the midpoint, add the two numbers together and divide by 2. This yields $\frac{-5 + 23}{2} = \frac{18}{2} = 9$. Grid in 9.

50. 1

Subject: Algebra

Getting to the Answer: Start by simplifying each inequality. The first inequality simplifies to $f > 3$, while the second inequality simplifies to $f < 5$. The value of f must be between 3 and 5; however, since f is an integer, the only possible value f can take is 4. There is only 1 possible value of f, so grid in 1.

51. 11

Subject: Algebra

Getting to the Answer: Combine like terms, then solve. In this equation, it is easier to move the c terms to the right side:

$$\begin{aligned} 20c + 36 &= 24c - 8 \\ 44 &= 4c \\ 11 &= c \end{aligned}$$

Grid in 11.

52. 12

Subject: Algebra

Getting to the Answer: Cross-multiply the proportion, then take the square root of both sides to get a by itself:

$$\begin{aligned} \frac{a}{6} &= \frac{24}{a} \\ a^2 &= 144 \\ a &= 12 \end{aligned}$$

Because $a > 0$, grid in 12.

53. .35

Subject: Arithmetic

Getting to the Answer: Remember that to add or subtract fractions, you need to find a common denominator. Here, the common denominator is 20. Once you convert both fractions to have denominators of 20, simply subtract and simplify, if possible.

$$\frac{3}{5} - \frac{1}{4}$$
$$\frac{12}{20} - \frac{5}{20} = \frac{7}{20}$$

Grid in 0.35, which is the decimal equivalent of $\frac{7}{20}$.

54. 1.33

Subject: Arithmetic

Getting to the Answer: Dividing by a fraction is like multiplying by the fraction's reciprocal. Take the first fraction and multiply by the reciprocal of the second fraction:

$$\frac{2}{3} \div \frac{1}{2} \rightarrow \frac{2}{3} \times \frac{2}{1} = \frac{4}{3}$$

Grid in 1.33, which is equivalent to $\frac{4}{3}$.

55. .667

Subject: Arithmetic

Getting to the Answer: Remember the order of operations: Here, multiplication should be done before subtraction:

$$\frac{5}{6} - \frac{1}{2} \times \frac{1}{3}$$
$$\frac{5}{6} - \frac{1}{6} = \frac{4}{6} = \frac{2}{3}$$

Grid in .667.

56. 29

Subject: Algebra

Getting to the Answer: Begin by simplifying both inequalities. Subtracting 8 from both sides of the first inequality gives $m < 14$, and adding 4 to both sides of the second inequality gives $n < 17$. Since m and n are both integers, the largest possible value of m is 13, and the largest possible value of n is 16. Thus, the largest possible value of $m + n$ is $13 + 16 = 29$. Grid in 29.

57. .125

Subject: Algebra

Getting to the Answer: Be sure to distribute on both sides of the equal sign first, then solve like you would any other equation:

$$\begin{aligned} 3(2x + 5) &= -2(x - 8) \\ 6x + 15 &= -2x + 16 \\ 8x &= 1 \\ x &= \frac{1}{8} \end{aligned}$$

Grid in the decimal equivalent of $\frac{1}{8}$, which is .125.

58. 212

Subject: Arithmetic

Getting to the Answer: Each of the 8 students needs a paintbrush, so the cost of 8 paintbrushes is $8 \times \$1.50 = \$12$. Each student needs 5 tubes of paint, meaning that $8 \times 5 = 40$ tubes of paint are needed. 40 tubes of paint costs $40 \times \$5 = \$200$. Thus, Bob spends $\$12 + \$200 = \$212$ on supplies for his class, so grid in 212.

59. 1962

Subject: Arithmetic

Getting to the Answer: If an airplane flies 436 miles per hour and the flight takes 4.5 hours, then the distance the airplane flies is simply 436×4.5. This product is 1,962, meaning the distance between Miami and Quito is 1,962 miles. Grid in 1962.

60. 36

Subject: Arithmetic

Getting to the Answer: The question tells you that the book club sends William a book each month, which would be 12 books over the course of a year. However, don't forget about the free book! If William receives a free book at the end of the year, then he receives 13 books total for the year. If you are computing the average price per book, you need to consider all 13 books. The answer, then, will simply be \$468 divided by 13, which is \$36. Grid in 36.

61. 21

Subject: Algebra

Getting to the Answer: If 4 of every 7 socks in Tammy's drawer are blue, then the other 3 socks must be yellow. Thus, the ratio of blue socks to yellow socks must be 4:3. If you know that there are 28 blue socks, then you can set up the following ratio to solve for the number of yellow socks: $\frac{4}{3} = \frac{28}{x}$. Cross-multiplying will yield $4x = 84$, and dividing by 4 will give you $x = 21$, meaning there are 21 yellow socks. Grid in 21.

62. 37

Subject: Arithmetic

Getting to the Answer: You know that Danielle read 13 books, and that Emma read 15 less than 3 times this amount. Here, that means that Emma read 15 less than 3(13) books, or $3(13) - 15 = 24$ books. The question asks for the number of books that Danielle and Emma read combined, which would be $13 + 24 = 37$ books, so grid in 37.

63. 8.42

Subject: Arithmetic

Getting to the Answer: First, consider which items are taxed and which aren't. The question tells you that food is taxed, so the salad and the soup will be taxed at 6%. Thus, these two items cost $\$3 + \$4 = \$7$, but you also need to consider the tax, which is $\$7(.06) = \$.42$. Including tax, these two items cost \$7.42. You also need to include the cost of the iced tea, which is \$1, giving you a total of \$8.42. Grid in 8.42.

64. 80

Subject: Algebra

Getting to the Answer: Use the information you are given in the question to construct a proportion. You know that the ratio of cars to trucks is 7:3 and there are 56 cars, so you can translate this information to the following proportion:

$$\frac{7}{3} = \frac{56}{x}$$
$$7x = 168$$
$$x = 24$$

Be sure you answer the right question, though. You are asked for the number of vehicles, not the number of trucks. To calculate the number of vehicles at Wally's, simply add the number of cars and trucks together: $56 + 24 = 80$ vehicles. Grid in 80.

65. 3

Subject: Arithmetic

Getting to the Answer: To determine how much liquid is used to make the cake, simply add the three numbers together. Remember to use a common denominator when adding or subtracting fractions. Also, converting mixed numbers to improper fractions first is usually a good idea.

$$\frac{5}{3} + \frac{1}{2} + \frac{5}{6} \Rightarrow \frac{10}{6} + \frac{3}{6} + \frac{5}{6} = \frac{18}{6} = 3$$

Grid in 3.

66. 10

Subject: Algebra

Getting to the Answer: Let c be the number of coffee mugs that Christine has. If Diane has four more than half of this number of mugs and they have a total of 19 mugs, then the following equation can be constructed:

$$c + \frac{1}{2}c + 4 = 19$$
$$\frac{3}{2}c + 4 = 19$$
$$\frac{3}{2}c = 15$$
$$c = 10$$

The question asks for the number of mugs that Christine has, so grid in 10.

67. 116

Subject: Arithmetic

Getting to the Answer: If one baseball team uses 5 bats, 9 gloves, and 15 baseballs in a typical game, then the team uses 29 pieces of equipment. To calculate how many pieces of equipment would be needed for 4 baseball teams, simply multiply this number by 4: $29 \times 4 = 116$ pieces of equipment. Grid in 116.

68. 325

Subject: Arithmetic

Getting to the Answer: Translate the problem to mathematical operations to get to the answer. You know that Adam's store has 50 less than three times the number of books that Barney's store has. Barney has 125 books, so Adam must have $125(3) - 50 = 325$ books. Grid in 325.

69. 750

Subject: Algebra

Getting to the Answer: Start by calculating how much gravel was used in the anti-skid material last year. You know that the ratio of gravel to salt was 3:2 and 300 tons of salt was used, so the following proportion can be set up: $\frac{3}{2} = \frac{x}{300}$. Multiplying by 2 and dividing by 3 will give you 450, so 450 tons of gravel were used. This isn't the correct answer, though! The question asks how much total material was used, so add up both numbers to get $300 + 450 = 750$ tons of material. Grid in 750.

70. 11

Subject: Arithmetic

Getting to the Answer: If a case of water costs \$3.99, then the price per bottle would simply be the price of the case divided by the number of bottles of water in the case. Here, that means you would take \$3.99 divided by 35. This gives you 0.114. The question asks you to round to the nearest cent and express your answer in cents. The price to the nearest cent is \$0.11, so you would grid in 11.

COUNTDOWN TO THE TEST

To calm any pretest jitters you may have, this chapter leads you through a helpful itinerary for the last week.

> ✔ **Emergency Plan**
>
> **Even if you're short on time, read this entire chapter. It tells you how to use your time wisely before, during, and after the test.**

The Week Before the Test

- Focus on strategy and backup plans.
- Practice the strategies you had the best success rate with.
- Decide and know **exactly** how you are going to approach each section and question type.
- Sit down and do practice problems in the Practice Sets, or complete extra drills you skipped the first time through.
- Start practicing waking up early and eating breakfast so that you will be alert in the morning on Test Day.

Two Days Before the Test

Do your last studying—a few more practice problems—and call it quits.

> ✔ **Things NOT to Do the Night Before the Test**
>
> - **Stay up all night watching all the *Friday the 13th* movies.**
> - **Eat a large, double anchovy, sausage, and pepperoni pizza with a case of chocolate soda.**
> - **Send away for brochures about clown school.**
> - **Start making flash cards.**
> - **Tattoo yourself.**

The Night Before the Test

Don't study. Get together the following items:

- Your admission/registration ticket
- Your ID
- A watch (choose one that is easy to read)
- Slightly dull No. 2 pencils (so they fill in the ovals faster)
- A pencil sharpener

- Erasers
- Clothes you will wear (Dress in layers! The climate at the test location may vary, as may your body temperature. Make sure you can warm up or cool down easily.)
- Snacks (easy to open or partially unwrapped)
- Money
- A packet of tissues

Know exactly where you're going and exactly how you're getting there.

Relax the night before the test. Read a good book, take a bubble bath, or watch TV. Get a good night's sleep. Go to bed at a reasonable hour and leave yourself extra time in the morning.

The Morning of the Test

Eat breakfast. Make it something substantial and nutritious, but don't deviate too much from your everyday pattern.

Dress in layers so that you can adjust to the temperature of the test room.

Read a newspaper or a magazine to warm up your brain before the test starts.

Be sure to get there early. Leave enough time to allow for traffic, mass transit delays, getting lost en route, and any other snag that could slow you down.

During the Test

Don't be shaken. If you find your confidence slipping, remind yourself of how well you've prepared. You know the structure of the test, you know the instructions, and you've studied for every question type.

Even if something goes really wrong, don't panic. If the test booklet is defective—two pages are stuck together or the ink has run—stay calm. Raise your hand and tell the proctor you need a new book. If you accidentally misgrid your answer page or put the answers in the wrong section, again don't panic. Raise your hand and tell the proctor. He or she may be able to arrange for you to regrid your test after it's over, when it won't cost you any time.

ONCE THE TEST IS OVER...

Put it out of your mind! Start thinking about more interesting things. Do something fun and relaxing that day. You might walk out of the SHSAT thinking that you blew it, but you probably didn't. You tend to remember the questions that stumped you, not the many that you knew.

If you want more help, want to know more about the SHSAT, or want to find out about Kaplan prep courses for the PSAT, SAT, and ACT, give us a call at 1-800-KAP-TEST. We're here to answer your questions and help you in any way we can. You can also check out our website at kaptest.com.

CHAPTER 20

Stress Management

CHAPTER OBJECTIVES

By the end of this chapter, you will be able to:

- Tame Test Day stress
- Prepare for success

The countdown has begun. Your date with the test is looming on the horizon. Anxiety is on the rise. The butterflies are flapping around in your stomach. Your thinking is getting cloudy. Maybe you think you won't be ready. Maybe you already know everything you need to, but you're going into panic mode anyway. Worst of all, you're not sure of what to do about it.

Don't panic! It is possible to tame that anxiety and stress—before and during the test. We'll show you how. You won't believe how quickly and easily you can deal with that killer anxiety.

MAKE THE MOST OF YOUR PREP TIME

Lack of control is one of the prime causes of stress. Research shows that if you don't have a sense of control over what's happening in your life, you can easily end up feeling helpless and hopeless. So just having concrete things to do and to think about—taking control—will help reduce your stress. This chapter shows you how to take control during the days leading up to taking the test.

> **✔ Avoid Must-y Thinking**
>
> **Let go of "must-y" thoughts, those notions that you must do something in a certain way—for example, "I must get a great score, or else!" or "I must meet everyone's expectations!"**

IDENTIFY THE SOURCES OF STRESS

In the space provided, jot down anything you identify as a source of your test-related stress. The idea is to pin down that free-floating anxiety so that you can take control of it. Here are some common examples to get you started:

- I always freeze up on tests.
- I'm nervous about the English Language Arts/Math section.
- I need a good/great score to go to Brooklyn Tech.
- My older brother/sister/best friend got in. I have to, too.
- People will be really disappointed if I don't get in.
- I'm afraid of losing my focus and concentration.
- I'm afraid I'm not spending enough time preparing.
- I study like crazy, but nothing seems to stick in my mind.
- I always run out of time and get panicky.
- I feel as though thinking is becoming like wading through thick mud.

Sources of Stress

______________________	______________________
______________________	______________________
______________________	______________________
______________________	______________________

Take a few minutes to think about the things you've just written down. Then rewrite them, listing the statements you most associate with your stress first and putting the least disturbing items last. Chances are, the top of the list is a fairly accurate description of how you react to test anxiety, both physically and mentally. The later items usually describe your fears (disappointing Mom and Dad, looking bad, etc.). As you write the list, you're forming a hierarchy of items so you can deal first with the anxiety provokers that affect you most. Very often, taking care of the major items from the top of the list goes a long way toward relieving overall testing anxiety. You probably won't have to bother with the worries you placed last.

> ✔ **Don't Do It in Bed**
>
> **Don't study on your bed, especially if you have problems with insomnia. Your mind might start to associate the bed with work, making it even harder for you to fall asleep.**

STRENGTHS AND AREAS OF OPPORTUNITY

Take one minute to list the areas of the test that you are good at. They can be general ("Reading") or specific ("Math Grid-In questions"). Put down as many as you can think of and, if possible, time yourself. Write for the entire time; don't stop writing until you've reached the one-minute stopping point.

> ✔ **Think Good Thoughts**
>
> **Create a set of positive but brief affirmations and mentally repeat them to yourself just before you fall asleep at night. (That's when your mind is very open to suggestion.) You'll find yourself feeling a lot more positive in the morning.**
>
> **Periodically repeating your affirmations during the day makes them more effective.**

Strong Test Subjects

Next, take one minute to list areas of the test you're not so good at, just plain bad at, have failed at, or keep failing at. Again, keep it to one minute and continue writing until you reach the cutoff. Don't be afraid to identify and write down your weak spots! In all probability, as you do both lists, you'll find you are strong in some areas and not so strong in others. Taking stock of your assets and liabilities lets you know the areas you don't have to worry about and the ones that will demand extra attention and effort.

Areas of Opportunity

Facing your weak spots gives you some distinct advantages. It helps a lot to find out where you need to spend extra effort. Increased exposure to tough material makes it more familiar and less intimidating. (After all, we mostly fear what we don't know and are probably afraid to face.) You'll feel better about yourself because you're dealing directly with areas of the test that bring on your anxiety. You can't help feeling more confident when you know you're actively strengthening your chances of earning a higher overall test score.

> **✓ Very Superstitious**
>
> **Stress expert Stephen Sideroff, PhD, tells of a client who always stressed out before, during, and even after taking tests. Yet, she always got outstanding scores. It became obvious that she was thinking superstitiously—subconsciously believing that the great scores were a result of her worrying. She also didn't trust herself and believed that if she didn't worry, she wouldn't study hard enough. Sideroff convinced her to take a risk and work on relaxing before her next test. She did, and her test results were still as good as ever—which broke her cycle of superstitious thinking.**

Now, go back to the "good" list and expand on it for two minutes. Take the general items on that first list and make them more specific; take the specific items and expand them into more general conclusions. Naturally, if anything new comes to mind, jot it down. Focus all of your attention and effort on your strengths. Don't underestimate yourself or your abilities. Give yourself full credit. At the same time, don't list strengths you don't really have; you'll only be fooling yourself.

Expanding from general to specific might go as follows. If you listed "reading" as a broad topic you feel strong in, you would then narrow your focus to include areas of this subject about which you are particularly knowledgeable. Your areas of strength might include identifying the main idea of a passage, locating key details, etc.

Whatever you know comfortably goes on your "good" list. Now, get ready, check your starting time, and start writing down items on your expanded "good" list.

> ✔ **Stress Tip**
>
> **Don't work in a messy or cramped area. Before you sit down to study, clear yourself a nice, open space. And make sure you have books, paper, pencils—whatever tools you will need—within easy reach before you sit down to study.**

Strong Test Subjects: An Expanded List

______________________	______________________
______________________	______________________
______________________	______________________
______________________	______________________

> ✔ **Ocean Dumping**
>
> **Visualize a beautiful beach, with white sand, blue skies, sparkling water, a warm sun, and seagulls. See yourself walking on the beach, carrying a small plastic pail. Stop at a good spot and put your worries and whatever may be bothering you into the pail. Drop it at the water's edge and watch it drift out to sea. When the pail is out of sight, walk on.**

After you've stopped, check your time. Did you find yourself going beyond the two minutes allotted? Did you write down more things than you thought you knew? Is it possible you know more than you've given yourself credit for? Could that mean you've found a number of areas in which you feel strong?

You just took an active step toward helping yourself. Notice any increased feelings of confidence? Enjoy them.

Here's another way to think about your writing exercise. Every area of strength and confidence you can identify is much like having a reserve of solid gold at Fort Knox. You'll be able to draw on your reserves as you need them. You can use your reserves to solve difficult questions, maintain confidence, and keep test stress and anxiety at a distance. The encouraging thing is that every time you recognize another area of strength, succeed at coming up with a solution, or get a good score on a test, you increase your reserves. And there is absolutely no limit to how much self-confidence you can have or how good you can feel about yourself.

IMAGINE YOURSELF SUCCEEDING

This next little group of exercises is both physical and mental. They're a natural follow-up to what you've just accomplished with your lists.

> **✔ Counseling**
>
> **Don't forget that your school probably has counseling available. If you can't conquer test stress on your own, make an appointment at the counseling center. That's what counselors are there for.**

First, find a comfortable chair and get yourself into a comfortable sitting position in a quiet setting. Wear loose clothes. If you wear glasses, take them off. Then, close your eyes and breathe in a deep, satisfying breath of air. Really fill your lungs until your rib cage is fully expanded and you can't take in any more. Then, exhale the air completely. Imagine you're blowing out a candle with your last little puff of air. Do this two or three more times, filling your lungs to their maximum and emptying them totally. Keep your eyes closed, comfortably but not tightly. Let your body sink deeper into the chair as you become even more comfortable.

With your eyes shut you can notice something very interesting. You're no longer dealing with the worrisome stuff going on in the world outside of you. Now you can concentrate on what happens *inside* you. The more you recognize your own physical reactions to stress and anxiety, the more you can do about them. You might not realize it, but you've begun to regain a sense of being in control.

Let images begin to form on the "viewing screens" on the back of your eyelids. You're experiencing visualizations from the place in your mind that makes pictures. Allow the images to come easily and naturally; don't force them. Imagine yourself in a relaxing situation. It might be in a special place you've visited before or one you've read about. It can be a fictional location that you create in your imagination, but a real-life memory of a place or situation you know is usually better. Make it as detailed as possible and notice as much as you can.

> **✔ Take a Hike, Pal**
>
> **When you're in the middle of studying and hit a wall, take a short, brisk walk. Breathe deeply and swing your arms as you walk. Clear your mind. (And don't forget to look for flowers that grow in the cracks of the sidewalk.)**

Stay focused on the images as you sink farther back into your chair. Breathe easily and naturally. You might have the sensation of stress or tension draining from your muscles and flowing downward, out your feet, and away from you.

Take a moment to check how you're feeling. Notice how comfortable you've become. Imagine how much easier it would be if you could take the test feeling this relaxed and in this state of ease. You've coupled the images of your special place with sensations of comfort and relaxation. You've also found a way to become relaxed simply by visualizing your own safe, special place.

Now, close your eyes and start remembering a real-life situation in which you did well on a test. If you can't come up with one, remember a situation in which you did something (academic or otherwise) that you were really proud of—a genuine accomplishment. Make the memory as detailed as possible. Think about the sights, the sounds, the smells, even the tastes associated with this remembered experience. Remember how confident you felt as you accomplished your goal. Now start thinking about the upcoming test. Keep your thoughts and feelings in line with that successful experience. Don't make comparisons between them. Just imagine taking the upcoming test with the same feelings of confidence and relaxed control.

✔ Play the Music

If you want to play music, keep it low and in the background. Music with a regular, mathematical rhythm—reggae, for example—aids the learning process. A recording of ocean waves is also soothing.

This exercise is a great way to bring the test down to earth. You should practice this exercise often, especially when the prospect of taking the exam starts to stress you out. The more you practice it, the more effective the exercise will be for you.

✔ Cyberstress

If you spend a lot of time in cyberspace anyway, do a search for the phrase *stress management*. There's a great deal of stress advice online, including material specifically for students.

EXERCISE YOUR FRUSTRATIONS AWAY

Whether it is jogging, walking, biking, mild aerobics, push-ups, or a pickup basketball game, physical exercise is a very effective way to stimulate both your mind and body and to improve your ability to think and concentrate. Ironically, a surprising number of students get out of the habit of regular exercise because they're spending so much time prepping for exams. Also, it's a medical fact that sedentary people get less oxygen to the blood, and hence to the head, than active people. You can live fine with a little less oxygen; you just can't think as well.

Any big test is a bit like a race. Thinking clearly at the end is just as important as having a quick mind early on. If you can't sustain your energy level in the last sections of the exam, there's a good chance you could lose focus and start making mistakes. You need a fit body that can weather the demands any big exam puts on you. Along with a good diet and adequate sleep, exercise is an important part of keeping yourself in fighting shape and thinking clearly for the long haul.

There's something else that happens when students don't make exercise an integral part of their test preparation. Like any organism in nature, you operate best if all your "energy systems" are in balance. Studying uses a lot of energy, but it's all mental. When you take a study break, do something active instead of raiding the fridge or staring at the TV. Take a 5- to 10-minute activity break for every 50 or 60 minutes that you study. The physical exertion gets your body active, which helps to keep your mind and body in sync. Then, when you finish studying for the night and go to bed, you won't lie there tense and unable to sleep because your head is overtired and your body wants to run a marathon.

One warning about exercise, however: it's not a good idea to exercise vigorously right before you go to bed. This could easily cause sleep onset problems. For the same reason, it's also not a good idea to study right up to bedtime. Make time for a "buffer period" before you go to bed: for 30 to 60 minutes, take a hot shower, meditate, or just relax.

✔ Nutrition and Stress: The Dos and Don'ts

Do eat:

- **Fruits and vegetables (raw is best, or just lightly steamed or nuked)**
- **Low-fat protein such as fish, skinless poultry, beans, and legumes (like lentils)**
- **Whole grains such as brown rice, whole wheat bread, and pastas (no bleached flour)**

Don't eat:

- **Refined sugar; sweet, high-fat snacks (simple carbohydrates like sugar make stress worse, and fatty foods lower your immunity)**
- **Salty foods (they can deplete potassium, which you need for nerve functions)**

THE DANGERS OF DRUGS

Using drugs (prescription or recreational) specifically to prepare for and take a big test is definitely self-defeating. (And if they're illegal drugs, you can end up with a bigger problem than the SHSAT on your hands.) Except for the drugs that occur naturally in your brain, every drug has major drawbacks—and a false sense of security is only one of them.

You may have heard that taking uppers helps you study by keeping you alert. If they're illegal, definitely forget about it. They wouldn't really work anyway, since amphetamines make it hard to retain information. Mild stimulants, such as coffee, cola, or over-the-counter caffeine pills can sometimes help as you study, since they keep you alert. On the other hand, they can also lead to agitation, restlessness, and insomnia. Some people can drink a pot of high-octane coffee and sleep like a baby. Others have one cup and start to vibrate. It all depends on your tolerance for caffeine. Remember, a little anxiety is a good thing. The adrenaline that gets pumped into your bloodstream helps you stay alert and think more clearly. But if there's too much anxiety, you can't think straight at all.

> **✔ The Relaxation Paradox**
>
> **Forcing relaxation is like asking yourself to flap your arms and fly. You can't do it, and every push and prod only gets you more frustrated. Relaxation is something you don't work at. You simply let it happen. Think about it. When was the last time you tried to force yourself to go to sleep and it worked?**

Instead, go for endorphins—the "natural morphine." Endorphins have no side effects, and they're free—you've already got them in your brain. It just takes some exercise to release them. Running around on the basketball court, bicycling, swimming, aerobics, power walking—these activities cause endorphins to occupy certain spots in your brain's neural synapses. In addition, exercise develops staying power and increases the oxygen transfer to your brain.

TAKE A DEEP BREATH...

Here's another natural route to relaxation and invigoration. It's a classic isometric exercise that you can do whenever you get stressed out—just before the test begins, even *during* the test. It's very simple and takes just a few minutes.

Close your eyes. Start with your eyes and—without holding your breath—gradually tighten every muscle in your body (but not to the point of pain) in the following sequence:

1. Close your eyes tightly.
2. Squeeze your nose and mouth together so that your whole face is scrunched up. (If it makes you self-conscious to do this in the test room, skip the face-scrunching part.)
3. Pull your chin into your chest, and pull your shoulders together.
4. Tighten your arms to your body, and then clench your hands into tight fists.
5. Pull in your stomach.
6. Squeeze your thighs and buttocks together and tighten your calves.
7. Stretch your feet, and then curl your toes (watch out for cramping in this part).

At this point, every muscle should be tightened. Now, relax your body, one part at a time, *in reverse order,* starting with your toes. Let the tension drop out of each muscle. The entire process might take five minutes from start to finish (maybe a couple of minutes during the test). This clenching and unclenching exercise should help you to feel very relaxed.

> **✔ Enlightenment**
>
> **A lamp with a 75-watt bulb is optimal for studying. But don't put it so close to your study material that you create a glare.**

AND KEEP BREATHING

Conscious attention to breathing is an excellent way of managing test stress (or any stress, for that matter). The majority of people who get into trouble during tests take shallow breaths. They breathe using only their upper chest and shoulder muscles, and they may even hold their breath for long periods of time. Conversely, the test taker who keeps breathing normally and rhythmically is likely to be more relaxed and in better control during the entire test experience.

So, now is the time to get into the habit of relaxed breathing. Do the next exercise to learn to breathe in a natural, easy rhythm. This is another technique you can use during the test to collect your thoughts and ward off excess stress. The entire exercise should take no more than three to five minutes.

With your eyes still closed, breathe in slowly and *deeply* through your nose. Hold the breath for a bit, and then release it through your mouth. The key is to breathe slowly and deeply by using your diaphragm (the big band of muscle that spans your body just above your waist) to draw air in and out naturally and effortlessly. Breathing with your diaphragm encourages relaxation and helps minimize tension. Try it and notice how relaxed and comfortable you feel.

QUICK TIPS FOR THE DAYS JUST BEFORE THE EXAM

- The best test takers do less and less as the test approaches. Taper off your study schedule and take it easy on yourself. You want to be relaxed and ready on the day of the test. Give yourself time off, especially on the evening before the exam. By then, if you've studied well, everything you need to know is firmly stored in your memory banks.
- Positive self-talk can be extremely liberating and invigorating, especially as the test looms closer. Tell yourself things such as "I choose to take this test," rather than "I have to"; "I will do well," rather than "I hope things go well"; "I can," rather than "I cannot." Be aware of negative, self-defeating thoughts and images, and immediately counter any you become aware of. Replace them with affirming statements that encourage your self-esteem and confidence. Create and practice visualizations that build on your positive statements.
- Get everything you will need together sooner rather than later. Have it all (including choice of clothing) laid out days in advance. Most importantly, know where the test will be held and the easiest, quickest way to get there. You will gain great peace of mind if you know that all the little details—gas in the car, directions, etc.—are firmly in your control before the day of the test.
- Experience the test site a few days in advance. This is very helpful if you are especially anxious. If at all possible, find out what room your part of the alphabet is assigned to and try to sit there (by yourself) for a while. Better yet, bring some practice material and do a section or two, if not an entire practice test, in that room. In this situation, familiarity generates comfort and confidence.

- Forego any practice on the day before the test. It's in your best interest to marshal your physical and psychological resources for 24 hours or so. Even racehorses are kept in the paddock and treated like royalty the day before a race. Keep the upcoming test out of your consciousness; go to a movie, take a pleasant hike, or just relax. Don't eat junk food or tons of sugar. And—of course—get plenty of rest the night before. Just don't go to bed too early. It's hard to fall asleep earlier than you're used to, and you don't want to lie there thinking about the test.

✔ Dress for Success

On the day of the test, wear loose layers. That way, you'll be prepared no matter what the temperature of the room is. (An uncomfortable temperature will just distract you from the job at hand.)

And, if you have an item of clothing that you tend to feel "lucky" or confident in—a shirt, a pair of jeans, whatever—wear it. A little totem couldn't hurt.

HANDLING STRESS DURING THE TEST

The biggest stress generator will be the test itself. Fear not; there are methods of quelling your stress during the test.

- Keep moving forward instead of getting bogged down in a difficult question. You don't have to get everything right to achieve a good score. The best test takers skip difficult material temporarily in search of the easier questions. They mark the questions that require extra time and thought. This strategy buys time and builds confidence so you can handle the tough questions later.
- Don't be thrown if other test takers seem to be working more furiously than you are. Continue to spend your time patiently thinking through your answers; it's going to lead to better results. Don't mistake the other people's sheer activity as a sign of progress and higher scores.
- Keep breathing! Weak test takers tend to forget to breathe properly as the test proceeds. They start holding their breath without realizing it, or they breathe erratically or arrhythmically. Improper breathing interferes with clear thinking.
- Some quick isometrics during the test—especially if concentration is wandering or energy is waning—can help. Try this: put your palms together and press intensely for a few seconds. Concentrate on the tension you feel through your palms, wrists, forearms, and up into your biceps and shoulders. Then, quickly release the pressure. Feel the difference as you let go. Focus on the warm relaxation that floods through the muscles. Now you're ready to return to the task.
- Here's another isometric that will relieve tension in both your neck and eye muscles. Slowly rotate your head from side to side, turning your head and eyes to look as far back over each shoulder as you can. Feel the muscles stretch on one side of your neck as they contract on the other. Repeat five times in each direction.

✔ What Are "Signs of a Winner," Alex?

Here's some advice from a Kaplan instructor who won big on *Jeopardy!*™ In the green room before the show, he noticed that the contestants who were quiet and "within themselves" were the ones who did really well on the show. The contestants who did not perform as well were the ones who were fact-cramming, talking a lot, and generally being manic before the show. Lesson: spend the final hours leading up to the test getting sleep, meditating, and generally relaxing.

PART 5

Practice Tests

SHSAT
Practice Test 1

SHSAT Practice Test 1

ANSWER SHEET

Scan Code

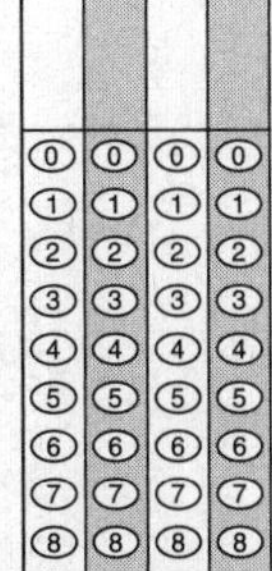

Please use this Answer Sheet only if the test will be scored via a webgrid/online scoring process. This Answer Sheet will NOT work if the test will be scanned.

For scanned exams, please refer to the Kaplan Answer Grid (which requires the use of a No. 2 pencil and is formatted for scanning machines).

Enrollment ID

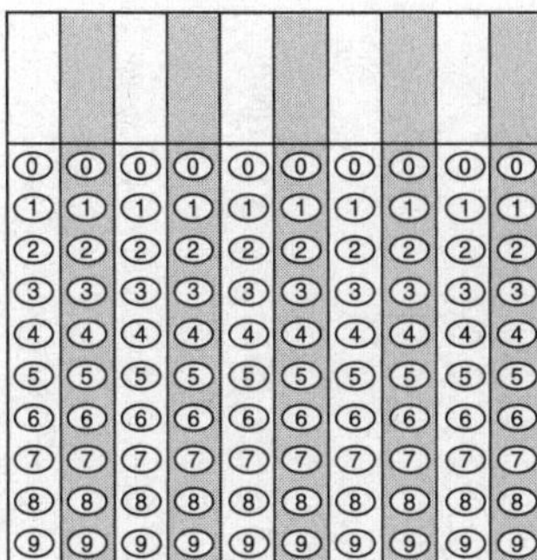

PART 1—ENGLISH LANGUAGE ARTS

1. A B C D
2. E F G H
3. A B C D
4. E F G H
5. A B C D
6. E F G H
7. A B C D
8. E F G H
9. A B C D
10. E F G H
11. A B C D
12. E F G H
13. A B C D
14. E F G H
15. A B C D
16. E F G H
17. A B C D
18. E F G H
19. A B C D
20. E F G H
21. A B C D
22. E F G H
23. A B C D
24. E F G H
25. A B C D
26. E F G H
27. A B C D
28. E F G H
29. A B C D
30. E F G H
31. A B C D
32. E F G H
33. A B C D
34. E F G H
35. A B C D
36. E F G H
37. A B C D
38. E F G H
39. A B C D
40. E F G H
41. A B C D
42. E F G H
43. A B C D
44. E F G H
45. A B C D
46. E F G H
47. A B C D
48. E F G H
49. A B C D
50. E F G H
51. A B C D
52. E F G H
53. A B C D
54. E F G H
55. A B C D
56. E F G H
57. A B C D

PART 2—MATHEMATICS

58. – 0 1 2 3 4 5 6 7 8 9
59. – 0 1 2 3 4 5 6 7 8 9
60. – 0 1 2 3 4 5 6 7 8 9
61. – 0 1 2 3 4 5 6 7 8 9
62. – 0 1 2 3 4 5 6 7 8 9

63. A B C D
64. E F G H
65. A B C D
66. E F G H
67. A B C D
68. E F G H
69. A B C D
70. E F G H
71. A B C D
72. E F G H
73. A B C D
74. E F G H
75. A B C D
76. E F G H
77. A B C D
78. E F G H
79. A B C D
80. E F G H
81. A B C D
82. E F G H
83. A B C D
84. E F G H
85. A B C D
86. E F G H
87. A B C D
88. E F G H
89. A B C D
90. E F G H
91. A B C D
92. E F G H
93. A B C D
94. E F G H
95. A B C D
96. E F G H
97. A B C D
98. E F G H
99. A B C D
100. E F G H
101. A B C D
102. E F G H
103. A B C D
104. E F G H
105. A B C D
106. E F G H
107. A B C D
108. E F G H
109. A B C D
110. E F G H
111. A B C D
112. E F G H
113. A B C D
114. E F G H

PRACTICE TEST 1

DIRECTIONS: Mark your answers on the separate sheet provided. You will receive credit only for answers marked on the answer grid. DO NOT MAKE ANY STRAY MARKS ON THE ANSWER GRID. You can write in the test booklet, or use the paper provided for scratchwork.

Part 1	Questions 1–57	90 minutes
Part 2	Questions 58–114	90 minutes

Marking Your Answers

Each question has only one correct answer. Select the **best** answer for each question. Your score is determined by the number of questions you answered correctly. **It is to your advantage to answer every question, even though you may not be certain which choice is correct.**

Planning Your Time

You have 180 minutes to complete the entire test. How you allot the time between the English Language Arts and Mathematics sections is up to you. **If you begin with the English Language Arts section, you may go on to the Mathematics section as soon as you are ready. Likewise, if you begin with the Mathematics section, you may go on to the English Language Arts section as soon as you are ready.** It is recommended that you do not spend more than 90 minutes on either section. If you complete the test before the allotted time (180 minutes) is over, you may go back to review questions in either section.

Work as rapidly as you can without making mistakes. Don't spend too much time on a difficult question. Return to it later if you have time.

Part 1 — English Language Arts

Suggested Time — 90 Minutes

57 Questions

Revising/Editing

Questions 1–11

IMPORTANT NOTE

The Revising/Editing section (Questions 1–11) is in two parts: Part A and Part B.

REVISING/EDITING Part A

DIRECTIONS: Read and answer each of the following questions. You will be asked to recognize and correct errors in sentences or short paragraphs. Mark the best answer for each question.

1. Read this paragraph.

> (1) A talented geographer, the professor, who teaches college students, is an expert at locating cities and countries on maps. (2) In his lectures, he explains about cartography, or map-making, which involves surveying the Earth's surface to represent its physical structures. (3) Geographers use maps that have different projections and can display Earth's various features, including mountains, the magnetic poles, and oceans. (4) Studying the field of geography provides knowledge about its connections to biology, sociology, and history, among other subjects.

Which sentence should be revised to correct a wordiness issue?

A. sentence 1

B. sentence 2

C. sentence 3

D. sentence 4

2. Read this paragraph.

> (1) After engineering students graduate from college, they spends most of the next five years working toward a graduate degree in computer science. (2) Their courses involve programming, which is the preparation of instructions that tell the computer which operations it needs to perform. (3) Students learn formulas as well as programs that translate complex computer languages. (4) With new advancements every day, the computer science field requires professionals to constantly learn about applying the latest technology.

Which sentence should be revised to correct a usage issue?

E. sentence 1
F. sentence 2
G. sentence 3
H. sentence 4

3. Read this sentence.

> The federal government provides low-interest loans that allow students of deferring payment until they graduate and begin to work.

Which edit should be made to correct this sentence?

A. change ***provides*** to **provide**
B. change ***allow*** to **allowed**
C. change ***of deferring*** to **to defer**
D. change ***begin to*** to **begin with**

4. Read this sentence.

> The helicopter, offering the advantages of flight without requiring large amounts of space for takeoff and landing, allows relatively easy access to remote places as islands, mountain villages, and snow-bound communities.

Which edit should be made to correct this sentence?

E. change ***advantages of*** to **advantages in**
F. change ***large amounts of space*** to **space in rather large amounts**
G. change ***allows relatively easy access to*** to **easily allows relative access for**
H. change ***remote places as*** to **places as remote as**

REVISING/EDITING Part B

DIRECTIONS: Read the passage below and answer the questions following it. You will be asked to improve the writing quality of the passage and to correct errors so that the passage follows the conventions of standard written English. You may reread the passage if you need to. Mark the **best** answer for each question.

Weaving

(1) Hand weaving, traditionally the province of home spinners and weavers, had been practiced at least since the Neolithic era, as evidenced by a Turkish burial cloth dating from 7000 B.C.E. (2) Silk weaving has been known in China since 3500 B.C.E. (3) By 700 C.E., looms were common in Africa, Asia, and Europe. (4) In particular, they were found throughout the Islamic world; indeed, weaving is an integral part of many cultures.

(5) In mythology, weaving is the province of women. (6) In Pre-Dynastic Egypt, Neith was the goddess of weaving; in Greece, the goddess Athena; for the Norse, it was Frigg, the wife of chief god Odin. (7) These, and other protectors of weavers, were variously deemed to also have influence over childbirth, wisdom, the creation of the stars, and fate itself. (8) Tale's about weaving are numerous. (9) Theseus emerges from the maze of the Minotaur by following Ariadne's woven thread. (10) Valkyries weave with thread made of human guts on looms weighted with human heads and arrows for shuttles, all the while chanting of war. (11) In the fable "The Old Man and Death," Aesop warns of being careful of what you wish for. (12) Sleeping Beauty pricks her finger on a spindle and is cursed. (13) Indeed, the English word *text* derives from the Latin word *textare*—weaving, as in "weaving a story."

(14) On the other hand, many modern things tell stories also. (15) In the Ukraine, the *rushnyk*, a ritual cloth, accompanies a person throughout his life; the newborn is placed immediately upon it and the dead are covered with it. (16) Not surprisingly, the tree of life being a recurring motif. (17) Navajo weaving often features a cross, symbol of Spider Woman, who gave the art of weaving to Navajo women. (18) Andean peoples, living as they do with nature, incorporate symbols for the sun and rivers. (19) As is often the case with weavers in general, a pattern or motif may be specific to the weaver herself, and can convey piety, cultural or family traditions, daily life, folklore characters, and even humor.

5. Which edit is needed to correct sentence 1?

   A. change ***traditionally*** to **in the past**

   B. change ***had been*** to **has been**

   C. change ***practiced*** to **practice**

   D. change ***at least since*** to **before**

6. Which is the best way to combine sentences 3 and 4 to clarify the relationship between ideas?

   E. By 700 C.E. looms were common in Africa, Asia, and Europe and evidence has shown that they could also be found throughout the Islamic world; indeed, weaving is an integral part of many cultures.

   F. As long ago as the year 700 C.E. looms were common in Africa, Asia, Europe, and were also common in parts of the Islamic world; indeed, weaving is an integral part of many cultures.

   G. By 700 C.E. looms were common in Africa, Asia, Europe, they were also found throughout the Islamic world; indeed, weaving is an integral part of many cultures.

   H. By 700 C.E. looms were common in Africa, Asia, and Europe, as well as throughout the Islamic world; indeed, weaving is an integral part of many cultures.

7. Which sentence would best follow and support sentence 4?

   A. Given the widespread use and long history of weaving, it is only to be expected that myths about the art abound.

   B. Cultures are reflections of people's beliefs and attitudes.

   C. Weaving materials include tree bark, cotton, and silk.

   D. Since weaving is done in so many cultures, it is a worldwide art.

8. What edit is needed to correct sentence 8?

   E. change ***Tale's*** to **Tales**

   F. change ***Tale's*** to **Tales'**

   G. change ***are*** to **is**

   H. change ***numerous*** to **many**

9. Which sentence is irrelevant to the argument in the passage and should be deleted?

   A. sentence 9

   B. sentence 10

   C. sentence 11

   D. sentence 12

10. Which revision of sentence 14 uses the most precise language?

    E. On the other hand, many modern woven patterns tell stories also.

    F. On the other hand, there are modern things that tell stories too.

    G. On the other hand, there are great modern woven patterns, too.

    H. On the other hand, many modern woven patterns somehow tell stories also.

11. Which edit is necessary to correct sentence 16?

    A. delete the word ***not***

    B. change ***being*** to **is**

    C. change ***recurring*** to **repeating**

    D. change ***motif*** to **motive**

Reading Comprehension

Questions 12–57

DIRECTIONS: Read each passage below and answer the questions following it. Base your answers **on information contained only in the passage.** You may reread a passage if you need to. Mark the **best** answer for each question.

The question of why dinosaurs became extinct has puzzled paleontologists since the first dinosaur fossil was found almost two centuries ago. These great reptiles dominated the Earth for almost 160 million years, but mysteriously died out approximately 65 million years ago. Various explanations for this disappearance have been offered, ranging from an epidemic to a sudden, catastrophic drop in temperature. But no theory has yet been conclusively proven.

In 1980, Luis Alvarez, a Nobel Prize-winning physicist, suggested a new explanation for the extinction of dinosaurs. According to Luis Alvarez and his geologist son Walter, a huge meteor crashed into the Earth's surface 65 million years ago, sending up a massive cloud of dust and rock particles. The cloud blocked out sunlight for a period of months or even years, disrupting plant growth and the global food chain. The lack of plants as a food source, coupled with a significant drop in temperature, resulted in the extinction of the dinosaurs.

Alvarez based his theory on an unusual piece of evidence. Geologists discovered that a thin layer of the metal iridium had been deposited all over the world at approximately the time the dinosaurs died out. Since iridium is rarely found on the Earth's surface, Alvarez reasoned that it had either come up from the Earth's core by volcanic action or been deposited by meteorite strikes from space. Because the iridium was deposited evenly in sediments worldwide, Alvarez found the meteorite theory more likely.

But paleontologists—scientists who study dinosaurs—scoffed at the Alvarez extinction theory. Neither Luis nor Walter Alvarez was a paleontologist, yet they claimed to have solved a mystery that had defied the efforts of paleontologists for over a century. Some scientists pointed out that, in order to create worldwide fallout of iridium on the scale suggested by Alvarez, the "doomsday" meteorite would have had to be about 5 miles in diameter, and its impact would have formed a crater perhaps a hundred miles wide. If such a meteorite had hit the Earth, where was the crater?

Finally, a decade after the cosmic extinction theory was first proposed, the crater was found. Lying on the northern edge of Mexico's Yucatan Peninsula, the crater is 110 miles wide. Long buried under sediment, it had actually been discovered in 1981 by oil geologists, but datings of nearby rock samples taken at that time suggested that it was significantly older than 65 million years. New samples of melted rock from the crater itself were recently analyzed by an advanced dating process, however, and were found to be 64.98 million years old. Many scientists now feel that, thanks to the Alvarez theory, the mystery of dinosaur extinction has finally been solved.

12. Which of the following best describes what this passage is about?

E. how recent advances in dating processes explain dinosaur extinction

F. the professional life of Luis Alvarez and his son Walter

G. the theories of paleontologists about why dinosaurs died out

H. the Alvarez theory that a giant meteor caused the extinction of the dinosaurs

13. Alvarez leaned toward the iridium layer being deposited by a meteorite rather than volcanic action because

A. the Yucatan crater provided proof of a meteor strike.
B. it was the only way in which a large enough dust and rock cloud could be generated to disrupt the food chain.
C. iridium was laid down in even sediments worldwide.
D. geologists agreed that iridium is rare on the surface of the earth.

14. The author indicates that opponents of the Alvarez theory criticized both Luis and Walter Alvarez for

E. publishing incomplete research.
F. being personally abrasive.
G. theorizing outside their own fields.
H. misinterpreting experimental data.

15. In the second paragraph, the author mentions the global food chain in order to

A. refute the theory that an epidemic was responsible for dinosaur extinction.
B. illustrate the importance of a clean atmosphere for life on Earth.
C. support the contention that dinosaurs were primarily plant-eaters.
D. explain how the cloud of dust caused the extinction of dinosaurs.

16. According to the author, the discovery of a layer of iridium in geologic sediments (lines 22–24) was considered unusual because

E. iridium had never been detected there before.
F. iridium is normally quite scarce at the Earth's surface.
G. few volcanoes had been active during the era when those sediments accumulated.
H. iridium usually only occurs in meteoric craters.

17. The Alvarez theory would most directly be strengthened by additional information concerning

A. the extraterrestrial origins of the Yucatan crater.
B. the number of dinosaur species indigenous to the Yucatan area.
C. the iridium content of the Yucatan crater.
D. the discovery of a crater of similar age in the Southern Hemisphere.

18. The last paragraph indicates that the Yucatan crater was

E. rejected by the majority of paleontologists.
F. pointed out by Luis and Walter Alvarez.
G. recognized only a decade after the Alvarez theory was proposed.
H. obscured by the lack of iridium at the site.

19. Based on the passage, it can be inferred that

A. the cause of dinosaur extinction has now been conclusively proven.
B. the Alvarez theory has gained proponents.
C. physicists are the scientists most concerned with dinosaur extinction.
D. 1981 dating of rock samples was more accurate than later dating.

Surgeons perform phenomenal feats. They replace clogged coronary arteries with blood vessels from the leg. They reconnect capillaries, tendons, and nerves to reattach severed fingers. They even refashion parts of intestines to create new bladders. But surgeons find it difficult to reconstruct complicated bones like the jawbone or those of the inner ear, and only rarely can they replace large bones lost to disease or injury.

The challenge stems from the nature of bones. Unlike other types of tissue, bones with one normal shape cannot be reworked into other shapes. Nor can doctors move large bones from one part of the body to another without severely disabling a person. Existing treatments for bone defects are all short-term and limited. Surgeons can replace some diseased joints with plastic or metal implants, but artificial hips or knees steadily loosen and must be reconstructed every few years.

Fortunately, surgeons are beginning to overcome these obstacles by creating bone substitutes from, of all things, muscle. The idea of making bones from muscle is not all that strange. Muscle, bone, fat, blood vessels, and bone marrow all develop in human embryos from the same loosely organized tissue. In 1987, scientists isolated a bone-inducing protein called osteogenin from cows. Osteogenin can make undifferentiated human tissue produce cartilage and bone. Few surgeons have used osteogenin because it is hard to control. If sprinkled directly onto a defect, for instance, the entire area might stiffen to bone if a tiny bit fell on the surrounding blood vessels and nerves.

More recently, plastic surgeons have circumvented that snag by prefabricating bones away from the immediate site of a defect. Flaps of animal thigh muscles are removed, placed in osteogenin-coated molds, and implanted in the same animal's abdomen to provide a suitable biologic environment for transforming muscle into bone. Within weeks, the molds yield tiny, perfectly detailed bone segments. So far, surgeons have made bones from muscles in small animals but have not yet tried the process in humans. For one thing, osteogenin is available only in small amounts. Secondly, the safety and effectiveness of the process must first be tested on larger animals.

20. Which of the following best describes the main point of this passage?

E. to outline the drawbacks and limitations of osteogenin

F. to explain the details of a procedure for growing bone tissue

G. to describe how medical procedures are approved for use on humans

H. to summarize recent major advances in reconstructive surgery

21. The fact that bones created from muscle tissue have been implanted in small animals, and large animals may be tested next, implies that

A. osteogenin bone replacement in humans can be tried only after extensive animal testing.

B. success in large animals assures success in human bone transplants.

C. all bones can be regenerated from undifferentiated muscle tissue.

D. cows are unique in producing osteogenin.

22. What is the most likely reason the author uses the word "challenge" in paragraph 2?

E. to argue how hard it is to learn how tissues like muscle, bone, and fat develop in the human embryo

F. to explain the problems of learning how to reconfigure the shapes of bones

G. to emphasize the issues with designing better types of plastic or metal substitutes for bone

H. to reference how difficult it is to find ways of reconstructing or replacing certain bones

23. The author claims that making bone from muscle tissue is not a strange idea because

 A. artificial joint and bone substitutes loosen or wear out over time.
 B. osteogenin-coated molds make it possible to grow bones in any shape desired.
 C. muscle and bone develop from the same undifferentiated tissue in embryos.
 D. large bones usually cannot be replaced at all.

24. According to the passage, all of the following statements about osteogenin are true **except**

 E. current supplies are limited.
 F. tests of its effectiveness have been limited.
 G. its application can be easily controlled.
 H. its safety for human use is undetermined.

25. The passage suggests that osteogenin-coated molds are placed inside the animal's abdomen during the bone growth procedure because

 A. the procedure needs a living environment in order to work properly.
 B. the abdominal muscles are the easiest to transform into bone.
 C. doctors cannot move large bones in the body without disabling the test subject.
 D. osteogenin is available only in small amounts.

26. The author of the passage expects that future experiments concerned with making bone from muscle will

 E. encounter no serious problems.
 F. be limited mostly to smaller animals.
 G. be hindered by surgeons opposed to the process.
 H. involve larger animals and perhaps humans.

27. What is the primary role of paragraph 3 in the structure of the passage?

 A. It explains how osteogenin can be used safely.
 B. It argues that replacing bone is more difficult than other procedures.
 C. It describes how a protein can turn other human tissue into bone.
 D. It indicates that artificial bones and joints do not last long.

Flexible body armor made from interlocking iron or steel rings was known as far back as the ancient Roman era. Used primarily as protection for elite heavy cavalry troops, various forms of so-called "chain mail" armor were relatively rare and expensive at that time, and less practical in many ways than the Roman infantryman's segmented steel breastplate. For centuries after the fall of Imperial Rome, the craft of fashioning mail armor fell into disuse. In the medieval period, however, the techniques were revived and became more popular than ever. By the fourteenth century, entire armies were often outfitted with practical and effective linked-metal armor suits.

The type of armor historians sometimes call "chain mail," but which was called by the people of the time merely "mail," had many advantages for the individual fighting man in the age of steel weapons. It combined the flexibility and suppleness of cloth with the impact-absorbing mass and cut resistance of rigid metal plates. Edged weapons, no matter how sharp, are incapable of slashing or sawing through a well-fashioned mail suit. Moreover, when struck with a blunt object, the links transfer much of the force through the mass of the garment, absorbing a significant amount of impact instead of allowing it to pass to the soft tissues beneath.

The process of manufacturing a mail shirt was very labor-intensive in preindustrial times. Each of the thousands of individual links that made up a full suit, or "harness," had to be individually cut from a coil of hand-drawn wire. The ends of each link were flattened and drilled with tiny holes, and then the link was added into the garment and riveted closed. By varying the pattern of interlocking links, the master mailer was able to grow or shrink the metal garment to "knit" sleeves, mittens, hoods, and other garments. Eventually, as improved stabbing and piercing weapons became more widespread, linked mail armor became obsolete and was relegated to the common foot soldier, the peasant recruit, or just discarded completely. For the nobility, the need for greater protection spurred the development of armors revolving around cleverly articulated rigid steel plates instead. Today, only a few examples of medieval-era linked metal armor suits remain.

28. Which of the following best describes what this passage is about?

E. the relationship between weapon and armor technology in the medieval era

F. the history and technology of medieval mail armor

G. the revival of Roman arms technology in the middle ages

H. the evolution of body armor through the ages

29. What is the most likely reason the author uses the word "master" in paragraph 3?

A. to emphasize that the mailers owned the mail shirts they made

B. to indicate that the makers of mail shirts were elders

C. to define the mailers as teachers

D. to describe the makers of mail shirts as experts

30. According to the passage, all of the following were steps in the process of creating a medieval-era mail suit **except**

E. flattening and drilling holes in the ends of each link.

F. varying the pattern of interlocking links to form contours.

G. cutting the individual links from a coil of wire.

H. suspending the completed mail suit from a leather harness.

31. Which of the following can be inferred from the passage about ancient Roman armor?
    - A. Ancient Roman linked mail armor was less effective than the armor made in the fourteenth century.
    - B. The improved stabbing and piercing weapons used by Rome's military opponents made flexible mail armor impractical for Roman troops.
    - C. Armor made from segmented steel plates was unsuitable for wear by cavalry troops.
    - D. The segmented breastplate was a more practical form of protection for infantry than flexible mail armor.

32. Which of the following is implied by the passage?
    - E. Steel plate armor was more flexible than mail armor.
    - F. Mail armor was less versatile than steel plate armor.
    - G. Steel plate armor was more effective against piercing weapons than mail armor.
    - H. Mail armor required less labor to create than steel plate armor.

33. The last paragraph of the passage suggests that only a few examples of medieval mail armor remain today because
    - A. the complex, multi-step process of creating mail armor has been mostly forgotten.
    - B. new developments in the technology of cutting and slashing weapons made mail obsolete.
    - C. medieval mail armor was less durable than other types of medieval armor.
    - D. mail armor was often discarded in favor of articulated steel plate armor.

34. Which of the following statements is best supported by the passage?
    - E. Linked-metal armor represented a practical solution to a technological need in a particular historical era.
    - F. Military technologies in the era of steel hand weapons succeeded primarily because of the existence of an adequate network of skilled craftsmen to support them.
    - G. The availability of practical mail armor was limited mainly to the fourteenth century.
    - H. Linked-metal armor was of such limited usefulness that it became obsolete as soon as the superior technology of articulated metal plates became widespread.

The following poem, "The Flying Gang" by Andrew Barton Paterson, was first published in 1891.

I served my time, in the days gone by,
In the railway's clash and clang,
And I worked my way to the end, and I
Was the head of the 'Flying Gang.'
'Twas a chosen band that was kept at hand
In case of an urgent need,
Was it south or north we were started forth,
And away at our utmost speed.
If word reached town that a bridge was down,
The imperious summons rang —
'Come out with the pilot engine sharp,
And away with the flying gang.'

Then a piercing scream and a rush of steam
As the engine moved ahead,
With a measured beat by the slum and street
Of the busy town we fled,
By the uplands bright and the homesteads white,
With the rush of the western gale,
And the pilot swayed with the pace we made
As she rocked on the ringing rail.
And the country children clapped their hands
As the engine's echoes rang,
But their elders said: 'There is work ahead
When they send for the flying gang.'

Then across the miles of the saltbush plain
That gleamed with the morning dew,
Where the grasses waved like the ripening grain
The pilot engine flew,
A fiery rush in the open bush
Where the grade marks seemed to fly,
And the order sped on the wires ahead,
The pilot *MUST* go by.
The Governor's special must stand aside,
And the fast express go hang,
Let your orders be that the line is free
For the boys of the flying gang.

35. The description in the first stanza (lines 1–12) helps establish a central idea of the poem by

- **A.** showing how the members of the flying gang were chosen.
- **B.** explaining the occupation of the narrator.
- **C.** comparing the work of the flying gang to the jobs performed by other railroad workers.
- **D.** implying that the narrator was required to travel long distances.

36. Read lines 5–6 from the first stanza.

> **'Twas a chosen band that was kept at hand**
> **In case of an urgent need,**

How do the lines contribute to the development of ideas in the stanza?

- **E.** The lines emphasize the immediacy and importance of the narrator's work.
- **F.** The lines indicate how musicians were an integral part of railroad work.
- **G.** The lines reveal the narrator's intention to persevere in a difficult situation.
- **H.** The lines show how the narrator began his employment at the railroad.

37. Which line from the poem best supports the idea that the flying gang was used for the largest, most important repairs the railroad needed?

- **A.** "I served my time, in the days gone by, In the railway's clash and clang," (lines 1–2)
- **B.** "And I worked my way to the end, and I Was the head of the 'Flying Gang.'" (lines 3–4)
- **C.** "If word reached town that a bridge was down, The imperious summons rang —" (lines 9–10)
- **D.** "'Come out with the pilot engine sharp, And away with the flying gang.'" (lines 11–12)

38. How does the poet develop the speaker's point of view in the second stanza (lines 13–24)?
 E. by describing the beautiful, desolate countryside through which the flying gang travels
 F. by showing how the train thrills the city dwellers as it moves through the town
 G. by illustrating all the preparations necessary before the flying gang can leave
 H. by contrasting the children's cheerful excitement with the adults' recognition of the job ahead

39. In the second stanza, what impact do the phrases "piercing scream," "rush of steam," and "she rocked on the ringing rail" have on the meaning of the poem?
 A. They suggest that the flying gang must urgently respond to its orders.
 B. They imply that the flying gang is very noisy when it works.
 C. They indicate the sounds that one might expect close to a railroad.
 D. They contrast the quiet of the countryside with the noise the train makes as it passes.

40. Which line from the poem best supports the idea that the children do not understand the work of the flying gang?
 E. "Then a piercing scream and a rush of steam As the engine moved ahead," (lines 13–14)
 F. "And the pilot swayed with the pace we made As she rocked on the ringing rail." (lines 19–20)
 G. "And the country children clapped their hands As the engine's echoes rang," (lines 21–22)
 H. "But their elders said: 'There is work ahead When they send for the flying gang.'" (lines 23–24)

41. Read lines 29–30.

 A fiery rush in the open bush
 Where the grade marks seemed to fly,

 Which of the following supports what is implied in these lines?
 A. "By the uplands bright and the homesteads white, With the rush of the western gale," (lines 17–18)
 B. "But their elders said: 'There is work ahead When they send for the flying gang.'" (lines 23–24)
 C. "Then across the miles of the saltbush plain That gleamed with the morning dew," (lines 25–26)
 D. "Let your orders be that the line is free For the boys of the flying gang." (lines 35–36)

42. How does the form of the poem contribute to its meaning?
 E. The use of an equal number of lines in each stanza emphasizes that each stage of the journey is equally important.
 F. The regular rhyme scheme and meter reflect the repetitive sound and motion of the train.
 G. The different stanzas are used to illustrate different aspects of the flying gang and its work.
 H. The first-person narrator is used to emphasize the dangerous conditions faced by the flying gang.

In 1880, Ferdinand de Lesseps attempted to finance the construction of a canal in Panama. This canal would link the Atlantic and Pacific Oceans by cutting across the Isthmus of Panama, the shortest distance between the two oceans. Ultimately, such a project would dramatically shorten many voyages. However, by 1888, de Lesseps had had enough. Some of the problems he faced were logistical in nature. For example, the volume of excavation that the canal would require was beyond the capabilities of the era's technology. Likewise, all materials to be used on the canal had to be imported, and communities to house the canal's workers had to be constructed from scratch.

The Isthmus of Panama also presented many environmental obstacles that had to be overcome before real progress could be made on the canal. The unique geology of the area resulted in frequent landslides, and tropical diseases plagued the workers. In fact, during the six years that the canal was being constructed, between 10,000 and 20,000 workers died from various diseases, most notably malaria and yellow fever. As a result of these hardships, de Lesseps was forced to abandon his project, though his company still retained the right to complete it.

Just after the turn of the century, the United States began taking an active interest in the Panama Canal. The United States had been mulling over the idea of investing in a canal in Nicaragua, but experts managed to convince American leaders that the Panama site was more suited for this type of project. However, de Lesseps's Compagnie Nouvelle refused to sell its contracts and equipment for less than $100 million. The Nicaraguan site was far less expensive. Finally, afraid that the Americans would decide on the Nicaraguan canal, the Compagnie Nouvelle agreed to sell for only $40 million. Now, America had only to convince Panama and Colombia—since at this time, Panama was under Colombian rule—to sell them the land. The Americans approached the Panamanians, who were eager to sell, but the Colombians refused. The Panamanians showed interest in staging a revolution, and the United States supported them by sending a battleship to Panama, which prevented any Colombians from invading.

America's next step was to control the rampant diseases of the area. Colonel William Crawford Gorgas helped to rid the Isthmus of yellow fever and to limit the outbreaks of malaria. Though this was a praiseworthy accomplishment, many of the obstacles that had faced de Lesseps remained. Landslides were still common, so a system of dredges was designed to remove debris from the locks that would be used to move ships across the canal. Once these problems were solved, it still took a decade and the labor of more than 70,000 workers to construct the canal, all at a cost of nearly half a billion dollars. The first ship passed through the canal on August 15, 1914, and throughout the twentieth century, nearly a million vessels have crossed the Isthmus via the Panama Canal.

43. This passage is primarily about

A. Central America in the late 1800s.

B. the Panamanian revolution.

C. the impact of the Panama Canal on international trade.

D. difficulties that were encountered in planning and constructing the Panama Canal.

44. Which word **best** describes Ferdinand de Lesseps?

E. greedy

F. practical

G. idealistic

H. relentless

45. The hardships that de Lesseps experienced in building his canal were

A. political in nature.

B. caused by financial problems.

C. made worse by the Nicaraguan government's stance.

D. mostly logistical and environmental.

46. According to the passage, which characteristic of Nicaragua made it a desirable canal site for the United States?

E. It was cheaper to build the canal in Nicaragua.

F. The Nicaraguan site was the shortest distance between the two oceans.

G. Experts recommended the Nicaraguan site.

H. Nicaraguans had nearly completed the canal already.

47. The United States experienced all of the following difficulties in constructing the Panama Canal **except**

A. the Panamanians did not want to allow the United States to build the canal.

B. diseases were rampant on the Isthmus.

C. the area had frequent landslides.

D. the Colombian government refused to allow the United States to buy the land for the canal.

48. Which of the following is a valid inference, based on the passage?

E. The United States spent much more to build the canal than was expected.

F. The diseases in the area were a major impediment to United States construction of the canal.

G. Ferdinand de Lesseps did not want the United States to have control over the canal.

H. The canal project damaged relations between the United States and Colombia.

49. From information in the passage, it can be inferred that

A. Colombia intended to build its own canal.

B. in de Lesseps' time, technology was adequate to excavate land for the canal.

C. a plan to build a canal in Nicaragua was abandoned because of endemic diseases in the country.

D. the Panamanian revolution was successful in separating Panama from Colombia.

50. What is the primary role of paragraph 3 in the structure of the passage?

E. It describes how the United States controlled diseases and built dredges.

F. It explains how the United States decided to complete the canal.

G. It offers details about why de Lesseps discontinued building the canal.

H. It illustrates how de Lesseps attempted to build a canal in the 1880s.

This passage is from the short story "The Adventure of the Speckled Band" by Sir Arthur Conan Doyle, which was originally published in 1892. In this excerpt, renowned detective Sherlock Holmes and his companion and chronicler Dr. Watson have received an early morning visit from a distraught woman, afraid for her life. The stepdaughter of Dr. Grimesby Roylott, she has witnessed the mysterious death of her sister and been ill-treated by her stepfather, a violent and unpredictable man, who has unexpectedly burst in on Holmes and Watson.

[O]ur door had been suddenly dashed open, and…a huge man had framed himself in the aperture. His costume was a peculiar mixture of the professional and of the agricultural, having a black top-hat, a long frock-coat, and a pair of high gaiters, with a hunting-crop swinging in his hand. So tall was he that his hat actually brushed the cross bar of the doorway, and his breadth seemed to span it across from side to side. A large face, seared with a thousand wrinkles, burned yellow with the sun, and marked with every evil passion, was turned from one to the other of us, while his deep-set, bile-shot eyes, and his high, thin, fleshless nose, gave him somewhat the resemblance to a fierce old bird of prey.

"Which of you is Holmes?" asked this apparition.

"My name, sir; but you have the advantage of me," said my companion quietly.

"I am Dr. Grimesby Roylott, of Stoke Moran."

"Indeed, Doctor," said Holmes blandly. "Pray take a seat."

"I will do nothing of the kind. My stepdaughter has been here. I have traced her. What has she been saying to you?"

"It is a little cold for the time of the year," said Holmes.

"What has she been saying to you?" screamed the old man furiously.

"But I have heard that the crocuses promise well," continued my companion imperturbably.

"Ha! You put me off, do you?" said our new visitor, taking a step forward and shaking his hunting-crop. "I know you, you scoundrel! I have heard of you before. You are Holmes, the meddler."

My friend smiled.

"Holmes, the busybody!"

His smile broadened.

"Holmes, the Scotland Yard Jack-in-office!"

Holmes chuckled heartily. "Your conversation is most entertaining," said he. "When you go out close the door, for there is a decided draught."

"I will go when I have said my say. Don't you dare to meddle with my affairs. I know that Miss Stoner has been here. I traced her! I am a dangerous man to fall foul of! See here." He stepped swiftly forward, seized the poker, and bent it into a curve with his huge brown hands.

"See that you keep yourself out of my grip," he snarled, and hurling the twisted poker into the fireplace he strode out of the room.

"He seems a very amiable person," said Holmes, laughing. "I am not quite so bulky, but if he had remained I might have shown him that my grip was not much more feeble than his own." As he spoke he picked up the steel poker and, with a sudden effort, straightened it out again.

"Fancy his having the insolence to confound me with the official detective force! This incident gives zest to our investigation, however, and I only trust that our little friend will not suffer from her imprudence in allowing this brute to trace her. And now, Watson, we shall order breakfast, and afterwards I shall walk down to Doctors' Commons, where I hope to get some data which may help us in this matter."

It was nearly one o'clock when Sherlock Holmes returned from his excursion. He held in his hand a sheet of blue paper, scrawled over with notes and figures.

"I have seen the will of the deceased wife," said he. "To determine its exact meaning I have been obliged to work out the present prices of the investments with which it is concerned. The total income, which at the time of the wife's death was little short of 1100 pounds, is now, through the fall in agricultural prices, not more than 750 pounds. Each daughter can claim an income of 250 pounds, in case of marriage. It is evident, therefore, that if both girls had married, this beauty would have had a mere pittance, while even one of them would cripple him to a very serious extent. My morning's work has not been wasted, since it has proved that he has the very strongest motives for standing in the way of anything of the sort. And now, Watson, this is too serious for dawdling, especially as the old man is aware that we are interesting ourselves in his affairs; so if you are ready, we shall call a cab and drive to Waterloo. I should be very much obliged if you would slip your revolver into your pocket. An Eley's No. 2 is an excellent argument with gentlemen who can twist steel pokers into knots. That and a tooth-brush are, I think, all that we need."

51. In paragraph 1, how do words like "peculiar," "bile-shot," and "fleshless" contribute to the meaning of the excerpt?

A. They demonstrate how Dr. Roylott is concerned for his stepdaughter.

B. They emphasize how Dr. Roylott is deathly ill.

C. They indicate that Dr. Roylott is about to inflict harm on Holmes.

D. They illustrate that Dr. Roylott is a threat to his stepdaughter.

52. Read paragraph 9.

> **"But I have heard that the crocuses promise well," continued my companion imperturbably.**

How does this exchange of dialogue contribute to the main purpose of the excerpt?

E. It establishes that this is a meeting between two satiric adversaries.

F. It illustrates the calmness of Holmes in the face of possible danger.

G. It highlights the somewhat unseasonable weather.

H. It describes the degree of Dr. Roylott's anger.

53. How does his stepdaughter speaking with Holmes influence Dr. Roylott's behavior?

A. It causes him to threaten Holmes in order to find out what his stepdaughter has said.

B. It causes him to burst into the room and physically assault both Holmes and Dr. Watson.

C. It causes him to furiously deny the accusations that his stepdaughter has made.

D. It causes him to threaten his stepdaughter's life if Holmes doesn't stop investigating.

54. In paragraph 10, how do the words "scoundrel" and "meddler" contribute to the meaning of the excerpt?

  E. They show that Dr. Roylott is a violent, unhinged person who does not care whom he attacks.

  F. They underline that Dr. Roylott knows enough about Holmes to view him as a threat.

  G. They emphasize that Dr. Roylott is taking care not to come across as potentially guilty.

  H. They reveal that Dr. Roylott knows who Holmes is and what he does for a living.

55. How do the various insults in paragraphs 10–14 contribute to the development of the plot?

  A. They reveal that Dr. Roylott will insult every man that he meets.

  B. They bolster the ever-increasing outrage that Holmes feels.

  C. They show that Dr. Roylott is trying and failing to make Holmes afraid of him.

  D. They illustrate that Holmes is calm until his profession is called into question.

56. Read paragraph 17.

> **"See that you keep yourself out of my grip," he snarled, and hurling the twisted poker into the fireplace he strode out of the room.**

Which statement best describes how the paragraph fits into the overall structure of the excerpt?

  E. It introduces a shift from the perspective of Dr. Roylott to that of Dr. Watson.

  F. It emphasizes that neither Dr. Roylott nor his stepdaughter can intimidate Holmes.

  G. It offers a practical explanation for why Holmes is not afraid of Dr. Roylott.

  H. It indicates that the conversation between Holmes and Dr. Roylott is now over.

57. Which sentence from the excerpt best illustrates how Dr. Roylott poses no actual threat to the safety of Holmes?

  A. "'Pray take a seat.'" (paragraph 5)

  B. "Holmes chuckled heartily. 'Your conversation is most entertaining,' said he." (paragraph 15)

  C. "'He seems a very amiable person,' said Holmes, laughing." (paragraph 18)

  D. "'...my grip was not much more feeble than his own.'" (paragraph 18)

IF TIME REMAINS, YOU MAY EITHER REVIEW THE ENGLISH LANGUAGE ARTS QUESTIONS IN PART 1, OR YOU MAY CONTINUE ON TO PART 2, THE MATHEMATICS SECTION.

PART 2 — MATHEMATICS

Suggested Time — 90 Minutes

57 QUESTIONS

IMPORTANT NOTES

(1) Formulas and definitions of mathematical terms and symbols are **not** provided.

(2) Diagrams other than graphs are **not** necessarily drawn to scale. Do not assume any relationship in a diagram unless it is specifically stated or can be figured out from the information given.

(3) Assume that a diagram is in one plane unless the problem specifically states that it is not.

(4) Graphs are drawn to scale. Unless stated otherwise, you can assume relationships according to appearance. For example, (on a graph) lines that appear to be parallel can be assumed to be parallel; likewise for concurrent lines, straight lines, collinear points, right angles, etc.

(5) Reduce all fractions to lowest terms.

GRID-IN PROBLEMS

QUESTIONS 58–62

DIRECTIONS: Solve each problem. On the answer sheet, write your answer in the boxes at the top of the grid. Start on the left side of each grid. Print only one number or symbol in each box. **DO NOT LEAVE A BOX BLANK IN THE MIDDLE OF AN ANSWER.** Under each box, fill in the circle that matches the number or symbol you wrote above. **DO NOT FILL IN A CIRCLE UNDER AN UNUSED BOX.**

58. $3{,}142 + 5{,}975 = ?$

59. What value of m makes the proportion $\frac{3m}{5} = \frac{12}{4}$ true?

60. Sidney is eating lunch at a salad restaurant where you can create your own salad. A base salad (lettuce plus four vegetables) costs $5.49. Each additional vegetable over 4 costs $0.55, and each protein costs $1.09. If Sidney creates a salad with 7 vegetables and 2 proteins, how much does his salad cost?

61. If $2x + 3y = 194$ and $x = 28$, what is the value of y?

62. If $x^2 - 25 = 0$ and $x < 0$, what is the value of x?

Multiple Choice Problems

Questions 63–114

DIRECTIONS: Solve each problem. Select the **best** answer from the choices given. Mark the letter of your answer on the answer sheet. You can do your figuring in the test booklet or on paper provided by the proctor. **DO NOT MAKE ANY MARKS ON YOUR ANSWER SHEET OTHER THAN FILLING IN YOUR ANSWER CHOICES.**

63. Solve for x: $x^3 = 2^6$

A. 1

B. 2

C. 4

D. 16

64. Population of City X, 1984–1988
(in Hundred Thousands)

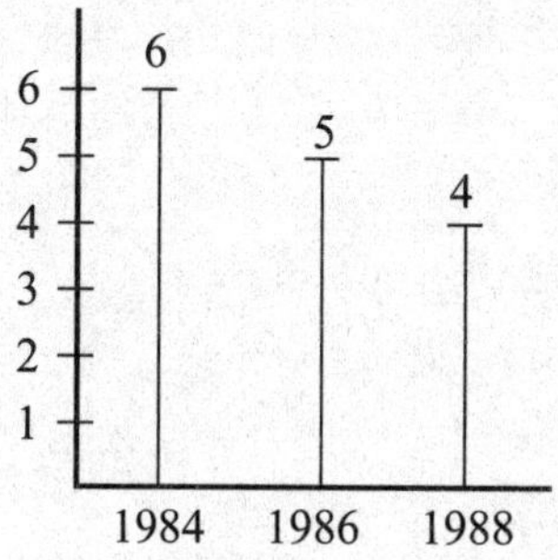

In the graph above, if the percent decrease from the 1986 population to the 1988 population was the same as the percent decrease from the 1988 population to the 1990 population, what was the 1990 population in City X?

E. 350,000

F. 320,000

G. 300,000

H. 280,000

65. If $2(x + y) = 8 + 2y$, then $x =$

A. 1

B. 2

C. 3

D. 4

66.

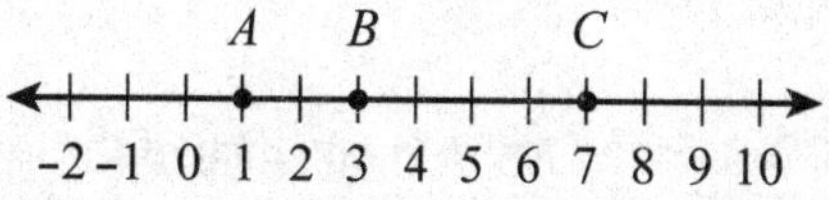

On the number line above, what is the distance from point B to the midpoint of AC?

E. 1

F. 2

G. 3

H. 4

67. A certain machine caps 5 bottles every 2 seconds. At this rate, how many bottles will be capped in 1 minute?

A. 10

B. 75

C. 150

D. 300

68. 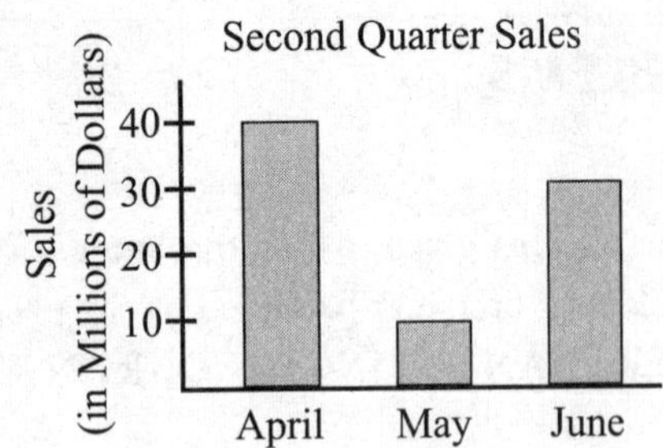

According to the graph above, April sales accounted for approximately what percent of the total second quarter sales?

E. $12\frac{1}{2}\%$

F. 25%

G. $37\frac{1}{2}\%$

H. 50%

69. If $a + b < 5$, and $a - b > 6$, which of the following pairs could be the values of a and b?

A. (1, 3)

B. (3, −2)

C. (4, −2)

D. (4, −3)

70. 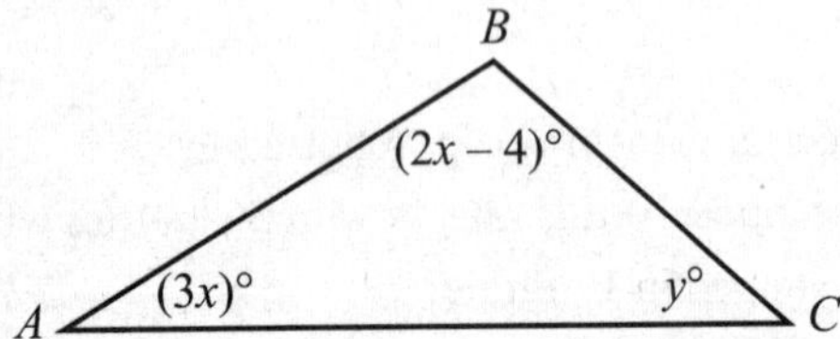

In the triangle above, if the measure of angle B is 60 degrees, then what is the value of y?

E. 24

F. 26

G. 28

H. 30

71. In a certain building, there are 10 floors and the number of rooms on each floor is R. If each room has exactly C chairs, which of the following expresses the total number of chairs in the building?

A. $\frac{10}{RC}$

B. $10RC$

C. $10R + C$

D. $10R + 10C$

72. If a "sump" number is defined as one in which the sum of the digits of the number is greater than the product of the digits of the same number, which of the following is a sump number?

E. 123

F. 222

G. 234

H. 411

73. If 4% of r is 6.2, then 20% of $r =$

A. 25

B. 26

C. 30

D. 31

74. At a certain school, the ratio of teachers to students is 1 to 10. Which of the following could be the total number of teachers and students?

E. 100

F. 121

G. 144

H. 222

75. Points A, B, C, D, E, F, G, and H are all on a straight line in that order. The distance between any two adjacent points is a constant. If the distance between points A and H is 56, what is the distance between points B and E?

A. 16

B. 18

C. 21

D. 24

76.

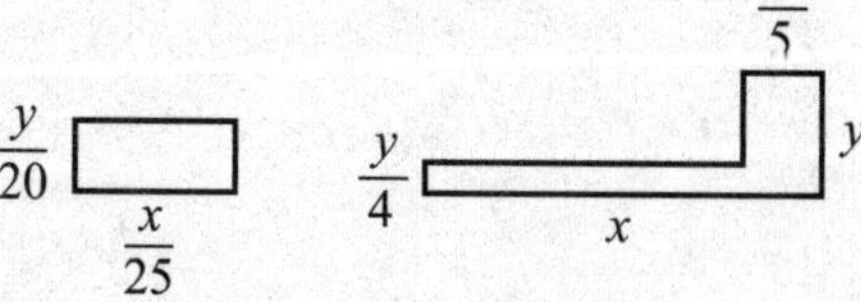

In the figures above, if rectangular tiles are used to completely cover the L-shaped bathroom floor without overlap, how many rectangular tiles are needed?

E. 125

F. 150

G. 175

H. 200

77. At an appliance store, if 63 stereos were sold during a one-month period, which of the following MUST be true?

A. At least one stereo was sold on each day of the month.

B. At least one stereo was sold on either a Monday, Wednesday, or Friday during the month.

C. At least two stereos were sold on each day of the month.

D. At least three stereos were sold on one day of the month.

78. If the ratio of a to b is 4 to 5 and the ratio of a to c is 2 to 7, what is the ratio of c to b?

E. $\frac{35}{8}$

F. $\frac{14}{5}$

G. $\frac{5}{7}$

H. $\frac{8}{35}$

79. If $x(b - c) = y + x$ and $2b = 3c = 7$, then $\frac{y}{x} =$

A. $\frac{1}{7}$

B. $\frac{1}{6}$

C. $\frac{1}{3}$

D. $\frac{5}{7}$

80. What is the greatest number of pieces that can result from slicing a spherical orange with 3 straight cuts?

E. 5

F. 6

G. 7

H. 8

81. The cost of a widget at store A is n dollars. When the store opened on Tuesday, it had $4y$ widgets available for sale. When the store closed on Tuesday, it had sold all of the widgets except for y widgets. What was the total cost of the widgets the store sold, in dollars?

A. ny

B. $2ny$

C. $3ny$

D. $2ny + n$

82.

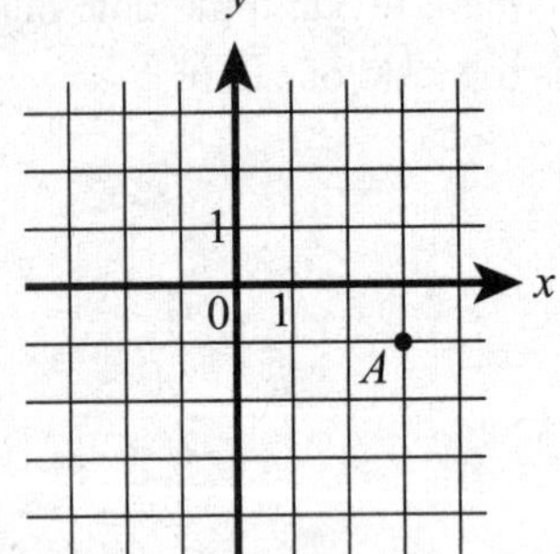

What is the slope of the line connecting point $(-1, 2)$ to point A?

E. $-\frac{3}{4}$

F. $-\frac{1}{2}$

G. $\frac{1}{2}$

H. $\frac{2}{3}$

83. The number $7^5 \times 6^5$ is what fraction of the number $7^4 \times 6^{10}$?

A. $\frac{1}{6^7}$

B. $\frac{1}{6^8}$

C. $\frac{7}{6^5}$

D. $\frac{7}{6^3}$

84. Jung's average (arithmetic mean) on 2 biology quizzes is 7. What should Jung's score on the next quiz be in order to have an average of 8 for the three quizzes?

E. 8

F. 8.5

G. 9

H. 10

85. How many three-digit integers less than 400 are there such that the sum of the hundreds and units digits is equal to the square of the tens' digit?

A. five

B. six

C. seven

D. eight

86. If a rectangle of perimeter 12 has a width that is 2 less than its length, what is its area?

E. 6

F. 8

G. 10

H. 20

87. In a recent survey, 80% of the people polled were registered voters and 75% of the registered voters voted in the last election. What fraction of all those surveyed were registered voters who did not vote in the last election?

A. $\frac{1}{10}$

B. $\frac{1}{5}$

C. $\frac{1}{4}$

D. $\frac{2}{5}$

88. In the 10-digit number, 7,346,285,5_6, the tens digit is missing. If the 10-digit number is a multiple of both 3 and 4, what is the missing digit?

E. 2

F. 3

G. 4

H. 5

89. What is the surface area of a cube with volume 27?

A. 24

B. 27

C. 36

D. 54

90. Education/Career Plans for Centerville High School Graduates

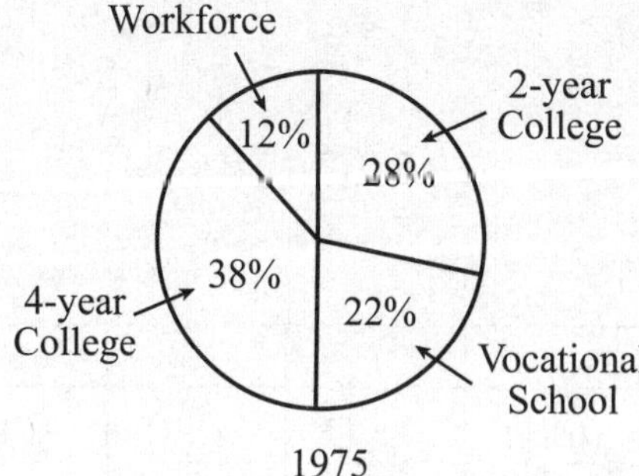

1975
Total Number of Graduates: 600

In 1975, how many graduates from Centerville High School chose either to enter the workforce or to continue their education at a vocational school?

E. 72

F. 132

G. 168

H. 204

91. If n, p, and x are positive integers, and $\frac{n}{p} = \frac{2}{x} + 2$, then $\frac{p}{n} =$

A. $\frac{1}{x+2}$

B. $\frac{2}{x+2}$

C. $\frac{x}{2(x+1)}$

D. $\frac{x}{2} + \frac{1}{2}$

92. A is the sum of the first 50 consecutive multiples of 3, and B is the sum of the first 50 consecutive multiples of 6. What percent of A is B?

E. 50%

F. 75%

G. 100%

H. 200%

93.

Brand of Orange Juice	Number of Respondents who Chose as Favorite
A	61
B	24
C	x
D	y

The table above depicts the results of a survey of 180 people, each of whom tried orange juice from each of brands A, B, C, and D. Each person was asked to select his or her favorite of the four brands and could not select more than one brand. If no brand was the favorite of more than 40 percent of all people, what is the smallest possible value of x?

A. 23

B. 24

C. 31

D. 36

94.

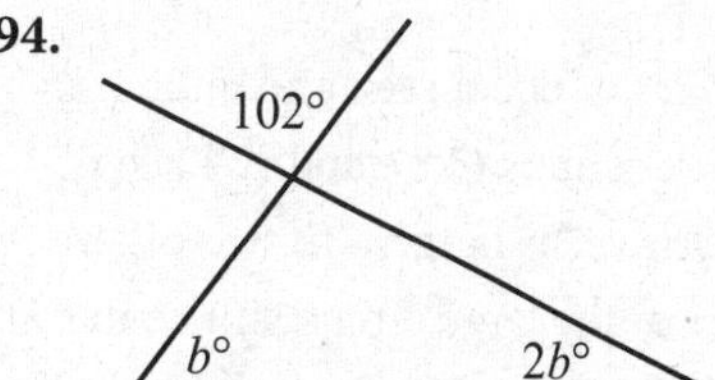

What is the value of b in the figure above?

E. 26

F. 28

G. 30

H. 31

95. 3, 8, 13, 18, 23, 28, 33, 38

From the sequence of numbers above, if a new sequence is created by increasing each odd-valued term by 3 and decreasing each even-valued term by 2, the sum of the terms of this new sequence is how much greater than the sum of the terms of the original sequence?

A. 4

B. 6

C. 8

D. 10

96. If $xyz \neq 0$, then $\frac{x^2y^3z^6}{x^6y^3z^2} =$

E. xyz

F. $\frac{z}{x}$

G. $\frac{z^2}{x^2}$

H. $\frac{z^4}{x^4}$

97.

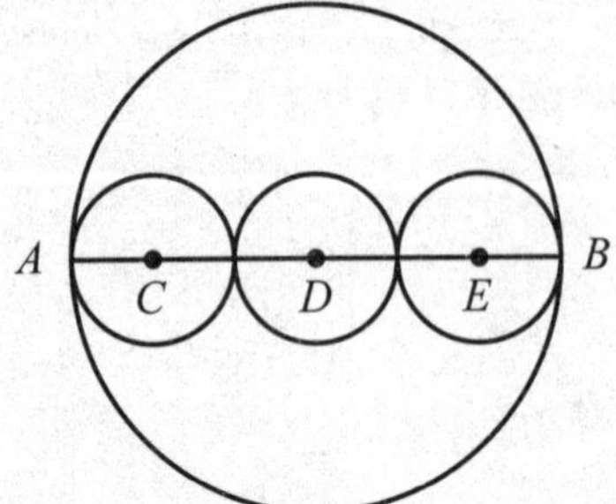

Three small circles of equal area are on line segment AB with centers C, D, and E. Each of the three small circles is tangent to two other circles. The area of the large circle with center D is 900π. What is the circumference of the circle with center C?

A. 5π

B. 10π

C. 20π

D. 40π

98.

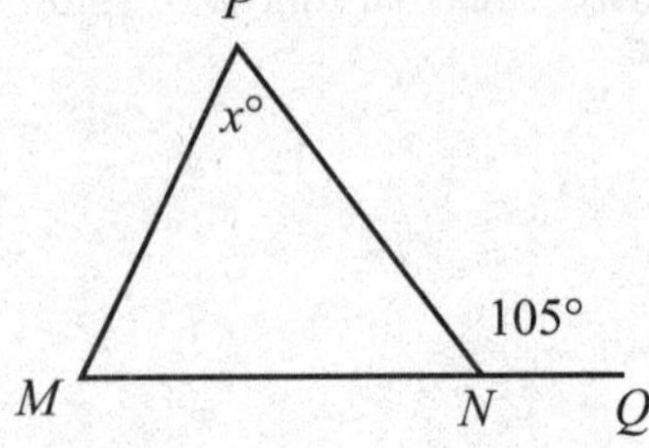

In the figure above, $\overline{MQ}$ is a straight line. If $PM = PN$, what is the value of x?

E. 30

F. 45

G. 60

H. 75

99.

x	0	1	2	3
y	$\frac{(0)(1)}{5}$	$\frac{(1)(4)}{5}$	$\frac{(4)(7)}{5}$	$\frac{(9)(10)}{5}$

Which of the following equations is a description of the relationship between x and y that is consistent with all of the information in the table above?

A. $y = \frac{3x+1}{5}$

B. $y = \frac{x(3x+1)}{5}$

C. $y = \frac{4x}{5}$

D. $y = \frac{x^2(3x+1)}{5}$

100. Set C is made up of a series of consecutive integers whose sum is a positive even number. If the smallest number in the set is -2, what is the least possible number of integers that could be in the set?

E. 4

F. 5

G. 6

H. 8

101.

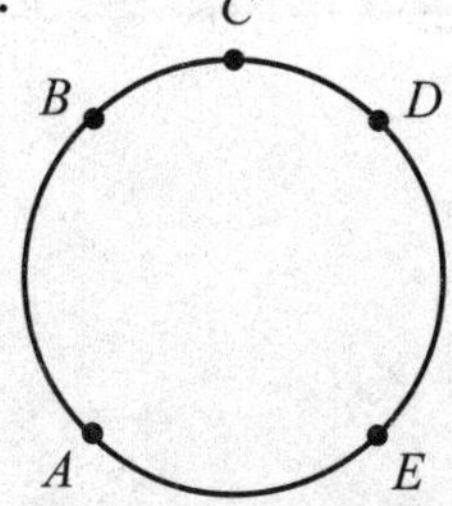

In the figure above, if points A, B, C, D, and E are on the circumference of a circle, what is the total number of different line segments that can be drawn to connect all possible pairs of the points shown?

A. 6

B. 8

C. 10

D. 15

102. If a solution of sugar and water contains 4 ounces of sugar and 16 ounces of water, how many ounces of water would need to evaporate in order to make the ratio of sugar to total solution 2 to 3?

E. 6

F. 7

G. 8

H. 14

103. If $k = 15$, what is $(4k + 30) - (2k + 15)$?

A. 15

B. 30

C. 45

D. 60

104. What is $\frac{4g - 150}{h}$ if $h = 100$ and $g = 300$?

E. 1.5

F. 10.5

G. 105

H. 1,000

105. If $x = 4$ and $y = 6$, what is $\frac{10x^2 - 6y}{\sqrt{x}}$?

A. 4

B. 44

C. 62

D. 114

106. What is $\frac{(3b + 2a) - c}{(b - a)}$ if $a = 10$, $b = 20$, and $c = 30$?

E. 1

F. 2

G. 3

H. 5

107. If $x = 2$, $y = 3$, and $z = 4$, then what is $\left(\frac{4y}{2x}\right)\left(\frac{9z}{3x}\right)$?

A. 6

B. 12

C. 18

D. 36

108. What is $\frac{lm}{lp} + l$ if $l = 24$, $m = 50$, and $p = 10$?

E. 5.1

F. 29

G. 240

H. 1,200

109. If $q = 5$, $r = 10$ and $s = 15$, what is $\frac{(qrs - 4rs)}{(qrs + qr)}$?

A. $\frac{3}{16}$

B. 1

C. $\frac{15}{8}$

D. $\frac{16}{3}$

110. If $x = \frac{1}{4} - \left(\frac{1}{2} - \frac{1}{3}\right)$, what is the value of x?

E. $-\frac{7}{12}$

F. $-\frac{5}{12}$

G. 0

H. $\frac{1}{12}$

111. If $x - \sqrt{2} = \sqrt{8}$, then what is the value of x?

A. $\sqrt{6}$

B. $2\sqrt{2}$

C. $\sqrt{10}$

D. $3\sqrt{2}$

112. If $x = 8 \div \sqrt{2}$, what is the value of x?

E. $\sqrt{2}$

F. $2\sqrt{2}$

G. 4

H. $4\sqrt{2}$

113. Solve for x: $x = \frac{9}{x}$, $x \geq 0$

A. 0

B. 1

C. 3

D. 9

114. If $x = \frac{1}{3}\left(\frac{1}{2} - \frac{1}{8}\right)$, what is the value of x?

E. $-\frac{1}{8}$

F. $\frac{1}{24}$

G. $\frac{1}{12}$

H. $\frac{1}{8}$

THIS IS THE END OF THE TEST. IF TIME REMAINS, YOU MAY CHECK YOUR ANSWERS TO PART 1 AND PART 2. BE SURE THAT THERE ARE NO STRAY MARKS, PARTIALLY FILLED ANSWER CIRCLES, OR INCOMPLETE ERASURES ON YOUR ANSWER SHEET.	STOP

ANSWER KEY

Practice Test 1—English Language Arts

1. A
2. E
3. C
4. H
5. B
6. H
7. A
8. E
9. C
10. E
11. B
12. H
13. C
14. G
15. D
16. F
17. C
18. G
19. B
20. F
21. A
22. H
23. C
24. G
25. A
26. H
27. C
28. F
29. D
30. H
31. D
32. G
33. D
34. E
35. B
36. E
37. C
38. H
39. A
40. H
41. D
42. F
43. D
44. F
45. D
46. E
47. A
48. H
49. D
50. F
51. D
52. F
53. A
54. F
55. C
56. H
57. D

ANSWER KEY

Practice Test 1—Mathematics

58. 9117
59. 5
60. 9.32
61. 46
62. −5
63. C
64. F
65. D
66. E
67. C
68. H
69. D
70. E
71. B
72. H
73. D
74. F
75. D
76. H
77. D
78. F
79. B
80. H
81. C
82. E
83. C
84. H
85. C
86. F
87. B
88. H
89. D
90. H
91. C
92. H
93. A
94. E
95. A
96. H
97. C
98. E
99. D
100. H
101. C
102. H
103. C
104. F
105. C
106. H
107. C
108. F
109. A
110. H
111. D
112. H
113. C
114. H

ANSWERS AND EXPLANATIONS

Part 1—English Language Arts

Revising/Editing Part A

1. A

Category: Knowledge of Language

Getting to the Answer: In sentence 1, the nonessential clause "who teaches college students" is redundant because the sentence uses the word "professor," which does not require additional explanation. **(A)** is correct. The sentences in **(B)**, **(C)**, and **(D)** do not have errors.

2. E

Category: Usage

Getting to the Answer: In sentence 1, the subject "students" is plural, so a plural verb is needed to match. Keep in mind that a verb might not always appear close to its subject due to intervening phrases. The sentence could be revised to read, "they spend." The correct choice is **(E)**. The sentences in **(F)**, **(G)**, and **(H)** use the correct verb tense.

3. C

Category: Usage

Getting to the Answer: Check to see that idioms are paired with the correct prepositions. **(C)** has the correct preposition, "to." **(A)** does not have correct subject-verb agreement. **(B)** makes an unnecessary switch to the past tense. **(D)** includes the wrong preposition, forming an incorrect idiom.

4. H

Category: Usage

Getting to the Answer: Check to see that idioms are matched with the correct prepositions. **(H)** is correct. The revision in **(E)** does not have the correct preposition. **(F)** would make the sentence wordy. **(G)** has the wrong preposition and makes the sentence confusing.

Revising/Editing Part B

5. B

Category: Usage

Getting to the Answer: The sentence discusses the history of weaving, starting with the Neolithic era. Since the rest of the passage is about both traditional and current weaving, it is clear that weaving continues today. Thus the verb should be in the present progressive tense, "has been," **(B)**. **(A)** makes an unnecessary change; "traditionally" and "in the past" say essentially the same thing, and "traditionally" is shorter. **(C)** changes the appropriate past tense to the present. **(D)** changes the meaning of the sentence, saying that weaving began before, not since, Neolithic times.

6. H

Category: Organization, Unity, and Cohesion

Getting to the Answer: Both sentences identify where looms were used, so it's not necessary to separate them. Since concision is important on the SHSAT, look for a revision that connects the sentences logically and concisely. **(H)** is the best revision. **(E)** is unnecessarily wordy. **(F)** not only changes the shorter phrase "By 700 C.E." to "As long ago as the year 700 C.E." but also changes the meaning with the addition of the phrase "parts of." **(G)** incorrectly connects two independent clauses with a comma.

7. A

Category: Topic Development

Getting to the Answer: All the sentences in this paragraph are about the history of weaving and how it is embedded in so many cultures. **(A)** continues this thought, supports sentence 4, and connects well with the following paragraph. **(B)** and **(C)** are off topic and do not belong here. **(D)** is redundant; we already know that weaving is practiced around the world.

8. E

Category: Punctuation

Getting to the Answer: The verb "are" tells you that "tale" is plural, but as written, it is possessive. **(E)** makes the proper revision. **(E)** makes the word a plural possessive, while **(F)** turns the plural verb into singular. **(H)** makes an unnecessary change; the word "numerous" is fine as is.

9. C

Category: Topic Development

Getting to the Answer: To determine which sentence is out of place, read in context and identify the Main Idea. This paragraph is about myths involving weaving, with several examples. Aesop's fable, however, is neither a myth nor about weaving; thus sentence 11, **(C)**, is irrelevant and should be deleted. All other sentences work well with the overall idea.

10. E

Category: Knowledge of Language

Getting to the Answer: Precise language clearly delivers the intended message and can also help the reader create a mental picture. The words "things," **(F)**, "great," **(G)**, and "somehow," **(H)**, are not precise. "Things" is too general, "great" can have a number of different meanings, and "somehow" is meaningless; everything happens somehow. The only precise wording is in **(E)**. Notice also how the words "woven patterns" create a mental picture.

11. B

Category: Usage

Getting to the Answer: The entire paragraph is in the present tense and sentence 16 is a fragment, so the word "being" needs to be changed to "is." **(B)** makes the necessary correction. Deleting the word "not," **(A)**, would change the meaning of the sentence. **(C)** is incorrect because there is no need to change "recurring" to "repeating"; they both mean the same thing. "Motive," **(D)**, the reason for an action, doesn't make sense in the sentence.

Reading Comprehension

Passage Analysis: This passage describes the Alvarez theory that dinosaurs became extinct due to a giant meteor strike. The first paragraph introduces the topic of dinosaur extinction and explains that paleontologists provided many theories of dinosaur extinction, but none had been proven. The second explains how a physicist named Luis Alvarez and his son, a geologist, proposed a new theory: that a meteor strike caused the temperature to drop and plants to die. The third paragraph provides their evidence: a layer of iridium across the whole Earth from the time when the dinosaurs died. Paragraph 4 states that paleontologists refused to believe them because no crater had been found, but Paragraph 5 describes how a crater was found a decade later in Mexico, solving the mystery.

12. H

Category: Global

Getting to the Answer: Overall, the passage explains how Luis Alvarez and his son came up with evidence to support the theory that a giant meteor caused dinosaurs to become extinct: **(H)**. Choice **(E)** is too narrow—the advance in dating processes is only mentioned in the last paragraph. **(F)** is Out of Scope and not supported by the passage. **(G)** is too general and also contradicts the passage: the only theory mentioned is that of Luis and Walter Alvarez, and they are not paleontologists.

13. C

Category: Detail

Getting to the Answer: Alvarez's theory is discussed in paragraph three, where it mentions that the iridium could have been laid down either by a meteor strike or by volcanic action. However, "Because the iridium was deposited evenly in sediments worldwide, Alvarez found the meteorite theory more likely" (lines 28–30). Match this with choice **(C)**. It is true that the Yucatan crater seems to support Alvarez's theory, but it was discovered 10 years after the theory was proposed, thus could not have been a reason for Alvarez's choice of a meteorite strike. Eliminate **(A)**. Since Alvarez initially considered the volcano causation, it must be true that he deemed such an event destructive enough to disrupt the food chain, making **(B)** incorrect. **(D)** is incorrect because there is no

support for geologist agreement, and even if it is true, it doesn't explain why Alvarez preferred the meteorite explanation.

14. G

Category: Detail

Getting to the Answer: Incomplete or improper research, **(E)**, and being abrasive, **(F)**, are not mentioned in the passage. **(H)** may be true, but it is not the reason why the Alvarez team was criticized. Neither Alvarez was a paleontologist; opponents of the Alvarez theory—who were paleontologists—criticized both Luis and Walter for theorizing about the field of paleontology. The answer is **(G)**.

15. D

Category: Inference

Getting to the Answer: The second paragraph explains the Alvarez theory of dinosaur extinction: a huge meteor crash created a cloud of dust, which disrupted plant photosynthesis. That disruption led to a lack of vegetation, which meant a break in the global food chain and thus no food for dinosaurs to eat. The answer is **(D)**.

16. F

Category: Detail

Getting to the Answer: According to paragraph 3, the discovery of the layer of iridium was significant because iridium is rarely found on the Earth's surface; Alvarez theorized that the iridium layer either came from the Earth's core or from a meteorite. The information matches **(F)**.

17. C

Category: Inference

Getting to the Answer: Finding and correctly dating the Yucatan crater helped strengthen the Alvarez theory. Establishing that there was iridium in the crater would even further strengthen the theory. The answer is **(C)**.

18. G

Category: Detail

Getting to the Answer: The Yucatan crater was discovered in 1981 by oil geologists. But it wasn't until a decade after the Alvarez theory was proposed that many scientists recognized the crater for its larger significance—as evidence for the Alvarez theory of dinosaur extinction. The answer is **(G)**.

19. B

Category: Inference

Getting to the Answer: **(A)** can be eliminated from the last sentence of the first paragraph, which states that "no theory has yet been conclusively proven" (line 9). There is no support for **(C)**, and the scientists most often mentioned in the passage are paleontologists. **(D)** is Opposite; the passage implies that the later sampling was more accurate. This leaves **(B)**, which is supported by the last sentence stating that "Many scientists now feel that, thanks to the Alvarez theory, the mystery of dinosaur extinction has finally been solved." Note, however, that "many scientists" and "feel that" are not the same as conclusively proven.

Passage Analysis: This passage describes how materials used to replace bone in living organisms have been made from muscles. The first paragraph explains that replacing bone is much more difficult for surgeons than many other procedures. The second paragraph explains that bones are difficult to work with because they cannot be moved or reshaped, and that artificial bones and joints do not last long. Paragraph 3 describes how a protein called osteogenin can cause other human tissues to turn into bone, but it is hard to control because it can turn unintended body parts into bone. Paragraph 4 describes how osteogenin can be used safely by removing muscle tissue from animals, coating it with osteogenin, putting it in a cast to shape it, and then placing it back in the animal while it develops.

20. F

Category: Global

Getting to the Answer: This is a Science passage, and Science passages tend to explain new discoveries or theories, so predict an answer that includes the right scope: to tell about the method of growing bones from muscle with osteogenin. This prediction matches **(F)**. **(E)** may be tempting until you recognize that the passage talks about benefits as well as limitations. **(G)** is too general and brings up a point that is only mentioned in one part of the passage. **(H)** is too broad; the passage is about bone growth specifically, not all reconstructive surgery.

21. A

Category: Inference

Getting to the Answer: Since the passage states that "surgeons have made bones from muscles in small animals but have not yet tried the process in humans" (lines 41–42), and "the safety and effectiveness of the process must first be tested on larger animals" (lines 44–45), it can be implied that scientists do not perform procedures on humans until they are first tried and evaluated in animals. This matches choice **(A)**. **(B)** and **(C)** are Extreme, with the words "assures success" and "all." The passage states that osteogenin has been isolated in cows, but that doesn't mean that it exists only in cows. It is possible that the protein may also be found in other animals, so **(D)** is incorrect.

22. H

Category: Function

Getting to the Answer: At the end of paragraph 1, the author talks about the difficulty of restructuring and replacing bones. This is what the word "challenge" in paragraph 2 refers back to; **(H)** is correct. The author does not mention tissue development in the human embryo until paragraph 3; **(E)** is incorrect. **(F)** is incorrect because the author indicates that it is impossible to reconfigure the shapes of bones. While the author mentions plastic and metal substitutes for bones, there is no discussion of designing better types; **(G)** is incorrect.

23. C

Category: Detail

Getting to the Answer: Paragraph 3 gives a list of the different types of tissues that develop from the same tissue in embryos to support the point that changing muscle to bone is not unusual. **(C)** is correct. **(A)** and **(D)** are Misused Details from other parts of the passage. **(B)** is true according to the passage, but it is not related to the reason why making bone from muscle is not a strange idea.

24. G

Category: Detail

Getting to the Answer: Information about osteogenin is spread over the last three paragraphs, so scan through the choices, eliminating based on the passage. **(G)**, "its application can be easily controlled," should strike you as false because the author says in paragraph 3 that osteogenin is hard to control—it might turn an entire area to bone if sprinkled on a defect. Since the question is asking for the answer that is *not* true, this is **(G)**.

25. A

Category: Inference

Getting to the Answer: The passage says that placing the mold in the animal's abdomen provides a "suitable biologic environment" for growth—in other words, it needs to be inside something that is alive, choice **(A)**. **(B)** contradicts the passage, which says that thigh muscles are used, not abdominal muscles. **(C)** and **(D)** are Misused Details from other parts of the passage.

26. H

Category: Inference

Getting to the Answer: The stem contains no line reference, but the only place the author talks about future experiments in making bone from muscle is the last paragraph. She says there that surgeons "have not yet tried the process in humans" and that it "must first be tested on larger animals." The author expects, therefore, that future experiments will "involve larger animals and perhaps humans," choice **(H)**. There's no evidence that future experiments will "encounter no serious problems," eliminating **(E)**, or that they will be "hindered by surgeons," choice **(G)**. And despite the fact that all experiments have so far been limited to smaller animals, **(F)**, it's clear that this isn't what the author expects in the future.

27. C

Category: Function

Getting to the Answer: In paragraph 3, the author describes how a protein called osteogenin can turn other human tissue into bone; **(C)** is correct. **(A)** is incorrect because paragraph 4, not paragraph 3, explains how osteogenin can be used safely. Paragraph 1 explains that replacing bone is more difficult than other procedures; **(B)** is incorrect. Finally, **(D)** is incorrect because paragraph 2 indicates that artificial bones and joints do not last long.

Passage Analysis: This passage describes how chain mail was created, how it works, and why it is no longer used. The first paragraph explains that chain mail was used by cavalry (horse) troops in the Roman era and again in the fourteenth century. Paragraph 2 describes how it could deflect sharp weapons and soften blunt strikes. The third paragraph explains that linking each part of the mail was difficult and labor-intensive, and that when better weapons were developed, it stopped being used.

28. F

Category: Global

Getting to the Answer: The passage begins with a history of chain mail armor, goes on to discuss how it works, and then describes why people stopped using it. In other words, the history and functionality of the armor, **(F)**, is the main point of the passage. **(G)** is too narrow, focusing only on one small part of the passage. **(E)** and **(H)** are too broad and focus on topics that are Out of Scope.

29. D

Category: Function

Getting to the Answer: In paragraph 3, the author states that the armor maker "was able to grow or shrink the metal garment to 'knit' sleeves, mittens, hoods, and other garments" (lines 35–36). Such an artisan must have been an expert at making chain mail; **(D)** is correct. **(A)** is incorrect because it is not mentioned in the paragraph. There is no indication that the armor makers were elders or teachers; **(B)** and **(C)** are incorrect.

30. H

Category: Detail

Getting to the Answer: Be careful with "EXCEPT" questions; the incorrect answers will all be found in the passage, while the right answer is the only one that is not found there. **(E)**, **(F)**, and **(G)** are all mentioned in the third paragraph as stages in the creation of a flexible mail armor suit. The answer is **(H)**.

31. D

Category: Inference

Getting to the Answer: The first paragraph tells us that chain mail was "less practical...than the Roman infantryman's segmented steel breastplate." **(D)** is a very close rephrasing of this idea and is the correct answer. **(A)** makes an unsupported comparison between Roman and fourteenth-century armor. **(B)** is a Distortion—the passage implies that "improved stabbing and piercing weapons" capable of defeating flexible mail did not come along until after the medieval period, so this could not be the reason that such armor was impractical for Roman troops. **(C)** is also unsupported—some cavalry may have preferred mail armor, but nowhere in the passage do we have evidence that segmented-plate armor was "unsuitable" for cavalry.

32. G

Category: Inference

Getting to the Answer: The passage implies in paragraph 3 that steel plate armor is more effective against piercing weapons than mail armor: "as improved stabbing and piercing weapons became more widespread, linked mail armor became obsolete.... [T]he need for greater protection spurred the development of armors [with] steel plates instead." The correct answer is **(G)**. **(F)** is contradicted in paragraph 3, which describes how mail could be "knit" in different shapes and sizes. In paragraph 2, "flexibility and suppleness" are described as advantages of mail armor, suggesting that steel plate armor is less flexible and ruling out **(E)**. Paragraph 3 indicates that mail armor was very labor-intensive to create, but does not mention the labor requirements of steel plate armor, so **(H)** is not implied.

33. D

Category: Inference

Getting to the Answer: The last paragraph says that mail armor was relegated (passed down) to the common troops, or just discarded, and the nobility started wearing articulated steel plate armor. It's reasonable to infer that this discarding resulted in fewer surviving examples of mail armor suits; the answer is **(D)**. Present-day awareness of the process, **(A)**, doesn't have any effect on how many medieval suits survived. **(B)** contradicts the passage, which says the obsolescence was due to piercing weapons, and it also isn't relevant to the question. There is no information in the passage about the durability of armors, **(C)**.

34. E

Category: Global

Getting to the Answer: (E) makes a statement that is well supported by the passage. Chain mail was, in fact, "a practical solution to a technological need" during the late medieval era, according to the last sentence in paragraph 1. So, this is the best answer. **(F)** makes too strong a point; we don't have sufficient evidence that a network of skilled craftsmen was always the primary reason for the success of older military technologies. **(G)** is also Extreme; we know that mail armor was widely available in the fourteenth century, but we aren't told that it was hard to get in, say, the thirteenth century. **(H)** incorrectly describes mail armor as being of "limited usefulness" and thus quickly becoming out-of-date; the passage actually says it was quite useful and was used for some time.

Poem Analysis: Written by Australian poet and journalist A. B. Paterson, "The Flying Gang" was first published in 1895. The poem describes a special railroad repair crew that was called out to do the most important, urgent repairs. The first stanza introduces the narrator, a person who, after long employment with the railroad, has become the head of the flying gang, and describes the type of repair the crew is used for. The second stanza describes the start of the flying gang's journey and the excitement generated by the gang's train as it rushes to the repair site. The third stanza continues this theme and emphasizes the importance of the flying gang—even the "fast express" and the "Governor's special" must wait to allow the train carrying the flying gang to pass.

35. B

Category: Global

Getting to the Answer: The first stanza introduces the narrator, who, after long employment with the railroad, is now head of "the flying gang," and goes on to explain what "the flying gang" is: a "chosen band ... kept at hand in case of an urgent need." In other words, "the flying gang" is a select group of workers who were reserved so they would be available for important repairs; **(B)** is correct. **(A)** is incorrect because, while the narrator worked for the railroad for a long time, the poem doesn't explain how the members of the flying gang were chosen. **(C)** is incorrect because the flying gang is described as "chosen," but no comparison is made with the work done by other railroad workers. **(D)** is incorrect because the stanza indicates the flying gang would travel in any direction "south or north" as quickly as it could with "utmost speed," but there is no indication that the gang is traveling long distances.

36. E

Category: Function

Getting to the Answer: The lines describe the flying gang as a select group of workers who were reserved so they would be available for important repairs, making **(E)** correct. **(F)** is incorrect because "band" refers to a group of railroad workers, not musicians. **(G)** is incorrect because the lines are a factual description, not a statement of the narrator's intentions. **(H)** is incorrect because the narrator is head of the flying gang after a long period of employment with the railroad, not at the beginning of his career.

37. C

Category: Inference

Getting to the Answer: The first stanza describes the flying gang as a special team of railroad repair experts. Lines 9–10 describe the type of job they would be called for—a broken bridge, a major repair that would prevent any trains from running—and how they would respond—with utmost speed. This matches **(C)**. **(A)** and **(B)** are incorrect because these lines describe the narrator's experience, not the type of work done by the flying gang. **(D)** is incorrect because it describes how the flying gang responds to the call, not the nature of the job they are called to do.

38. H

Category: Global

Getting to the Answer: Throughout the poem, the narrator is conveying the urgent, difficult work of the flying gang. The second stanza describes the flying gang responding to a call for an urgent repair. A special train,

the pilot engine, is used to speed the flying gang to the location where they are needed. The vivid description in the first part of the stanza reflects the excitement the fast-moving train creates; the children are happily clapping their hands as they see the train go by, but their "elders," the adults, know the flying gang is on its way to serious, urgent work. This matches **(H)**. **(E)** is incorrect because the beauty of the countryside is not the theme of the poem. **(F)** is incorrect because, while the train is exciting, that excitement is not the focus of the poem. **(G)** is incorrect because the preparations of the flying gang are not mentioned in the poem.

39. A

Category: Global

Getting to the Answer: The central theme of the poem is the urgent, important work of the flying gang. The phrases in the question are sharp descriptions that emphasize how quickly the flying gang travels to where they are needed, so **(A)** is correct. **(B)** is incorrect because the noise is made by the pilot engine on the trip to where the flying gang will work, not by the flying gang itself. **(C)** is incorrect because, while the sounds are made by a railroad, their importance to the poem is the urgency they convey. **(D)** is incorrect because, while there is an element of contrast between the noisy train and the calmer countryside, the central focus of the poem is the work of the flying gang.

40. H

Category: Inference

Getting to the Answer: The flying gang is heading to urgent, difficult work, but the children only see the exciting, speeding engine. The adults recognize what is ahead for the flying gang, but the children do not, so **(H)** is correct. **(E)** is incorrect because these lines describe the sounds the engine makes as it starts, and these sounds have nothing to do with the children. **(F)** is incorrect because it describes the motion of the speeding pilot engine, not the children. **(G)** is incorrect because children clapping their hands at a thrilling site does not indicate their misunderstanding. It is the following line that makes the misunderstanding clear.

41. D

Category: Inference

Getting to the Answer: The lines are emphasizing the rapid speed of the pilot engine, "the fiery rush," and the distance it's covering, the "grade marks" flying by, so **(D)** is correct. The pilot engine could only be moving so quickly if there were no other trains in the vicinity. **(A)** is incorrect because the "rush" being described is the winter gale blowing through. **(B)** is incorrect because these lines illustrate the elders' recognition of the hard work ahead, not of the speed at which the train is traveling. **(C)** is incorrect because it is a description of the lovely countryside, not the speed of the train.

42. F

Category: Function

Getting to the Answer: The rhyme and meter make the poem sound like a train, contributing to the theme of the urgency and importance of the work of the flying gang, so **(F)** is correct. **(E)** is incorrect because the poem is not describing different stages of the journey in different stanzas. **(G)** is incorrect because the stanzas are not describing different aspects of the work of the flying gang. **(H)** is incorrect because, although the poem opens with a first-person narrator, the narrator does not emphasize the dangers faced by the flying gang.

Passage Analysis: This passage describes the history of how the Panama Canal was built. This first paragraph describes how de Lesseps tried to build a canal to connect the Pacific and Atlantic Oceans in 1880, but was unable to complete it due to insufficient materials and technology. The second paragraph provides more details about why he quit: landslides and 10,000 to 20,000 deaths from diseases. Paragraph 3 explains how the United States decided to complete the canal around a decade later; de Lesseps asked for $100 million for his equipment and contracts, but settled on $40 million when it looked like the United States would build the canal in Nicaragua. It then explains that Panama was ruled by Colombia, and when Panama wanted to build the canal but Colombia did not, the United States sent a battleship to prevent the Colombians from invading. Paragraph 4 explains how the United States controlled the diseases, built dredges to avoid landslides, but still required a lot of money and labor to complete the canal.

43. D

Category: Global

Getting to the Answer: The passage focuses primarily on the history of the Panama Canal in the period before its construction and consists mainly of a list of the obstacles that builders faced. This outline is summarized in choice **(D)**. **(A)** is too broad. Choices **(B)** and **(C)** are only mentioned in one part of the passage and are therefore too narrow.

44. F

Category: Inference

Getting to the Answer: The only description of Ferdinand de Lesseps that is supported by the passage is **(F)**. The first paragraph explains that he wanted to create the canal to speed up travel from the Atlantic Ocean to the Pacific Ocean, but gave up on the project when it became unrealistic to complete it, indicating a practical approach. Nothing in the passage specifically supports or contradicts **(E)**. An idealistic or relentless person would likely continue to pursue the goal "against all odds," so choices **(G)** and **(H)** are contradicted by the fact that de Lesseps gave up on the project and made the practical decision to sell the equipment to the United States.

45. D

Category: Detail

Getting to the Answer: The first paragraph claims that de Lesseps faced environmental and logistical problems in building the canal. The answer is **(D)**. No political problems are mentioned in connection with de Lesseps, which eliminates **(A)**, and no mention is made of financial problems inhibiting the construction of de Lesseps's canal, which eliminates **(B)**. The Nicaraguan government had no influence on Panama's affairs, **(C)**.

46. E

Category: Detail

Getting to the Answer: **(E)** is the right answer, since the third paragraph of the passage says that the Nicaraguan site was far less expensive than the Panamanian site. **(F)** is Opposite; it is stated in paragraph 1 that the shortest distance between the Atlantic and Pacific Oceans was through Panama. Experts recommended Panama, not Nicaragua, which eliminates **(G)**. **(H)** is incorrect, because there is never any indication that the Nicaraguans had already begun the canal.

47. A

Category: Detail

Getting to the Answer: **(A)** is correct since the passage says that the Panamanians did want to allow the United States to construct the canal, but the Colombians did not. Remember that the question is asking which answer choice was *not* a difficulty. All of the other choices are described as obstacles to the Panama Canal's construction and are therefore not correct.

48. H

Category: Inference

Getting to the Answer: The third paragraph supports the inference in answer **(H)**. The United States positioned a battleship near Panama to prevent Colombian action against a Panamanian revolution and separation from Panama. It is a logical conclusion that this interference in Colombian affairs would damage relations between the United States and Colombia. The United States did spend "nearly half a billion dollars" to build the canal, but the passage does not indicate how this cost compared to the expected cost, so **(E)** is not supported. **(G)** is incorrect because no mention is made of how de Lesseps felt about U.S. control over the canal. Diseases are described in the last paragraph as being one of the obstacles that the United States overcame in the project, so **(F)** is also incorrect.

49. D

Category: Inference

Getting to the Answer: Though not explicitly stated, it must be true that the Panamanian Revolution successfully separated Panama from Colombia. After stating that the United States supported Panama against Colombia, the author writes about "America's next step" (line 46), indicating that the United States had started to build the canal. That would not have happened had Panama still been under Colombian rule. **(D)** is correct. There is no support for **(A)**, and **(B)** is contradicted by information

in the passage. **(C)** is incorrect because the Nicaraguan canal notion was abandoned not because of diseases in the country, but because experts deemed "that the Panama site was more suited for this type of project" (lines 30–31).

50. F

Category: Function

Getting to the Answer: In paragraph 3, the author explains how the United States decided to complete the canal; **(F)** is correct. **(E)** is incorrect because paragraph 4, not paragraph 3, describes how the United States controlled diseases and built dredges. The first and second paragraphs provide details about why de Lesseps discontinued building the canal; **(G)** is incorrect. Finally, **(H)** is incorrect because the first paragraph discusses how de Lesseps attempted to build a canal connecting the Pacific and Atlantic Oceans in the 1880s.

Passage Analysis: The excerpt begins shortly after a visit to Holmes by the distraught daughter of Dr. Grimesby Roylott. Paragraph 1 introduces Dr. Roylott, a large and threatening man who bursts into the room. Paragraphs 2 through 9 follow the prickly introductory conversation between Holmes and Roylott. The confrontation continues in paragraphs 10–15 with a furious Roylott calling Holmes every name he can think of. However, this verbal attack merely amuses Holmes. Paragraph 16 describes how Roylott threatens Holmes with violence by bending a poker. Paragraph 17 has Roylott warning Holmes to stay away. Paragraph 18 describes Holmes's amused reaction to Roylott and reveals Holmes's equal ability to bend an iron poker. Paragraph 19 features Holmes's opinion of the encounter with Roylott. Paragraph 20 describes Holmes's return from his visit to Doctors' Commons. Paragraph 21 explains the details of the wife's will and Holmes's plans to go to Waterloo.

51. D

Category: Detail

Getting to the Answer: In paragraph 1, the words "peculiar," "bile-shot," and "fleshless" help illustrate that Dr. Roylott is a threat to his stepdaughter. They paint a picture of an ugly, angry, unlikable person. Thus, **(D)** is correct and **(A)** is incorrect. While the words make for a visually unfavorable description of Dr. Roylott, they do not present the case that he is gravely ill; **(B)** is incorrect. While the physical description of Dr. Roylott presents him as an angry, evil person, his attempts to threaten Holmes come later in the story; **(C)** is incorrect.

52. F

Category: Global

Getting to the Answer: The exchange in paragraph 9 illustrates how Holmes maintains his calm in the face of being verbally threatened by Dr. Roylott; **(F)** is correct. Although Holmes is using wit to dismiss Dr. Roylott, that approach is not returned. Dr. Roylott shouts at Holmes. So, **(E)** is incorrect. That Holmes is discussing the weather and its effects on gardening is unimportant. Content aside, he is trying to dismiss Dr. Roylott's angry threats by treating this as an ordinary, everyday conversation; **(G)** is incorrect. Dr. Roylott's anger is not discussed in paragraph 9. The reaction of Holmes to that anger is touched upon, making **(H)** incorrect.

53. A

Category: Detail

Getting to the Answer: In response to learning that his stepdaughter has met with a famous detective, Dr. Roylott attempts to intimidate Holmes and then briefly tries to learn what his stepdaughter said to him; **(A)** is correct. While Dr. Roylott does burst into the room, he merely threatens Holmes and Dr. Watson. He does not physically attack them; **(B)** is incorrect. While Dr. Roylott attempts to learn what his stepdaughter has said to Holmes, Roylott does not deny anything; **(C)** is incorrect. Although he threatens Holmes if the detective does not stop his investigation, Dr. Roylott does not threaten his stepdaughter's life; **(D)** is incorrect.

54. F

Category: Detail

Getting to the Answer: In paragraph 10, words like "scoundrel" and "meddler" underline that Dr. Roylott knows that Holmes is a talented detective who could unearth the wrongs he has committed toward his stepdaughter. Thus, **(F)** is correct, and **(H)** is incorrect because it references only one of those things. While Dr. Roylott is violent, he is not totally unhinged. He does not physically attack Holmes or Dr. Watson. He merely threatens to do so; **(E)** is incorrect. Although Dr. Roylott is not taking care to come across as an innocent party, that is not how words like "scoundrel" and "meddler" contribute to the meaning of the excerpt. Instead, they reveal to the reader that Dr. Roylott has knowledge of Holmes's professional background; **(G)** is incorrect.

55. C

Category: Global

Getting to the Answer: The various insults show that Dr. Roylott is trying and failing to make Holmes afraid of him. Despite Dr. Roylott's repeated hounding, Holmes projects a calm face. Thus, **(C)** is correct. There is no evidence that Dr. Roylott insults every man that he meets. Indeed, his argument with Holmes is rooted in the fact that his stepdaughter has been speaking with Holmes; **(A)** is incorrect. Holmes keeps his calm regardless of what Dr. Roylott says or does; **(B)** and **(D)** are incorrect.

56. H

Category: Function

Getting to the Answer: In terms of the excerpt's structure, paragraph 17 serves to indicate that the conversation between Holmes and Dr. Roylott is over. Thus, **(H)** is correct. The excerpt is told entirely from the perspective of Dr. Watson; **(E)** is incorrect. There is nothing in the excerpt to suggest that Dr. Roylott and his stepdaughter are working together; **(F)** is incorrect. Although paragraph 17 has Dr. Roylott twist the fireplace poker, this section itself does not provide the practical explanation for why Holmes is not afraid of Dr. Roylott; **(G)** is incorrect. That comes in the next paragraph, when Holmes picks up the solid metal poker and straightens it out.

57. D

Category: Function

Getting to the Answer: Holmes revealing that "my grip was not much more feeble than his own" (paragraph 18) shows that he and Dr. Roylott would bring equal levels of physical strength to any fight. Thus, **(D)** is correct. While Holmes keeps a calm face when dealing with Dr. Roylott, the reader does not know if Holmes is merely bluffing or not until he unbends the poker. Since **(A)** and **(B)** occur before Holmes unbends the poker, they are incorrect. Likewise, "He seems a very amiable person" could be another instance of Holmes keeping his calm. It is only after that point that he picks up the twisted poker and unbends it. So, **(C)** is incorrect.

Part 2—Mathematics

58. 9117

Subject: Arithmetic

Getting to the Answer: Simply add these two numbers together, being sure to carry 1s when necessary. 3,142 + 5,975 = 9,117, so grid in **9117**.

59. 5

Subject: Algebra

Getting to the Answer: As with any proportion, cross-multiply and isolate the variable.

$$\frac{3m}{5} = \frac{12}{4}$$
$$12m = 60$$
$$m = 5$$

Grid in **5**.

60. 9.32

Subject: Arithmetic

Getting to the Answer: A salad with up to 4 vegetables costs $5.49. Each additional vegetable over 4 costs $0.55, so the 3 extra vegetables cost 3($0.55) = $1.65. 2 proteins cost 2($1.09) = $2.18. Thus, Sidney's salad costs $5.49 + $1.65 + $2.18 = $9.32. Grid in **9.32**.

61. 46

Subject: Algebra

Getting to the Answer: Start by substituting 28 in for x. This gives the equation $56 + 3y = 194$. From here, solve the equation for y by subtracting 46 from both sides and dividing by 3:

$$56 + 3y = 194$$
$$3y = 138$$
$$y = 46$$

Grid in **46**.

62. −5

Subject: Algebra

Getting to the Answer: Start by isolating the variable. Adding 25 to both sides will accomplish this:

$$x^2 - 25 = 0$$
$$x^2 = 25$$
$$x = \pm 5$$

Because x is negative, grid in **−5**.

63. C

Subject: Algebra

Getting to the Answer:

$$x^3 = 2^6$$
$$\left(x^3\right)^{\frac{1}{3}} = \left(2^6\right)^{\frac{1}{3}} \quad \text{Take the cube root of both sides.}$$
$$x = 2^{\frac{6}{3}} \quad \text{Divide the exponents.}$$
$$x = 2^2$$
$$x = 4, \textbf{(C)}$$

64. F

Subject: Algebra

Getting to the Answer: For this question, you have to know not only how to read graphs but how to find a percent decrease. The population in 1986 is 500,000, since the bar above 1986 reaches to 5 on the graph and the graph is in units of 100,000. The population in 1988 is 400,000. What's the percent decrease in population if it goes from 500,000 to 400,000? It works out like this:

$$\left(\frac{500{,}000 - 400{,}000}{500{,}000}\right) \times 100\% = \frac{100{,}000}{500{,}000} \times 100\%$$
$$= \frac{1}{5} \times 100\% = 20\%$$

If the percent decrease in population from 1988 to 1990 is the same as the percent decrease from 1986 to 1988, then from 1988 to 1990, the population also decreased by 20%. 20% of the 1988 population is 20% of 400,000, or 80,000, so the 1990 population is 400,000 − 80,000 = 320,000, **(F)**.

65. D

Subject: Algebra

Getting to the Answer: You want the value of x. Begin by distributing the 2 over the terms inside the parentheses on the left side of the equation. This gives you $2x + 2y = 8 + 2y$. Subtracting $2y$ from both sides results in $2x = 8$. Dividing both sides by 2 gives you $x = 4$, **(D)**.

66. E

Subject: Geometry

Getting to the Answer: Since point A is at 1 on the number line and point C is on 7, the distance between them is $7 - 1$, or 6. Half the distance from A to C is half of 6, or 3, and 3 units from either point A or point C is 4, since $1 + 3 = 4$ and $7 - 3 = 4$. Therefore, the point at 4 on the number line is the midpoint of AC, since a midpoint by definition divides a line in half. Point B is at 3, and the midpoint of AC is at 4, so the distance between them is 1, answer choice **(E)**.

67. C

Subject: Arithmetic

Getting to the Answer: The machine caps 5 bottles every 2 seconds, and we want to know how many bottles it caps in 1 minute, or 60 seconds. Multiplying 2 seconds by 30 gives you 60 seconds. If the machine caps 5 bottles in 2 seconds, how many bottles does it cap in 30×2 seconds? Multiply by the same factor of 30 to get $30 \times 5 = 150$ bottles, **(C)**.

68. H

Subject: Algebra

Getting to the Answer: The graph shows you the sales of all the toys for each month of the second quarter of a certain year, consisting of April, May, and June. If you look at the sales for those 3 months, you'll see that the bar for April goes up to 40, the bar for May goes up to 10, and the bar for June goes up to 30. The title on the vertical axis says "Sales (in millions of dollars)" so that's what those numbers represent: $40 million in sales for April, $10 million for May, and $30 million for June. $40 + 10 + 30 = 80$ million dollars total in sales for the 2nd quarter. The total sales were $80 million and the April sales were $40 million, and you want to know what percent of the total the April sales were. Since it says "of the total," the total, or $80 million, is the whole and the $40 million is the part, so using the formula PERCENT × WHOLE = PART you get PERCENT × 80 = 40, or PERCENT $= \frac{40}{80} = \frac{1}{2} = 50\%$, **(H)**.

69. D

Subject: Algebra

Getting to the Answer: The easiest way to do this problem is just to Backsolve. Since each pair of numbers in the answer choices represents possible values of a and b, just add up each a and b to see if $a + b < 5$, and subtract each b from each a to see if $a - b > 6$. If you do this, you'll find that in all 5 cases $a + b < 5$, but in only 1 case, **(D)**, is $a - b > 6$. In **(D)**, $a + b = 4 + (-3) = 1$ and $a - b = 4 - (-3) = 7$. Therefore, the answer is **(D)**.

If you think about the properties of negative and positive numbers (drawing a number line can help), you'll probably realize that the only way $a - b$ could be larger than $a + b$ is if b is a negative number, but that would only eliminate **(A)**. In some problems, your knowledge of math only helps you a little bit. In those cases, use the answer choices to solve the problem.

70. E

Subject: Geometry

Getting to the Answer: In the figure, angle B is labeled $(2x - 4)°$, and in the question stem, you're told that angle B measures 60 degrees. So, $2x - 4 = 60$, and $x = 32$. That means that angle A, which is labeled $(3x)°$, must measure 3×32, or 96°. Since the 3 angles of a triangle must add up to 180°, $60° + 96° + y° = 180°$, and $y = 24$, **(E)**.

71. B

Subject: Algebra

Getting to the Answer: This one is easier if you pick numbers for C and R. Suppose R is 2. Then there would be 2 rooms on each floor, and since there are 10 floors in the building, there would be 2×10 or 20 rooms altogether. If $C = 3$, then there are 3 chairs in each room. Since there are 20 rooms and 3 chairs per room there are $20 \times 3 = 60$ chairs altogether. Which answer choices are 60 when R is 2 and C is 3? Only $10RC$, **(B)**.

Alternatively, you don't have to pick numbers here if you think about the units of each variable. There are 10 floors, R rooms per floor, and C chairs per room. If you multiply 10 floors × R rooms/floor, the unit "floors" will cancel out, leaving you with $10R$ rooms, and if you multiply $10R$ rooms × C chairs/room, the unit "rooms" will cancel out, leaving $10RC$ chairs in the building. Again, this is answer choice **(B)**.

72. H

Subject: Algebra

Getting to the Answer: Here you have a strange word, "sump," which describes a number that has a certain relationship between the sum and the product of its digits. To solve this one, just find the sum and the product of the digits for each answer choice. You're told that for a sump number the sum of the digits should be greater than the product. **(H)**, 411, has a sum of 6 and a product of 4, so that's the one you're looking for. Be careful with answer **(E)**. The sum and product of the digits 1, 2, and 3 are both 6. However, a sump number requires that the sum be greater than, not equal to, the product. The answer is **(H)**.

73. D

Subject: Algebra

Getting to the Answer: You're given 4% of a number and you have to find 20% of that same number. 4% of r is just a certain fraction, $\frac{4}{100}$ to be exact, times r, and 20% of r is just $\frac{20}{100} \times r$. That means that 20% of r is 5 times as great as 4% of r, since $\frac{4}{100} \times 5$ is $\frac{20}{100}$. Since 4% of r is 6.2, then 20% of r must be 5×6.2, or 31, **(D)**. You could also have figured out the value of r and then found 20% of that value, but this takes a bit longer. 4% of r is the same as 4% $\times$ r, or $0.04r$. If $0.04r = 6.2$, then $r = \frac{6.2}{0.04} = 155$, and 20% of 155 is $0.2(155) = 31$, **(D)** again.

74. F

Subject: Arithmetic

Getting to the Answer: The ratio of teachers to students is 1 to 10, so there might be only 1 teacher and 10 students, or there might be 50 teachers and 500 students, or just about any number of teachers and students that are in the ratio 1 to 10. That means that the teachers and the students can be divided into groups of 11: one teacher and 10 students in each group. Think of it as a school with a large number of classrooms, all with 1 teacher and 10 students, for a total of 11 people in each room. So, the total number of teachers and students in the school must be a multiple of 11. If you look at the answer choices, you'll notice that 121, **(F)** is the only multiple of 11, so **(F)** must be correct.

75. D

Subject: Geometry

Getting to the Answer: Each of the 7 segments *AB*, *BC*, *CD*, *DE*, *EF*, *FG*, and *GH* has the same length. These 7 segments make up segment *AH*. Since the length of *AH* is 56, the length of each of the 7 small segments is $56 \div 7$, or 8. The distance between points *B* and *E* is the sum of the lengths of the 3 equal segments *BC*, *CD*, and *DE*, so the distance between points *B* and *E* is 3×8, or 24, **(D)**.

76. H

Subject: Geometry

Getting to the Answer: To figure out how many tiles are needed, you must break up the L-shaped floor into sections. This will allow you to work with rectangular areas instead of an odd shape. Break the room up like this:

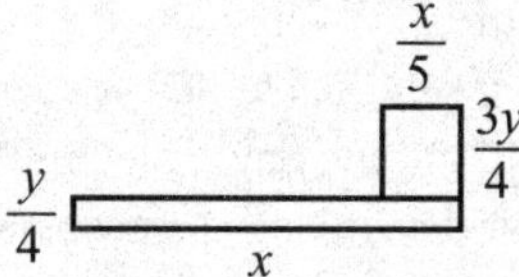

Now, you must find how many tiles are needed to cover each rectangle. Since you have the dimensions of each tile in terms of x and y, you can figure out how many tiles are needed by Picking Numbers for x and y. To make life easier, use $x = 25$ and $y = 20$. Now, calculate the dimensions of the tile and of the room and re-label the diagram:

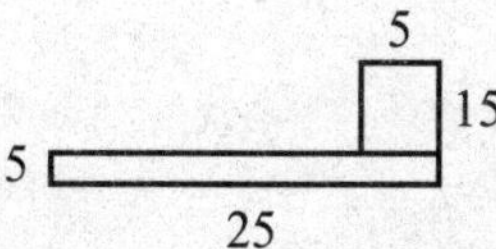

Now the tile is 1 by 1 and the room's two areas are 5 by 25 and 15 by 5. Find the areas of the 2 sections of the floor, add them together to get the total area of the bathroom floor, and, since the area of the tile is 1, you have your answer:

$$\begin{aligned} \text{Area} &= (5 \times 25) + (15 \times 5) \\ &= 125 + 75 \\ &= 200 \end{aligned}$$

You would normally divide this number by the area of one tile, but since the area of the tile is 1, then 200 divided by 1 = 200. The answer is **(H)**.

77. D

Subject: Arithmetic

Getting to the Answer: This is much more of a Logic problem than a math question, so you have to think it through carefully. Since you're asked which answer choice must be true, one way to do it is to go look at each answer choice and try to find a possible situation in which that choice is not true.

Start with **(A)**, which says that at least one stereo was sold on each day of the month. That's not necessarily true; maybe all 63 stereos were sold on one day and none the rest of the month. Cross out **(A)**. Move on to **(B)**. Do you know if a stereo was sold on a Monday, a Wednesday, or a Friday? What if all 63 were sold on a particular Tuesday? So, **(B)** is not necessarily true. The unlikely scenario of all 63 stereos being sold on one particular day is enough to eliminate **(C)** as well. This leaves you with only **(D)**, which must be correct.

Just to be sure, take a look at **(D)**. It says that at least 3 stereos were sold on one day. If all 63 were sold on one day, then on that day at least 3 stereos were sold. If the sale of stereos was more evenly distributed, would there necessarily be a day in which 3 or more stereos were sold? Since a month has at most 31 days, if 2 or fewer stereos were sold each day of the month, then at most only 62 stereos would have been sold in that month. In order for 63 stereos to be sold, there has to be at least one day in which 3 or more stereos were sold, so **(D)** is correct.

78. F

Subject: Arithmetic

Getting to the Answer: The first step to solving this problem is getting both ratios into a form that has the same value for a. If $a{:}b = 4{:}5$ and $a{:}c = 2{:}7$, you can make both values of a 4 by multiplying the entire $a{:}c$ ratio by 2. The new form of the ratio becomes 4:14. Now, you can compare b and c. Be careful, however, because the question asks for $c{:}b$, not the other way around. Therefore, the ratio is 14:5 or $\frac{14}{5}$, **(F)**.

79. B

Subject: Algebra

Getting to the Answer: Use algebra to find the solution to this problem. First, find the numerical values for b and c. Since $2b = 7$, divide both sides of the equation by 2 and you get $b = \frac{7}{2}$. Do the same thing with $3c = 7$, giving you $c = \frac{7}{3}$. Now, plug these values into the first equation:

$$x\left(\frac{7}{2}-\frac{7}{3}\right) = y + x$$

Now, solve for $\frac{y}{x}$:

$$x\left(\frac{7}{2}-\frac{7}{3}\right) - x = y$$

$$x\left(\frac{7}{2}-\frac{7}{3}-1\right) = y$$

$$x\left(\frac{21}{6}-\frac{14}{6}-\frac{6}{6}\right) = y$$

$$\frac{21}{6}-\frac{14}{6}-\frac{6}{6} = \frac{y}{x}$$

$$\frac{1}{6} = \frac{y}{x}, \textbf{(B)}$$

80. H

Subject: Geometry

Getting to the Answer: This one is hard to draw. Think logically and try to visualize the orange. The first cut breaks the orange into 2 pieces. If you cut the orange so that you cut the 2 halves into equal pieces, you have 4 equal quarters. Now, rotate the orange so that you can make another cut that is perpendicular to the first two. Your next cut can cut the quarters into 8 equal pieces. Therefore, 3 cuts can yield a maximum of 8 pieces, **(H)**.

81. C

Subject: Algebra

Getting to the Answer: Pick Numbers to solve this question. Suppose that n is 5 and y is 10. Then the cost of a widget is 5 dollars. At the start of the day, the store had $4y$, which is $4(10) = 40$ widgets. When the store closed, it had 10 widgets. The store must have sold $40 - 10 = 30$ widgets. The total cost of the widgets was

(\$5)(30) = \$150. Now, substitute 5 for n and 10 for y into each answer choice, and eliminate those that don't equal 150.

(A) $ny = 5(10) = 50$. Eliminate.

(B) $2ny = 2(5)(10) = 100$. Eliminate.

(C) $3ny = 3(5)(10) = 150$.

(D) $2ny + n = 2(5)(10) + 5 = 105$. Eliminate.

Now that all incorrect answer choices have been eliminated, we know that **(C)** must be correct.

82. E

Subject: Algebra

Getting to the Answer: The coordinates of point A are $(3, -1)$. Use the slope formula and the two given points to find the slope. The slope of the line containing the points $(-1, 2)$ and $(3, -1)$ is $\frac{2-(-1)}{-1-3} = \frac{3}{-4} = -\frac{3}{4}$, or **(E)**.

83. C

Subject: Arithmetic

Getting to the Answer: To solve this question, use the Law of Exponents. When you divide powers with the same base, subtract the exponents in the appropriate order and keep the same base.

Algebraically, if b is not 0, then $\frac{b^x}{b^y} = b^{x-y}$. The fraction that $7^5 \times 6^5$ is of $7^4 \times 6^{10}$ is:

$$\frac{7^5 \times 6^5}{7^4 \times 6^{10}} =$$

$$\frac{7^5}{7^4} \times \frac{6^5}{6^{10}} =$$

$$\left(7^{5-4}\right) \times \left(6^{5-10}\right) =$$

$$7^1 \times \left(6^{5-10}\right) =$$

$$7^1 \times 6^{-5} = \frac{7}{6^5}, \text{ or } \textbf{(C)}.$$

84. H

Subject: Algebra

$$\text{Average score} = \frac{\text{Sum of Scores}}{\text{Number of Quizzes}}$$

Getting to the Answer: If Jung wishes to get an average score of 8 on 3 quizzes, then $8 = \frac{\text{Sum of Scores}}{3}$ and Sum of Scores $= 8 \times 3 = 24$.

So, he needs to score a total of 24 points on all 3 tests. Since he had an average score of 7 on the first two quizzes $7 = \frac{\text{Sum of Scores on 2 Quizzes}}{2}$. Sum of scores on 2 quizzes = 7 times 2 = 14. If he scored a total of 14 points on the first 2 quizzes, and he needs to score a total of 24 points on all three quizzes, then he must score $24 - 14 = 10$ points on the third quiz. The answer is **(H)**.

85. C

Subject: Arithmetic

Getting to the Answer: The first thing you need to do is find what the tens digit can be. You are given that the sum of the other two digits must equal the square of the tens digit and that the hundreds digit must be 3, 2, or 1. Therefore, the greatest possible sum of the hundreds and ones digits is $3 + 9$, or 12. The square of the tens digit must be 12 or less, and the only perfect squares less than 12 are 0, 1, 4, and 9. Since there is no way the hundreds digit can equal 0, you can eliminate 0 as an option. The tens digit can either be $\sqrt{1} = 1$, $\sqrt{4} = 2$, or $\sqrt{9} = 3$. Now, count the combinations of numbers between 100 and 400 in which the sum of the hundreds digit and the units digit equals 1, 4, or 9. The easiest way to do this is to list the possibilities:

110, 123, 222, 321, 138, 237, 336

There are seven possibilities, **(C)**.

86. F

Subject: Geometry

Getting to the Answer: If a rectangle has a perimeter of 12 then $2(W + \ell) = 12$, where W is the width of the rectangle and ℓ is its length. If $2(W + \ell) = 12$, then $W + \ell = 6$. If the width is 2 less than the length, then $W = \ell - 2$. You can plug $\ell - 2$ for W into the equation

$W + \ell = 6$, so $W + \ell = 6$ becomes $(\ell - 2) + \ell = 6$, and so $2\ell - 2 = 6$, $2\ell = 8$, and $\ell = 4$. If the length is 4, then the width, which is 2 less, must be 2. The area of a rectangle with length 4 and width 2 is $4 \times 2 = 8$, **(F)**.

87. B

Subject: Arithmetic

Getting to the Answer: Whenever you have a percent problem that doesn't give you a definite amount and asks you a question like "What fraction of the total...?" you should pick a number for the total. Since you're dealing with percents here, and will be converting the percents to fractions, a good number for the total is 100. So, say that 100 people were polled. 80% of the 100 people were registered voters, so 80 people were registered voters. 75% of the registered voters voted in the last election, so 75% × 80, or 60 people, voted in the last election. If 60 of the 80 registered voters actually voted in the last election, then $80 - 60 = 20$ of the registered voters didn't vote in the last election. The fraction of the people surveyed who were registered but didn't vote is $\frac{20}{100}$, or $\frac{1}{5}$, answer choice **(B)**.

88. H

Subject: Arithmetic

Getting to the Answer: This question tests your knowledge of divisibility rules. In order for a number to be divisible by 3, the sum of its digits must be divisible by 3. In order for a number to be divisible by 4, the last two digits of the number must be divisible by 4. So, the sum of the digits of 7,346,285,5_6 must be a multiple of 3. $7 + 3 + 4 + 6 + 2 + 8 + 5 + 5 + x + 6 = x + 46$. We now know that the missing digit plus 46 is a multiple of 3. The nearest multiple of 3 is 48, which is 2 more than 46. That means that the missing digit could be 2. 51 and 54 are also multiples of 3, so the missing digit could also be 5 or 8 respectively. 8 is not an answer choice, and 26 is not a multiple of 4, so the correct answer is 5, **(H)**. Note that if the tens digit were a 5, the last two digits of the number would be 56, a multiple of 4. So, the number is a multiple of 4, and **(H)** is correct. If you can't remember the divisibility rules, you can always Backsolve.

89. D

Subject: Geometry

Getting to the Answer: The formula for the volume of a cube is $V = s^3$, where V is the volume of the cube and s is the length of a side of the cube. So, if the volume of a cube is 27, its sides must be of a length of 3, since $3^3 = 27$. There are six faces of equal area on a cube, so the surface area equals six times the area of a single face. If each face has a length of 3, then each of the six faces of the cube has an area of 3 times 3, or 9. The total surface area would be six times the area of one face. 6 times $9 = 54$, **(D)**.

90. H

Subject: Arithmetic

Getting to the Answer: The graph shows that, of the 600 graduates, 12% chose to enter the workforce, and 22% chose to go to vocational school. $12\% + 22\% = 34\%$. 34% of $600 = \frac{34}{100} \times 600 = 204$, so 204 graduates chose to enter the workforce or go to vocational school. The answer is **(H)**.

91. C

Subject: Algebra

Getting to the Answer: You need to find $\frac{p}{n}$ in terms of x. $\frac{p}{n}$ is the reciprocal of $\frac{n}{p}$, so combine the right side of the equation into one expression and then take its reciprocal.

You can combine $\frac{2}{x} + 2$ by rewriting the terms with a common denominator: $\frac{2}{x} + 2 = \frac{2}{x} + \frac{2x}{x} = \frac{2x+2}{x}$.

The reciprocal of this expression is $\frac{x}{2x+2}$ or $\frac{x}{2(x+1)}$, **(C)**.

If you didn't know how to solve it, you could have Picked Numbers. If $n = 6$ and $p = 2$, x must be 2. To find out which choice has the value of $\frac{p}{n}$ or $\frac{2}{6}$, plug in 2 for x in each choice; the only choice that yields a value of $\frac{2}{6}$ is **(C)**.

92. H

Subject: Arithmetic

Getting to the Answer: The multiples of 3 are the integers 3, 6, 9, 12... It is useful to think of the multiples of 3 this way: $1 \times 3, 2 \times 3, 3 \times 3, 4 \times 3\ldots$

A is the sum of the first 50 multiples of 3. The first 50 multiples of 3 are $1 \times 3, 2 \times 3, 3 \times 3, 4 \times 3, \cdots, 48 \times 3, 49 \times 3$, and 50×3. Factor out $1 + 2 + 3 + \cdots + 50$, and it becomes clear that $A = (1 + 2 + 3 + \cdots + 50) \times 3$

We also know that *B* is the sum of the first 50 multiples of 6, so $B = 1 \times 6 + 2 \times 6 + 3 \times 6 + \cdots + 50 \times 6 = (1 + 2 + 3 + \cdots + 50) \times 6$.

If we call the sum of the first 50 positive integers *Y*, then $A = 3Y$ and $B = 6Y$. To answer "What percent of *A* is *B*?" it may help to use another variable for that percent. Think of $x\%$ of $A = B$ or $\frac{x}{100} \times 3Y = 6Y$.

Divide both sides by $3Y$ to get $\frac{x}{100} = 2$. So $x = 200\%$, **(H)**.

93. A

Subject: Arithmetic

Getting to the Answer: To find the smallest possible value of *x*, find the greatest possible value of *y*. The largest that *y* can be is 40% of 180. 40% of $180 = 0.40 \times 180 = 72$. Plug in 72 for *y* and find *x*. $61 + 24 + x + 72 = 180$, $157 + x = 180$, and $x = 23$, **(A)**.

94. E

Subject: Geometry

Getting to the Answer: The angle marked 102 degrees is opposite the interior angle of the triangle at the top. Opposite angles are equal, so the interior angle at the top of the triangle has a measure of 102 degrees. The sum of the interior angles of a triangle is 180 degrees, so $b + 2b + 102 = 180$. Solve this equation for *b*.

$$\begin{aligned} b + 2b + 102 &= 180 \\ 3b + 102 &= 180 \\ 3b &= 78 \\ b &= 26, \textbf{(E)} \end{aligned}$$

95. A

Subject: Arithmetic

Getting to the Answer: The sequence that you're given has 8 numbers, 4 of which are odd and 4 of which are even. You want to know how the sum of those numbers would change if the individual numbers changed by various amounts. You don't need to start adding up the numbers in the sequence. You're only concerned with how the sum would change, not what its value is.

There are 4 odd numbers in the sequence. The question tells you that each odd-valued term will be increased by 3, so the sum will increase by 4×3, or 12. If each even valued term is decreased by 2, that's the same as decreasing 4 of the terms by 2 each, or the entire sequence by 4×2, or 8. So, the sum of the sequence will increase by 12 and decrease by 8. That's like adding 12 and then subtracting 8, which is the same as adding 4, **(A)**.

96. H

Subject: Algebra

Getting to the Answer: Simplify by canceling common factors from the numerator and the denominator. x^2 means 2 factors of *x*; x^6 means 6 factors of *x*. Canceling, you're left with 4 factors of *x*, or x^4, in the denominator. The y^3s cancel out. Canceling the common factors of *z*, you're left with z^4 in the numerator. Combining the terms in the numerator and the denominator gives you $\frac{z^4}{x^4}$, **(H)**.

97. C

Subject: Geometry

Getting to the Answer: The area of a circle with radius *r* is πr^2. The area of the large circle is 900π. So, $\pi r^2 = 900\pi$. Then $r^2 = 900$, and $r = 30$. The radius of the large circle is 30. So, the diameter of the large circle is 2×30, or 60. The diameters of the three identical small circles make up the diameter of the large circle, so the diameter of each small circle is one-third of 60, or 20. The circumference of a circle is π times the diameter, so the circumference of the small circle with center *C* is π times 20, or 20π. The answer is **(C)**.

98. E

Subject: Geometry

Getting to the Answer: $\angle PNM$ is supplementary to $\angle PNQ$, so $\angle PNM + 105° = 180°$, and $\angle PNM = 75°$. Since $PM = PN$, triangle MPN is isosceles and $\angle PMN = \angle PNM = 75°$. The interior angles of a triangle sum to 180°, so $75 + 75 + x = 180$, and $x = 30$, **(E)**.

99. D

Subject: Algebra

Getting to the Answer: Don't be thrown off by the unusual formatting. The values in the *y* row are just fractions that have multiplication in the numerator. Incorrect answer choices can be found by substituting the values from the table into the answer choices and seeing which choices do not give the correct value of *y*. Start with **(A)**: $\frac{3x+1}{5} = \frac{3(0)+1}{5} = \frac{1}{5}$. This answer is not 0, so eliminate choice **(A)**.

In **(B)**, the value of *y* does work out to the correct value of 0 when *x* is 0. It also works out to the correct value of $\frac{4}{5} = \frac{(1)(4)}{5}$ when *x* is 1. However, when *x* is 2, the value in the table is $\frac{(4)(7)}{5} = \frac{28}{5}$, while **(B)** shows that $\frac{x(3x+1)}{5} = \frac{2[3(2)+1]}{5} = \frac{(2)(7)}{5} = \frac{14}{5}$. Eliminate **(B)**.

(C) can be eliminated using either $x = 2$ or $x = 3$.

(D) works for all 4 values of *x* in the table and is correct.

Instead of substituting in values, you might also notice that answer choices **(B)** and **(D)** are the only equations that contain both a multiplication expression in the numerator and a denominator of 5. Looking back at the table, the first factor is always x^2 and the second is always $3x + 1$, which matches **(D)**.

100. H

Subject: Arithmetic

Getting to the Answer: Try out the answer choices. Since you know that the smallest integer in set *C* is −2, and the numbers are consecutive, you can make up set *C* given the number of elements for that answer choice. The set containing the least possible number of integers, in which the integers in the set also add up to a positive even number, will be the correct answer.

(E) Set *C* has 4 elements, so $C = \{-2, -1, 0, 1\}$. This adds up to −2, so eliminate **(E)**.

(F) Set *C* has 5 elements, so $C = \{-2, -1, 0, 1, 2\}$. This adds up to zero, and although zero is even, it is neither positive nor negative, so eliminate **(F)**.

(G) Set *C* has 6 elements, so $C = \{-2, -1, 0, 1, 2, 3\}$. This adds up to 3, which isn't even. Eliminate **(G)**.

(H) Set *C* has 8 elements, so $C = \{-2, -1, 0, 1, 2, 3, 4, 5\}$. This adds up to 12, which is positive and even, so **(H)** must be correct.

101. C

Subject: Geometry

Getting to the Answer: The easiest way to do this one is to just draw lines from each point and then add up the number of line segments drawn. From point *A*, draw one line to each of points *B*, *C*, *D*, and *E*. From point *B*, you already have a line to point *A*, so just draw a line to each of points *C*, *D*, and *E*. From point *C*, you have already drawn lines to *A* and *B*, so draw a line to point *D* and one to point *E*, and finally draw a line from point *D* to point *E*. (You've drawn a star inside a pentagon—very artistic!) Can you see any point that is unconnected to any other point? No, so just add up the number of lines you've already drawn—there are $4 + 3 + 2 + 1$, or 10, of them. The answer is **(C)**.

102. H

Subject: Algebra

Getting to the Answer: Mixture problems are very tricky. The important thing to look for in a mixture problem is which quantities stay the same and which quantities change. Here, the water is evaporating but the sugar is not. Therefore, the quantity of sugar will be unchanged. Start with 4 ounces of sugar and 16 ounces of water, and end with 4 ounces of sugar and an unknown quantity of water, which you can call *x* ounces. That means, in the end, the whole solution has a total of $4 + x$ ounces, since the solution is made up of only sugar and water. The final quantities of sugar and total solution are in the ratio of

2 to 3. That means that the ratio of 4 to $4 + x$ is equal to the ratio of 2 to 3, or $\frac{4}{4+x} = \frac{2}{3}$, which is just an algebraic equation that can be solved:

$$\begin{aligned} 4 \times 3 &= 2 \times (4 + x) \\ 12 &= 8 + 2x \\ 4 &= 2x \\ 2 &= x \end{aligned}$$

If there are 2 ounces of water left after starting with 16 ounces, then $16 - 2 = 14$ ounces must have evaporated, so the correct answer is 14, **(H)**.

103. C

Subject: Algebra

Getting to the Answer:

$$[4(15) + 30] - [2(15) + 15]$$
$$[60 + 30] - [30 - 15]$$
$$90 - 45$$
$$45, \textbf{(C)}$$

104. F

Subject: Algebra

Getting to the Answer:

$$\frac{4(300) - 150}{100}$$
$$\frac{1{,}200 - 150}{100}$$
$$\frac{1{,}050}{100}$$
$$10.5, \textbf{(F)}$$

105. C

Subject: Algebra

Getting to the Answer:

$$\frac{10(4)^2 - 6(6)}{\sqrt{4}}$$
$$\frac{10(16) - 36}{2}$$
$$\frac{160 - 36}{2}$$
$$\frac{124}{2}$$
$$62, \textbf{(C)}$$

106. H

Subject: Algebra

Getting to the Answer:

$$\frac{[(3)(20) + (2)(10)] - 30}{(20 - 10)}$$
$$\frac{(60 + 20) - 30}{10}$$
$$\frac{80 - 30}{10}$$
$$\frac{50}{10}$$
$$5, \textbf{(H)}$$

107. C

Subject: Algebra

Getting to the Answer:

$$\left[\frac{(4)(3)}{(2)(2)}\right]\left[\frac{(9)(4)}{(3)(2)}\right]$$
$$\left[\frac{12}{4}\right]\left[\frac{36}{6}\right]$$
$$[3][6]$$
$$18, \textbf{(C)}$$

108. F

Subject: Algebra

Getting to the Answer:

$$\left(\frac{lm}{lp}\right) + l$$
$$\left(\frac{m}{p}\right) + l \quad \text{Cancel the } l.$$
$$\left(\frac{50}{10}\right) + 24$$
$$5 + 24 = 29, \textbf{(F)}$$

109. A

Subject: Algebra

Getting to the Answer:

$$\frac{[(5)(10)(15)]-[(4)(10)(15)]}{[(5)(10)(15)]+[(5)(10)]}$$
$$\frac{750-600}{750+50}$$
$$\frac{150}{800}$$
$$\frac{3}{16}, \textbf{(A)}$$

Factoring out common terms before multiplying, then simplifying makes the calculation easier.

110. H

Subject: Algebra

Getting to the Answer:

$$x=\frac{1}{4}-\left(\frac{1}{2}-\frac{1}{3}\right)$$

$$x=\left(\frac{3}{3}\right)\frac{1}{4}-\left(\left(\frac{6}{6}\right)\frac{1}{2}-\left(\frac{4}{4}\right)\frac{1}{3}\right)$$ Express everything in terms of 12ths, LCD.

$$x=\frac{3}{12}-\left(\frac{6}{12}-\frac{4}{12}\right)$$

$$x=\frac{3}{12}-\left(\frac{2}{12}\right)$$ Work within the parentheses first.

$$x=\frac{1}{12}, \textbf{(H)}$$

111. D

Subject: Algebra

Getting to the Answer:

$$x-\sqrt{2}=\sqrt{8}$$
$$x-\sqrt{2}=\sqrt{4\times 2}$$
$$x-\sqrt{2}=2\sqrt{2}$$ $\sqrt{xy}=\sqrt{x}\sqrt{y}$
$$\left(x-\sqrt{2}\right)+\sqrt{2}=2\sqrt{2}+\sqrt{2}$$ Add $\sqrt{2}$ to both sides.
$$x=3\sqrt{2}, \textbf{(D)}$$

112. H

Subject: Algebra

Getting to the Answer:

$$x=8\div\sqrt{2}$$
$$x=\frac{8}{\sqrt{2}}$$ Dividing is the same thing as a fraction.
$$x=\frac{8}{\sqrt{2}}\times\frac{\sqrt{2}}{\sqrt{2}}$$ Rationalize the radical by multiplying the numerator and denominator by the square root of 2 and simplify.
$$x=4\sqrt{2}, \textbf{(H)}$$

113. C

Subject: Algebra

Getting to the Answer:

$$x=\frac{9}{x}$$
$$x\cdot x=\frac{9}{x}\cdot x$$ Multiply both sides by x, isolating the variable.
$$x^2=9$$
$$x=\pm 3$$ Because $x\geq 0$, we can discard -3.
$$x=3, \textbf{(C)}$$

114. H

Subject: Algebra

Getting to the Answer:

$$x=\frac{1}{3}\left(\frac{1}{2}-\frac{1}{8}\right)$$
$$x=\frac{1}{3}\left(\left(\frac{1}{2}\times\frac{4}{4}\right)-\frac{1}{8}\right)$$ Convert the units within the parentheses to 8, the LCD.
$$x=\frac{1}{3}\left(\frac{4}{8}-\frac{1}{8}\right)$$
$$x=\frac{1}{3}\left(\frac{3}{8}\right)=\frac{1}{8}, \textbf{(H)}$$

SHSAT
Practice Test 2

SHSAT Practice Test 2

ANSWER SHEET

Scan Code

Please use this Answer Sheet only if the test will be scored via a webgrid/online scoring process. This Answer Sheet will NOT work if the test will be scanned.

For scanned exams, please refer to the Kaplan Answer Grid (which requires the use of a No. 2 pencil and is formatted for scanning machines).

Enrollment ID

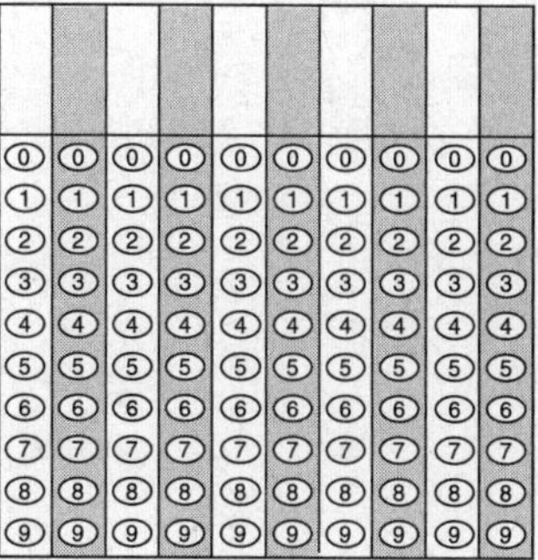

PART 1—ENGLISH LANGUAGE ARTS

1. Ⓐ Ⓑ Ⓒ Ⓓ	11. Ⓐ Ⓑ Ⓒ Ⓓ	21. Ⓐ Ⓑ Ⓒ Ⓓ	31. Ⓐ Ⓑ Ⓒ Ⓓ	41. Ⓐ Ⓑ Ⓒ Ⓓ	51. Ⓐ Ⓑ Ⓒ Ⓓ
2. Ⓔ Ⓕ Ⓖ Ⓗ	12. Ⓔ Ⓕ Ⓖ Ⓗ	22. Ⓔ Ⓕ Ⓖ Ⓗ	32. Ⓔ Ⓕ Ⓖ Ⓗ	42. Ⓔ Ⓕ Ⓖ Ⓗ	52. Ⓔ Ⓕ Ⓖ Ⓗ
3. Ⓐ Ⓑ Ⓒ Ⓓ	13. Ⓐ Ⓑ Ⓒ Ⓓ	23. Ⓐ Ⓑ Ⓒ Ⓓ	33. Ⓐ Ⓑ Ⓒ Ⓓ	43. Ⓐ Ⓑ Ⓒ Ⓓ	53. Ⓐ Ⓑ Ⓒ Ⓓ
4. Ⓔ Ⓕ Ⓖ Ⓗ	14. Ⓔ Ⓕ Ⓖ Ⓗ	24. Ⓔ Ⓕ Ⓖ Ⓗ	34. Ⓔ Ⓕ Ⓖ Ⓗ	44. Ⓔ Ⓕ Ⓖ Ⓗ	54. Ⓔ Ⓕ Ⓖ Ⓗ
5. Ⓐ Ⓑ Ⓒ Ⓓ	15. Ⓐ Ⓑ Ⓒ Ⓓ	25. Ⓐ Ⓑ Ⓒ Ⓓ	35. Ⓐ Ⓑ Ⓒ Ⓓ	45. Ⓐ Ⓑ Ⓒ Ⓓ	55. Ⓐ Ⓑ Ⓒ Ⓓ
6. Ⓔ Ⓕ Ⓖ Ⓗ	16. Ⓔ Ⓕ Ⓖ Ⓗ	26. Ⓔ Ⓕ Ⓖ Ⓗ	36. Ⓔ Ⓕ Ⓖ Ⓗ	46. Ⓔ Ⓕ Ⓖ Ⓗ	56. Ⓔ Ⓕ Ⓖ Ⓗ
7. Ⓐ Ⓑ Ⓒ Ⓓ	17. Ⓐ Ⓑ Ⓒ Ⓓ	27. Ⓐ Ⓑ Ⓒ Ⓓ	37. Ⓐ Ⓑ Ⓒ Ⓓ	47. Ⓐ Ⓑ Ⓒ Ⓓ	57. Ⓐ Ⓑ Ⓒ Ⓓ
8. Ⓔ Ⓕ Ⓖ Ⓗ	18. Ⓔ Ⓕ Ⓖ Ⓗ	28. Ⓔ Ⓕ Ⓖ Ⓗ	38. Ⓔ Ⓕ Ⓖ Ⓗ	48. Ⓔ Ⓕ Ⓖ Ⓗ	
9. Ⓐ Ⓑ Ⓒ Ⓓ	19. Ⓐ Ⓑ Ⓒ Ⓓ	29. Ⓐ Ⓑ Ⓒ Ⓓ	39. Ⓐ Ⓑ Ⓒ Ⓓ	49. Ⓐ Ⓑ Ⓒ Ⓓ	
10. Ⓔ Ⓕ Ⓖ Ⓗ	20. Ⓔ Ⓕ Ⓖ Ⓗ	30. Ⓔ Ⓕ Ⓖ Ⓗ	40. Ⓔ Ⓕ Ⓖ Ⓗ	50. Ⓔ Ⓕ Ⓖ Ⓗ	

PART 2—MATHEMATICS

58. 59. 60. 61. 62.

63. Ⓐ Ⓑ Ⓒ Ⓓ	72. Ⓔ Ⓕ Ⓖ Ⓗ	81. Ⓐ Ⓑ Ⓒ Ⓓ	90. Ⓔ Ⓕ Ⓖ Ⓗ	99. Ⓐ Ⓑ Ⓒ Ⓓ	108. Ⓔ Ⓕ Ⓖ Ⓗ
64. Ⓔ Ⓕ Ⓖ Ⓗ	73. Ⓐ Ⓑ Ⓒ Ⓓ	82. Ⓔ Ⓕ Ⓖ Ⓗ	91. Ⓐ Ⓑ Ⓒ Ⓓ	100. Ⓔ Ⓕ Ⓖ Ⓗ	109. Ⓐ Ⓑ Ⓒ Ⓓ
65. Ⓐ Ⓑ Ⓒ Ⓓ	74. Ⓔ Ⓕ Ⓖ Ⓗ	83. Ⓐ Ⓑ Ⓒ Ⓓ	92. Ⓔ Ⓕ Ⓖ Ⓗ	101. Ⓐ Ⓑ Ⓒ Ⓓ	110. Ⓔ Ⓕ Ⓖ Ⓗ
66. Ⓔ Ⓕ Ⓖ Ⓗ	75. Ⓐ Ⓑ Ⓒ Ⓓ	84. Ⓔ Ⓕ Ⓖ Ⓗ	93. Ⓐ Ⓑ Ⓒ Ⓓ	102. Ⓔ Ⓕ Ⓖ Ⓗ	111. Ⓐ Ⓑ Ⓒ Ⓓ
67. Ⓐ Ⓑ Ⓒ Ⓓ	76. Ⓔ Ⓕ Ⓖ Ⓗ	85. Ⓐ Ⓑ Ⓒ Ⓓ	94. Ⓔ Ⓕ Ⓖ Ⓗ	103. Ⓐ Ⓑ Ⓒ Ⓓ	112. Ⓔ Ⓕ Ⓖ Ⓗ
68. Ⓔ Ⓕ Ⓖ Ⓗ	77. Ⓐ Ⓑ Ⓒ Ⓓ	86. Ⓔ Ⓕ Ⓖ Ⓗ	95. Ⓐ Ⓑ Ⓒ Ⓓ	104. Ⓔ Ⓕ Ⓖ Ⓗ	113. Ⓐ Ⓑ Ⓒ Ⓓ
69. Ⓐ Ⓑ Ⓒ Ⓓ	78. Ⓔ Ⓕ Ⓖ Ⓗ	87. Ⓐ Ⓑ Ⓒ Ⓓ	96. Ⓔ Ⓕ Ⓖ Ⓗ	105. Ⓐ Ⓑ Ⓒ Ⓓ	114. Ⓔ Ⓕ Ⓖ Ⓗ
70. Ⓔ Ⓕ Ⓖ Ⓗ	79. Ⓐ Ⓑ Ⓒ Ⓓ	88. Ⓔ Ⓕ Ⓖ Ⓗ	97. Ⓐ Ⓑ Ⓒ Ⓓ	106. Ⓔ Ⓕ Ⓖ Ⓗ	
71. Ⓐ Ⓑ Ⓒ Ⓓ	80. Ⓔ Ⓕ Ⓖ Ⓗ	89. Ⓐ Ⓑ Ⓒ Ⓓ	98. Ⓔ Ⓕ Ⓖ Ⓗ	107. Ⓐ Ⓑ Ⓒ Ⓓ	

PRACTICE TEST 2

DIRECTIONS: Mark your answers on the separate sheet provided. You will receive credit only for answers marked on the answer grid. DO NOT MAKE ANY STRAY MARKS ON THE ANSWER GRID. You can write in the test booklet, or use the paper provided for scratchwork.

Part 1	Questions 1–57	90 minutes
Part 2	Questions 58–114	90 minutes

Marking Your Answers

Each question has only one correct answer. Select the **best** answer for each question. Your score is determined by the number of questions you answered correctly. **It is to your advantage to answer every question, even though you may not be certain which choice is correct.**

Planning Your Time

You have 180 minutes to complete the entire test. How you allot the time between the English Language Arts and Mathematics sections is up to you. **If you begin with the English Language Arts section, you may go on to the Mathematics section as soon as you are ready. Likewise, if you begin with the Mathematics section, you may go on to the English Language Arts section as soon as you are ready.** It is recommended that you do not spend more than 90 minutes on either section. If you complete the test before the allotted time (180 minutes) is over, you may go back to review questions in either section.

Work as rapidly as you can without making mistakes. Don't spend too much time on a difficult question. Return to it later if you have time.

PART 1 — ENGLISH LANGUAGE ARTS

Suggested Time — 90 Minutes

57 QUESTIONS

REVISING/EDITING

QUESTIONS 1–11

IMPORTANT NOTE

The Revising/Editing section (Questions 1–11) is in two parts: Part A and Part B.

REVISING/EDITING Part A

DIRECTIONS: Read and answer each of the following questions. You will be asked to recognize and correct errors in sentences or short paragraphs. Mark the **best** answer for each question.

1. Read this sentence.

> That the Superbowl was the most highly rated television show last week came as no surprise to the sponsor's whose commercials aired during the broadcast.

Which edit should be made to correct this sentence?

A. change ***most*** to **more**

B. insert a comma after ***week***

C. change ***sponsor's*** to **sponsors**

D. insert a comma after ***aired***

2. Read this sentence.

> The rock group attracts a multifarious audience; a surprisingly diverse group of people flock to their sold-out concerts.

Which edit should be made to correct this sentence?

E. change ***group attracts*** to **group attract**

F. change ***people flock*** to **people flocks**

G. change ***to their*** to **to there**

H. change ***concerts*** to **concert**

3. Read this paragraph.

> (1) James D. Watson studied biology as a graduate student at Indiana University, but the scientists there inspired him to pursue the fields of genetics and biochemistry instead. (2) In Copenhagen, he conducted research on DNA for his postdoctoral studies, but became discouraged due to his lack of success. (3) After hearing a speech by Maurice Wilkins, Watson renewed his interest in DNA and then collaborated in England with a biologist named Francis Crick to research and study the structure of the DNA molecule. (4) Rosalind Franklin's X-ray images of DNA helped Watson, Crick, and Wilkins earn the Nobel Prize in 1962.

Which sentence should be revised to correct a wordiness issue?

A. sentence 1
B. sentence 2
C. sentence 3
D. sentence 4

4. Read this paragraph.

> (1) The Siberian husky's good temperament, speed, and eagerness to cooperate make it a valuable dog in the Arctic regions. (2) Besides running for hundreds of miles in dogsled competitions the outgoing huskies have readily helped people in need. (3) For example, through the efforts of 20 heroic, courageous mushers, a life-saving serum was relayed by dogsled teams across the 674 miles of frigid Alaskan wilderness from Nenana to Nome in 1925 to save a town stricken with diphtheria. (4) In addition, during World War II, Siberian huskies served in the Army's Arctic Search and Rescue Unit.

Which sentence should be revised to correct a punctuation issue?

E. sentence 1
F. sentence 2
G. sentence 3
H. sentence 4

REVISING/EDITING Part B

DIRECTIONS: Read the passage below and answer the questions following it. You will be asked to improve the writing quality of the passage and to correct errors so that the passage follows the conventions of standard written English. You may reread the passage if you need to. Mark the **best** answer for each question.

Helium

(1) Pierre-Jules César Janssen first obtained evidence for the existence of the new element helium when studying a total solar eclipse in 1868. (2) He detected a yellow line on his spectroscope while observing the sun, and realized that, because of its wavelength, it could not be attributed to any element known at the time. (3) It was repeated by Norman Lockyer, who also concluded that no known element produced such a line. (4) However, other scientists were dubious, finding it unlikely that an element existed only on the sun. (5) In 1895, William Ramsay discovered helium on Earth after treating cleveite, a uranium mineral, with mineral acids. (6) After isolating the resulting gas, Ramsay sent samples to William Crookes and Norman Lockyer. (7) He identified it conclusively as the missing element helium. (8) It was Lockyer who named the element "helium," from the Greek word "helios," meaning "sun."

(9) The controversy concerning this new element is ironic, considering that helium is the second most abundant element in the universe (hydrogen is the first). (10) However, helium does not bind to Earth by gravitation, thus mostly appears in space. (11) On earth, it is created by the decay of radioactive elements, such as uranium and thorium. (12) Helium became trapped in natural gas and can be extracted for commercial use. (13) Helium is a nonrenewable resource. (14) Once extracted, it quickly returns to space.

(15) The most common application for liquid helium is in cryogenics, a branch of physics dealing with very low temperatures. (16) Among other uses, helium is employed to cool superconducting magnets in devices such as MRI scanners. (17) It is also used to grow crystals for silicon wafers. (18) In nonscientific endeavors, helium is the gas that makes balloons and blimps rise. (19) Inhaling helium changes the sound of one's voice to a flat, high-pitched one. (20) Rare though helium is on Earth, several large gas fields with helium have been found in the United States. (21) Until recently, scientist's had been concerned that helium is in very short supply.

5. Which revision of sentence 3 uses the most precise language?

   A. Norman Lockyer did another of the same, which also concluded that no known element produced such a line.

   B. Janssen's experiment was repeated by Norman Lockyer, who also concluded that no known element produced such a line.

   C. The fact that no known element produced it was concluded by Norman Lockyer.

   D. Norman Lockyer did it and again concluded that no known element produced such a line.

6. What edit is needed to correct sentence 7?

   E. change ***He*** to **Lockyer**

   F. change ***He*** to **Janssen**

   G. change ***it*** to **them**

   H. change ***it*** to **those**

7. What edit is needed to correct sentence 12?

   A. change ***became*** to **becomes**

   B. change ***trapped*** to **released**

   C. change ***can be*** to **will be**

   D. change ***commercial use*** to **used for commercial reasons**

8. What is the best way to combine sentences 13 and 14 to clarify the relationship between ideas?

   E. Helium is a nonrenewable resource, once extracted, it quickly returns to space.

   F. Helium quickly returns to space after having been extracted and because of this is a nonrenewable resource.

   G. Helium is a nonrenewable resource; once extracted, it quickly returns to space.

   H. Helium is a nonrenewable resource; quickly returning to space after extraction.

9. What transition should be added to the beginning of sentence 19?

   A. Similarly

   B. In contrast

   C. It has also been known that

   D. In addition

10. What edit is necessary to correct sentence 21?

    E. change ***Until*** to **Before**

    F. change ***scientist's*** to **scientists**

    G. change ***had been*** to **has been**

    H. change ***concerned*** to **unconcerned**

11. Which concluding sentence should be added after sentence 21 to support the argument presented in the passage?

    A. New research indicates that it can collect in large quantities in gas fields and can also be released by volcanic eruptions.

    B. There have been frequent scientific discussions about this concern.

    C. The concern is unwarranted.

    D. In reality, there is enough helium on the sun to fill Earth's needs.

Reading Comprehension

Questions 12–57

DIRECTIONS: Read each passage below and answer the questions following it. Base your answers **on information contained only in the passage.** You may reread a passage if you need to. Mark the **best** answer for each question.

It was a particularly cold winter in Springfield, Massachusetts. Luther Gulick, head of the Physical Education department at the School for Christian Workers, faced with a rowdy class, called James Naismith to his office. The conversation that followed would change the future of sports.

Gulick ordered Naismith to invent an indoor game that would provide "athletic distraction" for the eighteen members of an especially rambunctious group of students. Naismith initially responded by trying to bring outdoor games, like soccer, indoors. However, as his two-week deadline drew closer, he remembered a game from his childhood that required skill and precision: just the kind of activity this situation called for. This game became the inspiration for an entirely new sport. He gathered his students in the YMCA gymnasium. His equipment consisted of two peach baskets and a soccer ball. The date was Dec. 21, 1891. Basketball was born.

Although the first basketball game was played by a group of men, women quickly became interested in this new sport. A few weeks later, the first women's basketball team was created by a nearby school's teachers who saw Dr. Naismith's students playing. By the next year, the first women's college team was formed at Smith College in Northampton, Massachusetts.

In general, basketball was played solely for recreation until 1946, when the owners of the United States' biggest arenas began to consider the idea of professional basketball. The Basketball Association of America was formed in part to fill seats on days when there were no professional hockey or college basketball matches.

Basketball continued to change throughout the twentieth century, and with it, many of James Naismith's rules. For example, in 1980, following a rule change, the first three-point shot was scored by Western Carolina's Ronnie Carr. Additionally, basketball is now played five-on-five, whereas the first game was played with nine to a side. However, at its core, the game has stayed close to the one envisioned by its creator over one hundred years ago.

12. What is this passage primarily about?

    E. the history of women's basketball
    F. sports in the twentieth century
    G. the life of Dr. James Naismith
    H. the evolution of basketball

13. It can be inferred that prior to the formation of the Basketball Association of America, basketball was played in arenas

    A. by women's teams only.
    B. by college teams only.
    C. by professional teams only.
    D. only when there were no professional hockey matches.

14. Which of the following is **not** mentioned in the passage as an example of a way in which basketball has changed since its inception?

    E. There are fewer players on a side now.

    F. There has been a change in scoring procedures.

    G. The slam dunk is now a common practice.

    H. Initially, basketball was played only by men, but now anyone can play.

15. The passage implies that Luther Gulick wanted Dr. Naismith to create a new game because

    A. he wanted a game that spectators would come to watch in his arena.

    B. outdoor games like soccer had become too commonplace.

    C. he had been inspired by a childhood game.

    D. he wanted his students to channel their energy in a healthy direction.

16. From the passage, it is reasonable to assume that the owners of the largest U.S. arenas formed a professional league

    E. in order to increase their profits.

    F. because they realized that basketball could easily be converted from an outdoor into an indoor game.

    G. because professional hockey and college basketball games rarely filled these arenas.

    H. to capitalize on the popularity of the three-point shot.

17. Ronnie Carr is responsible for which important moment?

    A. He ordered a subordinate to invent basketball.

    B. He scored the first three-point shot in a basketball game.

    C. He formed the Basketball Association of America.

    D. He invented the game of basketball.

18. All of the following describe the game that Dr. Naismith invented **except**

    E. it involved elaborate and expensive equipment.

    F. it involved skill.

    G. it could be played indoors.

    H. precision was required.

Most of human prehistory has left behind no convincing trace of art at all. Perhaps our remote ancestors painted their bodies, but if that was the first art, it wouldn't have survived for us to know about. The oldest known artworks were created more or less simultaneously in Europe, Africa, and Australia, with some further recent discoveries of old art in Asia and the Americas as well. Early art itself assumed many forms, ranging from wood and bone carving, engraving, bas relief, and three-dimensional sculpture to painting and music. Best known to modern Europeans are the cave paintings of so-called Cro-Magnon people from France and Spain, who lived in the era termed the Paleolithic (from about 40,000 to 10,000 years ago).

We think of cave art as made by "cavemen," a term that immediately evokes images of hairy brutes, partly draped in animal furs. In fact, the Cro-Magnons lived far from caves, as well as within them; we think of them as cavemen only because the garbage they left in caves is more likely to have been preserved than other artifacts. From their garbage, burials, and art, we know that they had needles, buttons, sewn clothing, and parkas, and were probably as warmly dressed as modern Eskimos. They marked their caves with trail signs called claviforms, which warned Cro-Magnon tourists to stay on the right-hand side of wide passages, to look for art in concealed niches, and to avoid bumping their heads in places with low ceilings. Their footprints are still on the cave floors, their handprints and marks of their scaffolding still on the cave walls. Visiting some of the sites, you get the vivid sense that the artists walked off the job only yesterday.

But why did the Cro-Magnons create cave art in the first place? Archaeologists used to debate various interpretations: that the paintings represented mindless copies of nature by savage people, or magical rites to ensure success at hunting, or depictions of myths, and so on. Such theories became less popular when anthropologists began to ask present-day tribal Australian aborigines and African Bushmen why they create their own rock art. The reasons turned out to be ones that any future art historian would be very unlikely to guess. The same image—for example, a fish painted by aboriginal Australians—has been painted for different reasons on different occasions. Some fish paintings serve to mark a tribal territory, others tell a story ("I caught this big fish"), and still others have religious significance. It shouldn't surprise us that the Cro-Magnons' motives may have been equally varied, given all the evidence for their modern mentality.

19. Which of the following best describes what this passage is about?

A. Research on present-day tribal people can tell us about humans in the prehistoric era.

B. Early humans were not all that different in their lifestyle and technology from present-day Eskimos.

C. The art and artifacts left behind by early humans suggest that they were not as primitive as popular images portray them.

D. The artistic creations of the cave dwellers included not only paintings, but also crafts, tools, sculpture, and music.

20. What is the primary role of paragraph 2 in the passage?

E. It considers the many forms of early art.

F. It discusses the debate surrounding the interpretations of art created by the Cro-Magnons.

G. It suggests that the Cro-Magnons may have had varying motives for creating art.

H. It introduces some examples of early art created by the Cro-Magnons.

21. It can be inferred that more Cro-Magnon artifacts have been found in caves than elsewhere primarily because the majority of

    A. Cro-Magnon people lived in caves.
    B. artifacts in other locations are more likely to have decayed.
    C. trail signs led archaeologists to many cave sites.
    D. archaeologists are more likely to prefer cave sites.

22. According to paragraph 3, the theories mentioned "became less popular" when scientists discovered that

    E. the Cro-Magnons were more advanced than the Neanderthals.
    F. the rock art produced today serves several different functions.
    G. many painted images were used by the Cro-Magnons as trail signs.
    H. Cro-Magnon paintings were not as important as was once believed.

23. The description of the fish painted by aboriginal Australians in the last paragraph suggests that

    A. most rock paintings were used to mark tribal boundaries.
    B. animals are depicted more often than people in early rock art.
    C. it is difficult to generalize about the motivations of prehistoric artists.
    D. the images used by Cro-Magnon and Australian aboriginal artists served the same functions.

24. The Cro-Magnon's use of claviforms implies that the Cro-Magnon people of France and Spain were

    E. surprisingly similar in many ways to modern humans.
    F. dependent on hunting far more than on agriculture.
    G. not the same people who are commonly called "cavemen."
    H. artistically more sophisticated than many later civilizations.

25. What is the most likely reason the author uses the word "convincing" in paragraph 1?

    A. to show that human prehistoric art is undependable
    B. to propose that human prehistoric art is more irresistible than today's art
    C. to suggest that art remaining from human prehistory is truthful
    D. to illustrate that few credible examples of human prehistoric art exist

26. From the passage it can be inferred that the impetus to create art was

    E. localized to caves.
    F. dependent on a modern mentality.
    G. essentially universal.
    H. a development of the Paleolithic era.

The following poem, "The Song of Wandering Aengus" by William Butler Yeats, was first published in 1899.

I went out to the hazel wood,
Because a fire was in my head,
And cut and peeled a hazel wand,
And hooked a berry to a thread;
And when white moths were on the wing,
And moth-like stars were flickering out,
I dropped the berry in a stream
And caught a little silver trout.

When I had laid it on the floor
I went to blow the fire a-flame,
But something rustled on the floor,
And someone called me by my name:
It had become a glimmering girl
With apple blossom in her hair
Who called me by my name and ran
And faded through the brightening air.

Though I am old with wandering
Through hollow lands and hilly lands,
I will find out where she has gone,
And kiss her lips and take her hands;
And walk among long dappled grass,
And pluck till time and times are done,
The silver apples of the moon,
The golden apples of the sun.

27. How does the form of "The Song of Wandering Aengus" contribute to its meaning?

A. The poem is written as an elegy to illuminate the speaker's sadness over the death of a former lover.

B. The poem is written as an epic to celebrate the heroism of the trout's process of becoming a girl.

C. The poem is written as a lament to highlight the speaker's grief in misplacing the trout.

D. The poem is written as a lyric to better express the speaker's emotions, deepening the meaning.

28. Read line 2.

Because a fire was in my head,

How does this line contribute to the development of a central idea of the poem?

E. This line explains that Aengus has a headache.

F. This line alludes to a fire-like burning in Aengus's scalp.

G. This line implies Aengus's burning passion of love.

H. This line describes Aengus's sorrow over unrequited love.

29. What impact does the phrase "And cut and peeled a hazel wand" (line 3) have on the meaning of the poem?

A. It symbolizes how Aengus prepared fruit.

B. It illustrates how Aengus typically relieves headaches.

C. It reveals the magical rod Aengus uses for the transformation.

D. It explains that Aengus is fishing with a small tree limb.

30. Which line from the poem best supports the idea that Aengus is mortal?

E. "And moth-like stars were flickering out," (line 6)

F. "Though I am old with wandering" (line 17)

G. "And pluck till time and times are done," (line 22)

H. "The silver apples of the moon," (line 23)

31. How does the poet develop the speaker's experiences in the second stanza (lines 9–16)?
   - A. The poet spotlights Aengus's immortality as a Celtic god.
   - B. The poet demonstrates how the passing of the days has aged Aengus.
   - C. The poet explains how Aengus witnessed a fish transform into a girl.
   - D. The poet exposes Aengus's life-long, unattainable yearning for a lost love.

32. Read lines 6 and 16.

   And moth-like stars were flickering out, (line 6)
   And faded through the brightening air. (line 16)

   What impact do lines 6 and 16 have on the meaning of the poem?
   - E. These lines indicate that Aengus is fishing in the early morning.
   - F. These lines show that Aengus is fishing in the afternoon.
   - G. These lines prove that Aengus is fishing in the evening.
   - H. These lines illustrate that Aengus is fishing late at night.

33. Read lines 12–13.

   And someone called me by my name:
   It had become a glimmering girl

   What impact do these lines have on the meaning of the poem?
   - A. They illustrate the first meeting of two lovers.
   - B. They tell of a magical transformation.
   - C. They share the narrator's surprise.
   - D. They recount a fishing trip.

34. Which detail from the poem reflects the idea of love slipping away?
   - E. "I went to blow the fire a-flame," (line 10)
   - F. "But something rustled on the floor," (line 11)
   - G. "It had become a glimmering girl" (line 13)
   - H. "And faded through the brightening air." (line 16)

Most scholars agree that, due to the political climate in Europe in the period prior to the First World War, a conflict of some kind was inevitable. Several circumstances contributed in the long-term to the breakout of war. However, these circumstances only served to set the stage for war. The missing ingredient was a spark that would ignite the volatile situation. It came in the form of an assassin's bullet on June 28, 1914.

At that time, Bosnia-Herzegovina was a province of Austria-Hungary. Many Bosnians resented Austrian rule, and there was a widespread desire for independence. When Archduke Franz Ferdinand, the heir to the Austro-Hungarian throne, announced plans to visit Bosnia, a terrorist organization known as the "Black Hand" made plans to assassinate him. The Archduke's decision to visit Bosnia was, by all accounts, foolhardy, since everyone knew that he would quite possibly become an assassin's target. However, the visit went as planned. As Ferdinand's entourage arrived in the Sarajevo train station, members of the "Black Hand" were already lining the path to City Hall, his destination.

As the motorcade passed the central police station, "Black Hand" member Nedeljko Cabrinovic tossed a grenade at the Archduke's vehicle. When the driver saw the object coming toward him, he accelerated. The grenade exploded under the next car. The Archduke's driver drove so quickly the rest of the way that none of the terrorists were able to attack his car. Ferdinand then attended the official reception at City Hall. Afterward, when he found out that the passengers in the second car had been badly injured, the Archduke insisted on visiting the hospital where they were being cared for. When one of his staff argued that this might be dangerous, he was quickly overruled. On the way to the hospital, the driver took a wrong turn. Realizing his mistake, he stopped and began reversing. Just then, one of the conspirators, Gavrilo Princip, happened to be walking down the same road. The car moved slowly in reverse and came within five feet of the waiting Princip, who fired several times into the car, killing the Archduke. This was the spark needed to inflame the tense situation in Europe. Within months, the entire continent would be engulfed in war.

35. Which of the following best describes what the passage is about?

- **A.** Europe in the early twentieth century
- **B.** Archduke Ferdinand's assassination
- **C.** long-term circumstances that contributed to the outbreak of World War I
- **D.** the Bosnian drive for independence

36. According to the passage, which of the following is a correct statement concerning the "Black Hand"?

- **E.** It was dedicated to securing the freedom of Austria from the Bosnians.
- **F.** Its members included Princip, Cabrinovic, and Ferdinand.
- **G.** Members of the "Black Hand" killed the Austrian heir with a hand grenade.
- **H.** It was a group that used assassination to achieve its goals.

37. According to the passage, each of the following mistakes led to Archduke Franz Ferdinand's death **except**

- **A.** visiting Bosnia.
- **B.** taking a wrong turn.
- **C.** allowing Nedeljko Cabrinovic to ride in the Archduke's car.
- **D.** visiting injured members of the Archduke's entourage.

38. After passing the central police station, why did Ferdinand's driver start driving faster?

E. He saw an object thrown at the vehicle.
F. There was a change in the posted speed limit just after the station.
G. The Archduke was running late for his reception at City Hall.
H. He was attempting to make up for time he had lost by taking a wrong turn.

39. The passage suggests that

A. Princip and Ferdinand had confronted one another in the past.
B. only one member of the "Black Hand" was in Sarajevo on June 28, 1914.
C. the driver of Ferdinand's vehicle was a "Black Hand" operative.
D. the "Black Hand" wanted Ferdinand dead because he was from the Austrian royal family.

40. Which of the following is a reasonable assumption about World War I based on the passage?

E. When war erupted, Bosnia and Austria were on the same side.
F. The war's only cause was the assassination of Franz Ferdinand.
G. World War I was completely avoidable.
H. The death of Archduke Ferdinand was an important contributing factor to the outbreak of war.

41. According to the passage, the assassination of Archduke Ferdinand was the result of

A. a carefully planned strategy.
B. an unforeseen coincidence.
C. a confrontation with a group of Black Hand activists.
D. a bomb thrown into his car.

42. Based on the information in the passage, Archduke Ferdinand's decision to visit Bosnia was

E. ill-conceived.
F. important to maintaining Austrian control.
G. a friendly, good-will gesture.
H. welcomed by the majority of Bosnians.

This passage is from the short story "The Masque of the Red Death" by Edgar Allan Poe, which was originally published in 1842.

The "Red Death" had long devastated the country. No pestilence had ever been so fatal, or so hideous. Blood was its Avatar and its seal—the madness and the horror of blood. There were sharp pains, and sudden dizziness, and then profuse bleeding at the pores, with dissolution. The scarlet stains upon the body and especially upon the face of the victim, were the pest ban which shut him out from the aid and from the sympathy of his fellow-men. And the whole seizure, progress, and termination of the disease, were incidents of half an hour.

But Prince Prospero was happy and dauntless and sagacious. When his dominions were half depopulated, he summoned to his presence a thousand hale and light-hearted friends from among the knights and dames of his court, and with these retired to the deep seclusion of one of his castellated abbeys. This was an extensive and magnificent structure, the creation of the prince's own eccentric yet august taste. A strong and lofty wall girdled it in. This wall had gates of iron. The courtiers, having entered, brought furnaces and massy hammers and welded the bolts.

They resolved to leave means neither of ingress nor egress to the sudden impulses of despair or of frenzy from within. The abbey was amply provisioned. With such precautions the courtiers might bid defiance to contagion. The external world could take care of itself. In the meantime it was folly to grieve or to think. The prince had provided all the appliances of pleasure. There were buffoons, there were improvisatori, there were ballet-dancers, there were musicians, there was Beauty, there was wine. All these and security were within. Without was the "Red Death."

It was toward the close of the fifth or sixth month of his seclusion that the Prince Prospero entertained his thousand friends at a masked ball of the most unusual magnificence. [. . .]

And the revel went whirlingly on, until at length there commenced the sounding of midnight upon the clock. And then the music ceased, as I have told; and the evolutions of the waltzers were quieted; and there was an uneasy cessation of all things as before. But now there were twelve strokes to be sounded by the bell of the clock; and thus it happened, perhaps, that more of thought crept, with more of time, into the meditations of the thoughtful among those who reveled. And thus too, it happened, that before the last echoes of the last chime had utterly sunk into silence, there were many individuals in the crowd who had found leisure to become aware of the presence of a masked figure which had arrested the attention of no single individual before. And the rumor of this new presence having spread itself whisperingly around, there arose at length from the whole company a buzz, or murmur, of horror, and of disgust.

In an assembly of phantasms such as I have painted, it may well be supposed that no ordinary appearance could have excited such sensation. In truth the masquerade license of the night was nearly unlimited; but the figure in question had out-Heroded Herod, and gone beyond the bounds of even the prince's indefinite decorum. There are chords in the hearts of the most reckless which cannot be touched without emotion. Even with the utterly lost, to whom life and death are equally jests, there are matters of which no jest can be made. The whole company, indeed, seemed now deeply to feel that in the costume and bearing of the stranger neither wit nor propriety existed. The figure was tall and gaunt, and shrouded from head to foot in the habiliments of the grave. The mask which concealed the visage was made so nearly to resemble the countenance of a stiffened corpse that the closest scrutiny must have had difficulty in detecting the cheat. And yet all this might have been endured, if not approved, by the mad revellers around. But the mummer had gone so far as to assume the type of the Red Death. His vesture was dabbled in blood—and his broad brow, with all the features of the face, was besprinkled with the scarlet horror.

When the eyes of the Prince Prospero fell upon this spectral image (which, with a slow and solemn movement, as if more fully to sustain its role, stalked to and fro among the waltzers) he was seen to be convulsed, in the first moment with a strong shudder either of terror or distaste; but, in the next, his brow reddened with rage.

43. How does paragraph 1 contribute to the plot of the excerpt?

A. The paragraph offers a historical context for how others have avoided the Red Death.

B. The paragraph explains the symptoms of a disease that is no longer cause for concern.

C. The paragraph introduces a disease that a country tries unsuccessfully to avoid.

D. The paragraph illustrates how the courtiers plan to eliminate the spread of the disease.

44. Which sentence from the excerpt best supports the idea that the country over which Prince Prospero rules has suffered major losses?

E. "When his dominions were half depopulated, he summoned to his presence a thousand hale and light-hearted friends..." (lines 13–15)

F. "They resolved to leave means neither of ingress nor egress to the sudden impulses of despair or of frenzy from within." (lines 23–25)

G. "And the whole seizure, progress, and termination of the disease, were incidents of half an hour." (lines 9–11)

H. "And the rumor of this new presence having spread itself whisperingly around, there arose at length from the whole company a buzz, or murmur, of horror, and of disgust." (lines 52–56)

45. The phrase "the scarlet stains upon the body and especially upon the face of the victim, were the pest ban which shut him out from the aid and from the sympathy of his fellow-men," (lines 6–9) in paragraph 1 shows that a person who shows symptoms of the Red Death is

A. carefully tended to by others.

B. gravely ill but likely to recover.

C. shunned by all.

D. sick for a long time.

46. Read this text from paragraph 2.

> **A strong and lofty wall girdled it in. This wall had gates of iron. The courtiers, having entered, brought furnaces and massy hammers and welded the bolts.**

These details convey a central idea in the excerpt by showing that the courtiers are hoping to

E. secure the abbey from attack since it was a building that was particularly vulnerable to assault.

F. keep out any rival princes and other dignitaries from both nearby and remote provinces.

G. separate themselves from the common people, who were considered to be of lower status.

H. ensure that no one entered or left, thus preventing the Red Death from spreading to them.

47. Read this text from paragraph 3.

> **The external world could take care of itself. In the meantime it was folly to grieve or to think. The prince had provided all the appliances of pleasure.**

How do these sentences contribute to the development of the plot?

A. They illustrate that the prince is unconcerned for his people's welfare outside of the abbey.

B. They show that the prince is focused on remaining humble and frugal.

C. They explain that the prince is resigned to give up his pleasure-seeking ways.

D. They note that the prince is secure in his ability to meet all of his people's needs.

48. Read this text from paragraph 4.

> **It was toward the close of the fifth or sixth month of his seclusion that the Prince Prospero entertained his thousand friends at a masked ball of the most unusual magnificence.**

Which statement best describes how the sentence fits into the overall structure of the excerpt?

E. It indicates a shift to the realization that the Red Death is already present within the abbey.

F. It emphasizes a shift from analysis of the courtiers' behavior to the behavior of the prince.

G. It introduces the idea that time has passed while foreshadowing a momentous event.

H. It provides a transition to the observation that the courtiers dislike being secluded.

49. In paragraph 4, how do the words "uneasy," "silence," and "masked figure" contribute to the meaning of the excerpt?

A. They illustrate a sense of anger.

B. They highlight a sense of foreboding.

C. They demonstrate a sense of revelry.

D. They allude to a sense of disdain.

50. How does paragraph 4 contribute to the central idea of the excerpt?

E. It condemns those who try to protect themselves against a fatal disease.

F. It discusses the medical symptoms of the Red Death.

G. It highlights the inevitability of death.

H. It emphasizes the foolishness of revelry.

Although it took the publication of his now-famous novel *Animal Farm* in 1945 to finally establish British writer George Orwell's reputation for shrewd political commentary, this well-known satire did not mark the beginning of Orwell's writing career. Indeed, by the time Orwell achieved any fame, he had been writing seriously for nearly fifteen years. In the decade preceding his completion of *Animal Farm*, for example, Orwell struggled mightily to make ends meet as a writer, and he was forced to settle for commissions that paid his bills but lacked the creative possibilities he sought. In fact, right up to his final bedridden days, much of Orwell's life was marked by struggle of one kind or another.

Born in 1903, Orwell grew up in England and was educated at Eton College, where he first began to write, expressing his dissatisfaction with his schooling experiences in various essays published in the college periodicals. Once free of his academic responsibilities in 1922, Orwell chose to go abroad as an administrator for the Indian Imperial Police in Burma. Again, Orwell struggled, this time with the clash resulting from his job responsibilities as a bureaucrat of the British government and his growing disillusionment with the concept of imperialism. In fact, it was during these conflicted years that Orwell first began to experience the intense feelings of disenchantment with large state bureaucracies that fill the pages of his later, and most popular, literary works, as well as a series of essays he published upon his return to England in 1928. In 1930, Orwell began his literary career in earnest, and he soon became a regular contributor to a number of lesser-known periodicals. In late 1936, already a committed socialist, Orwell was sent to Spain to report on the civil war. Once in Spain, however, Orwell quickly abandoned his responsibilities as a journalist and decided to join the communist Republican Army in its struggle against the Nationalists. After more than 100 days on the frontlines, Orwell was promoted to second lieutenant, given command of more than 30 men, and wounded by a sniper. In these years abroad, seemingly constantly thrust into violent clashes, Orwell found his political sensibilities changing.

By the time he returned to England in 1938, he had grown cynical about communism, a change that alienated his left-wing publishers but inspired his crowning literary achievement, the wholly pessimistic and satirical novel *Nineteen Eighty-Four,* which depicts the threat of political tyranny in the future. Orwell, however, would not live to experience the tremendous impact of this final work, as one last struggle, tuberculosis, claimed his life just months after the novel's release in 1949.

51. Which of the following best tells what this passage is about?

A. how Orwell struggled during his experiences abroad

B. how Orwell finally became an enormously successful writer

C. why Orwell found little success as a writer early in his career

D. how Orwell's literary career was consistently marked by struggle

52. All of the following are given as characteristics of Orwell's writing **except**

E. satirical.

F. politically shrewd.

G. creative.

H. cynical.

53. What does the passage imply about Orwell's political sentiments before he went to Burma?

A. He was already a firmly established socialist.

B. He was not opposed to British imperialism.

C. He sympathized with his left-wing publishers.

D. He was an ardent supporter of democracy.

54. Which of the following best describes what is suggested by the author's statement that "Orwell found his political sensibilities changing" (line 45)?

E. Orwell found the Spanish Civil War difficult to understand.

F. Orwell no longer believed in British imperialism.

G. Orwell lost the support of his left-wing publishers.

H. Orwell was no longer committed to the communist party.

55. What is the most likely reason the author uses the word "commissions" in paragraph 1?

A. to emphasize that Orwell was a part of many administrative organizations

B. to illustrate the groups of people Orwell interacted with

C. to show that Orwell received small payments for his work

D. to communicate the writing tasks Orwell received during his early career

56. According to the passage, Orwell's novel *Animal Farm* can best be described as

E. a crowning literary achievement.

F. a mocking commentary.

G. influenced by Orwell's experiences abroad.

H. depicting political tyranny.

57. The passage states that Orwell's cynicism about communism

A. motivated him to write his best, and final, novel.

B. endeared him to left-wing publishers.

C. was unfortunate, given his previous achievements.

D. led to a greater appreciation of the global political system.

IF TIME REMAINS, YOU MAY EITHER REVIEW THE ENGLISH LANGUAGE ARTS QUESTIONS IN PART 1, OR YOU MAY CONTINUE ON TO PART 2, THE MATHEMATICS SECTION.

PART 2 — MATHEMATICS

Suggested Time — 90 Minutes

57 QUESTIONS

IMPORTANT NOTES

(1) Formulas and definitions of mathematical terms and symbols are **not** provided.
(2) Diagrams other than graphs are **not** necessarily drawn to scale. Do not assume any relationship in a diagram unless it is specifically stated or can be figured out from the information given.
(3) Assume that a diagram is in one plane unless the problem specifically states that it is not.
(4) Graphs are drawn to scale. Unless stated otherwise, you can assume relationships according to appearance. For example, (on a graph) lines that appear to be parallel can be assumed to be parallel; likewise for concurrent lines, straight lines, collinear points, right angles, etc.
(5) Reduce all fractions to lowest terms.

GRID-IN PROBLEMS

QUESTIONS 58–62

DIRECTIONS: Solve each problem. On the answer sheet, write your answer in the boxes at the top of the grid. Start on the left side of each grid. Print only one number or symbol in each box. **DO NOT LEAVE A BOX BLANK IN THE MIDDLE OF AN ANSWER.** Under each box, fill in the circle that matches the number or symbol you wrote above. **DO NOT FILL IN A CIRCLE UNDER AN UNUSED BOX.**

58. If $\frac{2x+1}{4} = \frac{12}{20}$, what is the value of x?

59. What value of f makes the equation $5f + 25 = 450$ true?

60. If n is a positive integer, what is one value of n that satisfies the inequality $-3n + 5 \geq -1$?

61. If $\frac{2}{5} = \frac{d}{115}$, what is the value of d?

62. Samantha grows carrots, peppers, and onions in her garden. She has twice as many carrots as peppers, and she has three times as many onions as carrots. If Samantha grew 36 onions, how many total vegetables did Samantha grow?

Multiple Choice Problems

Questions 63–114

DIRECTIONS: Solve each problem. Select the best answer from the choices given. Mark the letter of your answer on the answer sheet. You can do your figuring in the test booklet or on paper provided by the proctor. **DO NOT MAKE ANY MARKS ON YOUR ANSWER SHEET OTHER THAN FILLING IN YOUR ANSWER CHOICES.**

63. If $4x = (3y)^2$ and $x = 36$, where y is a positive number, what is the value of y?

A. 2

B. 4

C. $4\sqrt{3}$

D. 27

64. If $\sqrt{m+9} - 1 = 3$, what is the value of m?

E. 5

F. 7

G. 12

H. 15

65. If $x \square y$ is defined by the expression $(x - y)^x + (x + y)^y$, what is the value of $4 \square 2$?

A. 52

B. 44

C. 28

D. 20

66. A college class is made up of f freshmen and s sophomores. If 5 freshmen drop this class, the number of sophomores in the class is 3 times the number of freshmen. Which of the following equations represents s in terms of f?

E. $s = \dfrac{f-5}{3}$

F. $s = \dfrac{f+5}{3}$

G. $s = 3(f - 5)$

H. $s = 3(f + 5)$

67.

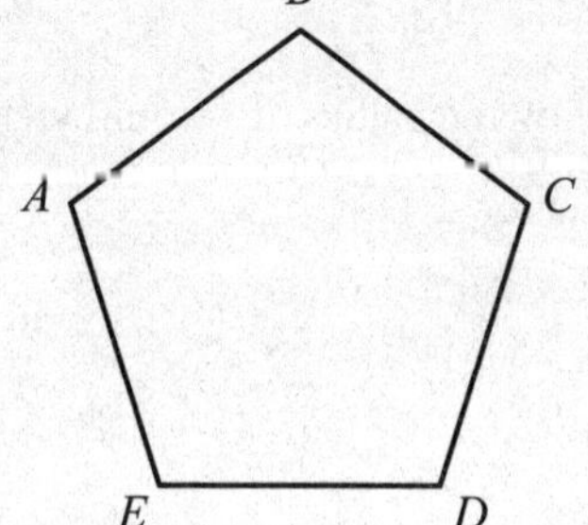

In pentagon $ABCDE$ shown above, each side is 1 centimeter. If a particle starts at point A and travels clockwise 723 centimeters along $ABCDE$, at which point will the particle stop?

A. A

B. B

C. C

D. D

68. In a coordinate plane, if points A $(p, 3)$ and B $(6, p)$ lie on a line with a slope of 2, what is the value of p?

E. 2

F. 3

G. 4

H. 5

69. Sixty cookies were to be equally distributed to x campers. When 8 campers did not want the cookies, the other campers each received 2 more cookies. Which of the following equations could be used to find the number of campers, x?

A. $x^2 - 8x - 240 = 0$

B. $x^2 - 8x + 240 = 0$

C. $x^2 + 8x - 240 = 0$

D. $x^2 + 8x + 240 = 0$

70. Which of the following values of s would yield the smallest value for $4 + \frac{1}{s}$?

E. $\frac{1}{4}$

F. $\frac{1}{2}$

G. 1

H. 4

71. If an integer is randomly chosen from the first 50 positive integers, what is the probability that an integer with a digit of 3 is selected?

A. $\frac{7}{25}$

B. $\frac{3}{10}$

C. $\frac{8}{25}$

D. $\frac{2}{5}$

72. If $4x + 2 = 26$, then $4x + 8 =$

E. 32

F. 34

G. 36

H. 38

73. If a certain train fare costs $5.00 for the first 10 miles of service, $0.25 per mile for the next 40 miles, and $0.10 per mile for each additional mile, what would the train fare be to travel a total distance of 100 miles?

A. $15.00

B. $17.50

C. $20.00

D. $25.00

74.

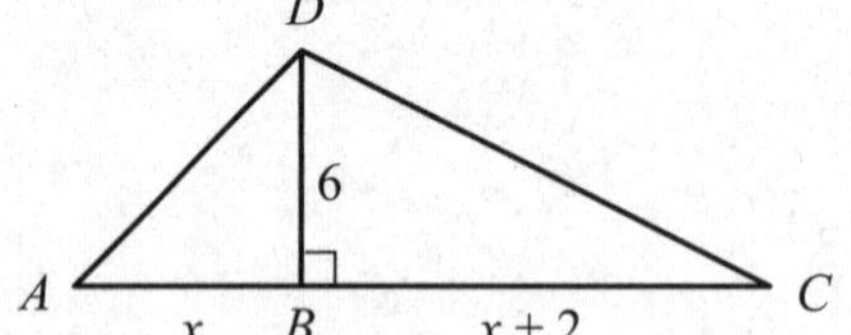

In the figure above, triangle ADC has an area of 24, and the lengths of AB and BC are x and $x + 2$, respectively. If the length of BD is 6, what is the value of x?

E. 1

F. 2

G. 3

H. 4

75. If $-1 < y < 0$, which of the following is the greatest?

A. y^2

B. $1 - y$

C. $1 + y$

D. $2y$

76. Tariq has $10 and wants to buy 21 oranges at $0.30 each and 12 apples at $0.50 each. If there is no sales tax, how much more money does he need?

E. $2.00

F. $2.30

G. $2.60

H. $12.00

77. If Thomas went shopping with $15 and ended up with a debt of $5, how much money did he spend?

A. $5

B. $10

C. $15

D. $20

78. If $2x + 2x + 14 = 2x + 2x + 2x + 6$, then what is the value of x?

E. 3

F. 4

G. 5

H. 7

79.

Which estimate is the closest to the percent of the area of the rectangle above that is shaded?

A. 40%

B. 50%

C. 55%

D. 60%

80. A booklet contains 116 pages, which were supposed to be numbered beginning with page 1. Because of a printing error, only pages 1 through 87, inclusive, were numbered. If someone wants to number the remaining pages of a single booklet by hand, how many digits will that person have to write?

E. 46

F. 58

G. 64

H. 75

81.

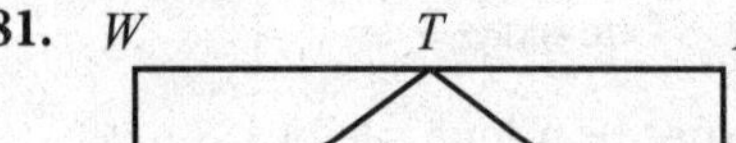

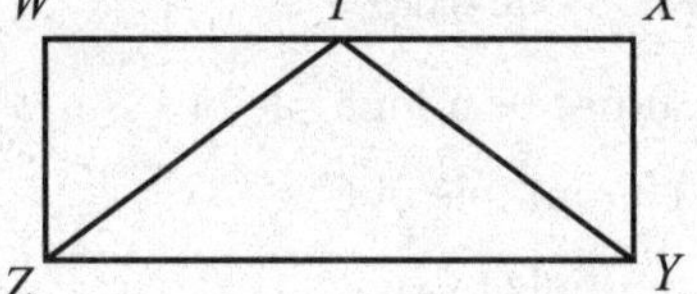

In rectangle $WXYZ$ in the figure above, the length of WZ is 6 and the rectangle has an area of 96. Point T is the midpoint of WX. What is the perimeter of triangle TYZ?

A. 28

B. 30

C. 36

D. 48

82. When 368 is divided by 7, the remainder is x. What is the remainder when 368 is divided by $3x$?

E. 0

F. 3

G. 5

H. 8

83. In a room of 33 students, 12 are taking geography, 14 are taking history, and 5 are taking both geography and history. How many of these students are not taking either geography or history?

A. 7

B. 10

C. 12

D. 14

84. The ratio of the positive integer x to the positive integer y is 7 to 5. Which of the following statements MUST be true?

E. $x + y$ cannot be a multiple of 18.

F. $x + y$ is a multiple of 6.

G. xy is a multiple of 70.

H. $x - y$ can be an odd integer.

85. 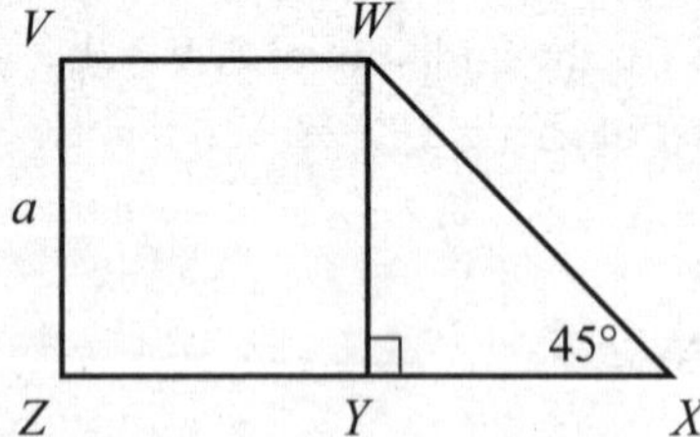

In the figure above, $VWYZ$ is a square. What is the perimeter of the entire figure?

A. $5a$

B. $(3+\sqrt{2})a$

C. $5a+\sqrt{2}$

D. $(4+\sqrt{2})a$

86. As long as $x \neq 3$, what do you get when you divide $x^2 - 9$ by $x - 3$?

E. $x - 6$

F. $x - 3$

G. x

H. $x + 3$

87. There are a total of 256 people at a party. If, after every 5 minutes, half of the people present leave, how many people will still remain after 20 minutes?

A. 80

B. 64

C. 32

D. 16

88. 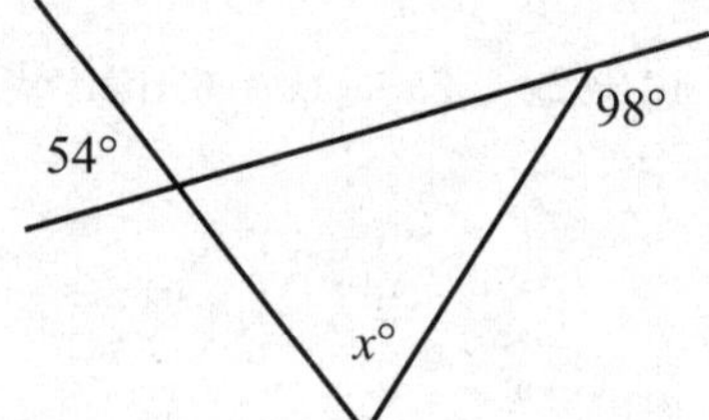

In the figure above, what is the value of x?

E. 24

F. 28

G. 36

H. 44

89. The average (arithmetic mean) of 16 numbers is 3. The average of these 16 numbers and a seventeenth number is 4. What is the seventeenth number?

A. 12

B. 17

C. 18

D. 20

90. One box contains 3 balls, one of which is red. A second box contains 4 balls, one of which is red. If Pilar draws one ball at random from each box, what is the probability that both balls are red?

E. $\frac{1}{14}$

F. $\frac{1}{12}$

G. $\frac{1}{7}$

H. $\frac{2}{7}$

91. If a, b, and c are positive numbers and $abc = b^2$, which of the following must equal b?

A. ac

B. ab

C. bc

D. $\frac{a}{c}$

92. The spare change on a dresser is composed of pennies, nickels, and dimes. If the ratio of pennies to nickels is 2:3 and the ratio of pennies to dimes is 3:4, what is the ratio of nickels to dimes?

E. 9:8

F. 5:7

G. 4:5

H. 3:4

93. If $5a - b = 9$ and $3a + b = 15$, then $a + b =$

A. 3

B. 5

C. 7

D. 9

94. If x is a positive integer, then $5x - x^2$ must be

E. positive.

F. negative.

G. even.

H. a perfect square.

95.

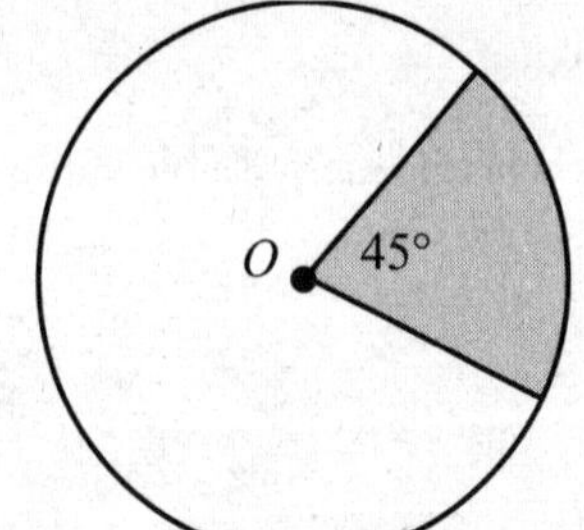

If the area of the shaded region in the circle above is 2π, what is the diameter of circle O?

A. 4

B. 8

C. 16

D. 4π

96. A certain deck of cards contains r cards. After the cards are distributed evenly among s people, 8 cards are left over. In terms of r and s, how many cards did each person receive?

E. $\frac{s}{8-r}$

F. $\frac{r-8}{s}$

G. $\frac{r}{s} - 8$

H. $s - 8r$

97. Which of the following points lies on the same line as the points with coordinates (2, 6) and (4, 3)?

A. (1, 7)

B. (2, 8)

C. (3, 5)

D. (6, 0)

98. If $3\sqrt{x} = 15$, what is x?

E. 0

F. $\sqrt{5}$

G. 9

H. 25

99. If $|7 + r| = 3$, then what is one possible value of r?

A. −10

B. −7

C. −3

D. 4

100. $\frac{1}{y} = \frac{x}{3}$, and $y = \frac{1}{5}$. What is the value of x?

E. $\frac{1}{15}$

F. $\frac{3}{5}$

G. $\frac{5}{3}$

H. 15

101. $x - \frac{7}{10} = y$, and $y = 2$. What is the value of x?

A. $-\frac{3}{10}$

B. $\frac{9}{10}$

C. $\frac{13}{10}$

D. $\frac{27}{10}$

102. $20 - (y - x) = 30 - (x - y)$, and $x = 4$. What is the value of y?

E. −9

F. −1

G. 1

H. Cannot be determined from the information given.

103. If $\frac{x}{10} - \frac{y}{5} + \frac{1}{6} = \frac{1}{15}$ and $y = 1$, then what does x equal?

A. $\frac{2}{3}$

B. $\frac{5}{7}$

C. 1

D. 3

104. If $y \div 7 = x - 3 \times 5$ and $y = 21$, what is the value of x?

E. $\frac{6}{5}$

F. $\frac{18}{5}$

G. 16

H. 18

105. If $-x - 9 = -y^2$ and $y = 4$, what is the value of x?

A. -25

B. -7

C. $\sqrt{13}$

D. 7

106. If $x = 4y^2 + |-5|$, what is the value of y in terms of x?

E. $\frac{x-5}{4}$

F. $\sqrt{\frac{x-5}{4}}$

G. $\sqrt{\frac{x+5}{4}}$

H. $\frac{x+5}{4}$

107. If $x = 4(3 - y)(2^2 - 1)$, what is the value of y in terms of x?

A. $\frac{x-6}{4}$

B. $\frac{x}{4} - 3$

C. $4 - \frac{x}{3}$

D. $3 - \frac{x}{12}$

108. If $x = 3y(2 - |-4|) + y(3 - |-2|)$, what is the value of y in terms of x?

E. $-\frac{x}{5}$

F. $-5x$

G. $-x$

H. $\frac{x}{23}$

109. If $\frac{1}{x} = x - \frac{3}{x}$, $x \geq 0$, what is the value of x?

A. 0

B. 1

C. 2

D. 3

110. If $|r + 7| = 6$ and $|2r - 2| = 4$, what is the value of r?

E. -13

F. -10

G. -1

H. 1

111. For how many positive integers x is $\frac{130}{x}$ an integer?

A. 8

B. 7

C. 6

D. 5

112. $x + \frac{3}{4} = 2y$, and $y = \frac{1}{6}$. What is the value of x?

E. $-\frac{5}{12}$

F. $\frac{1}{4}$

G. $\frac{13}{12}$

H. $\frac{27}{12}$

113. If $x = \sqrt{y} + 2$, what is the value of y in terms of x?

A. $\sqrt{x-2}$

B. $\sqrt{x} - 2$

C. $x - 2$

D. $(x - 2)^2$

114.

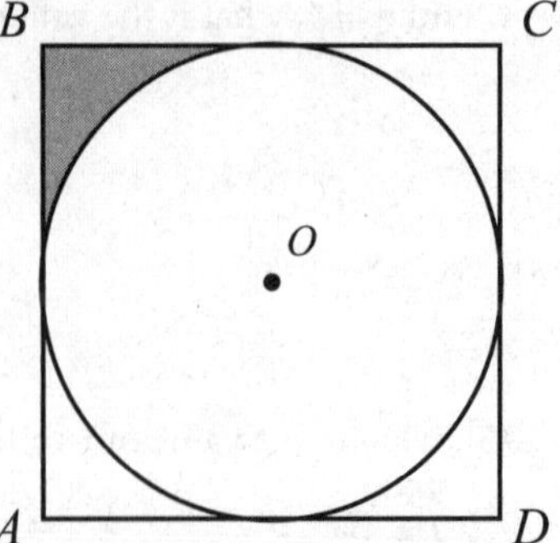

In the figure above, circle O is inscribed in square $ABCD$. If the circumference of circle O is 4π, what is the area of the shaded region?

E. $\pi - 2$

F. $4 - \pi$

G. $4 + \pi$

H. $16 - 4\pi$

THIS IS THE END OF THE TEST. IF TIME REMAINS, YOU MAY CHECK YOUR ANSWERS TO PART 2 AND PART 1. BE SURE THAT THERE ARE NO STRAY MARKS, PARTIALLY FILLED ANSWER CIRCLES, OR INCOMPLETE ERASURES ON YOUR ANSWER SHEET.	**STOP**

ANSWER KEY

Practice Test 2—English Language Arts

1. C
2. F
3. C
4. F
5. B
6. F
7. A
8. G
9. D
10. F
11. A
12. H
13. B
14. G
15. D
16. E
17. B
18. E
19. C
20. H
21. B
22. F
23. C
24. E
25. D
26. G
27. D
28. G
29. D
30. F
31. C
32. E
33. B
34. H
35. B
36. H
37. C
38. E
39. D
40. H
41. B
42. E
43. C
44. E
45. C
46. H
47. A
48. G
49. B
50. G
51. D
52. G
53. B
54. H
55. D
56. F
57. A

ANSWER KEY

Practice Test 2—Mathematics

58. .7
59. 85
60. 0, 1, or 2
61. 46
62. 54
63. B
64. F
65. A
66. G
67. D
68. H
69. A
70. H
71. A
72. E
73. C
74. G
75. B
76. F
77. D
78. F
79. D
80. H
81. C
82. H
83. C
84. F
85. D
86. H
87. D
88. H
89. D
90. F
91. A
92. E
93. D
94. G
95. B
96. F
97. D
98. H
99. A
100. H
101. D
102. F
103. C
104. H
105. D
106. F
107. D
108. E
109. C
110. G
111. A
112. E
113. D
114. F

ANSWERS AND EXPLANATIONS

Part 1—English Language Arts

Revising/Editing Part A

1. C

Category: Usage

Getting to the Answer: Be sure that an apostrophe indicates possession or a contraction. "Sponsors" should not be possessive, so **(C)** is correct. The revision in **(A)** would incorrectly switch to the comparative form, but the superlative "most" refers to all television shows that aired last week. **(B)** introduces an unnecessary comma. The comma in **(D)** would interrupt the flow of the sentence.

2. F

Category: Usage

Getting to the Answer: Be sure that the verb agrees with the subject in number. The subject of a sentence might not be the noun closest to the main verb. "Group of people" begins with a singular noun, requiring the singular verb form, so **(F)** is correct. The revision in **(E)** incorrectly removes the singular form. **(G)** contains the wrong word. **(H)** would refer to a specific concert, but the sentence discusses all of the concerts.

3. C

Category: Knowledge of Language

Getting to the Answer: Using two words with the same meaning in one sentence is redundant. "Research" and "study" mean the same thing, so sentence 3 should be revised to fix the issue. **(C)** is correct. **(A)**, **(B)**, and **(D)** do not have wordiness issues.

4. F

Category: Sentence Structure and Formation

Getting to the Answer: In sentence two, place a comma after "competitions" to separate the introductory phrase from the rest of the sentence. **(F)** is correct. The sentences in **(E)**, **(G)**, and **(H)** have correct punctuation.

Revising/Editing Part B

5. B

Category: Knowledge of Language

Getting to the Answer: The word "it" is vague and could refer to anything. To make the meaning clear and precise, it's necessary to specifically refer to Janssen's experiment, as **(B)** does. **(B)** also turns a passive sentence into an active one, making it even clearer. **(A)** deletes the necessary word "experiment," and **(C)** is not only passive but also deletes reference to Lockyer's experiment. **(D)** retains the vague word "it."

6. E

Category: Usage

Getting to the Answer: Every pronoun must have a clear antecedent or the sentence will be confusing. To whom does "He" refer? In context, it has to be either Crookes or Lockyer. Since only Lockyer is in the answer choices, **(E)** must be correct. **(F)** is incorrect because it is not Janssen to whom the samples were sent. **(G)** and **(H)** incorrectly change the singular "it" to a plural pronoun, which doesn't match the singular "element."

7. A

Category: Usage

Getting to the Answer: Read the sentence in context; all verbs in the paragraph are in the present tense. **(A)** makes the necessary change by putting "became" in the present. **(B)** and **(C)** change the meaning of the sentence, and **(D)** is wordy.

8. G

Category: Organization, Unity, and Cohesion

Getting to the Answer: Since both sentences describe the same property of helium—why it is a nonrenewable resource—they can be combined with a simple semicolon joining two independent clauses. **(G)** does just that. **(E)**

incorrectly joins the two with a comma, while **(F)**, though grammatically correct, is confusing and wordy. **(H)** makes the second sentence a dependent clause, but then incorrectly joins it with the first by a semicolon.

9. D

Category: Organization, Unity, and Cohesion

Getting to the Answer: This sentence is another example of the non-scientific uses of helium, and as such requires a continuation rather than a contrast phrase. The words "In addition" provide continuation, making **(D)** correct. **(A)** is a continuation word but indicates more of the same, and inhaling helium is not the same as using helium in blimps and balloons. **(B)** is a contrast phrase, and **(C)** is wordy.

10. F

Category: Punctuation

Getting to the Answer: The problem with this sentence is the possessive word "scientist's," which should be a non-possessive, plural word. **(F)** corrects this mistake. **(E)** and **(H)** change the meaning of the sentence, and **(G)** creates a verb error.

11. A

Category: Topic Development

Getting to the Answer: Sentence 21, starting with the words "Until recently," indicates that something new has changed scientists' thinking. A concluding sentence describing that new event is needed to bring the thought to a logical end. **(A)** provides that conclusion. **(B)** adds nothing to the idea, and without the concluding sentence, there is no support for **(C)**. **(D)** is also unsupported and confuses helium on the sun with helium on Earth.

Reading Comprehension

Passage Analysis: This passage describes how basketball was created and follows the pathway it took to become the game it is today. The first paragraph sets the stage for basketball's creation: Gulick wanted to keep a rowdy class busy. Paragraph 2 explains how Naismith adapted a game from his youth, which became basketball. The third paragraph describes the game's introduction to colleges and women's teams. Paragraph 4 discusses how professional basketball was used as a backup for other sports. And the last paragraph details how basketball has continued to change.

12. H

Category: Global

Getting to the Answer: **(H)** is correct because the passage discusses the changes that have occurred since basketball was invented. **(E)** is incorrect because women's basketball is only mentioned in one paragraph. **(F)** is too general; only one sport is mentioned. **(G)** is incorrect since only a small part of Dr. Naismith's life is discussed.

13. B

Category: Inference

Getting to the Answer: As your Roadmap shows, the formation of the Basketball Association of America is discussed in paragraph 4, where it states that professional basketball was programmed "to fill seats on days when there were no professional hockey or college basketball matches." That statement supports the inference that college basketball teams were already playing games in large stadiums, a match for choice **(B)**. There is no support for **(A)**, and professional teams, **(C)**, didn't exist before the Association was formed. **(D)** is a Misused Detail; professional hockey matches were played but there is no suggestion that professional basketball was programmed only when there were no hockey matches.

14. G

Category: Detail

Getting to the Answer: (G) is correct because slam dunks are never mentioned in the passage. **(E)** is incorrect because the last paragraph mentions that there are now four fewer players per side than in the days of Naismith. **(F)** is also incorrect because the passage states that a rule change resulted in the three-point shot. **(H)** is incorrect because women began playing basketball after Dr. Naismith's students were seen playing it.

15. D

Category: Inference

Getting to the Answer: (D) is correct because the passage says that Gulick wanted an athletic distraction for a rowdy group of students. **(A)** is incorrect since the passage does not refer to Gulick as an arena owner. **(B)** is incorrect because outdoor games could not be played because of the weather, not because of their commonplace nature. **(C)** is incorrect since the only childhood game mentioned in the passage served to inspire Naismith, not Gulick.

16. E

Category: Inference

Getting to the Answer: (E) is correct. The passage says that the owners wanted to fill seats. You can infer that more people in attendance results in more money for the arena owners. **(F)** is incorrect because basketball began as an indoor sport. **(G)** is incorrect since there is no reason to believe that attendance was not high on days when these games were played. **(H)** is incorrect because the three-point shot did not come into existence until 1980.

17. B

Category: Detail

Getting to the Answer: (B) is correct, according to the last paragraph of the passage. **(A)** is incorrect because it was Gulick who gave these orders. **(C)** is incorrect since the inventor of the BAA is not mentioned in the passage. **(D)** refers to Naismith, not Carr.

18. E

Category: Detail

Getting to the Answer: (E) is correct, because the only pieces of equipment used to play Naismith's original version of the game were convenient things like peach baskets and balls from other sports. **(F)** and **(H)** are incorrect because the activity that inspired Naismith, according to paragraph 2, required precision and skill. **(G)** is incorrect because the main stipulation of Naismith's assignment was to create an indoor game.

Passage Analysis: This passage explores the creation of art by early peoples for a variety of purposes. The first paragraph explains when and where early art was created, focusing on Cro-Magnon art. The second paragraph refutes popular misconceptions about prehistoric peoples, showing that they had more skills and resources than many believe. The third paragraph explores reasons why early art may have been created, suggesting that Australian aborigines and African Bushmen may provide information: that art is created for a variety of reasons.

19. C

Category: Global

Getting to the Answer: The information in each of the three paragraphs (that ancient art exists, that it includes a variety of forms in addition to paintings, and that paintings can have various meanings) all contribute to the point that ancient humans were probably more sophisticated than most people think. All the remaining answers are true according to the passage, but they are too narrow. **(A)** is a detail pulled from the last paragraph. **(B)** is a too-narrow detail from the second paragraph. **(D)** is a detail that appears only in paragraph 2. The correct answer, therefore, is **(C)**.

20. H

Category: Function

Getting to the Answer: In paragraph 2, the author introduces some examples of early art created by the Cro-Magnons, including clothing and trail signs; **(H)** is correct. The first paragraph considers the many forms of early art in a broad sense, making **(E)** incorrect. **(F)** and **(G)** are incorrect because the third paragraph discusses the debate surrounding the interpretations of art created by the Cro-Magnons and suggests that the Cro-Magnons may have had varying motives for creating art.

21. B

Category: Inference

Getting to the Answer: This question asks you to make an inference. If, as lines 21–22 say, "garbage...left in caves is more likely to have been preserved than other artifacts," it's almost the same as saying that "artifacts in other locations are more likely to have decayed." **(B)** is correct. **(A)** is incorrect because the author actually says that Cro-Magnons lived both in caves and far from them; she says nothing about the "majority" of them. Archaeologists found trail signs inside caves, not outside them as **(C)** suggests. The author says nothing about what sites archaeologists are more likely to prefer, so **(D)** infers too much.

22. F

Category: Inference

Getting to the Answer: In this question, you have to make an inference—but remember, don't go overboard. What did archaeologists formerly believe? They believed that the paintings were of the animals most often hunted by Cro-Magnons. But now, scientists have discovered that similar paintings made by Aborigines are made for a variety of reasons, choice **(F)**. **(E)** and **(H)** are Out of Scope, with information not mentioned in the passage. **(G)** is true according to the passage but is not given as a reason why scientists changed their interpretations.

23. C

Category: Inference

Getting to the Answer: The author doesn't say that Cro-Magnon and aboriginal art served the same functions, but that, because we know that aboriginal artists paint for many reasons, we shouldn't oversimplify the motivations of Cro-Magnon artists. The correct answer is **(C)**. **(A)** is too narrow; the author's big point is not about "tribal boundaries." The author says nothing about depictions of people in early rock art, so **(B)** is incorrect. **(D)** makes a larger point, but it is too Extreme.

24. E

Category: Inference

Getting to the Answer: Check the passage if you don't remember that "claviforms" are trail signs. The point that the passage makes about claviforms is that they warn visitors about hazards in the same way that modern humans use warning signs. The correct answer is **(E)**. Hunting and agriculture are not related to claviforms, which eliminates **(F)**. **(G)** contradicts the passage, which says that the people commonly called "cavemen" did make claviforms. The passage doesn't bring up the issue of their artistic sophistication in this part, so **(H)** is incorrect.

25. D

Category: Function

Getting to the Answer: In the first paragraph, the author is emphasizing the scarceness of art discoveries from early prehistory, which matches **(D)**. **(A)** and **(B)** are incorrect because the author does not see any credible prehistoric art left. There is no indication of the truthfulness or falsity of prehistoric art, making **(C)** incorrect.

26. G

Category: Inference

Getting to the Answer: Though the passage focuses on Cro-Magnon French and German cave art, early on the author makes the sweeping declaration that "The oldest known artworks were created more or less simultaneously in Europe, Africa, and Australia, with some further recent discoveries of old art in Asia and the Americas as well" (lines 5–8). Since there was likely no contact between people of these varied regions, it can be assumed that the impetus to create art was a universal urge, present in all peoples regardless of their location, as **(G)** states. **(E)** is Opposite and **(F)** is a Misused Detail about modern mentality (line 55). The passage states that prior to producing the cave art of the Paleolithic era, it is possible that people painted their bodies. Thus art would have existed before that time, so **(H)** is incorrect.

Poem Analysis: Published in 1899, "The Song of Wandering Aengus" has several themes, but overall, it is a love story. In Celtic mythology (a field in which Yeats, an Irish poet, was very interested and knowledgeable), Aengus is the god of love and beauty, but in this poem, he seems to be a love-struck mortal. The first stanza introduces the narrator, Aengus, going into the woods on a fishing trip, during which he lands "a little silver trout." The second stanza describes the startling transformation of the trout into a beautiful girl, who calls his name and then immediately runs away. In the third stanza, Aengus describes his futile search for the girl, even into his old age, and his hopes for when—and if—he ever finds her. The moon and sun signify the passing days, and the apples give a sense of the magic of nature.

27. D

Category: Function

Getting to the Answer: A lyric poem is usually written in the first person "I" and expresses the speaker's emotions. Because of its use of personal pronouns and emotional language, this is a lyric poem, which, incidentally, was put to music much later; **(D)** is correct. The poem does not focus on a death, grief, or a heroic event, making **(A)**, **(B)**, and **(C)** incorrect.

28. G

Category: Global

Getting to the Answer: Keep the overall theme in mind: the fire must refer to love, which is often called a "burning passion," foreshadowing the progression of the poem. So, **(G)** is correct. **(E)** and **(F)** are too literal and improbable, making them incorrect. **(H)** is incorrect because the fire in Aengus's head is described before Aengus meets the girl, so he has yet to experience the sorrow of unrequited love.

29. D

Category: Detail

Getting to the Answer: In line 3, Aengus "cut and peeled a hazel wand" to use as a fishing rod. To serve as a fishing rod, it must have been a relatively small and thin stick, such as a small limb from a hazel tree that he could cut and peel; **(D)** is correct. **(A)**, **(B)** and **(C)** are incorrect because there is no evidence in the poem that Aengus is preparing fruit to eat, has a headache, or is creating a magical rod to use later in the poem.

30. F

Category: Inference

Getting to the Answer: In the third stanza, Aengus notes that his wandering ages him, which indicates his mortality. Thus, **(F)** is correct. **(E)** is incorrect because the stars flickering out describes the time of day, not Aengus's mortality. **(G)** and **(H)** are incorrect because lines 22–23 describe an action that Aengus plans to do once he finds the girl.

31. C

Category: Global

Getting to the Answer: In the second stanza, the poet illustrates how Aengus saw the transformation of a fish into a girl; **(C)** is correct. The poet shows how the passing of days has aged Aengus in his lifelong, unattainable yearning for a lost love in the third stanza, making **(B)** and **(D)** incorrect. **(A)** is incorrect because the poem never specifically mentions Aengus's status as a god, though he is considered to be one in Celtic mythology.

32. E

Category: Detail

Getting to the Answer: Though the time of day (or night) is not explicitly mentioned, Yeats writes that "moth-like stars were flickering out" (line 6) and that the girl "faded through the brightening air" (line 16). These two descriptors seem to describe the early morning; **(E)** is correct. Stars do not fade in the afternoon, making **(F)** incorrect. If the action took place in the evening or late at night, the air would not be becoming brighter; **(G)** and **(H)** are incorrect.

33. B

Category: Detail

Getting to the Answer: Lines 12–13 ("And someone called me by my name: It had become a glimmering girl") highlight the most important action in the poem, which is the magical transformation from fish to girl; **(B)** is correct. The first meeting between Aengus and the girl occurs in the third stanza, and while Aengus may immediately fall in love, there is not enough information to determine whether the girl falls in love, too; **(A)** is incorrect. It seems likely that the narrator might be surprised, but this is not the central idea of the poem, making **(C)** incorrect. The entire poem speaks of far more than an ordinary fishing trip; **(D)** is incorrect.

34. H

Category: Detail

Getting to the Answer: The girl "faded through the brightening air" (line 16) after running away. Later in the third stanza, Aengus is still searching for her, making **(H)** correct. **(E)** is incorrect because Aengus had not yet met the girl in line 10. **(F)** and **(G)** are incorrect because these two lines signal the transformation of the trout into the "glimmering girl" and not the idea of love slipping away.

Passage Analysis: This passage describes the events that led to the beginning of World War I. The first paragraph states that the world was already at the brink of war when an assassination set it off in 1914. The second paragraph explains the political situation in Bosnia-Herzegovina, where the "Black Hand" was making plans to assassinate Archduke Ferdinand. The third paragraph describes how the planned assassination attempt failed, but, after several members of the Archduke's party were injured, the Archduke's car took a wrong turn to where a member of the "Black Hand," Princip, could shoot him.

35. B

Category: Global

Getting to the Answer: The main focus of the passage is the events of June 28, 1914, the day Franz Ferdinand was assassinated. Therefore, **(B)** is correct. **(A)** is incorrect because it is too broad. **(C)** is also too broad: the long-term circumstances are mentioned, but never discussed in depth. **(D)** is incorrect since the drive for independence is only a detail that explains the assassination of Ferdinand.

36. H

Category: Detail

Getting to the Answer: (H) is the only answer consistent with the passage. **(E)** is incorrect: the group is described as dedicated to freeing Bosnia from Austrian control. **(F)** is incorrect because, while Princip and Cabrinovic were members of the "Black Hand," Ferdinand was not. **(G)** is incorrect because the hand grenade attack missed the Archduke, who was later killed by a bullet.

37. C

Category: Detail

Getting to the Answer: Remember that this question is asking for the answer choice NOT supported by the passage. **(C)** is correct because the passage never mentions Cabrinovic riding in the car with the Archduke. The rest of the answer choices are listed as mistakes in the passage and are therefore incorrect.

38. E

Category: Detail

Getting to the Answer: (E) is correct; the passage claims the driver accelerated when he saw the grenade that Cabrinovic had thrown coming toward him. **(F)** and **(G)** contradict the passage, since there is no mention of a speed limit or the group running late. **(H)** is incorrect because the wrong turn did not occur until later in the day.

39. D

Category: Inference

Getting to the Answer: (D) is correct: the passage explains that the Bosnians were unhappy with Austrian rule. **(A)** is incorrect because the passage does not mention any previous encounters between Princip and Ferdinand, and there is no evidence to suggest that the two had previously met one another. **(B)** is incorrect because two members are mentioned in the passage: Princip and Cabrinovic. **(C)** is incorrect because the driver attempted to save Ferdinand by speeding up to avoid the grenade.

40. H

Category: Inference

Getting to the Answer: (H) is correct because the assassination is referred to as a spark that set off an explosive situation. **(E)** is incorrect because the Bosnians wanted independence from Austria. Therefore, it is unreasonable to assume that they would fight on the same side. **(F)** is incorrect since the passage states that there were several contributing factors to the outbreak of war. **(G)** is incorrect because the first paragraph explains that "a conflict of some kind was inevitable."

41. B

Category: Detail

Getting to the Answer: Despite the carefully laid plans of the Black Hand, the Archduke was not assassinated as planned, that is, by members lying in wait along the motorcade path. The actual assassination was an unforeseen coincidence; Gavrilo Princip "happened to be walking down the same road" (line 41) where the Archduke's car had stopped and was backing up to correct a wrong turn. Thus the opportunity for the assassination was an unforeseen coincidence, choice **(B)**. A coincidence is the opposite of a carefully-planned strategy; eliminate **(A)**. Princip is described as walking along; there is no support that he was part of a group in that area, making **(C)** incorrect. **(D)** is incorrect because Princip "fired several times into the car" (lines 43–44), indicating a gun, not a bomb.

42. E

Category: Detail

Getting to the Answer: Lines 17–18 answer this question: "The Archduke's decision to visit Bosnia was, by all accounts, foolhardy." A foolhardy decision—reckless or rash—is certainly ill-conceived. Match this with choice **(E)**. There is nothing in the passage supporting **(F)** or **(G)**, and since the author states that "Many Bosnians resented Austrian rule, and there was a widespread desire for independence" (lines 11–13), **(H)** is also incorrect.

Passage Analysis: In this cautionary horror story by Edgar Allan Poe, a thousand of Prince Prospero's titled friends gather in his locked, fortified abbey. They are attempting to shield themselves from contact with the fatal Red Death disease. Paragraph 1 describes the scourge of the Red Death and how quickly and ruthlessly it kills its victims. Paragraph 2 introduces the happy and wise Prince Prospero, the light-hearted friends at his abbey, and how the abbey is bolted shut. Paragraph 3 describes the joys and frivolities the Prince provides within the abbey and the courtiers' determination to make merry, while outside the Red Death continues to stalk. Paragraph 4 introduces a masked figure who appears at midnight. Paragraph 5 describes the masked figure, and paragraph 6 discusses the prince's reaction. It can be inferred from the horrified response of the revelers and the prince's anger that they all recognize this figure as the Red Death. All their precautions have failed.

43. C

Category: Global

Getting to the Answer: The first paragraph introduces a disease called the Red Death, along with its symptoms. The paragraph describes the prince's country attempting to avoid the Red Death and ultimately failing; **(C)** is correct. **(A)** is incorrect because the first paragraph does not explain how others have avoided the Red Death. While the first paragraph explains the disease's symptoms, it does not suggest that it is no longer a cause for concern; **(B)** is incorrect. Paragraphs 2 and 3, not paragraph 1, illustrate how the courtiers intend to stop the spread of the Red Death; **(D)** is incorrect.

44. E

Category: Detail

Getting to the Answer: The second paragraph mentions that the Red Death has caused the prince's dominions to be "half depopulated," suggesting massive numbers of his citizens have died; **(E)** is correct. **(F)** is incorrect because this sentence details the courtiers locking themselves in the abbey as a means of preventing anyone from entering or exiting. **(G)** is incorrect because this statement notes how the symptoms of the Red Death progress. Finally, **(H)** is incorrect because these lines illustrate the reaction of the courtiers to the presence of the Red Death, not the devastating toll the disease has taken on the prince's country.

45. C

Category: Function

Getting to the Answer: In paragraph 1, Poe writes that "the scarlet stains upon the body and especially upon the face of the victim, were the pest ban which shut him out from the aid and from the sympathy of his fellow-men" (lines 6–9), meaning that the victim was left to suffer and die alone; **(C)** is correct. **(A)** is incorrect because the passage states that a victim's scarlet stains "shut him out from the aid and from the sympathy of his fellow-men" (lines 8–9). **(B)** is incorrect because it is contradicted by the statement "No pestilence had ever been so fatal" (line 2). **(D)** is incorrect because paragraph 1 states that the entire incident would last half an hour: "And the whole seizure, progress, and termination of the disease, were incidents of half an hour" (lines 9–11).

46. H

Category: Global

Getting to the Answer: Upon entering, the courtiers "welded the bolts," essentially locking themselves in the abbey, to shield themselves from the Red Death; **(H)** is correct. Both **(E)** and **(F)** are incorrect because there is no attack and no rival princes are mentioned. Since the guests were the "knights and dames of his court," it is likely true that they did not mix with the common people, but this is not the reason they secluded themselves in the abbey; **(G)** is incorrect.

47. A

Category: Global

Getting to the Answer: The prince's notion that "the external world could take care of itself" shows that he is unconcerned with the people outside of the abbey; **(A)** is correct. The excerpt states that the prince "provided all the appliances of pleasure," which offers no evidence that the prince is humble or frugal, that he has given up his pleasure-seeking ways, or that he can meet all of his people's needs. Thus, **(B)** and **(C)** are incorrect. **(D)** is incorrect because the Prince provided appliances of pleasure to only some of his people—those that were invited into the abbey—not all of his people.

48. G

Category: Function

Getting to the Answer: The fourth paragraph begins by stating how many months the courtiers have been secluded and also foreshadows the masked ball to come; **(G)** is correct. **(E)** is incorrect because the Red Death does not make an appearance until later in paragraph 4. **(F)** is incorrect because the prince's behavior was analyzed in paragraph 2. There is no indication that the courtiers dislike being secluded; **(H)** is incorrect.

49. B

Category: Detail

Getting to the Answer: Poe, the master of the macabre, is known for his ability to draw word pictures of horror, foreboding, and fear. The words used in paragraph 4—uneasy, silence, and masked figure—combine to create a sense of horror and foreboding; something terrible is going to happen. Thus, **(B)** is correct. Nowhere is anger mentioned or implied; eliminate **(A)**. **(C)** is incorrect because revelry (noisy festivities) is opposite of the tone. **(D)** is incorrect because Poe describes the characters as happy, sagacious, and light-hearted, but not disdainful.

50. G

Category: Global

Getting to the Answer: In paragraph 4, Poe writes that "the music ceased" (line 40) and "there were many individuals in the crowd who had found leisure to become aware of the presence of a masked figure" (lines 49–51). These lines show that even with all of their precautions, the courtiers could not escape death; **(G)** is correct. Poe is not generally condemning people who try to protect themselves against disease; **(E)** is incorrect. **(F)** is incorrect because the medical symptoms of the Red Death are discussed in paragraph 1, not paragraph 4, and this is not a central idea of the excerpt. While the prince and revelers are foolish to think they can avoid the plague, their mistake is only in relation to the Red Death, not to revelry in general; **(H)** is incorrect.

Passage Analysis: The Main Idea of this passage is that struggles marked George Orwell's life and efforts to become a successful writer. Paragraph 1 suggests that Orwell struggled in his life and as a writer long before the publication of his enormously successful novel *Animal Farm*. Paragraph 2 describes Orwell's background and the beginning of his writing career. Paragraph 3 describes the growing disillusionment with communism that inspired Orwell's final and most popular novel.

51. D

Category: Global

Getting to the Answer: First, identify a common theme running through the entire passage. In this case, each paragraph focuses in one way or another on the struggles Orwell experienced in his life. Look for an answer choice that best captures this focus. **(D)** is correct. **(A)** is a Misused Detail; this passage describes Orwell's struggles abroad in Burma and Spain, but this is not the focus of the passage as a whole. **(B)** is also a Misused Detail; Orwell's success achieved late in his career is mentioned, but this is not the focus of the entire passage. **(C)** is Out of Scope—the passage never explores *why* Orwell's early literary efforts failed to establish a successful career for him.

52. G

Category: Detail

Getting to the Answer: Because the entire passage describes various characteristics of Orwell's writing, use the answer choices to direct your research of the passage's content. In addition, be wary of wordings taken directly from the text that do not accurately apply to the question. **(G)** is correct. Although the passage mentions that Orwell sought "creative possibilities," his writing is never specifically described as creative. **(E)** is mentioned in paragraphs 1 and 3. **(F)** is mentioned in paragraph 1. **(H)** is mentioned in paragraph 3; the adjective "cynical" can be inferred from the statement that Orwell's pessimistic and satirical final novel was inspired by his increasingly cynical views regarding communism.

53. B

Category: Inference

Getting to the Answer: While Orwell's political sentiments are not specifically mentioned in paragraph 2's description of his work as an administrator in Burma, the author has included important clues regarding Orwell's beliefs. In lines 25–26, for example, the author states that in Burma, Orwell experienced a "growing disillusionment with the concept of imperialism"; this information, coupled with the fact that Orwell had volunteered for service in the Indian Imperial Police, suggests that before he went to Burma, Orwell did not have significant problems with British imperialism. Look for an answer choice that draws a similar conclusion. **(B)** is correct. **(A)** is Out of Scope as the passage never mentions when Orwell became a socialist. **(C)** is incorrect because the passage never describes the political relationship between Orwell and his publishers before he went to Burma. **(D)** is also Out of Scope since the passage never explores Orwell's views on democracy.

54. H

Category: Inference

Getting to the Answer: Although you may not be able to clearly grasp the author's meaning behind the cited words simply by reading them, use their context in the passage for clarification. In this case, the sentence that follows the cited words states that Orwell had grown "cynical about communism"; look for an answer choice that takes this information into account. **(H)** does so and is therefore correct. **(E)** is a Distortion; the cited words are referring to Orwell's political sensibilities, not directly to his understanding of the war. **(F)** is a Misused Detail; the cited words come in paragraph 3 and are not connected with the author's description of Orwell's disillusionment with imperialism in paragraph 2. **(G)** is also a Distortion because the fact that Orwell lost the support of his publishers was a result of his changing political sensibilities, not the change itself.

55. D

Category: Function

Getting to the Answer: In paragraph 1, the passage states that these commissions "paid his bills but lacked the creative possibilities he sought" (lines 11–12). This, coupled with the fact that Orwell was a writer, leads you to predict that Orwell was writing for money; **(D)** is correct. While a commission can refer to an organization or to groups of people, neither fits the context of the sentence; **(A)** and **(B)** are incorrect. There is no indication that Orwell's payments were small, so **(C)** is incorrect.

56. F

Category: Detail

Getting to the Answer: First, re-familiarize yourself with the author's description of *Animal Farm* in the opening paragraph. The author states that this novel established Orwell's reputation for "shrewd political commentary" and describes the book as a "well-known satire." Look for the answer choice that takes this information into account. **(F)** is correct; the word "commentary" is used in the author's description, while the word "mocking" can be inferred from the description of the book as a satire. **(E)** is a Distortion; it is Orwell's *Nineteen Eighty-Four* that is referred to as his "crowning achievement." **(G)** is incorrect because the passage never mentions what exactly influenced *Animal Farm*. **(H)** is a Distortion; again, it is *Nineteen Eighty-Four* that is described as "depicting political tyranny."

57. A

Category: Detail

Getting to the Answer: Lines 47–49 state that Orwell's cynicism about communism "inspired his crowning literary achievement," which matches **(A)**. Choice **(B)** is Opposite because Orwell's cynicism alienated his left-wing publishers. **(C)** and **(D)** are Out of Scope; they are not supported by the information in the passage.

Part 2—Mathematics

58. .7

Subject: Algebra

Getting to the Answer: As with any proportion, start by cross-multiplying, then perform the necessary algebra to isolate x:

$$\frac{2x+1}{4} = \frac{12}{20}$$
$$40x + 20 = 48$$
$$40x = 28$$
$$x = \frac{28}{40} = \frac{7}{10}$$

Grid in **.7**.

59. 85

Subject: Algebra

Getting to the Answer: Solve the given equation for f:

$$5f + 25 = 450$$
$$5f = 425$$
$$f = 85$$

Grid in **85**.

60. 0, 1, or 2

Subject: Algebra

Getting to the Answer: Inequalities can be solved just like equations. Remember that if you multiply or divide by a negative number, then the direction of the inequality changes!

$$-3n + 5 \geq -1$$
$$-3n \geq -6$$
$$n \leq 2$$

Since you know that n is a positive integer less than or equal to 2, there are three possible answers that may be gridded in: **0, 1, or 2**.

61. 46

Subject: Algebra

Getting to the Answer: Whenever you see a proportion, cross-multiply and solve for the desired variable:

$$\frac{2}{5} = \frac{d}{115}$$
$$5d = 230$$
$$d = 46$$

Grid in **46**.

62. 54

Subject: Arithmetic

Getting to the Answer: The question states that Samantha grew 36 onions. If she grew 36 onions, then this number is three times the number of carrots she grew. Thus, she grew 12 carrots. The number of carrots is twice the number of peppers she grew, so she grew 6 peppers. Combined, she grew $36 + 12 + 6 = 54$ total vegetables, so grid in **54**.

63. B

Subject: Algebra

Getting to the Answer: Substitute 36 for x.

$$4x = (3y)^2 \rightarrow 4(36) = (3y)^2$$

$$144 = (3y)^2 \rightarrow \sqrt{144} = \sqrt{(3y)^2}$$ Take the square root of both sides to simplify variable term.

$$12 = 3y \rightarrow 4 = y$$ Divide by 3 to solve for y. (You know $12 = 3y$ because y is positive.) The answer is **(B)**.

64. F

Subject: Algebra

Getting to the Answer:

$$\begin{aligned}\sqrt{m+9}-1 &= 3\\ \sqrt{m+9} &= 4\\ \left(\sqrt{m+9}\right)^2 &= (4)^2\\ m+9 &= 16\\ m &= 7, \textbf{(F)}\end{aligned}$$

You could also Backsolve and find the answer in seconds!

65. A

Subject: Algebra

Getting to the Answer: Since $x \square y$ means $(x - y)^x + (x + y)^y$, to find $4 \square 2$, just plug 4 in for x and 2 in for y, then simplify. $(4 - 2)^4 + (4 + 2)^2 = 2^4 + 6^2 = 16 + 36 = 52$, which is answer **(A)**.

66. G

Subject: Algebra

Getting to the Answer: Try Picking Numbers. If $f = 10$, then there are 10 freshmen in the class. If 5 freshmen drop the class, then there are $10 - 5$, or 5, freshmen left in the class. The number of sophomores is 3 times the number of freshmen left, or $3 \times 5 = 15$. So, there are 15 sophomores in the class and $s = 15$. Which of the answer choices work with $f = 10$ and $s = 15$? All you have to do is plug in those numbers into the 5 choices. Only **(G)** works, so therefore **(G)** is the correct answer.

To do it algebraically, just translate one step at a time. There are f freshmen in the class, but if 5 freshmen drop the class, there are $f - 5$ freshmen left. The number of sophomores is 3 times the number of freshmen left, or 3 times $f - 5$, or $3(f - 5)$. So, $s = 3(f - 5)$, **(G)**.

67. D

Subject: Arithmetic

Getting to the Answer: If the particle travels from A to B to C to D to E and then back to A, it has traveled 5 centimeters, since each side of the pentagon measures 1 centimeter. If it goes all the way around the pentagon again, it has traveled another 5 centimeters, for a total of 10 centimeters. In fact, every time the particle makes a complete revolution around the pentagon (from point A back to point A again) it travels an additional 5 centimeters. So, if the number of centimeters the particle has traveled is a multiple of 5, the particle must be at point A. The number 723 is 3 more than a multiple of 5. If the particle had gone 720 centimeters it would be at point A; since it has gone 3 more centimeters it must be at point D. The answer is **(D)**.

68. H

Subject: Geometry

Getting to the Answer: The slope of a line is defined as the change in the y-coordinate divided by the change in the x-coordinate. As you go from point A to point B, the x-coordinate goes from p to 6 and the y-coordinate goes from 3 to p, so the change in the x-coordinate is $6 - p$ and the change in the y-coordinate is $p - 3$. You can make this into an equation: $\frac{p-3}{6-p} = 2$, and solve this equation for p. That would give you $p = 5$, **(H)**. You could also plug the 4 possible values for p into the expression to see which one gives you 2 as a result. Either way, **(H)** is correct.

69. A

Subject: Algebra

Getting to the Answer: If 60 cookies are distributed among x campers, then each camper gets $\frac{60}{x}$ cookies. When the same number of cookies is divided among fewer campers, then each camper gets 2 more than $\frac{60}{x}$ cookies, or $\frac{60}{x} + 2$. This number of cookies per camper is also equal to 60 cookies divided by 8 less than the original number of campers, or $\frac{60}{x-8}$. This gives us the

equation $\frac{60}{x} + 2 = \frac{60}{x-8}$. Unfortunately, this equation is not in the same form as the equations in the answer choices so you'll have to do some algebra:

$$\frac{60}{x} + 2 = \frac{60}{x-8}$$

$$\frac{60+2x}{x} = \frac{60}{x-8}$$

$$(60+2x)(x-8) = 60x$$

$$60x - 480 + 2x^2 - 16x = 60x$$

$$2x^2 - 16x - 480 = 0$$

$x^2 - 8x - 240 = 0$, or answer choice **(A)**

70. H

Subject: Arithmetic

Getting to the Answer: When would $4 + \frac{1}{s}$ have the smallest possible value? Certainly if s, and its reciprocal, were negative, $4 + \frac{1}{s}$ would be smaller than 4, since adding a negative number is like subtracting a positive number. However, none of the answer choices are negative, so $4 + \frac{1}{s}$ will be greater than 4. However, it will be as small as possible when $\frac{1}{s}$ is as small as possible. To find the value of $\frac{1}{s}$, remember that dividing by a fraction is the same as multiplying by the reciprocal of the fraction. If $s = \frac{1}{4}$, then $\frac{1}{s} = \frac{1}{\frac{1}{4}} = 1 \times \frac{4}{1} = 4$. If you do that, you'll probably notice that as s gets larger, its reciprocal gets smaller, so $\frac{1}{s}$ is smallest when s is largest, in this case, when $s = 4$. The answer is **(H)**.

71. A

Subject: Arithmetic

Getting to the Answer: If an integer is chosen randomly from the first 50 integers, the probability of choosing any particular number is 1 divided by 50, and the probability of choosing an integer with a digit of 3 is the number of integers with a digit of 3, divided by 50. The integers 3, 13, 23, 30, 31, 32, 33, 34, 35, 36, 37, 38, 39, and 43 are the only integers with 3s in them, for a total of 14 different integers, so the probability is $\frac{7}{25}$, or **(A)**.

72. E

Subject: Algebra

Getting to the Answer: The important thing to remember here is that when solving an algebraic equation, you have to do the same thing to both sides of the equation. You're given an equation with $4x + 2$ on the left side of the equal sign and the question asks about $4x + 8$. To make $4x + 2$ look like $4x + 8$, just add 6. But since you've added 6 to the left side of the equation, you have to add 6 to the right side of the equation also. Adding 6 to the right side of the equation gives you 26 + 6, or 32, answer choice **(E)**.

A more mathematical way of expressing what you just did is to write it out like this:

$$\begin{array}{r} 4x+2 = 26 \\ +6 = +6 \\ \hline 4x+8 = 32 \end{array}$$

73. C

Subject: Arithmetic

Getting to the Answer: First, figure out how many miles will be traveled at each price. There are 100 miles total, and the first 10 cost a flat rate of \$5.00. That leaves 90 miles, 40 of which cost \$0.25 per mile. The last 50 miles cost \$0.10 per mile. Now, find out how much each segment costs and add them together:

$$\$5 + 40(\$0.25) + 50(\$0.10) =$$
$$\$5 + \$10 + \$5 = \$20, \textbf{(C)}$$

74. G

Subject: Geometry

Getting to the Answer: The formula for the area of a triangle is Area $= \frac{1}{2}$ base × height. In this problem, you are told that the area of the triangle is 24 and that the height is 6. You can also tell from the diagram that the base is equal to $x + (x + 2)$. Now, substitute these values into the area formula:

$$\begin{aligned} 24 &= \frac{1}{2}(x+x+2)(6) \\ 48 &= (x+x+2)(6) \\ 8 &= (x+x+2) \\ 6 &= 2x \\ x &= 3, \text{or } \textbf{(G)} \end{aligned}$$

75. B

Subject: Algebra

Getting to the Answer: Since you're given that y is between -1 and 0, why not pick an appropriate number for y and plug it into each answer choice? Try $y = -\frac{1}{2}$. Then **(A)** is $y^2 = \left(-\frac{1}{2}\right)^2 = \frac{1}{4}$, **(B)** is $1 - y = 1 - \left(-\frac{1}{2}\right) = 1\frac{1}{2}$, **(C)** is $1 + y = 1 + \left(-\frac{1}{2}\right) = \frac{1}{2}$, and **(D)** is $2y = 2\left(-\frac{1}{2}\right) = -1$. **(B)** is the greatest, and therefore the correct answer.

76. F

Subject: Arithmetic

Getting to the Answer: First, find out how much money Tariq's purchase will cost. 21 oranges at 30 cents each will cost 21 × \$0.30 = \$6.30. 12 apples at 50 cents each will cost 12 × \$0.50 = \$6.00. The total purchase would cost \$6.30 + \$6.00, or \$12.30. Since Tariq only has \$10, he needs \$12.30 − \$10.00, or \$2.30 more, **(F)**.

77. D

Subject: Arithmetic

Getting to the Answer: If Thomas wound up in debt, it means that he spent more money than he actually had, so the correct answer must be greater than the amount of money he had to start with, \$15. Therefore, eliminate **(A)**, **(B)**, and **(C)**. If he has a debt of \$5, then he must have spent all the money he had, or \$15, and then borrowed another \$5 and spent that also. So, he spent a total of \$15 + \$5, or \$20, **(D)**.

78. F

Subject: Algebra

Getting to the Answer: Notice that in the equation $2x + 2x + 14 = 2x + 2x + 2x + 6$, $2x + 2x$ appears on both sides. Subtracting $2x + 2x$ from both sides results in:

$$\begin{aligned} 14 &= 2x + 6 \\ 8 &= 2x \\ 4 &= x, \textbf{(F)} \end{aligned}$$

79. D

Subject: Algebra

Getting to the Answer: Use Makeshift Measuring. The shaded area on the left is half, or 50%, of the area of the rectangle. You can fold your paper in half or measure with a corner to check that both sides are the same length. Because the shaded area on the right represents a bit more than half, you can eliminate **(A)** and **(B)**. Now, look at the shaded part on the right. It is about $\frac{1}{5}$ of the right side, or $\frac{1}{10}$ of the whole rectangle, which is another 10%. The total area is 50% + 10% = 60%, answer choice **(D)**.

80. H

Subject: Arithmetic

Getting to the Answer: The person must write the digits of each of the integers 88 through 116, inclusive. Each of the integers 88 through 99, inclusive, contains 2 digits and each of the integers 100 through 116, inclusive, contains 3 digits. If a and b are integers and $a < b$, then the number of integers from a through b, inclusive, is $b - a + 1$. Among the integers 88 through 99, inclusive, there are 99 − 88 + 1 = 12 integers. There are 2 digits in each of the integers 88 through 99, inclusive, for a total of 24 digits. Among the integers 100 through 116, inclusive, there are 116 − 100 + 1 = 17 integers. There are 3 digits in each of the integers 100 through 116, inclusive, for a total of 51 digits. So, the total number of digits that must be written is 24 + 51 = 75, **(H)**.

81. C

Subject: Geometry

Getting to the Answer: The perimeter of any polygon is the sum of the lengths of its sides. The area of any rectangle is length × width. The area of rectangle *WXYZ* is 96 and *WZ* (which is the width of rectangle *WXYZ*) is 6. *YZ*, the length, must then be $YZ \times 6 = 96$, or $YZ = \frac{96}{6} = 16$. *YZ* is the length of one side of triangle *TYZ*. Opposite sides of a rectangle are equal, so *WX* also has a length of 16. Since *T* is the midpoint of *WX*, the lengths of *WT* and *TX* are each half of 16, or 8.

Triangle *WTZ* is a right triangle. Leg *WZ* is 6 and leg *WT* is 8, so this right triangle is a multiple of the 3-4-5 right triangle in which each member of the 3:4:5 ratio is multiplied by 2. So, the length of hypotenuse *ZT* is 2 × 5, or 10. Right triangle *XTY* is identical to right triangle *WTZ*, so the length of hypotenuse *TY* is also 10. Since *TY* is 10, *YZ* is 16, and *ZT* is 10, the perimeter of triangle *TYZ* is 10 + 16 + 10 = 36, **(C)**.

82. H

Subject: Algebra

Getting to the Answer: When 368 is divided by 7, the result is 52 with a remainder of 4, so *x* is 4. 3*x* is 3(4), or 12, and 368 divided by 12 equals 30 with a remainder of 8, **(H)**.

83. C

Subject: Arithmetic

Getting to the Answer: To find the number of students who are not taking either geography, history, or both, first find the number of students taking either geography or history and then subtract this number from the total number of students in the room. In order to find the number of students taking either geography or history, add the number of students taking geography and the number of students taking history and then subtract the number of students taking both geography and history.

So, the number of students taking either geography or history is 12 + 14 − 5, which is 21. Since 21 students are taking either geography or history, the number of students that are not taking either geography or history is 33 − 21 = 12, **(C)**.

84. F

Subject: Arithmetic

Getting to the Answer: Pick Numbers to eliminate the incorrect answer choices. Begin with **(E)**. No matter what $x + y$ is, if you scaled up the numbers in the ratio by multiplying them both by 18, the sum would be a multiple of 18. So the statement is false. Eliminate **(E)**.

Now, look at **(F)**. If *x* is 7 and *y* is 5, then $x + y$ is 7 + 5 or 12. This answer is a multiple of 6. If *x* is 2 × 7 or 14 and *y* is 2 × 5 or 10, then $x + y$ is 14 + 10 or 24. This answer is also a multiple of 12. It turns out that $x + y$ is always a multiple of 12 and, therefore, a multiple of 6. **(F)** is correct.

85. D

Subject: Geometry

Getting to the Answer: The key to solving this problem is to realize that triangle *WXY* is an isosceles right triangle. If one of its angles is 90 degrees and the other is 45 degrees as indicated, the remaining angle must also be 45 degrees and *WY* = *XY*. In this figure, because *VWYZ* is a square, both *WY* and *XY* are equal to *a*.

An isosceles right triangle has side lengths in the ratio of $x : x : x\sqrt{2}$, so the length of the hypotenuse of *WXY* is $a\sqrt{2}$.

Add up the three sides of the square and one leg and the hypotenuse of the right triangle to find the perimeter:

$$3a + a + a\sqrt{2} =$$
$$4a + a\sqrt{2} =$$
$$\left(4 + \sqrt{2}\right)a, \text{ or } \textbf{(D)}$$

86. H

Subject: Algebra

Getting to the Answer: Get familiar with classic expressions like $x^2 - 9$. The expression $x^2 - 9$ factors out to $(x + 3)(x - 3)$. The entire expression looks like this: $\frac{x^2-9}{x-3} = \frac{(x+3)(x-3)}{x-3} = x + 3$, or **(H)**. If you have trouble factoring expressions like this one, you can Pick Numbers for *x* and plug that number back into each of the answer choices until you find the matching correct answer.

87. D

Subject: Arithmetic

Getting to the Answer: Since something happens every 5 minutes at this party, look at each five-minute interval. At first, there are 256 people. After 5 minutes, half of them leave. That means that 128 people leave and 128 people are left after 5 minutes. 5 minutes after that, or 10 minutes after the party started, half the remaining people leave. That means that half of 128, or 64, people leave and 64 are left after 10 minutes. 15 minutes after the party started, half the remaining 64, or 32, people leave and 32 people are left. Finally, 20 minutes after the start, half of 32, or 16, people leave, and so, ultimately, only 16 people are left at the party. **(D)** is correct.

88. H

Subject: Geometry

Getting to the Answer: Here, the angle marked $x°$ is in a triangle with 2 other unknown angles. However, one of those unknown angles of the triangle, the one just above the $x°$ angle, lies on a straight line with an angle measuring 98°. Therefore, that angle must measure $180° - 98° = 82°$. The third angle in the triangle is opposite a 54° angle that is formed by the intersection of 2 straight lines, so the third angle of the triangle must also measure 54°. The 3 angles of a triangle add up to 180°, so $54° + 82° + x° = 180°$, and $x = 44$, **(H)**.

89. D

Subject: Algebra

Getting to the Answer: Use the average formula in the rearranged form: Sum of the Terms = Average × Number of Terms. The sum of the 16 terms is 3×16, or 48. When the seventeenth number joins the group, the average of all 17 numbers is 4, so the sum of all 17 numbers is 4×17, or 68. The sum of all 17 numbers is equal to the sum of the first sixteen numbers plus the seventeenth number. Let x equal the unknown number, and solve: $68 = 48 + x$, $x = 20$, **(D)**.

90. F

Subject: Arithmetic

Getting to the Answer: To find the probability that two events will occur together, simply multiply together the probabilities of the two events. Remember the probability formula: $\text{Probability} = \frac{\text{Number of desired outcomes}}{\text{Number of possible outcomes}}$.

In the first box, the chance of drawing a red ball is one in three. The probability of drawing a red ball in the second box is one in four. So, the probability of drawing a red ball from each box is $\frac{1}{3} \times \frac{1}{4} = \frac{1}{12}$. **(F)** is correct.

91. A

Subject: Algebra

Divide both sides of the equation $abc = b^2$ by b:

$$\frac{abc}{b} = \frac{b^2}{b}$$
$$ac = b$$

(A) is correct.

92. E

Subject: Arithmetic

Getting to the Answer: Don't fall into the "obvious answer" trap of just taking the number of nickels and the number of dimes from the two ratios to come up with 3:4. To find the ratio of nickels to dimes, you need to get the two ratios in proportion to one another by getting the same number of pennies in each. Multiplying the first ratio by 3 gives you 6:9; multiplying the second by 2 gives you 6:8. Since the number corresponding to pennies is now the same in each ratio, the ratio of nickels to dimes can now be found. The ratio of nickels to dimes is 9:8, **(E)**.

93. D

Subject: Algebra

Add the two equations to cancel out b:

$$\begin{aligned} 5a - b &= 9 \\ +3a + b &= 15 \\ 8a &= 24 \\ a &= 3 \end{aligned}$$

If $a = 3$, then $b = 15 - 3a = 15 - 9 = 6$.
So, $a + b = 3 + 6 = 9$, **(D)**.

94. G

Subject: Algebra

You should Pick Numbers. You need to try several positive integer values for x to find which choice must be true. If $x = 1$, the expression equals 4, so you can eliminate **(F)**; if $x = 2$, the expression equals 6, so **(H)** can be eliminated; if $x = 5$, the expression equals 0, so **(E)** can be eliminated. This leaves **(G)** as the correct answer.

95. B

Subject: Geometry

Getting to the Answer: The shaded region in this question is a sector of a circle with an interior angle of 45 degrees. Determine what fraction of the circle the sector occupies by dividing its interior angle by 360. $\frac{45^\circ}{360^\circ} = \frac{1}{8}$. So, we know the sector has an area that is $\frac{1}{8}$ of the area of the entire circle. We are told that the area of the shaded region is 2π. Setting up a proportion will allow you to solve from here. $\frac{1}{8} = \frac{2\pi}{x}$. So, the area of the entire circle is 16π. That means that $\pi r^2 = 16\pi$. Therefore, the radius, r, is 4. The diameter is twice the radius, so $d = 8$ and **(B)** is correct.

96. F

Subject: Algebra

Getting to the Answer: When the r cards are distributed, there are 8 left over, so the number of cards distributed is $r - 8$. Divide the number of cards distributed by the number of people. Since there are s people, each person gets $\frac{r-8}{s}$ cards, **(F)**.

97. D

Subject: Algebra

Getting to the Answer: Find the slope between (2, 6) and (4, 3). Then check the answer choices, finding the slope between the given point and (2, 6). If it is the same as the slope between (2, 6) and (4, 3), then all three points lie on the same line. The formula for the slope is $\frac{\text{Change in } y\text{-coordinates}}{\text{Change in } x\text{-coordinates}}$. So, the slope between (2, 6) and (4, 3) is $\frac{6-3}{2-4} = -\frac{3}{2}$.

Check the answer choices, finding the slope between the given point and (2, 6):

(A) (1, 7) Slope $= \frac{7-6}{1-2} = -\frac{1}{1}$. Eliminate.

(B) (2, 8) Slope $= \frac{8-6}{2-2}$ = Undefined. Eliminate.

(C) (3, 5) Slope $= \frac{5-6}{3-2} = -\frac{1}{1}$. Eliminate.

(D) (6, 0) Slope $= \frac{0-6}{6-2} = -\frac{6}{4} = -\frac{3}{2}$. This is the same as the slope between (2, 6) and (4, 3), so **(D)** also lies on the same line. The correct answer is **(D)**.

98. H

Subject: Algebra

Getting to the Answer:

$$\begin{aligned} 3\sqrt{x} &= 15 \\ \sqrt{x} &= 5 \\ x &= 25, \textbf{(H)} \end{aligned}$$

99. A

Subject: Algebra

Getting to the Answer:

$$\begin{aligned} |7+r| &= 3 \\ 7+r &= 3 \quad \text{or} \quad 7+r = -3 \\ r &= -4 \quad \text{or} \quad r = -10 \\ r &= -10 \quad \text{is } \textbf{(A)} \end{aligned}$$

You could also use Backsolving here.

100. H

Subject: Algebra

Getting to the Answer: Substitute $\frac{1}{5}$ for y.

$$\frac{1}{y} = \frac{x}{3} \rightarrow \frac{1}{\left(\frac{1}{5}\right)} = \frac{x}{3}$$

$$\frac{1}{\left(\frac{1}{5}\right)} = 1 \div \frac{1}{5} = 5$$ Simplify the fraction within a fraction.

$$5 = \frac{x}{3} \rightarrow 15 = x$$ Multiply by 3 to solve for x. The answer is 15, or **(H)**.

101. D

Subject: Algebra

Getting to the Answer: Substitute 2 for *y*:

$x - \frac{7}{10} = y \rightarrow x - \frac{7}{10} = 2$

$x - \frac{7}{10} = 2 \rightarrow x = 2 + \frac{7}{10}$ Add $\frac{7}{10}$ to both sides to isolate the variable.

$x = \frac{20}{10} + \frac{7}{10}$ Change 2 into a fraction and add to $\frac{7}{10}$.

$x = \frac{27}{10}$, **(D)**

102. F

Subject: Algebra

Getting to the Answer: Substitute 4 for *x*:

$20 - (y - x) = 30 - (x - y) \rightarrow 20 - (y - 4) = 30 - (4 - y)$

$20 - (y - 4) = 30 - (4 - y) \rightarrow$ $20 - y + 4 = 30 - 4 + y$ Distribute the negative signs.

$24 - y = 26 + y \rightarrow -2 = 2y$ $y = -1$, or **(F)** Add *y* and subtract 26 from both sides to isolate variable.

103. C

Subject: Algebra

Getting to the Answer: Substitute 1 for *y*:

$\frac{x}{10} - \frac{y}{5} + \frac{1}{6} = \frac{1}{15} \rightarrow$

$\frac{x}{10} - \frac{1}{5} + \frac{1}{6} = \frac{1}{15}$ LCM of 5, 6, 10 and 15 is 30.

$\frac{x}{10} - \frac{1}{5} + \frac{1}{6} = \frac{1}{15} \rightarrow$

$\frac{3x}{30} - \frac{6}{30} + \frac{5}{30} = \frac{2}{30}$

$\frac{3x}{30} - \frac{6}{30} + \frac{5}{30} = \frac{2}{30} \rightarrow$

$\frac{3x}{30} = \frac{2}{30} + \frac{6}{30} - \frac{5}{30}$ Add $\frac{6}{30}$ and subtract $\frac{5}{30}$ to isolate the variable.

$\frac{3x}{30} = \frac{2}{30} + \frac{6}{30} - \frac{5}{30} \rightarrow$

$\frac{3x}{30} = \frac{3}{30}$

$3x = 3 \rightarrow x = 1$ Divide by 3 to solve for *x*; the answer is 1, or **(C)**.

104. H

Subject: Algebra

Getting to the Answer: Substitute 21 for *y*:

$y \div 7 = x - 3 \cdot 5 \rightarrow 21 \div 7 = x - 3 \cdot 5$

$21 \div 7 = x - 3 \cdot 5 \rightarrow 3 = x - 15$ Simplify both sides using PEMDAS.

$3 = x - 15 \rightarrow x = 18$, **(H)** Add 15 to both sides to solve for *x*.

105. D

Subject: Algebra

Getting to the Answer: Substitute 4 for *y*:

$-x - 9 = -y^2 \rightarrow -x - 9 = -(4)^2$

$-x - 9 = -(4)^2 \rightarrow -x - 9 = -16$ Simplify following PEMDAS.

$-x - 9 = -16 \rightarrow -x = -7$ Add 9 to both sides to isolate the variable.

$-x = -7 \rightarrow x = 7$, **(D)** Divide both sides by -1 to solve for *x*.

106. F

Subject: Algebra

Getting to the Answer:

$x = 4y^2 + |-5|$

$x = 4y^2 + 5$

$x - 5 = 4y^2$

$\frac{x-5}{4} = y^2$

$\sqrt{\frac{x-5}{4}} = y$, **(F)**

107. D

Subject: Algebra

Getting to the Answer:

$$\begin{aligned} x &= 4(3-y)(2^2-1) \\ x &= (12-4y)(4-1) \\ x &= (12-4y)(3) \\ x &= 36-12y \\ x-36 &= -12y \\ \frac{x-36}{-12} &= y \\ \frac{-x}{12}+3 &= y \\ 3-\frac{x}{12} &= y, \textbf{(D)} \end{aligned}$$

108. E

Subject: Algebra

Getting to the Answer:

$$\begin{aligned} x &= 3y(2-|-4|)+y(3-|-2|) \\ x &= 3y(-2)+y(1) \\ x &= -6y+y \\ x &= -5y \\ -\frac{x}{5} &= y, \textbf{(E)} \end{aligned}$$

109. C

Subject: Algebra

Getting to the Answer:

$\frac{1}{x} = x-\frac{3}{x}$

$x\left(\frac{1}{x}\right) = x\left(x-\frac{3}{x}\right)$ Multiply both sides by x.

$1 = x^2-3$

$1+3 = x^2-3+3$ Add 3 to both sides, isolating the variable.

$4 = x^2$

$\sqrt{4} = \sqrt{x^2}$ Take the square root of both sides

$\pm 2 = x$ Since $x \geq 0$, we can discard -2.

$x = 2$, **(C)**

110. G

Subject: Algebra

Getting to the Answer: Backsolving would be a great way to solve this problem. If you'd rather solve it algebraically, remember that there are two possibilities when dealing with an equation involving absolute value.

$$\begin{aligned} |r+7| &= 6 \\ r+7 &= 6 \quad \text{or} \quad r+7 = -6 \\ r &= -1 \quad \text{or} \quad r = -13 \end{aligned}$$

$$\begin{aligned} |2r-2| &= 4 \\ 2r-2 &= 4 \quad \text{or} \quad 2r-2 = -4 \\ 2r &= 6 \quad \text{or} \quad 2r = -2 \\ r &= 3 \quad \text{or} \quad r = -1 \end{aligned}$$

The value of r that is common to both solution sets is $r = -1$, **(G)**.

111. A

Subject: Arithmetic

Getting to the Answer: $\frac{130}{x}$ will be an integer whenever x evenly divides into 130. So, you need to find all of the numbers that will divide evenly into 130—that is, all of the factors of 130. The easiest way to do that is to write down all of the factor pairs of 130:

$130 = 1 \times 130$, 2×65, 5×26, and 10×13. That makes 8 numbers that divide evenly into 130, **(A)**.

112. E

Subject: Algebra

Getting to the Answer: Substitute $\frac{1}{6}$ for y:

$x+\frac{3}{4} = 2y \rightarrow x+\frac{3}{4} = 2\frac{1}{6}$

$x+\frac{3}{4} = \frac{1}{3} \rightarrow x = \frac{1}{3}-\frac{3}{4}$ Subtract $\frac{3}{4}$ from both sides to isolate the variable.

$x = \frac{4}{12}-\frac{9}{12}$

$x = \frac{5}{12}$, **(E)**

113. D

Subject: Algebra

Getting to the Answer:

$$x = \sqrt{y} + 2$$
$$x - 2 = \sqrt{y}$$
$$(x-2)^2 = y, \textbf{(D)}$$

114. F

Subject: Geometry

Getting to the Answer: The shaded region is one of four equal pieces left when the circle is subtracted from the square. So, to find the area of the shaded region, you must subtract the area of the circle from the area of the square and then take one fourth of this difference.

You're told that the circumference of the circle is 4π. You also know that the circumference C of a circle is related to its radius r by the formula $C = 2\pi r$. So here, $4\pi = 2\pi r$ and $r = 2$. The area of the circle is πr^2 which equals $\pi(2)^2$ or 4π. To find the area of the square, you must know the length of its side. If you draw in the diameter of the circle whose endpoints are the point where the circle touches side BC of the square and the point where the circle touches side AD of the square, you'll see that the side of the square is equal in length to the diameter of the circle. The radius of the circle is 2, so its diameter, which is twice the radius, is 2×2 or 4. Since the side of the square is 4, its area is its side squared or 4^2 which is 16. The area of the square is 16 and the area of the circle is 4π, so the area outside the circle and inside the square is $16 - 4\pi$, and the area of the shaded region is $\frac{16-4\pi}{4} = 4 - \pi$, **(F)**.